core
JavaServer™
Faces

DAVID GEARY
CAY HORSTMANN

PRENTICE
HALL
PTR

Prentice Hall PTR, Upper Saddle River, NJ 07458
www.phptr.com

Sun Microsystems Press
A Prentice Hall Title

Prentice Hall PTR offers excellent discounts on this book when ordered in quantity for bulk purchases or special sales. For more information, please contact U.S. Corporate and Government Sales, 1-800-382-3419, corpsales@pearsontechgroup.com. For sales outside of the U.S., please contact International Sales, 1-317-581-3793, international@pearsontechgroup.com.

Acquisitions Editor: *Gregory G. Doench*
Editorial Assistant: *Raquel Kaplan*
Production Supervision: *Patti Guerrieri*
Cover Design Director: *Jerry Votta*
Cover Designer: *Anthony Gemmellaro*
Art Director: *Gail Cocker-Bogusz*
Manufacturing Manager: *Alexis R. Heydt*
Marketing Manager: *Chris Guzikowski*

Sun Microsystems Press Publisher: *Myrna Rivera*

Second Printing

ISBN 0-13-146305-5

Sun Microsystems Press
A Prentice Hall Title

About Prentice Hall Professional Technical Reference

With origins reaching back to the industry's first computer science publishing program in the 1960s, and formally launched as its own imprint in 1986, Prentice Hall Professional Technical Reference (PH PTR) has developed into the leading provider of technical books in the world today. Our editors now publish over 200 books annually, authored by leaders in the fields of computing, engineering, and business.

Our roots are firmly planted in the soil that gave rise to the technical revolution. Our bookshelf contains many of the industry's computing and engineering classics: Kernighan and Ritchie's *C Programming Language*, Nemeth's *UNIX System Administration Handbook*, Horstmann's *Core Java*, and Johnson's *High-Speed Digital Design*.

PH PTR acknowledges its auspicious beginnings while it looks to the future for inspiration. We continue to evolve and break new ground in publishing by providing today's professionals with tomorrow's solutions.

Contents

Preface

When we heard about JavaServer™ Faces (JSF) at the 2002 Java One conference, we were very excited. Both of us had extensive experience with client-side Java programming, and had lived to tell the tale—David in *Graphic Java*, and Cay in *Core Java*, both published by Sun Microsystems Press. When we first tried web programming with servlets and JavaServer Pages (JSP), we found it to be rather unintuitive and tedious. JavaServer *Faces* promised to put a friendly face in front of a web application, allowing programmers to think about text fields and menus instead of fretting over page flips and request parameters. Each of us proposed a book project to the publisher, who promptly suggested that we should jointly write the Sun Microsystems Press book on this technology.

It took the JSF expert group (of which David is a member) another two years to release the JSF 1.0 specification and reference implementation. (A maintenance release, called JSF 1.1, followed shortly thereafter. It introduced no new features.) This release fulfills many of the original promises. You really can design web user interfaces by putting components on a form and linking them to Java objects, without having to write any code at all. The framework was designed for tool support, and the first batch of drag-and-drop GUI builders is now emerging. The framework is extensible—you are not limited to the standard set of HTML components, and you can even use completely different rendering technologies, to support, for example, wireless devices. And finally, unlike competing technologies that let you tumble down a deep cliff once you step beyond the glitz, JSF supports the hard stuff—separation of presentation and business logic, navigation, connections with external services, and configuration management.

Of course, the initial version of JSF is far from perfect. Some of the APIs are awkward. We supply you with utility classes in the com.corejsf.util package to reduce your pain. Also, there are fewer components than we originally expected. While JSF has a powerful and convenient data table component, some useful components such as tabbed panes, scrollers, file uploads, and so on, were not included for lack of time. In the book, we show you how to implement these features. Of course, we expect the next release of JSF to remedy many of these shortcomings.

We are still excited about JSF, and we hope you will share this excitement when you learn how this technology makes you a more effective web application developer.

About This Book

This book is suitable for web developers whose main focus is user interface design, as well as for programmers who implement reusable components for web applications. This is in stark contrast to the official JSF specification, a dense and pompously worded document whose principal audience is framework implementors, as well as long-suffering book authors.

The first half of the book, extending to the middle of Chapter 6, focuses on the JSF *tags*. These tags are similar to HTML form tags. They are the basic building blocks for JSF user interfaces. No programming is required for use of to use the tags. We only assume only basic HTML skills for web pages and standard Java programming for the business logic.

The first part of the book covers these topics:

• Setting up your programming environment (Chapter 1)

• Connecting JSF tags to application logic (Chapter 2)

• Navigating between pages (Chapter 3)

• Using the standard JSF tags (Chapters 4 and 5)

• Converting and validating input (Chapter 6)

Starting with the final sections of Chapter 6, we begin JSF programming in earnest. You will learn how to perform advanced tasks, and how to extend the JSF framework. Here are the main topics of the second part:

• Implementing custom converters and validators (Chapter 6)

• Event handling (Chapter 7)

• Including common content among multiple pages (Chapter 8)

• Implementing custom components (Chapter 9)

• Connecting to databases and other external services (Chapter 10)

- Supporting wireless clients (Chapter 11)

We end the book with a chapter that aims to answer common questions of the form "How do I....?" We encourage you to have a peek at that chapter as soon as you become comfortable with the basics of JSF. There are helpful notes on debugging and logging, and we also give you implementation details and working code for features that are missing from JSF 1.0/1.1, such as file uploads, popup menus, and a pager component for long tables.

JSF is built on top of servlets and JSP, but from the point of view of the JSF developer, these technologies merely form the low-level plumbing. While it can't hurt to be familiar with other web technologies such as servlets, JSP, or Struts, we do not assume any such knowledge.

Required Software

All software that you need for this book is freely available. You need the Java Software Development Kit from Sun Microsystems, a servlet container such as Tomcat, and, of course, a JSF implementation, such as Sun's reference implementation. The software runs identically on Linux, Mac OS X, Solaris, and Windows. We used the 1.4.2 J2SE and Tomcat 5.0.19 on both Linux and Mac OS X to develop the code examples in the book.

We also expect that integrated environments will become commercially available in the near future.

Web Support

The web page for this book is http://corejsf.com. It contains

- The source code for all examples in this book
- Useful reference material that we felt is more effective in browseable form than in print
- A list of known errors in the book and the code
- A form for submitting corrections and suggestions

Acknowledgments

First and foremost, we'd like to thank Greg Doench, our editor at Prentice Hall, who has shepherded us through this project, never losing his nerve in spite of numerous delays and complications. Thanks to Mary Lou Nohr for editing the manuscript, and to Patti Guerrieri for her production work. We very much appreciate our reviewers who have done a splendid job, finding errors and suggesting improvements in various drafts of the manuscript. They are:

- Larry Brown, Johns Hopkins University
- Frank Cohen, PushToTest
- Rob Gordon, Crooked Furrow Farm
- Marty Hall, author of *Core Java Servlets and JavaServer Pages*
- Jeff Markham, Markham Software Company
- Angus McIntyre, IBM Corporation
- John Muchow, author of *Core J2ME*
- Sergei Smirnov, principal architect of Exadel JSF Studio
- Roman Smolgovsky, Flytecomm
- Stephen Stelting, Sun Microsystems, Inc.
- Christopher Taylor, Nanshu Densetsu
- Michael Yuan, author of *Enterprise J2ME*

Finally, thanks to our families and friends who have supported us through this project and who share our relief that it is finally completed.

core
JavaServer™
Faces

GETTING STARTED

Topics in This Chapter

Chapter 1

Why JavaServer Faces

Judging from the job advertisements in employment web sites, there are currently two popular techniques for developing web applications.

- The "rapid development" style, using a visual development environment such as Microsoft ASP.NET.
- The "hard-core coding" style, writing lots of code to support a high-performance back end such as J2EE (the Java 2 Enterprise Edition).

As we write this book, development teams face a difficult choice. J2EE is an attractive platform. It is highly scalable. It is portable to multiple platforms. It is supported by many vendors. On the other hand, ASP.NET makes it easy to create attractive user interfaces without tedious programming. Of course, programmers want both: a high-performance back end and easy user-interface programming.

The promise of JavaServer Faces is to bring rapid user-interface development to server-side Java.

If you are familiar with client-side Java development, you can think of JSF as "Swing for server-side applications." If you have experience with JavaServer Pages (JSP), you will find that JSF provides much of the plumbing that JSP developers have to implement by hand. If you already know a server-side framework such as Struts, you will find that JSF uses a similar architecture.

NOTE: You need *not* know anything about Swing, JSP, or Struts in order to use this book. We assume basic familiarity only with Java and HTML.

JSF has these parts:

- A set of prefabricated UI components
- An event-driven programming model
- A component model that enables third-party developers to supply additional components

JSF contains all the necessary code for event handling and component organization. Application programmers can be blissfully ignorant of these details and spend their effort on the application logic.

For the promise of JSF to be fully realized, we need integrated development environments that generate JSF applications. As we write this chapter, these IDEs are just beginning to be developed. For that reason, we start this tutorial chapter by showing you how to compose a JSF application by hand. When reading the instructions in this chapter, consider that many of the steps can and will be automated in the future.

Software Installation

You need the following software packages to get started.

- The Java SDK 1.4.1 or higher (http://java.sun.com/j2se)
- The Tomcat servlet container (http://jakarta.apache.org/tomcat/).
- The JavaServer Faces reference implementation (http://java.sun.com/j2ee/javaserverfaces)
- The sample code for this book, available at http://corejsf.com

We assume that you already installed the Java SDK and that you are familiar with the SDK tools. For more information on the Java SDK, see *Horstmann & Cornell, Core Java, Sun Microsystems Press, 2003.*

In this chapter, we describe how to use JSF with Tomcat 5. Tomcat is a *servlet container*: a program that serves web pages and executes servlets—Java programs that process web requests. JavaServer Faces is built on top of the servlet technology, but you need not know anything about servlets to build JSF applications.

Download and unzip Tomcat, the JSF reference implementation, and the sample code. Place them into directories of your choice. (As always, it is best to avoid path names with spaces, such as c:\Program Files.)

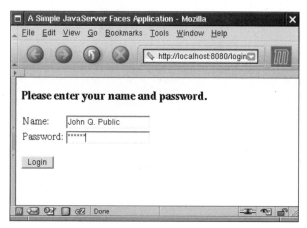

Figure 1–3   A Login Screen

Of course, in a real web application, this screen would be beautified by a skilled web designer.

The file that describes the login screen is essentially an HTML file with a few additional tags—see Listing 1–1. Its visual appearance can be easily improved by a graphic artist who need not have any programming skills.

Listing 1–1   `login/index.jsp`

```
1.  <html>
2.     <%@ taglib uri="http://java.sun.com/jsf/core" prefix="f" %>
3.     <%@ taglib uri="http://java.sun.com/jsf/html" prefix="h" %>
4.
5.     <f:view>
6.        <head>
7.           <title>A Simple JavaServer Faces Application</title>
8.        </head>
9.        <body>
10.          <h:form>
11.             <h3>Please enter your name and password.</h3>
12.             <table>
13.                <tr>
14.                   <td>Name:</td>
15.                   <td>
16.                      <h:inputText value="#{user.name}"/>
17.                   </td>
18.                </tr>
19.                <tr>
20.                   <td>Password:</td>
```

Listing 1–1	login/index.jsp (cont.)

```
21.                   <td>
22.                       <h:inputSecret value="#{user.password}"/>
23.                   </td>
24.               </tr>
25.           </table>
26.           <p>
27.               <h:commandButton value="Login" action="login"/>
28.           </p>
29.       </h:form>
30.   </body>
31.   </f:view>
32. </html>
```

We discuss the contents of this file in detail later in this chapter. For now, note the following points:

- A number of the tags are standard HTML tags: body, table, and so on.
- Some tags have *prefixes*, such as f:view and h:inputText. These are JSF tags. The two taglib declarations declare the JSF tag libraries.
- The h:inputText, h:inputSecret, and h:commandButton tags correspond to the text field, password field, and submit button in Figure 1–3.
- The input fields are linked to object properties. For example, the attribute value="#{user.name}" tells the JSF implementation to link the text field with the name property of a user object. We discuss this linkage in more detail later in this chapter.

When the user enters the name and password and clicks the login button, a welcome screen appears (see Figure 1–4).

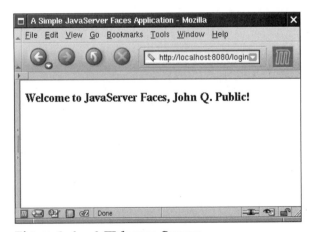

Figure 1–4   A Welcome Screen

The welcome message contains the user name. The password is ignored for now.

The purpose of this application is, of course, not to impress anyone, but merely to illustrate the various pieces that are necessary to produce a JSF application.

Ingredients

Our sample application consists of the following ingredients:

- Pages that define the login and welcome screens. We call them index.jsp and welcome.jsp.

- A *bean* that manages the user data (in our case, username and password). A bean is simply a Java class that exposes properties, usually by following a simple naming convention for the getter and setter methods. The code is in the file UserBean.java—see Listing 1–2. Note that the class is contained inside the com.corejsf package.

- A configuration file for the application that lists bean resources and navigation rules. By default, this file is called faces-config.xml.

- Miscellaneous files that are needed to keep the servlet container happy: the web.xml file and an index.html file that redirects the user to the correct URL for the login page.

More advanced JSF applications have the same structure, but they can contain additional Java classes, such as event handlers, validators, and custom components.

Listing 1–2 login/WEB-INF/classes/com/corejsf/UserBean.java

```
1. package com.corejsf;
2.
3. public class UserBean {
4.    private String name;
5.    private String password;
6.
7.    // PROPERTY: name
8.    public String getName() { return name; }
9.    public void setName(String newValue) { name = newValue; }
10.
11.   // PROPERTY: password
12.   public String getPassword() { return password; }
13.   public void setPassword(String newValue) { password = newValue; }
14. }
```

Directory Structure

A JSF application is deployed as a *WAR file*: a zipped file with extension .war and a directory structure that follows a standardized layout:

    HTML and JSP files

WEB-INF/

    configuration files

    classes/

        class files

    lib/

        library files

For example, the WAR file of our sample application has the directory structure shown in Figure 1–5. Note that the UserBean class is in the package com.corejsf. The META-INF directory is automatically produced by the JAR program when the WAR file is created.

Figure 1–5   Directory Structure
         of the Sample WAR File

To minimize confusion, we package our application source in the exact same directory structure as a WAR file, except that the classes directory contains the source files (see Figure 1–6).

login
├── index.html
├── index.jsp
├── welcome.jsp
└── WEB-INF
    ├── faces-config.xml
    ├── web.xml
    └── classes
        └── com
            └── corejsf
                └── UserBean.java

**Figure 1–6   Directory Structure
of the Sample Application**

Build Instructions

We now walk you through the steps required for building JSF applications with your bare hands. At the end of this chapter, we show you how to automate this process.

1. Launch a command shell.

2. Change to the ch1/login/WEB-INF/classes directory inside *corejsf-examples*, the directory that contains the sample code for this book.

3. Run the command

    javac com/corejsf/UserBean.java

    (On Windows, use backslashes instead: javac com\corejsf\UserBean.java.)

4. Make a ch1/login/WEB-INF/lib directory. Into that directory, copy the following files:

    jsf/lib/jsf-api.jar
    jsf/lib/jsf-impl.jar
    tomcat/server/lib/commons-digester.jar
    tomcat/server/lib/commons-beanutils.jar
    tomcat/webapps/jsp-examples/WEB-INF/lib/jstl.jar
    tomcat/webapps/jsp-examples/WEB-INF/lib/standard.jar

5. Change to the ch1/login directory.

6. Run the command

    jar cvf login.war .

    (Note the period at the end of the command, indicating the current directory.)

7. Copy the `login.war` file to the directory *tomcat*/webapps.

8. Now point your browser to

   http://localhost:8080/login

   The application should start up at this point.

TIP: If you are very impatient, you can use two shortcuts. Copy the six library JAR files into the *tomcat*/common/lib directory and restart the server. Then you don't have to place the libraries into the WEB-INF/lib directory of your applications. Moreover, you can bypass the WAR file—simply copy the entire login directory (including its subdirectories) to the *tomcat*/webapps directory. Remember to compile the source files in the WEB-INF/classes directory.

For more complex programs that reference the JSF libraries, the compilation step is more complex. Your class path must include the following JAR files:

tomcat/common/lib/servlet-api.jar
tomcat/common/lib/jsp-api.jar
jsf/lib/jsf-api.jar
jsf/lib/jsf-impl.jar

A typical compilation command would look like this:

```
javac -classpath .:tomcat/common/lib/servlet-api.jar
    :tomcat/common/lib/jsp-api.jar:jsf/lib/jsf-api.jar
    com/corejsf/*.java
```

The entire command needs to be placed on a single line.

(On Windows, use semicolons to separate the path elements.)

Sample Application Analysis

Web applications have two parts: the *presentation layer* and the *business logic*. The presentation layer is concerned with the look of the application. In the context of a browser-based application, the look is determined by the HTML tags that specify layout, fonts, images, and so on. The business logic is implemented in the Java code that determines the behavior of the application.

Some web technologies intermingle HTML and code. That approach is seductive since it is easy to produce simple applications in a single file. But for serious applications, mixing markup and code poses considerable problems. Professional web designers know about graphics design, but they typically rely on tools that translate their vision into HTML. They would certainly not want to deal with embedded code. On the other hand, programmers are notoriously unqualified when it comes to graphic design. (The example programs in this book bear ample evidence.) Thus, for designing professional web applications, it is important to *separate* the presentation from the business logic. This allows both web designers and programmers to focus on their core competences.

In the context of JSF, the application code is contained in *beans*, and the design is contained in web pages. We look at beans first.

Beans

A Java *bean* is a class that exposes properties and events to an environment such as JSF. A *property* is a named value of a given type that can be read and/or written. The simplest way to define a property is to use a standard naming convention for the reader and writer methods, namely, the familiar get/set convention. The first letter of the property name is changed to upper case in the method names.

For example, the UserBean class has two properties: name and password, both of type String.

```
public class UserBean {
    public String getName() { . . . }
    public void setName(String newValue) {. . . }
    public String getPassword() { . . . }
    public void setPassword(String newValue) { . . . }
    . . .
}
```

The get/set methods can carry out arbitrary actions. In many cases, they simply get or set an instance field. But they might also access a database or a JNDI directory.

NOTE: According to the bean specification, it is legal to omit a read or write method. For example, if getPassword is omitted, then password is a write-only property. That might indeed be desirable for security reasons. However, JSF 1.0 deals poorly with this situation. For now, it is best to give read/write access to all bean properties.

In JSF applications, you use beans for all data that needs to be accessible from a page. The beans are the conduits between the user interface and the back end of the application.

JSF Pages

You need a JSF page for each browser screen. Depending on your development environment, JSF pages typically have extension .jsp or .jsf. At the time of this writing, the extension .jsp requires less configuration effort when used with Tomcat. For that reason, we use the .jsp extension in the examples of this book.

 NOTE: The extension of the page *files* is .jsp or .jsf, whereas in the preferred configuration, the extension of the page *URLs* is .faces. For example, when the browser requests the URL http://localhost:8080/login/index.faces, the URL extension .faces is *mapped* to the file extension.jsp and the servlet container loads the file index.jsp. This process sounds rather byzantine, but it is necessary to implement JSF on top of the servlet technology.

Let's have a second look at the first page of our sample application in Listing 1–1. The page starts out with the tag library declarations

```
<%@ taglib uri="http://java.sun.com/jsf/core" prefix="f" %>
<%@ taglib uri="http://java.sun.com/jsf/html" prefix="h" %>
```

The JSF implementation defines two sets of tags. The core tags are independent of the rendering technology. For example, you need the f:view tag both for HTML pages and for pages that are rendered by a cell phone. The HTML tags generate HTML specific markup. If you want your web application to render pages for an alternative client technology, you must use a different tag library. (We discuss support for alternative client technologies in Chapter 11.)

NOTE: You can choose any prefixes for tags, such as h:inputText and f:view. However, we use f for the core tags and h for the HTML tags.

Much of the page is similar to an HTML form. Note the following differences:

- All JSF tags are contained inside an f:view tag.
- Instead of using an HTML form tag, you enclose all of the JSF components inside an h:form tag.
- Instead of using the familiar input HTML tags, use h:inputText, h:inputSecret, and h:commandButton.

We discuss all standard JSF tags and their attributes in Chapters 4 and 5. In the first three chapters, we can get by with input fields and command buttons.

The input field values are bound to properties of a bean property:

```
<h:inputText value="#{user.name}"/>
```

You will see the definition of the user bean in the next section. The #{...} delimiters are explained in Chapter 2.

When the page is displayed, the getName method is called to obtain the current property value. When the page is submitted, the setName method is invoked to set the value that the user entered.

The h:commandButton tag has an action attribute whose value is used when specifying navigation rules.

```
<h:commandButton value="Login" action="login"/>
```

We discuss navigation rules in the next section. The value attribute is the string that is displayed on the button.

The second JSF page of our application is even simpler than the first. It merely uses the h:outputText tag to display the user name—see Listing 1–3.

Listing 1–3   login/welcome.jsp

```
 1. <html>
 2.    <%@ taglib uri="http://java.sun.com/jsf/core" prefix="f" %>
 3.    <%@ taglib uri="http://java.sun.com/jsf/html" prefix="h" %>
 4.
 5.    <f:view>
 6.       <head>
 7.          <title>A Simple JavaServer Faces Application</title>
 8.       </head>
 9.       <body>
10.          <h3>
11.             Welcome to JavaServer Faces,
12.             <h:outputText value="#{user.name}"/>!
13.          </h3>
14.       </body>
15.    </f:view>
16. </html>
```

> NOTE: We use a plain and old-fashioned format for our JSF pages so that they are as easy to read as possible.

XML-savvy readers will want to do a better job. First, it is desirable to use proper XML for the tag library declarations, eliminating the <%...%> tags. Moreover, you will want to emit a proper DOCTYPE declaration for the generated HTML document.

The following format solves both issues:

```
<?xml version="1.0" ?>
<jsp:root version="2.0"
   xmlns:jsp="http://java.sun.com/JSP/Page"
   xmlns:f="http://java.sun.com/jsf/core"
   xmlns:h="http://java.sun.com/jsf/html">
   <f:view>
      <f:verbatim><![CDATA[<!DOCTYPE html
         PUBLIC "-//W3C//DTD XHTML 1.0 Transitional//EN"
         "http://www.w3.org/TR/xhtml1/DTD/xhtml1-transitional.dtd">]]>
      </f:verbatim>
      <html xmlns="http://www.w3.org/1999/xhtml">
         <head>
            <title>A Simple Java Server Faces Application</title>
         </head>
         <body>
            <h:form>
               . . .
            </h:form>
         </body>
      </html>
   </f:view>
</jsp:root>
```

If you use an XML-aware editor, you should seriously consider this form.

 CAUTION: You sometimes see naive page authors produce documents that start with an HTML DOCTYPE declaration, like this:

```
<!DOCTYPE HTML PUBLIC "-//W3C//DTD HTML 4.01 Transitional//EN">
<html>
   <%@ taglib uri="http://java.sun.com/jsf/html" prefix="h" %>
   <%@ taglib uri="http://java.sun.com/jsf/core" prefix="f" %>
   <f:view>

   . . .
```

This may have been acceptable at one time, but nowadays, it is quite reprehensible. Plainly, this document is *not* an "HTML 4.01 Transitional" document. It merely aims to produce such a document. Many XML editors and tools don't take it kindly when you lie about the document type. Therefore, either omit the DOCTYPE altogether or follow the outline given in the preceding note.

Navigation

To complete our JSF application, we need to specify the navigation rules. A navigation rule tells the JSF implementation which page to send back to the browser after a form has been submitted.

In this case, navigation is simple. When the user clicks the "Login" button, we want to navigate from the index.jsp page to welcome.jsp. You specify this navigation rule in the faces-config.xml file:

```
<navigation-rule>
    <from-view-id>/index.jsp</from-view-id>
    <navigation-case>
        <from-outcome>login</from-outcome>
        <to-view-id>/welcome.jsp</to-view-id>
    </navigation-case>
</navigation-rule>
```

The from-outcome value matches the action attribute of the command button of the index.jsp page:

```
<h:commandButton value="Login" action="login"/>
```

In addition to the navigation rules, the faces-config.xml file contains the bean definitions. Here is the definition of the user bean.

```
<managed-bean>
    <managed-bean-name>user</managed-bean-name>
    <managed-bean-class>
        com.corejsf.UserBean
    </managed-bean-class>
    <managed-bean-scope>session</managed-bean-scope>
</managed-bean>
```

You can use the bean name, user, in the attributes of the user interface components. For example, index.jsp contains the tag

```
<h:inputText value="#{user.name}"/>
```

The value attribute refers to the name property of the user bean. (The #{...} delimiters denote the fact that user.name is a "value binding expression." We explain this syntax in Chapter 2.)

The managed-bean-class tag simply specifies the bean class, in our case, com.corejsf.UserBean. Finally, the scope is set to session. That means that the bean object is available for one user across multiple pages. Different users who use the web application are given different instances of the bean object.

Listing 1–4 shows the complete faces-config.xml file.

Listing 1–4   login/WEB-INF/faces-config.xml

```
1. <?xml version="1.0"?>
2.
3. <!DOCTYPE faces-config PUBLIC
4.    "-//Sun Microsystems, Inc.//DTD JavaServer Faces Config 1.0//EN"
5.    "http://java.sun.com/dtd/web-facesconfig_1_0.dtd">
6.
7. <faces-config>
8.    <navigation-rule>
9.       <from-view-id>/index.jsp</from-view-id>
10.       <navigation-case>
11.          <from-outcome>login</from-outcome>
12.          <to-view-id>/welcome.jsp</to-view-id>
13.       </navigation-case>
14.    </navigation-rule>
15.
16.    <managed-bean>
17.       <managed-bean-name>user</managed-bean-name>
18.       <managed-bean-class>com.corejsf.UserBean</managed-bean-class>
19.       <managed-bean-scope>session</managed-bean-scope>
20.    </managed-bean>
21. </faces-config>
```

Servlet Configuration

When you deploy a JSF application inside an application server, you need to supply a configuration file named web.xml. Fortunately, you can use the same web.xml file for most JSF applications. Listing 1–5 shows the file.

Listing 1–5   login/WEB-INF/web.xml

```
1. <?xml version="1.0"?>
2.
3. <!DOCTYPE web-app PUBLIC
4.    "-//Sun Microsystems, Inc.//DTD Web Application 2.3//EN"
5.    "http://java.sun.com/dtd/web-app_2_3.dtd">
6.
7. <web-app>
8.    <servlet>
9.       <servlet-name>Faces Servlet</servlet-name>
10.       <servlet-class>javax.faces.webapp.FacesServlet</servlet-class>
11.       <load-on-startup>1</load-on-startup>
12.    </servlet>
13.
```

Listing 1–5   login/WEB-INF/web.xml (cont.)

```
14.    <servlet-mapping>
15.        <servlet-name>Faces Servlet</servlet-name>
16.        <url-pattern>*.faces</url-pattern>
17.    </servlet-mapping>
18.
19.    <welcome-file-list>
20.        <welcome-file>index.html</welcome-file>
21.    </welcome-file-list>
22. </web-app>
```

The only remarkable aspect of this file is the *servlet mapping*. All JSF pages are processed by a special servlet that is a part of the JSF implementation code. To ensure that the correct servlet is activated when a JSF page is requested, the JSF URLs have a special format. In our configuration, they have an extension .faces. For example, you cannot simply point your browser to http://localhost:8080/login/index.jsp. The URL has to be http://localhost:8080/login/index.faces. The servlet container uses the servlet mapping rule to activate the JSF servlet, which strips off the faces suffix and loads the index.jsp page.

 NOTE: You can also define a *prefix mapping* instead of the .faces extension mapping. Use the following directive in your web.xml file:

```
<servlet-mapping>
    <servlet-name>Faces Servlet</servlet-name>
    <url-pattern>/faces/*</url-pattern>
</servlet-mapping>
```

Then use the URL http://localhost:8080/login/faces/index.jsp. That URL activates the JSF servlet, which then strips off the faces prefix and loads the file /login/index.jsp.

NOTE: If you want to use a .jsf extension for JSF page files, then you need to configure your web application so that it invokes the JSP servlet for files with that extension. In Tomcat, you use the following mapping in the web.xml file:

```
<servlet-mapping>
    <servlet-name>jsp</servlet-name>
    <url-pattern>*.jsf</url-pattern>
</servlet-mapping>
```

You now need to tell the JSF implementation to map the .faces extension of the URLs to the .jsf extension of the associated files.

```
<context-param>
    <param-name>javax.faces.DEFAULT_SUFFIX</param-name>
```

```
    <param-value>.jsf</param-value>
</context-param>
```

Note that this configuration affects only the web developers, not the users of your web application. The URLs still have a `.faces` extension or `/faces` prefix.

The Welcome File

Many web designers rely on web servers to load the `index.html` or `index.jsp` page when they are given a directory URL. Unfortunately, that mechanism doesn't work smoothly with JSF pages. For example, if a user visits the URL http://localhost:8080/login, then Tomcat should *not* load `index.jsp`. Doing so would skip the JavaServer Faces processing phase.

To overcome this issue, you can supply an `index.html` file that automatically redirects the user to the start of the application, using the proper faces URL. Listing 1–6 shows such an index file.

Listing 1–6	login/index.html

```
1. <html>
2.    <head>
3.       <meta http-equiv="Refresh" content= "0; URL=index.faces"/>
4.       <title>Start Web Application</title>
5.    </head>
6.    <body>
7.       <p>Please wait for the web application to start.</p>
8.    </body>
9. </html>
```

Finally, it is a good idea to specify `index.html` as the "welcome file" in `web.xml`. See the `welcome-file` tag in Listing 1–5 on page 18.

> NOTE: The `index.html` file redirects the browser to the `index.faces` URL. It is slightly more efficient to use a JSP forward action instead. Create a page, say, `start.jsp`, that contains the line
>
> `<jsp:forward page="/index.faces"/>`
>
> Then set this page as the `welcome-file` in the `web.xml` configuration file.

Visual Development Environments

We produced the JSF pages and configuration files for this application with a text editor. However, we expect that many JSF programmers will use visual development environments once they become available. A visual environment displays a graphical representation of the components and allows a designer to drag and drop components from a palette. Figure 1–7 shows a prerelease of Sun Java Studio Creator (http://www.sun.com/software/products/jscreator). The component palette is in the lower-left corner. You drag the components onto the center of the window and customize them with the property sheet in the upper-right corner. The environment produces the corresponding JSF tags automatically (see Figure 1–8).

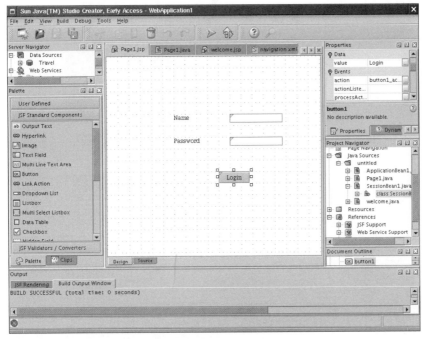

Figure 1–7   Visual JSF Development Environment

Moreover, visual environments give you graphical interfaces for specifying the navigation rules and beans—see Figure 1–9. Those environments automatically produce the faces-config.xml file.

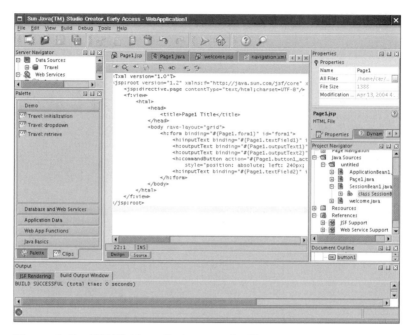

Figure 1–8   JSF Markup Is Automatically Generated

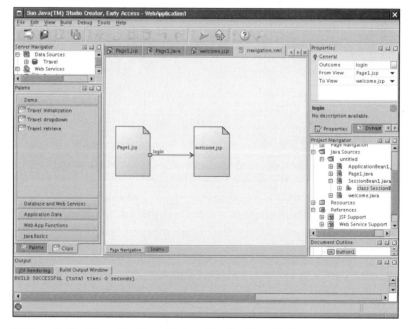

Figure 1–9   Visually Specifying Navigation Rules

JSF Framework Services

Now that you have seen your first JSF application, it is easier to explain the services that the JSF framework offers to developers. Figure 1–10 gives a high-level overview of the JSF architecture. As you can see, the JSF framework is responsible for interacting with client devices, and it provides tools for tying together the visual presentation, application logic, and business logic of a web application. However, the scope of JSF is restricted to the presentation tier. Database persistence, web services, and other back-end connections are outside the scope of JSF.

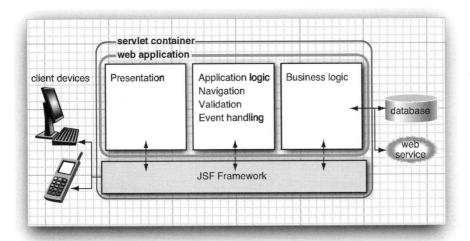

Figure 1–10   High-Level Overview of the JSF Framework

Here are the most important services that the JSF framework provides.

- Model-View-Controller Architecture

    All software applications let users manipulate certain data, such as shopping carts, travel itineraries, or whatever data are required in a particular problem domain. These data are called the *model*. Just like an artist creates a painting of a model in a studio, a software developer produces *views* of the data model. In a web application, HTML (or a similar rendering technology) is used to paint these views.

    JSF connects the view and the model. As you have seen, a view component can be wired to a bean property of a model object, such as

    ```
    <h:inputText value="#{user.name}"/>
    ```

Moreover, JSF operates as the *controller* that reacts to the user by processing action and value change events, routing them to code that updates the model or the view. For example, you may want to invoke a method to check whether a user is allowed to log in. Use the following JSF tag:

```
<h:commandButton value="Login" action="#{user.check}"/>
```

When the button is clicked and the form is submitted to the server, the JSF implementation invokes the `check` method of the `user` bean. That method can perform arbitrary updates to the model, and it returns the navigation ID of the next page to be displayed. We discuss this mechanism further in Chapter 3.

Thus, JSF implements the classical model-view-controller architecture.

- Data Conversion

  Users enter data into web forms as text. Business objects want data as numbers, dates, or other data types. As explained in Chapter 6, JSF makes it easy to specify and customize conversion rules.

- Validation and Error Handling

  JSF makes it easy to attach validation rules for fields such as "this field is required" or "this field must be a number." Of course, when users enter invalid data, you need to display appropriate error messages. JSF takes away much of the tedium of this programming task. We cover validation in Chapter 6.

- Internationalization

  JSF manages internationalization issues such as character encodings and the selection of resource bundles. We cover resource bundles in Chapter 2.

- Custom Components

  Component developers can develop sophisticated components that page designers simply drop into their pages. For example, suppose a component developer produces a calendar component with all the usual bells and whistles. You just use it in your page, with a command such as

  ```
  <acme:calendar value="#{flight.departure}" startOfWeek="Mon"/>
  ```

  Chapter 9 covers custom components in detail.

- Alternative Renderers

  By default, JSF generates markup for HTML pages. But it is easy to extend the JSF framework to produce markup for another page description language such as WML or XUL. In Chapter 11, we show you how to use JSF to communicate with J2ME-powered cell phones.

- Tool Support

  JSF is optimized for use with automated tools. As these tools mature in the coming years, we believe that JSF will be the must-have framework for developing web interfaces with Java.

Behind the Scenes

Now that you have read about the "what" and the "why" of JavaServer Faces, you may be curious just how the JSF framework does its job.

Let us look behind the scenes of our sample application. We'll start at the point when the browser first connects to http://localhost:8080/login/index.faces. The JSF servlet initializes the JSF code and reads the index.jsp page. That page contains tags such as f:form and h:inputText. Each tag has an associated *tag handler* class. When the page is read, the tag handlers are executed. The JSF tag handlers collaborate with each other to build a *component tree* (see Figure 1–11).

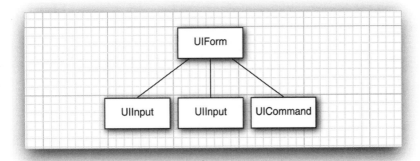

Figure 1–11   Component Tree of the Sample Application

The component tree is a data structure that contains Java objects for all user interface elements on the JSF page. For example, the two UIInput objects correspond to the h:inputText and h:inputSecret fields in the JSF file.

Rendering Pages

Next, the HTML page is *rendered*. All text that is not a JSF tag is simply passed through. The h:form, h:inputText, h:inputSecret, and h:commandButton tags are converted to HTML.

As we just discussed, each of these tags gives rise to an associated component. Each component has a *renderer* that produces HTML output, reflecting the component state. For example, the renderer for the component that corresponds to the h:inputText tag produces the following output:

```
<input type="text" name="unique ID" value="current value"/>
```

This process is called *encoding*. The renderer of the UIInput object asks the framework to look up the unique ID of the HTML element and the current value of the expression user.name. By default, ID strings (such as _id0:_id1) are assigned by the framework.

The encoded page is sent to the browser, and the browser displays it in the usual way (see Figure 1–12).

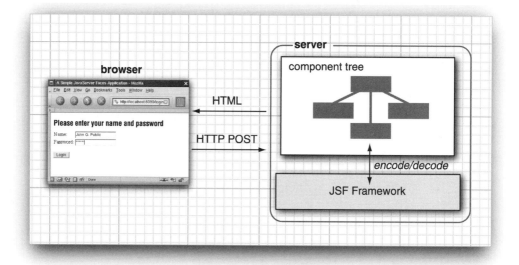

Figure 1–12   Encoding and Decoding JSF Pages

> TIP: Select View->Page source from the browser menu to see the HTML output of the rendering process. Figure 1–13 shows a typical output. This is useful for debugging JSF problems.

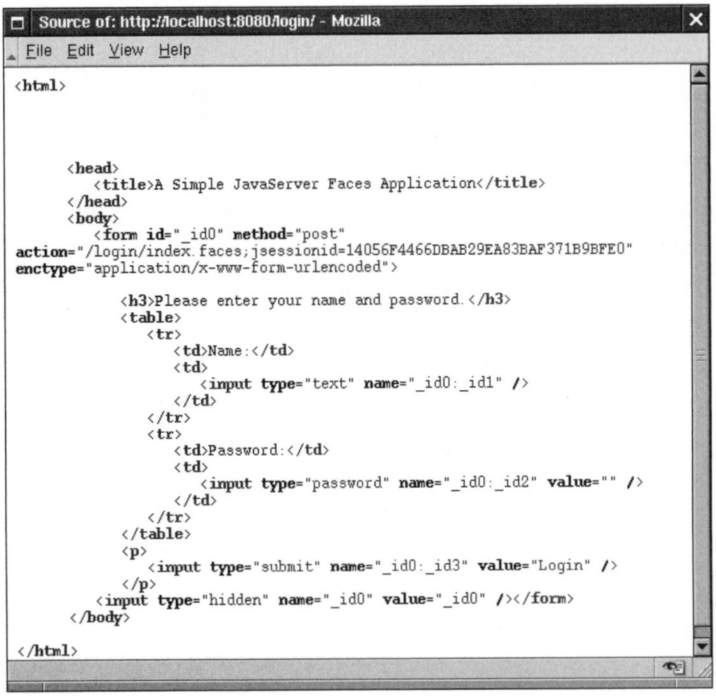

```
┌─────────────────────────────────────────────────────────────────┐
│ □  Source of: http://localhost:8080/login/ - Mozilla          ✕  │
├─────────────────────────────────────────────────────────────────┤
│ ▲ File  Edit  View  Help                                          │
├─────────────────────────────────────────────────────────────────┤
│ <html>                                                         ▲  │
│                                                                   │
│                                                                   │
│         <head>                                                    │
│           <title>A Simple JavaServer Faces Application</title>    │
│         </head>                                                   │
│         <body>                                                    │
│           <form id="_id0" method="post"                          │
│ action="/login/index.faces;jsessionid=14056F4466DBAB29EA83BAF371B9BFE0" │
│ enctype="application/x-www-form-urlencoded">                      │
│                                                                   │
│               <h3>Please enter your name and password.</h3>      │
│               <table>                                             │
│                 <tr>                                             │
│                   <td>Name:</td>                                 │
│                   <td>                                           │
│                     <input type="text" name="_id0:_id1" />       │
│                   </td>                                           │
│                 </tr>                                            │
│                 <tr>                                             │
│                   <td>Password:</td>                             │
│                   <td>                                           │
│                     <input type="password" name="_id0:_id2" value="" /> │
│                   </td>                                           │
│                 </tr>                                            │
│               </table>                                           │
│               <p>                                               │
│                 <input type="submit" name="_id0:_id3" value="Login" /> │
│               </p>                                              │
│             <input type="hidden" name="_id0" value="_id0" /></form> │
│           </body>                                                │
│                                                                   │
│ </html>                                                        ▼  │
│                                                              🐭⃠  │
└─────────────────────────────────────────────────────────────────┘
```

Figure 1–13   Viewing the Source of the Login Page

Decoding Requests

After the page is displayed in the browser, the user fills in the form fields and clicks the "Login" button. The browser sends the *form data* back to the web server, formatted as a "POST request." This is a special format, defined as part of the HTTP protocol. The POST request contains the URL of the form (/login/index.faces), as well as the form data.

NOTE: The URL for the POST request is the same as that of the request that renders the form. Navigation to a new page occurs after the form has been submitted.

The form data is a string of ID/value pairs, such as

```
_id0:_id1=me&_id0:_id2=secret&_id0:_id3=Login&_id0=_id0
```

As part of the normal servlet processing, the form data is placed in a hash table that all components can access.

Next, the JSF framework gives each component a chance to inspect that hash table, a process called *decoding*. Each component decides on its own how to interpret the form data.

The login form has three component objects: two UIInput objects that correspond to the text fields on the form and a UICommand object that corresponds to the submit button.

- The UIInput components update the bean properties referenced in the value attributes: they invoke the setter methods with the values that the user supplied.

- The UICommand component checks whether the button was clicked. If so, it fires an *action event* to launch the login action referenced in the action attribute. That event tells the navigation handler to look up the successor page, welcome.jsp.

Now the cycle repeats.

You have just seen the two most important processing steps of the JSF framework: encoding and decoding. However, the processing sequence (also called the "life cycle") is a bit more intricate. If everything goes well, you don't need to worry about the intricacies of the life cycle. However, when an error occurs, you will definitely want to understand what the framework does. In the next section, we look at the life cycle in greater detail.

The Life Cycle

The JSF specification defines six distinct *phases*, as shown in Figure 1–14. The normal flow of control is shown with solid lines; alternative flows are shown with dashed lines.

The *Restore View* phase retrieves the component tree for the requested page if it was displayed previously or constructs a new component tree if it is displayed for the first time. If the page was displayed previously, all components are set to their prior state. This means that JSF automatically retains form information. For example, when a user posts illegal data that are rejected during decoding, the old inputs are redisplayed so that the user can correct them.

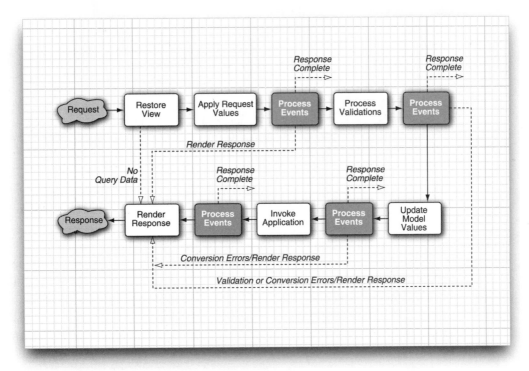

Figure 1–14   The JavaServer Faces Life Cycle

If the request has no query data, the JSF implementation skips ahead to the Render Response phase. This happens when a page is displayed for the first time. Otherwise, the next phase is the *Apply Request Values* phase. In this phase, the JSF implementation iterates over the component objects in the component tree. Each component object checks which request values belong to it and stores them.

> NOTE: In addition to extracting request information, the "Apply Request Values" phase adds events to an event queue when a command button or link has been clicked. We discuss event handling in detail in Chapter 7. As you can see in Figure 1–14, events can be executed after each phase. In specialized situations, an event handler can "bail out" and skip to the Render Response phase or even terminate request processing altogether.

In the *Process Validations* phase, the submitted string values are first converted to "submitted values," which can be objects of any type. When you design a JSF page, you can attach *validators* that perform correctness checks on the local values. If validation passes, the JSF life cycle proceeds normally. However, when conversion or validation errors occur, the JSF implementation invokes the Render Response phase directly, redisplaying the current page so that the user has another chance to provide correct inputs.

> **NOTE:** To many programmers, this is the most surprising aspect of the JSF life cycle. If a converter or validator fails, the current page is simply redisplayed. You should add tags to display the validation errors so that your users know why they see the old page again. See Chapter 6 for details.

After the converters and validators have done their work, it is assumed that it is safe to update the model data. During the *Update Model* phase, the local values are used to update the beans that are wired to the components.

In the *Invoke Application* phase, the action method of the button or link component that caused the form submission is executed. That method can carry out arbitrary application processing. It returns an outcome string that is passed to the navigation handler. The navigation handler looks up the next page.

Finally, the *Render Response* phase encodes the response and sends it to the browser. When a user submits a form, clicks on a link, or otherwise generates a new request, the cycle starts anew.

You have now seen the basic mechanisms that make the JSF magic possible. In the following chapters, we examine the various parts of the life cycle in more detail.

Automation of the Build Process with Ant

The manual build process that we described earlier in this chapter can become tedious if you need to do it over and over. In this section, we describe how you can automate the process. The material in this section is not required for working with JSF—feel free to skip it if the manual build process doesn't bother you.

We recommend the Ant tool for automating the building and deployment of JSF applications. Ant is not required to work with JSF, but we find it convenient and easy to learn. In fact, you need not know much about Ant at all if you simply want to use the build script that we prepared.

Download Ant from http://ant.apache.org and install it in a directory of your choice. The page http://ant.apache.org/resources.html contains links to tutorials and other information about Ant.

Ant takes directions from a *build file*. By default, the build file is named build.xml. We provide a build.xml file for building JSF applications. This file is contained inside the root of the corejsf-examples directory. The build.xml file contains the instructions for compiling, copying, zipping, and deploying to Tomcat, described in XML syntax.

The file is rather long and we won't reproduce it in its entirety. Listing 1–7 contains the most important elements.

Listing 1–7　`build.xml`

```
1.  <project default="install">
2.
3.      <property file="build.properties"/>
4.      <property name="appdir" value="${basedir}/${app}"/>
5.      <property name="builddir" value="${appdir}/build"/>
6.      <basename property="appname" file="${appdir}"/>
7.      <property name="warfile" value="${builddir}/${appname}.war"/>
8.
9.      <path id="classpath">
10.         <pathelement location="${servlet.api.jar}"/>
11.         <pathelement location="${jsp.api.jar}"/>
12.         <fileset dir="${builddir}/WEB-INF/lib">
13.             <include name="*.jar"/>
14.         </fileset>
15.     </path>
16.
17.     <target name="init">
18.         <tstamp/>
19.         <fail unless="app" message="Run ant -Dapp=..."/>
20.     </target>
21.
22.     <target name="prepare" depends="init"
23.         description="Create build directory.">
24.         <mkdir dir="${builddir}"/>
25.     </target>
26.
27.     <target name="copy" depends="prepare"
28.         description="Copy files to build directory.">
29.         <copy todir="${builddir}">
30.             <fileset dir="${appdir}">
31.                 <exclude name="**/*.java"/>
32.                 <exclude name="build/**"/>
33.             </fileset>
34.         </copy>
35.         <copy todir="${builddir}/WEB-INF/lib">
36.             <fileset dir="${jsf.lib.dir}" includes="${jsf.libs}"/>
37.             <fileset dir="${jstl.lib.dir}" includes="${jstl.libs}"/>
38.             <fileset dir="${commons.lib.dir}" includes="${commons.libs}"/>
39.         </copy>
40.     </target>
```

Listing 1–7   `build.xml (cont.)`

```
1.    <target name="compile" depends="copy"
1.        description="Compile source files.">
1.        <javac
1.            srcdir="${appdir}/WEB-INF/classes"
1.            destdir="${builddir}/WEB-INF/classes"
1.            debug="true"
1.            deprecation="true">
1.            <include name="**/*.java"/>
1.            <classpath refid="classpath"/>
1.        </javac>
1.    </target>
1.
1.    <target name="war" depends="compile"
1.        description="Build WAR file.">
1.        <delete file="${warfile}"/>
1.        <jar jarfile="${warfile}" basedir="${builddir}"/>
1.    </target>
1.
1.    <target name="install" depends="war"
1.        description="Deploy web application.">
1.        <copy file="${warfile}" todir="${tomcat.dir}/webapps"/>
1.    </target>
1.
1. </project>
```

To use this build file, you must customize the `build.properties` file that is contained in the same directory (see Listing 1–8). The default file looks like this.

Listing 1–8   `build.properties`

```
1. jsf.dir=/usr/local/jsf-1_0
2. tomcat.dir=/usr/local/jakarta-tomcat-5.0.19
3.
4. username=me
5. password=secret
6. manager.url=http://localhost:8080/manager
7.
8. jsp.api.jar=${tomcat.dir}/common/lib/jsp-api.jar
9. jsp.api.jar=${jsp.lib.dir}/jsp-api.jar
10.
11. jsf.lib.dir=${jsf.dir}/lib
12. jstl.lib.dir=${tomcat.dir}/webapps/jsp-examples/WEB-INF/lib
13. commons.lib.dir=${tomcat.dir}/server/lib
14.
15. jsf.libs=jsf-api.jar,jsf-impl.jar
16. jstl.libs=jstl.jar,standard.jar
17. commons.libs=commons-beanutils.jar,commons-digester.jar
```

You need to change the directories for Tomcat and JSF to match your local installation. Simply edit the first two lines of build.properties. On Windows, remember to use forward slashes for file separators.

Now you are ready to build the sample application (see Figure 1–15).

1. Open a command shell and change into the corejsf-examples directory.

2. Run the command

   apache-ant/bin/ant -Dapp=ch1/login

   Here, *apache-ant* is the directory into which you installed Ant, such as c:\apache-ant-1.6.1.

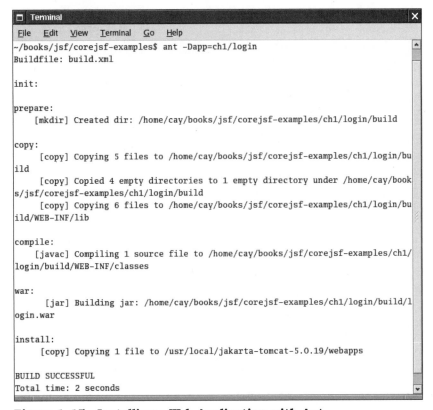

```
Terminal                                                            X
File   Edit   View   Terminal   Go   Help
~/books/jsf/corejsf-examples$ ant -Dapp=ch1/login
Buildfile: build.xml

init:

prepare:
    [mkdir] Created dir: /home/cay/books/jsf/corejsf-examples/ch1/login/build

copy:
    [copy] Copying 5 files to /home/cay/books/jsf/corejsf-examples/ch1/login/bu
ild
    [copy] Copied 4 empty directories to 1 empty directory under /home/cay/book
s/jsf/corejsf-examples/ch1/login/build
    [copy] Copying 6 files to /home/cay/books/jsf/corejsf-examples/ch1/login/bu
ild/WEB-INF/lib

compile:
    [javac] Compiling 1 source file to /home/cay/books/jsf/corejsf-examples/ch1/
login/build/WEB-INF/classes

war:
    [jar] Building jar: /home/cay/books/jsf/corejsf-examples/ch1/login/build/l
ogin.war

install:
    [copy] Copying 1 file to /usr/local/jakarta-tomcat-5.0.19/webapps

BUILD SUCCESSFUL
Total time: 2 seconds
```

Figure 1–15   Installing a Web Application with Ant

 TIP: You'll be running ant all the time. We suggest that you add the apache-ant/bin directory to the PATH environment variable.

> NOTE: Our Ant script is a bit different from the scripts of the sample applications in the JSF distribution. We use a single script that can build almost all applications in the book. You use the -Dapp=... flag to specify the name of the application that you want to build. We think that approach is better than supplying lots of nearly identical scripts. Note that you call the script from the *corejsf-examples* directory, not the directory of the application.

Using the Deployment Manager with Ant

The build.xml file of the preceding section exactly imitates the manual deployment process by copying the WAR file to the Tomcat directory. This deployment method relies on the "auto deploy" feature of Tomcat. When "auto deploy" is turned on, Tomcat checks the timestamp of the WAR file before fulfilling a web request. When the WAR file has changed, Tomcat discards the old pages and Java classes and reads the new versions from the WAR file. This behavior is activated by default, but you can turn it off by editing the *tomcat/* conf/server.xml file.

In our experience, automatic deployment works well most of the time, but there are occasional glitches. Sometimes, there is a slight delay before the new version of the application becomes available. Occasionally, you will find that Tomcat is in an inconsistent state, and you have to restart it.

We prefer to use the Tomcat deployment manager instead. The build.xml file in in the corejsf-examples directory defines several tasks for this purpose (which are not shown in Listing 1–7). You need to carry out several configuration steps to activate them.

1. Edit the file *tomcat*/conf/tomcat-users.xml. Anywhere inside the tomcat-users tag add the tag

   ```
   <user username="me" password="secret" roles="manager"/>
   ```

   This tag defines a user who is allowed to add and remove web applications. Of course, if your computer is publicly accessible, you should use secure values for the username and password.

2. If you changed the manager username and password, edit the build.properties file and update the username and password settings.

3. Copy the following file to the *apache-ant*/lib directory:

   tomcat/server/lib/catalina-ant.jar

   This file is required by the Ant tasks for installing web applications.

When you want to deploy a new web application, first make sure that Tomcat is running. Then issue the command

apache-ant/bin/ant -Dapp=ch1/login deploy

Your application will now be deployed to the servlet container.

 TIP: If Ant complains that it does not know the deploy task, double-check that you added catalina-ant.jar to the *apache-ant*/lib directory.

If your application is already deployed and you try to deploy it again, the deploy task throws an exception. In that case, you need to undeploy it first. Use the command

apache-ant/bin/ant -Dapp=ch1/login undeploy

Then deploy the application again.

 TIP: We found it tedious to remember whether our application was currently deployed or not. Our Ant script contains a task redeploy that automatically undeploys and redeploys an application. However, undeploying a nonexistent application throws an exception that terminates Ant. We overcame that problem by using the handy ant-contrib library from http://ant-contrib.sourceforge.net. If you want to use the redeploy task, you need to download and install the library. Next, copy the JAR file in the lib subdirectory of the ant-contrib installation into the *apache-ant*/lib directory. Then simply issue the command

apache-ant/bin/ant -Dapp=*chapter/appname* redeploy

You need not worry whether or not the application was previously deployed.

MANAGED BEANS

Topics in This Chapter

Chapter 2

A central theme of web application design is the separation of presentation and business logic. JSF uses *beans* to achieve this separation. JSF pages refer to bean properties, and the business logic is contained in the bean implementation code. Because beans are so fundamental to JSF programming, we discuss them in detail in this chapter.

The first half of the chapter discusses the essential features of beans that every JSF developer needs to know. We then present an example program that puts these essentials to work. The remaining sections cover more technical aspects about bean configuration and value binding expressions. You can safely skip these sections when you first read this book, and return to them when the need arises.

Definition of a Bean

According to the JavaBeans specification (available at http://java.sun.com/products/javabeans/), a Java Bean is "a reusable software component that can be manipulated in a builder tool." That is a pretty broad definition, and indeed, as you will see in this chapter, beans are used for a wide variety of purposes.

At first glance, a bean seems to be similar to an object. However, beans serve a different purpose. Objects are created and manipulated inside a Java program when the program calls constructors and invokes methods. However, beans can be configured and manipulated *without programming*.

> NOTE: You may wonder where the term "bean" comes from. Well, Java is a synonym for coffee (at least in the United States), and coffee is made from beans that encapsulate its flavor. You may find the analogy cute or annoying, but the term has stuck.

The "classic" application for JavaBeans is a user-interface builder. A palette window in the builder tool contains component beans such as text fields, sliders, check boxes, and so on. Instead of writing user interface code, a user-interface designer drags and drops component beans into a form and customizes them, by selecting property values from a dialog (see Figure 2–1).

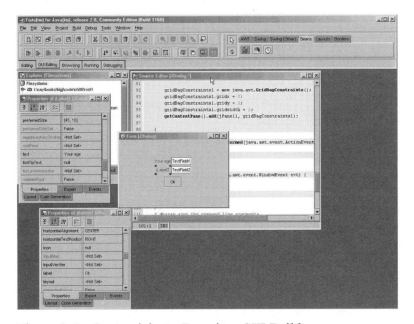

Figure 2–1   Customizing a Bean in a GUI Builder

In the context of JavaServer Faces, beans go beyond user interface components. You use beans whenever you need to wire up Java classes with web pages or configuration files.

Consider the login application in Chapter 1. A UserBean instance is configured in the faces-config.xml file:

```
<managed-bean>
   <managed-bean-name>user</managed-bean-name>
   <managed-bean-class>com.corejsf.UserBean</managed-bean-class>
   <managed-bean-scope>session</managed-bean-scope>
</managed-bean>
```

This means: Construct an object of the class com.corejsf.UserBean, give it the name user, and keep it alive for the duration of the *session*, that is, for all requests that originate from the same client.

Once the bean has been defined, it can be accessed by JSF components. For example, this input field reads and updates the password property of the user bean.

```
<h:inputSecret value="#{user.password}"/>
```

As you can see, the JSF developer does not need to write any code to construct and manipulate the user bean.

In a JSF application, beans are commonly used for the following purposes:

*   For user interface components (traditional user interface beans)
*   For tying together the behavior of a web form (called "backing beans")
*   For business objects whose properties are displayed on web pages
*   For services such as external data sources that need to be configured when an application is assembled

Because beans are so ubiquitous, we now turn to a review of those parts of the JavaBeans specification that are relevant to JSF programmers.

Bean Properties

Bean classes need to follow specific programming conventions in order to expose features that tools can use. We discuss these conventions in this section.

The most important features of a bean are the properties that it exposes. A *property* is any attribute of a bean that has

*   a name
*   a type
*   methods for getting and/or setting the property value

For example, the UserBean class of the preceding chapter has a property with name password and type String. The methods getPassword and setPassword access the property value.

Some programming languages, in particular Visual Basic and C#, have direct support for properties. However, in Java, a bean is simply a class that follows certain coding conventions.

The JavaBeans specification puts a single demand on a bean class: It must have a default constructor, that is, a constructor without parameters. However, in order to define properties, a bean must either use a *naming pattern* for property getters and setters, or it must define property descriptors. The latter approach is quite tedious and not commonly used, and we will not discuss it here. See *Horstmann & Cornell, Core Java vol. 2 ch. 8, Sun Microsystems Press 2003* for more information.

Defining properties with naming patterns is straightforward. Consider the following pair of methods:

```
T getFoo()
void setFoo(T newValue)
```

The pair corresponds to a read-write property with type T and name foo. If you only have the first method, then the property is read-only. If you only have the second method, then the property is write-only.

The method names and signatures must match the pattern precisely. The method name must start with get or set. A get method must have no parameters. A set method must have one parameter and no return value. A bean class can have other methods, but they do not yield bean properties.

Note that the name of the property is the "decapitalized" form of the part of the method name that follows the get or set prefix. For example, getFoo gives rise to a property named foo, with the first letter turned into lower case. However, if the first *two* letters after the prefix are upper case, then the first letter stays unchanged. For example, the method name getURL defines a property URL, and not uRL.

For properties of type boolean, you have a choice of prefixes for the method that reads the property. Both

```
boolean isConnected()
```

and

```
boolean getConnected()
```

are valid names for the reader of the connected property.

 NOTE: The JavaBean specification also defines indexed properties, specified by method sets such as the following:

```
T[] getFoo()
T getFoo(int index)
void setFoo(T[] newArray)
void setFoo(int index, T newValue)
```

However, JSF provides no support for accessing the indexed values.

The JavaBeans specification is silent on the *behavior* of the getter and setter methods. In many situations, these methods will simply manipulate an instance field. But they may equally well carry out more sophisticated operations, such as database lookups, data conversion, validation, and so on.

A bean class may have other methods beyond property getters and setters. Of course, those methods do not give rise to bean properties.

Value Binding Expressions

Many JSF user interface components have an attribute value that lets you specify either a value or a *binding* to a value that is obtained from a bean property. For example, you can specify a direct value.

```
<h:outputText value="Hello, World!"/>
```

Or you can specify a value binding.

```
<h:outputText value="#{user.name}"/>
```

In most situations, a value binding expression such as #{user.name} describes a property. Note that the binding can be used both for reading and writing when it is used in an input component, such as

```
<h:inputText value="#{user.name}"/>
```

The property getter is invoked when the component is rendered. The property setter is invoked when the user response is processed.

We will discuss the syntax of value binding expressions in detail starting on page 60.

 NOTE: JSF value binding expressions are different from the JSTL/JSP 2.0 expression language. A JSTL expression always invokes property getters. For that reason, JSF uses the #{...} delimiters instead of the JSTL ${...} syntax.

Message Bundles

When you implement a web application, it is a good idea to collect all message strings in a central location. This process makes it easier to keep messages consistent and, crucially, makes it easier to localize your application for other locales

JSF simplifies this process. First, you collect your message strings in a file in the time-honored "properties" format:

```
currentScore=Your current score is:
guessNext=Guess the next number in the sequence!
```

 NOTE: Look into the API documentation of the load method of the java.util.Properties class for a precise description of the file format.

Save the file together with your classes, for example, in WEB-INF/classes/com/core-jsf/messages.properties. You can choose any directory path and file name, but you must use the extension .properties.

Add the f:loadBundle element to your JSF page, like this:

```
<f:loadBundle basename="com.corejsf.messages" var="msgs"/>
```

This element loads the messages in the bundle into a map variable with the name msgs, and stores that variable in request scope. (The base name looks like a class name, and indeed the properties file is loaded by the class loader.)

You can now use value binding expressions to access the message strings:

```
<h:outputText value="#{msgs.guessNext}"/>
```

That's all there is to it! When you are ready to localize your application for another locale, you simply supply localized bundle files.

When you localize a bundle file, you need to add a locale suffix to the file name: an underscore followed by the lowercase two-letter ISO-639 language code. For example, German strings would be in com/corejsf/messages_de.properties.

 NOTE: You can find a listing of all two- and three-letter ISO-639 language codes at http://www.loc.gov/standards/iso639-2/.

As part of the internationalization support in Java, the bundle that matches the current locale is automatically loaded. The default bundle without a locale prefix is used as a fallback when the appropriate localized bundle is not available. (See Chapter 10 of *Horstmann & Cornell, Core Java vol. 2* for a detailed description of Java internationalization.)

 NOTE: When you prepare translations, keep one oddity in mind: message bundle files are not encoded in UTF-8. Instead, Unicode characters beyond 127 are encoded as \uxxxx escape sequences. The Java SDK utility native2ascii can create these files.

You can have multiple bundles for a particular locale. For example, you may want to have separate bundles for commonly used error messages.

Once you have prepared your message bundles, you need to decide how to set the locale of your application. You have three choices:

- You can add a locale attribute to the f:view element, for example,

  ```
  <f:view locale="de">
  ```

- You can set the default and supported locales in WEB-INF/faces-config.xml (or another application configuration resource):

```
<faces-config>
  <application>
    <locale-config>
      <default-locale>en</default-locale>
      <supported-locale>de</supported-locale>
    </locale-config>
  </application>
</faces-config>
```

When a browser connects to your application, it usually includes an Accept-Language value in the HTTP header (see http://www.w3.org/International/ questions/qa-accept-lang-locales.html). JSF reads the header and finds the best match among the supported locales. You can test this feature by setting the preferred language in your browser—see Figure 2–2.

- You can call the setLocale method of the UIViewRoot object:

```
UIViewRoot viewRoot = FacesContext.getCurrentInstance().getViewRoot();
viewRoot.setLocale(new Locale("de"));
```

See chapter 7 for more information.

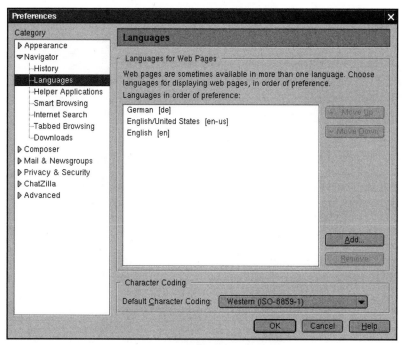

Figure 2–2   Selecting the Preferred Language

A Sample Application

After all these rather abstract rules and regulations, it is time for a concrete example. The application presents a series of quiz questions. Each question displays a sequence of numbers and asks the participant to guess the next number of the sequence.

For example, Figure 2–3 asks for the next number in the sequence

    3 1 4 1 5

You often find puzzles of this kind in tests that purport to measure intelligence. To solve the puzzle, you need to find the pattern. In this case, we have the first digits of π.

Type in the next number in the sequence (9), and the score goes up by one.

NOTE: There is a Java-compatible mnemonic for the digits of π: "Can I have a small container of coffee?" Count the letters in each word, and you get 3 1 4 1 5 9 2 6. See http://dir.yahoo.com/Science/Mathematics/Numerical_Analysis/ Numbers/Specific_Numbers/Pi/Mnemonics/ for more elaborate memorization aids.

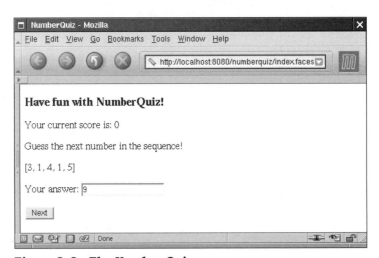

Figure 2–3   The Number Quiz

In this example, we place the quiz questions in the faces-config.xml file. Of course in a real application, you would be more likely to store this information in a database, but the purpose of the example is to demonstrate how to configure beans that have complex structure.

We start out with a ProblemBean class. A ProblemBean has two properties: solution, of type int, and sequence, of type ArrayList—see Listing 2–1.

Listing 2–1 numberquiz/WEB-INF/classes/com/corejsf/ProblemBean.java

```
 1. package com.corejsf;
 2. import java.util.ArrayList;
 3.
 4. public class ProblemBean {
 5.    private ArrayList sequence;
 6.    private int solution;
 7.
 8.    public ProblemBean() {}
 9.
10.    public ProblemBean(int[] values, int solution) {
11.       sequence = new ArrayList();
12.       for (int i = 0; i < values.length; i++)
13.          sequence.add(new Integer(values[i]));
14.       this.solution = solution;
15.    }
16.
17.    // PROPERTY: sequence
18.    public ArrayList getSequence() { return sequence; }
19.    public void setSequence(ArrayList newValue) { sequence = newValue; }
20.
21.    // PROPERTY: solution
22.    public int getSolution() { return solution; }
23.    public void setSolution(int newValue) { solution = newValue; }
24. }
```

Next, we define a bean for the quiz with the following properties:

- problems: a write-only property to set the quiz problems
- score: a read-only property to get the current score
- current: a read-only property to get the current quiz problem
- answer: a property to get and set the answer that the user provides

The problems property is unused in this sample program—we initialize the problem set in the QuizBean constructor. However, on page 57, you will see how to set up the problem set inside faces-config.xml, without having to write any code.

The current property is used to display the current problem. However, the value of the current property is a ProblemBean object, and we cannot directly display that object in a text field. We perform a second property access to get the number sequence:

```
<h:outputText value="#{quiz.current.sequence}"/>
```

The value of the sequence property is an ArrayList. When it is displayed, it is converted to a string by a call to the toString method. The result is a string of the form

```
[3, 1, 4, 1, 5]
```

Finally, we do a bit of dirty work with the answer property. We tie the answer property to the input field.

```
<h:inputText value="#{quiz.answer}"/>
```

When the input field is displayed, the getter is called, and we define the getAnswer method to return an empty string.

When the form is submitted, the setter is called with the value that the user typed into the input field. We define setAnswer to check the answer, update the score, and advance to the next problem.

```
public void setAnswer(String newValue) {
    try {
        int answer = Integer.parseInt(newValue.trim());
        if (getCurrent().getSolution() == answer) score++;
        currentIndex = (currentIndex + 1) % problems.size();
    }
    catch (NumberFormatException ex) {
    }
}
```

Strictly speaking, it is a bad idea to put code into a property setter that is unrelated to the task of setting the property. Updating the score and advancing to the next problem should really be contained in a handler for the button action. However, we have not yet discussed button actions, so we use the flexibility of the setter method to our advantage.

Another weakness of our sample application is that we haven't yet covered how to stop at the end of the quiz. Instead, we just wrap around to the beginning, letting the user rack up a higher score. You will learn in the next chapter how to do a better job. Remember—the point of this application is to show you how to configure and use beans.

Finally, note that we use message bundles for internationalization. Try switching your browser language to German, and the program will appear as in Figure 2–4.

This finishes our sample application. Figure 2–5 shows the directory structure. The remaining code is in Listings 2–2 through 2–6.

Figure 2–4   Viel Spaß mit dem Zahlenquiz!

Figure 2–5   The Directory Structure
            of the Number Quiz Example

Listing 2–2   numberquiz/index.jsp

```
1. <html>
2.    <%@ taglib uri="http://java.sun.com/jsf/html" prefix="h" %>
3.    <%@ taglib uri="http://java.sun.com/jsf/core" prefix="f" %>
4.
5.    <f:view>
6.       <f:loadBundle basename="com.corejsf.messages" var="msgs"/>
7.       <head>
8.          <title><h:outputText value="#{msgs.title}"/></title>
9.       </head>
```

Listing 2–2   numberquiz/index.jsp (cont.)

```
10.      <body>
11.        <h:form>
12.          <h3>
13.            <h:outputText value="#{msgs.heading}"/>
14.          </h3>
15.          <p>
16.            <h:outputText value="#{msgs.currentScore}"/>
17.            <h:outputText value="#{quiz.score}"/>
18.          </p>
19.          <p>
20.            <h:outputText value="#{msgs.guessNext}"/>
21.          </p>
22.          <p>
23.            <h:outputText value="#{quiz.current.sequence}"/>
24.          </p>
25.          <p>
26.            <h:outputText value="#{msgs.answer}"/>
27.            <h:inputText value="#{quiz.answer}"/></p>
28.          <p>
29.            <h:commandButton value="#{msgs.next}" action="next"/>
30.          </p>
31.        </h:form>
32.      </body>
33.    </f:view>
34. </html>
```

Listing 2–3   numberquiz/WEB-INF/classes/com/corejsf/QuizBean.java

```
1. package com.corejsf;
2. import java.util.ArrayList;
3.
4. public class QuizBean {
5.    private ArrayList problems = new ArrayList();
6.    private int currentIndex;
7.    private int score;
8.
9.    public QuizBean() {
10.      problems.add(
11.        new ProblemBean(new int[] { 3, 1, 4, 1, 5 }, 9)); // pi
12.      problems.add(
13.        new ProblemBean(new int[] { 1, 1, 2, 3, 5 }, 8)); // fibonacci
14.      problems.add(
15.        new ProblemBean(new int[] { 1, 4, 9, 16, 25 }, 36)); // squares
16.      problems.add(
```

Listing 2–3	numberquiz/WEB-INF/classes/com/corejsf/QuizBean.java (cont.)

```
17.        new ProblemBean(new int[] { 2, 3, 5, 7, 11 }, 13)); // primes
18.      problems.add(
19.        new ProblemBean(new int[] { 1, 2, 4, 8, 16 }, 32)); // powers of 2
20.    }
21.
22.    // PROPERTY: problems
23.    public void setProblems(ArrayList newValue) {
24.      problems = newValue;
25.      currentIndex = 0;
26.      score = 0;
27.    }
28.
29.    // PROPERTY: score
30.    public int getScore() { return score; }
31.
32.    // PROPERTY: current
33.    public ProblemBean getCurrent() {
34.      return (ProblemBean) problems.get(currentIndex);
35.    }
36.
37.    // PROPERTY: answer
38.    public String getAnswer() { return ""; }
39.    public void setAnswer(String newValue) {
40.      try {
41.        int answer = Integer.parseInt(newValue.trim());
42.        if (getCurrent().getSolution() == answer) score++;
43.        currentIndex = (currentIndex + 1) % problems.size();
44.      }
45.      catch (NumberFormatException ex) {
46.      }
47.    }
48. }
```

Listing 2–4	quizbean/WEB-INF/faces-config.xml

```
1. <?xml version="1.0"?>
2.
3. <!DOCTYPE faces-config PUBLIC
4.   "-//Sun Microsystems, Inc.//DTD JavaServer Faces Config 1.0//EN"
5.   "http://java.sun.com/dtd/web-facesconfig_1_0.dtd">
6.
7. <faces-config>
8.   <application>
9.     <locale-config>
10.       <default-locale>en</default-locale>
```

Listing 2–4	quizbean/WEB-INF/faces-config.xml (cont.)

```
11.          <supported-locale>de</supported-locale>
12.        </locale-config>
13.      </application>
14.
15.      <navigation-rule>
16.        <from-view-id>/index.faces</from-view-id>
17.        <navigation-case>
18.          <from-outcome>next</from-outcome>
19.          <to-view-id>/index.faces</to-view-id>
20.        </navigation-case>
21.      </navigation-rule>
22.
23.      <managed-bean>
24.        <managed-bean-name>quiz</managed-bean-name>
25.        <managed-bean-class>com.corejsf.QuizBean</managed-bean-class>
26.        <managed-bean-scope>session</managed-bean-scope>
27.      </managed-bean>
28.    </faces-config>
```

Listing 2–5	quizbean/WEB-INF/classes/com/corejsf/messsages.properties

```
1. title=NumberQuiz
2. heading=Have fun with NumberQuiz!
3. currentScore=Your current score is:
4. guessNext=Guess the next number in the sequence!
5. answer=Your answer:
6. next=Next
```

Listing 2–6	quizbean/WEB-INF/classes/com/corejsf/messsages_de.properties

```
1. title=Zahlenquiz
2. heading=Viel Spa\u00df mit dem Zahlenquiz!
3. currentScore=Ihre Punktzahl:
4. guessNext=Raten Sie die n\u00e4chste Zahl in der Folge!
5. answer=Ihre Antwort:
6. next=Weiter
```

Backing Beans

Sometimes, it is convenient to design a bean that contains some or all component objects of a web form. Such a bean is called a *backing bean* for the web form.

For example, we can turn the QuizBean into a backing bean by adding properties for the component on the form:

```
public class QuizBean {
   private UIOutput scoreComponent;
   private UIInput answerComponent;

   // PROPERTY: scoreComponent
   public UIOutput getScoreComponent() { return scoreComponent; }
   public void setScoreComponent(UIOutput newValue) { scoreComponent = newValue; }

   // PROPERTY: answerComponent
   public UIInput getAnswerComponent() { return answerComponent; }
   public void setAnswerComponent(UIInput newValue) { answerComponent = newValue; }
   ...
}
```

Output components belong to the UIOutput class and input components belong to the UIInput class. We will discuss these classes in greater detail in Chapter 9.

Why would you want such a bean? As we show in Chapters 6 and 7, it is sometimes necessary for validators and event handlers to have access to the actual components on a form. Moreover, visual JSF development environments generally use backing beans. These environments automatically generate the property getters and setters for all components that are dragged onto a form.

When you use a backing bean, you need to wire up the components on the form to those on the bean. You use the binding attribute for this purpose:

```
<h:outputText binding="#{quiz.scoreComponent}"/>
```

When the component tree for the form is built, the getScoreComponent method of the backing bean is called, but it returns null. As a result, an output component is constructed and installed into the backing bean with a call to setScoreComponent.

Backing beans have their uses, but they can also be abused. You should not use the user interface components as a repository for business data. If you use backing beans for your forms, you should still use beans for business objects.

Bean Scopes

For the convenience of the web application programmer, a servlet container provides separate scopes, each of which manages a table of name/value bindings. These scopes typically hold beans and other objects that need to be available in different components of a web application.

Request Scope

The *request scope* is short-lived. It starts when an HTTP request is submitted and ends when the response is sent back to the client. The f:loadBundle tag places the bundle variable in request scope. You would place an object into request scope only if you wanted to forward it to another processing phase inside the current request.

> **NOTE:** If a request is *forwarded* to another request, all name/value pairs stored in the request scope are carried over to the new request. On the other hand, if a request is *redirected*, the request data are lost.

Session Scope

Recall that the HTTP protocol is *stateless*. The browser sends a request to the server, the server returns a response, and then neither the browser nor the server has any obligation to keep any memory of the transaction. This simple arrangement works well for retrieving basic information, but it is unsatisfactory for server-side applications. For example, in a shopping application, you want the server to remember the contents of the shopping cart.

For that reason, servlet containers augment the HTTP protocol to keep track of a *session*, that is, repeated connections by the same client. There are various methods for session tracking. The simplest method uses *cookies*: name/value pairs that a server sends to a client, hoping to have them returned in subsequent requests (see Figure 2–6).

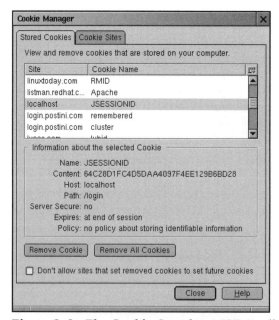

Figure 2–6   The Cookie Sent by a JSF Application

As long as the client doesn't deactivate cookies, the server receives a session identifier with each subsequent request.

Application servers use fallback strategies, such as *URL rewriting*, for dealing with those clients that don't return cookies. URL rewriting adds a session identifier to an URL, which looks somewhat like this:

```
http://corejsf.com/login/index.jsp;jsessionid=64C28D1FC...D28
```

Session tracking with cookies is completely transparent to the web developer, and the standard JSF tags automatically perform URL rewriting if a client does not use cookies.

The *session scope* persists from the time that a session is established until session termination. A session terminates if the web application invokes the `invalidate` method on the `HttpSession` object or if it times out.

Web applications typically place most of their beans into session scope.

For example, a `UserBean` can contain information about users that is accessible throughout the entire session. A `ShoppingCartBean` can be filled up gradually during the requests that make up a session.

Application Scope

Finally, the *application scope* persists for the entire duration of the web application. That scope is shared among all requests and all sessions.

You can see in Chapter 10 how to use the application scope for global beans such as LDAP directories.

Configuring Beans

This section describes how you can configure a bean in a configuration file. The details are rather technical. You may want to have a glance at this section and return to it when you need to configure beans with complex properties.

The most commonly used configuration file is `WEB-INF/faces-config.xml`. However, you can also place configuration information inside the following locations:

- Files named `META-INF/faces-config.xml` inside any JAR files loaded by the external context's class loader. (You use this mechanism if you deliver reusable components in a JAR file.)

- Files listed in the `javax.faces.CONFIG_FILES` initialization parameter inside `WEB-INF/web.xml`. For example,

```
<web-app>
   <context-param>
      <param-name>javax.faces.CONFIG_FILES</param-name>
```

```
        <param-value>WEB-INF/navigation.xml,WEB-INF/beans.xml</param-value>
    </context-param>
    ...
</web-app>
```

(This mechanism is attractive for builder tools because it separates navigation, beans, etc.)

For simplicity, we use WEB-INF/faces-config.xml in this chapter.

A bean is defined with a managed-bean element inside the top-level faces-config element. Minimally, you must specify the name, class, and scope of the bean.

```
<faces-config>
    <managed-bean>
        <managed-bean-name>user</managed-bean-name>
        <managed-bean-class>com.corejsf.UserBean</managed-bean-class>
        <managed-bean-scope>session</managed-bean-scope>
    </managed-bean>
</faces-config>
```

The scope can be request, session, application, or none. The none scope denotes an object that is not kept in one of the three scope maps. You use objects with scope none as building blocks when wiring up complex beans.

Setting Property Values

Let us start with a simple example. Here we customize a UserBean instance:

```
<managed-bean>
    <managed-bean-name>user</managed-bean-name>
    <managed-bean-class>com.corejsf.UserBean</managed-bean-class>
    <managed-bean-scope>session</managed-bean-scope>
    <managed-property>
        <property-name>name</property-name>
        <value>me</value>
    </managed-property>
    <managed-property>
        <property-name>password</property-name>
        <value>secret</value>
    </managed-property>
</managed-bean>
```

When the user bean is first looked up, it is constructed with the UserBean() default constructor. Then the setName and setPassword methods are executed.

To initialize a property with null, use a null-value element. For example,

```
<managed-property>
    <property-name>password</property-name>
    <null-value/>
</managed-property>
```

Initializing Lists and Maps

A special syntax initializes values that are of type List or Map. Here is an example of a list:

```
<list-entries>
    <value-class>java.lang.Integer</value.class>
    <value>3</value>
    <value>1</value>
    <value>4</value>
    <value>1</value>
    <value>5</value>
</list-entries>
```

Here we use the java.lang.Integer wrapper type since a List cannot hold values of primitive type.

The list can contain a mixture of value and null-value elements. The value-class is optional. If it is omitted, a list of java.lang.String objects is produced.

A map is more complex. You specify optional key-class and value-class elements (again, with a default of java.lang.String). Then you provide a sequence of map-entry elements, each of which has a key element followed by a value or null-value element.

Here is an example:

```
<map-entries>
    <key-class>java.lang.Integer</key-class>
    <map-entry>
        <key>1</key>
        <value>George Washington</value>
    </map-entry>
    <map-entry>
        <key>3</key>
        <value>Thomas Jefferson</value>
    </map-entry>
    <map-entry>
        <key>16</key>
        <value>Abraham Lincoln</value>
    </map-entry>
    <map-entry>
        <key>26</key>
        <value>Theodore Roosevelt</value>
    </map-entry>
</map-entries>
```

You can use list-entries and map-entries elements to initialize either a managed-bean or a managed-property, provided that the bean or property type is a List or Map.

Figure 2–7 shows a *syntax diagram* for the managed-bean element and all of its child elements. Simply follow the arrows to see which constructs are legal inside a managed-bean element. For example, the second graph tells you that a managed-property element starts with zero or more description elements, followed by zero or more display-name elements, zero or more icons, then a mandatory property-name, an optional property-class, and exactly one of the elements value, null-value, values, or map-entries.

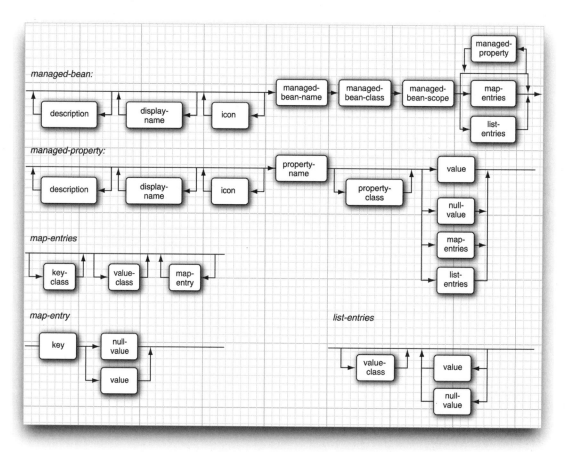

Figure 2–7   Syntax Diagram for managed-bean **Elements**

Chaining Bean Definitions

You can achieve more complex arrangements by using value binding expressions inside the value element to chain beans together. Consider the quiz bean in the numberquiz application.

The quiz contains a collection of problems, represented as the write-only problems property. You can configure it with the following instructions:

```
<managed-bean>
   <managed-bean-name>quiz</managed-bean-name>
   <managed-bean-class>com.corejsf.QuizBackingBean</managed-bean-class>
   <managed-bean-scope>session</managed-bean-scope>
   <managed-property>
      <property-name>problems</property-name>
      <list-entries>
         <value-class>com.corejsf.ProblemBean</value-class>
         <value>#{problem1}</value>
         <value>#{problem2}</value>
         <value>#{problem3}</value>
         <value>#{problem4}</value>
         <value>#{problem5}</value>
      </list-entries>
   </managed-property>
</managed-bean>
```

Of course, now we must define beans with names problem1 through problem5, like this:

```
<managed-bean>
   <managed-bean-name>problem1</managed-bean-name>
   <managed-bean-class>
      com.corejsf.ProblemBean
   </managed-bean-class>
   <managed-bean-scope>none</managed-bean-scope>
      <managed-property>
         <property-name>sequence</property-name>
         <list-entries>
            <value-class>java.lang.Integer</value-class>
            <value>3</value>
            <value>1</value>
            <value>4</value>
            <value>1</value>
            <value>5</value>
         </list-entries>
      </managed-property>
```

```
      <managed-property>
         <property-name>solution</property-name>
         <value>9</value>
      </managed-property>
   </managed-bean>
```

When the quiz bean is requested, then the creation of the beans problem1 through problem5 is triggered automatically. You need not worry about the order in which you specify managed beans.

Note that the problem beans have scope none since they are never requested from a JSP page.

When you wire beans together, make sure that their scopes are compatible. Table 2–1 lists the permissible combinations.

Table 2–1   Compatible Bean Scopes

When defining a bean of this scope...	...you can use beans of these scopes
none	none
application	none, application
session	none, application, session
request	none, application, session, request

String Conversions

You specify property values and elements of lists or maps with a value element that contains a string. The enclosed string needs to be converted to the type of the property or element. For primitive types, this conversion is straightforward. For example, you can specify a boolean value with the string true or false.

For other property types, the JSF implementation attempts to locate a matching PropertyEditor. If a property editor exists, its setAsText method is invoked to convert strings to property values. Property editors are heavily used for client-side beans, to convert between property values and a textual or graphical representation that can be displayed in a property sheet (see Figure 2–8).

Defining a property editor is somewhat involved, and we refer the interested reader to *Horstmann & Cornell, Core Java, volume 2 chapter 8, Sun Microsystems Press 2002.*

Figure 2–8 A Property Sheet in a GUI Builder

Note that the rules are fairly restrictive. For example, if you have a property of type URL, you cannot simply specify the URL as a string, even though there is a constructor URL(String). You would need to supply a property editor for the URL type or reimplement the property type as String.

Table 2–2 summarizes these conversion rules. They are identical to the rules for the jsp:setProperty action of the JSP specification.

Table 2–2 String Conversions

Target Type	Conversion
int, byte, short, long, float, double, or the corresponding wrapper type	The valueOf method of the wrapper type, or 0 if the string is empty.
boolean or Boolean	The result of Boolean.valueOf, or false if the string is empty.
char or Character	The first character of the string, or (char) 0 if the string is empty
String or Object	A copy of the string; new String("") if the string is empty.
bean property	A type that calls the setAsText method of the property editor if it exists. If the property editor doesn't exist or it throws an exception, the property is set to null if the string is empty. An error occurs otherwise

---

NOTE: You now know how to use value binding expressions inside your JSF pages. Sometimes, you need to evaluate a value binding expression in your Java code. Use a sequence of statements such as the following:

```
FacesContext context = FacesContext.getCurrentInstance();
ValueBinding binding =
    context.getApplication().createValueBinding("#{user.name}");
String name = (String) binding.getValue(context);
```

See Chapter 9 for more information.

The Syntax of Value Binding Expressions

In this section, we discuss the syntax for value binding expressions in gruesome detail. This section is intended for reference. Feel free to skip it at first reading.

Let us start with an expression of the form a.b. For now, we'll assume that we already know the object to which a refers. If a is an array, a list, or a map, then special rules apply—see the next subsection. If a is any other object, then b must be the name of a property of a. The exact meaning of a.b depends on whether the expression is used in *rvalue mode* or *lvalue mode*.

This terminology is used in the theory of programming languages to denote that an expression on the *right-hand side* of an assignment is treated differently from an expression on the *left-hand side*.

Consider the assignment

```
left = right;
```

A compiler generates different code for the left and right expressions. The right expression is evaluated in rvalue mode and yields a value. The left expression is evaluated in lvalue mode and stores a value in a location.

The same phenomenon happens when you use a value binding expression in a user interface component:

```
<h:inputText value="#{user.name}"/>
```

When the text field is rendered, the expression user.name is evaluated in rvalue mode, and the getName method is called. During decoding, the same expression is evaluated in lvalue mode, and the setName method is called.

In general, the expression a.b in rvalue mode is evaluated by calling the property getter, whereas a.b in lvalue mode calls the property setter.

Using Brackets

Just as in JavaScript, you can use brackets instead of the dot notation. That is, the following three expressions all have the same meaning:

```
a.b
a["b"]
a['b']
```

For example, user.password, user["password"], and user['password'] are equivalent expressions.

Why would anyone write user["password"] when user.password is much easier to type? There are a number of reasons.

- When you access an array or map, the [] notation is more intuitive.

- You can use the [] notation with strings that contain periods or dashes, for example, msgs["error.password"].

- The [] notation allows you to dynamically compute a property: a[b.propname].

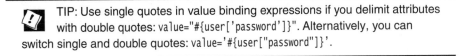

TIP: Use single quotes in value binding expressions if you delimit attributes with double quotes: value="#{user['password']}". Alternatively, you can switch single and double quotes: value='#{user["password"]}'.

Map and List Expressions

The value binding expression language goes beyond bean property access. For example, let m be an object of any class that implements the Map interface. Then m["key"] (or the equivalent m.key) is a binding to the associated value. In rvalue mode, the value

```
m.get("key")
```

is fetched. In lvalue mode, the statement

```
m.put("key", right);
```

is executed. Here, right is the "right-hand side" value that is assigned to m.key.

You can also access a value of any object of a class that implements the List interface (such as an ArrayList). You specify an integer index for the list position. For example, a[i] (or, if you prefer, a.i) binds the ith element of the list a. Here i can be an integer or a string that can be converted to an integer. The same rule applies for array types. As always, index values start at zero.

Table 2–3 summarizes these evaluation rules.

Table 2–3   Evaluating the Value Binding Expression a.b

Type of a	Type of b	lvalue mode	rvalue mode
null	any	error	null
any	null	error	null
Map	any	a.put(b, right)	a.get(b)
List	convertible to int	a.set(b, right)	a.get(b)
array	convertible to int	a[b]	a[b]
bean	any	call setter of property with name b.toString()	call getter of property with name b.toString()

CAUTION: Unfortunately, value bindings do not work for indexed properties. If p is an indexed property of a bean b and i is an integer, then b.p[i] does not access the ith value of the property. It is simply a syntax error. This deficiency is inherited from the JSTL expression language.

Resolving the Initial Term

Now you know how an expression of the form a.b is resolved. The rules can be applied repetitively to expressions such as a.b.c.d (or, of course, a['b'].c["d"]). We still need to discuss the meaning of the initial term a.

In the examples, you have seen so far, the initial term referred to a bean that was configured in the faces-config.xml file, or to a message bundle map. Those are indeed the most common situations. But it is also possible to specify other names.

There are a number of predefined objects. Table 2–4 shows the complete list. For example,

```
header['User-Agent']
```

is the value of the User-Agent parameter of the HTTP request that identifies the user's browser.

If the initial term is not one of the predefined objects, the JSF implementation looks for it in the *request, session,* and *application scopes,* in that order. Those scopes are map objects that are managed by the servlet container. For example, when you define a managed bean, its name and value are added to the appropriate scope map.

Table 2–4 Predefined Objects in the Value Binding Expression Language

Variable Name	Meaning
header	a Map of HTTP header parameters, containing only the first value for each name
headerValues	a Map of HTTP header parameters, yielding a String[]array of all values for a given name
param	a Map of HTTP request parameters, containing only the first value for each name
paramValues	a Map of HTTP request parameters, yielding a String[]array of all values for a given name
cookie	a Map of the cookie names and values of the current request
initParam	a Map of the initialization parameters of this web application. Initialization parameters are discussed in Chapter 10.
requestScope	a Map of all request scope attributes
sessionScope	a Map of all session scope attributes
applicationScope	a Map of all application scope attributes
facesContext	The FacesContext instance of this request. This class is discussed in Chapter 6
view	The UIViewRoot instance of this request. This class is discussed in Chapter 7

Finally, if the name is still not found, it is passed to the VariableResolver of the JSF application. The default variable resolver looks up managed-bean elements in a configuration resource, typically the faces-config.xml file.

Consider, for example, the expression

```
#{user.password}
```

The term user is not one of the predefined objects. When it is encountered for the first time, it is not an attribute name in request, session, or application scope. Therefore, the variable resolver processes the faces-config.xml entry.

```
<managed-bean>
    <managed-bean-name>user</managed-bean-name>
    <managed-bean-class>com.corejsf.UserBean</managed-bean-class>
    <managed-bean-scope>session</managed-bean-scope>
</managed-bean>
```

It calls the default constructor of the class `com.corejsf.UserBean`. Next, it adds an association to the `sessionScope` map. Finally, it returns the object as the result of the lookup.

When the term `user` needs to be resolved again in the same session, it is located in the session scope.

Composite Expressions

You can use a limited set of operators inside value binding expressions:

- arithmetic operators + - * / %. The last two operators have alphabetic variants `div` and `mod`.

- relational operators < <= > >= == != and their alphabetic variants `lt` `le` `gt` `ge` `eq` `ne`. (The first four variants are required for XML safety.)

- logical operators && || ! and their alphabetic variants `and` `or` `not`. (The first variant is required for XML safety.)

- the `empty` operator. The expression `empty a` is `true` if `a` is `null`, an array or `String` of length 0, or a `Collection` or `Map` of size 0.

- the ternary ?: selection operator

Operator precedence follows the same rules as in Java. The `empty` operator has the same precedence as the unary - and ! operators.

Generally, you don't want to do a lot of expression computation in web pages—that would violate the separation of presentation and business logic. However, occasionally the presentation layer can benefit from operators. For example, suppose you want to hide a component when the `hide` property of a bean is true. To hide a component, you set its `rendered` attribute to `false`. Inverting the bean value requires the ! (or `not`) operator:

```
<h:inputText rendered="#{!bean.hide}" ... />
```

Finally, you can concatenate plain strings and value binding expressions, simply by placing them next to each other. Consider, for example,

```
<h:outputText value="#{messages.greeting}, #{user.name}!"/>
```

The statement concatenates four strings: the string returned from #{messages.greeting}, the string consisting of a comma and a space, the string returned from #{user.name}, and the string "!".

You have now seen all the rules that are applied to resolve value binding expressions. Of course, in practice, most expressions are simply of the form #{bean.property}. Just come back to this section when you need to tackle a more complex expression.

Method Binding Expressions

A *method binding expression* denotes an object together with a method that can be applied to it.

For example, here is a typical use of a method binding expression.

```
<h:commandButton action="#{user.checkPassword}"/>
```

We assume that user is a value of type UserBean and checkPassword is a method of that class. The method binding expression is simply a convenient way of describing a method invocation that needs to be carried out at some future time.

When the expression is evaluated, the method is applied to the object.

In our example, the command button component will call user.checkPassword() and pass the returned string to the navigation handler.

Syntax rules for method binding expressions are similar to those of value binding expressions. All but the last component are used to determine an object. The last component must be the name of a method that can be applied to that object.

Four component attributes can take a method binding expression:

- action (see Chapter 3)
- validator (see Chapter 6)
- actionListener (see Chapter 7)
- valueChangeListener (see Chapter 7)

The parameter and return types of the method depend on the context in which the method binding is used. For example, an action must be bound to a method with no parameters and return type String, whereas an actionListener is bound to a method with one parameter of type ActionEvent and return type void. The code that invokes the method binding is responsible for supplying parameter values and processing the return value.

NAVIGATION

Topics in This Chapter

Chapter 3

In this short chapter, we discuss how you configure the navigation of your web application. In particular, you will learn how your application can move from one page to the next, depending on user actions and the outcomes of decisions in the business logic.

Static Navigation

Consider what happens when the user of a web application fills out a web page. The user might fill in text fields, click on radio buttons, or select list entries.

All of these edits happen inside the user's browser. When the user clicks a button that posts the form data, the changes are transmitted to the server.

At that time, the web application analyzes the user input and must decide which JSF page to use for rendering the response. The *navigation handler* is responsible for selecting the next JSF page.

In a simple web application, page navigation is static. That is, clicking a particular button always selects a fixed JSF page for rendering the response. You have seen in Chapter 1 how to wire up static navigation between JSF pages in the `faces-config.xml` file.

You simply give each button an `action` attribute, for example,

```
<h:commandButton label="Login" action="login"/>
```

NOTE: As you will see in Chapter 4, navigation actions can also be attached to hyperlinks.

The action must match an *outcome* in a navigation rule:

```
<navigation-rule>
   <from-view-id>/index.jsp</from-view-id>
   <navigation-case>
     <from-outcome>login</from-outcome>
     <to-view-id>/welcome.jsp</to-view-id>
   </navigation-case>
</navigation-rule>
```

This rule simply states that the login action navigates to /welcome.jsp if it occurred inside /index.jsp.

Note that the view ID strings must start with a /. The extension should match the file extension (.jsp), not the URL extension. For example, if you use a from-view-id of /index.faces, then the rule will not work.

If you pick the action strings carefully, you can group multiple navigation rules together. For example, you may have buttons with action logout sprinkled throughout your application's pages. You can have all of these buttons navigate to the logout.jsp page with the single rule

```
<navigation-rule>
   <navigation-case>
     <from-outcome>logout</from-outcome>
     <to-view-id>/logout.jsp</to-view-id>
   </navigation-case>
</navigation-rule>
```

This rule applies to all pages because no from-view-id element was specified.

You can merge navigation rules with the same from-view-id, for example,

```
<navigation-rule>
   <from-view-id>/index.jsp</from-view-id>
   <navigation-case>
     <from-outcome>login</from-outcome>
     <to-view-id>/welcome.jsp</to-view-id>
   </navigation-case>
   <navigation-case>
     <from-outcome>signup</from-outcome>
     <to-view-id>/newuser.jsp</to-view-id>
   </navigation-case>
</navigation-rule>
```

This merging seems like a good idea, even though it is not required.

> CAUTION: If no navigation rule matches a given action, then the current page is simply redisplayed.

Dynamic Navigation

In most web applications, navigation is not static. The page flow doesn't just depend on which button you click, but also on the inputs that you provide. For example, submitting a login page may have two outcomes: success or failure. The outcome depends on a computation, namely, whether the username and password are legitimate.

To implement dynamic navigation, the submit button must have a *method reference*, such as

```
<h:commandButton label="Login" action="#{loginController.verifyUser}"/>
```

In our example, loginController references a bean of some class, and that class must have a method named verifyUser.

A method reference in an action attribute has no parameters and a return type String. For example, the verifyUser method should look somewhat like this:

```
String verifyUser() {
    if (...)
        return "success";
    else
        return "failure";
}
```

The method returns an outcome string such as "success" or "failure". The navigation handler uses the returned string to look up a matching navigation rule.

> NOTE: An action method may return null to indicate that the same page should be redisplayed.

In summary, here are the steps that are carried out whenever the user clicks a command button whose action attribute is a method reference.

- The specified bean is retrieved.
- The referenced method is called.

- The resulting string is passed to the navigation handler. (As explained on page 82, the navigation handler also receives the method reference string.)
- The navigation handler looks up the next page.

Thus, to implement branching behavior, you supply a reference to a method in an appropriate bean class. You have wide latitude about where to place that method. The best approach is to find a class that has all of the data that you need for decision making.

Let us work through this process in an actual application. Our sample program presents the user with a sequence of quiz questions (see Figure 3–1).

Figure 3–1   A Quiz Question

When the user clicks the "Check answer" button, the application checks whether the user provided the correct answer. If not, the user has one additional chance to answer the same problem (see Figure 3–2).

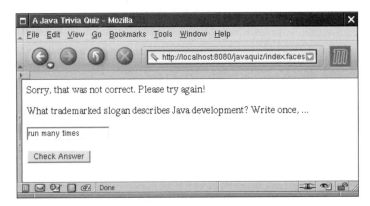

Figure 3–2   One Wrong Answer: Try Again

After two wrong answers, the next problem is presented (see Figure 3–3).

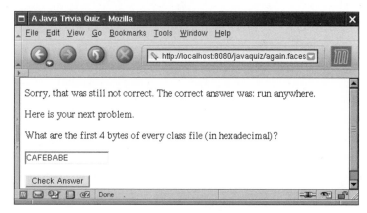

Figure 3–3   Two Wrong Answers: Move On

And, of course, after a correct answer, the next problem is presented as well. Finally, after the last problem, a summary page displays the score and invites the user to start over (see Figure 3–4).

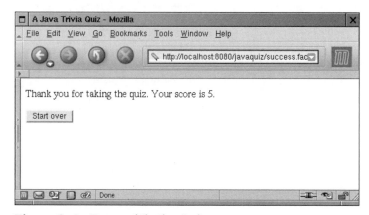

Figure 3–4   Done with the Quiz

Our application has two classes. The Problem class, shown in Listing 3–1, describes a single problem, with a question, an answer, and a method to check whether a given response is correct.

Listing 3–1   javaquiz/WEB-INF/classes/com/corejsf/Problem.java

```
1. package com.corejsf;
2.
3. public class Problem {
4.    private String question;
5.    private String answer;
6.
7.    public Problem(String question, String answer) {
8.       this.question = question;
9.       this.answer = answer;
10.   }
11.
12.   public String getQuestion() { return question; }
13.
14.   public String getAnswer() { return answer; }
15.
16.   // override for more sophisticated checking
17.   public boolean isCorrect(String response) {
18.      return response.trim().equalsIgnoreCase(answer);
19.   }
20. }
```

The QuizBean class describes a quiz that consists of a number of problems. A Quiz-Bean instance also keeps track of the current problem and the total score of a user. You will find the complete code in Listing 3–2.

In this example, the QuizBean is the appropriate class for holding the navigation methods. That bean has all the knowledge about the user's actions, and it can determine which page should be displayed next.

Have a glance at the code inside the answerAction method of the QuizBean class. The method returns one of the strings "success" or "done" if the user answered the question correctly, "again" after the first wrong answer, and "failure" or "done" after the second wrong try.

```
public String answerAction() {
   tries++;
   if (problems[currentProblem].isCorrect(response)) {
      score++;
      if (currentProblem == problems.length - 1) {
         return "done";
      }
      else {
         nextProblem();
```

```
            return "success";
        }
    }
    else if (tries == 1) {
        return "again";
    }
    else {
        if (currentProblem == problems.length - 1) {
            return "done";
        }
        else {
            nextProblem();
            return "failure";
        }
    }
}
```

We attach the answerAction method reference to the buttons on each of the pages. For example, the index.jsp page contains the following element:

```
<h:commandButton value="Check answer" action="#{quiz.answerAction}"/>
```

Here, quiz is the QuizBean instance that is defined in faces-config.xml.

Figure 3–5 shows the directory structure of the application. Listing 3–3 shows the main quiz page index.jsp. The more.jsp and failure.jsp pages are omitted. They differ from index.jsp only in the message at the top of the page.

The done.jsp page in Listing 3–4 shows the final score and invites the user to play again. Pay attention to the command button on that page. It looks as if we could use static navigation, since clicking the "Start over" button always returns to the index.jsp page. However, we use a method reference.

```
<h:commandButton value="Start over"
    action="#{quiz.startOverAction}"/>
```

The startOverAction method carries out useful work that needs to take place to reset the game. It resets the score and reshuffles the response items.

```
public String startOverAction() {
    startOver();
    return "startOver";
}
```

In general, action methods have two roles:

- to carry out the model updates that are a consequence of the user action
- to tell the navigation handler where to go next

NOTE: As you will see in Chapter 7, you can also attach action listeners to buttons. When the button is clicked, the code in the `processAction` method of the action listener is executed. However, action listeners do not interact with the navigation handler.

Listing 3–5 shows the application configuration file with the navigation rules. Because we selected our outcome strings so that they uniquely determine the successor web page, we can use a single navigation rule:

```
<navigation-rule>
   <navigation-case>
      <from-outcome>success</from-outcome>
      <to-view-id>/success.jsp</to-view-id>
   </navigation-case>
   <navigation-case>
      <from-outcome>again</from-outcome>
      <to-view-id>/again.jsp</to-view-id>
   </navigation-case>

   ...
</navigation-rule>
```

Figure 3–6 shows the transition diagram.

Finally, Listing 3–6 shows the message strings.

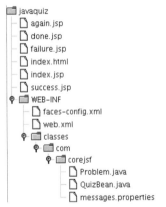

**Figure 3–5   Directory Structure
of the Java Quiz Application**

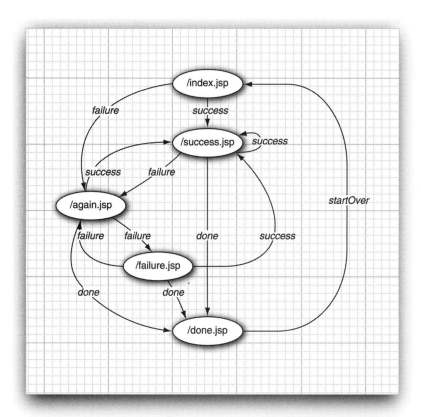

Figure 3–6   The Transition Diagram of the Java Quiz Application

Listing 3–2   javaquiz/WEB-INF/classes/com/corejsf/QuizBean.java

```
1. package com.corejsf;
2.
3. public class QuizBean {
4.    private int currentProblem;
5.    private int tries;
6.    private int score;
7.    private String response;
8.    private String correctAnswer;
9.
10.   // here, we hardwire the problems. In a real application,
11.   // they would come from a database
12.   private Problem[] problems = {
```

Listing 3–2 javaquiz/WEB-INF/classes/com/corejsf/QuizBean.java (cont.)

```
13.        new Problem(
14.            "What trademarked slogan describes Java development? Write once, ...",
15.            "run anywhere"),
16.        new Problem(
17.            "What are the first 4 bytes of every class file (in hexadecimal)?",
18.            "CAFEBABE"),
19.        new Problem(
20.            "What does this statement print? System.out.println(1+\"2\");",
21.            "12"),
22.        new Problem(
23.            "Which Java keyword is used to define a subclass?",
24.            "extends"),
25.        new Problem(
26.            "What was the original name of the Java programming language?",
27.            "Oak"),
28.        new Problem(
29.            "Which java.util class describes a point in time?",
30.            "Date")
31.    };
32.
33.    public QuizBean() { startOver(); }
34.
35.    // PROPERTY: question
36.    public String getQuestion() {
37.        return problems[currentProblem].getQuestion();
38.    }
39.
40.    // PROPERTY: answer
41.    public String getAnswer() { return correctAnswer; }
42.
43.    // PROPERTY: score
44.    public int getScore() { return score; }
45.
46.    // PROPERTY: response
47.    public String getResponse() { return response; }
48.    public void setResponse(String newValue) { response = newValue; }
49.
50.    public String answerAction() {
51.        tries++;
52.        if (problems[currentProblem].isCorrect(response)) {
53.            score++;
54.            nextProblem();
55.            if (currentProblem == problems.length) return "done";
56.            else return "success";
57.        }
58.        else if (tries == 1) {
59.            return "again";
```

Listing 3–2 javaquiz/WEB-INF/classes/com/corejsf/QuizBean.java (cont.)

```
60.       }
61.       else {
62.          nextProblem();
63.          if (currentProblem == problems.length) return "done";
64.          else return "failure";
65.       }
66.    }
67.
68.    public String startOverAction() {
69.       startOver();
70.       return "startOver";
71.    }
72.
73.    private void startOver() {
74.       currentProblem = 0;
75.       score = 0;
76.       tries = 0;
77.       response = "";
78.    }
79.
80.    private void nextProblem() {
81.       correctAnswer = problems[currentProblem].getAnswer();
82.       currentProblem++;
83.       tries = 0;
84.       response = "";
85.    }
86. }
```

Listing 3–3 javaquiz/index.jsp

```
1. <html>
2.    <%@ taglib uri="http://java.sun.com/jsf/core" prefix="f" %>
3.    <%@ taglib uri="http://java.sun.com/jsf/html" prefix="h" %>
4.
5.    <f:view>
6.       <f:loadBundle basename="com.corejsf.messages" var="msgs"/>
7.       <head>
8.          <title><h:outputText value="#{msgs.title}"/></title>
9.       </head>
10.       <body>
11.          <h:form>
12.             <p>
13.                <h:outputText value="#{quiz.question}"/>
14.             </p>
15.             <p>
16.                <h:inputText value="#{quiz.response}"/>
```

Listing 3–3   javaquiz/index.jsp (cont.)

```
17.          </p>
18.          <p>
19.            <h:commandButton value="#{msgs.answerButton}"
20.                action="#{quiz.answerAction}"/>
21.          </p>
22.        </h:form>
23.      </body>
24.    </f:view>
25. </html>
```

Listing 3–4   javaquiz/done.jsp

```
1. <html>
2.    <%@ taglib uri="http://java.sun.com/jsf/core" prefix="f" %>
3.    <%@ taglib uri="http://java.sun.com/jsf/html" prefix="h" %>
4.    <f:view>
5.      <f:loadBundle basename="com.corejsf.messages" var="msgs"/>
6.      <head>
7.        <title><h:outputText value="#{msgs.title}"/></title>
8.      </head>
9.      <body>
10.        <h:form>
11.          <p>
12.            <h:outputText value="#{msgs.thankYou}"/>
13.            <h:outputText value="#{msgs.score}"/>
14.            <h:outputText value="#{quiz.score}"/>.
15.          </p>
16.          <p>
17.            <h:commandButton value="#{msgs.startOverButton}"
18.                action="#{quiz.startOverAction}"/>
19.          </p>
20.        </h:form>
21.      </body>
22.    </f:view>
23. </html>
```

Listing 3–5   javaquiz/WEB-INF/faces-config.xml

```
1. <?xml version="1.0"?>
2.
3. <!DOCTYPE faces-config PUBLIC
4.  "-//Sun Microsystems, Inc.//DTD JavaServer Faces Config 1.0//EN"
5.  "http://java.sun.com/dtd/web-facesconfig_1_0.dtd">
6.
```

Listing 3–5   javaquiz/WEB-INF/faces-config.xml (cont.)

```
 7. <faces-config>
 8.    <navigation-rule>
 9.       <navigation-case>
10.          <from-outcome>success</from-outcome>
11.          <to-view-id>/success.jsp</to-view-id>
12.          <redirect/>
13.       </navigation-case>
14.       <navigation-case>
15.          <from-outcome>again</from-outcome>
16.          <to-view-id>/again.jsp</to-view-id>
17.       </navigation-case>
18.       <navigation-case>
19.          <from-outcome>failure</from-outcome>
20.          <to-view-id>/failure.jsp</to-view-id>
21.       </navigation-case>
22.       <navigation-case>
23.          <from-outcome>done</from-outcome>
24.          <to-view-id>/done.jsp</to-view-id>
25.       </navigation-case>
26.       <navigation-case>
27.          <from-outcome>startOver</from-outcome>
28.          <to-view-id>/index.jsp</to-view-id>
29.       </navigation-case>
30.    </navigation-rule>
31.
32.    <managed-bean>
33.       <managed-bean-name>quiz</managed-bean-name>
34.       <managed-bean-class>com.corejsf.QuizBean</managed-bean-class>
35.       <managed-bean-scope>session</managed-bean-scope>
36.    </managed-bean>
37.
38. </faces-config>
```

Listing 3–6   javaquiz/WEB-INF/classes/com/corejsf/messages.properties

```
1. title=A Java Trivia Quiz
2. answerButton=Check Answer
3. startOverButton=Start over
4. correct=Congratulations, that is correct.
5. notCorrect=Sorry, that was not correct. Please try again!
6. stillNotCorrect=Sorry, that was still not correct.
7. correctAnswer=The correct answer was:
8. score=Your score is
9. thankYou=Thank you for taking the quiz.
```

Advanced Navigation Issues

The techniques of the preceding sections should be sufficient for most practical navigation needs. In this section, we describe the remaining rules for the navigation elements that can appear in the faces-config.xml file. Figure 3–7 shows a syntax diagram of the valid elements.

 NOTE: As you saw in Chapter 2, it is also possible to place the navigation information into configuration files other than the standard faces-config.xml file.

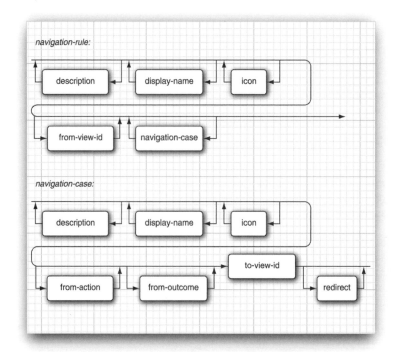

Figure 3–7 Syntax Diagram for Navigation Elements

As you can see from the syntax diagram, each navigation-rule and navigation-case element can have arbitrary description, display-name, and icon elements. These elements are intended for use in builder tools, and we do not discuss them further.

Redirection

If you add a redirect element after to-view-id, then the JSP container terminates the current request and sends an HTTP redirect to the client. The redirect response tells the client which URL to use for the next page.

Redirecting the page is slower than forwarding because another round trip to the browser is involved. However, the redirection gives the browser a chance to update its address field.

Figure 3–6 shows how the address field changes when you add a redirection element as follows:

```
<navigation-case>
    <from-outcome>success</from-outcome>
    <to-view-id>/success.jsp</to-view-id>
    <redirect/>
</navigation-case>
```

Without redirection, the original URL (`localhost:8080/javaquiz/index.faces`) is unchanged when the user moves from the `/index.jsp` page to the `/success.jsp` face. With redirection, the browser displays the new URL (`localhost:8080/java-quiz/success.faces`).

Figure 3–8   Redirection Updates the URL in the Browser

 TIP: Use the `redirect` element for pages that the user might want to bookmark.

Wildcards

You can use *wildcards* in the `from-view-id` element of a navigation rule, for example:

```
<navigation-rule>
    <from-view-id>/secure/*</from-view-id>
    <navigation-case>
        . . .
    </navigation-case>
</navigation-rule>
```

This rule applies to all pages that start with the prefix /secure/. Only a single * is allowed, and it must be at the end of the ID string.

If there are multiple matching wildcard rules, the longest match is taken.

> ▣ NOTE: Instead of leaving out a `from-view-id` element, you can also use one of the following to specify a rule that applies to all pages:
>
> `<from-view-id>/*</from-view-id>`
>
> or
>
> `<from-view-id>*</from-view-id>`

Using `from-action`

The structure of the `navigation-case` element is more complex than we previously discussed. In addition to the `from-outcome` element, there is also a `from-action` element. That flexibility can be useful if you have two separate actions with the same action string, or two action method references that return the same action string.

For example, suppose that in our quiz application, the `startOverAction` returns the string `"again"` instead of `"startOver"`. The same string can be returned by the `answerAction`. To differentiate between the two navigation cases, you can use a `from-action` element. The contents of the element must be identical to the method reference string of the `action` attribute.

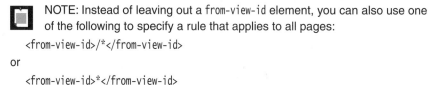

```
<navigation-case>
  <from-action>#{quiz.answerAction}</from-action>
  <from-outcome>again</from-outcome>
  <to-view-id>/again.jsp</to-view-id>
</navigation-case>
<navigation-case>
  <from-action>#{quiz.startOverAction}</from-action>
  <from-outcome>again</from-outcome>
  <to-view-id>/index.jsp</to-view-id>
</navigation-case>
```

> ▣ NOTE: The navigation handler does *not* invoke the method inside the #{...} delimiters. The method has been invoked before the navigation handler kicks in. The navigation handler merely uses the `from-action` string as a key to find a matching navigation case.

The Navigation Algorithm

We finish this chapter with a description of the precise algorithm that the navigation handler uses to resolve ambiguous situations. Feel free to skip this section for now and come back when you have to decipher rules produced by other programmers or automated tools.

The algorithm has three inputs:

- The *outcome*, that is, the value of an action attribute or the string resulting from the invocation of a method reference.
- The *view ID* of the current view
- The *action*, that is, the literal value of the action attribute in the component that triggered the navigation.

The first of two phases is to find the matching navigation-rule, following these steps.

- If the outcome is null, return immediately and redisplay the current page.
- Merge all navigation rules with the same from-view-id value.
- Try to find a navigation rule whose from-view-id value matches the view ID exactly. If such a rule exists, take it.
- Consider all navigation rules whose from-view-id values end with a wildcard suffix, such as secure. For each such rule, check whether the prefix (after removing the *) is identical to the corresponding prefix of the view ID. If there are matching rules, take the one with the longest matching prefix.
- If there is a rule without a from-view-id, take it.
- If there is no match at all, redisplay the current page.

The second of two phases is to consider all navigation-case elements in the matching navigation rule (which may consist of several merged navigation-rule elements with matching from-view-id.values).

Follow these steps to find the matching case.

- If a case has both matching from-outcome and from-action, take it.
- Otherwise, if a case has matching from-outcome and no from-action, take it.
- Otherwise, if a case has matching from-action and no from-outcome, take it.
- Otherwise, if there is a case with neither from-outcome or from-action, take it.
- If there is no match at all, redisplay the current page.

Naturally, we recommend that you do not create tricky navigation rules in your own programs. As long as you stay away from wildcards and from-action elements, you won't need to know about the gory details of the navigation algorithm.

Standard JSF Tags

Topics in This Chapter

Chapter 4

Development of compelling JSF applications requires a good grasp of the JSF tag libraries—core and HTML—that represent a combined total of 43 tags. Because of their prominence in the JSF framework, this chapter and the next— Data Tables—provide in-depth coverage of those tags, their attributes, and how you can best use them.

Even simple JSF pages use tags from both libraries. Many JSF pages have a structure similar to this:

```
<%@ taglib uri="http://java.sun.com/jsf/core" prefix="f" %>
<%@ taglib uri="http://java.sun.com/jsf/html" prefix="h" %>

<f:view>
    <h:form>
        ...
    </h:form>
</f:view>
```

To use the JSF tag libraries, you must import them with taglib directives, as in the preceding code fragment. You can choose any name you want for the prefixes. The convention is f and h, for the core and HTML libraries, respectively.

This chapter starts with a brief look at the core library. That library, with 18 tags, is smaller than its HTML sibling, which has 25. It's also considerably simpler than the HTML library. Because of that simplicity and because most of the core tags are discussed elsewhere in this book, the overwhelming majority of this chapter focuses on the HTML library.

We begin our exploration of the HTML library with a look at common attributes shared by most JSF HTML tags. Then we discuss each tag individually with attribute tables for reference and useful code examples that you can adapt to your own applications.

 NOTE: The core library has 2.8 attributes per tag—the HTML library has 26.2.

An Overview of the JSF Core Tags

The core library is the poor stepchild of the HTML library—the former exists entirely to support the latter. The core tags are listed in Table 4–1.

Table 4–1   JSF Core Tags

Tag	Description
view	Creates the top-level view
subview	Creates a subview of a view
facet	Adds a facet to a component
attribute	Adds an attribute (key/value) to a component
param	Adds a parameter to a component
actionListener	Adds an action listener to a component
valueChangeListener	Adds a valuechange listener to a component
converter	Adds an arbitrary converter to a component
convertDateTime	Adds a datetime converter to a component
convertNumber	Adds a number converter to a component
validator	Adds a validator to a component
validateDoubleRange	Validates a double range for a component's value
validateLength	Validates the length of a component's value
validateLongRange	Validates a long range for a component's value
loadBundle	Loads a resource bundle, stores properties as a Map
selectitems	Specifies items for a select one or select many component
selectitem	Specifies an item for a select one or select many component
verbatim	Adds markup to a JSF page

Most of the core tags represent *objects you add to components*:

- Attributes
- Listeners
- Converters
- Validators
- Facets
- Parameters
- Select items

The core library also contains tags for defining views and subviews, loading resource bundles, and adding arbitrary text to a page.

All of the core tags are discussed at length elsewhere in this book.

NOTE: All tag attributes, except for var and id, accept value reference expressions. The majority of those expressions represent value bindings; a handful represent method bindings.

An Overview of the JSF HTML Tags

JSF HTML tags represent the following kinds of components:

- Inputs
- Outputs
- Commands
- Selection
- Others

The Others category includes forms, messages, and components that layout other components. Table 4–2 lists all the HTML tags.

Table 4–2 JSF HTML Tags

Tag	Description
form	HTML form
inputText	Single-line text input control
inputTextarea	Multiline text input control
inputSecret	Password input control

Table 4–2   JSF HTML Tags (cont.)

Tag	Description
inputHidden	Hidden field
outputLabel	Label for another component for accessibility
outputLink	HTML anchor
outputFormat	Like outputText, but formats compound messages
outputText	Single-line text output
commandButton	Button: submit, reset, or pushbutton
commandLink	Link that acts like a pushbutton
message	Displays the most recent message for a component
messages	Displays all messages
graphicImage	Displays an image
selectOneListbox	Single-select listbox
selectOneMenu	Single-select menu
selectOneRadio	Set of radio buttons
selectBooleanCheckbox	Checkbox
selectManyCheckbox	Set of checkboxes
selectManyListbox	Multiselect listbox
selectManyMenu	Multiselect menu
panelGrid	HTML table
panelGroup	Two or more components that are laid out as one
dataTable	A feature-rich table control
column	Column in a dataTable

We can group the HTML tags in the following categories:

- Inputs (`input`...)
- Outputs (`output`...)
- Commands (`commandButton` and `commandLink`)
- Selections (`checkbox`, `listbox`, `menu`, `radio`)
- Layouts (`panelGrid`)
- Data Table (`dataTable`); see Chapter 5
- Errors and messages (`message`, `messages`)

The JSF HTML tags share common attributes, HTML pass-through attributes, and attributes that support dynamic HTML.

NOTE: The HTML tags may seem overly verbose; for example, `selectManyListbox` could be more efficiently expressed as `multiList`. But those verbose names correspond to a component/renderer combination, so `selectManyListbox` represents a `selectMany` component paired with a `listbox` renderer. Knowing the type of component a tag represents is crucial if you want to access components programmatically.

NOTE: Both JSF and Struts developers implement web pages with JSP custom tags. But Struts tags generate HTML directly, whereas JSF tags represent a component and renderer that generate HTML. That key difference makes it easy to adapt JSF applications to alternative display technologies, as we'll see when we implement a wireless JSF application in Chapter 11.

Common Attributes

Three types of tag attributes are shared among multiple HTML component tags:

- Basic
- HTML 4.0
- DHTML events

Let's look at each type.

Basic Attributes

As you can see from Table 4–3, basic attributes are shared by the majority of JSF HTML tags.

Table 4–3 Basic HTML Tag Attributes[a]

Attribute	Component Types	Description
id	A (25)	Identifier for a component
binding	A (25)	Reference to the component that can be used in a backing bean
rendered	A (25)	A boolean; false suppresses rendering
styleClass	A (23)	Cascading stylesheet (CSS) class name
value	I, O, C (19)	A component's value, typically a value binding
valueChangeListener	I (11)	A method binding to a method that responds to value changes
converter	I,O (15)	Converter class name
validator	I (11)	Class name of a validator that's created and attached to a component
required	I (11)	A boolean; if true, requires a value to be entered in the associated field

a. A = all, I = input, O = output, C = commands, (*n*) = number of tags with attribute

The id and binding attributes, applicable to all HTML tags, reference a component—the former is used primarily by page authors, and the latter is used by Java developers.

The value and converter attributes let you specify a component value and a means to convert it from a string to an object, or vice versa.

The validator, required, and valueChangeListener attributes are available for input components so that you can validate values and react to changes to those values. See Chapter 6 for more information about validators and converters.

The ubiquitous rendered and styleClass attributes affect how a component is rendered.

Let's take a brief look at these important attributes.

IDs and Bindings

The versatile id attribute lets you do the following:

- Access JSF components from other JSF tags
- Obtain component references in Java code
- Access HTML elements with scripts

In this section we discuss the first two tasks listed above. See "Form Elements and JavaScript" on page 97 for more about the last task.

The id attribute lets page authors reference a component from another tag. For example, an error message for a component can be displayed like this:

```
<h:inputText id="name".../>
<h:message for="name"/>
```

You can also use component identifiers to get a component reference in your Java code. For example, you could access the name component in a listener, like this:

```
UIComponent component = event.getComponent().findComponent("name");
```

The preceding call to findComponent has a caveat: the component that generated the event and the name component must be in the same form (or data table). There is a better way to access a component in your Java code. Define the component as an instance field of a class. Provide property getters and setters for the component. Then use the binding attribute, which you specify in a JSF page like this:

```
<h:outputText binding="#{form.statePrompt}".../>
```

The binding attribute is specified with a value reference expression. That expression refers to a read-write bean property. See Chapter 2 for more information about the binding attribute. The JSF implementation sets the property to the component, so you can programatically manipulate components.

You can also *programmatically create a component that will be used in lieu of the component specified in the JSF page.* For example, the form bean's statePrompt property could be implemented like this:

```
private UIComponent statePrompt = new UIOutput();
public UIComponent getStatePrompt() { return statePrompt; }
public void setStatePrompt(UIComponent statePrompt) {...}
```

When the #{form.statePrompt} value binding is first encountered, the JSF framework calls Form.getStateOutput(). If that method returns null—as is typically the case—the JSF implementation creates the component specified in the JSF page.

But *if that method returns a reference to a component*—as is the case in the preceding code fragment—*that component is used instead.*

Values, Converters, and Validators

Inputs, outputs, commands, and data tables all have values. Associated tags in the HTML library, such as h:inputText and h:dataTable, come with a value attribute. You can specify values with a string, like this:

```
<h:outputText value="William"/>
```

Most of the time you'll use a value binding, for example:

```
<h:outputText value="#{customer.name}"/>
```

The converter attribute, shared by inputs and outputs, lets you attach a converter to a component. Input tags also have a validator attribute that you can use to attach a validator to a component. Converters and validators are discussed at length in Chapter 6.

Rendering and Styles

You can use CSS styles, either inline (style) or classes (styleClass), to influence how components are rendered. Most of the time you'll specify string constants instead of value bindings for the style and styleClass attributes; for example:

```
<h:outputText value="#{customer.name}" styleClass="emphasis"/>
<h:outputText value="#{customer.id}" style="border: thin solid blue"/>
```

Value bindings are useful when you need programmatic control over styles. You can also control whether components are rendered at all with the rendered attribute. That attribute comes in handy in all sorts of situations, for example, an optional table column.

 TIP: Instead of using a hardwired style, it's better to use a stylesheet. Define a CSS style such as

```
.prompts {
    color:red;
}
```

Place it in a stylesheet, say, styles.css. Add a link element inside the head element in your JSF page:

```
<link href="styles.css" rel="stylesheet" type="text/css"/>
```

Then use the styleClass attribute:

```
<h:outputText value="#{msgs.namePrompt}" styleClass="prompts"/>
```

Now you can change the appearance of all prompts simply by updating the stylesheet.

> **TIP:** Remember, you can use operators in value reference expressions. For example, you might have a view that acts as a tabbed pane by optionally rendering a panel depending on the selected tab. In that case, you could use `h:panelGrid` like this:
>
> ```
> <h:panelGrid rendered='#{bean.selectedTab == "Movies"}'/>
> ```
>
> The preceding code renders the movies panel when the `Movies` tab is selected.

HTML 4.0 Attributes

JSF HTML tags have appropriate HTML 4.0 pass-through attributes. Those attribute values are passed through to the generated HTML element. For example, `<h:inputText value="#{form.name.last}" size="25".../>` generates this HTML: `<input type="text" size="25".../>`. Notice that the `size` attribute is passed through to HTML.

The HTML 4.0 attributes are listed in Table 4–4.

Table 4–4   HTML 4.0 Pass-through Attributes[a]

Attribute	Description
accesskey (14)	A key, typically combined with a system-defined metakey, that gives focus to an element
accept (1)	Comma-separated list of content types for a form
accept-charset (1)	Comma- or space-separated list of character encodings for a form. The accept-charset attribute is specified with the JSF HTML attribute named acceptcharset.
alt (4)	Alternative text for nontextual elements such as images or applets
border (4)	Pixel value for an element's border width
charset (3)	Character encoding for a linked resource
coords (2)	Coordinates for an element whose shape is a rectangle, circle, or polygon
dir (18)	Direction for text. Valid values are ltr (left to right) and rtl (right to left).
disabled (11)	Disabled state of an input element or button
hreflang (2)	Base language of a resource specified with the href attribute; hreflang may only be used with href.

Table 4–4   HTML 4.0 Pass-through Attributes[a] (cont.)

Attribute	Description
lang (20)	Base language of an element's attributes and text
maxlength (2)	Maximum number of characters for text fields
readonly (11)	Read-only state of an input field; text can be selected in a read-only field but not edited
rel (2)	Relationship between the current document and a link specified with the href attribute
rev (2)	Reverse link from the anchor specified with href to the current document. The value of the attribute is a space-separated list of link types.
rows (1)	Number of visible rows in a text area. h:dataTable has a rows attribute, but it's not an HTML pass-through attribute.
shape (2)	Shape of a region. Valid values: default, rect, circle, poly. (default signifies the entire region)
size (4)	Size of an input field
style (23)	Inline style information
tabindex (14)	Numerical value specifying a tab index
target (3)	The name of a frame in which a document is opened
title (22)	A title, used for accessibility, that describes an element. Visual browsers typically create tooltips for the title's value
type (4)	Type of a link; for example, "stylesheet"
width (3)	Width of an element

a. (n) = number of tags with attribute

The attributes listed in Table 4–4 are defined in the HTML specification, which you can access on line at http://www.w3.org/TR/REC-html40. That web site is an excellent resource for deep digging into HTML.

DHTML Events

Client-side scripting is useful for all sorts of tasks, such as syntax validation or rollover images, and it is easy to use with JSF. HTML attributes that support scripting, such as onclick and onchange are referred to as dynamic HTML

(DHTML) event attributes. JSF supports DHTML event attributes for nearly all of the JSF HTML tags. Those attributes are listed in Table 4–5.

Table 4–5   DHTML Event Attributes[a]

Attribute	Description
onblur (14)	Element loses focus
onchange (11)	Element's value changes
onclick (17)	Mouse button is clicked over the element
ondblclick (18)	Mouse button is double-clicked over the element
onfocus (14)	Element receives focus
onkeydown (18)	Key is pressed
onkeypress (18)	Key is pressed and subsequently released
onkeyup (18)	Key is released
onmousedown (18)	Mouse button is pressed over the element
onmousemove (18)	Mouse moves over the element
onmouseout (18)	Mouse leaves the element's area
onmouseover (18)	Mouse moves onto an element
onmouseup (18)	Mouse button is released
onreset (1)	Form is reset
onselect (11)	Text is selected in an input field
onsubmit (1)	Form is submitted

a.   (*n*) = number of tags with attribute

The DHTML event attributes listed in Table 4–5 let you associate client-side scripts with events. Typically, JavaScript is used as a scripting language, but you can use any scripting language you like. See the HTML specification for more details.

> TIP: You'll probably add client-side scripts to your JSF pages soon after you start using JSF. One common use is to submit a request when an input's value is changed so that value change listeners are immediately notified of the change, like this: `<h:selectOneMenu onchange="submit()"...>`

Forms

Web applications run on form submissions, and JSF applications are no exception. Table 4–6 lists all h:form attributes.

Table 4–6   Attributes for h:form

Attributes	Description
binding, id, rendered, styleClass	Basic attributes[a]
accept, acceptcharset, dir, enctype, lang, style, target, title	HTML 4.0[b] attributes
onblur, onchange, onclick, ondblclick, onfocus, onkeydown, onkeypress, onkeyup, onmousedown, onmousemove, onmouseout, onmouseover, onreset, onsubmit	DHTML events[c]

a. See Table 4–3 on page 90 for information about basic attributes.
b. See Table 4–4 on page 93 for information about HTML 4.0 attributes.
c. See Table 4–5 on page 95 for information about DHTML event attributes.

Although the HTML form tag has method and action attributes, h:form does not. Because you can save state in the client—an option that is implemented as a hidden field—posting forms with the GET method is disallowed. The contents of that hidden field can be quite large and may overrun the buffer for request parameters, so all JSF form submissions are implemented with the POST method. Also, if you don't specify navigation, JSF form submissions post to the current page (through the Faces servlet), although the actual page that's loaded as a result of a form submit can (and typically does) change as a result of actions that are fired on behalf of command components. See Chapter 2 for more details about actions.

The h:form tag generates an HTML form element. For example, if, in a JSF page named /index.jsp, you use an h:form tag with no attributes, the Form renderer generates HTML like this:

```
<form id="_id0" method="post" action="/forms/faces/index.jsp"
                enctype="application/x-www-form-urlencoded">
```

h:form comes with a full complement of DHTML event attributes. You can also specify the style or styleClass attributes for h:form. Those styles will then be applied to all output elements contained in the form.

Finally, the id attribute is passed through to the HTML form element. If you don't specify the id attribute explicitly, a value is generated by the JSF implementation, as is the case for all generated HTML elements. The id attribute is often explicitly specified for forms so that it can be referenced from stylesheets or scripts.

Form Elements and JavaScript

Java*Server* Faces is all about *server*-side components, but it's also designed to work with scripting languages, such as JavaScript. For example, the application shown in Figure 4–1 uses JavaScript to confirm that a password field matches a password confirm field. If the fields don't match, a JavaScript dialog is displayed. If they do match, the form is submitted.

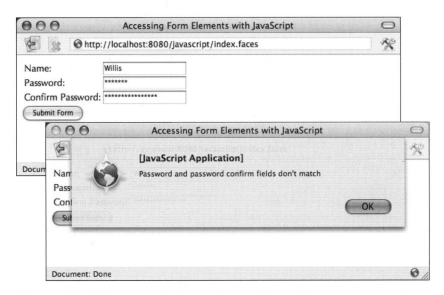

Figure 4–1   Using JavaScript to Access Form Elements

We use the id attribute to assign names to the relevant HTML elements so that we can access them with JavaScript:

```
<h:form id="registerForm">
    ...
    <h:inputText id="password".../>
    <h:inputText id="passwordConfirm".../>
    ...
    <h:commandButton type="button"
                     onclick="checkPassword(this.form)"/>
    ...
</h:form>
```

When the button is clicked, a JavaScript function—checkPassword—is invoked. That function follows:

```
function checkPassword(form) {
    var password = form["registerForm:password"].value;
    var passwordConfirm = form["registerForm:passwordConfirm"].value;

    if (password == passwordConfirm)
        form.submit();
    else
        alert("Password and password confirm fields don't match");
}
```

Notice the syntax used to access form elements. You might think you could access the form elements with a simpler syntax, like this:

```
documents.forms.registerForm.password
```

But that won't work. Let's look at the HTML produced by the preceding code to find out why:

```
<form id="registerForm" method="post"
    action="/javascript/faces/index.jsp"
    enctype="application/x-www-form-urlencoded">
    ...
    <input id="registerForm:password"
        type="text" name="registerForm:password"/>
    ...
    <input type="button" name="registerForm:_id5"
        value="Submit Form" onclick="checkPassword(this.form)"/>
    ...
</form>
```

All form controls generated by JSF have names that conform to *formName:componentName*, where *formName* represents the name of the control's form and *componentName* represents the control's name. If you don't specify id attributes, the JSF framework creates identifiers for you, as you can see from the button in the preceding HTML fragment. Therefore, to access the password field in the preceding example, you must do this instead:

```
documents.forms.registerForm["registerForm:password"].value
```

The directory structure for the application shown in Figure 4–1 is shown in Figure 4–2. The JSF page is listed in Listing 4–1 and the English resource bundle is listed in Listing 4–2.

```
javascript
  index.html
  index.jsp
  styles.css
  WEB-INF
    web.xml
    classes
      com
        corejsf
          messages.properties
```

**Figure 4–2   The JavaScript Example
Directory Structure**

Listing 4–1   javascript/index.jsp

```
1.  <html>
2.    <%@ taglib uri="http://java.sun.com/jsf/core" prefix="f" %>
3.    <%@ taglib uri="http://java.sun.com/jsf/html" prefix="h" %>
4.    <f:view>
5.      <f:loadBundle basename="com.corejsf.messages" var="msgs"/>
6.      <head>
7.        <title>
8.          <h:outputText value="#{msgs.windowTitle}"/>
9.        </title>
10.     </head>
11.     <body>
12.       <h:form id="registerForm">
13.         <table>
14.           <tr>
15.             <td>
16.               <h:outputText value="#{msgs.namePrompt}"/>
17.             </td>
18.             <td>
19.               <h:inputText/>
20.             </td>
21.           </tr>
22.           <tr>
23.             <td>
24.               <h:outputText value="#{msgs.passwordPrompt}"/>
25.             </td>
26.             <td>
27.               <h:inputSecret id="password"/>
28.             </td>
29.           </tr>
30.           <tr>
```

Listing 4–1	javascript/index.jsp (cont.)

```
31.                    <td>
32.                        <h:outputText value="#{msgs.confirmPasswordPrompt}"/>
33.                    </td>
34.                    <td>
35.                        <h:inputSecret id="passwordConfirm"/>
36.                    </td>
37.                </tr>
38.            </table>
39.            <h:commandButton type="button" value="Submit Form"
40.                onclick="checkPassword(this.form)"/>
41.        </h:form>
42.    </body>
43.    <script type="text/javascript">
44.    <!--
45.        function checkPassword(form) {
46.            var password = form["registerForm:password"].value;
47.            var passwordConfirm = form["registerForm:passwordConfirm"].value;
48.
49.            if(password == passwordConfirm)
50.                form.submit();
51.            else
52.                alert("Password and password confirm fields don't match");
53.        }
54.    -->
55.    </script>
56.    </f:view>
57. </html>
```

Listing 4–2	javascript/WEB-INF/classes/com/corejsf/messages.properties

```
1. windowTitle=Accessing Form Elements with JavaScript
2. namePrompt=Name:
3. passwordPrompt=Password:
4. confirmPasswordPrompt=Confirm Password:
```

Text Fields and Text Areas

Text inputs are the mainstay of most web applications. JSF supports three varieties represented by the following tags:

- h:inputText
- h:inputSecret
- h:inputTextarea

Since the three tags use similar attributes, Table 4–7 lists attributes for all three.

Table 4–7 Attributes for h:inputText, h:inputSecret **and** h:inputTextarea

Attributes	Description
cols	For h:inputTextarea only—number of columns
immediate	Process validation early in the life cycle
redisplay	For h:inputSecret only—when true, the input field's value is redisplayed when the web page is reloaded
required	Require input in the component when the form is submitted
rows	For h:inputTextarea only—number of rows
valueChangeListener	A specified listener that's notified of value changes
binding, converter, id, rendered, required, styleClass, value, validator	Basic attributes[a]
accesskey, alt, dir, disabled, lang, maxlength, readonly, size, style, tabindex, title	HTML 4.0 pass-through attributes[b]—alt, maxlength, and size do not apply to h:inputTextarea
onblur, onchange, onclick, ondblclick, onfocus, onkeydown, onkeypress, onkeyup, onmousedown, onmousemove, onmouseout, onmouseover, onselect	DHTML events[c]

a. See Table 4–3 on page 90 for information about basic attributes.
b. See Table 4–4 on page 93 for information about HTML 4.0 attributes.
c. See Table 4–5 on page 95 for information about DHTML event attributes.

All three tags have immediate, required, value, and valueChangeListener attributes. The immediate attribute is used primarily for value changes that affect the user interface and is rarely used by these three tags. Instead, it is more commonly used by other input components such as menus and listboxes. See Chapter 7 for more information about the immediate attribute.

Three attributes in Table 4–7 are each applicable to only one tag: cols, rows, and redisplay. The rows and cols attributes are used with h:inputTextarea to specify the number of rows and columns, respectively, for the text area. The redisplay attribute, used with h:inputSecret, is a boolean that determines whether a secret field retains its value—and therefore redisplays it—when the field's form is resubmitted.

Table 4–8 shows sample uses of the h:inputText and h:inputSecret tags.

Table 4–8   h:inputText **and** h:inputSecret **Examples**

Example	Result
`<h:inputText value="#{form.testString}" readonly="true"/>`	12345678901234567890
`<h:inputSecret value="#{form.passwd}" redisplay="true"/>`	********** (shown after an unsuccessful form submit)
`<h:inputSecret value="#{form.passwd}" redisplay="false"/>`	 (shown after an unsuccessful form submit)
`<h:inputText value="inputText" style="color: Yellow; background: Teal;"/>`	inputText
`<h:inputText value="1234567" size="5"/>`	123456
`<h:inputText value="1234567890" maxlength="6" size="10"/>`	123456

The first example in Table 4–8 produces the following HTML:

```
<input type="text" name="_id0:_id4" value="12345678901234567890"
    readonly="readonly"/>
```

The input field is read-only, so our form bean only defines a getter method:

```
private String testString = "12345678901234567890";
public String getTestString() {
    return testString;
}
```

The h:inputSecret examples illustrate the use of the redisplay attribute. If that attribute is true, the text field stores its value between requests and therefore the value is redisplayed when the page reloads. If redisplay is false, the value is discarded and is not redisplayed.

The size attribute specifies the number of visible characters in a text field. But because most fonts are variable width, the size attribute is not precise, as you can see from the fifth example in Table 4–8, which specifies a size of 5 but displays six characters. The maxlength attribute specifies the maximum number of characters a text field will display. That attribute is precise. Both size and maxlength are HTML pass-through attributes.

Table 4–9 shows examples of the h:inputTextarea tag.

Table 4–9 h:inputTextarea **Examples**

Example	Result
<h:inputTextarea rows="5"/>	
<h:inputTextarea cols="5"/>	
<h:inputTextarea value="123456789012345" rows="3" cols="10"/>	456789012345
<h:inputTextarea value="#{form.dataInRows}" rows="2" cols="15"/>	line one line two line three

The h:inputTextarea has cols and rows attributes to specify the number of columns and rows, respectively, in the text area. The cols attributes is analogous to the size attribute for h:inputText and is also imprecise.

If you specify one long string for h:inputTextarea's value, the string will be placed in its entirety in one line, as you can see from the third example in Table 4–9. If you want to put data on separate lines, you can insert new line characters ('\n') to force a line break; for example, the last example in Table 4–9 accesses the dataInRows property of a backing bean. That property is implemented like this:

```
private String dataInRows = "line one\nline two\nline three";
public void setDataInRows(String newValue) {
    dataInRows = newValue;
}
public String getDataInRows() {
    return dataInRows;
}
```

Using Text Fields and Text Areas

Let's take a look at a complete example that uses text fields and text areas. The application shown in Figure 4–3 uses h:inputText, h:inputSecret, and h:inputTextarea to collect personal information from a user. Those components' values are wired to bean properties, which are accessed in a Thank You page that redisplays the information the user entered.

Three things are noteworthy about the following application. First, the JSF pages reference a user bean (com.corejsf.UserBean). Second, the h:inputTextarea tag transfers the text entered in a text area to the model (in this case, the user bean) as one string with embedded newlines ('\n'). We display that string by using the HTML <pre> element to preserve that formatting. Third, for illustration, we use the style attribute to format output. A more industrial-strength application would presumably use stylesheets exclusively to make global style changes easier to manage.

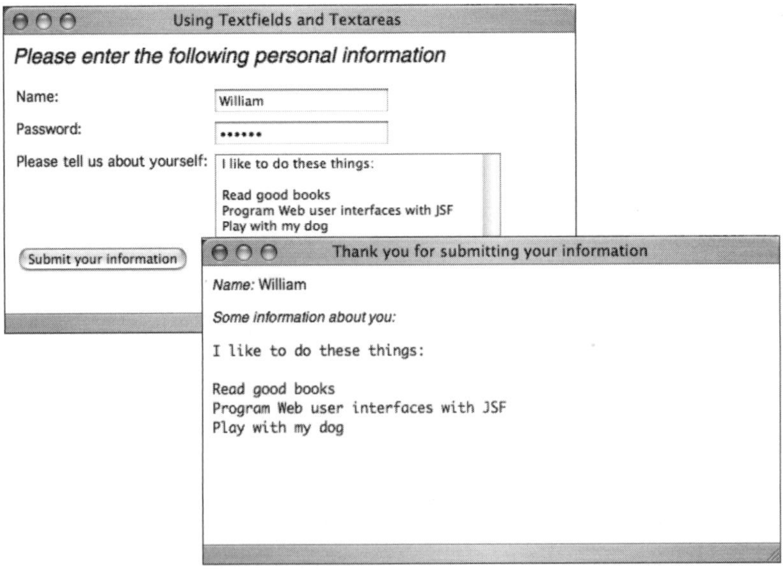

Figure 4–3   Using Text Fields and Text Areas

Figure 4–4 shows the directory structure for the application shown in Figure 4–3. Listing 4–3 through Listing 4–7 show the pertinent JSF pages, managed beans, faces configuration file, and resource bundle.

Figure 4–4 **Directory Structure**
of the Text Fields and Text Areas Example

Listing 4–3 `personalData/index.jsp`

```
1. <html>
2.    <%@ taglib uri="http://java.sun.com/jsf/core" prefix="f" %>
3.    <%@ taglib uri="http://java.sun.com/jsf/html" prefix="h" %>
4.    <f:view>
5.       <f:loadBundle basename="com.corejsf.messages" var="msgs"/>
6.       <head>
7.          <title>
8.             <h:outputText value="#{msgs.indexWindowTitle}"/>
9.          </title>
10.      </head>
11.      <body>
12.         <h:outputText value="#{msgs.indexPageTitle}"
13.            style="font-style: italic; font-size: 1.5em"/>
14.         <h:form>
15.            <table>
16.               <tr>
17.                  <td>
18.                     <h:outputText value="#{msgs.namePrompt}"/>
19.                  </td>
20.                  <td>
21.                     <h:inputText value="#{user.name}"/>
22.                  </td>
23.               </tr>
24.               <tr>
25.                  <td>
```

Listing 4–3   personalData/index.jsp (cont.)

```
26.                    <h:outputText value="#{msgs.passwordPrompt}"/>
27.                 </td>
28.                 <td>
29.                    <h:inputSecret value="#{user.password}"/>
30.                 </td>
31.              </tr>
32.              <tr>
33.                 <td>
34.                    <h:outputText value="#{msgs.tellUsPrompt}"/>
35.                 </td>
36.                 <td>
37.                    <h:inputTextarea value="#{user.aboutYourself}" rows="5"
38.                       cols="35"/>
39.                 </td>
40.              </tr>
41.           </table>
42.           <h:commandButton value="#{msgs.submitPrompt}" action="thankYou"/>
43.        </h:form>
44.     </body>
45.  </f:view>
46. </html>
```

Listing 4–4   personalData/thankYou.jsp

```
1. <html>
2.    <%@ taglib uri="http://java.sun.com/jsf/core" prefix="f" %>
3.    <%@ taglib uri="http://java.sun.com/jsf/html" prefix="h" %>
4.    <f:view>
5.       <f:loadBundle basename="com.corejsf.messages" var="msgs"/>
6.       <head>
7.          <title>
8.             <h:outputText value="#{msgs.thankYouWindowTitle}"/>
9.          </title>
10.       </head>
11.       <body>
12.          <h:outputText value="#{msgs.namePrompt}" style="font-style: italic"/>
13.          <h:outputText value="#{user.name}"/>
14.          <br/>
15.          <h:outputText value="#{msgs.aboutYourselfPrompt}"
16.             style="font-style: italic"/>
17.          <br/>
18.          <pre><h:outputText value="#{user.aboutYourself}"/></pre>
19.       </body>
20.    </f:view>
21. </html>
```

Listing 4–5 personalData/WEB-INF/classes/com/corejsf/UserBean.java

```
1. package com.corejsf;
2.
3. public class UserBean {
4.    private String name;
5.    private String password;
6.    private String aboutYourself;
7.
8.    // PROPERTY: name
9.    public String getName() { return name; }
10.   public void setName(String newValue) { name = newValue; }
11.
12.   // PROPERTY: password
13.   public String getPassword() { return password; }
14.   public void setPassword(String newValue) { password = newValue; }
15.
16.   // PROPERTY: aboutYourself
17.   public String getAboutYourself() { return aboutYourself;}
18.   public void setAboutYourself(String newValue) { aboutYourself = newValue; }
19. }
```

Listing 4–6 personalData/WEB-INF/faces-config.xml

```
1. <?xml version="1.0"?>
2.
3. <!DOCTYPE faces-config PUBLIC
4. "-//Sun Microsystems, Inc.//DTD JavaServer Faces Config 1.0//EN"
5. "http://java.sun.com/dtd/web-facesconfig_1_0.dtd">
6.
7. <faces-config>
8.
9.    <navigation-rule>
10.      <from-view-id>/index.jsp</from-view-id>
11.      <navigation-case>
12.         <from-outcome>thankYou</from-outcome>
13.         <to-view-id>/thankYou.jsp</to-view-id>
14.      </navigation-case>
15.   </navigation-rule>
16.
17.   <managed-bean>
18.      <managed-bean-name>user</managed-bean-name>
19.      <managed-bean-class>com.corejsf.UserBean</managed-bean-class>
20.      <managed-bean-scope>session</managed-bean-scope>
21.   </managed-bean>
22.
23. </faces-config>
```

Listing 4–7	personalData/WEB-INF/classes/com/corejsf/messages.properties

```
1. indexWindowTitle=Using Textfields and Textareas
2. thankYouWindowTitle=Thank you for submitting your information
3. thankYouPageTitle=Thank you!
4. indexPageTitle=Please enter the following personal information
5. namePrompt=Name:
6. passwordPrompt=Password:
7. tellUsPrompt=Please tell us about yourself:
8. aboutYourselfPrompt=Some information about you:
9. submitPrompt=Submit your information
```

Displaying Text and Images

JSF applications use the following tags to display text and images:

- h:outputText
- h:outputFormat
- h:graphicImage

The h:outputText tag is one of JSF's simplest tags. With only a handful of attributes, it does not typically generate an HTML element. Instead, it generates mere text—with one exception: if you specify the style or styleClass attributes, h:outputText will generate an HTML span element. Also, h:outputText and h:outputFormat have one attribute that is unique among all JSF HTML tags: escape. By default, the escape attribute is false, but if you set it to true, the following characters > < & are converted to < > and & respectively. Changing those characters helps prevent cross-site scripting attacks. See http://www.cert.org/advisories/CA-2000-02.html for more information about cross-site scripting attacks. Table 4–10 lists all h:outputText attributes.

Table 4–10 Attributes for h:outputText

Attributes	Description
escape	If set to true, escapes <, >, and & characters. Default value is false.
binding, converter, id, rendered, styleClass, value	Basic attributes[a]
style, title	HTML 4.0[b]

a. See Table 4–3 on page 90 for information about basic attributes.
b. See Table 4–4 on page 93 for information about HTML 4.0 attributes.

The h:outputFormat tag formats a compound message with parameters specified in the body of the tag; for example:

```
<h:outputFormat value="{0} is {1} years old">
    <f:param value="Bill"/>
    <f:param value="38"/>
</h:outputFormat>
```

In the preceding code fragment, the compound message is {0} is {1} years old and the parameters, specified with f:param tags, are Bill and 38. The output of the preceding code fragment is: Bill is 38 years old. The h:outputFormat tag uses a java.text.MessageFormat instance to format it's output.

Table 4–11 lists all attributes for h:outputFormat.

Table 4–11   Attributes for h:outputFormat

Attributes	Description
escape	If set to true, escapes <, >, and & characters. Default value is false.
binding, converter, id, rendered, styleClass, value	Basic attributes[a]
style, title	HTML 4.0[b]

a. See Table 4–3 on page 90 for information about basic attributes.
b. See Table 4–4 on page 93 for information about HTML 4.0 attributes.

The h:graphicImage tag lets you use a context-relative path—meaning relative to the web application's top-level directory—to display images. h:graphicImage generates an HTML img element.

Table 4–12 shows all the attributes for h:graphicImage.

Table 4–12   Attributes for h:graphicImage

Attributes	Description
binding, id, rendered, styleClass, value	Basic attributes[a]
alt, dir, height, ismap, lang, longdesc, style, title, url, usemap, width	HTML 4.0[b]
onblur, onchange, onclick, ondblclick, onfocus, onkeydown, onkeypress, onkeyup, onmousedown, onmousemove, onmouseout, onmouseover, onmouseup	DHTML events[c]

a. See Table 4–3 on page 90 for information about basic attributes.
b. See Table 4–4 on page 93 for information about HTML 4.0 attributes.
c. See Table 4–5 on page 95 for information about DHTML event attributes.

Table 4–13 shows some examples of using h:outputText and h:graphicImage.

Table 4–13   h:outputText **and** h:graphicImage **Examples**

Example	Result
`<h:outputText value="#{form.testString}"/>`	12345678901234567890
`<h:outputText value="Number #{form.number}"/>`	Number 1000
`<h:outputText` `value="<input type='text' value='hello'/>"/>`	hello
`<h:outputText escape="true"` `value="<input type='text' value='hello'/>"/>`	`<input type="text" value="hello">`
`<h:graphicImage value="/tjefferson.jpg"/>`	
`<h:graphicImage value="/tjefferson.jpg"` `style="border: thin solid black"/>`	

The third and fourth examples in Table 4–13 illustrate use of the escape attribute. If the value for h:outputText is `<input type='text' value='hello'/>` and the escape attribute is false—as is the case for the third example in Table 4–13—the h:outputText tag generates an HTML input element. Unintentional generation of HTML elements is exactly the sort of mischief that enables miscreants to carry out cross-site scripting attacks. With the escape attribute set to true—as in the fourth example in Table 4–13—that output is transformed to harmless text, thereby thwarting a potential attack.

The final two examples in Table 4–13 show you how to use h:graphicImage.

Hidden Fields

JSF provides support for hidden fields with h:inputHidden. Table 4–14 lists all attributes for h:inputHidden.

Table 4–14 Attributes for h:inputHidden

Attributes	Attributes
binding, converter, id, immediate, required, validator, value, valueChangeListener	Basic attributes[a]

a. See Table 4–3 on page 90 for information about basic attributes.

Buttons and Links

Buttons and links are ubiquitous among web applications, and JSF provides the following tags to support them:

*   h:commandButton
*   h:commandLink
*   h:outputLink

The h:commandButton and h:commandLink actions both represent JSF command components—the JSF framework fires action events and invokes actions when a button or link is activated. See Chapter 7 for more information about event handling for command components.

The h:outputLink tag generates an HTML anchor element that points to a resource such as an image or a web page. Clicking on the generated link takes you to the designated resource without further involving the JSF framework.

Table 4–15 lists the attributes shared by h:commandButton and h:commandLink.

Table 4–15 Attributes for h:commandButton **and** h:commandLink

Attribute	Description
action	*If specified as a string:* Directly specifies an outcome used by the navigation handler to determine the JSF page to load next as a result of activating the button or link
	If specified as a method binding: The method has this signature: String methodName(); the string represents the outcome
actionListener	A method binding that refers to a method with this signature: void methodName(ActionEvent)

Table 4–15   Attributes for h:commandButton **and** h:commandLink **(cont.)**

Attribute	Description
charset	For h:commandLink only—The character encoding of the linked reference
image	For h:commandButton only—A context-relative path to an image displayed in a button. If you specify this attribute, the HTML input's type will be image.
immediate	A boolean. If false (the default), actions and action listeners are invoked at the end of the request life cycle; if true, actions and action listeners are invoked at the beginning of the life cycle. See Chapter 6 for more information about the immediate attribute.
type	*For h:commandButton:* The type of the generated input element: button, submit, or reset. The default, unless you specify the image attribute, is submit. *For h:commandLink:* The content type of the linked resource; for example, text/html, image/gif, or audio/basic
value	The label displayed by the button or link. You can specify a string or a value reference expression.
accesskey, alt, binding, id, lang, rendered, styleClass, value	Basic attributes[a]
coords (h:commandLink only), dir, disabled, hreflang (h:commandLink only), lang, readonly, rel (h:commandLink only), rev (h:commandLink only), shape (h:commandLink only), style, tabindex, target (h:commandLink only), title, type	HTML 4.0[b]
onblur, onchange, onclick, ondblclick, onfocus, onkeydown, onkeypress, onkeyup, onmousedown, onmousemove, onmouseout, onmouseover, onmouseup, onselect	DHTML events[c]

a. See Table 4–3 on page 90 for information about basic attributes.
b. See Table 4–4 on page 93 for information about HTML 4.0 attributes.
c. See Table 4–5 on page 95 for information about DHTML event attributes.

Using Command Buttons

The h:commandButton tag generates an HTML input element whose type is button, image, submit, or reset, depending on the attributes you specify. Table 4–16 illustrates some uses of h:commandButton.

Table 4–16 h:commandButton **Examples**

Example	Result
`<h:commandButton value="submit" type="submit"/>`	submit
`<h:commandButton value="reset"` `   type="reset"/>`	reset

`<h:commandButton value="click this button..."`
`   onclick="alert('button clicked')"`
`   type="button"/>`
	click this button to execute JavaScript

`<h:commandButton value="disabled"` `   disabled="#{not form.buttonEnabled}"/>`	disabled
`<h:commandButton value="#{form.buttonText}"` `   type="reset"/>`	press me

The third example in Table 4–16 generates a push button—an HTML input element whose type is button—that does not result in a form submit. The only way to attach behavior to a push button is to specify a script for one of the DHTML event attributes, as we did for onclick in the example.

> CAUTION: h:graphicImage and h:commandButton can both display images, but the way in which you specify the image is not consistent between the two tags. h:commandButton requires a context path, whereas the context path is added automatically by h:graphicImage. For example, for an application named myApp, here's how you specify the same image for each tag:
>
> `<h:commandButton image="/myApp/imageFile.jpg"/>`
> `<h:graphicImage value="/imageFile.jpg"/>`

The h:commandLink tag generates an HTML anchor element that acts like a form submit button. Table 4–17 shows some h:commandLink examples.

Table 4–17   `h:commandLink` **Examples**

Example	Result
| ```
<h:commandLink>
   <h:outputText value="register"/>
</h:commandLink>
``` | register |
| ```
<h:commandLink style="font-style: italic">
   <h:outputText value="#{msgs.linkText}"/>
</h:commandLink>
``` | *click here to register* |
| ```
<h:commandLink>
   <h:outputText value="#{msgs.linkText}"/>
   <h:graphicImage value="/registration.jpg"/>
</h:commandLink>
``` | <br>click here to register |
| ```
<h:commandLink value="welcome"
   actionListener="#{form.useLinkValue}"
   action="#{form.followLink}">
``` | welcome |
| ```
<h:commandLink>
   <h:outputText value="welcome"/>
   <f:param name="outcome" value="welcome"/>
</h:commandLink>
``` | welcome |

`h:commandLink` generates JavaScript to make links act like buttons. For example, here is the HTML generated by the first example in Table 4–17:

```
<a href="#"
onclick="document.forms['_id0']['_id0:_id2'].value='_id0:_id2';document.forms['_id0']
.submit()">register</a>
```

When the link is clicked, the anchor element's value is set to the `h:commandLink`'s client ID and the enclosing form is submitted. That submission sets the JSF life cycle in motion and, because the `href` attribute is '#', the current page will be reloaded unless an action associated with the link returns a non-`null` outcome. See Chapter 3 for more information about JSF navigation.
```

You can place as many JSF HTML tags as you want in the body of an h:commandLink tag—each corresponding HTML element is part of the link. So, for example, if you click on either the text or image in the third example in Table 4–17, the link's form will be submitted.

The next-to-last example in Table 4–17 attaches an action listener, in addition to an action, to a link. The last example in Table 4–17 embeds an f:param tag in the body of the h:commandLink tag. When you click on the link, a request parameter with the name and value specified with the f:param tag is created by the link. You can use that request parameter any way you like. Chapter 7 tells you how to use request parameters to affect navigation outcomes.

Both h:commandButton and h:commandLink submit requests and subsequently invoke the JSF life cycle. Although those tags are useful, sometimes you just need a link that simply loads a resource without invoking the JSF life cycle. In that case, you can use the h:outputLink tag. Table 4–18 lists all attributes for h:outputLink.

Table 4–18 Attributes for h:outputLink

Attributes	Description
accesskey, binding, converter, id, lang, rendered, styleClass, value	Basic attributes[a]
charset, coords, dir, hreflang, lang, rel, rev, shape, style, tabindex, target, title, type	HTML 4.0[b]
onblur, onchange, onclick, ondblclick, onfocus, onkeydown, onkeypress, onkeyup, onmousedown, onmousemove, onmouseout, onmouseover, onmouseup	DHTML events[c]

a. See Table 4–3 on page 90 for information about basic attributes.
b. See Table 4–4 on page 93 for information about HTML 4.0 attributes.
c. See Table 4–5 on page 95 for information about DHTML event attributes.

Like h:commandLink, h:outputLink generates an HTML anchor element. But unlike h:commandLink, h:outputLink does not generate JavaScript to make the link act like a submit button. The value of the h:outputLink value attribute is used for the anchor's href attribute, and the contents of the h:outputLink body are used to populate the body of the anchor element. Table 4–19 shows some h:outputLink examples.

Table 4–19   h:outputLink **Examples**

Example	Result

`<h:outputLink value="http://java.net">`
`  <h:graphicImage value="java-dot-net.jpg"/>`
`  <h:outputText value="java.net"/>`
`</h:outputLink>`	

`<h:outputLink value="#{form.welcomeURL}">`
`  <h:outputText value="#{form.welcomeLinkText}"/>`
`</h:outputLink>`
	go to welcome page

`<h:outputLink value="#introduction">`
`  <h:outputText value="Introduction"`
`    style="font-style: italic"/>`
`</h:outputLink>`
	Introduction

`<h:outputLink value="#conclusion"`
`  title="Go to the conclusion">`
`  <h:outputText value="Conclusion"/>`
`</h:outputLink>`
	Conclusion
	Go to the conclusion

`<h:outputLink value="#toc"`
`  title="Go to the table of contents">`
`  <f:verbatim>`
`    <h2>Table of Contents</h2>`
`  </f:verbatim>`
`</h:outputLink>`
	Table of Contents

The first example in Table 4–19 is a link to http://java.net. The second example uses properties stored in a bean for the link's URL and text. Those properties are implemented like this:

```
private String welcomeURL = "/outputLinks/faces/welcome.jsp";
    public String getWelcomeURL() {
        return welcomeURL;
    }
    private String welcomeLinkText = "go to welcome page";
    public String getWelcomeLinkText() {
        return welcomeLinkText;
    }
```

The last three examples in Table 4–19 are links to named anchors in the same JSF page. Those anchors look like this:

```
<a name="introduction">Introduction</a>
...
<a name="toc">Table of Contents</a>
...
<a name="conclusion">Conclusion</a>
...
```

Notice that the last example in Table 4–19 uses f:verbatim. You cannot simply place text inside the h:outputLink tag. For example, <h:outputLink...>Introduction</ h:outputLink> would not work correctly—the text would appear outside the link. The remedy is to place the text inside a component, either with h:outputText or with f:verbatim. Generally, you use h:outputText for text, f:verbatim for HTML—see the first and last examples in Table 4–19.

Using Command Links

Now that we've discussed the details of JSF tags for buttons and links, let's take a look at a complete example. Figure 4–5 shows the application discussed in "Using Text Fields and Text Areas" on page 104 with two links that let you select either English or German locales. When a link is activated, an action changes the view's locale and the JSF implementation reloads the current page.

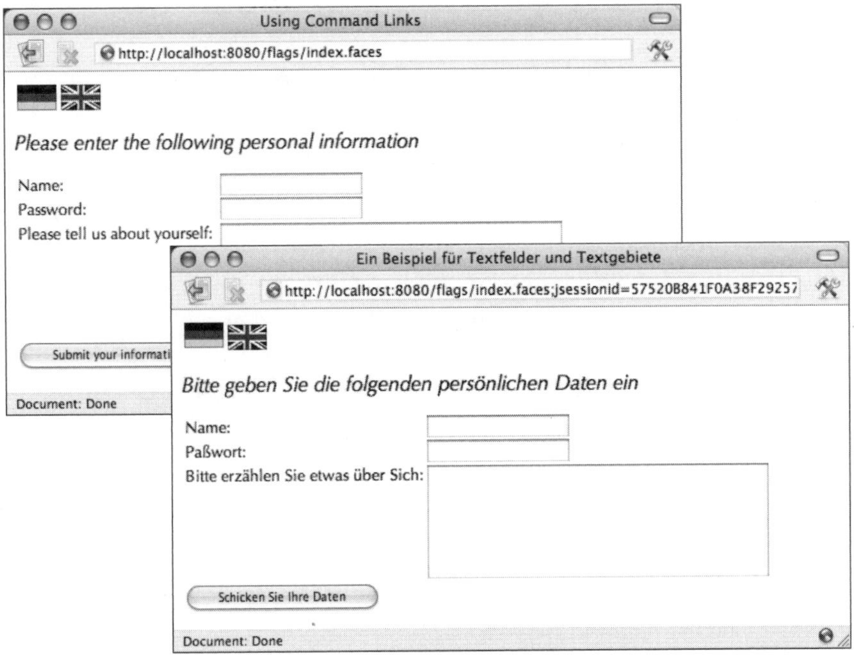

Figure 4–5   Using Command Links to Change Locales

The two links are implemented like this:

```
<h:form>
    ...
    <h:commandLink action="#{localeChanger.germanAction}">
        <h:graphicImage value="/german_flag.gif"
            style="border: 0px"/>
    </h:commandLink>

    <h:commandLink action="#{localeChanger.englishAction}">
        <h:graphicImage value="/britain_flag.gif"
            style="border: 0px"/>
    </h:commandLink>
    ...
</h:form>
```

Both links specify an image, request parameter, and an action method. Those methods look like this:

```
public class ChangeLocaleBean {
    public String germanAction() {
        FacesContext context = FacesContext.getCurrentInstance();
        context.getViewRoot().setLocale(Locale.GERMAN);
        return null;
    }
    public String englishAction() {
        FacesContext context = FacesContext.getCurrentInstance();
        context.getViewRoot().setLocale(Locale.ENGLISH);
        return null;
    }
}
```

Both actions set the locale of the view. And because we have not specified any navigation for this application, the JSF implementation will reload the current page after the form is submitted. When the page is reloaded, it is localized for English or German and the page redisplays accordingly.

Figure 4–6 shows the directory structure for the application and Listing 4–8 through Listing 4–10 show the associated JSF pages and the faces configuration file.

```
flags
    britain_flag.gif
    german_flag.gif
    index.html
    index.jsp
    styles.css
    thankYou.jsp
WEB-INF
    faces-config.xml
    web.xml
    classes
        messages_de.properties
        messages_en.properties
        com
            corejsf
                ChangeLocaleBean.java
                UserBean.java
```

**Figure 4–6   Directory Structure
of the Text Fields and Text Areas Example**

Listing 4–8   flags/index.jsp

```jsp
1.  <html>
2.    <%@ taglib uri="http://java.sun.com/jsf/core" prefix="f" %>
3.    <%@ taglib uri="http://java.sun.com/jsf/html" prefix="h" %>
4.    <f:view>
5.      <f:loadBundle basename="messages" var="msgs"/>
6.      <head>
7.        <link href="styles.css" rel="stylesheet" type="text/css"/>
8.        <title>
9.          <h:outputText value="#{msgs.indexWindowTitle}"/>
10.       </title>
11.     </head>
12.     <body>
13.       <h:form>
14.         <table>
15.           <tr>
16.             <td>
17.               <h:commandLink immediate="true"
18.                   action="#{localeChanger.germanAction}">
19.                 <h:graphicImage value="/german_flag.gif"
20.                     style="border: 0px"/>
21.               </h:commandLink>
22.             </td
23.             <td>
24.               <h:commandLink immediate="true"
25.                   action="#{localeChanger.englishAction}">
```

Listing 4–8 flags/index.jsp (cont.)

```
26.                        <h:graphicImage value="/britain_flag.gif"
27.                            style="border: 0px"/>
28.                        </h:commandLink>
29.                    </td>
30.                </tr>
31.            </table>
32.            <p>
33.                <h:outputText value="#{msgs.indexPageTitle}"
34.                    style="font-style: italic; font-size: 1.3em"/>
35.            </p>
36.            <table>
37.                <tr>
38.                    <td>
39.                        <h:outputText value="#{msgs.namePrompt}"/>
40.                    </td>
41.                    <td>
42.                        <h:inputText value="#{user.name}"/>
43.                    </td>
44.                </tr>
45.                <tr>
46.                    <td>
47.                        <h:outputText value="#{msgs.passwordPrompt}"/>
48.                    </td>
49.                    <td>
50.                        <h:inputSecret value="#{user.password}"/>
51.                    </td>
52.                </tr>
53.                <tr>
54.                    <td style="vertical-align: top">
55.                        <h:outputText value="#{msgs.tellUsPrompt}"/>
56.                    </td>
57.                    <td>
58.                        <h:inputTextarea value="#{user.aboutYourself}" rows="5"
59.                            cols="35"/>
60.                    </td>
61.                </tr>
62.                <tr>
63.                    <td>
64.                        <h:commandButton value="#{msgs.submitPrompt}"
65.                            action="thankYou"/>
66.                    </td>
67.                </tr>
68.            </table>
69.        </h:form>
70.    </body>
71. </f:view>
72. </html>
```

Listing 4–9 flags/WEB-INF/classes/com/corejsf/UserBean.java

```
1. package com.corejsf;
2.
3. public class UserBean {
4.    private String name;
5.    private String password;
6.    private String aboutYourself;
7.
8.    // PROPERTY: name
9.    public String getName() { return name; }
10.   public void setName(String newValue) { name = newValue; }
11.
12.   // PROPERTY: password
13.   public String getPassword() { return password; }
14.   public void setPassword(String newValue) { password = newValue; }
15.
16.   // PROPERTY: aboutYourself
17.   public String getAboutYourself() { return aboutYourself;}
18.   public void setAboutYourself(String newValue) { aboutYourself = newValue; }
19. }
```

Listing 4–10 flags/WEB-INF/faces-config.xml

```
1. <?xml version="1.0"?>
2.
3. <!DOCTYPE faces-config PUBLIC
4. "-//Sun Microsystems, Inc.//DTD JavaServer Faces Config 1.0//EN"
5. "http://java.sun.com/dtd/web-facesconfig_1_0.dtd">
6.
7. <faces-config>
8.
9.    <navigation-rule>
10.      <from-view-id>/index.jsp</from-view-id>
11.      <navigation-case>
12.        <from-outcome>thankYou</from-outcome>
13.        <to-view-id>/thankYou.jsp</to-view-id>
14.      </navigation-case>
15.   </navigation-rule>
16.
17.   <managed-bean>
18.      <managed-bean-name>localeChanger</managed-bean-name>
19.      <managed-bean-class>com.corejsf.ChangeLocaleBean</managed-bean-class>
20.      <managed-bean-scope>session</managed-bean-scope>
21.   </managed-bean>
22.
```

Listing 4–10   flags/WEB-INF/faces-config.xml (cont.)

```
23.    <managed-bean>
24.        <managed-bean-name>user</managed-bean-name>
25.        <managed-bean-class>com.corejsf.UserBean</managed-bean-class>
26.        <managed-bean-scope>session</managed-bean-scope>
27.    </managed-bean>
28.
29. </faces-config>
```

Selection Tags

JavaServer Faces has seven tags for making selections:

- h:selectBooleanCheckbox
- h:selectManyCheckbox
- h:selectOneRadio
- h:selectOneListbox
- h:selectManyListbox
- h:selectOneMenu
- h:selectManyMenu

Table 4–20 shows examples of each tag listed above.

Table 4–20   Selection Tag Examples

Tag	Generated HTML	Examples
h:selectBooleanCheckbox	`<input type="checkbox">`	Receive email: ☑

h:selectManyCheckbox	`<table>`
	
	...
	
	`<label>`
	
	`<input type="checkbox"/>`
	
	`</label>`
	
	...
	
	`</table>`
		☐ Red ☑ Blue ☐ Yellow

Table 4–20   Selection Tag Examples (cont.)

Tag	Generated HTML	Examples

h:selectOneRadio	```<table>```
	
	```...```
	
	```<label>```
	
	``` <input type="radio"/>```
	
	```</label>```
	
	```...```
	
	```</table>```
		○ High School
		◉ Bachelor's
		○ Master's
		○ Doctorate

h:selectOneListbox	```<select>```
	
	``` <option value="Cheese">```
	
	``` Cheese```
	
	``` </option>```
	
	```...```
	
	```</select>```
		Cheese
		Pickle
		Mustard
		Lettuce

h:selectManyListbox	```<select multiple>```
	
	``` <option value="Cheese">```
	
	``` Cheese```
	
	``` </option>```
	
	```...```
	
	```</select>```
		Cheese
		Pickle
		Mustard
		Lettuce
		Onions

h:selectOneMenu	```<select size="1">```
	
	``` <option value="Cheese">```
	
	``` Cheese```
	
	``` </option>```
	
	```...```
	
	```</select>```
		Pickle
		Cheese
		Pickle
		Mustard
		Lettuce
		Onions

h:selectManyMenu	```<select multiple size="1">```
	
	``` <option value="Sunday">```
	
	``` Sunday```
	
	``` </option>```
	
	```...```
	
	```</select>```
		Sunday
		Monday
		Tuesday
		Wednesday

The h:selectBooleanCheckbox is the simplest selection tag—it renders a checkbox you can wire to a boolean bean property. You can also render a set of checkboxes with h:selectManyCheckbox.

Tags whose names begin with selectOne let you select one item from a collection. The selectOne tags render sets of radio buttons, single-select menus, or listboxes. The selectMany tags render sets of checkboxes, multiselect menus, or listboxes.

All selection tags share an almost identical set of attributes, listed in Table 4–21.

Table 4–21   Attributes for h:selectBooleanCheckbox, h:selectManyCheckbox, h:selectOneRadio, h:selectOneListbox, h:selectManyListbox, h:selectOneMenu, h:selectManyMenu

Attributes	Description
disabledClass	CSS class for disabled elements—for h:selectOneRadio and h:selectManyCheckbox only
enabledClass	CSS class for enabled elements—for h:selectOneRadio and h:selectManyCheckbox only
layout	Specification for how elements are laid out: LINE_DIRECTION (horizontal) or PAGE_DIRECTION (vertical)—for h:selectOneRadio and h:selectManyCheckbox only
binding, converter, id, immediate, styleClass, required, rendered, validator, value, valueChangeListener	Basic attributes[a]
accesskey, border, dir, disabled, lang, readonly, style, size, tabindex, title	HTML 4.0[b]—border is applicable to h:selectOneRadio and h:selectManyCheckbox only. size is applicable to h:selectOneListbox and h:selectManyListbox only.
onblur, onchange, onclick, ondblclick, onfocus, onkeydown, onkeypress, onkeyup, onmousedown, onmousemove, onmouseout, onmouseover, onmouseup, onselect	DHTML events[c]

a. See Table 4–3 on page 90 for information about basic attributes.
b. See Table 4–4 on page 93 for information about HTML 4.0 attributes.
c. See Table 4–5 on page 95 for information about DHTML event attributes.

Checkboxes and Radio Buttons

Two JSF tags represent checkboxes:

- h:selectBooleanCheckbox
- h:selectManyCheckbox

h:selectBooleanCheckbox represents a single checkbox that you can wire to a boolean bean property. Here is an example.

Contact me ☑

In your JSF page, you do this:

```
<h:selectBooleanCheckbox value="#{form.contactMe}"/>
```

In your backing bean, provide a read-write property:

```
private boolean contactMe;
public void setContactMe(boolean newValue) {
    contactMe = newValue;
}
public boolean getContactMe() {
    return contactMe;
}
```

The generated HTML looks something like this:

```
<input type="checkbox" name="_id2:_id7"/>
```

You can create a group of checkboxes with h:selectManyCheckbox. As the tag name implies, you can select one or more of the checkboxes in the group. You specify that group within the body of h:selectManyCheckbox, either with one or more f:selectItem tags or one f:selectItems tag. See "Items" on page 130 for more information about those core tags. For example, here's a group of checkboxes for selecting colors.

The h:selectManyCheckbox tag looks like this:

```
<h:selectManyCheckbox value="#{form.colors}">
    <f:selectItem itemValue="Red"/>
    <f:selectItem itemValue="Blue"/>
    <f:selectItem itemValue="Yellow"/>
    <f:selectItem itemValue="Green"/>
    <f:selectItem itemValue="Orange"/>
</h:selectManyCheckbox>
```

The checkboxes are specified with f:selectItem tags. See "f:selectItem" on page 130 for more information on that tag.

h:selectManyCheckbox generates an HTML table element; for example, here's the generated HTML for our color example:

```
<table>
    <tr>
        <td>
            <label for="_id2:_id14">
                <input name="_id2:_id14" value="Red" type="checkbox">Red</input>
            </label>
        </td>
    </tr>
    ...
</table>
```

Each color is an input element, wrapped in a label for accessibility purposes. That label is placed in a td element.

Radio buttons are implemented with h:selectOneRadio. Here is an example.

○ High School ○ Bachelor's ● Master's ○ Doctorate

The h:selectOneRadio value attribute specifies the currently selected item. Once again, we use multiple f:selectItem tags to populate the radio buttons:

```
<h:selectOneRadio value="#{form.education}">
    <f:selectItem itemValue="High School" itemLabel="High School"/>
    <f:selectItem itemValue="Bachelor's" itemLabel="Bachelor's"/>
    <f:selectItem itemValue="Master's" itemLabel="Master's"/>
    <f:selectItem itemValue="Doctorate" itemLabel="Doctorate"/>
</h:selectOneRadio>
```

Like h:selectManyCheckbox, h:selectOneRadio generates an HTML table. Here's the table generated by the preceding tag:

```
<table>
    <tr>
        <td>
            <label for="_id2:_id14">
                <input name="_id2:_id14" value="High School" type="radio">
                    High School
                </input>
            </label>
        </td>
    </tr>
    ...
</table>
```

Besides generating HTML tables, h:selectOneRadio and h:selectManyCheckbox have something else in common—a handful of attributes unique to those two tags.

- border
- enabledClass
- disabledClass
- layout

The border attribute specifies the width of the border. For example, here are radio buttons and checkboxes with borders of 1 and 2, respectively.

enabledClass and disabledClass specify CSS classes used when the checkboxes or radio buttons are enabled or disabled, respectively. For example, the following picture shows an enabled class with an italic font style, blue color, and yellow background.

The layout attribute can be either lineDirection (horizontal) or pageDirection (vertical). For example, the following checkboxes on the left have a pageDirection layout and the checkboxes on the right are lineDirection.

NOTE: You might wonder why layout attribute values aren't horizontal and vertical, instead of lineDirection and pageDirection, respectively. Although lineDirection and pageDirection are indeed horizontal and vertical for Latin-based languages, that's not always the case for other languages. For example, a Chinese browser that displays text top to bottom could regard lineDirection as vertical and pageDirection as horizontal.

Menus and Listboxes

Menus and listboxes are represented by the following tags:

- h:selectOneListbox
- h:selectManyListbox
- h:selectOneMenu
- h:selectManyMenu

The attributes for the preceding tags are listed in Table 4–21 on page 124, so that discussion is not repeated here.

Menu and listbox tags generate HTML select elements. The menu tags add a size="1" attribute to the select element. That size designation is all that separates menus and listboxes.

Here's a single-select listbox.

The corresponding listbox tag looks like this:

```
<h:selectOneListbox value="#{form.year}" size="5">
    <f:selectItem itemValue="1900" itemLabel="1900"/>
    <f:selectItem itemValue="1901" itemLabel="1901"/>
    ...
</h:selectOneListbox>
```

Notice that we've used the size attribute to specify the number of visible items. The generated HTML looks like this:

```
<select name="_id2:_id11" size="5">
    <option value="1900">1900</option>
    <option value="1901">1901</option>
    ...
</select>
```

Use h:selectManyListbox for multiselect listboxes like this one.

The listbox tag looks like this:

```
<h:selectManyListbox value="#{form.languages}">
    <f:selectItem itemValue="English" itemLabel="English"/>
    <f:selectItem itemValue="French" itemLabel="French"/>
    <f:selectItem itemValue="Italian" itemLabel="Italian"/>
    <f:selectItem itemValue="Spanish" itemLabel="Spanish"/>
    <f:selectItem itemValue="Russian" itemLabel="Russian"/>
</h:selectManyListbox>
```

This time we don't specify the size attribute, so the listbox grows to accommodate all its items. The generated HTML looks like this:

```
<select name="_id2:_id11" multiple>
    <option value="English">English</option>
    <option value="French">French</option>
    ...
</select>
```

Use h:selectOneMenu and h:selectManyMenu for menus. A single-select menu looks like this.

h:selectOneMenu created the preceding menu:

```
<h:selectOneMenu value="#{form.day}">
    <f:selectItem itemValue="Sunday" itemLabel="Sunday"/>
    <f:selectItem itemValue="Monday" itemLabel="Monday"/>
    <f:selectItem itemValue="Tuesday" itemLabel="Tuesday"/>
    <f:selectItem itemValue="Wednesday" itemLabel="Wednesday"/>
    <f:selectItem itemValue="Thursday" itemLabel="Thursday"/>
    <f:selectItem itemValue="Friday" itemLabel="Friday"/>
    <f:selectItem itemValue="Saturday" itemLabel="Saturday"/>
</h:selectOneMenu>
```

Here's the generated HTML:

```
<select name="_id2:_id17" size="1">
    <option value="Sunday">Sunday</option>
    ...
</select>
```

h:selectManyMenu is used for multiselect menus. That tag generates HTML that looks like this:

```
<select name="_id2:_id17" multiple size="1">
    <option value="Sunday">Sunday</option>
    ...
</select>
```

That HTML does not yield consistent results among browsers. For example, here's h:selectManyMenu on Internet Explorer (left) and Netscape (right).

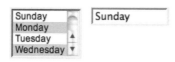

> ![NOTE icon] **NOTE:** In HTML, the distinction between menus and listboxes is artificial. Menus and listboxes are both HTML `select` elements. The only distinction: menus always have a `size="1"` attribute.
>
> Browsers consistently render single-select menus as drop-down lists, as expected. But they do not consistently render multiple select menus, specified with `size="1"` and `multiple` attributes. Instead of rendering a drop-down list with multiple selection, as you might expect, browsers render absurdities such as tiny scrollbars that are nearly impossible to manipulate (Windows IE)—as shown above—or no scrollbar at all, leaving you to navigate with arrow keys (Mozilla).

Starting with "Selection Tags" on page 122, we've consistently used multiple f:selectItem tags to populate select components. Now that we're familiar with the fundamentals of selection tags, let's take a closer look at f:selectItem and the related f:selectItems tag.

Items

All selection tags except h:selectBooleanCheckbox use f:selectItem or f:selectItems to specify their items. Let's look at those core tags, starting with f:selectItem.

f:selectItem

You use f:selectItem to specify single selection items, like this:

```
<h:selectOneMenu value="#{form.condiments}">
    <f:selectItem itemValue="Cheese" itemLabel="Cheese"/>
    <f:selectItem itemValue="Pickle" itemLabel="Pickle"/>
    <f:selectItem itemValue="Mustard" itemLabel="Mustard"/>
    <f:selectItem itemValue="Lettuce" itemLabel="Lettuce"/>
    <f:selectItem itemValue="Onions" itemLabel="Onions"/>
</h:selectOneMenu>
```

The values—Cheese, Pickle, etc.—are transmitted as request parameter values when a selection is made from the menu and the menu's form is subsequently submitted. Those values are also used as labels for the menu items. Sometimes you want to specify different values for request parameter values and item labels, so f:selectItem also has an itemLabel attribute:

```
<h:selectOneMenu value="#{form.condiments}">
    <f:selectItem itemValue="1" itemLabel="Cheese"/>
    <f:selectItem itemValue="2" itemLabel="Pickle"/>
    <f:selectItem itemValue="3" itemLabel="Mustard"/>
    <f:selectItem itemValue="4" itemLabel="Lettuce"/>
    <f:selectItem itemValue="5" itemLabel="Onions"/>
</h:selectOneMenu>
```

In the preceding code, the item values are strings. "Binding the value Attribute" on page 136 shows you how to use different data types for item values.

In addition to labels and values, you can also supply item descriptions and specify an item's disabled state:

```
<f:selectItem itemLabel="Cheese" itemValue="#{form.cheeseValue}"
        itemDescription="used to be milk"
          itemDisabled="true"/>
```

Item descriptions are for tools only—they do not affect the generated HTML. The disabled attribute, however, is passed to HTML. The f:selectItem tag has the following attributes:

Table 4–22   Attributes for f:selectItem

Attribute	Description
binding	Component binding—see Chapter 2 for more information about component bindings.
id	Component ID
itemDescription	Description used by tools only
itemDisabled	Boolean value that sets the item's disabled property
itemLabel	Text shown by the item
itemValue	Item's value, which is passed to the server as a request parameter
value	Value binding expression that points to a SelectItem instance

You can use f:selectItem's value attribute to access SelectItem instances created in a bean:

```
<f:selectItem value="#{form.cheeseItem}"/>
```

The value binding expression for the value attribute points to a method that returns a javax.faces.model.SelectItem instance:

```
public SelectItem getCheeseItem() {
    return new SelectItem("Cheese");
}
```

javax.faces.model.SelectItem

- `SelectItem(Object value)`
  Creates a `SelectItem` with a value. The item label is obtained by applying `toString()` to the value.
- `SelectItem(Object value, String label)`
  Creates a `SelectItem` with a value and a label.
- `SelectItem(Object value, String label, String description)`
  Creates a `SelectItem` with a value, label, and description.
- `SelectItem(Object value, String label, String description, boolean disabled)`
  Creates a `SelectItem` with a value, label, description, and disabled state.

f:selectItems

As we saw in "f:selectItem" on page 130, `f:selectItem` is versatile, but it's tedious for specifying more than a few items. The first code fragment in "f:selectItem" on page 130 can be reduced to the following with `f:selectItems`:

```
<h:selectOneRadio>
    <f:selectItems value="#{form.condiments}"/>
</h:selectOneRadio>
```

The value binding expression `#{form.condiments}` could point to an array of `SelectItem` instances:

```
private SelectItem[] condiments = {
    new SelectItem(new Integer(1), "Cheese"),
    new SelectItem(new Integer(2), "Pickle"),
    new SelectItem(new Integer(3), "Mustard"),
    new SelectItem(new Integer(4), "Lettuce"),
    new SelectItem(new Integer(5), "Onions")
};

public SelectItem[] getCondiments() {
    return condiments;
}
```

The `f:selectItems` value attribute must be a value binding expression that points to one of the following:

- A single `SelectItem` instance
- A collection of `SelectItem` instances
- An array of `SelectItem` instances
- A map whose entries represent `SelectItem` labels and values

If you specify a map, the JSF implementation creates a SelectItem instance for every entry in the map. The entry's key is used as the item's label, and the entry's value is used as the item's value. For example, here are condiments specified with a map:

```
private Map condiments = null;

public Map getCondiments() {
    if(condiments == null) {
        condiments = new HashMap();
        condiments.put("Cheese",  new Integer(1)); // key,value
        condiments.put("Pickle",  new Integer(2));
        condiments.put("Mustard", new Integer(3));
        condiments.put("Lettuce", new Integer(4));
        condiments.put("Onions",  new Integer(5));
    }
    return condiments;
}
```

Note that you cannot specify item descriptions or disabled status when you use a map.

 NOTE: A single f:selectItems tag is usually better than multiple f:selectItem tags. If the number of items changes, you have to modify only Java code if you use f:selectItems, whereas f:selectItem may require you to modify both Java code and JSF pages.

 NOTE: If you use SelectItem, you couple your code to the JSF API. This makes the Map alternative seemingly attractive.

 CAUTION: If you use a Map for select items, JSF turns map keys into item labels and map values into item values. When a user selects an item, the JSF implementation returns a value in your map, not a key. That makes it painful to dig out the corresponding key.

 CAUTION: If you use a Map for select items, pay attention to the item ordering. If you use a TreeMap, the values (which are the keys of the map) are sorted alphabetically. For example, days of the week would be neatly arranged as Friday Monday Saturday Sunday Thursday Tuesday Wednesday.

NOTE: It's a SCAM: Can't remember what you can specify for the
`f:selectItems` value attribute? <u>S</u>ingle select item; <u>C</u>ollection of select items;
<u>A</u>rray of select items; <u>M</u>ap.

Item Groups

You can group menu or listbox items together, like this.

Here are the JSF tags that define the listbox:

```
<h:selectManyListbox>
    <f:selectItems value="#{form.menuItems}"/>
</h:selectManyListbox>
```

The `menuItems` property is a `SelectItem` array:

```
public SelectItem[] getMenuItems() { return menuItems; }
```

The `menuItems` array is instantiated like this:

```
private static SelectItem[] menuItems = { burgers,  beverages, condiments };
```

The burgers, beverages, and condiments variables are `SelectItemGroup` instances that are
instantiated like this:

```
private SelectItemGroup burgers =
    new  SelectItemGroup("Burgers", // value
            "burgers on the menu", // description
            false, // disabled
            burgerItems); // select items

    private SelectItemGroup beverages =
        new  SelectItemGroup("Beverages", // value
```

```
                    "beverages on the menu", // description
                    false, // disabled
                    beverageItems); // select items

    private SelectItemGroup condiments =
        new  SelectItemGroup("Condiments", // value
                    "condiments on the menu", // description
                    false, // disabled
                    condimentItems); // select items
```

Notice we're using SelectItemGroups to populate an array of SelectItems. We can do that because SelectItemGroup extends SelectItem. The groups are created and initialized like this:

```
private SelectItem[] burgerItems = {
    new SelectItem("Qwarter pounder"),
    new SelectItem("Single"),
    new SelectItem("Veggie"),
};
private SelectItem[] beverageItems = {
    new SelectItem("Coke"),
    new SelectItem("Pepsi"),
    new SelectItem("Water"),
    new SelectItem("Coffee"),
    new SelectItem("Tea"),
};
private SelectItem[] condimentItems = {
    new SelectItem("cheese"),
    new SelectItem("pickle"),
    new SelectItem("mustard"),
    new SelectItem("lettuce"),
    new SelectItem("onions"),
};
```

SelectItemGroup instances encode HTML optgroup elements. For example, the preceding code generates the following HTML:

```
<select name="_id0:_id1" multiple size="16">
    <optgroup label="Burgers">
        <option value="1"  selected>Qwarter pounder</option>
        <option value="2">Single</option>
        <option value="3">Veggie</option>
    </optgroup>

    <optgroup label="Beverages">
        <option value="4"  selected>Coke</option>
        <option value="5">Pepsi</option>
        <option value="6">Water</option>
```

```
        <option value="7">Coffee</option>
        <option value="8">Tea</option>
    </optgroup>

    <optgroup label="Condiments">
        <option value="9">cheese</option>
        <option value="10">pickle</option>
        <option value="11">mustard</option>
        <option value="12">lettuce</option>
        <option value="13">onions</option>
    </optgroup>
</select>
```

> **NOTE:** The HTML 4.01 specification does not allow nested optgroup elements, which would be useful for things like cascading menus. The specification does mention that future HTML versions may support that behavior.

javax.faces.model.SelectItemGroup

- SelectItemGroup(String label)

  Creates a group with a label, but no selection items

- SelectItemGroup(String label, String description, boolean disabled, SelectItem[] items)

  Creates a group with a label, a description (which is ignored by the JSF 1.0 Reference Implementation), a boolean that disables all of the items when true, and an array of select items used to populate the group

- setSelectItems(SelectItem[] items)

  Sets a group's array of SelectItems

Binding the value Attribute

In all likelihood, whether you're using a set of checkboxes, a menu, or a listbox, you'll want to keep track of selected items. For that purpose, you can exploit selectOne and selectMany tags, which have value attributes that represent selected items. For example, you can specify a selected item with the h:selectOneRadio value attribute, like this:

```
<h:selectOneRadio value="#{form.education}">
    <f:selectItems value="#{form.educationItems}"/>
</h:selectOneRadio>
```

The #{form.education} value reference expression refers to the education property of a bean named form. That property is implemented like this:

```
private Integer education = null;
public Integer getEducation() {
    return education;
}
public void setEducation(Integer newValue) {
    education = newValue;
}
```

Notice that the education property type is Integer. That means the radio buttons must have Integer values. Those radio buttons are specified with f:selectItems, with a value attribute that points to the educationItems property of the form bean:

```
private SelectItem[] educationItems = {
    new SelectItem(new Integer(1), "High School"), // value, label
    new SelectItem(new Integer(2), "Bachelors"),
    new SelectItem(new Integer(3), "Masters"),
    new SelectItem(new Integer(4), "PHD")
};
public SelectItem[] getEducationItems() {
    return educationItems;
}
```

In the preceding example, we arbitrarily chose Integer to represent education level. You can choose any type you like as long as the properties for items and selected item have matching types.

You can keep track of multiple selections with a selectMany tag. Those tags also have a value attribute that lets you specify one or more selected items. That attribute's value must be an array or list of convertible types.

Let's take a look at some different data types. We'll use h:selectManyListbox to let a user choose multiple condiments:

```
<h:selectManyListbox value="#{form.condiments}">
    <f:selectItems value="#{form.condimentItems}"/>
</h:selectManyListbox>
```

Here are the condimentItems and condiments properties:

```
private static SelectItem[] condimentItems = {
    new SelectItem(new Integer(1), "Cheese"),
    new SelectItem(new Integer(2), "Pickle"),
    new SelectItem(new Integer(3), "Mustard"),
    new SelectItem(new Integer(4), "Lettuce"),
    new SelectItem(new Integer(5), "Onions"),
};
```

```
public SelectItem[] getCondimentItems() {
   return condimentItems;
}

private Integer[] condiments;
public void setCondiments(Integer[] newValue) {
   condiments = newValue;
}
public Integer[] getCondiments() {
   return condiments;
}
```

Instead of an Integer array for the condiments property, we could have used the corresponding primitive type, int:

```
private int[] condiments;
public void setCondiments(int[] newValue) {
   condiments = newValue;
}
public int[] getCondiments() {
   return condiments;
}
```

If you use strings for item values, you can use a string array or list of strings for your selected items property:

```
private static SelectItem[] condimentItems = {
   new SelectItem("cheese", "Cheese"),
   new SelectItem("pickle", "Pickle"),
   new SelectItem("mustard", "Mustard"),
   new SelectItem("lettuce", "Lettuce"),
   new SelectItem("onions", "Onions"),
};
public SelectItem[] getCondimentItems() {
   return condimentItems;
}

private String[] condiments;
public void setCondiments(String[] newValue) {
   condiments = newValue;
}
public String[] getCondiments() {
   return condiments;
}
```

The preceding condiments property is an array of strings. You could use a list instead:

```
private List condiments = null;
public List getCondiments() {
    if(condiments == null) {
        condiments = new LinkedList();
        condiments.add(new SelectItem("cheese", "Cheese"));
        condiments.add(new SelectItem("pickle", "Pickle"));
        condiments.add(new SelectItem("mustard", "Mustard"));
        condiments.add(new SelectItem("lettuce", "Lettuce"));
        condiments.add(new SelectItem("onions", "Onions"));
    }
    return condiments;
}
public void setCondiments(List newValue) {
    selectedCondiments = newValue;
}
```

Finally, you can specify user-defined types for selected items. If you do, you must provide a converter so that the JSF implementation can convert the strings on the client to objects on the server.

> **NOTE:** If you use application-specific objects in selection lists, you must implement a converter and either register it for your application-specific class, or specify the converter ID with the tag's converter attribute. If you do not provide a converter, the JSF implementation will create conversion errors when it tries to convert strings to instances of your class, and your model values will not be updated. See Chapter 6 for more information on converters.

All Together: Checkboxes, Radio Buttons, Menus, and Listboxes

We close out our section on selection tags with an example that exercises nearly all of those tags. That example, shown in Figure 4–7, implements a form requesting personal information. We use an h:selectBooleanCheckbox to determine whether the user wants to receive email, and h:selectOneMenu lets the user select the best day of the week for us to call. The year listbox is implemented with h:selectOneListbox; the language checkboxes are implemented with h:selectManyCheckbox; the education level is implemented with h:selectOneRadio.

When the user submits the form, JSF navigation takes us to a JSF page that shows the data the user entered.

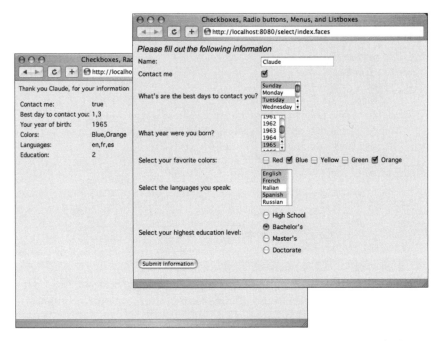

Figure 4–7   Using Checkboxes, Radio Buttons, Menus, and Listboxes

The directory structure for the application shown in Figure 4–7 is shown in Figure 4–8. The JSF pages, RegisterForm bean, faces configuration file and resource bundle are listed in Listing 4–11 through Listing 4–15.

Figure 4–8   The Directory Structure

Listing 4–11   `select/index.jsp`

```
1.  <html>
2.     <%@ taglib uri="http://java.sun.com/jsf/core" prefix="f" %>
3.     <%@ taglib uri="http://java.sun.com/jsf/html" prefix="h" %>
4.     <f:view>
5.        <head>
6.           <link href="styles.css" rel="stylesheet" type="text/css"/>
7.           <f:loadBundle basename="com.corejsf.messages" var="msgs"/>
8.           <title>
9.              <h:outputText value="#{msgs.indexWindowTitle}"/>
10.          </title>
11.       </head>
12.
13.       <body>
14.          <h:outputText value="#{msgs.indexPageTitle}" styleClass="emphasis"/>
15.          <h:form>
16.             <table>
17.                <tr>
18.                   <td>
19.                      <h:outputText value="#{msgs.namePrompt}"/>
20.                   </td>
21.                   <td>
22.                      <h:inputText value="#{form.name}"/>
23.                   </td>
24.                </tr>
25.                <tr>
26.                   <td>
27.                      <h:outputText value="#{msgs.contactMePrompt}"/>
28.                   </td>
29.                   <td>
30.                      <h:selectBooleanCheckbox value="#{form.contactMe}"/>
31.                   </td>
32.                </tr>
33.                <tr>
34.                   <td>
35.                      <h:outputText value="#{msgs.bestDayPrompt}"/>
36.                   </td>
37.                   <td>
38.                      <h:selectManyMenu value="#{form.bestDaysToContact}">
39.                         <f:selectItems value="#{form.daysOfTheWeekItems}"/>
40.                      </h:selectManyMenu>
41.                   </td>
42.                </tr>
43.                <tr>
44.                   <td>
45.                      <h:outputText value="#{msgs.yearOfBirthPrompt}"/>
```

Listing 4–11   select/index.jsp (cont.)

```
46.                    </td>
47.                    <td>
48.                      <h:selectOneListbox size="5" value="#{form.yearOfBirth}">
49.                        <f:selectItems value="#{form.yearItems}"/>
50.                      </h:selectOneListbox>
51.                    </td>
52.                  </tr>
53.                  <tr>
54.                    <td>
55.                      <h:outputText value="#{msgs.colorPrompt}"/>
56.                    </td>
57.                    <td>
58.                      <h:selectManyCheckbox value="#{form.colors}">
59.                        <f:selectItems value="#{form.colorItems}"/>
60.                      </h:selectManyCheckbox>
61.                    </td>
62.                  </tr>
63.                  <tr>
64.                    <td>
65.                      <h:outputText value="#{msgs.languagePrompt}"/>
66.                    </td>
67.                    <td>
68.                      <h:selectManyListbox value="#{form.languages}">
69.                        <f:selectItems value="#{form.languageItems}"/>
70.                      </h:selectManyListbox>
71.                    </td>
72.                  </tr>
73.                  <tr>
74.                    <td>
75.                      <h:outputText value="#{msgs.educationPrompt}"/>
76.                    </td>
77.                    <td>
78.                      <h:selectOneRadio value="#{form.education}"
79.                        layout="PAGE_DIRECTION">
80.                        <f:selectItems value="#{form.educationItems}"/>
81.                      </h:selectOneRadio>
82.                    </td>
83.                  </tr>
84.                </table>
85.                <h:commandButton value="#{msgs.buttonPrompt}"
86.                  action="showInformation"/>
87.            </h:form>
88.            <h:messages/>
89.        </body>
90.    </f:view>
91. </html>
```

Listing 4–12 `select/showInformation.jsp`

```
1.  <html>
2.  <%@ taglib uri="http://java.sun.com/jsf/core" prefix="f" %>
3.  <%@ taglib uri="http://java.sun.com/jsf/html" prefix="h" %>
4.  <f:view>
5.     <head>
6.        <f:loadBundle basename="com.corejsf.messages" var="msgs"/>
7.        <link href="styles.css" rel="stylesheet" type="text/css"/>
8.
9.        <title>
10.           <h:outputText value="#{msgs.indexWindowTitle}"/>
11.        </title>
12.     </head>
13.
14.     <body>
15.        <h:outputFormat value="#{msgs.thankYouLabel}">
16.           <f:param value="#{form.name}"/>
17.        </h:outputFormat>
18.        <p>
19.        <table>
20.           <tr>
21.              <td><h:outputText value="#{msgs.contactMeLabel}"/></td>
22.              <td><h:outputText value="#{form.contactMe}"/></td>
23.           </tr>
24.
25.           <tr>
26.              <td><h:outputText value="#{msgs.bestDayLabel}"/></td>
27.              <td><h:outputText value="#{form.bestDaysConcatenated}"/></td>
28.           </tr>
29.
30.           <tr>
31.              <td><h:outputText value="#{msgs.yearOfBirthLabel}"/></td>
32.              <td><h:outputText value="#{form.yearOfBirth}"/></td>
33.           </tr>
34.
35.           <tr>
36.              <td><h:outputText value="#{msgs.languageLabel}"/></td>
37.              <td><h:outputText value="#{form.languagesConcatenated}"/></td>
38.           </tr>
39.
40.           <tr>
41.              <td><h:outputText value="#{msgs.colorLabel}"/></td>
42.              <td><h:outputText value="#{form.colorsConcatenated}"/></td>
43.           </tr>
44.
```

Listing 4–12	select/showInformation.jsp (cont.)

```
45.              <tr>
46.                  <td><h:outputText value="#{msgs.educationLabel}"/></td>
47.                  <td><h:outputText value="#{form.education}"/></td>
48.              </tr>
49.          </table>
50.        </body>
51.    </f:view>
52. </html>
```

Listing 4–13	select/WEB-INF/com/classes/corejsf/RegisterForm.java

```
1. package com.corejsf;
2.
3. import java.text.DateFormatSymbols;
4. import java.util.ArrayList;
5. import java.util.Calendar;
6. import java.util.List;
7.
8. import javax.faces.model.SelectItem;
9.
10. public class RegisterForm {
11.    private String name;
12.    private boolean contactMe;
13.    private Integer[] bestDaysToContact;
14.    private Integer yearOfBirth;
15.    private String[] colors = null;
16.    private String[] languages = null;
17.    private int education;
18.
19.    // PROPERTY: name
20.    public String getName() {
21.       return name;
22.    }
23.    public void setName(String newValue) {
24.       name = newValue;
25.    }
26.
27.    // PROPERTY: contactMe
28.    public boolean getContactMe() {
29.       return contactMe;
30.    }
31.    public void setContactMe(boolean newValue) {
32.       contactMe = newValue;
33.    }
34.
```

Listing 4–13   select/WEB-INF/com/classes/corejsf/RegisterForm.java (cont.)

```
35.   // PROPERTY: bestDaysToContact
36.   public Integer[] getBestDaysToContact() {
37.      return bestDaysToContact;
38.   }
39.   public void setBestDaysToContact(Integer[] newValue) {
40.      bestDaysToContact = newValue;
41.   }
42.
43.   // PROPERTY: yearOfBirth
44.   public Integer getYearOfBirth() {
45.      return yearOfBirth;
46.   }
47.   public void setYearOfBirth(Integer newValue) {
48.      yearOfBirth = newValue;
49.   }
50.
51.   // PROPERTY: colors
52.   public String[] getColors() {
53.      return colors;
54.   }
55.   public void setColors(String[] newValue) {
56.      colors = newValue;
57.   }
58.
59.   // PROPERTY: languages
60.   public String[] getLanguages() {
61.      return languages;
62.   }
63.   public void setLanguages(String[] newValue) {
64.      languages = newValue;
65.   }
66.
67.   // PROPERTY: education
68.   public int getEducation() {
69.      return education;
70.   }
71.   public void setEducation(int newValue) {
72.      education = newValue;
73.   }
74.
75.   // PROPERTY: yearItems
76.   public List getYearItems() {
77.      return birthYears;
78.   }
79.
```

Listing 4–13 select/WEB-INF/com/classes/corejsf/RegisterForm.java (cont.)

```
80.    // PROPERTY: daysOfTheWeekItems
81.    public SelectItem[] getDaysOfTheWeekItems() {
82.       return daysOfTheWeek;
83.    }
84.
85.    // PROPERTY: languageItems
86.    public SelectItem[] getLanguageItems() {
87.       return languageItems;
88.    }
89.
90.    // PROPERTY: colorItems
91.    public SelectItem[] getColorItems() {
92.       return colorItems;
93.    }
94.
95.    // PROPERTY: educationItems
96.    public SelectItem[] getEducationItems() {
97.       return educationItems;
98.    }
99.
100.   // PROPERTY: bestDaysConcatenated
101.   public String getBestDaysConcatenated() {
102.      return concatenate(bestDaysToContact);
103.   }
104.
105.   // PROPERTY: languagesConcatenated
106.   public String getLanguagesConcatenated() {
107.      return concatenate(languages);
108.   }
109.
110.   // PROPERTY: colorsConcatenated
111.   public String getColorsConcatenated() {
112.      return concatenate(colors);
113.   }
114.
115.   private static String concatenate(Object[] values) {
116.      if (values == null)
117.         return "";
118.      StringBuffer r = new StringBuffer();
119.      for (int i = 0; i < values.length; ++i) {
120.         if (i > 0)
121.            r.append(',');
122.         r.append(values[i].toString());
123.      }
```

Listing 4–13	select/WEB-INF/com/classes/corejsf/RegisterForm.java (cont.)

```
124.        return r.toString();
125.    }
126.
127.    private static final int HIGH_SCHOOL = 1;
128.    private static final int BACHELOR = 2;
129.    private static final int MASTER = 3;
130.    private static final int DOCTOR = 4;
131.
132.    private static SelectItem[] colorItems = new SelectItem[]{
133.        new SelectItem("Red"),
134.        new SelectItem("Blue"),
135.        new SelectItem("Yellow"),
136.        new SelectItem("Green"),
137.        new SelectItem("Orange") };
138.
139.    private static SelectItem[] languageItems = new SelectItem[]{
140.        new SelectItem("en", "English"),
141.        new SelectItem("fr", "French"),
142.        new SelectItem("it", "Italian"),
143.        new SelectItem("es", "Spanish"),
144.        new SelectItem("ru", "Russian") };
145.
146.    private static SelectItem[] educationItems = new SelectItem[]{
147.        new SelectItem(new Integer(HIGH_SCHOOL), "High School"),
148.        new SelectItem(new Integer(BACHELOR), "Bachelor's"),
149.        new SelectItem(new Integer(MASTER), "Master's"),
150.        new SelectItem(new Integer(DOCTOR), "Doctorate") };
151.
152.    private static List birthYears;
153.    private static SelectItem[] daysOfTheWeek;
154.    static {
155.        birthYears = new ArrayList();
156.        for (int i = 1900; i < 2000; ++i) {
157.            birthYears.add(new SelectItem(new Integer(i)));
158.        }
159.
160.        DateFormatSymbols symbols = new DateFormatSymbols();
161.        String[] weekdays = symbols.getWeekdays();
162.        daysOfTheWeek = new SelectItem[7];
163.        for (int i = Calendar.SUNDAY; i <= Calendar.SATURDAY; i++) {
164.            daysOfTheWeek[i - 1] = new SelectItem(new Integer(i), weekdays[i]);
165.        }
166.    }
167. }
```

Listing 4–14 select/WEB-INF/classes/com/corejsf/messages.properties

```
1. indexWindowTitle=Checkboxes, Radio buttons, Menus, and Listboxes
2. indexPageTitle=Please fill out the following information
3.
4. namePrompt=Name:
5. contactMePrompt=Contact me
6. bestDayPrompt=What's the best day to contact you?
7. yearOfBirthPrompt=What year were you born?
8. buttonPrompt=Submit information
9. languagePrompt=Select the languages you speak:
10. educationPrompt=Select your highest education level:
11. emailAppPrompt=Select your email application:
12. colorPrompt=Select your favorite colors:
13.
14. thankYouLabel=Thank you {0}, for your information
15. contactMeLabel=Contact me:
16. bestDayLabel=Best day to contact you:
17. yearOfBirthLabel=Your year of birth:
18. colorLabel=Colors:
19. languageLabel=Languages:
20. educationLabel=Education:
```

Listing 4–15 select/WEB-INF/faces-config.xml

```
1. <?xml version="1.0"?>
2.
3. <!DOCTYPE faces-config PUBLIC
4.    "-//Sun Microsystems, Inc.//DTD JavaServer Faces Config 1.0//EN"
5.    "http://java.sun.com/dtd/web-facesconfig_1_0.dtd">
6.
7. <faces-config>
8.    <navigation-rule>
9.       <navigation-case>
10.          <from-outcome>showInformation</from-outcome>
11.          <to-view-id>/showInformation.jsp</to-view-id>
12.       </navigation-case>
13.    </navigation-rule>
14.
15.    <managed-bean>
16.       <managed-bean-name>form</managed-bean-name>
17.       <managed-bean-class>com.corejsf.RegisterForm</managed-bean-class>
18.       <managed-bean-scope>session</managed-bean-scope>
19.    </managed-bean>
20. </faces-config>
```

Messages

During the JSF life cycle, any object can create a message and add it to a queue of messages maintained by the faces context. At the end of the life cycle—in the render response phase—you can display those messages in a view. Typically, messages are associated with a particular component and indicate either conversion or validation errors.

Although error messages are usually the most prevalent message type in a JSF application, messages come in four varieties:

- Information
- Warning
- Error
- Fatal

All messages can contain a summary and a detail. For example, a summary might be Invalid Entry and a detail might be The number entered was greater than the maximum.

JSF applications use two tags to display messages in JSF pages: h:messages and h:message.

The h:messages tag displays all messages that were stored in the faces context during the course of the JSF life cycle. You can restrict those messages to global messages—meaning messages not associated with a component—by setting h:message's globalOnly attribute to true. By default, that attribute is false.

The h:message tag displays a single message for a particular component. That component is designated with h:message's mandatory for attribute. If more than one message has been stored in the Faces context for a component, h:message shows only the last message that was created.

h:message and h:messages share many attributes. Table 4–23 lists all attributes for both tags.

Table 4–23   Attributes for h:message **and** h:messages

Attributes	Description
for	The ID of the component whose message is displayed— applicable only to h:message
errorClass	CSS class applied to error messages
errorStyle	CSS style applied to error messages
fatalClass	CSS class applied to fatal messages
fatalStyle	CSS style applied to fatal messages

Table 4–23   Attributes for h:message **and** h:messages **(cont.)**

Attributes	Description
globalOnly	Instruction to display only global messages—applicable only to h:messages. Default: false
infoClass	CSS class applied to information messages
infoStyle	CSS style applied to information messages
layout	Specification for message layout: table or list—applicable only to h:messages
showDetail	A boolean that determines whether message details are shown. Defaults are false for h:messages, true for h:message.
showSummary	A boolean that determines whether message summaries are shown. Defaults are true for h:messages, false for h:message.
tooltip	A boolean that determines whether message details are rendered in a tooltip; the tooltip is only rendered if showDetail and showSummary are true
warnClass	CSS class for warning messages
warnStyle	CSS style for warning messages
binding, id, rendered, styleClass	Basic attributes[a]
style, title	HTML 4.0[b]

a. See Table 4–3 on page 90 for information about basic attributes.
b. See Table 4–4 on page 93 for information about HTML 4.0 attributes.

The majority of the attributes in Table 4–23 represent CSS classes or styles that h:message and h:messages apply to particular types of messages.

You can also specify whether you want to display a message's summary or detail, or both, with the showSummary and showDetail attributes, respectively.

The h:messages layout attribute can be used to specify how messages are laid out, either as a list or a table. If you specify true for the tooltip attribute and you've also set showDetail and showSummary to true, the message's detail will be wrapped in a tooltip that's shown when the mouse hovers over the error message.

Now that we have a grasp of message fundamentals, let's take a look at an application that uses the h:message and h:messages tags. The application shown in Figure 4–9 contains a simple form with two text fields. Both text fields have required attributes. Moreover, the Age text field is wired to an integer property, so it's value is converted automatically by the JSF framework. Figure 4–9 shows the error messages generated by the JSF framework when we neglect to specify a value for the Name field and provide the wrong type of value for the Age field.

Figure 4–9   Displaying Messages

At the top of the JSF page we use h:messages to display all messages. We use h:message to display messages for each input field.

```
<h:form>
    <h:messages layout="table" errorClass="errors"/>
    ...
    <h:inputText id="name" required="true"/>
    <h:message for="name" errorClass="errors"/>
    ...
    <h:inputText id="date" value="#{form.date}" required="true"/>
    <h:message for="date" errorClass="errors"/>
    ...
</form>
```

Both tags in our example specify a CSS class named errors, which is defined in styles.css. That class definition looks like this:

```
.errors {
    font-style: italic;
}
```

We've also specified layout="table" for the h:messages tag. If we had omitted that attribute (or alternatively specified layout="list"), the output would look like this:

The list layout encodes the error messages, one after the other, as text, whereas the table layout puts the messages in an HTML table element, one row per message. Most of the time you will probably prefer the table layout (even though it's not the default) because it's easier to read.

Figure 4–10 shows the directory structure for the application shown in Figure 4–9. Listing 4–16 through Listing 4–18 list the JSP page, resource bundle, and stylesheet for the application.

Figure 4–10   Directory Structure for the Messages Example

Listing 4–16   `messages/index.jsp`

```
1. <html>
2.    <%@ taglib uri="http://java.sun.com/jsf/core" prefix="f" %>
3.    <%@ taglib uri="http://java.sun.com/jsf/html" prefix="h" %>
4.    <f:view>
5.       <f:loadBundle basename="com.corejsf.messages" var="msgs"/>
6.       <head>
7.          <link href="styles.css" rel="stylesheet" type="text/css"/>
```

Listing 4–16　messages/index.jsp (cont.)

```
8.          <title>
9.              <h:outputText value="#{msgs.windowTitle}"/>
10.         </title>
11.     </head>
12.     <body>
13.       <h:form>
14.           <h:outputText value="#{msgs.greeting}" styleClass="emphasis"/>
15.           <br/>
16.           <h:messages errorClass="errors"/>
17.           <br/>
18.           <table>
19.             <tr>
20.               <td>
21.                 <h:outputText value="#{msgs.namePrompt}"/>
22.               </td>
23.               <td>
24.                 <h:inputText id="name"
25.                     value="#{user.name}" required="true"/>
26.               </td>
27.               <td>
28.                 <h:message for="name" errorClass="errors"/>
29.               </td>
30.             </tr>
31.             <tr>
32.               <td>
33.                 <h:outputText value="#{msgs.agePrompt}"/>
34.               </td>
35.               <td>
36.                 <h:inputText id="age"
37.                     value="#{user.age}" required="true" size="3"/>
38.               </td>
39.               <td>
40.                 <h:message for="age" errorClass="errors"/>
41.               </td>
42.             </tr>
43.           </table>
44.           <br/>
45.           <h:commandButton value="#{msgs.submitPrompt}"/>
46.       </h:form>
47.     </body>
48.   </f:view>
49. </html>
```

Listing 4–17	messages/WEB-INF/classes/com/corejsf/messages.properties

```
1. windowTitle=Using h:messages and h:message
2. greeting=Please fill out the following information
3. namePrompt=Name:
4. agePrompt=Age:
5. submitPrompt=Submit form
```

Listing 4–18	messages/styles.css

```
1. .errors {
2.    font-style: italic;
3. }
4. .emphasis {
5.    font-size: 1.3em;
6. }
```

> NOTE: By default, h:messages shows message summaries but not details. h:message, on the other hand, shows details but not summaries. If you use h:messages and h:message together, as we did in the preceding example, summaries will appear at the top of the page, with details next to the appropriate input field.

Panels

Throughout this chapter we've used HTML tables to align form prompts and input fields. Creating table markup by hand is tedious and error prone, so let's see how we can alleviate some of that tediousness with h:panelGrid, which generates an HTML table element. You can specify the number of columns in the table with the columns attribute, like this:

```
<h:panelGrid columns="3">
    ...
</h:panelGrid>
```

The columns attribute is not mandatory—if you don't specify it, the number of columns defaults to 1. h:panelGrid places components in columns from left to right and top to bottom. For example, if you have a panel grid with three columns and nine components, you'll wind up with three rows, each containing three columns. If you specify three columns and ten components, you'll have four rows and in the last row only the first column will contain a component—the tenth component.

Table 4–24 lists h:panelGrid attributes.

Table 4–24 Attributes for h:panelGrid

Attributes	Description
bgcolor	Background color for the table
border	Width of the table's border
cellpadding	Padding around table cells
cellspacing	Spacing between table cells
columnClasses	Comma-separated list of CSS classes for columns
columns	Number of columns in the table
footerClass	CSS class for the table footer
frame	Specification for sides of the frame surrounding the table that are to be drawn; valid values: none, above, below, hsides, vsides, lhs, rhs, box, border
headerClass	CSS class for the table header
rowClasses	Comma-separated list of CSS classes for columns
rules	Specification for lines drawn between cells; valid values: groups, rows, columns, all
summary	Summary of the table's purpose and structure used for non-visual feedback such as speech
binding, id, rendered, style-Class, value	Basic attributes[a]
dir, lang, style, title, width	HTML 4.0[b]
onclick, ondblclick, onkeydown, onkeypress, onkeyup, onmouse-down, onmousemove, onmouseout, onmouseover, onmouseup	DHTML events[c]

a. See Table 4–3 on page 90 for information about basic attributes.
b. See Table 4–4 on page 93 for information about HTML 4.0 attributes.
c. See Table 4–5 on page 95 for information about DHTML event attributes.

You can specify CSS classes for different parts of the table: header, footer, rows, and columns. The columnClasses and rowClasses specify lists of CSS classes that are applied to columns and rows, respectively. If those lists contain fewer class names than rows or columns, the CSS classes are reused. That makes it possible to specify classes like this: rowClasses="evenRows, oddRows" and columnClasses="evenColumns, oddColumns".

The cellpadding, cellspacing, frame, rules, and summary attributes are HTML pass-through attributes that apply only to tables. See the HTML 4.0 specification for more information.

h:panelGrid is often used in conjunction with h:panelGroup, which groups two or more components so they are treated as one. For example, you might group an input field and it's error message, like this:

```
<h:panelGrid columns="2">
    ...
    <h:panelGroup>
        <h:inputText id="name" value="#{user.name}">
        <h:message for="name"/>
    </h:panelGroup>
    ...
</h:panelGrid>
```

Grouping the text field and error message puts them in the same table cell. Without that grouping, the error message component would occupy its own cell. In the absence of an error message, the error message component produces no output, but still takes up a cell, so you wind up with an empty cell.

h:panelGroup is a simple tag with only a handful of attributes. Those attributes are listed in Table 4–25.

Table 4–25   Attributes for h:panelGroup

Attributes	Description
binding, id, rendered, styleClass	Basic Attributes
style	HTML 4.0[a]

a. See Table 4–4 on page 93 for information about HTML 4.0 attributes.

Figure 4–11 shows a simple example that uses h:panelGrid and h:panelGroup. The application contains a form that asks for the user's name and age. We've added a required validator—with h:inputText's required attribute—to the name field and used an h:message tag to display the corresponding error when that constraint is violated. We've placed no restrictions on the Age text field. Notice that those constraints require three columns in the first row—one each for the name prompt, text field, and error message—but only two in the second: the age prompt and text field. Since h:panelGrid allows only one value for its columns attribute, we can resolve this column quandary by placing the name text field and error message in a panel group, and because those two components will be treated as one, we actually have only two columns in each row.

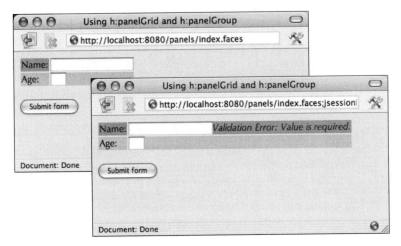

Figure 4–11 **Using** h:panelGrid **and** h:panelGroup

The directory structure for the application shown in Figure 4–11 is shown in Figure 4–12. Listings 4–19 through 4–21 shows the JSF page and related files.

Figure 4–12 Directory Structure for the Panels Example

Listing 4–19   `panels/index.jsp`

```
1.  <html>
2.     <%@ taglib uri="http://java.sun.com/jsf/core" prefix="f" %>
3.     <%@ taglib uri="http://java.sun.com/jsf/html" prefix="h" %>
4.     <f:view>
5.        <f:loadBundle basename="com.corejsf.messages" var="msgs"/>
6.        <head>
7.        <link href="styles.css" rel="stylesheet" type="text/css"/>
8.           <title>
9.              <h:outputText value="#{msgs.windowTitle}"/>
10.          </title>
11.       </head>
12.
13.       <body>
14.          <h:form>
15.             <h:panelGrid columns="2" rowClasses="oddRows,evenRows">
16.                <h:outputText value="#{msgs.namePrompt}"/>
17.                <h:panelGroup>
18.                   <h:inputText id="name" required="true"/>
19.                   <h:message for="name" errorClass="errors"/>
20.                </h:panelGroup>
21.                <h:outputText value="#{msgs.agePrompt}"/>
22.                <h:inputText size="3"/>
23.             </h:panelGrid>
24.             <br/>
25.             <h:commandButton value="#{msgs.submitPrompt}"/>
26.          </h:form>
27.       </body>
28.    </f:view>
29. </html>
```

Listing 4–20   `panels/WEB-INF/classes/com/corejsf/messages.properties`

```
1. windowTitle=Using h:panelGrid and h:panelGroup
2. namePrompt=Name:
3. agePrompt=Age:
4. submitPrompt=Submit form
```

Listing 4–21 panels/styles.css

```css
1. body {
2.     background: #eee;
3. }
4. .errors {
5.     font-style: italic;
6. }
7. .evenRows {
8.     background: PowderBlue;
9. }
10. .oddRows {
11.     background: MediumTurquoise;
12. }
```

DATA TABLES

Topics in This Chapter

Chapter 5

HTML tables are popular for laying out content in Web applications. JSF lets you lay out components with the h:dataTable tag. This chapter shows you how to make the most out of that tag.

The Data Table Tag

The h:dataTable tag iterates over *data* to create an HTML *table*. Here's how you use it:

```
<h:dataTable value='#{items}' var='item'>
    <h:column>
        <%-- left column components --%>
        <h:outputText value='#{item.propertyName}'/>
    </h:column>

    <h:column>
        <%-- next column components --%>
        <h:outputText value='#{item.anotherPropertyName}'/>
    </h:column>

    <%-- add more columns, as desired --%>
</h:dataTable>
```

The value attribute represents the data over which h:dataTable iterates; that data must be one of the following:

- an array
- an instance of java.util.List
- an instance of java.sql.ResultSet
- an instance of javax.servlet.jsp.jstl.sql.Result
- an instance of javax.faces.model.DataModel

As h:dataTable iterates, it makes each item in the array, list, result set, etc., available within the body of the tag. The name of the item is specified with h:dataTable's var attribute. In the preceding code fragment, each item (item) of a collection (items) is made available in turn as h:dataTable iterates over the collection. You use properties from the current item to populate columns for the current row.

You can also specify any Java object for h:dataTable's value attribute, although the usefulness of doing so is questionable. If that object is a scalar (meaning it's not a collection of some sort), h:dataTable iterates once, making the object available in the body of the tag.

The body of h:dataTable tags can contain only h:column tags; h:dataTable ignores all other component tags. Each column can contain an unlimited number of components in addition to optional header and footer components.

h:dataTable pairs a UIData component with a Table renderer. That combination provides robust table generation that includes support for CSS styles, database access, custom table models, and more. Let's start our h:dataTable exploration with a simple table.

A Simple Table

Figure 5–1 shows a table of names.

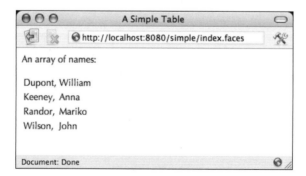

Figure 5–1   A Simple Table

The directory structure for the application shown in Figure 5–1 is shown in Figure 5–2. The application's JSF page is given in Listing 5–1.

```
simple
    index.html
    index.jsp
WEB-INF
        faces-config.xml
        web.xml
    classes
        com
            corejsf
                Name.java
                TableData.java
                messages.properties
```

**Figure 5–2 The Directory Structure
for the Simple Example**

Listing 5–1 simple/index.jsp

```
1. <html>
2.    <%@ taglib uri="http://java.sun.com/jsf/core"  prefix="f" %>
3.    <%@ taglib uri="http://java.sun.com/jsf/html"  prefix="h" %>
4.    <f:view>
5.       <head>
6.          <f:loadBundle basename="com.corejsf.messages" var="msgs"/>
7.          <title>
8.             <h:outputText value="#{msgs.windowTitle}"/>
9.          </title>
10.      </head>
11.      <body>
12.         <h:outputText value="#{msgs.pageTitle}"/>
13.         <p>
14.         <h:form>
15.            <h:dataTable value="#{tableData.names}"
16.                         var="name">
17.               <h:column>
18.                  <h:outputText value="#{name.last}"/>
19.                  <f:verbatim>,</f:verbatim>
20.               </h:column>
21.
22.               <h:column>
23.                  <h:outputText value="#{name.first}"/>
24.               </h:column>
25.            </h:dataTable>
26.         </h:form>
27.      </body>
28.   </f:view>
29. </html>
```

In Listing 5–1 we use h:dataTable to iterate over an array of names. The last name followed by a comma is placed in the left column and the first name is placed in the right column. Notice that we enclose the comma in an f:verbatim tag. Anytime you specify template text—meaning anything other than a JSF tag—inside of a component that renders its children, you must wrap that template text in the body of an f:verbatim tag. The following JSF HTML tags represent components that render their children.

- h:dataTable
- h:panelGrid
- h:panelGroup
- h:commandLink
- h:outputLink

If you place template text in the body of any of the preceding tags, you must enclose that template text in an f:verbatim tag (or alternatively, produce that template text with an h:outputText tag).

The array of names in this example is instantiated by a bean, which is managed by JSF. That bean is an instance of com.corejsf.TableData, which is listed in Listing 5–3. Listing 5–2 shows the Name class, and the faces configuration file and message resource bundle are listed in Listing 5–4 and Listing 5–5, respectively.

Listing 5–2 simple/WEB-INF/classes/com/corejsf/Name.java

```
 1. package com.corejsf;
 2.
 3. public class Name {
 4.    private String first;
 5.    private String last;
 6.
 7.    public Name(String first, String last) {
 8.       this.first = first;
 9.       this.last = last;
10.    }
11.
12.    public void setFirst(String newValue) { first = newValue; }
13.    public String getFirst() { return first; }
14.
15.    public void setLast(String newValue) { last = newValue; }
16.    public String getLast() { return last; }
17. }
```

Listing 5–3 simple/WEB-INF/classes/com/corejsf/TableData.java

```java
1. package com.corejsf;
2.
3. public class TableData {
4.    private static final Name[] names = new Name[] {
5.       new Name("William", "Dupont"),
6.       new Name("Anna", "Keeney"),
7.       new Name("Mariko", "Randor"),
8.       new Name("John", "Wilson")
9.    };
10.
11.    public Name[] getNames() { return names;}
12. }
```

Listing 5–4 simple/WEB-INF/faces_config.xml

```xml
1. <?xml version="1.0"?>
2.
3. <!DOCTYPE faces-config PUBLIC
4.    "-//Sun Microsystems, Inc.//DTD JavaServer Faces Config 1.0//EN"
5.    "http://java.sun.com/dtd/web-facesconfig_1_0.dtd">
6.
7. <faces-config>
8.    <managed-bean>
9.       <managed-bean-name>tableData</managed-bean-name>
10.       <managed-bean-class>com.corejsf.TableData</managed-bean-class>
11.       <managed-bean-scope>session</managed-bean-scope>
12.    </managed-bean>
13. </faces-config>
```

Listing 5–5 simple/WEB-INF/classes/com/corejsf/messages.properties

```
1. windowTitle=A Simple Table
2. pageTitle=An array of names:
```

The table in Figure 5–1 is intentionally vanilla. Throughout this chapter we'll see how to add bells and whistles, such as CSS styles and column headers, to tables, but first let's take a short tour of h:dataTable attributes.

> CAUTION: h:dataTable data is row oriented; for example, the list of names in Listing 5–3 correspond to table rows, but the names say nothing about what's stored in each column—it's up to the page author to specify column content. Row-oriented data might be different from what you're used to; Swing table models, for example, keep track of what's in each row *and* column.

h:dataTable Attributes

h:dataTable attributes are listed in Table 5–1.

Table 5–1   Attributes for h:dataTable

Attribute	Description
bgcolor	Background color for the table
border	Width of the table's border
cellpadding	Padding around table cells
cellspacing	Spacing between table cells
columnClasses	Comma-separated list of CSS classes for columns
first	Index of the first row shown in the table
footerClass	CSS class for the table footer
frame	Specification for sides of the frame surrounding the table should be drawn; valid values: none, above, below, hsides, vsides, lhs, rhs, box, border
headerClass	CSS class for the table header
rowClasses	Comma-separated list of CSS classes for rows
rules	Specification for lines drawn between cells; valid values: groups, rows, columns, all
summary	Summary of the table's purpose and structure used for non-visual feedback such as speech
var	The name of the variable created by the data table that represents the current item in the value
binding, id, rendered, styleClass, value	Basic attributes
dir, lang, style, title, width	HTML 4.0
onclick, ondblclick, onkeydown, onkeypress, onkeyup, onmousedown, onmousemove, onmouseout, onmouseover, onmouseup	DHTML events

The binding, id, and rendered attributes are discussed in Chapter 4.

h:dataTable also comes with a full complement of DHTML event and HTML 4.0 pass-through attributes. You can read more about those attributes in Chapter 4.

The first attribute specifies the index of the first visible row in the table. The value attribute points to the data over which h:dataTable iterates. At the start of each iteration, h:dataTable creates a request-scoped variable that you name with h:dataTable's var attribute. Within the body of the h:dataTable tag you can reference the current item with that name.

Headers and Footers

If you display a list of names as we did in "A Simple Table" on page 162, you need to distinguish last names from first names. You can do that with a column header, as shown in Figure 5–3.

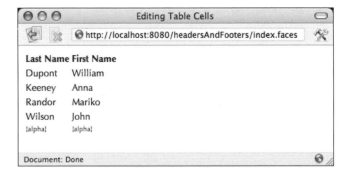

Figure 5–3 Specifying Column Headers and Footers

Besides headers, the table columns in Figure 5–3 also contain footers that indicate the data type of their respective columns; in this case, both columns are [alpha], for alphanumeric.

Column headers and footers are specified with facets, as shown below:

```
<h:dataTable>
    ...
    <h:column>
        <f:facet name="header">
            <%-- header components go here --%>
        </f:facet>

        <%-- column components go here --%>

        <f:facet name="footer">
            <%-- footer components go here --%>
```

```
        </f:facet>
      </h:column>
      ...
    </h:dataTable>
```

h:dataTable places the components specified for the header and footer facets in the HTML table's header and footer, respectively.

The full code for the JSF page shown in Figure 5–3 is given in Listing 5–6. The application's resource bundle is shown in Listing 5–7. The directory structure for the application is identical to the one shown in Figure 5–2 on page 163. You'll notice we've used the style attribute for output components to format column headers and footers. See Chapter 4 for more information about the style attribute in general and "Styles for Rows and Columns" on page 177 for more about CSS style classes and JSF tables.

Listing 5–6 headersAndFooters/index.jsp

```
1.  <html>
2.    <%@ taglib uri="http://java.sun.com/jsf/core"  prefix="f" %>
3.    <%@ taglib uri="http://java.sun.com/jsf/html"  prefix="h" %>
4.    <f:view>
5.      <head>
6.        <title>
7.          <f:loadBundle basename="com.corejsf.messages" var="msgs"/>
8.          <h:outputText value="#{msgs.windowTitle}"/>
9.        </title>
10.     </head>
11.     <body>
12.       <h:form>
13.         <h:dataTable value="#{tableData.names}" var="name">
14.           <h:column>
15.             <f:facet name="header">
16.               <h:outputText value="#{msgs.lastnameColumn}"
17.                 style="font-weight: bold"/>
18.             </f:facet>
19.             <h:outputText value="#{name.last}"/>
20.             <f:facet name="footer">
21.               <h:outputText value="#{msgs.alphanumeric}"
22.                 style="font-size: .75em"/>
23.             </f:facet>
24.           </h:column>
25.           <h:column>
```

Listing 5–6	headersAndFooters/index.jsp (cont.)

```
26.               <f:facet name="header">
27.                  <h:outputText value="#{msgs.firstnameColumn}"
28.                     style="font-weight: bold"/>
29.               </f:facet>
30.               <h:outputText value="#{name.first}"/>
31.               <f:facet name="footer">
32.                  <h:outputText value="#{msgs.alphanumeric}"
33.                     style="font-size: .75em"/>
34.               </f:facet>
35.            </h:column>
36.         </h:dataTable>
37.      </h:form>
38.   </body>
39. </f:view>
40. </html>
```

Listing 5–7	headersAndFooters/WEB-INF/classes/com/corejsf/messages.properties

```
1. windowTitle=Editing Table Cells
2. lastnameColumn=Last Name
3. firstnameColumn=First Name
4. editColumn=Edit
5. alphanumeric=[alpha]
```

> **TIP:** To place multiple components in a table header or footer, you must group them in an h:panelGroup tag, or place them in a container component with h:panelGrid or h:dataTable. If you place multiple components in a facet, only the first component will be displayed.

JSF Components in Table Cells

To this point, we've used only output components in table columns, but you can place any JSF component in a table column. Figure 5–4 shows an application that uses a variety of components in a table.

h:dataTable iterates over data, so the table shown in Figure 5–4 provides a list of integers for that purpose; the current integer populates components in the Number, Textfields, Buttons, Links, and Menu columns.

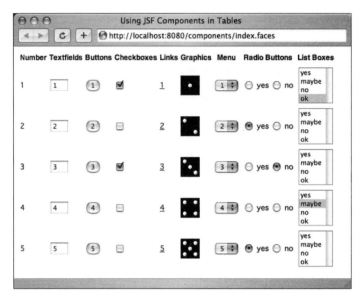

Figure 5–4   JSF Components in Table Cells

Components in a table are no different from components outside tables; you can manipulate them in any manner you desire, including conditional rendering with the rendered attribute, handling events, and the like.

The directory structure for the application shown in Figure 5–4 is shown in Figure 5–5. The JSF page, faces configuration file and property resource bundle are given in Listing 5–8 through Listing 5–10.

Figure 5–5   The Directory Structure for the Components Example

Listing 5–8	components/index.jsp

```
1. <html>
2.    <%@ taglib uri="http://java.sun.com/jsf/core"  prefix="f" %>
3.    <%@ taglib uri="http://java.sun.com/jsf/html"  prefix="h" %>
4.    <f:view>
5.       <head>
6.          <link href="styles.css" rel="stylesheet" type="text/css"/>
7.          <title>
8.             <f:loadBundle basename="com.corejsf.messages" var="msgs"/>
9.             <h:outputText value="#{msgs.windowTitle}"/>
10.         </title>
11.      </head>
12.      <body>
13.         <h:form>
14.            <h:dataTable value="#{numberList}" var="number">
15.               <h:column>
16.                  <f:facet name="header">
17.                     <h:outputText value="#{msgs.numberHeader}"/>
18.                  </f:facet>
19.                  <h:outputText value="#{number}"/>
20.               </h:column>
21.               <h:column>
22.                  <f:facet name="header">
23.                     <h:outputText value="#{msgs.textfieldHeader}"/>
24.                  </f:facet>
25.                  <h:inputText value="#{number}" size="3"/>
26.               </h:column>
27.               <h:column>
28.                  <f:facet name="header">
29.                     <h:outputText value="#{msgs.buttonHeader}"/>
30.                  </f:facet>
31.                  <h:commandButton value="#{number}"/>
32.               </h:column>
33.               <h:column>
34.                  <f:facet name="header">
35.                     <h:outputText value="#{msgs.checkboxHeader}"/>
36.                  </f:facet>
37.                  <h:selectBooleanCheckbox value="false"/>
38.               </h:column>
39.               <h:column>
40.                  <f:facet name="header">
41.                     <h:outputText value="#{msgs.linkHeader}"/>
42.                  </f:facet>
43.                  <h:commandLink>
44.                     <h:outputText value="#{number}"/>
45.                  </h:commandLink>
```

Listing 5–8   components/index.jsp (cont.)

```
46.          </h:column>
47.          <h:column>
48.            <f:facet name="header">
49.              <h:outputText value="#{msgs.graphicHeader}"/>
50.            </f:facet>
51.            <h:graphicImage value="images/dice#{number}.gif"
52.              style="border: 0px"/>
53.          </h:column>
54.          <h:column>
55.            <f:facet name="header">
56.              <h:outputText value="#{msgs.menuHeader}"/>
57.            </f:facet>
58.            <h:selectOneMenu>
59.              <f:selectItem itemLabel="#{number}" itemValue="#{number}"/>
60.            </h:selectOneMenu>
61.          </h:column>
62.          <h:column>
63.            <f:facet name="header">
64.              <h:outputText value="#{msgs.radioHeader}"/>
65.            </f:facet>
66.            <h:selectOneRadio layout="LINE_DIRECTION" value="nextMonth">
67.              <f:selectItem itemValue="yes" itemLabel="yes"/>
68.              <f:selectItem itemValue="no" itemLabel="no" />
69.            </h:selectOneRadio>
70.          </h:column>
71.          <h:column>
72.            <f:facet name="header">
73.              <h:outputText value="#{msgs.listboxHeader}"/>
74.            </f:facet>
75.            <h:selectOneListbox size="3">
76.              <f:selectItem itemValue="yes" itemLabel="yes"/>
77.              <f:selectItem itemValue="maybe" itemLabel="maybe"/>
78.              <f:selectItem itemValue="no" itemLabel="no" />
79.              <f:selectItem itemValue="ok" itemLabel="ok" />
80.            </h:selectOneListbox>
81.          </h:column>
82.        </h:dataTable>
83.      </h:form>
84.    </body>
85.  </f:view>
86. </html>
```

Listing 5–9	components/WEB-INF/faces-config.xml

```
 1. <?xml version="1.0"?>
 2.
 3. <!DOCTYPE faces-config PUBLIC
 4.    "-//Sun Microsystems, Inc.//DTD JavaServer Faces Config 1.0//EN"
 5.    "http://java.sun.com/dtd/web-facesconfig_1_0.dtd">
 6.
 7. <faces-config>
 8.    <managed-bean>
 9.       <managed-bean-name>numberList</managed-bean-name>
10.       <managed-bean-class>java.util.ArrayList</managed-bean-class>
11.       <managed-bean-scope>session</managed-bean-scope>
12.       <list-entries>
13.          <value>1</value>
14.          <value>2</value>
15.          <value>3</value>
16.          <value>4</value>
17.          <value>5</value>
18.       </list-entries>
19.    </managed-bean>
20. </faces-config>
```

Listing 5–10	components/WEB-INF/classes/com/corejsf/messages.properties

```
 1. windowTitle=Using JSF Components in Tables
 2.
 3. numberHeader=Number
 4. textfieldHeader=Textfields
 5. buttonHeader=Buttons
 6. checkboxHeader=Checkboxes
 7. linkHeader=Links
 8. menuHeader=Menu
 9. graphicHeader=Graphics
10. radioHeader=Radio Buttons
11. listboxHeader=List Boxes
```

Editing Table Cells

To edit table cells, you merely provide an input component for the cell(s) you want to edit. The application shown in Figure 5–6 allows editing of all its cells. You click on a checkbox to edit a row and then click on the Save Changes button to save your changes. From top to bottom, Figure 5–6 shows a cell being edited.

Figure 5–6   Editing Table Cells

The table cells in Figure 5–6 use an input component when the cell is being edited and an output component when it's not. Here's how that's implemented:

```
<h:dataTable value="#{tableData.names}" var="name">
    <%-- checkbox column --%>
    <h:column>
        <f:facet name="header">
            <h:outputText value="#{msgs.editColumn}"
                style="font-weight: bold"/>
        </f:facet>

        <h:selectBooleanCheckbox value="#{name.editable}"
            onclick="submit()"/>
    </h:column>
```

```
<%-- last name column --%>
<h:column>
    ...
    <h:inputText value='#{name.last}'
        rendered='#{name.editable}'
        size='10'/>

    <h:outputText value='#{name.last}'
        rendered='#{not name.editable}'/>
</h:column>
    ...
</h:dataTable>
<p>
<h:commandButton value="#{msgs.saveChangesButtonText}"/>
```

The preceding code fragment lists only the code for the checkbox and last name columns. The value of the checkbox corresponds to whether the current name is editable; if so, the checkbox is checked. Two components are specified for the last name column: an h:inputText and an h:outputText. If the name is editable, the input component is rendered. If the name is not editable, the output component is rendered.

The full listing for the JSF page shown in Figure 5–6 is given in Listing 5–11. The messages resource bundle for the application is shown in Listing 5–12. The directory structure for the application is the same as the one shown in Figure 5–2 on page 163.

Listing 5–11	edit/index.jsp

```
1.  <html>
2.     <%@ taglib uri="http://java.sun.com/jsf/core"  prefix="f" %>
3.     <%@ taglib uri="http://java.sun.com/jsf/html"  prefix="h" %>
4.     <f:view>
5.        <head>
6.           <title>
7.              <f:loadBundle basename="com.corejsf.messages" var="msgs"/>
8.              <h:outputText value="#{msgs.windowTitle}"/>
9.           </title>
10.       </head>
11.       <body>
12.          <h:form>
13.             <h:dataTable value="#{tableData.names}" var="name">
14.                <h:column>
15.                   <f:facet name="header">
16.                      <h:outputText value="#{msgs.editColumn}"
17.                         style="font-weight: bold"/>
```

| Listing 5-11 | edit/index.jsp (cont.) |

```
18.                  </f:facet>
19.                  <h:selectBooleanCheckbox value="#{name.editable}"
20.                     onclick="submit()"/>
21.               </h:column>
22.               <h:column>
23.                  <f:facet name="header">
24.                     <h:outputText value="#{msgs.lastnameColumn}"
25.                        style="font-weight: bold"/>
26.                  </f:facet>
27.                  <h:inputText value="#{name.last}" rendered="#{name.editable}"
28.                     size="10"/>
29.                  <h:outputText value="#{name.last}"
30.                     rendered="#{not name.editable}"/>
31.               </h:column>
32.               <h:column>
33.                  <f:facet name="header">
34.                     <h:outputText value="#{msgs.firstnameColumn}"
35.                        style="font-weight: bold"/>
36.                  </f:facet>
37.                  <h:inputText value="#{name.first}"
38.                     rendered="#{name.editable}" size="10"/>
39.                  <h:outputText value="#{name.first}"
40.                     rendered="#{not name.editable}"/>
41.               </h:column>
42.            </h:dataTable>
43.            <p>
44.            <h:commandButton value="#{msgs.saveChangesButtonText}"/>
45.         </h:form>
46.      </body>
47.   </f:view>
48. </html>
```

| Listing 5-12 | edit/WEB-INF/classes/com/corejsf/messages.properties |

```
1. windowTitle=Editing Table Cells
2. lastnameColumn=Last Name
3. firstnameColumn=First Name
4. editColumn=Edit
5. alphanumeric=[alpha]
6. saveChangesButtonText=Save Changes
```

> NOTE: Table cell editing, as illustrated in "Editing Table Cells" on page 173 works for all valid types of table data: Java objects, arrays, lists, result sets, and results. However, for database tables, the *result set* associated with a table must be *updatable* for the JSF implementation to update the database.

Styles for Rows and Columns

h:dataTable has attributes that specify CSS classes for the following:

- The table as a whole (styleClass)
- Column headers and footers (headerClass and footerClass)
- Individual columns (columnClasses)
- Individual rows (rowClasses)

The table shown in Figure 5–7 uses the styleClass, headerClass, and rowClasses attributes.

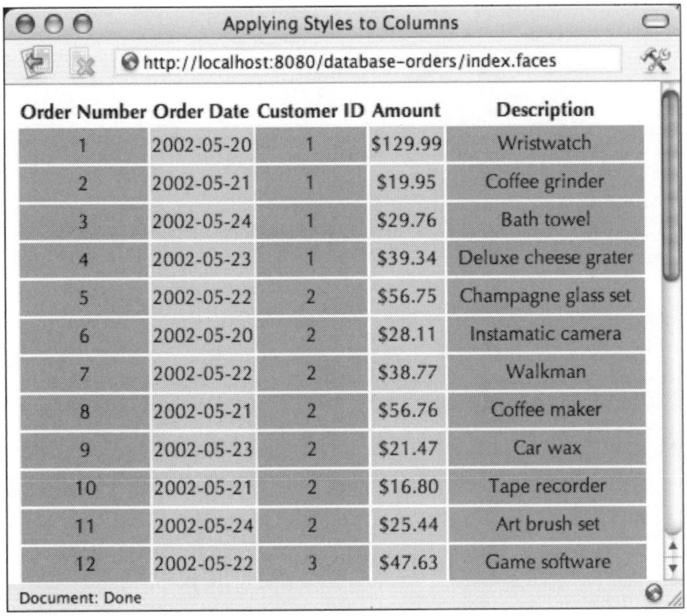

Order Number	Order Date	Customer ID	Amount	Description
1	2002-05-20	1	$129.99	Wristwatch
2	2002-05-21	1	$19.95	Coffee grinder
3	2002-05-24	1	$29.76	Bath towel
4	2002-05-23	1	$39.34	Deluxe cheese grater
5	2002-05-22	2	$56.75	Champagne glass set
6	2002-05-20	2	$28.11	Instamatic camera
7	2002-05-22	2	$38.77	Walkman
8	2002-05-21	2	$56.76	Coffee maker
9	2002-05-23	2	$21.47	Car wax
10	2002-05-21	2	$16.80	Tape recorder
11	2002-05-24	2	$25.44	Art brush set
12	2002-05-22	3	$47.63	Game software

Figure 5–7 Applying Styles by Column

NOTE: The `h:dataTable` `rowClasses` and `columnClasses` attributes are mutually exclusive. If you specify both, `columnClasses` has priority.

Styles by Column

Here's how the CSS classes in Figure 5–7 are specified:

```
<link href="styles.css" rel="stylesheet" type="text/css"/>
...
<h:dataTable value="#{order.all}" var="order"
    styleClass="orders"
    headerClass="ordersHeader"
    columnClasses="evenColumn,oddColumn">
```

Those CSS classes are listed below.

```
.orders {
    border: thin solid black;
}
.ordersHeader {
    text-align: center;
    font-style: italic;
    color: Snow;
    background: Teal;
}
.evenColumn {
    height: 25px;
    text-align: center;
    background: MediumTurquoise;
}
.oddColumn {
    text-align: center;
    background: PowderBlue;
}
```

We only specified two column classes, but notice we have five columns. In that case, `h:dataTable` reuses the column classes, starting with the first. By specifying only the first two column classes, we can set the CSS classes for even and odd columns.

Styles by Row

You can use the `rowClasses` attribute to specify CSS classes by rows instead of columns, as illustrated by Figure 5–8. That data table is implemented like this:

```
<link href='styles.css' rel='stylesheet' type='text/css'/>
...
<h:dataTable value="#{order.all}" var="order"
    styleClass="orders"
    headerClass="ordersHeader"
    rowClasses="evenRow,oddRow">
```

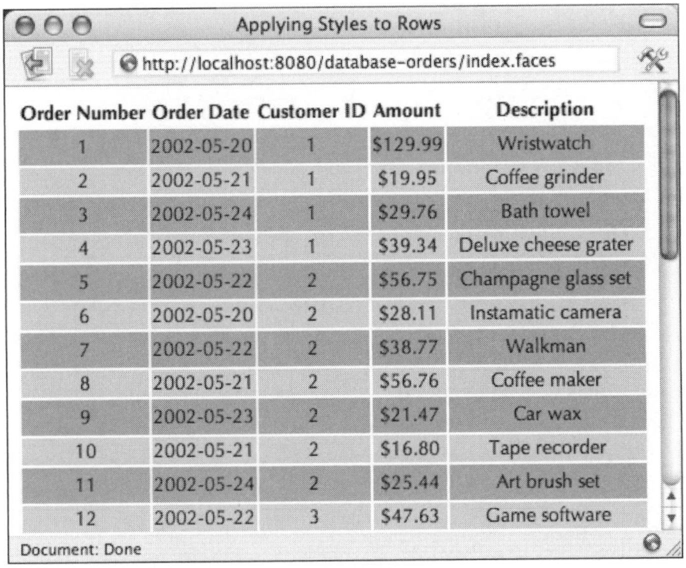
Applying Styles to Rows
http://localhost:8080/database-orders/index.faces
Order Number Order Date Customer ID Amount Description
1 2002-05-20 1 $129.99 Wristwatch
2 2002-05-21 1 $19.95 Coffee grinder
3 2002-05-24 1 $29.76 Bath towel
4 2002-05-23 1 $39.34 Deluxe cheese grater
5 2002-05-22 2 $56.75 Champagne glass set
6 2002-05-20 2 $28.11 Instamatic camera
7 2002-05-22 2 $38.77 Walkman
8 2002-05-21 2 $56.76 Coffee maker
9 2002-05-23 2 $21.47 Car wax
10 2002-05-21 2 $16.80 Tape recorder
11 2002-05-24 2 $25.44 Art brush set
12 2002-05-22 3 $47.63 Game software
Document: Done

Figure 5–8 Specifying Styles by Row

Like column classes, `h:dataTable` reuses row classes when the number of classes is less than the number of rows. In the preceding code fragment, we've taken advantage of this feature to specify CSS classes for even and odd rows.

> CAUTION: We use color names, such as PowderBlue and MediumTurquoise, in our style classes for the sake of illustration. You should prefer the equivalent hex constants because they are portable, whereas color names are not.

Database Tables

In chapter 10, we show you how to connect to a database and perform queries. In this section, we show you how to display the results of a database query.

Figure 5–9 shows a JSF application that displays a database table.

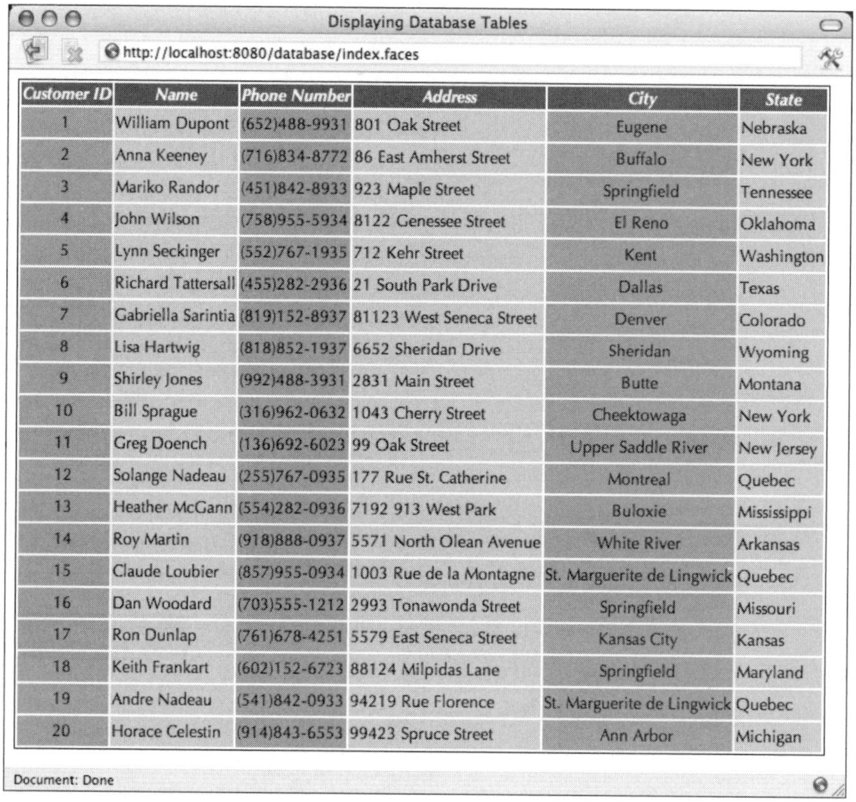

Customer ID	Name	Phone Number	Address	City	State
1	William Dupont	(652)488-9931	801 Oak Street	Eugene	Nebraska
2	Anna Keeney	(716)834-8772	86 East Amherst Street	Buffalo	New York
3	Mariko Randor	(451)842-8933	923 Maple Street	Springfield	Tennessee
4	John Wilson	(758)955-5934	8122 Genessee Street	El Reno	Oklahoma
5	Lynn Seckinger	(552)767-1935	712 Kehr Street	Kent	Washington
6	Richard Tattersall	(455)282-2936	21 South Park Drive	Dallas	Texas
7	Gabriella Sarintia	(819)152-8937	81123 West Seneca Street	Denver	Colorado
8	Lisa Hartwig	(818)852-1937	6652 Sheridan Drive	Sheridan	Wyoming
9	Shirley Jones	(992)488-3931	2831 Main Street	Butte	Montana
10	Bill Sprague	(316)962-0632	1043 Cherry Street	Cheektowaga	New York
11	Greg Doench	(136)692-6023	99 Oak Street	Upper Saddle River	New Jersey
12	Solange Nadeau	(255)767-0935	177 Rue St. Catherine	Montreal	Quebec
13	Heather McGann	(554)282-0936	7192 913 West Park	Buloxie	Mississippi
14	Roy Martin	(918)888-0937	5571 North Olean Avenue	White River	Arkansas
15	Claude Loubier	(857)955-0934	1003 Rue de la Montagne	St. Marguerite de Lingwick	Quebec
16	Dan Woodard	(703)555-1212	2993 Tonawonda Street	Springfield	Missouri
17	Ron Dunlap	(761)678-4251	5579 East Seneca Street	Kansas City	Kansas
18	Keith Frankart	(602)152-6723	88124 Milpidas Lane	Springfield	Maryland
19	Andre Nadeau	(541)842-0933	94219 Rue Florence	St. Marguerite de Lingwick	Quebec
20	Horace Celestin	(914)843-6553	99423 Spruce Street	Ann Arbor	Michigan

Figure 5–9 Displaying a Database Table

The JSF page shown in Figure 5–9 uses `h:dataTable` like this:

```
<h:dataTable value="#{customer.all}" var="customer"
    styleClass="customers"
    headerClass="customersHeader"
    columnClasses="custid,name">
            <h:column>
        <f:facet name="header">
            <h:outputText value="#{msgs.customerIdHeader}"/>
        </f:facet>
                <h:outputText value="#{customer.Cust_ID}"/>
    </h:column>
```

```
<h:column>
    <f:facet name="header">
        <h:outputText value="#{msgs.nameHeader}"/>
    </f:facet>
            <h:outputText value="#{customer.Name}"/>
</h:column>
...
</h:dataTable>
```

The customer bean is a managed bean that knows how to connect to a database and perform a query of all customers in the database. The CustomerBean.all method performs that query and returns a JSTL Result object.

The preceding JSF page accesses column data by referencing column names; for example, #{customer.Cust_ID} references the Cust_ID column. In this example, we've strictly adhered to a column's capitalization, but we weren't required to; for example, #{customer.CuSt_Id} would work equally well in the preceding code.

The directory structure for the database example is shown in Figure 5–10. Listings for the application are given in Listing 5–13 through Listing 5–16.

**Figure 5–10   The Directory Structure
                for the Database Example**

Listing 5–13 database/index.jsp

```
1.  <html>
2.  <%@ taglib uri="http://java.sun.com/jsf/core"  prefix="f" %>
3.  <%@ taglib uri="http://java.sun.com/jsf/html"  prefix="h" %>
4.  <f:view>
5.     <head>
6.        <link href="styles.css" rel="stylesheet" type="text/css"/>
7.        <f:loadBundle basename="com.corejsf.messages" var="msgs"/>
8.        <title>
9.           <h:outputText value="#{msgs.pageTitle}"/>
10.       </title>
11.    </head>
12.    <body>
13.       <h:form>
14.          <h:dataTable value="#{customer.all}" var="customer"
15.             styleClass="customers"
16.             headerClass="customersHeader" columnClasses="custid,name">
17.             <h:column>
18.                <f:facet name="header">
19.                   <h:outputText value="#{msgs.customerIdHeader}"/>
20.                </f:facet>
21.                <h:outputText value="#{customer.Cust_ID}"/>
22.             </h:column>
23.             <h:column>
24.                <f:facet name="header">
25.                   <h:outputText value="#{msgs.nameHeader}"/>
26.                </f:facet>
27.                <h:outputText value="#{customer.Name}"/>
28.             </h:column>
29.             <h:column>
30.                <f:facet name="header">
31.                   <h:outputText value="#{msgs.phoneHeader}"/>
32.                </f:facet>
33.                <h:outputText value="#{customer.Phone_Number}"/>
34.             </h:column>
35.             <h:column>
36.                <f:facet name="header">
37.                   <h:outputText value="#{msgs.addressHeader}"/>
38.                </f:facet>
39.                <h:outputText value="#{customer.Street_Address}"/>
40.             </h:column>
41.             <h:column>
42.                <f:facet name="header">
43.                   <h:outputText value="#{msgs.cityHeader}"/>
44.                </f:facet>
```

Listing 5–13 database/index.jsp (cont.)

```
45.                <h:outputText value="#{customer.City}"/>
46.             </h:column>
47.             <h:column>
48.                <f:facet name="header">
49.                   <h:outputText value="#{msgs.stateHeader}"/>
50.                </f:facet>
51.                <h:outputText value="#{customer.State}"/>
52.             </h:column>
53.          </h:dataTable>
54.       </h:form>
55.     </body>
56.   </f:view>
57. </html>
```

Listing 5–14 database/WEB-INF/classes/com/corejsf/CustomerBean.java

```
1. package com.corejsf;
2.
3. import java.sql.Connection;
4. import java.sql.ResultSet;
5. import java.sql.SQLException;
6. import java.sql.Statement;
7. import javax.naming.Context;
8. import javax.naming.InitialContext;
9. import javax.naming.NamingException;
10. import javax.servlet.jsp.jstl.sql.Result;
11. import javax.servlet.jsp.jstl.sql.ResultSupport;
12. import javax.sql.DataSource;
13.
14. public class CustomerBean {
15.    private Connection conn;
16.
17.    public void open() throws SQLException, NamingException {
18.       if (conn != null) return;
19.       Context ctx = new InitialContext();
20.       DataSource ds = (DataSource) ctx.lookup("java:comp/env/jdbc/test");
21.       conn = ds.getConnection();
22.    }
23.
24.    public Result getAll() throws SQLException, NamingException {
25.       try {
26.          open();
27.          Statement stmt = conn.createStatement();
28.          ResultSet result = stmt.executeQuery("SELECT * FROM Customers");
```

Listing 5–14   database/WEB-INF/classes/com/corejsf/CustomerBean.java (cont.)

```
29.        return ResultSupport.toResult(result);
30.      } finally {
31.        close();
32.      }
33.    }
34.
35.    public void close() throws SQLException {
36.      if (conn == null) return;
37.      conn.close();
38.      conn = null;
39.    }
40. }
```

Listing 5–15   database/WEB-INF/faces-config.xml

```
1. <?xml version="1.0"?>
2.
3. <!DOCTYPE faces-config PUBLIC
4.    "-//Sun Microsystems, Inc.//DTD JavaServer Faces Config 1.0//EN"
5.    "http://java.sun.com/dtd/web-facesconfig_1_0.dtd">
6.
7. <faces-config>
8.    <managed-bean>
9.       <managed-bean-name>customer</managed-bean-name>
10.       <managed-bean-class>com.corejsf.CustomerBean</managed-bean-class>
11.       <managed-bean-scope>session</managed-bean-scope>
12.    </managed-bean>
13. </faces-config>
```

Listing 5–16   database/WEB-INF/classes/com/corejsf/messages.properties

```
1. pageTitle=Displaying Database Tables
2. customerIdHeader=Customer ID
3. nameHeader=Name
4. phoneHeader=Phone Number
5. addressHeader=Address
6. cityHeader=City
7. stateHeader=State
8. refreshFromDB=Read from database
```

JSTL Result vs. Result Sets

The value you specify for h:dataTable can be, among other things, an instance of javax.servlet.jsp.jstl.Result or an instance of java.sql.Result—as was the case in "Database Tables" on page 179. h:dataTable wraps instances of those objects in instances of ResultDataModel and ResultSetDataModel, respectively. So how do the models differ? And which should you prefer?

If you've worked with result sets, you know they are fragile objects that require a good deal of programmatic control. The JSTL Result class is a bean that wraps a result set and implements that programmatic control for you; results are thus easier to deal with than are result sets. On the other hand, wrapping a result set in a result involves some overhead involved in creating the Result object; your application may not be able to afford the performance penalty.

In the application discussed in "Database Tables" on page 179, we follow our own advice and return a JSTL Result object from the CustomerBean.all method.

Table Models

When you use a Java object, array, list, result set, or JSTL result object to represent table data, h:dataTable wraps those objects in a model that extends the javax.faces.model.DataModel class. All of those model classes, listed below, reside in the javax.faces.model package:

- ArrayDataModel
- ListDataModel
- ResultDataModel
- ResultSetDataModel
- ScalarDataModel

h:dataTable deals with the models listed above; it never directly accesses the object—array, list, etc.—you specify with the value attribute. You can, however, access those objects yourself with the DataModel.getWrappedObject method. That method comes in handy for adding and removing table rows.

Editing Table Models

It's easy to add and delete table rows with two methods provided by all data models: getWrappedObject() and setWrappedObject(). Let's see how it works with an application, shown in Figure 5–11, that allows users to delete rows from a table.

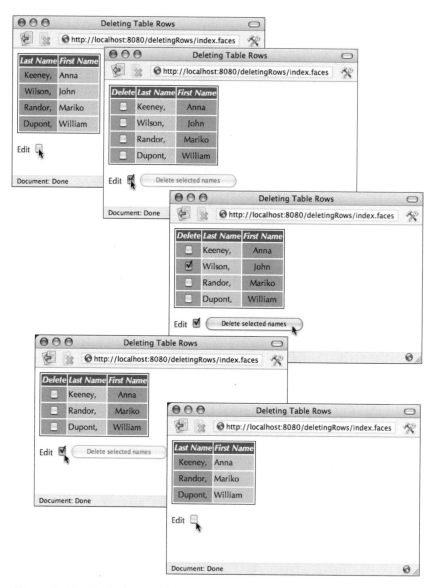

Figure 5–11 Deleting Table Rows

Going from top to bottom, Figure 5–11 shows the deletion of a single row. When a user activates the Delete selected names button, the JSF implementation invokes an action listener method that deletes the selected rows. That method looks like this:

```
public String deleteNames() {
    if (!getAnyNamesMarkedForDeletion())
        return null;

    Name[] currentNames = (Name[]) model.getWrappedData();
    Name[] newNames = new Name[currentNames.length -
        getNumberOfNamesMarkedForDeletion()];

    for(int i= 0, j = 0; i < currentNames.length; ++i) {
        Name name = (Name) currentNames[i];
            if (!name.isMarkedForDeletion()) {
            newNames[j++] = name;
        }
    }
    model.setWrappedData(newNames);
    return null;
    }
}
```

The deleteNames method obtains a reference to the current set of names by calling the model's getWrappedData method. Then it creates a new array whose size is the size of the current array minus the number of names that have been marked for deletion. Subsequently, the method adds each of the current names to the new array, leaving out names that were marked for deletion. Finally, the method calls the model's setWrappedData method to reset the model with the new array of names.

The JSF implementation invokes the TableData.deleteNames method when the Delete selected names button is activated. The deleteNames method obtains a reference to the current array of names by invoking the data model's getWrappedObject method. The deleteNames method subsequently creates a new array—without the names marked for deletion—that it pushes to the model with the setWrappedObject method.

Although the preceding example doesn't illustrate adding rows, it does illustrate the principle: Get the current object wrapped by the model with getWrapped-Object(), modify it (by adding or deleting rows), and then reset the wrapped object with setWrappedObject().

Figure 5–12 shows the directory structure for the application. Listing 5–17 through Listing 5–19 list the pertinent files from the application shown in Figure 5–11.

 NOTE: Calling the model's `setWrappedData()` to reset the model's data is one way to delete rows. We could've also reset the model itself, like this:

```
model = new ArrayDataModel(newNames);
```

```
deletingRows
├─ index.html
├─ index.jsp
├─ styles.css
└─ WEB-INF
   ├─ faces-config.xml
   ├─ web.xml
   └─ classes
      └─ com
         └─ corejsf
            ├─ Name.java
            ├─ TableData.java
            └─ messages.properties
```

**Figure 5–12   The Directory Structure
for the Delete Example**

Listing 5–17	`delete/index.jsp`

```
1.  <html>
2.     <%@ taglib uri="http://java.sun.com/jsf/core"  prefix="f" %>
3.     <%@ taglib uri="http://java.sun.com/jsf/html"  prefix="h" %>
4.     <f:view>
5.        <head>
6.           <link href="styles.css" rel="stylesheet" type="text/css"/>
7.           <f:loadBundle basename="com.corejsf.messages" var="msgs"/>
8.           <title>
9.              <h:outputText value="#{msgs.windowTitle}"/>
10.          </title>
11.       </head>
12.       <body>
13.          <h:form>
14.             <h:dataTable value="#{tableData.names}" var="name"
15.                styleClass="names" headerClass="namesHeader"
16.                columnClasses="last,first">
17.                <h:column rendered="#{tableData.editable}">
18.                   <f:facet name="header">
19.                      <h:outputText value="#{msgs.deleteColumnHeader}"/>
20.                   </f:facet>
21.                   <h:selectBooleanCheckbox value="#{name.markedForDeletion}"
22.                      onchange="submit()"/>
23.                </h:column>
```

Listing 5–17   delete/index.jsp (cont.)

```
24.              <h:column>
25.                 <f:facet name="header">
26.                    <h:outputText value="#{msgs.lastColumnHeader}"/>
27.                 </f:facet>
28.                 <h:outputText value="#{name.last}"/>
29.                 <f:verbatim>,</f:verbatim>
30.              </h:column>
31.              <h:column>
32.                 <f:facet name="header">
33.                    <h:outputText value="#{msgs.firstColumnHeader}"/>
34.                 </f:facet>
35.                 <h:outputText value="#{name.first}"/>
36.              </h:column>
37.           </h:dataTable>
38.           <p>
39.           <h:outputText value="#{msgs.editPrompt}"/>
40.           <h:selectBooleanCheckbox onchange="submit()"
41.              value="#{tableData.editable}"/>
42.           <h:commandButton value="#{msgs.deleteButtonText}"
43.              rendered="#{tableData.editable}"
44.              action="#{tableData.deleteNames}"
45.              disabled="#{not tableData.anyNamesMarkedForDeletion}"/>
46.        </h:form>
47.     </body>
48.  </f:view>
49. </html>
```

Listing 5–18   delete/WEB-INF/classes/com/corejsf/Name.java

```
1. package com.corejsf;
2.
3. public class Name {
4.    private String first;
5.    private String last;
6.    private boolean markedForDeletion = false;
7.
8.    public Name(String first, String last) {
9.       this.first = first;
10.      this.last = last;
11.   }
12.
```

Listing 5–18   delete/WEB-INF/classes/com/corejsf/Name.java

```
13.    public void setFirst(String newValue) { first = newValue; }
14.    public String getFirst() { return first; }
15.
16.    public void setLast(String newValue) { last = newValue; }
17.    public String getLast() { return last; }
18.
19.    public boolean isMarkedForDeletion() { return markedForDeletion; }
20.    public void setMarkedForDeletion(boolean newValue) {
21.       markedForDeletion = newValue;
22.    }
23. }
```

Listing 5–19   delete/WEB-INF/classes/com/corejsf/TableData.java

```
1. package com.corejsf;
2.
3. import javax.faces.model.DataModel;
4. import javax.faces.model.ArrayDataModel;
5.
6. public class TableData {
7.    private boolean editable = false;
8.    private ArrayDataModel model = null;
9.
10.    private static final Name[] names = {
11.       new Name("Anna", "Keeney"),
12.       new Name("John", "Wilson"),
13.       new Name("Mariko", "Randor"),
14.       new Name("William", "Dupont"),
15.    };
16.
17.    public TableData() { model = new ArrayDataModel(names); }
18.
19.    public DataModel getNames() { return model; }
20.
21.    public boolean isEditable() { return editable; }
22.    public void setEditable(boolean newValue) { editable = newValue; }
23.
24.    public String deleteNames() {
25.       if (!getAnyNamesMarkedForDeletion())
26.          return null;
27.
28.       Name[] currentNames = (Name[]) model.getWrappedData();
29.       Name[] newNames = new Name[currentNames.length
30.          - getNumberOfNamesMarkedForDeletion()];
```

Listing 5–19 `delete/WEB-INF/classes/com/corejsf/TableData.java (cont.)`

```
31.
32.    for(int i = 0, j = 0; i < currentNames.length; ++i) {
33.        Name name = (Name) currentNames[i];
34.        if (!name.isMarkedForDeletion()) {
35.            newNames[j++] = name;
36.        }
37.    }
38.    model.setWrappedData(newNames);
39.    return null;
40. }
41.
42. public int getNumberOfNamesMarkedForDeletion() {
43.     Name[] currentNames = (Name[]) model.getWrappedData();
44.     int cnt = 0;
45.
46.     for(int i = 0; i < currentNames.length; ++i) {
47.         Name name = (Name) currentNames[i];
48.         if (name.isMarkedForDeletion())
49.             ++cnt;
50.     }
51.     return cnt;
52. }
53.
54. public boolean getAnyNamesMarkedForDeletion() {
55.     Name[] currentNames = (Name[]) model.getWrappedData();
56.     for(int i = 0; i < currentNames.length; ++i) {
57.         Name name = (Name) currentNames[i];
58.         if (name.isMarkedForDeletion())
59.             return true;
60.     }
61.     return false;
62. }
63. }
```

We've seen how to perform simple manipulation of a data model. Sometimes, a little more sophistication is required, for example, when you sort or filter a model's data.

Sorting and Filtering

To sort or filter tables with h:dataTable, you need to implement a table model that decorates one of the table models listed on page 185. Figure 5–13 shows what it means to decorate a table model.

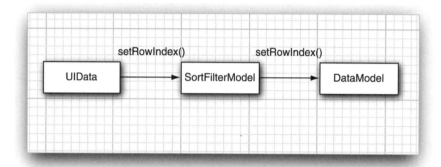

Figure 5–13 Data Model Filter

Instances of UIData—the component associated with h:dataTable—invoke methods on their model. When you decorate the model, those method calls are intercepted by a model of your own—one that mostly just forwards method calls to the original model. Typically, sorting models override the setRowIndex method to return a sorted index instead of the original model's index. Let's see how that works.

Figure 5–14 shows an application that sorts table columns.

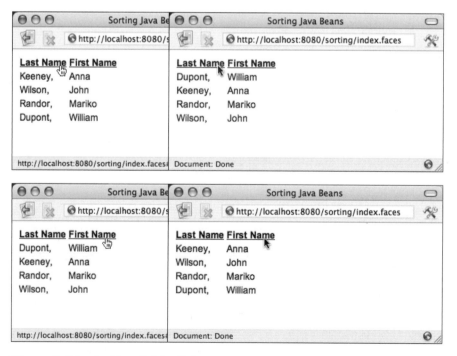

Figure 5–14   Sorting Table Columns

The application shown in Figure 5–14 sorts table columns by decorating a table data model. First, we specify the h:dataTable's value attribute like this:

```
<h:dataTable value="#{tableData.names}" var="name" ...>
   ...
```

The TableData.getNames method returns a data model:

```
public class TableData {
   private DataModel filterModel= null;
   private static final Name[] names = {
      new Name("Anna","Keeney"),
      new Name("John","Wilson"),
      newName("Mariko", "Randor"),
      newName("William", "Dupont"),
   };

   public TableData() {
      ArrayDataModel model = new ArrayDataModel(names);
      filterModel = new SortFilterModel(model);
   }
   public DataModel getNames() {
      return filterModel;
   }
}
```

When the tableData object is created, it creates an ArrayDataModel instance, passing it the array of names. That is the *original* model. Then the TableData constructor wraps that model in a *sorting* model. When the getNames method is subsequently called to populate the data table, that method returns the sorting model. The sorting model is implemented like this:

```
public class SortFilterModel extends DataModel {
   private DataModel model;
   private Row[] rows;
   ...
   public SortFilterModel(DataModel model) {
      this.model = model;
      int rowCnt = model.getRowCount();
      if (rowCnt != -1) {
         rows = new Row[rowCnt];
         for (int i = 0; i < rowCnt; ++i) {
         rows[i] = new Row(i);
      }
   }
   public void setRowIndex(int rowIndex) {
      if (rowIndex == -1 || rowIndex >= model.getRowCount()) {
         model.setRowIndex(rowIndex);
      }
```

```
    else {
        model.setRowIndex(rows[rowIndex].row);
    }
  }
  ...
}
```

Notice that we create our own array of indices that represent sorted indices. We return a sorted index from the setRowIndex method when the indicated index is in range.

So how does the sorting happen? The SortFilterModel class provides two methods, sortByFirst() and sortByLast():

```
public String sortByLast() {
    Arrays.sort(rows, byLast);
    return null;
}

public String sortByFirst() {
    Arrays.sort(rows, byFirst);
    return null;
}
```

The byLast and byFirst variables are comparators. The former compares last names and the latter compares first names. You can see the implementation of the comparators in Listing 5–21 on page 196.

The directory structure for the sorting example is shown in Figure 5–15. Listing 5–20 through Listing 5–26 provide full listings of the application.

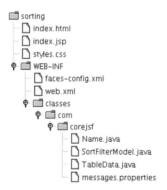

**Figure 5–15   The Directory Structure
for the Sorting Example**

Listing 5–20   `sort/index.jsp`

```
1. <html>
2.    <%@ taglib uri="http://java.sun.com/jsf/core"  prefix="f" %>
3.    <%@ taglib uri="http://java.sun.com/jsf/html"  prefix="h" %>
4.    <f:view>
5.       <head>
6.          <link href="site.css" rel="stylesheet" type="text/css"/>
7.          <f:loadBundle basename="com.corejsf.messages" var="msgs"/>
8.          <title>
9.             <h:outputText value="#{msgs.windowTitle}"/>
10.          </title>
11.       </head>
12.       <body>
13.          <h:form>
14.             <h:dataTable value="#{tableData.names}" var="name"
15.                styleClass="names" headerClass="namesHeader"
16.                columnClasses="last,first">
17.                <h:column>
18.                   <f:facet name="header">
19.                      <h:commandLink action="#{tableData.names.sortByLast}">
20.                         <h:outputText value="#{msgs.lastColumnHeader}"/>
21.                      </h:commandLink>
22.                   </f:facet>
23.                   <h:outputText value="#{name.last}"/>
24.                   <f:verbatim>,</f:verbatim>
25.                </h:column>
26.                <h:column>
27.                   <f:facet name="header">
28.                      <h:commandLink action="#{tableData.names.sortByFirst}">
29.                         <h:outputText value="#{msgs.firstColumnHeader}"/>
30.                      </h:commandLink>
31.                   </f:facet>
32.                   <h:outputText value="#{name.first}"/>
33.                </h:column>
34.             </h:dataTable>
35.          </h:form>
36.       </body>
37.    </f:view>
38. </html>
```

Listing 5–21 sort/WEB-INF/classes/com/corejsf/SortFilterModel.java

```
1. package com.corejsf;
2.
3. import java.util.Arrays;
4. import java.util.Comparator;
5. import javax.faces.model.DataModel;
6. import javax.faces.model.DataModelListener;
7.
8. public class SortFilterModel extends DataModel {
9.    private DataModel model;
10.   private Row[] rows;
11.
12.   private static Comparator byLast = new
13.      Comparator() {
14.         public int compare(Object o1, Object o2) {
15.            Row r1 = (Row) o1;
16.            Row r2 = (Row) o2;
17.            Name n1 = (Name) r1.getData();
18.            Name n2 = (Name) r2.getData();
19.            return n1.getLast().compareTo(n2.getLast());
20.         }
21.   };
22.
23.   private static Comparator byFirst = new
24.      Comparator() {
25.         public int compare(Object o1, Object o2) {
26.            Row r1 = (Row) o1;
27.            Row r2 = (Row) o2;
28.            Name n1 = (Name) r1.getData();
29.            Name n2 = (Name) r2.getData();
30.            return n1.getFirst().compareTo(n2.getFirst());
31.         }
32.   };
33.
34.   private class Row {
35.      private int row;
36.      public Row(int row) {
37.         this.row = row;
38.      }
39.      public Object getData() {
40.         int originalIndex = model.getRowIndex();
41.         model.setRowIndex(row);
42.         Object thisRowData = model.getRowData();
```

```
43.          model.setRowIndex(originalIndex);
44.          return thisRowData;
45.       }
46.    }
47.
48.    public SortFilterModel(DataModel model) {
49.       this.model = model;
50.       int rowCnt = model.getRowCount();
51.       if (rowCnt != -1) {
52.          rows = new Row[rowCnt];
53.          for(int i=0; i < rowCnt; ++i) {
54.             rows[i] = new Row(i);
55.          }
56.       }
57.    }
58.
59.    public String sortByLast() {
60.       Arrays.sort(rows, byLast);
61.       return null;
62.    }
63.
64.    public String sortByFirst() {
65.       Arrays.sort(rows, byFirst);
66.       return null;
67.    }
68.
69.    public void setRowIndex(int rowIndex) {
70.       if (rowIndex == -1 || rowIndex >= model.getRowCount()) {
71.          model.setRowIndex(rowIndex);
72.       }
73.       else {
74.          model.setRowIndex(rows[rowIndex].row);
75.       }
76.    }
77.
78.    // The following methods delegate directly to the
79.    // decorated model
80.
81.    public boolean isRowAvailable() {
82.       return model.isRowAvailable();
83.    }
84.    public int getRowCount() {
85.       return model.getRowCount();
```

Listing 5–21   sort/WEB-INF/classes/com/corejsf/SortFilterModel.java (cont.)

```
86.    }
87.    public Object getRowData() {
88.        return model.getRowData();
89.    }
90.    public int getRowIndex() {
91.        return model.getRowIndex();
92.    }
93.    public Object getWrappedData() {
94.        return model.getWrappedData();
95.    }
96.    public void setWrappedData(Object data) {
97.        model.setWrappedData(data);
98.    }
99.    public void addDataModelListener(DataModelListener listener) {
100.       model.addDataModelListener(listener);
101.   }
102.   public DataModelListener[] getDataModelListeners() {
103.       return model.getDataModelListeners();
104.   }
105.   public void removeDataModelListener(DataModelListener listener) {
106.       model.removeDataModelListener(listener);
107.   }
108. }
```

Listing 5–22   sort/WEB-INF/classes/com/corejsf/Name.java

```
1. package com.corejsf;
2.
3. public class Name {
4.    private String first;
5.    private String last;
6.
7.    public Name(String first, String last) {
8.        this.first = first;
9.        this.last = last;
10.   }
11.
12.   public void setFirst(String newValue) { first = newValue; }
13.   public String getFirst() { return first; }
14.
15.   public void setLast(String newValue) { last = newValue; }
16.   public String getLast() { return last; }
17. }
```

Listing 5–23 sort/WEB-INF/classes/com/corejsf/TableData.java

```
 1. package com.corejsf;
 2.
 3. import javax.faces.model.DataModel;
 4. import javax.faces.model.ArrayDataModel;
 5.
 6. public class TableData {
 7.    private DataModel filterModel = null;
 8.    private static final Name[] names = {
 9.       new Name("Anna", "Keeney"),
10.       new Name("John", "Wilson"),
11.       new Name("Mariko", "Randor"),
12.       new Name("William", "Dupont"),
13.    };
14.
15.    public TableData() {
16.       ArrayDataModel model = new ArrayDataModel(names);
17.       filterModel = new SortFilterModel(model);
18.    }
19.    public DataModel getNames() {
20.       return filterModel;
21.    }
22. }
```

Listing 5–24 sort/WEB-INF/faces-config.xml

```
 1. <?xml version="1.0"?>
 2.
 3. <!DOCTYPE faces-config PUBLIC
 4. "-//Sun Microsystems, Inc.//DTD JavaServer Faces Config 1.0//EN"
 5. "http://java.sun.com/dtd/web-facesconfig_1_0.dtd">
 6.
 7. <faces-config>
 8.    <managed-bean>
 9.       <managed-bean-name>tableData</managed-bean-name>
10.       <managed-bean-class>com.corejsf.TableData</managed-bean-class>
11.       <managed-bean-scope>session</managed-bean-scope>
12.    </managed-bean>
13. </faces-config>
```

Listing 5–25   sort/WEB-INF/styles.css

```
1. .names {
2.    border: thin solid black;
3. }
4. .namesHeader {
5.    text-align: center;
6.    font-style: italic;
7.    color: Snow;
8.    background: Teal;
9. }
10. .last {
11.    height: 25px;
12.    text-align: center;
13.    background: MediumTurquoise;
14. }
15. .first {
16.    text-align: left;
17.    background: PowderBlue;
18. }
```

Listing 5–26   sort/WEB-INF/classes/com/corejsf/messages.properties

```
1. windowTitle=Sorting Java Beans
2. pageTitle=An array of names:
3. firstColumnHeader=First Name
4. lastColumnHeader=Last Name
```

---

javax.faces.model.DataModel

- `int getRowCount()`

  Returns the total number of rows, if known; otherwise, it returns -1. The ResultSetDataModel always returns -1 from this method.

- `Object getRowData()`

  Returns the data associated with the current row

- `boolean isRowAvailable()`

  Returns true if there is valid data at the current row index

- `int getRowIndex()`
  Returns the index of the current row

- `void setRowIndex(int index)`
  Sets the current row index and updates the scoped variable representing the current item in the collection (that variable is specified with the `var` attribute of `h:dataTable`)

- `void addDataModelListener(DataModelListener listener)`
  Adds a data model listener that's notified when the row index changes

- `void removeDataModelListener(DataModelListener listener)`
  Removes a data model listener

- `void setWrappedData(Object obj)`
  Sets the object that a data model wraps

- `Object getWrappedData()`
  Returns a data model's wrapped data

Scrolling Techniques

There are two ways to scroll through tables with lots of rows: with a scrollbar or with some other type of control that moves through the rows. We explore both techniques in this section.

Scrolling with a Scrollbar

Scrolling with a scrollbar is the simplest solution; simply wrap your `h:dataTable` in an HTML `div`, like this:

```
<div style="overflow:auto; width:100%; height:200px">
    <h:dataTable...>
        <h:column>
            ...
        </h:column>
        ...
    </h:dataTable>
</div>
```

The application shown in Figure 5–16 is identical to the application discussed in "Database Tables" on page 179, except that the data table is placed in a scrollable DIV as shown above.

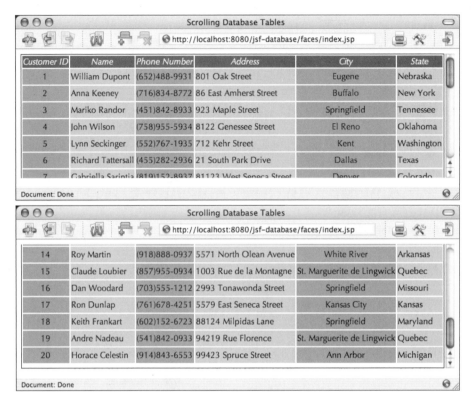

Figure 5–16   Scrolling Tables with Scrollable DIVs

Scrollbars are nice from a usability standpoint, but they can be expensive for large tables because all the table data is loaded at once. A less resource-intensive alternative is to scroll through tables with page widgets, an approach that requires only one page of data at a time.

Scrolling with Page Widgets

Scrolling with page widgets is more efficient than scrolling with a scrollable DIV, but it is also considerably more complex. In Chapter 12, we show you how to implement a pager widget that you can use with any table created with h:dataTable. Figure 5–17 shows an example of that pager.

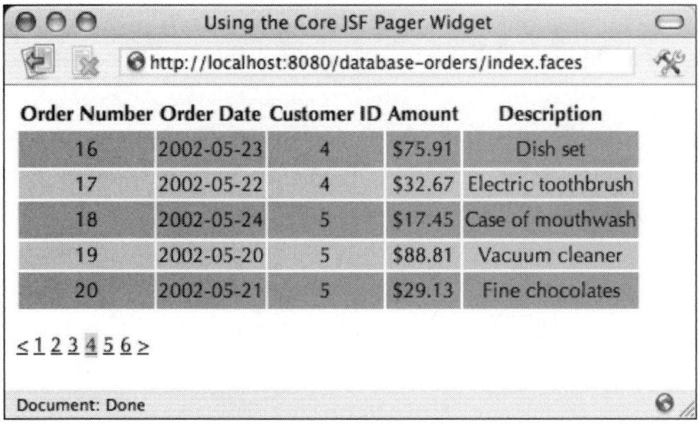

Figure 5–17   Scrolling with the Core JSF Pager

The application shown in Figure 5–17 uses a data table that displays customer orders from a database. See Chapter 12 for implementation details of the pager widget.

CONVERSION
AND VALIDATION

Topics in This Chapter

Chapter 6

In this chapter, we discuss how form data is converted to Java objects and how the conversion results are checked for correctness. The JSF container carries out these steps before updating the model, so you can rest assured that invalid inputs will never end up in the business logic.

We first look at the concepts behind conversion and validation process. Then we discuss the standard tags that JSF provides for conversion and validation. These tags suffice for the most common needs. Next, you see how to supply your own conversion and validation code for more complex scenarios. Finally, you learn how to implement custom tags—reusable converters and validators that can be configured by page authors.

Overview of the Conversion and Validation Process

Let us look at user input in slow motion as it travels from the browser form to the beans that make up the business logic.

First, the user fills in a field of a web form. When the user clicks the submit button, the browser sends the form data to the server. We call this value the *request value*.

In the "Apply Request Values" phase, the request values are stored in component objects. (Recall that each input tag of the JSF page has a corresponding component object.) The value that is stored in the component object is called the *submitted value*.

Of course, all request values are *strings*—after all, the client browser simply sends the strings that the user supplies. On the other hand, the web application deals with arbitrary types, such as int, Date, or even more sophisticated types. A *conversion* process transforms the incoming strings to those types. In the next section, we discuss conversion in detail.

The converted values are not immediately transmitted to the beans that make up the business logic. Instead, they are first stored inside the component objects as *local values*. After conversion, the local values are *validated*. Page designers can specify validation conditions, for example, that certain fields should have a minimum or maximum length. We begin our discussion of validation on page 217. After all local values have been validated, the "Update Model Values" phase starts, and the local values are stored in beans, as specified by their value references.

You may wonder why JSF bothers with local values at all. Couldn't one simply store the request values directly in the model?

JSF uses a two-step approach to make it easier to preserve model integrity. As all programmers know only too well, users will enter wrong information with distressing regularity. Suppose some of the model values had been updated before the first user error was detected. The model might then be in an inconsistent state, and it would be tedious to bring it back to its old state.

For that reason, JSF first converts and validates all user input. If errors are found, the page is simply redisplayed so that the user can try again. The "Update Model Values" phase starts only if all validations are successful.

Figure 6–1 shows the journey of a field value from the browser to the server-side component object and finally to the model bean.

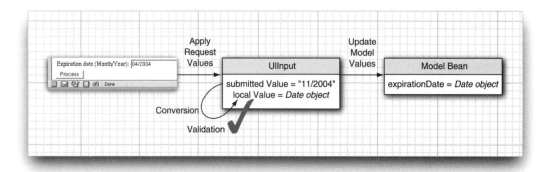

Figure 6–1   A Value Travels from the Browser to the Model

Using Standard Converters

In the following sections, we cover the converters and validators that are a part of the JSF library. Later in this chapter, you learn how to supply your own validation code if your needs go beyond the basics.

Conversion of Numbers and Dates

A web application stores data of many types, but the web user interface deals exclusively with strings. For example, suppose the user needs to edit a Date object that is stored in the business logic. First, the Date object is converted to a string that is sent to the client browser to be displayed inside a textfield. The user then edits the textfield. The resulting string is returned to the server and must be converted back to a Date object.

The same situation holds, of course, for primitive types such as int, double, or boolean. The user of the web application edits strings, and the JSF container needs to convert the string to the type required by the application.

To see a typical use of a built-in converter, imagine a web application that is used to process payments (see Figure 6–2). The payment data includes

- the amount to be charged
- the credit card number
- the credit card expiration date

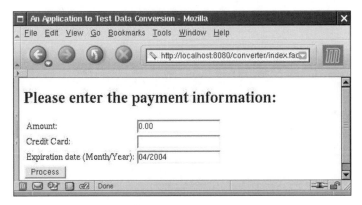

Figure 6–2   Processing payments

We attach a converter to the textfield and tell it to format the current value with at least two digits after the decimal point:

```
<h:inputText value="#{payment.amount}">
   <f:convertNumber minFractionDigits="2"/>
</h:inputText>
```

The f:convertNumber converter is one of the standard converters supplied by the JSF implementation.

The second field in this screen does not use a converter. (Later in this chapter, we attach a custom converter.) The third field uses an f:datetime converter whose pattern attribute is set to the string MM/yyyy. (The pattern string format is documented in the API documentation for the java.text.SimpleDateFormat class.)

```
<h:inputText value="#{payment.date}">
   <f:convertDateTime pattern="MM/yyyy"/>
</h:inputText>
```

In the result.jsp page, we show the inputs that the user provided, using a different converter for the payment amount:

```
<h:outputText value="#{payment.amount}">
   <f:convertNumber type="currency"/>
</h:outputText>
```

This converter automatically supplies a currency symbol and decimal separators (see Figure 6–3).

Figure 6–3   Displaying the Payment Information

Converters and Attributes

Tables 6–1 and 6–2 show the standard converters and their attributes.

NOTE: If you use a value binding whose type is either a primitive type or BigInteger/BigDecimal, then you don't need to specify any converter. The JSF implementation automatically picks a standard converter. However, you need to specify an explicit converter for Date values.

Table 6-1 Attributes of the f:convertNumber **tag**

Attribute	Type	Value
type	String	number (default), currency, or percent
pattern	String	Formatting pattern, as defined in java.text.DecimalFormat
maxFractionDigits	int	Maximum number of digits in the fractional part
minFractionDigits	int	Minimum number of digits in the fractional part
maxIntegerDigits	int	Maximum number of digits in the integer part
minIntegerDigits	int	Minimum number of digits in the integer part
integerOnly	boolean	True if only the integer part is parsed (default: false)
groupingUsed	boolean	True if grouping separators are used (default: true)
locale	java.util.Locale	Locale whose preferences are to be used for parsing and formatting
currencyCode	String	ISO 4217 currency code to use when converting currency values
currencySymbol	String	Currency symbol to use when converting currency values

Table 6–2 Attributes of the f:convertDateTime **tag**

Attribute	Type	Value
type	String	date (default), time, or both
dateStyle	String	default, short, medium, long, or full
timeStyle	String	default, short, medium, long, or full
pattern	String	Formatting pattern, as defined in java.text.SimpleDateFormat
locale	java.util.Locale	Locale whose preferences are to be used for parsing and formatting
timeZone	java.util.TimeZone	Time zone to use for parsing and formatting

The converter *Attribute*

An alternate syntax for attaching a converter to a component is to add the converter attribute to the component tag. You specify the ID of the converter like this:

```
<h:outputText value="#{payment.date}" converter="javax.faces.DateTime"/>
```

This is equivalent to using f:convertDateTime with no attributes:

```
<h:outputText value="#{payment.date}">
   <f:convertDateTime/>
</h:outputText>
```

All JSF implementations must define a set of converters with predefined IDs:

- javax.faces.DateTime (used by f:convertDateTime)
- javax.faces.Number (used by f:convertNumber)
- javax.faces.Boolean, javax.faces.Byte, javax.faces.Character, javax.faces.Double, javax.faces.Float, javax.faces.Integer, javax.faces.Long, javax.faces.Short (automatically used for primitive types and their wrapper classes)
- javax.faces.BigDecimal, javax.faces.BigInteger (automatically used for BigDecimal/BigInteger)

Additional converter IDs can be configured in an application configuration file—see page 226 for details.

CAUTION: When the value of the `converter` attribute is a string, then the value indicates the ID of a converter. However, if it is a value binding expression, then its value must be a *converter object*—an object of a class that implements the `Converter` interface. That interface is introduced on page 223.

Conversion Errors

When a conversion error occurs, the following actions are the result:

- The component whose conversion failed posts a *message* and declares itself invalid. (You see in the next section how to display the message.)
- The JSF implementation redisplays the current page immediately after the "Process Validations" phase has completed.

This behavior is generally desirable. If a user provides an illegal input for, say, a field that requires an integer, then the web application should not try to use that illegal input. The JSF implementation automatically redisplays the current page, giving the user another chance to enter the value correctly.

However, you should avoid overly restrictive conversion options for *input* fields. For example, consider the "amount" field in our example. Had we used a currency format, then the current value would have been nicely formatted. But suppose a user enters 100 (without a leading $ sign). The currency formatter will complain that the input is not a legal currency value. That's too strict for human use.

To overcome this problem, you can program a custom converter. A custom converter can format a value prettily, yet be lenient when interpreting human input. Custom converters are described later in this chapter.

TIP: When gathering input from the user, you should either use a lenient converter or simply redesign your form to be more user friendly. For example, rather than forcing users to format the expiration date as MM/yyyy, you can supply two input fields, one for the month and another for the year.

Displaying Error Messages

Of course, it is important that the user be able to see the messages that are caused by conversion and validation errors. You should add `h:message` tags whenever you use converters and validators.

Normally, you want to show the error messages next to the components that reported them (see Figure 6–4). Give an ID to the component, and reference that ID in the h:message tag.

```
<h:inputText id="amount" value="#{payment.amount}"/>
<h:message for="amount"/>
```

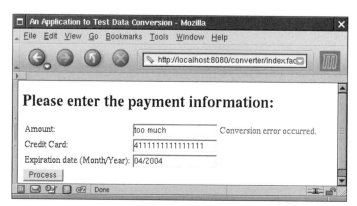

Figure 6–4   Displaying a Conversion Error Message

The h:message tag takes a number of attributes to describe the appearance of the message—see Chapter 4 for details. Here, we discuss only the attributes that are of particular interest for error reporting.

A message has two parts: *summary* and *detail*. By default, the h:message tag shows the detail and hides the summary. If you want to show the summary message instead, use these attributes:

```
<h:message for="amount" showSummary="true" showDetail="false"/>
```

> CAUTION: If you use a standard converter, display either the summary message or the detail message, but not both—for some errors, the messages are identical. You don't want your users to ponder an error message that reads "Conversion error occurred. Conversion error occurred."

You use the styleClass or style attribute to change the appearance of the error message:

```
<h:messages styleClass="errorMessage"/>
```

or

```
<h:message for="amount" style="color:red"/>
```

We recommend that you use styleClass and a stylesheet instead of a hard-coded style.

Displaying All Error Messages

It is uncommon to have multiple messages for one component, but it can happen. The h:message tag produces only the *first* message. Unfortunately, you don't know whether the first message is the most useful one for the user. While no tag shows all messages for a particular component, you can show a listing of all messages from all components with the h:messages tag.

By default, the h:messages tag shows the message summary but not the message detail. This behavior is opposite from that of the h:message tag.

For h:messages, you usually want to set the layout attribute to "table" so that the messages are lined up vertically. Otherwise they are simply concatenated.

```
<h:messages layout="table"/>
```

 TIP: Whenever you create a message, make sure it ends with a period and a space, to ensure a neat appearance when messages are concatenated.

However, we find it difficult to believe that anyone would actually use the h:messages tag in a form with multiple input fields. Suppose a user happened to fill in two fields incorrectly. The h:messages tag would display two "Conversion error occurred" messages, with no indication of the offending fields.

 TIP: The h:messages tag is useful for debugging. Whenever your JSF application stalls at a particular page and is unwilling to move on, add a <h:messages/> tag to see if a failed conversion or validation is the culprit.

Changing the Text of Standard Error Messages

As you saw in Figure 6–4, the default error message for a conversion error is "Conversion error occurred." If you think that your audience is unfamiliar with the concept of data conversion, you may want to change this message.

Set up a message bundle, as explained in Chapter 2. Add the replacement message, using the key javax.faces.component.UIInput.CONVERSION. For example,

```
javax.faces.component.UIInput.CONVERSION=Please correct your input.
```

Then set the base name of the bundle in a configuration file (such as faces-config.xml):

```
<faces-config>
  <application>
    <message-bundle>com.corejsf.messages</message-bundle>
  </application>
  ...
</faces-config>
```

A Complete Converter Example

We are now ready for our first complete example. Figure 6–5 shows the directory structure of the application. This web application simply asks the user to supply payment information (Listing 6–1), and then displays the formatted information on a confirmation screen (Listing 6–2). The messages are in Listing 6–3 and the bean class is in Listing 6–4.

Figure 6–5 Directory Structure of the Converter Sample

Listing 6–1   converter/index.jsp

```
1. <html>
2.    <%@ taglib uri="http://java.sun.com/jsf/core" prefix="f" %>
3.    <%@ taglib uri="http://java.sun.com/jsf/html" prefix="h" %>
4.    <f:view>
5.       <head>
6.          <link href="styles.css" rel="stylesheet" type="text/css"/>
7.          <f:loadBundle basename="com.corejsf.messages" var="msgs"/>
8.          <title><h:outputText value="#{msgs.title}"/></title>
9.       </head>
10.      <body>
11.         <h:form>
12.            <h1><h:outputText value="#{msgs.enterPayment}"/></h1>
13.            <h:panelGrid columns="3">
14.               <h:outputText value="#{msgs.amount}"/>
15.               <h:inputText id="amount" value="#{payment.amount}">
```

Listing 6–1 converter/index.jsp (cont.)

```
16.                 <f:convertNumber minFractionDigits="2"/>
17.              </h:inputText>
18.              <h:message for="amount" styleClass="errorMessage"/>
19.
20.              <h:outputText value="#{msgs.creditCard}"/>
21.              <h:inputText id="card" value="#{payment.card}"/>
22.              <h:panelGroup/>
23.
24.              <h:outputText value="#{msgs.expirationDate}"/>
25.              <h:inputText id="date" value="#{payment.date}">
26.                 <f:convertDateTime pattern="MM/yyyy"/>
27.              </h:inputText>
28.              <h:message for="date" styleClass="errorMessage"/>
29.           </h:panelGrid>
30.           <h:commandButton value="#{msgs.process}" action="process"/>
31.        </h:form>
32.     </body>
33.  </f:view>
34. </html>
```

Listing 6–2 converter/result.jsp

```
1. <html>
2.    <%@ taglib uri="http://java.sun.com/jsf/core" prefix="f" %>
3.    <%@ taglib uri="http://java.sun.com/jsf/html" prefix="h" %>
4.    <f:view>
5.       <head>
6.          <link href="styles.css" rel="stylesheet" type="text/css"/>
7.          <f:loadBundle basename="com.corejsf.messages" var="msgs"/>
8.          <title><h:outputText value="#{msgs.title}"/></title>
9.       </head>
10.      <body>
11.         <h:form>
12.            <h1><h:outputText value="#{msgs.paymentInformation}"/></h1>
13.            <h:panelGrid columns="2">
14.               <h:outputText value="#{msgs.amount}"/>
15.               <h:outputText value="#{payment.amount}">
16.                  <f:convertNumber type="currency"/>
17.               </h:outputText>
18.
19.               <h:outputText value="#{msgs.creditCard}"/>
20.               <h:outputText value="#{payment.card}"/>
21.
```

Listing 6–2 converter/result.jsp (cont.)

```
22.            <h:outputText value="#{msgs.expirationDate}"/>
23.            <h:outputText value="#{payment.date}">
24.               <f:convertDateTime pattern="MM/yyyy"/>
25.            </h:outputText>
26.         </h:panelGrid>
27.         <h:commandButton value="Back" action="back"/>
28.      </h:form>
29.   </body>
30. </f:view>
31. </html>
```

Listing 6–3 converter/WEB-INF/classes/com/corejsf/messages.properties

```
1. title=An Application to Test Data Conversion
2. enterPayment=Please enter the payment information:
3. amount=Amount:
4. creditCard=Credit Card:
5. expirationDate=Expiration date (Month/Year):
6. process=Process
7. paymentInformation=Payment information
```

Listing 6–4 converter/WEB-INF/classes/com/corejsf/PaymentBean.java

```
1. package com.corejsf;
2.
3. import java.util.Date;
4.
5. public class PaymentBean {
6.    private double amount;
7.    private String card = "";
8.    private Date date = new Date();
9.
10.   // PROPERTY: amount
11.   public void setAmount(double newValue) { amount = newValue; }
12.   public double getAmount() { return amount; }
13.
14.   // PROPERTY: card
15.   public void setCard(String newValue) { card = newValue; }
16.   public String getCard() { return card; }
17.
18.   // PROPERTY: date
19.   public void setDate(Date newValue) { date = newValue; }
20.   public Date getDate() { return date; }
21. }
```

Using Standard Validators

It's difficult to imagine a Web application that does not perform a healthy dose of data validation. Since validation is so pervasive, it should be easy to use and extend. JavaServer Faces fits the bill in both respects by providing a handful of standard validators and affording you a simple mechanism for implementing your own validators.

A key role of validation is to protect the model. Because JSF uses separate phases for processing validations and updating model values, you can be assured that the model is not put into an inconsistent state if some of the inputs cannot be validated.

Validating String Lengths and Numeric Ranges

It's easy to use JSF validators within JSF pages—simply add validator tags to the body of a component tag, like this:

```
<h:inputText id="card" value="#{payment.card}">
    <f:validateLength minimum="13"/>
</h:inputText>
```

The preceding code fragment adds a validator to a text field; when the text field's form is submitted, the validator makes sure that the string contains at least 13 characters. When validation fails (in this case, when the string has 12 or fewer characters), validators generate error messages associated with the guilty component. These messages can later be displayed in a JSF page by the h:message or h:messages tag.

NOTE: JavaServer Faces 1.0 does not explicitly support client-side validation. All validation occurs on the server after the user has submitted the form data. If you want validation to occur inside the browser, you need to supply custom tags that contain the appropriate JavaScript commands. See Chapter 12 for details.

JavaServer Faces has built-in mechanisms that let you carry out the following validations:

- Checking the length of a string
- Checking limits for a numerical value (for example, > 0 or ≤ 100)
- Checking that a value has been supplied

Table 6–3 lists the standard validators that are provided with JSF. You saw the string length validator in the preceding section. To validate numerical input, you use a range validator. For example,

```
<h:inputText id="amount" value="#{payment.amount}">
   <f:validateLongRange minimum="10" maximum="10000"/>
</h:inputText>
```

The validator checks that the supplied value is ≥ 10 and ≤ 10000.

Table 6–3   Standard Validators

JSP Tag	Validator Class	Attributes	Validates
f:validateDoubleRange	DoubleRangeValidator	minimum, maximum	a double value within an optional range
f:validateLongRange	LongRangeValidator	minimum, maximum	a long value within an optional range
f:validateLength	LengthValidator	minimum, maximum	a String with a minimum and maximum number of characters

All the standard validator tags have minimum and maximum attributes. You need to supply one or both of these attributes.

Checking for Required Values

To check that a value is supplied, you do not nest a validator inside the input component tag. Instead, you supply the attribute required="true":

```
<h:inputText id="date" value="#{payment.date}" required="true"/>
```

All JSF input tags support the required attribute. You can combine the required attribute with a nested validator:

```
<h:inputText id="card" value="#{payment.card}" required="true">
   <f:validateLength minimum="13"/>
</h:inputText>
```

CAUTION: If the required attribute is not set and a user supplies a blank input, then no validation occurs at all! Instead, the blank input is interpreted as a request to leave the existing value unchanged.

Displaying Validation Errors

Validation errors are handled in the same way as conversion errors. A message is added to the component that failed validation, the component is invalidated, and the current page is redisplayed immediately after the "Process Validations" phase has completed.

You use the h:message or h:messages tag to display the validation errors. For details see the section on displaying conversion errors on page 211.

You can override the default validator messages shown in Table 6–4. Define a message bundle for your application, and supply messages with the appropriate keys, as shown on page 213.

Table 6–4   Standard Validation Error Messages

Resource ID	Default Text	Reported by
javax.faces.component.UIInput.REQUIRED	Validation Error: Value is required.	UIInput with required attribute when value is missing
javax.faces.validator.NOT_IN_RANGE	Validation Error: Specified attribute is not between the expected values of {0} and {1}.	DoubleRangeValidator and Long-RangeValidator when value is out of range and both minimum and maximum are specified
javax.faces.validator.DoubleRangeValidator.MAXIMUM javax.faces.validator.LongRangeValidator.MAXIMUM	Validation Error: Value is greater than allowable maximum of '{0}'.	DoubleRangeValidator or LongRangeValidator when value is out of range and only maximum is specified

Table 6–4   Standard Validation Error Messages (cont.)

Resource ID	Default Text	Reported by
`javax.faces.validator.DoubleRangeValidator.MINIMUM` `javax.faces.validator.LongRangeValidator.MINIMUM`	Validation Error: Value is less than allowable minimum of '{0}'.	`DoubleRangeValidator` or `LongRangeValidator` when value is out of range and only `minimum` is specified
`javax.faces.validator.DoubleRangeValidator.TYPE` `javax.faces.validator.LongRangeValidator.TYPE`	Validation Error: Value is not of the correct type.	`DoubleRangeValidator` or `LongRangeValidator` when value cannot be converted to `double` or `long`
`javax.faces.validator.LengthValidator.MAXIMUM`	Validation Error: Value is greater than allowable maximum of "{0}".	`LengthValidator` when string length is greater than `maximum`
`javax.faces.validator.LengthValidator.MINIMUM`	Validation Error: Value is less than allowable minimum of "{0}".	`LengthValidator` when string length is less than `minimum`

Bypassing Validation

As you saw in the preceding examples, validation errors (as well as conversion errors) force a redisplay of the current page. This behavior can be problematic with certain navigation actions. Suppose, for example, you add a "Cancel" button to a page that contains required fields. If the user simply clicks Cancel, leaving a required field blank, then the validation mechanism kicks in and forces the current page to be redisplayed.

It would be unreasonable to expect your users to fill in required fields before they are allowed to cancel their input. Fortunately, a bypass mechanism is available. If a command has the `immediate` attribute set, then the command is executed during the "Apply Request Values" phase.

Thus, you would implement a Cancel button like this:

```
<h:commandButton value="Cancel" action="cancel" immediate="true"/>
```

A Complete Validation Example

The following sample application shows a form that employs all of the standard JSF validation checks: required fields, string length, and numeric limits. The application makes sure that values are entered in all fields, the amount is between $10 and $10,000, the credit card number has at least 13 characters, and the PIN is a number between 1000 and 9999. Figure 6–6 shows typical validation error messages. A Cancel button is also provided to demonstrate the validation bypass.

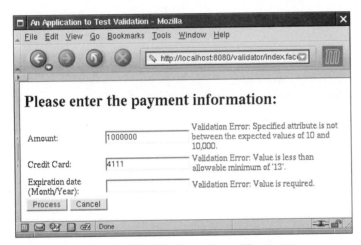

Figure 6–6   Typical Validation Error Messages

Figure 6–7 shows the directory structure of the application. Listing 6–5 contains the JSF page with the validators.

Figure 6–7   Directory Structure
of the Validation Example

Listing 6–5 `validator/index.jsp`

```
1.  <html>
2.     <%@ taglib uri="http://java.sun.com/jsf/core" prefix="f" %>
3.     <%@ taglib uri="http://java.sun.com/jsf/html" prefix="h" %>
4.     <f:view>
5.        <head>
6.           <link href="styles.css" rel="stylesheet" type="text/css"/>
7.           <f:loadBundle basename="com.corejsf.messages" var="msgs"/>
8.           <title><h:outputText value="#{msgs.title}"/></title>
9.        </head>
10.       <body>
11.          <h:form>
12.             <h1><h:outputText value="#{msgs.enterPayment}"/></h1>
13.             <h:panelGrid columns="3">
14.                <h:outputText value="#{msgs.amount}"/>
15.                <h:inputText id="amount" value="#{payment.amount}"
16.                   required="true">
17.                   <f:convertNumber minFractionDigits="2"/>
18.                   <f:validateDoubleRange minimum="10" maximum="10000"/>
19.                </h:inputText>
20.                <h:message for="amount" styleClass="errorMessage"/>
21.
22.                <h:outputText value="#{msgs.creditCard}"/>
23.                <h:inputText id="card" value="#{payment.card}"
24.                   required="true">
25.                   <f:validateLength minimum="13"/>
26.                </h:inputText>
27.                <h:message for="card" styleClass="errorMessage"/>
28.
29.                <h:outputText value="#{msgs.expirationDate}"/>
30.                <h:inputText id="date" value="#{payment.date}"
31.                   required="true">
32.                   <f:convertDateTime pattern="MM/yyyy"/>
33.                </h:inputText>
34.                <h:message for="date" styleClass="errorMessage"/>
35.             </h:panelGrid>
36.             <h:commandButton value="Process" action="process"/>
37.             <h:commandButton value="Cancel" action="cancel" immediate="true"/>
38.          </h:form>
39.       </body>
40.    </f:view>
41. </html>
```

Programming with Custom Converters and Validators

JSF standard converters and validators cover a lot of bases, but many Web applications must go further. For example, you may need to convert to types other than numbers and dates or perform application-specific validation such as checking a credit card.

In the following sections, we show you how to implement application-specific converters and validators. These implementations require a moderate amount of programming.

Implementing Custom Converter Classes

A *converter* is a class that converts between strings and objects. A converter must implement the Converter interface, which has the following two methods:

```
Object getAsObject(FacesContext context, UIComponent component, String newValue)
String getAsString(FacesContext context, UIComponent component, Object value)
```

The first method converts a string into an object of the desired type, throwing a ConverterException if the conversion cannot be carried out. This method is called when a string is submitted from the client, typically in a text field. The second method converts an object into a string representation to be displayed in the client interface.

To illustrate these methods, we develop a custom converter for credit card numbers. Our converter allows users to enter a credit card number with or without spaces. That is, we accept inputs of the following forms:

```
1234567890123456
1234 5678 9012 3456
```

Listing 6–6 shows the code for the custom converter. The getAsObject method of the converter simply strips out all characters that are not digits. It then creates an object of type CreditCard. If an error was found, then we generate a FacesMessage object and throw a ConverterException. We will discuss these steps in the next section.

The getAsString method of our converter makes an effort to format the credit card number in a way that is pleasing to the eye of the user. The digits are separated into the familiar patterns, depending on the credit card type. Table 6–5 shows the most common credit card formats.

Table 6–5   Credit Card Formats

Card Type	Digits	Format
MasterCard	16	5xxx xxxx xxxx xxxx
Visa	16	4xxx xxxx xxxx xxxx
Visa	13	4xxx xxx xxx xxx
Discover	16	6xxx xxxx xxxx xxxx
American Express	15	37xx xxxxxx xxxxx
American Express	22	3xxxxx xxxxxxxx xxxxxxxx
Diners Club, Carte Blanche	14	3xxxx xxxx xxxxx

In this example, the CreditCard class is trivial; it contains just the credit card number—see Listing 6–7. We could have left the credit card number as a String object, reducing the converter to a formatter. However, most converters have a target type other than String. To make it easier for you to reuse this example, we use a distinct target type.

Listing 6–6   converter2/WEB-INF/classes/com/coresjf/CreditCardConverter.java

```
1. package com.corejsf;
2.
3. import javax.faces.application.FacesMessage;
4. import javax.faces.component.UIComponent;
5. import javax.faces.context.FacesContext;
6. import javax.faces.convert.Converter;
7. import javax.faces.convert.ConverterException;
8.
9. public class CreditCardConverter implements Converter {
10.     public Object getAsObject(FacesContext context, UIComponent component,
11.         String newValue) throws ConverterException {
12.         StringBuffer buffer = new StringBuffer(newValue);
13.         boolean foundInvalidCharacter = false;
14.         char invalidCharacter = '\0';
15.         int i = 0;
16.         while (i < buffer.length() && !foundInvalidCharacter) {
17.             char ch = buffer.charAt(i);
18.             if (Character.isDigit(ch))
19.                 i++;
20.             else if (Character.isWhitespace(ch))
21.                 buffer.deleteCharAt(i);
```

Listing 6–6 converter2/WEB-INF/classes/com/coresjf/CreditCardConverter.java (cont.)

```
22.      else {
23.         foundInvalidCharacter = true;
24.         invalidCharacter = ch;
25.      }
26.   }
27.
28.   if (foundInvalidCharacter) {
29.      FacesMessage message = com.corejsf.util.Messages.getMessage(
30.            "com.corejsf.messages", "badCreditCardCharacter",
31.            new Object[]{ new Character(invalidCharacter) });
32.      message.setSeverity(FacesMessage.SEVERITY_ERROR);
33.      throw new ConverterException(message);
34.   }
35.
36.   return new CreditCard(buffer.toString());
37. }
38.
39. public String getAsString(FacesContext context, UIComponent component,
40.       Object value) throws ConverterException {
41.   // length 13: xxxx xxx xxx xxx
42.   // length 14: xxxxx xxxx xxxxx
43.   // length 15: xxxx xxxxxx xxxxx
44.   // length 16: xxxx xxxx xxxx xxxx
45.   // length 22: xxxxxx xxxxxxxx xxxxxxxx
46.   String v = value.toString();
47.   int[] boundaries = null;
48.   int length = v.length();
49.   if (length == 13)
50.      boundaries = new int[]{ 4, 7, 10 };
51.   else if (length == 14)
52.      boundaries = new int[]{ 5, 9 };
53.   else if (length == 15)
54.      boundaries = new int[]{ 4, 10 };
55.   else if (length == 16)
56.      boundaries = new int[]{ 4, 8, 12 };
57.   else if (length == 22)
58.      boundaries = new int[]{ 6, 14 };
59.   else
60.      return v;
61.   StringBuffer result = new StringBuffer();
62.   int start = 0;
63.   for (int i = 0; i < boundaries.length; i++) {
64.      int end = boundaries[i];
```

Listing 6–6	converter2/WEB-INF/classes/com/coresjf/CreditCardConverter.java (cont.)

```
65.         result.append(v.substring(start, end));
66.         result.append(" ");
67.         start = end;
68.      }
69.      result.append(v.substring(start));
70.      return result.toString();
71.   }
72. }
```

Listing 6–7	converter2/WEB-INF/classes/com/corejsf/CreditCard.java

```
1. package com.corejsf;
2.
3. public class CreditCard{
4.    private String number;
5.
6.    public CreditCard(String number) { this.number = number; }
7.    public String toString() { return number; }
8. }
```

One mechanism for specifying converters involves a symbolic ID that you register with the JSF application. We will use the ID com.corejsf.CreditCard for our credit card converter. The following entry to faces-config.xml associates the converter ID with the class that implements the converter:

```
<converter>
   <converter-id>com.corejsf.CreditCard</converter-id>
   <converter-class>com.corejsf.CreditCardConverter</converter-class>
</converter>
```

Now we can use the f:converter tag and specify the converter ID:

```
<h:inputText value="#{payment.card}">
   <f:converter converterId="com.corejsf.CreditCard"/>
</h:inputText>
```

Or, more succinctly, use the converter attribute.

```
<h:inputText value="#{payment.card}" converter="com.corejsf.CreditCard"/>
```

You can also access a converter without defining it in a configuration file. Use the converter attribute with a value binding expression that yields the converter object:

```
<h:outputText value="#{payment.card}" converter="#{bb.convert}"/>
```

Here, the bb bean must have a convert property of type Converter.

If you like, you can implement the property getter so that it returns an inner class object:

```
public class BackingBean {
    ...
    public Converter getConvert() {
        return new Converter() {
            public Object getAsObject(FacesContext context, UIComponent component,
                String newValue) throws ConverterException { ... }
            public String getAsString(FacesContext context, UIComponent component,
                Object value) throws ConverterException { ... }
        };
    }
}
```

This approach is convenient because the conversion methods can access the bean's private data.

Alternatively, if you are confident that your converter is appropriate for all conversions between String and CreditCard objects, then you can register it as the default converter for the CreditCard class:

```
<converter>
    <converter-for-class>com.corejsf.CreditCard</converter-for-class>
    <converter-class>com.corejsf.CreditCardConverter</converter-class>
</converter>
```

Now you don't have to mention the converter any longer. It is automatically used whenever a value reference has the type CreditCard. For example, consider the tag

```
<h:inputText value="#{payment.card}"/>
```

When the JSF implementation converts the request value, it notices that the target type is CreditCard, and it locates the converter for that class. This is the ultimate in converter convenience for the page author!

API   javax.faces.convert.Converter

- Object getAsObject(FacesContext context, UIComponent component, String value)
  Converts the given string value into an object that is appropriate for storage in the given component.

- `String getAsString(FacesContext context, UIComponent component, Object value)`
  Converts the given object, which is stored in the given component, into a string representation.

Reporting Conversion Errors

When a converter detects an error, it should throw a `ConverterException`. For example, the `getAsObject` method of our credit card converter checks whether the credit card contains characters other than digits or separators. If it finds an invalid character, it signals an error:

```
if (foundInvalidCharacter) {
   FacesMessage message = new FacesMessage(
      "Conversion error occurred. ", "Invalid card number. ");
   message.setSeverity(FacesMessage.SEVERITY_ERROR);
   throw new ConverterException(message);
}
```

The `FacesMessage` object contains the summary and detail messages that can be displayed with message tags.

 javax.faces.application.FacesMessage

- `FacesMessage(FacesMessage.Severity severity, String summary, String detail)`
  Constructs a message with the given severity, summary, and detail. The severity is one of the constants `SEVERITY_ERROR`, `SEVERITY_FATAL`, `SEVERITY_INFO`, or `SEVERITY_WARN` in the `FacesMessage` class.

- `FacesMessage(String summary, String detail)`
  Constructs a message with severity `SEVERITY_INFO` and the given summary and detail.

- `void setSeverity(FacesMessage.Severity severity)`
  Sets the severity to the given level. The severity is one of the constants `SEVERITY_ERROR`, `SEVERITY_FATAL`, `SEVERITY_INFO`, or `SEVERITY_WARN` in the `FacesMessage` class.

javax.faces.convert.ConverterException

- `ConverterException(FacesMessage message)`
- `ConverterException(FacesMessage message, Throwable cause)`
  These constructors create exceptions whose `getMessage` method returns the summary of the given message and whose `getFacesMessage` method returns the given message.

- `ConverterException()`
- `ConverterException(String detailMessage)`
- `ConverterException(Throwable cause)`
- `ConverterException(String detailMessage, Throwable cause)`

  These constructors create exceptions whose `getMessage` method returns the given detail message and whose `getFacesMessage` method returns `null`.

- `FacesMessage getFacesMessage()`

  Returns the `FacesMessage` with which this exception object was constructed, or `null` if none was supplied.

Getting Error Messages from Resource Bundles

Of course, for proper localization, you will want to retrieve the error messages from a message bundle.

Doing that involves some busywork with locales and class loaders:

1. Get the current locale.

   ```
   FacesContext context = FacesContext.getCurrentInstance();
   UIViewRoot viewRoot = context.getViewRoot();
   Locale locale = viewRoot.getLocale();
   ```

2. Get the current class loader. You need it to locate the resource bundle.

   ```
   ClassLoader loader = Thread.currentThread().getContextClassLoader();
   ```

3. Get the resource bundle with the given name, locale, and class loader.

   ```
   ResourceBundle bundle = ResourceBundle.getBundle(bundleName, locale, loader);
   ```

4. Get the resource string with the given ID from the bundle.

   ```
   String resource = bundle.getString(resourceId);
   ```

However, there are several wrinkles to the process. We actually need two message strings: one for the summary and one for the detail messages. By convention, the resource ID of a detail message is obtained by addition of the string "_detail" to the summary key. For example,

```
badCreditCardCharacter=Invalid card number.
badCreditCardCharacter_detail=The card number contains invalid characters.
```

Moreover, converters are usually part of a reusable library. It is a good idea to allow a specific application to override messages. (You saw on page 213 how to override the standard converter messages.) Therefore, you should first attempt to locate the messages in the application-specific message bundle before retrieving the default messages.

Recall that an application can supply a bundle name in a configuration file, such as

```
<faces-config>
  <application>
    <message-bundle>com.mycompany.myapp.messages</message-bundle>
  </application>
  ...
</faces-config>
```

The following code snippet retrieves that bundle name:

```
Application app = context.getApplication();
String appBundleName = app.getResourceBundle();
```

Look up your resources in this bundle before going to the library default.

Finally, you may want some messages to provide detailed information about the nature of the error. For example, you want to tell the user which character in the credit card number was objectionable. Message strings can contain placeholders {0}, {1}, and so on; for example:

```
The card number contains the invalid character {0}.
```

The java.text.MessageFormat class can substitute values for the placeholders:

```
Object[] params = ...;
MessageFormat formatter = new MessageFormat(resource, locale);
String message = formatter.format(params);
```

Here, the params array contains the values that should be substituted. Primitive type values need to be wrapped into objects of the appropriate wrapper classes, such as new Character(invalidCharacter). (For more information about the MessageFormat class, see *Horstmann & Cornell, Core Java 5th ed. vol. 2, ch. 10, Sun Microsystems Press 2002.*)

Ideally, much of this busywork should have been handled by the JSF framework. Of course, you can find the relevant code in the innards of the reference implementation, but the framework designers chose not to make it available to JSF programmers.

We provide the package com.corejsf.util with convenience classes that implement these missing pieces. Feel free to use these classes in your own code.

The com.corejsf.util.Messages class has a static method, getMessage, that returns a FacesMessage with a given bundle name, resource ID, and parameters:

```
FacesMessage message
  = com.corejsf.util.Messages.getMessage(
```

```
"com.corejsf.messages", "badCreditCardCharacter",
new Object[] { new Character(invalidCharacter) });
```

You can pass `null` for the parameter array if the message doesn't contain place-holders.

Our implementation follows the JSF convention of displaying missing resources as ???*resourceId*???. See Listing 6–8 for the source code.

 NOTE: If you prefer to reuse the standard JSF message for conversion errors, simply call

```
FacesMessage message = com.corejsf.util.Messages.getMessage(
    "javax.faces.Messages", "javax.faces.component.UIInput.CONVERSION", null);
```

---

javax.faces.context.FacesContext

- `static FacesContext getCurrentInstance()`

  Gets the context for the request that is being handled by the current thread, or `null` if the current thread does not handle a request.

- `UIViewRoot getViewRoot()`

  Gets the root component for the request described by this context.

javax.faces.component.UIViewRoot

- `Locale getLocale()`

  Gets the locale for rendering this view.

Listing 6–8 converter2/WEB-INF/classes/com/corejsf/util/Messages.java

```
1. package com.corejsf.util;
2.
3. import java.text.MessageFormat;
4. import java.util.Locale;
5. import java.util.MissingResourceException;
6. import java.util.ResourceBundle;
7. import javax.faces.application.Application;
8. import javax.faces.application.FacesMessage;
9. import javax.faces.component.UIViewRoot;
10. import javax.faces.context.FacesContext;
11.
```

Listing 6–8 converter2/WEB-INF/classes/com/corejsf/util/Messages.java (cont.)

```
12. public class Messages {
13.    public static FacesMessage getMessage(String bundleName, String resourceId,
14.       Object[] params) {
15.       FacesContext context = FacesContext.getCurrentInstance();
16.       Application app = context.getApplication();
17.       String appBundle = app.getMessageBundle();
18.       Locale locale = getLocale(context);
19.       ClassLoader loader = getClassLoader();
20.       String summary = getString(appBundle, bundleName, resourceId,
21.          locale, loader, params);
22.       if (summary == null) summary = "???" + resourceId + "???";
23.       String detail = getString(appBundle, bundleName, resourceId + "_detail",
24.          locale, loader, params);
25.       return new FacesMessage(summary, detail);
26.    }
27.
28.    public static String getString(String bundle, String resourceId,
29.          Object[] params) {
30.       FacesContext context = FacesContext.getCurrentInstance();
31.       Application app = context.getApplication();
32.       String appBundle = app.getMessageBundle();
33.       Locale locale = getLocale(context);
34.       ClassLoader loader = getClassLoader();
35.       return getString(appBundle, bundle, resourceId, locale, loader, params);
36.    }
37.
38.    public static String getString(String bundle1, String bundle2,
39.          String resourceId, Locale locale, ClassLoader loader,
40.          Object[] params) {
41.       String resource = null;
42.       ResourceBundle bundle;
43.
44.       if (bundle1 != null) {
45.          bundle = ResourceBundle.getBundle(bundle1, locale, loader);
46.          if (bundle != null)
47.             try {
48.                resource = bundle.getString(resourceId);
49.             } catch (MissingResourceException ex) {
50.             }
51.       }
52.       if (resource == null) {
53.          bundle = ResourceBundle.getBundle(bundle2, locale, loader);
54.          if (bundle != null)
```

Listing 6–8 converter2/WEB-INF/classes/com/corejsf/util/Messages.java (cont.)

```
55.            try {
56.                resource = bundle.getString(resourceId);
57.            } catch (MissingResourceException ex) {
58.            }
59.        }
60.
61.        if (resource == null) return null; // no match
62.        if (params == null) return resource;
63.
64.        MessageFormat formatter = new MessageFormat(resource, locale);
65.        return formatter.format(params);
66.    }
67.
68.    public static Locale getLocale(FacesContext context) {
69.        Locale locale = null;
70.        UIViewRoot viewRoot = context.getViewRoot();
71.        if (viewRoot != null) locale = viewRoot.getLocale();
72.        if (locale == null) locale = Locale.getDefault();
73.        return locale;
74.    }
75.
76.    public static ClassLoader getClassLoader() {
77.        ClassLoader loader = Thread.currentThread().getContextClassLoader();
78.        if (loader == null) loader = ClassLoader.getSystemClassLoader();
79.        return loader;
80.    }
81. }
```

The Custom Converter Sample Application

Here are the remaining pieces of our next sample application. Figure 6–8 shows the directory structure. Listings 6–9 and 6–10 show the input and result pages. Look at the inputText and outputText tags for the credit card numbers to see the two styles of specifying a custom converter. (Both converter specifications could have been omitted if the converter had been registered to be the default for the CreditCard type.) The custom converter is defined in faces-config.xml (Listing 6–11). The messages.properties file—shown in Listing 6–12—contains the error message for the credit card converter. Finally, Listing 6–13 shows the payment bean with three properties of type double, Date, and CreditCard.

**Figure 6–8   Directory Structure
of the Custom Converter Example**

Listing 6–9   converter2/index.jsp

```
1.  <html>
2.     <%@ taglib uri="http://java.sun.com/jsf/core" prefix="f" %>
3.     <%@ taglib uri="http://java.sun.com/jsf/html" prefix="h" %>
4.     <f:view>
5.        <head>
6.           <link href="styles.css" rel="stylesheet" type="text/css"/>
7.           <f:loadBundle basename="com.corejsf.messages" var="msgs"/>
8.           <title><h:outputText value="#{msgs.title}"/></title>
9.        </head>
10.       <body>
11.          <h:form>
12.             <h1><h:outputText value="#{msgs.enterPayment}"/></h1>
13.             <h:panelGrid columns="3">
14.                <h:outputText value="#{msgs.amount}"/>
15.                <h:inputText id="amount" value="#{payment.amount}">
16.                   <f:convertNumber minFractionDigits="2"/>
17.                </h:inputText>
18.                <h:message for="amount" styleClass="errorMessage"/>
19.
20.                <h:outputText value="#{msgs.creditCard}"/>
21.                <h:inputText id="card" value="#{payment.card}">
22.                   <f:converter converterId="com.corejsf.CreditCard"/>
23.                </h:inputText>
24.                <h:message for="card" styleClass="errorMessage"/>
25.
```

Listing 6–9	converter2/index.jsp (cont.)

```
26.                <h:outputText value="#{msgs.expirationDate}"/>
27.                <h:inputText id="date" value="#{payment.date}">
28.                    <f:convertDateTime pattern="MM/yyyy"/>
29.                </h:inputText>
30.                <h:message for="date" styleClass="errorMessage"/>
31.            </h:panelGrid>
32.            <h:commandButton value="Process" action="process"/>
33.        </h:form>
34.    </body>
35.  </f:view>
36. </html>
```

Listing 6–10	converter2/result.jsp

```
1. <html>
2.   <%@ taglib uri="http://java.sun.com/jsf/core" prefix="f" %>
3.   <%@ taglib uri="http://java.sun.com/jsf/html" prefix="h" %>
4.   <f:view>
5.     <head>
6.       <link href="styles.css" rel="stylesheet" type="text/css"/>
7.       <f:loadBundle basename="com.corejsf.messages" var="msgs"/>
8.       <title><h:outputText value="#{msgs.title}"/></title>
9.     </head>
10.    <body>
11.      <h:form>
12.        <h1><h:outputText value="#{msgs.paymentInformation}"/></h1>
13.        <h:panelGrid columns="2">
14.          <h:outputText value="#{msgs.amount}"/>
15.          <h:outputText value="#{payment.amount}">
16.              <f:convertNumber type="currency"/>
17.          </h:outputText>
18.
19.          <h:outputText value="#{msgs.creditCard}"/>
20.          <h:outputText value="#{payment.card}"
21.              converter="com.corejsf.CreditCard"/>
22.
23.          <h:outputText value="#{msgs.expirationDate}"/>
24.          <h:outputText value="#{payment.date}">
25.              <f:convertDateTime pattern="MM/yyyy"/>
26.          </h:outputText>
27.        </h:panelGrid>
28.        <h:commandButton value="Back" action="back"/>
29.      </h:form>
30.    </body>
31.  </f:view>
32. </html>
```

Listing 6–11   converter2/WEB-INF/faces-config.xml

```
 1. <?xml version="1.0"?>
 2.
 3. <!DOCTYPE faces-config PUBLIC
 4.    "-//Sun Microsystems, Inc.//DTD JavaServer Faces Config 1.0//EN"
 5.    "http://java.sun.com/dtd/web-facesconfig_1_0.dtd">
 6.
 7. <faces-config>
 8.    <application>
 9.       <message-bundle>com.corejsf.messages</message-bundle>
10.    </application>
11.
12.    <navigation-rule>
13.       <from-view-id>/index.jsp</from-view-id>
14.       <navigation-case>
15.          <from-outcome>process</from-outcome>
16.          <to-view-id>/result.jsp</to-view-id>
17.       </navigation-case>
18.    </navigation-rule>
19.
20.    <navigation-rule>
21.       <from-view-id>/result.jsp</from-view-id>
22.       <navigation-case>
23.          <from-outcome>back</from-outcome>
24.          <to-view-id>/index.jsp</to-view-id>
25.       </navigation-case>
26.    </navigation-rule>
27.
28.    <converter>
29.       <converter-id>com.corejsf.CreditCard</converter-id>
30.      <converter-class>com.corejsf.CreditCardConverter</converter-class>
31.    </converter>
32.
33.    <managed-bean>
34.       <managed-bean-name>payment</managed-bean-name>
35.       <managed-bean-class>com.corejsf.PaymentBean</managed-bean-class>
36.       <managed-bean-scope>session</managed-bean-scope>
37.    </managed-bean>
38. </faces-config>
```

Listing 6–12 converter2/WEB-INF/classes/com/corejsf/messages.properties

```
 1. badCreditCardCharacter=Invalid card number.
 2. badCreditCardCharacter_detail=The card number contains the invalid character {0}.
 3. title=An Application to Test Data Conversion
 4. enterPayment=Please enter the payment information:
 5. amount=Amount:
 6. creditCard=Credit Card:
 7. expirationDate=Expiration date (Month/Year):
 8. process=Process
 9. paymentInformation=Payment information
```

Listing 6–13 converter2/WEB-INF/classes/com/corejsf/PaymentBean.java

```
 1. package com.corejsf;
 2. import java.util.Date;
 3.
 4. public class PaymentBean {
 5.    private double amount;
 6.    private CreditCard card = new CreditCard("");
 7.    private Date date = new Date();
 8.
 9.    // PROPERTY: amount
10.    public void setAmount(double newValue) { amount = newValue; }
11.    public double getAmount() { return amount; }
12.
13.    // PROPERTY: card
14.    public void setCard(CreditCard newValue) { card = newValue; }
15.    public CreditCard getCard() { return card; }
16.
17.    // PROPERTY: date
18.    public void setDate(Date newValue) { date = newValue; }
19.    public Date getDate() { return date; }
20. }
```

Implementing Custom Validator Classes

Implementing custom validator classes is a two-step process, similar to the
process you saw in the preceding section:

1. Implement a validator by implementing the javax.faces.validator.Validator
    interface.

2. Register your validator in a configuration file (such as faces-config.xml).

The Validator interface defines only one method:

```
void validate(FacesContext context, UIComponent component)
```

If validation fails, simply generate a FacesMessage that describes the error, construct a ValidatorException from the message, and throw it.

```
if (validation fails) {
    FacesMessage message = ...;
    message.setSeverity(FacesMessage.SEVERITY_ERROR);
    throw new ValidatorException(message);
}
```

The process is completely analogous to the reporting of conversion errors, except that you throw a ValidatorException instead of a ConverterException.

For example, Listing 6–14 shows a validator that checks the digits of a credit card, using the Luhn formula. Figure 6–9 shows the application at work. As described on page 229, we use the convenience class com.corejsf.util.Messages to locate the message strings in a resource bundle.

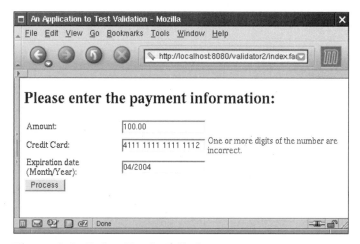

Figure 6–9   Luhn Check Failed

NOTE: The Luhn formula—developed by a group of mathematicians in the late 1960s—verifies and generates credit card numbers, as well as Social Insurance numbers for the Canadian government. The formula can detect whether a digit is entered wrongly or whether two digits were transposed. See the web site http://www.merriampark.com/anatomycc.htm for more information about the Luhn formula. For debugging, it is handy to know that the number 4111 1111 1111 1111 passes the Luhn check.

`javax.faces.validator.Validator`

- void validate(FacesContext context, UIComponent component)

  Validates the component to which this validator is attached. If there is a validation error, throw a ValidatorException.

Listing 6–14   validator2/WEB-INF/classes/com/corejsf/CreditCardValidator.java

```java
 1. package com.corejsf;
 2.
 3. import javax.faces.application.FacesMessage;
 4. import javax.faces.component.UIComponent;
 5. import javax.faces.context.FacesContext;
 6. import javax.faces.validator.Validator;
 7. import javax.faces.validator.ValidatorException;
 8.
 9. public class CreditCardValidator implements Validator {
10.    public void validate(FacesContext context, UIComponent component,
11.        Object value) {
12.       if(value == null) return;
13.       String cardNumber;
14.       if (value instanceof CreditCard)
15.          cardNumber = value.toString();
16.       else
17.          cardNumber = getDigitsOnly(value.toString());
18.       if(!luhnCheck(cardNumber)) {
19.          FacesMessage message
20.             = com.corejsf.util.Messages.getMessage(
21.                "com.corejsf.messages", "badLuhnCheck", null);
22.          message.setSeverity(FacesMessage.SEVERITY_ERROR);
23.          throw new ValidatorException(message);
24.       }
25.    }
26.
27.    private static boolean luhnCheck(String cardNumber) {
28.       int sum = 0;
29.
30.       for(int i = cardNumber.length() - 1; i >= 0; i -= 2) {
31.          sum += Integer.parseInt(cardNumber.substring(i, i + 1));
32.          if(i > 0) {
33.             int d = 2 * Integer.parseInt(cardNumber.substring(i - 1, i));
34.             if(d > 9) d -= 9;
35.             sum += d;
36.          }
37.       }
```

Listing 6–14	validator2/WEB-INF/classes/com/corejsf/CreditCardValidator.java (cont.)

```
38.
39.     return sum % 10 == 0;
40.   }
41.
42.   private static String getDigitsOnly(String s) {
43.     StringBuffer digitsOnly = new StringBuffer ();
44.     char c;
45.     for(int i = 0; i < s.length (); i++) {
46.       c = s.charAt (i);
47.       if (Character.isDigit(c)) {
48.         digitsOnly.append(c);
49.       }
50.     }
51.     return digitsOnly.toString ();
52.   }
53. }
```

Registering Custom Validators

Now that we've created a validator, we need to register it in a configuration file (such as faces-config.xml), like this:

```
<validator>
  <validator-id>com.corejsf.CreditCard</validator-id>
  <validator-class>com.corejsf.CreditCardValidator</validator-class>
</validator>
```

You can use custom validators with the f:validator tag; for example, the following code fragment uses the credit card validator discussed above:

```
<h:inputText id="card" value="#{payment.card}" required="true">
  <f:converter converterId="com.corejsf.CreditCard"/>
  <f:validator validatorId="com.corejsf.CreditCard"/>
</h:inputText>
```

The validatorId specified for f:validator must correspond to a validator ID specified in the configuration file. The f:validator tag uses the validator ID to look up the corresponding class, creates an instance of that class if necessary, and invokes its validate method.

> **NOTE:** JSF uses separate name spaces for converter and validator IDs. Thus, it is ok to have both a converter and a validator with ID `com.core-jsf.CreditCard`.

> **NOTE:** JSF registers its three standard validators with IDs `javax.faces.LongRange`, `javax.faces.DoubleRange`, and `javax.faces.Length`.

The remainder of the sample application is straightforward. Figure 6–10 shows the directory structure, and Listing 6–15 contains the JSF page.

```
validator2
    index.html
    index.jsp
    result.jsp
    styles.css
    WEB-INF
        faces-config.xml
        web.xml
        classes
            com
                corejsf
                    CreditCard.java
                    CreditCardConverter.java
                    CreditCardValidator.java
                    PaymentBean.java
                    messages.properties
                    util
                        Messages.java
```

**Figure 6–10   The Directory Structure
of the Luhn Check Example**

Listing 6–15   `validator2/index.jsp`

```
1.  <html>
2.     <%@ taglib uri="http://java.sun.com/jsf/core" prefix="f" %>
3.     <%@ taglib uri="http://java.sun.com/jsf/html" prefix="h" %>
4.     <f:view>
5.        <head>
6.           <link href="styles.css" rel="stylesheet" type="text/css"/>
7.           <f:loadBundle basename="com.corejsf.messages" var="msgs"/>
8.           <title><h:outputText value="#{msgs.title}"/></title>
9.        </head>
10.       <body>
```

Listing 6–15	validator2/index.jsp (cont.)

```
11.        <h:form>
12.          <h1><h:outputText value="#{msgs.enterPayment}"/></h1>
13.          <h:panelGrid columns="3">
14.            <h:outputText value="#{msgs.amount}"/>
15.            <h:inputText id="amount" value="#{payment.amount}">
16.              <f:convertNumber minFractionDigits="2"/>
17.            </h:inputText>
18.            <h:message for="amount" styleClass="errorMessage"/>
19.
20.            <h:outputText value="#{msgs.creditCard}"/>
21.            <h:inputText id="card" value="#{payment.card}" required="true">
22.              <f:converter converterId="com.corejsf.CreditCard"/>
23.              <f:validator validatorId="com.corejsf.CreditCard"/>
24.            </h:inputText>
25.            <h:message for="card" styleClass="errorMessage"/>
26.
27.            <h:outputText value="#{msgs.expirationDate}"/>
28.            <h:inputText id="date" value="#{payment.date}">
29.              <f:convertDateTime pattern="MM/yyyy"/>
30.            </h:inputText>
31.            <h:message for="date" styleClass="errorMessage"/>
32.          </h:panelGrid>
33.          <h:commandButton value="Process" action="process"/>
34.        </h:form>
35.      </body>
36.    </f:view>
37. </html>
```

The f:validator tag is useful for simple validators that don't have parameters, such as the credit validator discussed above. If you need a validator with properties that can be specified in a JSF page, you should implement a custom tag for your validator. You see how to do that later in this chapter.

Validating with Bean Methods

In the preceding section, you saw how to implement a validation class. However, you can also add the validation method to an existing class and invoke it through a method reference, like this:

```
<h:inputText id="card" value="#{payment.card}"
  required="true" validator="#{payment.luhnCheck}"/>
```

The payment bean must then have a method with the exact same signature as the validate method of the Validator interface:

```
public class PaymentBean {
    ...
    public void luhnCheck(FacesContext context, UIComponent component, Object value) {
        ... // same code as in the preceding example
    }
}
```

Why would you want to do this? There is one major advantage. The validation method can access other instance fields of the class. You will see an example in the next section.

On the downside, this approach makes it more difficult to move a validator to a new web application, so you would probably only use it for application-specific scenarios.

> CAUTION: The value of the `validator` attribute is a *method reference*, whereas the seemingly similar `converter` attribute specifies a *converter ID* (if it is a string) or *converter object* (if it is a value binding). As Emerson said, a foolish consistency is the hobgoblin of little minds.

Validating Relationships Between Multiple Components

The validation mechanism in JSF was designed to validate a *single* component. However, in practice, you often need to ensure that related components have reasonable values before letting the values propagate into the model. For example, as we noted earlier, it is not a good idea to ask users to enter a date into a single textfield. Instead, you would use three different textfields, for the day, month, and year, as in Figure 6–11.

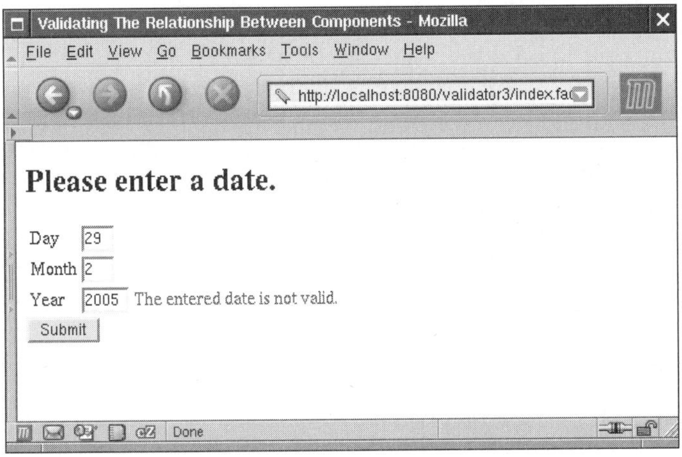

Figure 6–11   Validating a Relationship Involving Three Components

If the user enters an illegal date, such as February 30, you would like to show a validation error and prevent the illegal data from entering the model.

The trick is to attach the validator to the last of the components. By the time its validator is called, the preceding components passed validation and had their local values set. The last component has passed conversion, and the converted value is passed as the Object parameter of the validation method.

Of course, you need to have access to the other components. You can easily achieve that access by using a backing bean that contains all components of the current form (see Listing 6–16). Simply attach the validation method to the backing bean:

```
public class BackingBean {
    private UIInput dayInput;
    private UIInput monthInput;
    ...
    public void validateDate(FacesContext context, UIComponent component,
        Object value) {
        int d = ((Integer) dayInput.getLocalValue()).intValue();
        int m = ((Integer) monthInput.getLocalValue()).intValue();
        int y = ((Integer) value).intValue();

        if (!isValidDate(d, m, y)) {
            FacesMessage message = ...;
            throw new ValidatorException(message);
        }
    }
    ...
}
```

Note that the value lookup is a bit asymmetric. The last component does not yet have the local value set since it has not passed validation.

Figure 6–12 shows the application's directory structure. Listing 6–17 shows the JSF page. Note the converter property of the last input field. Also note the use of the binding attributes that bind the input components to the backing bean.

**Figure 6–12 Directory Structure
of the Date Validation Example**

Listing 6–16 validator3/WEB-INF/classes/com/corejsf/BackingBean.java

```
1. package com.corejsf;
2.
3. import javax.faces.application.FacesMessage;
4. import javax.faces.component.UIComponent;
5. import javax.faces.component.UIInput;
6. import javax.faces.context.FacesContext;
7. import javax.faces.validator.ValidatorException;
8.
9. public class BackingBean {
10.    private int day;
11.    private int month;
12.    private int year;
13.    private UIInput dayInput;
14.    private UIInput monthInput;
15.    private UIInput yearInput;
16.
17.    // PROPERTY: day
18.    public int getDay() { return day; }
19.    public void setDay(int newValue) { day = newValue; }
20.
21.    // PROPERTY: month
22.    public int getMonth() { return month; }
23.    public void setMonth(int newValue) { month = newValue; }
24.
25.    // PROPERTY: year
26.    public int getYear() { return year; }
27.    public void setYear(int newValue) { year = newValue; }
28.
```

```
29.   // PROPERTY: dayInput
30.   public UIInput getDayInput() { return dayInput; }
31.   public void setDayInput(UIInput newValue) { dayInput = newValue; }
32.
33.   // PROPERTY: monthInput
34.   public UIInput getMonthInput() { return monthInput; }
35.   public void setMonthInput(UIInput newValue) { monthInput = newValue; }
36.
37.   // PROPERTY: yearInput
38.   public UIInput getYearInput() { return yearInput; }
39.   public void setYearInput(UIInput newValue) { yearInput = newValue; }
40.
41.   public void validateDate(FacesContext context, UIComponent component,
42.      Object value) {
43.      int d = ((Integer) dayInput.getLocalValue()).intValue();
44.      int m = ((Integer) monthInput.getLocalValue()).intValue();
45.      int y = ((Integer) value).intValue();
46.
47.      if (!isValidDate(d, m, y)) {
48.         FacesMessage message
49.            = com.corejsf.util.Messages.getMessage(
50.               "com.corejsf.messages", "invalidDate", null);
51.         message.setSeverity(FacesMessage.SEVERITY_ERROR);
52.         throw new ValidatorException(message);
53.      }
54.   }
55.
56.   private static boolean isValidDate(int d, int m, int y) {
57.      if (d < 1 || m < 1 || m > 12) return false;
58.      if (m == 2) {
59.         if (isLeapYear(y)) return d <= 29;
60.         else return d <= 28;
61.      }
62.      else if (m == 4 || m == 6 || m == 9 || m == 11)
63.         return d <= 30;
64.      else
65.         return d <= 31;
66.   }
67.
68.   private static boolean isLeapYear(int y) {
69.      return y % 4 == 0 && (y % 400 == 0 || y % 100 != 0);
70.   }
71. }
```

Listing 6–17   `validator3/index.jsp`

```
 1. <html>
 2.    <%@ taglib uri="http://java.sun.com/jsf/core" prefix="f" %>
 3.    <%@ taglib uri="http://java.sun.com/jsf/html" prefix="h" %>
 4.    <f:view>
 5.       <head>
 6.          <link href="styles.css" rel="stylesheet" type="text/css"/>
 7.          <f:loadBundle basename="com.corejsf.messages" var="msgs"/>
 8.          <title><h:outputText value="#{msgs.title}"/></title>
 9.       </head>
10.       <body>
11.          <h:form>
12.             <h1><h:outputText value="#{msgs.enterDate}"/></h1>
13.             <h:panelGrid columns="3">
14.                <h:outputText value="#{msgs.day}"/>
15.                <h:inputText value="#{bb.day}" binding="#{bb.dayInput}"
16.                   size="2" required="true"/>
17.                <h:panelGroup/>
18.
19.                <h:outputText value="#{msgs.month}"/>
20.                <h:inputText value="#{bb.month}" binding="#{bb.monthInput}"
21.                   size="2" required="true"/>
22.                <h:panelGroup/>
23.
24.                <h:outputText value="#{msgs.year}"/>
25.                <h:inputText id="year" value="#{bb.year}"
26.                   binding="#{bb.yearInput}" size="4" required="true"
27.                   validator="#{bb.validateDate}"/>
28.                <h:message for="year" styleClass="errorMessage"/>
29.             </h:panelGrid>
30.             <h:commandButton value="#{msgs.submit}" action="submit"/>
31.          </h:form>
32.       </body>
33.    </f:view>
34. </html>
```

An alternative approach is to attach the validator to a *hidden input field* that
comes after all other fields on the form.

```
<h:inputHidden id="datecheck" validator="#{bb.validateDate}"
   value="needed"/>
```

The hidden field is rendered as a hidden HTML input field. When the field
value is posted back, the validator kicks in. (It is essential that you supply some
field value. Otherwise, the component value is never updated.) With this

approach, the validation function is more symmetrical since all other form components already have their local values set.

>  NOTE: It would actually be worthwhile to write a custom date component that renders three input fields and has a single value of type Date. That single component could then be validated easily. However, the technique of this section is useful for any form that needs validation across fields.

Implementing Custom Tags

The custom converters and validators of the preceding section have a shortcoming: they do not allow parameters. For example, we may want to specify a separator character for the credit card converter so that the page designer can choose whether to use dashes or spaces to separate the digit groups. In other words, custom converters should have the same capabilities as the standard f:convertNumber and f:convertDateTime tags. Specifically, we would like page designers to use tags such as the following:

```
<h:outputText value="#{payment.card}">
   <corejsf:convertCreditcard separator="-"/>
</h:outputText>
```

To achieve this, we need to implement a *custom tag*. Custom tags require a significant amount of programming, but the payback is a reusable tag that is convenient for page authors.

Custom Converter Tags

The same basic process is used to produce custom tags for converters, validators, or components, but there are minor variations for these three tag categories. For simplicity, we first discuss the steps needed for converter tags and later tell you how validator and component tags differ. The process is somewhat byzantine, and you may find it helpful to refer to Figure 6–13 as we discuss each step.

> NOTE: Custom tags use the Java Server Pages tag library mechanism. For more information on JSP custom tags, see chapter 15 of the J2EE 1.4 tutorial at http://java.sun.com/j2ee/1.4/docs/tutorial/doc/index.html.

You need to produce a TLD (tag library descriptor) file that describes one or more tags and their attributes. Place that file into the WEB-INF directory. Listing 6–18 shows the TLD file that describes our convertCreditcard custom tag.

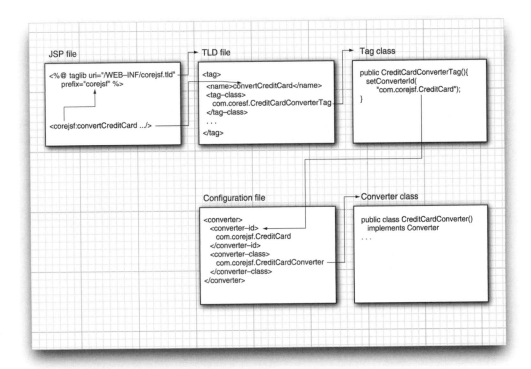

Figure 6–13   Locating a Converter

Listing 6–18   `converter3/WEB-INF/converter3.tld`

```
1. <?xml version="1.0" encoding="ISO-8859-1" ?>
2. <!DOCTYPE taglib
3.   PUBLIC "-//Sun Microsystems, Inc.//DTD JSP Tag Library 1.2//EN"
4.   "http://java.sun.com/dtd/web-jsptaglibrary_1_2.dtd">
5. <taglib>
6.    <tlib-version>1.0</tlib-version>
7.    <jsp-version>1.2</jsp-version>
8.    <short-name>converter3</short-name>
9.    <uri>http://corejsf.com/converter3</uri>
10.   <tag>
11.      <name>convertCreditcard</name>
12.      <tag-class>com.corejsf.CreditCardConverterTag</tag-class>
13.      <attribute>
14.         <name>separator</name>
15.      </attribute>
16.   </tag>
17. </taglib>
```

The entries in this file should be self-explanatory. The purpose of the file is to specify the class name for the tag handler (com.corejsf.ConvertCreditCardTag) and the permitted attributes of the tag (in our case, separator). Note the uri tag that identifies the tag library.

You reference the TLD identifier in a taglib directive of the JSF page, such as

```
<%@ taglib uri="http://corejsf.com/converter3" prefix="corejsf" %>
```

This is entirely analogous to the taglib directives that define the standard f and h prefixes in every JSF page.

 NOTE: You can choose arbitrary names for the TLD files—only the .tld extension matters. The JSF implementation searches for TLD files in the following locations:

- The WEB-INF directory
- The META-INF directory

The latter is useful if you want to package your converters as reusable JAR files.

Next, implement a *tag handler class*. That class is needed for three purposes:

1. To specify the converter or validator class
2. To gather the tag attributes
3. To configure a converter or validator object, using the gathered attributes

For a converter, the tag handler class should be a subclass of ConverterTag. As you see later, the handlers for custom validators need to subclass ValidatorTag, and custom component handlers need to subclass either UIComponentTag or UIComponentBodyTag.

Your tag handler class must specify a setter method for each tag attribute. For example,

```
public class ConvertCreditCardTag extends ConverterTag {
   private String separator;
   public void setSeparator(String newValue) {
      separator = newValue;
   }
   . . .
}
```

When the tag is parsed in the JSF page, the setters are called for all attributes that are present in the tag.

Moreover, the tag handler must specify and configure the actual converter, validator, or component object. The details depend on the type of the tag.

For a converter, you set the symbolic ID of the converter class in the tag handler constructor, like this:

```
public ConvertCreditCardTag() {
    setConverterId("com.corejsf.CreditCard");
}
```

Of course, the ID must be associated with a converter class in a configuration file (such as faces-config.xml).

To configure a converter instance with the tag attributes, override the createConverter method. First call the superclass method to obtain a converter object. This object will have the correct type—the superclass method used the converter ID that you supplied in the tag class constructor.

Then set the attributes of that object. For example,

```
public Converter createConverter() throws JspException {
    CreditCardConverter converter =
        (CreditCardConverter) super.createConverter();
    converter.setSeparator(eval(separator));

    return converter;
}
```

This method sets the separator property of the enhanced CreditCardConverter.

As with most JSF tag attributes, we want to allow both literal strings and #{...} expressions for the attribute value. In the latter case, we need to evaluate the value binding. Unfortunately, this common task is rather tedious, as you can see from the code in the eval method.

```
public static String eval(String expression) {
    if (expression != null && UIComponentTag.isValueReference(expression)) {
        FacesContext context = FacesContext.getCurrentInstance();
        Application app = context.getApplication();
        return "" + app.createValueBinding(expression).getValue(context);
    }
    else return expression;
}
```

NOTE: This eval method only handles expressions whose values are of type String. If the expression has a value other than String, you need a different method, such as

```
public static Integer evalInteger(String expression) {
```

```
    if (expression == null) return null;
    if (UIComponentTag.isValueReference(expression)) {
        FacesContext context = FacesContext.getCurrentInstance();
        Application app = context.getApplication();
        Object r = app.createValueBinding(expression).getValue(context);
        if (r == null) return null;
        else if (r instanceof Integer) return (Integer) r;
        else return new Integer(r.toString());
    }
    else return new Integer(expression);
}
```

Finally, you need to define a release method for each tag handler class that resets all instance fields to their defaults:

```
public void release() {
    separator = null;
}
```

This method is necessary because the JSF implementation may cache tag handler objects and reuse them for parsing tags. If a tag handler is reused, it should not have leftover settings from a previous tag.

Listing 6–19 shows the complete tag class.

API   **javax.faces.webapp.ConverterTag**

- void setConverterId(String id)

  Sets the ID of this converter. The ID is used for lookup of the converter class.

- protected void createConverter()

  Override this method to customize the converter, by setting the properties specified by the tag attributes.

- void release()

  Clears the state of this tag so that it can be reused.

API   **javax.faces.webapp.UIComponentTag**

- static boolean isValueReference(String s)

  Returns true if s is a value binding expression.

javax.faces.application.Application

- ValueBinding createValueBinding(String expression)

  Constructs a ValueBinding object that can be used to access and modify the given value binding expression.

 javax.faces.el.ValueBinding

- Object getValue(FacesContext context)

  Returns the value of the value binding expression represented by this object.

Listing 6–19	converter3/WEB-INF/classes/com/corejsf/ CreditCardConverterTag.java

```java
1. package com.corejsf;
2.
3. import javax.faces.application.Application;
4. import javax.faces.context.FacesContext;
5. import javax.faces.convert.Converter;
6. import javax.faces.webapp.ConverterTag;
7. import javax.faces.webapp.UIComponentTag;
8. import javax.servlet.jsp.JspException;
9.
10. public class CreditCardConverterTag extends ConverterTag {
11.     private String separator;
12.
13.     public CreditCardConverterTag() {
14.         setConverterId("com.corejsf.CreditCard");
15.     }
16.
17.     // PROPERTY: separator
18.     public void setSeparator(String newValue) {
19.         separator = newValue;
20.     }
21.     public Converter createConverter() throws JspException {
22.         CreditCardConverter converter =
23.             (CreditCardConverter) super.createConverter();
24.         converter.setSeparator(eval(separator));
25.
```

Listing 6–19	converter3/WEB-INF/classes/com/corejsf/ CreditCardConverterTag.java (cont.)

```
26.       return converter;
27.    }
28.
29.    public void release() {
30.       separator = null;
31.    }
32.
33.    public static String eval(String expression) {
34.       if (expression != null && UIComponentTag.isValueReference(expression)) {
35.          FacesContext context = FacesContext.getCurrentInstance();
36.          Application app = context.getApplication();
37.          return "" + app.createValueBinding(expression).getValue(context);
38.       }
39.       else return expression;
40.    }
41. }
```

Saving and Restoring State

The JSF implementation saves and restores *all* objects in the current view between requests. This includes converters, validators, and event listeners. You need to enable state saving for your converter classes.

When your application saves the state on the server, then the view objects are simply held in memory. However, when the state is saved on the client, then the view objects are encoded and stored in a hidden field, in a very long string that looks like this:

```
<input type="hidden" name="com.sun.faces.VIEW"
    value="rO0ABXNyACBjb20uc3VuLmZhY2VzLnV0aWwuVHJlZVN0cnVjdHVyZRRmG0QclWAgAgAETAAI...
    ...4ANXBwcHBwcHBwcHBwcHBxAH4ANXEAfgA1cHBwcHQABnN1Ym1pdHVxAH4ALAAAAAA=" />
```

Saving state on the client is required to support users who turn off cookies.

You have two choices for state saving. The easy choice is to make your converter class serializable. Simply implement the Serializable interface and follow the usual rules for Java serialization. (For more information on Java serialization, see *Horstmann & Cornell, Core Java 6th ed. vol. 1, ch. 12.*)

In the case of the credit card converter, we have a single instance field of type String, which is a serializable type. Therefore, we only need to implement the Serializable interface:

```
public class CreditCardConverter implements Converter, Serializable { ... }
```

The second choice is to supply a default constructor and implement the State-Holder interface. This is more work for the programmer, but it can yield a slightly more efficient encoding of the object state. Frankly, for small objects such as the credit card converter, this second choice is not worth the extra trouble.

In the interest of completeness, we describe the technique, using the standard DateTimeConverter as an example.

In the saveState method of the StateHolder interface, construct a serializable object that describes the instance fields. The obvious choice is an array of objects that holds the instance fields. In the restoreState method, restore the instance fields from that object.

```
public class DateTimeConverter implements Converter, StateHolder {
    public Object saveState(FacesContext context) {
        Object[] values = new Object[6];
        values[0] = dateStyle;
        values[1] = locale;
        values[2] = pattern;
        values[3] = timeStyle;
        values[4] = timeZone;
        values[5] = type;
        return values;
    }
    public void restoreState(FacesContext context, Object state) {
        Object[] values = (Object[]) state;
        dateStyle = (String) values[0];
        locale = (Locale) values[1];
        pattern = (String) values[2];
        timeStyle = (String) values[3];
        timeZone = (TimeZone) values[4];
        type = (String) values[5];
    }
    ...
}
```

Moreover, the StateHolder interface also requires you to add a transient property. If the property is set, this particular object will not be saved. (At the time of this writing, this property seems unused in the JSF framework.) The property is the analog of the transient keyword used in Java serialization.

```
public class DateTimeConverter implements Converter, StateHolder {
    private boolean transientFlag; // "transient" is a reserved word
    public boolean isTransient() { return transientFlag; }
    public void setTransient(boolean newValue) { transientFlag = newValue; }
    ...
}
```

CAUTION: Converters, validators, and event listeners that implement neither the `Serializable` nor the `StateHolder` interface are skipped when the view is saved.

NOTE: Here is an easy experiment to verify that converters must save their state. Configure the `converter3` application to save state on the client by adding this parameter to `web.xml`:

```
<context-param>
    <param-name>javax.faces.STATE_SAVING_METHOD</param-name>
    <param-value>client</param-value>
</context-param>
```

Comment out the `Serializable` interface of the `CreditCardConverter` class. To the `result.jsp` page, add the button

```
<h:commandButton value="Submit"/>
```

Enter a credit card number in index.jsp, click the "Process" button, and see the number formatted with dashes: 4111-1111-1111-1111. Click the "Submit" button and see the dashes disappear.

`javax.faces.component.StateHolder`

- `Object saveState(FacesContext context)`
  Returns a `Serializable` object that saves the state of this object.

- `void restoreState(FacesContext context, Object state)`
  Restores the state of this object from the given state object, which is a copy of an object previously obtained from calling saveState.

- `void setTransient(boolean newValue)`
- `boolean isTransient()`
  Set and get the transient property. When this property is set, the state is not saved.

The Sample Application

This completes the discussion of the custom converter example. Figure 6–14 shows the directory structure. Most files are unchanged from the preceding example. However, `result.jsp` calls the custom converter—see Listing 6–20.

The tag handler is in Listing 6–21. The modified converter and configuration file are in Listings 6–22 and 6–23.

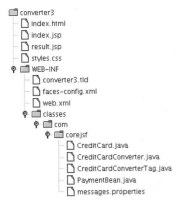

converter3
- index.html
- index.jsp
- result.jsp
- styles.css
- WEB-INF
  - converter3.tld
  - faces-config.xml
  - web.xml
  - classes
    - com
      - corejsf
        - CreditCard.java
        - CreditCardConverter.java
        - CreditCardConverterTag.java
        - PaymentBean.java
        - messages.properties

**Figure 6–14   Directory Structure
                of the Custom Converter Program**

Listing 6–20   converter3/result.jsp

```
1. <html>
2.    <%@ taglib uri="http://java.sun.com/jsf/core" prefix="f" %>
3.    <%@ taglib uri="http://java.sun.com/jsf/html" prefix="h" %>
4.    <%@ taglib uri="http://corejsf.com/converter3" prefix="corejsf" %>
5.    <f:view>
6.       <head>
7.          <link href="styles.css" rel="stylesheet" type="text/css"/>
8.          <f:loadBundle basename="com.corejsf.messages" var="msgs"/>
9.          <title><h:outputText value="#{msgs.title}"/></title>
10.      </head>
11.      <body>
12.         <h:form>
13.            <h1><h:outputText value="#{msgs.paymentInformation}"/></h1>
14.            <h:panelGrid columns="2">
15.               <h:outputText value="#{msgs.amount}"/>
16.               <h:outputText value="#{payment.amount}">
17.                  <f:convertNumber type="currency"/>
18.               </h:outputText>
19.
20.               <h:outputText value="#{msgs.creditCard}"/>
21.               <h:outputText value="#{payment.card}">
22.                  <corejsf:convertCreditcard separator="-"/>
23.               </h:outputText>
24.
25.               <h:outputText value="#{msgs.expirationDate}"/>
26.               <h:outputText value="#{payment.date}">
27.                  <f:convertDateTime pattern="MM/yyyy"/>
28.               </h:outputText>
29.            </h:panelGrid>
30.            <h:commandButton value="#{msgs.back}" action="back"/>
31.         </h:form>
32.      </body>
33.   </f:view>
34. </html>
```

Listing 6–21	converter3/WEB-INF/classes/com/corejsf/ CreditCardConverterTag.java

```java
1. package com.corejsf;
2.
3. import javax.faces.application.Application;
4. import javax.faces.context.FacesContext;
5. import javax.faces.convert.Converter;
6. import javax.faces.webapp.ConverterTag;
7. import javax.faces.webapp.UIComponentTag;
8. import javax.servlet.jsp.JspException;
9.
10. public class CreditCardConverterTag extends ConverterTag {
11.    private String separator;
12.
13.    public CreditCardConverterTag() {
14.       setConverterId("com.corejsf.CreditCard");
15.    }
16.
17.    // PROPERTY: separator
18.    public void setSeparator(String newValue) {
19.       separator = newValue;
20.    }
21.
22.    public Converter createConverter() throws JspException {
23.       CreditCardConverter converter =
24.          (CreditCardConverter) super.createConverter();
25.
26.       converter.setSeparator(eval(separator));
27.
28.       return converter;
29.    }
30.
31.    public void release() {
32.       separator = null;
33.    }
34.
35.    public static String eval(String expression) {
36.       if (expression != null && UIComponentTag.isValueReference(expression)) {
37.          FacesContext context = FacesContext.getCurrentInstance();
38.          Application app = context.getApplication();
39.          return "" + app.createValueBinding(expression).getValue(context);
40.       }
41.       else return expression;
42.    }
43. }
44.
```

Listing 6–22 | converter3/WEB-INF/classes/com/corejsf/CreditCardConverter.java

```
1.  package com.corejsf;
2.
3.  import java.io.Serializable;
4.  import javax.faces.component.UIComponent;
5.  import javax.faces.context.FacesContext;
6.  import javax.faces.convert.Converter;
7.  import javax.faces.convert.ConverterException;
8.
9.  public class CreditCardConverter implements Converter, Serializable {
10.     private String separator;
11.
12.     // PROPERTY: separator
13.     public void setSeparator(String newValue) { separator = newValue; }
14.
15.     public Object getAsObject(
16.        FacesContext context,
17.        UIComponent component,
18.        String newValue)
19.        throws ConverterException {
20.        StringBuffer buffer = new StringBuffer(newValue);
21.        int i = 0;
22.        while (i < buffer.length()) {
23.           if (Character.isDigit(buffer.charAt(i)))
24.              i++;
25.           else
26.              buffer.deleteCharAt(i);
27.        }
28.        return new CreditCard(buffer.toString());
29.     }
30.
31.     public String getAsString(
32.        FacesContext context,
33.        UIComponent component,
34.        Object value)
35.        throws ConverterException {
36.        // length 13: xxxx xxx xxx xxx
37.        // length 14: xxxxx xxxx xxxxx
38.        // length 15: xxxx xxxxxx xxxxx
39.        // length 16: xxxx xxxx xxxx xxxx
40.        // length 22: xxxxxx xxxxxxxx xxxxxxxx
41.        if (!(value instanceof CreditCard))
42.           throw new ConverterException();
43.        String v = ((CreditCard) value).toString();
```

Listing 6–22	converter3/WEB-INF/classes/com/corejsf/CreditCardConverter.java (cont.)

```
44.        String sep = separator;
45.        if (sep == null) sep = " ";
46.        int[] boundaries = null;
47.        int length = v.length();
48.        if (length == 13)
49.           boundaries = new int[] { 4, 7, 10 };
50.        else if (length == 14)
51.           boundaries = new int[] { 5, 9 };
52.        else if (length == 15)
53.           boundaries = new int[] { 4, 10 };
54.        else if (length == 16)
55.           boundaries = new int[] { 4, 8, 12 };
56.        else if (length == 22)
57.           boundaries = new int[] { 6, 14 };
58.        else
59.           return v;
60.        StringBuffer result = new StringBuffer();
61.        int start = 0;
62.        for (int i = 0; i < boundaries.length; i++) {
63.           int end = boundaries[i];
64.           result.append(v.substring(start, end));
65.           result.append(sep);
66.           start = end;
67.        }
68.        result.append(v.substring(start));
69.        return result.toString();
70.     }
71.
72. }
```

Listing 6–23 converter3/WEB-INF/faces-config.xml

```
1. <?xml version="1.0"?>
2.
3. <!DOCTYPE faces-config PUBLIC
4.   "-//Sun Microsystems, Inc.//DTD JavaServer Faces Config 1.0//EN"
5.   "http://java.sun.com/dtd/web-facesconfig_1_0.dtd">
6.
7. <faces-config>
8.    <navigation-rule>
9.       <from-view-id>/index.jsp</from-view-id>
10.      <navigation-case>
11.         <from-outcome>process</from-outcome>
12.         <to-view-id>/result.jsp</to-view-id>
13.      </navigation-case>
14.   </navigation-rule>
15.
16.   <navigation-rule>
17.      <from-view-id>/result.jsp</from-view-id>
18.      <navigation-case>
19.         <from-outcome>back</from-outcome>
20.         <to-view-id>/index.jsp</to-view-id>
21.      </navigation-case>
22.   </navigation-rule>
23.
24.   <converter>
25.      <converter-id>com.corejsf.CreditCard</converter-id>
26.     <converter-class>com.corejsf.CreditCardConverter</converter-class>
27.   </converter>
28.
29.   <converter>
30.     <converter-for-class>com.corejsf.CreditCard</converter-for-class>
31.     <converter-class>com.corejsf.CreditCardConverter</converter-class>
32.   </converter>
33.
34.   <managed-bean>
35.      <managed-bean-name>payment</managed-bean-name>
36.      <managed-bean-class>com.corejsf.PaymentBean</managed-bean-class>
37.      <managed-bean-scope>session</managed-bean-scope>
38.   </managed-bean>
39. </faces-config>
```

Supplying Parameters Without Custom Tags

Generally, you will want to implement a tag handler in order to supply configuration parameters to a converter. However, as you have seen, implementing custom tags is not for the faint of heart. In a pinch, you can use an alternative mechanism. Every JSF component can store arbitrary attributes. You can set an attribute of the component to be validated; use the f:attribute tag. Your converter can then retrieve the attribute from its component. Here is how that technique would work to set the separator string for the credit card converter.

When attaching the converter, also nest an f:attribute tag inside the component:

```
<h:outputText value="#{payment.card}">
  <f:converter converterId="CreditCard"/>
  <f:attribute name="separator" value="-"/>
</h:outputText>
```

In the converter, retrieve the attribute as follows:

```
separator = (String) component.getAttributes().get("separator");
```

This method avoids the implementation of a custom tag but adds complexity in the page markup.

 javax.faces.component.UIComponent

*   Map getAttributes()
    Returns a mutable map of all attributes and properties of this component.

Custom Validator Tags

In the preceding sections, you saw how to implement a custom converter that offers page authors the same convenience as the standard JSF tags. In this section, you will see how to provide a custom validator.

The steps for providing a custom validator are almost the same as those for a custom converter:

1. Produce a TLD file and reference it in your JSF pages.
2. Implement a tag handler class that extends the ValidatorTag class, gathers the attributes that the TLD file advertises, and passes them to a validator object.
3. Implement a validator class that implements the Validator interface. Supply the validate method in the usual way, by throwing a ValidatorException if an error is detected. Implement the Serializable or StateHolder interface to save and restore the state of validator objects.

As an example, let us do a thorough job validating credit card numbers (see Listing 6–23). We want to carry out three checks:

1.   The user has supplied a value.

2.   The number conforms to the Luhn formula.

3.   The number starts with a valid prefix.

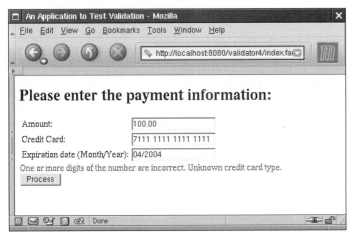

Figure 6–15   Thoroughly Validating a Credit Card Number

A credit card's prefix indicates card type; for example, a prefix between 51 and 55 is reserved for MasterCard, and a prefix of 4 indicates Visa. We could write custom code for this purpose, but instead we chose to implement a more general (and more useful) validator that validates arbitrary regular expressions. We use that validator in the following way:

```
<corejsf:validateRegex expression="[3-6].*"
    errorDetail="#{msgs.unknownType}"/>
```

The regular expression [3-6].* denotes any string that starts with the digits 3 through 6. Of course, we could easily design a more elaborate regular expression that does a more careful check.

You will find the validator code in Listing 6–24. When reading through the code, keep in mind that the moral of the story here has nothing to do with regular expressions per se. Instead, the story is about what validators do when their component's data is invalid: they generate a faces message, wrap it inside a validator exception, and throw it.

By default, the validator displays an error message that complains about failing to match a regular expression. If your application's audience includes users who are unfamiliar with regular expressions, you will want to change the message. We give you attributes errorSummmary and errorDetail for this purpose.

We use a custom tag so that we can supply parameters to the validator. Implementing a custom tag for a validator is similar to creating a custom converter tag, which we described earlier in this chapter. However, the custom validator tag must extend the ValidatorTag class.

You can find the implementation of the RegexValidatorTag class in Listing 6–25.

NOTE: Supplying the tag handler methods seems unreasonably repetitive, particularly for tags with many attributes. Turn to Chapter 12 for tips on how to minimize the drudgery.

Figure 6–16 shows the application's directory structure. Listing 6–28 shows the JSF page with the triple validation of the credit card field.

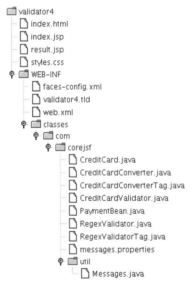

```
validator4
    index.html
    index.jsp
    result.jsp
    styles.css
 WEB-INF
        faces-config.xml
        validator4.tld
        web.xml
     classes
         com
             corejsf
                CreditCard.java
                CreditCardConverter.java
                CreditCardConverterTag.java
                CreditCardValidator.java
                PaymentBean.java
                RegexValidator.java
                RegexValidatorTag.java
                messages.properties
             util
                Messages.java
```

**Figure 6–16   Directory Structure
    of the Thoroughly Validating Application**

Listing 6–26 shows faces-config.xml. Note the mapping of the validator ID to the validator class. The validator tag class is defined in the tag library descriptor file (Listing 6–27).

javax.faces.webapp.ValidatorTag

- void setValidatorId(String id)

  Sets the ID of this validator. The ID is used to look up the validator class.

- protected void createValidator()

  Override this method to customize the validator, by setting the properties specified by the tag attributes.

Listing 6–24	validator4/WEB-INF/classes/com/corejsf/RegexValidator.java

```java
1.  package com.corejsf;
2.
3.  import java.io.Serializable;
4.  import java.text.MessageFormat;
5.  import java.util.Locale;
6.  import java.util.regex.Pattern;
7.  import javax.faces.application.FacesMessage;
8.  import javax.faces.component.UIComponent;
9.  import javax.faces.context.FacesContext;
10. import javax.faces.validator.Validator;
11. import javax.faces.validator.ValidatorException;
12.
13. public class RegexValidator implements Validator, Serializable {
14.    private String expression;
15.    private Pattern pattern;
16.    private String errorSummary;
17.    private String errorDetail;
18.
19.    public void validate(FacesContext context, UIComponent component,
20.          Object value) {
21.       if (value == null) return;
22.       if (pattern == null) return;
23.       if(!pattern.matcher(value.toString()).matches()) {
24.
25.          Object[] params = new Object[] { expression, value };
26.          Locale locale = context.getViewRoot().getLocale();
27.          String summary;
28.          if (errorSummary == null)
29.             summary = com.corejsf.util.Messages.getString(
30.                "com.corejsf.messages", "badRegex", params);
31.          else
32.             summary = new MessageFormat(errorSummary, locale).format(params);
```

Listing 6–24 validator4/WEB-INF/classes/com/corejsf/RegexValidator.java (cont.)

```
33.        String detail;
34.        if (errorDetail == null)
35.           detail = com.corejsf.util.Messages.getString(
36.              "com.corejsf.messages", "badRegex_detail", params);
37.        else
38.           detail = new MessageFormat(errorDetail, locale).format(params);
39.        FacesMessage message = new FacesMessage(FacesMessage.SEVERITY_ERROR,
40.           summary, detail);
41.        throw new ValidatorException(message);
42.     }
43.  }
44.
45.  // PROPERTY: expression
46.  public void setExpression(String newValue) {
47.     expression = newValue;
48.     pattern = Pattern.compile(expression);
49.  }
50.
51.  // PROPERTY: errorSummary
52.  public void setErrorSummary(String newValue) {
53.     errorSummary = newValue;
54.  }
55.
56.  // PROPERTY: errorDetail
57.  public void setErrorDetail(String newValue) {
58.     errorDetail = newValue;
59. }
```

Listing 6–25   validator4/WEB-INF/classes/com/corejsf/RegexValidatorTag.java

```java
1. package com.corejsf;
2.
3. import javax.faces.application.Application;
4. import javax.faces.context.FacesContext;
5. import javax.faces.validator.Validator;
6. import javax.faces.webapp.UIComponentTag;
7. import javax.faces.webapp.ValidatorTag;
8. import javax.servlet.jsp.JspException;
9.
10. public class RegexValidatorTag extends ValidatorTag {
11.    private String expression;
12.    private String errorSummary;
13.    private String errorDetail;
14.
15.    public RegexValidatorTag() {
16.       setValidatorId("com.corejsf.Regex");
17.    }
18.
19.    // PROPERTY: expression
20.    public void setExpression(String newValue) {
21.       expression = newValue;
22.    }
23.
24.    // PROPERTY: errorSummary
25.    public void setErrorSummary(String newValue) {
26.       errorSummary = newValue;
27.    }
28.
29.    // PROPERTY: errorDetail
30.    public void setErrorDetail(String newValue) {
31.       errorDetail = newValue;
32.    }
33.    public Validator createValidator() throws JspException {
34.       RegexValidator validator = (RegexValidator) super.createValidator();
35.
36.       validator.setExpression(eval(expression));
37.       validator.setErrorSummary(eval(errorSummary));
38.       validator.setErrorDetail(eval(errorDetail));
39.
```

Listing 6-25	validator4/WEB-INF/classes/com/corejsf/RegexValidatorTag.java (cont.)

```
40.      return validator;
41.    }
42.
43.    public void release() {
44.      expression = null;
45.      errorSummary = null;
46.      errorDetail = null;
47.    }
48.
49.    public static String eval(String expression) {
50.      if (expression != null && UIComponentTag.isValueReference(expression)) {
51.        FacesContext context = FacesContext.getCurrentInstance();
52.        Application app = context.getApplication();
53.        return "" + app.createValueBinding(expression).getValue(context);
54.      }
55.      else return expression;
56.    }
57. }
58.
```

Listing 6-26	validator4/WEB-INF/faces-config.xml

```
1. <?xml version="1.0"?>
2.
3. <!DOCTYPE faces-config PUBLIC
4.   "-//Sun Microsystems, Inc.//DTD JavaServer Faces Config 1.0//EN"
5.   "http://java.sun.com/dtd/web-facesconfig_1_0.dtd">
6.
7. <faces-config>
8.   <navigation-rule>
9.     <from-view-id>/index.jsp</from-view-id>
10.     <navigation-case>
11.       <from-outcome>process</from-outcome>
12.       <to-view-id>/result.jsp</to-view-id>
13.     </navigation-case>
14.   </navigation-rule>
15.
```

Listing 6–26 `validator4/WEB-INF/faces-config.xml (cont.)`

```
16.   <navigation-rule>
17.      <from-view-id>/result.jsp</from-view-id>
18.      <navigation-case>
19.         <from-outcome>back</from-outcome>
20.
21.         <to-view-id>/index.jsp</to-view-id>
22.      </navigation-case>
23.   </navigation-rule>
24.
25.   <converter>
26.      <converter-id>com.corejsf.CreditCard</converter-id>
27.    <converter-class>com.corejsf.CreditCardConverter</converter-class>
28.   </converter>
29.
30.   <converter>
31.      <converter-for-class>com.corejsf.CreditCard</converter-for-class>
32.    <converter-class>com.corejsf.CreditCardConverter</converter-class>
33.   </converter>
34.
35.   <validator>
36.      <validator-id>com.corejsf.CreditCard</validator-id>
37.    <validator-class>com.corejsf.CreditCardValidator</validator-class>
38.   </validator>
39.
40.   <validator>
41.      <validator-id>com.corejsf.Regex</validator-id>
42.      <validator-class>com.corejsf.RegexValidator</validator-class>
43.   </validator>
44.
45.   <managed-bean>
46.      <managed-bean-name>payment</managed-bean-name>
47.      <managed-bean-class>com.corejsf.PaymentBean</managed-bean-class>
48.      <managed-bean-scope>session</managed-bean-scope>
49.   </managed-bean>
50. </faces-config>
```

Listing 6–27 `validator4/WEB-INF/validator4.tld`

```
1. <?xml version="1.0" encoding="ISO-8859-1" ?>
2. <!DOCTYPE taglib
3.   PUBLIC "-//Sun Microsystems, Inc.//DTD JSP Tag Library 1.2//EN"
4.   "http://java.sun.com/dtd/web-jsptaglibrary_1_2.dtd">
5. <taglib>
6.   <tlib-version>1.0</tlib-version>
7.   <jsp-version>1.2</jsp-version>
8.   <short-name>validator4</short-name>
9.   <uri>http://corejsf.com/validator4</uri>
10.  <tag>
11.    <name>validateRegex</name>
12.    <tag-class>com.corejsf.RegexValidatorTag</tag-class>
13.    <attribute>
14.      <name>expression</name>
15.    </attribute>
16.    <attribute>
17.      <name>errorSummary</name>
18.    </attribute>
19.    <attribute>
20.      <name>errorDetail</name>
21.    </attribute>
22.  </tag>
23. </taglib>
```

Listing 6–28 validator4/index.jsp

```
1. <html>
2.    <%@ taglib uri="http://java.sun.com/jsf/core" prefix="f" %>
3.    <%@ taglib uri="http://java.sun.com/jsf/html" prefix="h" %>
4.    <%@ taglib uri="http://corejsf.com/validator4" prefix="corejsf" %>
5.    <f:view>
6.       <head>
7.          <link href="styles.css" rel="stylesheet" type="text/css"/>
8.          <f:loadBundle basename="com.corejsf.messages" var="msgs"/>
9.          <title><h:outputText value="#{msgs.title}"/></title>
10.      </head>
11.      <body>
12.         <h:form>
13.            <h1><h:outputText value="#{msgs.enterPayment}"/></h1>
14.            <h:panelGrid columns="2">
15.               <h:outputText value="#{msgs.amount}"/>
16.               <h:inputText id="amount" value="#{payment.amount}">
17.                  <f:convertNumber minFractionDigits="2"/>
18.               </h:inputText>
19.
20.               <h:outputText value="#{msgs.creditCard}"/>
21.               <h:inputText id="card" value="#{payment.card}" required="true">
22.                  <f:validator validatorId="com.corejsf.CreditCard"/>
23.                  <corejsf:validateRegex expression="[3-6].*"
24.                     errorDetail="#{msgs.unknownType}"/>
25.               </h:inputText>
26.
27.               <h:outputText value="#{msgs.expirationDate}"/>
28.               <h:inputText id="date" value="#{payment.date}">
29.                  <f:convertDateTime pattern="MM/yyyy"/>
30.               </h:inputText>
31.            </h:panelGrid>
32.            <h:messages styleClass="errorMessage"
33.               showSummary="false" showDetail="true"/>
34.            <br/>
35.            <h:commandButton value="Process" action="process"/>
36.         </h:form>
37.      </body>
38.   </f:view>
39. </html>
```

As you have seen, JavaServer Faces provides extensive and extensible support for conversion and validation. You can use JSF standard converter and validators with one line of code in your JSF pages, or you can implement your own, complete with a custom tag, if needed.

EVENT HANDLING

Topics in This Chapter

Chapter 7

Web applications often need to respond to user events, such as selecting items from a menu or clicking a button. For example, you might want to respond to the selection of a country in an address form by changing the locale and reloading the current page to better accommodate your users.

Typically, you register event handlers with components; for example, you might register a value change listener with a menu in a JSF page like this:

```
<h:selectOneMenu valueChangeListener="#{form.countryChanged}"...>
    ...
</h:selectOneMenu>
```

In the preceding code, the method binding #{form.countryChanged} references the countryChanged method of a bean named form. That method is invoked by the JSF implementation after the user makes a selection from the menu. Exactly when that method is invoked is one topic of discussion in this chapter.

JSF supports three kinds of events:

* Value change events
* Action events
* Phase events

Value change events are fired by input components—such as h:inputText, h:selectOneRadio, and h:selectManyMenu—when the component's value changes and the enclosing form is submitted.

Action events are fired by command components, for example, `h:commandButton` and `h:commandLink`, when the button or link is activated. Phase events are routinely fired by the JSF life cycle. If you want to handle events, you need to have a basic understanding of that life cycle. Let's see how it works.

Life-Cycle Events

Requests in JSF applications are fielded by the JSF implementation—typically with a controller servlet—which in turn executes the JSF life cycle.

The JSF life cycle is shown in Figure 7–1.

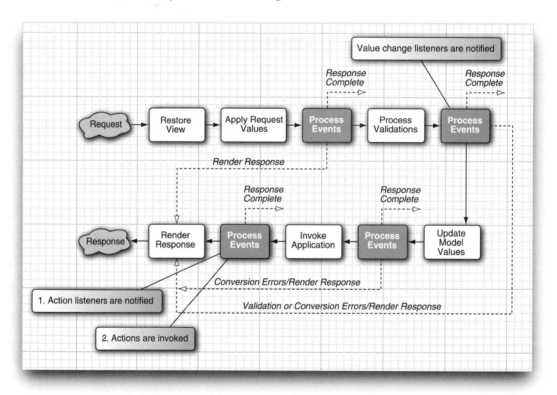

Figure 7–1   JSF Life Cycle

The JSF life cycle consists of the following phases:

*   Restore View
*   Apply Request Values
*   Process Validations

- Update Model Values
- Invoke Application
- Render Response

The Restore View phase recreates the server-side component tree when you revisit a JSF page. The Apply Request Values phase copies *request parameters* into component *submitted values*. The Process Validations phase first converts those submitted values and validates the converted value. The Update Model Values phase copies (converted and validated) values to the model, which is typically denoted in JSF pages with value reference expressions, such as:

```
<h:inputText value="#{user.name}"/>
```

The Invoke Application phase invokes action listeners and actions, in that order, for command components. You can register an action listener and an action with a component like this:

```
<h:commandButton action="#{bean.action}" actionListener="#{bean.listener}".../>
```

In that case, the JSF implementation will invoke the bean's `listener` method followed by the `action` method.

Finally, the Render Response phase saves state and loads the next view. For JSP-based applications the JSF navigation handler forwards or redirects to another JSP page. Forwarding is the default behavior, but you can specify redirects with the `redirect` element in a faces configuration file.

Starting with the Apply Request Values phases, events can be created and placed on an event queue during each life-cycle phase. After those phases, the JSF implementation broadcasts queued events to registered listeners. Those events and their associated listeners are the focus of this chapter.

> NOTE: Event listeners can affect the JSF life cycle in one of three ways: 1. Let the life cycle proceed normally; 2. Call `FacesContext.renderResponse()` to skip the rest of the life cycle up to Render Response; 3. Call `FacesContext.responseComplete()` to skip the rest of the life cycle entirely. See "Immediate Components" on page 292 for an example of using `FacesContext.renderResponse()`.

Value Change Events

Components in a web application often depend on each other. For example, in the application shown in Figure 7–2, the value of the State prompt depends on the country menu's value. You can keep dependent components in synch with value change events, which are fired by input components after their new value has been validated and the enclosing form is submitted.

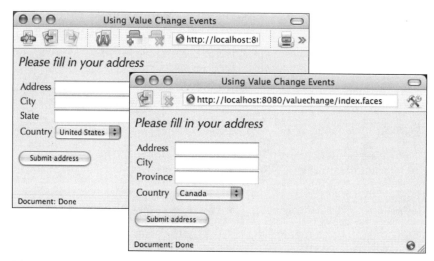

Figure 7–2   Using Value Change Events

The application shown in Figure 7–2 attaches a value change listener to the country menu and uses the onchange attribute to force a form submit after the menu's value is changed:

```
<h:selectOneMenu value="#{form.country}" onchange="submit()"
    valueChangeListener="#{form.countryChanged}">
    <f:selectItems value="#{form.countryNames}"/>
</h:selectOneMenu>
```

When a user selects a country from the menu, the JavaScript submit function is invoked to submit the menu's form, which subsequently invokes the JSF life cycle. After the Process Validations phase, the JSF implementation invokes the form bean's countryChanged method. That method changes the view root's locale, according to the new country value:

```
private static final String US = "United States";
...
public void countryChanged(ValueChangeEvent event) {
    FacesContext context = FacesContext.getCurrentInstance();
```

```
        if (US.equals((String)event.getNewValue()))
            context.getViewRoot().setLocale(Locale.US);
        else
            context.getViewRoot().setLocale(Locale.CANADA);
    }
}
```

Like all value change listeners, the preceding listener is passed a value change event. The listener uses that event to access the component's new value. The ValueChangeEvent class extends FacesEvent, both of which reside in the javax.faces.event package. The most commonly used methods from those classes are listed below.

API   **javax.faces.event.ValueChangeEvent**

- UIComponent getComponent()

  Returns the input component that triggered the event.

- Object getNewValue()

  Returns the component's new value, after the value has been converted and validated.

- Object getOldValue()

  Returns the component's previous value.

API   **javax.faces.event.FacesEvent**

- void queue()

  Queues the event for delivery at the end of the current life-cycle phase.

- PhaseId getPhaseId()

  Returns the phase identifier corresponding to the phase during which the event is delivered.

- void setPhaseId(PhaseId)

  Sets the phase identifier corresponding to the phase during which the event is delivered.

The directory structure for the application in Figure 7–2 is shown in Figure 7–3 and the application is listed in Listing 7–1 through Listing 7–5.

Figure 7–3   Directory Structure for the Value Change Example

Listing 7–1	valuechange/index.jsp

```
 1. <html>
 2.    <%@ taglib uri="http://java.sun.com/jsf/core" prefix="f" %>
 3.    <%@ taglib uri="http://java.sun.com/jsf/html" prefix="h" %>
 4.    <f:view>
 5.       <link href="styles.css" rel="stylesheet" type="text/css"/>
 6.       <f:loadBundle basename="com.corejsf.messages" var="msgs"/>
 7.       <head>
 8.          <title>
 9.             <h:outputText value="#{msgs.windowTitle}"/>
10.          </title>
11.       </head>
12.
13.       <body>
14.          <h:outputText value="#{msgs.pageTitle}" styleClass="emphasis"/>
15.          <p/>
16.          <h:form>
17.             <h:panelGrid columns="2">
18.                <h:outputText value="#{msgs.streetAddressPrompt}"/>
19.                <h:inputText value="#{form.streetAddress}" id="streetAddress"/>
20.
21.                <h:outputText value="#{msgs.cityPrompt}"/>
22.                <h:inputText value="#{form.city}"/>
23.
24.                <h:outputText value="#{msgs.statePrompt}"/>
25.                <h:inputText value="#{form.state}"/>
26.                <h:outputText value="#{msgs.countryPrompt}"/>
27.
28.                <h:selectOneMenu value="#{form.country}"
29.                   onchange="submit()"
```

Listing 7–1   valuechange/index.jsp (cont.)

```
30.                     valueChangeListener="#{form.countryChanged}">
31.                 <f:selectItems value="#{form.countryNames}"/>
32.             </h:selectOneMenu>
33.         </h:panelGrid>
34.         <p/>
35.         <h:commandButton value="#{msgs.submit}"/>
36.     </h:form>
37.     </body>
38.   </f:view>
39. </html>
```

Listing 7–2   valuechange/WEB-INF/classes/com/corejsf/RegisterForm.java

```
1. package com.corejsf;
2.
3. import java.util.ArrayList;
4. import java.util.Collection;
5. import java.util.Locale;
6. import javax.faces.context.FacesContext;
7. import javax.faces.event.ValueChangeEvent;
8. import javax.faces.model.SelectItem;
9.
10. public class RegisterForm {
11.    private String streetAddress;
12.    private String city;
13.    private String state;
14.    private String country;
15.
16.    private static final String US = "United States";
17.    private static final String CANADA = "Canada";
18.    private static final String[] COUNTRY_NAMES = { US, CANADA };
19.    private static ArrayList countryItems = null;
20.
21.    // PROPERTY: countryNames
22.    public Collection getCountryNames() {
23.       if(countryItems == null) {
24.          countryItems = new ArrayList();
25.          for (int i = 0; i < COUNTRY_NAMES.length; ++i) {
26.             countryItems.add(new SelectItem(COUNTRY_NAMES[i]));
27.          }
28.       }
29.       return countryItems;
30.    }
31.
```

Listing 7–2 valuechange/WEB-INF/classes/com/corejsf/RegisterForm.java (cont.)

```
32.    // PROPERTY: streetAddress
33.    public void setStreetAddress(String newValue) { streetAddress = newValue; }
34.    public String getStreetAddress() { return streetAddress; }
35.
36.    // PROPERTY: city
37.    public void setCity(String newValue) { city = newValue; }
38.    public String getCity() { return city; }
39.
40.    // PROPERTY: state
41.    public void setState(String newValue) { state = newValue; }
42.    public String getState() { return state; }
43.
44.    // PROPERTY: country
45.    public void setCountry(String newValue) { country = newValue; }
46.    public String getCountry()              { return country; }
47.
48.    public void countryChanged(ValueChangeEvent event) {
49.        FacesContext context = FacesContext.getCurrentInstance();
50.
51.        if(US.equals((String) event.getNewValue()))
52.            context.getViewRoot().setLocale(Locale.US);
53.        else
54.            context.getViewRoot().setLocale(Locale.CANADA);
55.    }
56. }
```

Listing 7–3 valuechange/WEB-INF/faces-config.xml

```
1. <?xml version="1.0"?>
2.
3. <!DOCTYPE faces-config PUBLIC
4.    "-//Sun Microsystems, Inc.//DTD JavaServer Faces Config 1.0//EN"
5.    "http://java.sun.com/dtd/web-facesconfig_1_0.dtd">
6.
7. <faces-config>
8.    <managed-bean>
9.        <managed-bean-name>form</managed-bean-name>
10.       <managed-bean-class>com.corejsf.RegisterForm</managed-bean-class>
11.       <managed-bean-scope>session</managed-bean-scope>
12.    </managed-bean>
13. </faces-config>
```

Listing 7–4 | valuechange/WEB-INF/classes/com/corejsf/messages_en_US.properties

```
1. windowTitle=Using Value Change Events
2. pageTitle=Please fill in your address
3.
4. streetAddressPrompt=Address
5. cityPrompt=City
6. statePrompt=State
7. countryPrompt=Country
8. submit=Submit address
```

Listing 7–5 | valuechange/WEB-INF/classes/com/corejsf/messages_en_CA.properties

```
1. windowTitle=Using Value Change Events
2. pageTitle=Please fill in your address
3.
4. streetAddressPrompt=Address
5. cityPrompt=City
6. statePrompt=Province
7. countryPrompt=Country
8. submit=Submit address
```

Action Events

Action events are fired by command components—buttons, links, etc.—when the component is activated. As we saw in "Life-Cycle Events" on page 274, action events are fired during the Invoke Application phase, near the end of the life cycle.

You typically attach action listeners to command components in JSF pages. For example, you can add an action listener to a link like this:

```
<h:commandLink actionListener="#{bean.linkActivated}">
    ...
</h:commandLink>
```

Command components submit requests when they are activated, so there's no need to use onchange to force form submits as we did with value change events in "Value Change Events" on page 275. When you activate a command or link, the surrounding form is submitted and the JSF implementation subsequently fires action events.

It's important to distinguish between *action listeners* and *actions*. In a nutshell, actions are designed for business logic and participate in navigation handling, whereas action listeners typically perform user interface logic and do not participate in navigation handling.

Action listeners often work in concert with actions when an action needs information about the user interface. For example, the application shown in Figure 7–4 uses an action and an action listener to react to mouse clicks by forwarding to a JSF page. If you click on a president's face, the application forwards to a JSF page with information about that president. Note that an action alone cannot implement that behavior—an action can *navigate* to the appropriate page, but it can't *determine* the appropriate page because it knows nothing about the image button in the user interface or the mouse click.

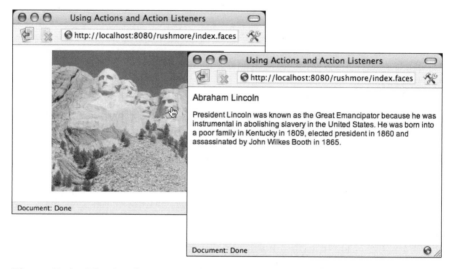

Figure 7–4   The Rushmore Application

The application shown in Figure 7–4 uses a button with an image, like this:

```
<h:commandButton image="mountrushmore.jpg"
    actionListener="#{rushmore.listen}"
        action="#{rushmore.act}"/>
```

When you click on a president, a listener—which has access to the mouse click coordinates—determines which president was selected. But the listener can't affect navigation, so it stores an outcome corresponding to the selected president in an instance field:

```
public class Rushmore {
    private String outcome;
    private Rectangle washingtonRect = new Rectangle(70,30,40,40);
    private Rectangle jeffersonRect  = new Rectangle(115,45,40,40);
    private Rectangle rooseveltRect  = new Rectangle(135,65,40,40);
    private Rectangle lincolnRect     = new Rectangle(175,62,40,40);
```

```
public void listen(ActionEvent e) {
   FacesContext context = FacesContext.getCurrentInstance();
   String clientId = e.getComponent().getClientId(context);
   Map requestParams = context.getExternalContext().
                       getRequestParameterMap();
   int x = new Integer((String)requestParams.get(clientId + ".x")).intValue();
   int y = new Integer((String)requestParams.get(clientId + ".y")).intValue();

   outcome = null;

   if(washingtonRect.contains(new Point(x,y)))
      outcome = "washington";

   if(jeffersonRect.contains(new Point(x,y)))
      outcome = "jefferson";

   if(rooseveltRect.contains(new Point(x,y)))
      outcome = "roosevelt";

   if(lincolnRect.contains(new Point(x,y)))
      outcome = "lincoln";
}
}
```

The action associated with the button uses the outcome to affect navigation:

```
public String act() {
   return outcome;
}
```

Note that the JSF implementation always invokes action listeners before actions.

NOTE: JSF insists that you separate user interface logic and business logic by refusing to give actions access to events or the components that fire them. In the preceding example, the action cannot access the client ID of the component that fired the event, information that is necessary for extraction of mouse click coordinates from the request parameters. Because the action knows nothing about the user interface, we must add an action listener to the mix to implement the required behavior.

The directory structure for the application shown in Figure 7–4 is shown in Figure 7–5. The code listings for the application are shown in Listing 7–6 through Listing 7–13.

rushmore
  index.html
  index.jsp
  jefferson.jsp
  lincoln.jsp
  mountrushmore.jpg
  roosevelt.jsp
  styles.css
  washington.jsp
  WEB-INF
    faces-config.xml
    web.xml
    classes
      com
        corejsf
          Rushmore.java
          messages.properties

**Figure 7–5   Rushmore Example
Directory Structure**

Listing 7–6	rushmore/index.jsp

```
1. <html>
2.    <%@ taglib uri="http://java.sun.com/jsf/core" prefix="f" %>
3.    <%@ taglib uri="http://java.sun.com/jsf/html" prefix="h" %>
4.    <f:view>
5.       <head>
6.          <link href="styles.css" rel="stylesheet" type="text/css"/>
7.          <f:loadBundle basename="com.corejsf.messages" var="msgs"/>
8.          <title>
9.             <h:outputText value="#{msgs.windowTitle}"/>
10.         </title>
11.      </head>
12.      <body>
13.         <h:form style="text-align: center">
14.            <h:commandButton image="mountrushmore.jpg"
15.               actionListener="#{rushmore.listen}"
16.               action="#{rushmore.act}"/>
17.         </h:form>
18.      </body>
19.   </f:view>
20. </html>
```

Listing 7–7 `rushmore/lincoln.jsp`

```
1.  <html>
2.     <%@ taglib uri="http://java.sun.com/jsf/core" prefix="f" %>
3.     <%@ taglib uri="http://java.sun.com/jsf/html" prefix="h" %>
4.     <f:view>
5.        <head>
6.           <link href="site.css" rel="stylesheet" type="text/css"/>
7.           <f:loadBundle basename="com.corejsf.messages" var="msgs"/>
8.           <title>
9.              <h:outputText value="#{msgs.windowTitle}"/>
10.          </title>
11.       </head>
12.
13.       <body>
14.          <h:form>
15.             <h:outputText value="#{msgs.lincolnPageTitle}"
16.                styleClass="presidentPageTitle"/>
17.             <p/>
18.             <h:outputText value="#{msgs.lincolnDiscussion}"
19.                styleClass="presidentDiscussion"/>
20.          </h:form>
21.       </body>
22.    </f:view>
23. </html>
```

Listing 7–8 `rushmore/jefferson.jsp`

```
1.  <html>
2.     <%@ taglib uri="http://java.sun.com/jsf/core" prefix="f" %>
3.     <%@ taglib uri="http://java.sun.com/jsf/html" prefix="h" %>
4.     <f:view>
5.        <head>
6.           <link href="site.css" rel="stylesheet" type="text/css"/>
7.           <f:loadBundle basename="com.corejsf.messages" var="msgs"/>
8.           <title>
9.              <h:outputText value="#{msgs.windowTitle}"/>
10.          </title>
11.       </head>
12.
13.
```

Listing 7–8   rushmore/jefferson.jsp (cont.)

```
14.      <body>
15.         <h:form>
16.            <h:outputText value="#{msgs.jeffersonPageTitle}"
17.               styleClass="presidentPageTitle"/>
18.            <p/>
19.            <h:outputText value="#{msgs.jeffersonDiscussion}"
20.               styleClass="presidentDiscussion"/>
21.         </h:form>
22.      </body>
23.   </f:view>
24. </html>
```

Listing 7–9   rushmore/roosevelt.jsp

```
1. <html>
2.    <%@ taglib uri="http://java.sun.com/jsf/core" prefix="f" %>
3.    <%@ taglib uri="http://java.sun.com/jsf/html" prefix="h" %>
4.    <f:view>
5.       <head>
6.          <link href="site.css" rel="stylesheet" type="text/css"/>
7.          <f:loadBundle basename="com.corejsf.messages" var="msgs"/>
8.          <title>
9.             <h:outputText value="#{msgs.windowTitle}"/>
10.         </title>
11.      </head>
12.
13.      <body>
14.         <h:form>
15.            <h:outputText value="#{msgs.rooseveltPageTitle}"
16.               styleClass="presidentPageTitle"/>
17.            <p/>
18.            <h:outputText value="#{msgs.rooseveltDiscussion}"
19.               styleClass="presidentDiscussion"/>
20.         </h:form>
21.      </body>
22.   </f:view>
23. </html>
```

Listing 7–10 `rushmore/washington.jsp`

```jsp
1. <html>
2.   <%@ taglib uri="http://java.sun.com/jsf/core" prefix="f" %>
3.   <%@ taglib uri="http://java.sun.com/jsf/html" prefix="h" %>
4.   <f:view>
5.     <head>
6.       <link href="site.css" rel="stylesheet" type="text/css"/>
7.       <f:loadBundle basename="com.corejsf.messages" var="msgs"/>
8.       <title>
9.         <h:outputText value="#{msgs.windowTitle}"/>
10.      </title>
11.    </head>
12.
13.    <body>
14.      <h:form>
15.        <h:outputText value="#{msgs.washingtonPageTitle}"
16.          styleClass="presidentPageTitle"/>
17.        <p/>
18.        <h:outputText value="#{msgs.washingtonDiscussion}"
19.          styleClass="presidentDiscussion"/>
20.      </h:form>
21.    </body>
22.  </f:view>
23. </html>
```

Listing 7–11 `rushmore/WEB-INF/classes/com/corejsf/Rushmore.java`

```java
1. package com.corejsf;
2.
3. import java.awt.Point;
4. import java.awt.Rectangle;
5. import java.util.Map;
6. import javax.faces.context.FacesContext;
7. import javax.faces.event.ActionEvent;
8.
9. public class Rushmore {
10.    private String outcome = null;
11.    private Rectangle washingtonRect = new Rectangle(70, 30, 40, 40);
12.    private Rectangle jeffersonRect = new Rectangle(115, 45, 40, 40);
13.    private Rectangle rooseveltRect = new Rectangle(135, 65, 40, 40);
14.    private Rectangle lincolnRect = new Rectangle(175, 62, 40, 40);
15.
```

Listing 7-11   rushmore/WEB-INF/classes/com/corejsf/Rushmore.java (cont.)

```
16.    public void listen(ActionEvent e) {
17.       FacesContext context = FacesContext.getCurrentInstance();
18.       String clientId = e.getComponent().getClientId(context);
19.       Map requestParams = context.getExternalContext().getRequestParameterMap();
20.
21.       int x = new Integer((String) requestParams.get(clientId + ".x"))
22.          .intValue();
23.       int y = new Integer((String) requestParams.get(clientId + ".y"))
24.          .intValue();
25.
26.       outcome = null;
27.
28.       if (washingtonRect.contains(new Point(x, y)))
29.          outcome = "washington";
30.
31.       if (jeffersonRect.contains(new Point(x, y)))
32.          outcome = "jefferson";
33.
34.       if (rooseveltRect.contains(new Point(x, y)))
35.          outcome = "roosevelt";
36.
37.       if (lincolnRect.contains(new Point(x, y)))
38.          outcome = "lincoln";
39.    }
40.
41.    public String act() {
42.       return outcome;
43.    }
44. }
```

Listing 7-12   rushmore/WEB-INF/faces-config.xml

```
 1. <?xml version="1.0"?>
 2.
 3. <!DOCTYPE faces-config PUBLIC
 4. "-//Sun Microsystems, Inc.//DTD JavaServer Faces Config 1.0//EN"
 5. "http://java.sun.com/dtd/web-facesconfig_1_0.dtd">
 6. <faces-config>
 7.    <navigation-rule>
 8.       <from-view-id>/index.jsp</from-view-id>
 9.       <navigation-case>
10.          <from-outcome>washington</from-outcome>
11.          <to-view-id>/washington.jsp</to-view-id>
12.       </navigation-case>
```

Listing 7–12	rushmore/WEB-INF/faces-config.xml (cont.)

```
13.        <navigation-case>
14.            <from-outcome>jefferson</from-outcome>
15.            <to-view-id>/jefferson.jsp</to-view-id>
16.        </navigation-case>
17.        <navigation-case>
18.            <from-outcome>roosevelt</from-outcome>
19.            <to-view-id>/roosevelt.jsp</to-view-id>
20.        </navigation-case>
21.        <navigation-case>
22.            <from-outcome>lincoln</from-outcome>
23.            <to-view-id>/lincoln.jsp</to-view-id>
24.        </navigation-case>
25.    </navigation-rule>
26.
27.    <managed-bean>
28.        <managed-bean-name>rushmore</managed-bean-name>
29.        <managed-bean-class>com.corejsf.Rushmore</managed-bean-class>
30.        <managed-bean-scope>session</managed-bean-scope>
31.    </managed-bean>
32.
33. </faces-config>
```

Listing 7–13	rushmore/WEB-INF/classes/com/corejsf/messages.properties

```
1. windowTitle=Mt. Rushmore Tabbed Pane
2. jeffersonTabText=Jefferson
3. rooseveltTabText=Roosevelt
4. lincolnTabText=Lincoln
5. washingtonTabText=Washington
6.
7. jeffersonTooltip=Thomas Jefferson
8. rooseveltTooltip=Theodore Roosevelt
9. lincolnTooltip=Abraham Lincoln
10. washingtonTooltip=George Washington
11.
12. lincolnDiscussion=President Lincoln was known as the Great Emancipator because \
13. he was instrumental in abolishing slavery in the United States. He was born \
14. into a poor family in Kentucky in 1809, elected president in 1860 and \
15. assassinated by John Wilkes Booth in 1865.
16.
```

```
17. washingtonDiscussion=George Washington was the first president of the United \
18. States. He was born in 1732 in Virginia and was elected Commander in Chief of \
19. the Continental Army in 1775 and forced the surrender of Cornwallis at Yorktown \
20. in 1781. He was inaugurated on April 30, 1789.
21.
22. rooseveltDiscussion=Theodore Roosevelt was the 26th president of the United \
23. States. In 1901 he became president after the assassination of President \
24. McKinley. At only 42 years of age, he was the youngest president in US history.
25.
26. jeffersonDiscussion=Thomas Jefferson, the 3rd US president, was born in \
27. 1743 in Virginia. Jefferson was tall and awkward, and was not known as a \
28. great public speaker. Jefferson became minister to France in 1785, after \
29. Benjamin Franklin held that post. In 1796, Jefferson was a reluctant \
30. presidential candiate, and missed winning the election by a mere three votes. \
31. He served as president from 1801-1809.
```

Event Listener Tags

Up to now, we've added action and value change listeners to components with the actionListener and valueChangeListener *attributes*, respectively. However, you can also add action and value change listeners to a component with the f:actionListener and f:valueChangeListener *tags*. Typically, you use those tags when you need multiple action or value change listeners for a single component.

In Listing 7–1 on page 278, we defined a menu like this:

```
<h:selectOneMenu value="#{form.country}" onchange="submit()"
    valueChangeListener="#{form.countryChanged}">
    <f:selectItems value="#{form.countryNames}"/>
</h:selectOneMenu>
```

Alternatively, we could use f:valueChangeListener, like this:

```
<h:selectOneMenu value="#{form.country}" onchange="submit()">
    <f:valueChangeListener type="com.corejsf.CountryListener"/>
    <f:selectItems value="#{form.countryNames}"/>
</h:selectOneMenu>
```

Notice the difference between the values specified for the valueChangeListener attribute and the f:valueChangeListener tag. The former specifies a method binding, whereas the latter specifies a Java class. For example, the class referred to in the previous code fragment looks like this:

```
public class CountryListener implements ValueChangeListener {
    private static final String US = "United States";
```

```
public void processValueChange(ValueChangeEvent event) {
    FacesContext context = FacesContext.getCurrentInstance();

    if (US.equals((String) event.getNewValue()))
        context.getViewRoot().setLocale(Locale.US);
    else
        context.getViewRoot().setLocale(Locale.CANADA);
    }
}
```

Like all listeners specified with f:valueChangeListener, the preceding class implements the ValueChangeListener interface. That class defines a single method: void processValueChange(ValueChangeEvent).

The f:actionListener tag is analogous to f:valueChangeListener—the former also has a type attribute that specifies a class name; the class must implement the Action-Listener interface. For example, in Listing 7–6 on page 284, we defined a button like this:

```
<h:commandButton image="mountrushmore.jpg"
    actionListener="#{rushmore.listen}"
    action="#{rushmore.act}"/>
```

Instead of using the actionListener attribute to define our listener, we could have used the f:actionListener tag instead:

```
<h:commandButton image="mountrushmore.jpg" action="#{rushmore.act}">
    <f:actionListener type="com.corejsf.RushmoreListener"/>
</h:commandButton>
```

The class specified by f:actionListener in the preceding code fragment looks like this:

```
public class ChangeLocaleBean implements ActionListener {
    public void processAction(ActionEvent e) {
        FacesContext context = FacesContext.getCurrentInstance();
        Map requestParams = context.getExternalContext().getRequestParameterMap();
        String locale = (String) requestParams.get("locale");

        if ("english".equals(locale))
            context.getViewRoot().setLocale(Locale.UK);
        else if("german".equals(locale))
            context.getViewRoot().setLocale(Locale.GERMANY);
    }
}
```

Action listener classes must implement the ActionListener interface, which defines a processAction method.

You can also specify multiple listeners with multiple f:actionListener or f:value-ChangeListener tags per component. For example, we could add another action listener to our previous example like this:

```
<h:commandButton image="mountrushmore.jpg" action="#{rushmore.act}">
    <f:actionListener type="com.corejsf.RushmoreListener"/>
    <f:actionListener type="com.corejsf.ActionLogger"/>
</h:commandButton>
```

In the preceding code fragment, the ActionLogger class is a simple action listener that logs action events.

If you specify multiple listeners for a component, as we did in the preceding code fragment, the listeners are invoked in the following order:

1. The listener specified by the listener attribute

2. Listeners specified by listener tags, in the order they are declared

---

API javax.faces.event.ValueChangeListener

*   void processValueChange(ValueChangeEvent)
    Processes a value change event.

API javax.faces.event.ActionListener

*   void processAction(ActionEvent)
    Processes an action event.

> **NOTE:** You may wonder why you must specify a method binding for listeners when you use the actionListener and valueChangeListener attributes and why you must use a class name for listeners specified with f:actionListener and f:valueChangeListener tags. The truth is that the mismatch between listener attributes and tags was an oversight on the part of the JSF Expert Group.

Immediate Components

In "Life-Cycle Events" on page 274 we saw that value change events are normally fired after the Process Validations phase and action events are normally fired after the Invoke Application phase. Typically, that's the preferred behavior—you usually want to be notified of value changes only when they are valid, and actions should be invoked after all submitted values have been transmitted to the model.

But sometimes you want value change events or action events to fire at the beginning of the life cycle to bypass validation for one or more components. In "Using Immediate Input Components" and "Using Immediate Command Components" on page 295 we make compelling arguments for such behavior. For now, let's look at the mechanics of how immediate events are delivered, as illustrated by Figure 7–6.

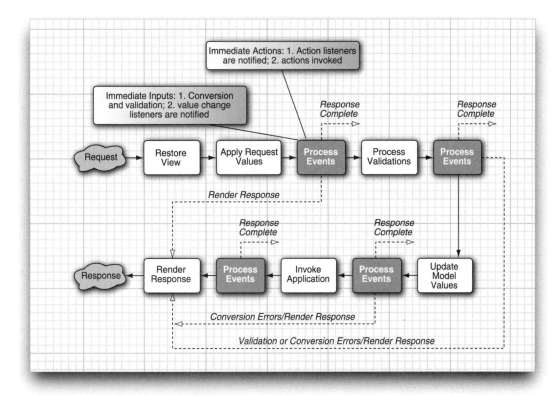

Figure 7–6   Immediate Components

Immediate events are fired after the Apply Request Values phase. For input components, conversion and validation are performed after the Apply Request Values phase and value change events are subsequently fired. For command components, action listeners are invoked, followed by actions; that process kicks in the navigation handler and circumvents the rest of the life cycle up to Render Response.

Using Immediate Input Components

Figure 7–7 shows the value change example discussed in "Value Change Events" on page 275. Recall that the application uses a value change listener to change the view's locale, which in turn changes the localized state prompt according to the selected locale.

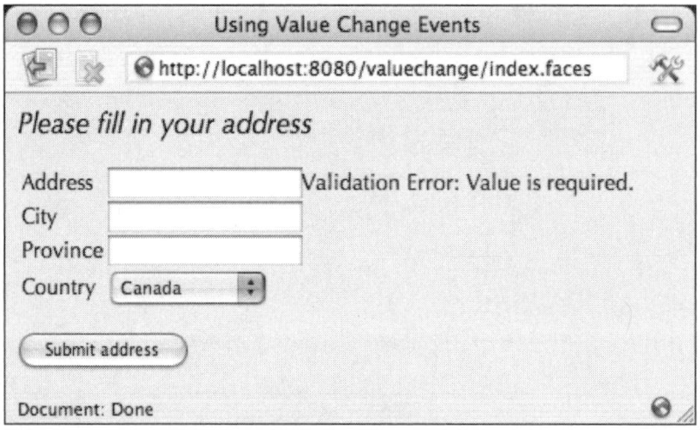

Figure 7–7   An Immediate Need

Here we've made a seemingly innocuous change to that application: we added a required validator to the Address field and added a message tag to the form. But that validation results in an error when we select a country without filling in the Address field (recall that the country menu submits its form when its value is changed).

The problem is this: We want validation to kick in when the submit button is activated, but not when the country is changed. How can we specify validation for one but not the other?

The solution is to make the country menu an *immediate* component. Immediate input components perform conversion and validation and subsequently deliver value change events at the beginning of the JSF life cycle—after the Apply Request Values phase—instead of after Process Validations.

We specify immediate components with the immediate attribute, which is available to all input and command components:

```
<h:selectOneMenu value="#{form.country}" onchange="submit()" immediate="true"
   valueChangeListener="#{form.countryChanged}">
   <f:selectItems value="#{form.countryNames}"/>
</h:selectOneMenu>
```

With the immediate attribute set to true, our menu fires value change events after Apply Request Values, well before any other input components are validated. You may wonder what good that does us if the other validations happen later instead of sooner—after all, the validations will still be performed and the validation error will still be displayed. To prevent validations for the other components in the form, we have one more thing to do: call the faces context renderResponse method at the end of our value change listener, like this:

```
private static final String US = "United States";
...
public void countryChanged(ValueChangeEvent event) {
    FacesContext context = FacesContext.getCurrentInstance();

    if(US.equals(event.getNewValue()))
        context.getViewRoot().setLocale(Locale.US);
    else
        context.getViewRoot().setLocale(Locale.CANADA);

    context.renderResponse();
}
}
```

The call to renderResponse() skips the rest of the life cycle—including validation of the rest of the input components in the form—up to Render Response. Thus, the other validations are skipped and the response is rendered normally (in this case, the current page is redisplayed).

To summarize, you can skip validation when a value change event fires by doing the following:

1.   Adding an immediate attribute to your input tag

2.   Calling FacesContext.renderResponse() at the end of your listener

Using Immediate Command Components

In Chapter 4 we discussed an application, shown in Figure 7–8, that uses command links to change locales.

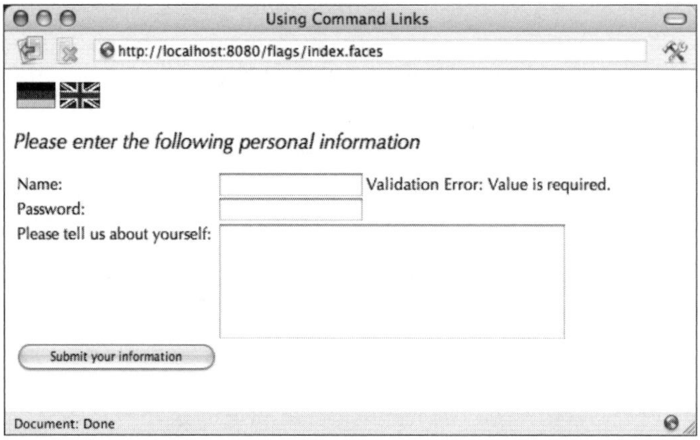

Figure 7–8   Changing Locales with Links

If we add a required validator to one of the input fields in the form, we'll have the same problem we had with the application discussed in "Using Immediate Input Components" on page 294: the validation error will appear when we just want to change the locale by clicking on a link. This time, however, we need an immediate *command* component instead of an immediate *input* component. All we need to do is add an `immediate` attribute to our `h:commandLink` tag, like this:

```
<h:commandLink actionListener="#{localeChanger.changeLocale}" immediate="true">
    <h:graphicImage value="/german_flag.gif" style="border: 0px"/>
    <f:param name="locale" value="german"/>
</h:commandLink>
```

Unlike value change events, we do not need to modify our listener to invoke `FacesContext.renderResponse()`, because all actions, immediate or not, proceed directly to the Render Response phase, regardless of when they are fired.

Phase Events

The JSF implementation fires events, known as phase events, before and after each life-cycle phase. Those events are handled by phase listeners. Unlike value change and action listeners that you attach to individual components, you specify phase listeners in a faces configuration file, like this:

```
<faces-config>
    <lifecycle>
        <phase-listener>com.corejsf.PhaseTracker</phase-listener>
    </lifecycle>
</faces-config>
```

The preceding code fragment specifies only one listener, but you can specify as many as you want. Listeners are invoked in the order in which they are specified in the configuration file.

You implement phase listeners by means of the PhaseListener interface from the javax.faces.event package. That interface defines three methods:

- PhaseId getPhaseId()
- void afterPhase(PhaseEvent)
- void beforePhase(PhaseEvent)

The getPhaseId method tells the JSF implementation when to deliver phase events to the listener; for example, getPhaseId() could return PhaseId.APPLY_REQUEST_VALUES. In that case, beforePhase() and afterPhase() would be called once per life cycle: before and after the Apply Request Values phase. You could also specify PhaseId.ANY_PHASE, which really means *all phases*—your phase listener's beforePhase and afterPhase methods will be called six times per life cycle: once each for each life-cycle phase.

Phase listeners are useful for debugging and for highly specialized behavior. For example, if you use JSF components in another web application framework such as Struts, you might want to update that framework's locale after the Apply Request Values phase, when JSF internally sets its locale.

Phase listeners can be useful for debugging, as illustrated by the application shown in Figure 7–9.

The application shown in Figure 7–9 has a single phase listener that logs messages with a logger, like this:

```
public class PhaseTracker implements PhaseListener {
    ...
    private static final Logger logger = Logger.getLogger("com.corejsf.phases");
    ...
    public void beforePhase(PhaseEvent e) {
        logger.info("BEFORE " + e.getPhaseId());
    }
    public void afterPhase(PhaseEvent e) {
        logger.info("AFTER " + e.getPhaseId());
    }
}
```

The phase ID for the listener is set with a listbox that's defined like this:

```
<h:selectOneListbox
    valueChangeListener="#{form.phaseChange}">
    <f:selectItems value="#{form.phases}"/>
</h:selectOneListbox>
```

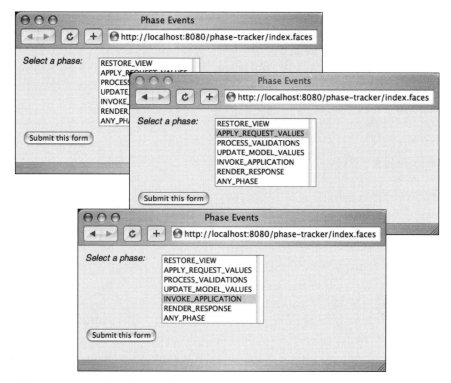

Figure 7–9   Using Phase Listeners

When you select a phase and activate the submit button, the phase listener's
phase ID is set by a value change listener:

```
public class FormBean {
    ...
    // VALUE CHANGE LISTENER: phaseChange
    public void phaseChange(ValueChangeEvent e) {
        // get a reference to the current lifecycle
        ...
        PhaseListener[] listeners = lifecycle.getPhaseListeners();
        for (int i = 0; i < listeners.length; ++i) {
            PhaseListener listener = listeners[i];
            if (listener instanceof com.corejsf.PhaseTracker)
                ((com.corejsf.PhaseTracker) listener).setPhase((String)
                                                     e.getNewValue());
        }
    }
}
```

The top picture in Figure 7–9 shows the application at startup—nothing is selected in the listbox. Because we set the listener's default phase to PhaseId.ANY_PHASE, the listener will be invoked before and after every phase until something is selected in the listbox and the form is submitted. Let's see what output the listener writes to the servlet container log file at application startup:

```
INFO: BEFORE RESTORE_VIEW 1
INFO: AFTER RESTORE_VIEW 1
INFO: BEFORE RENDER_RESPONSE 6
INFO: AFTER RENDER_RESPONSE 6
```

Why wasn't the listener notified of phases two (Apply Request Values) through five (Invoke Application)? When the application is started, there's no view to restore because the JSF page has not been loaded before. Without a component tree, there's no sense in processing validations, updating model values, or invoking actions, so the JSF life cycle skips directly to rendering the response. That's the last time that will happen for this application until it's reloaded by the servlet container. If you activate the submit button without selecting a phase, you'll see this output:

```
INFO: BEFORE RESTORE_VIEW 1
INFO: AFTER RESTORE_VIEW 1
INFO: BEFORE APPLY_REQUEST_VALUES 2
INFO: AFTER APPLY_REQUEST_VALUES 2
INFO: BEFORE PROCESS_VALIDATIONS 3
INFO: AFTER PROCESS_VALIDATIONS 3
INFO: BEFORE UPDATE_MODEL_VALUES 4
INFO: AFTER UPDATE_MODEL_VALUES 4
INFO: BEFORE INVOKE_APPLICATION 5
INFO: AFTER INVOKE_APPLICATION 5
INFO: BEFORE RENDER_RESPONSE 6
INFO: AFTER RENDER_RESPONSE 6
```

Now you can see that the listener is notified of all phases because we've set the default phase to PhaseId.ANY_PHASE.

Next, we select Apply Request Values from the listbox and activate the submit button, as shown in the middle picture in Figure 7–9. Here's the listener's output for that form submit:

```
INFO: BEFORE RESTORE_VIEW 1
INFO: AFTER RESTORE_VIEW 1
INFO: BEFORE APPLY_REQUEST_VALUES 2
INFO: AFTER APPLY_REQUEST_VALUES 2
INFO: BEFORE PROCESS_VALIDATIONS 3
```

You might have expected only the Apply Request Values output. Why was our listener notified before and after Restore View and before Process Validations? First, when the form was submitted, the listener's phase was still ANY_PHASE. So when the life cycle began, our listener was interested in all phases and was notified accordingly.

Second, remember that the phase ID for our listener is set with a value change listener, and recall from Figure 7–1 on page 274 that value change listeners are invoked after the Process Validations phase. At the end of Process Validations, the value change listener set the phase listener's phase to APPLY_REQUEST_VALUES. Since Apply Request Values has already executed, our listener was not notified for the remainder of the life cycle. If you click the submit button once again, you'll see the output you expect because the listener's phase ID was set to Apply Request Values from the beginning of the life cycle:

```
INFO: BEFORE APPLY_REQUEST_VALUES 2
INFO: AFTER APPLY_REQUEST_VALUES 2
```

Finally, we select Invoke Application and submit the form. That produces the following output:

```
INFO: BEFORE APPLY_REQUEST_VALUES 2
INFO: AFTER APPLY_REQUEST_VALUES 2
INFO: BEFORE INVOKE_APPLICATION 5
INFO: AFTER INVOKE_APPLICATION 5
```

Does the output make sense this time? When the life cycle starts, the listener's phase ID is Apply Request Values, so the listener is notified of that phase. Later in the life cycle—after Process Validation—the value change listener changes the listener's phase ID to INVOKE_APPLICATION. Subsequently, the listener is notified of the Invoke Application phase. If you click the submit button again, you'll see this output:

```
INFO: BEFORE INVOKE_APPLICATION 5
INFO: AFTER INVOKE_APPLICATION 5
```

The directory structure for the phase listener example is shown in Figure 7–10. The application shown in Figure 7–9 is listed in Listing 7–14 through Listing 7–19.

TIP: You can use the phase tracker in your own applications to see when events are fired: any log messages you generate will be mixed with the phase tracker messages. To use the phase tracker, make sure the class file is in your WAR file and you've declared the listener in web.xml as we did in Listing 7–17.

**Figure 7–10   Phase Listener Example
Directory Structure**

Listing 7–14   phase-tracker/index.jsp

```
1.  <html>
2.     <%@ taglib uri="http://java.sun.com/jsf/core" prefix="f" %>
3.     <%@ taglib uri="http://java.sun.com/jsf/html" prefix="h" %>
4.     <f:view>
5.        <head>
6.           <link href="styles.css" rel="stylesheet" type="text/css"/>
7.           <f:loadBundle basename="com.corejsf.messages" var="msgs"/>
8.           <title>
9.              <h:outputText value="#{msgs.indexWindowTitle}"/>
10.          </title>
11.       </head>
12.       <body>
13.          <h:form>
14.             <h:panelGrid columns="2" columnClasses="phaseFormColumns">
15.                <h:outputText value="#{msgs.phasePrompt}"/>
16.
17.                <h:selectOneListbox valueChangeListener="#{form.phaseChange}">
18.                   <f:selectItems value="#{form.phases}"/>
19.                </h:selectOneListbox>
20.
21.                <h:commandButton value="#{msgs.submitPrompt}"/>
22.             </h:panelGrid>
23.          </h:form>
24.       </body>
25.    </f:view>
26. </html>
```

Listing 7–15   phase-tracker/WEB-INF/classes/com/corejsf/FormBean.java

```
 1. package com.corejsf;
 2.
 3. import javax.faces.FactoryFinder;
 4. import javax.faces.event.PhaseListener;
 5. import javax.faces.event.ValueChangeEvent;
 6. import javax.faces.lifecycle.Lifecycle;
 7. import javax.faces.lifecycle.LifecycleFactory;
 8. import javax.faces.model.SelectItem;
 9.
10. public class FormBean {
11.    private SelectItem[] phases = {
12.       new SelectItem("RESTORE_VIEW"),
13.       new SelectItem("APPLY_REQUEST_VALUES"),
14.       new SelectItem("PROCESS_VALIDATIONS"),
15.       new SelectItem("UPDATE_MODEL_VALUES"),
16.       new SelectItem("INVOKE_APPLICATION"),
17.       new SelectItem("RENDER_RESPONSE"),
18.       new SelectItem("ANY_PHASE"),
19.    };
20.
21.    public SelectItem[] getPhases() { return phases; }
22.
23.    public void phaseChange(ValueChangeEvent e) {
24.       LifecycleFactory factory = (LifecycleFactory)FactoryFinder.getFactory(
25.          FactoryFinder.LIFECYCLE_FACTORY);
26.       Lifecycle lifecycle = factory.getLifecycle(LifecycleFactory.
27.          DEFAULT_LIFECYCLE);
28.
29.       PhaseListener[] listeners = lifecycle.getPhaseListeners();
30.       for (int i = 0; i < listeners.length; ++i) {
31.          PhaseListener listener = listeners[i];
32.          if(listener instanceof com.corejsf.PhaseTracker)
33.             ((com.corejsf.PhaseTracker) listener).setPhase(
34.                (String) e.getNewValue());
35.       }
36.    }
37. }
```

Listing 7-16 phase-tracker/WEB-INF/classes/com/corejsf/PhaseTracker.java

```java
1. package com.corejsf;
2.
3. import java.util.logging.Logger;
4. import javax.faces.context.FacesContext;
5. import javax.faces.event.PhaseEvent;
6. import javax.faces.event.PhaseListener;
7. import javax.faces.event.PhaseId;
8.
9. public class PhaseTracker implements PhaseListener {
10.    private static final String PHASE_PARAMETER ="com.corejsf.phaseTracker.phase";
11.    private static final Logger logger = Logger.getLogger("com.corejsf.phases");
12.    private static String phase = null;
13.
14.    public void setPhase(String newValue) { phase = newValue; }
15.
16.    public PhaseId getPhaseId() {
17.       if(phase == null) {
18.          FacesContext context = FacesContext.getCurrentInstance();
19.          phase = (String)context.getExternalContext().getInitParameter(
20.                                          PHASE_PARAMETER);
21.       }
22.       PhaseId phaseId = PhaseId.ANY_PHASE;
23.
24.       if(phase != null) {
25.          if("RESTORE_VIEW".equals(phase))
26.             phaseId = PhaseId.RESTORE_VIEW;
27.          else if("APPLY_REQUEST_VALUES".equals(phase))
28.             phaseId = PhaseId.APPLY_REQUEST_VALUES;
29.          else if("PROCESS_VALIDATIONS".equals(phase))
30.             phaseId = PhaseId.PROCESS_VALIDATIONS;
31.          else if("UPDATE_MODEL_VALUES".equals(phase))
32.             phaseId = PhaseId.UPDATE_MODEL_VALUES;
33.          else if("INVOKE_APPLICATION".equals(phase))
34.             phaseId = PhaseId.INVOKE_APPLICATION;
35.          else if("RENDER_RESPONSE".equals(phase))
36.             phaseId = PhaseId.RENDER_RESPONSE;
37.          else if("ANY_PHASE".equals(phase))
38.             phaseId = PhaseId.ANY_PHASE;
39.       }
40.       return phaseId;
41.    }
42.    public void beforePhase(PhaseEvent e) {
43.       logger.info("BEFORE " + e.getPhaseId());
44.    }
45.    public void afterPhase(PhaseEvent e) {
46.       logger.info("AFTER " + e.getPhaseId());
47.    }
48. }
```

Listing 7–17   phase-tracker/WEB-INF/faces-config.xml

```
1. <?xml version="1.0"?>
2.
3. <!DOCTYPE faces-config PUBLIC
4.    "-//Sun Microsystems, Inc.//DTD JavaServer Faces Config 1.0//EN"
5.    "http://java.sun.com/dtd/web-facesconfig_1_0.dtd">
6.
7. <faces-config>
8.    <managed-bean>
9.       <managed-bean-name>form</managed-bean-name>
10.      <managed-bean-class>com.corejsf.FormBean</managed-bean-class>
11.      <managed-bean-scope>session</managed-bean-scope>
12.   </managed-bean>
13.
14.   <lifecycle>
15.      <phase-listener>com.corejsf.PhaseTracker</phase-listener>
16.   </lifecycle>
17. </faces-config>
```

Listing 7–18   phase-tracker/WEB-INF/classes/com/corejsf/messages.properties

```
1. indexWindowTitle=Phase Events
2. phasePrompt=Select a phase:
3. submitPrompt=Submit this form
```

Listing 7–19   phase-tracker/styles.css

```
1. body {
2.    background: #eee;
3. }
4. .phaseFormColumns {
5.    vertical-align: top;
6.    font-style: italic;
7.    font-size: 1.1em;
8. }
9. .columns {
10.   vertical-align: top;
11. }
```

Putting It All Together

We close out this chapter with an example of a poor man's implementation of a tabbed pane. That example demonstrates event handling and advanced aspects of using JSF HTML tags. Those advanced uses include the following:

- Nesting h:panelGrid tags
- Using facets

- Specifying tab indexing
- Adding tooltips to components with the title attribute
- Dynamically determining style classes
- Using action listeners
- Optional rendering
- Statically including JSF pages

JSF 1.0/1.1 does not have a tabbed pane component, so if you want a tabbed pane in your application, you have two choices: implement a custom component or use existing tags—in conjunction with a backing bean—to create an ad hoc tabbed pane. Figure 7–11 shows the latter. The former is discussed in Chapter 9.

The tabbed pane shown in Figure 7–11 is implemented entirely with existing JSF HTML tags and a backing bean; no custom renderers or components are used. The JSF page for the tabbed pane looks like this:

```
...
<h:form>
    <%-- Tabs --%>
    <h:panelGrid styleClass="tabbedPane" columnClasses="displayPanel">
        <f:facet name="header">
            <h:panelGrid columns="4" styleClass="tabbedPaneHeader">
                <h:commandLink tabindex="1"
                    title="#{tp.jeffersonTooltip}"
                    styleClass="#{tp.jeffersonStyle}"
                    actionListener="#{tp.jeffersonAction}">

                    <h:outputText value="#{msgs.jeffersonTab}"/>
                </h:commandLink>
                ...
            </h:panelGrid>
        </f:facet>

        <%-- Main panel --%>
        <%@ include file="jefferson.jsp" %>
        <%@ include file="roosevelt.jsp" %>
        <%@ include file="lincoln.jsp" %>
        <%@ include file="washington.jsp" %>
    </h:panelGrid>
</h:form>
...
```

The tabbed pane is implemented with h:panelGrid. Because we don't specify the columns attribute, the panel has one column. The panel's header—defined with an f:facet tag—contains the tabs, which are implemented with another h:panelGrid that contains h:commandLink tags for each tab. The only row in the outer panel contains the content associated with the selected tab.

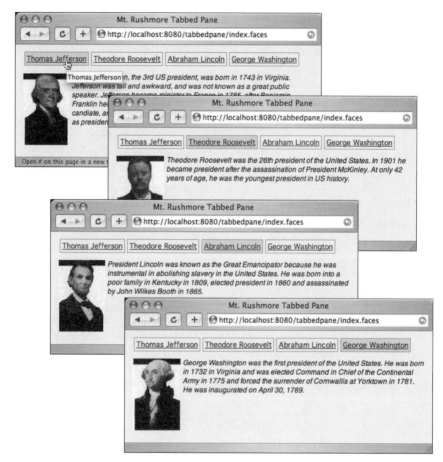

Figure 7–11   A Poor Man's Tabbed Pane

When a user selects a tab, the associated action listener for the command link is invoked and modifies the data stored in the backing bean. Because we use a different CSS style for the selected tab, the styleClass attribute of each h:commandLink tag is pulled from the backing bean with a value reference expression.

As you can see from the top picture in Figure 7–11, we've used the title attribute to associate a tooltip with each tab. Another accessibility feature is the ability to move from one tab to another with the keyboard instead of the mouse. We implemented that feature simply by specifying the tabindex attribute for each h:commandLink.

The content associated with each tab is statically included with the JSP include directive. For our application, that content is merely a picture and some text, but you could modify the included JSF pages to contain any set of appropriate components. Notice that even though all the JSF pages representing content are included, only the content associated with the current tab is rendered. That's accomplished with the rendered attribute; for example, jefferson.jsp looks like this:

```
<h:panelGrid columns="2" columnClasses="presidentDiscussionColumn"
    rendered="#{tp.jeffersonCurrent}">
    <h:graphicImage value="/images/jefferson.jpg"/>
    <h:outputText value="#{msgs.jeffersonDiscussion}" styleClass="tabbedPaneContent"/>
</h:panelGrid>
```

Figure 7–12 shows the directory structure for the tabbed pane application and Listing 7–20 through Listing 7–28 lists those files.

> NOTE: The JSF reference implementation contains a samples directory that holds a handful of sample applications. One of those applications, contained in jsf-components.war, is a tabbed pane component. Although the sample components are provided largely as proof-of-concept, you may find them useful as a starting point for your own custom components.

Figure 7–12 Tabbed Pane
Directory Structure

Listing 7–20	tabbedpane/index.jsp

```
1.  <html>
2.     <%@ taglib uri="http://java.sun.com/jsf/core"  prefix="f" %>
3.     <%@ taglib uri="http://java.sun.com/jsf/html"  prefix="h" %>
4.
5.     <f:view>
6.        <head>
7.           <link href="styles.css" rel="stylesheet" type="text/css"/>
8.           <f:loadBundle basename="com.corejsf.messages" var="msgs"/>
9.           <title>
10.             <h:outputText value="#{msgs.windowTitle}"/>
11.          </title>
12.       </head>
13.       <body>
14.          <h:form>
15.             <h:panelGrid styleClass="tabbedPane" columnClasses="displayPanel">
16.                <%-- Tabs --%>
17.
18.                <f:facet name="header">
19.                   <h:panelGrid columns="5" styleClass="tabbedPaneHeader">
20.
21.                      <h:commandLink tabindex="1"
22.                               title="#{tp.jeffersonTooltip}"
23.                            styleClass="#{tp.jeffersonStyle}"
24.                         actionListener="#{tp.jeffersonAction}">
25.
26.                         <h:outputText value="#{msgs.jeffersonTabText}"/>
27.                      </h:commandLink>
28.
29.                      <h:commandLink tabindex="2"
30.                               title="#{tp.rooseveltTooltip}"
31.                            styleClass="#{tp.rooseveltStyle}"
32.                         actionListener="#{tp.rooseveltAction}">
33.
34.                         <h:outputText value="#{msgs.rooseveltTabText}"/>
35.                      </h:commandLink>
36.
37.                      <h:commandLink tabindex="3"
38.                               title="#{tp.lincolnTooltip}"
39.                            styleClass="#{tp.lincolnStyle}"
40.                         actionListener="#{tp.lincolnAction}">
41.
42.                         <h:outputText value="#{msgs.lincolnTabText}"/>
43.                      </h:commandLink>
44.
```

Listing 7–20	tabbedpane/index.jsp (cont.)

```
45.                    <h:commandLink tabindex="4"
46.                            title="#{tp.washingtonTooltip}"
47.                        styleClass="#{tp.washingtonStyle}"
48.                   actionListener="#{tp.washingtonAction}">
49.
50.                       <h:outputText value="#{msgs.washingtonTabText}"/>
51.                     </h:commandLink>
52.                   </h:panelGrid>
53.                 </f:facet>
54.
55.                 <%-- Tabbed pane content --%>
56.
57.                 <%@ include file="washington.jsp" %>
58.                 <%@ include file="roosevelt.jsp" %>
59.                 <%@ include file="lincoln.jsp" %>
60.                 <%@ include file="jefferson.jsp" %>
61.             </h:panelGrid>
62.         </h:form>
63.       </body>
64.     </f:view>
65. </html>
```

Listing 7–21	tabbedpane/jefferson.jsp

```
1. <h:panelGrid columns='2' columnClasses='presidentDiscussionColumn'
2.           rendered='#{tp.jeffersonCurrent}'>
3.
4.    <h:graphicImage value='/images/jefferson.jpg'/>
5.    <h:outputText value='#{msgs.jeffersonDiscussion}'
6.          styleClass='tabbedPaneContent'/>
7.
8. </h:panelGrid>
```

Listing 7–22	tabbedpane/roosevelt.jsp

```
1. <h:panelGrid columns='2' columnClasses='presidentDiscussionColumn'
2.           rendered='#{tp.rooseveltCurrent}'>
3.
4.    <h:graphicImage value='/images/roosevelt.jpg'/>
5.    <h:outputText value='#{msgs.rooseveltDiscussion}'
6.          styleClass='tabbedPaneContent'/>
7.
8. </h:panelGrid>
```

Listing 7–23 tabbedpane/lincoln.jsp

```
1. <h:panelGrid columns='2' columnClasses='presidentDiscussionColumn'
2.             rendered='#{tp.lincolnCurrent}'>
3.
4.    <h:graphicImage value='/images/lincoln.jpg'/>
5.    <h:outputText value='#{msgs.lincolnDiscussion}'
6.             styleClass='tabbedPaneContent'/>
7.
8. </h:panelGrid>
```

Listing 7–24 tabbedpane/washington.jsp

```
1. <h:panelGrid columns='2' columnClasses='presidentDiscussionColumn'
2.             rendered='#{tp.washingtonCurrent}'>
3.
4.    <h:graphicImage value='/images/washington.jpg'/>
5.    <h:outputText value='#{msgs.washingtonDiscussion}'
6.             styleClass='tabbedPaneContent'/>
7.
8. </h:panelGrid>
```

Listing 7–25 tabbedpane/WEB-INF/classes/com/corejsf/messages.properties

```
1. windowTitle=Mt. Rushmore Tabbed Pane
2. lincolnTooltip=Abraham Lincoln
3. lincolnTabText=Abraham Lincoln
4. lincolnDiscussion=President Lincoln was known as the Great Emancipator because \
5. he was instrumental in abolishing slavery in the United States. He was born \
6. into a poor family in Kentucky in 1809, elected president in 1860 and \
7. assassinated by John Wilkes Booth in 1865.
8.
9. washingtonTooltip=George Washington
10. washingtonTabText=George Washington
11. washingtonDiscussion=George Washington was the first president of the United \
12. States. He was born in 1732 in Virginia and was elected Commander in Chief of \
13. the Continental Army in 1775 and forced the surrender of Cornwallis at Yorktown \
14. in 1781. He was inaugurated on April 30, 1789.
15.
16. rooseveltTooltip=Theodore Roosevelt
17. rooseveltTabText=Theodore Roosevelt
18. rooseveltDiscussion=Theodore Roosevelt was the 26th president of the United \
19. States. In 1901 he became president after the assassination of President \
20. McKinley. At only 42 years of age, he was the youngest president in US history.
21.
```

Listing 7–25	tabbedpane/WEB-INF/classes/com/corejsf/messages.properties (cont.)

```
22. jeffersonTooltip=Thomas Jefferson
23. jeffersonTabText=Thomas Jefferson
24. jeffersonDiscussion=Thomas Jefferson, the 3rd US president, was born in \
25. 1743 in Virginia. Jefferson was tall and awkward, and was not known as a \
26. great public speaker. Jefferson became minister to France in 1785, after \
27. Benjamin Franklin held that post. In 1796, Jefferson was a reluctant \
28. presidential candiate, and missed winning the election by a mere three votes. \
29. He served as president from 1801-1809.
```

Listing 7–26	tabbedpane/styles.css

```
1.  body {
2.    background: #eee;
3.  }
4.  .tabbedPaneHeader {
5.    vertical-align: top;
6.    text-align: left;
7.    padding: 2px 2px 0px 2px;
8.  }
9.  .tabbedPaneText {
10.    font-size: 1.0em;
11.    font-style: regular;
12.    padding: 3px;
13.    border: thin solid CornflowerBlue;
14.  }
15.  .tabbedPaneTextSelected {
16.    font-size: 1.0em;
17.    font-style: regular;
18.    padding: 3px;
19.    background: PowderBlue;
20.    border: thin solid CornflowerBlue;
21.  }
22.  .tabbedPane {
23.    vertical-align: top;
24.    text-align: left;
25.  }
26.  .displayPanel {
27.    vertical-align: top;
28.    text-align: left;
29.  }
30.  .tabbedPaneContent {
31.    width: 100%;
32.    height: 100%;
33.    font-style: italic;
```

Listing 7–26 tabbedpane/styles.css (cont.)

```
34.    vertical-align: top;
35.    text-align: left;
36.    font-size: 1.2m;
37. }
38. .presidentDiscussionColumn {
39.    vertical-align: top;
40.    text-align: left;
41. }
```

Listing 7–27 tabbedpane/WEB-INF/faces-config.xml

```
1. <?xml version="1.0"?>
2.
3. <!DOCTYPE faces-config PUBLIC
4. "-//Sun Microsystems, Inc.//DTD JavaServer Faces Config 1.0//EN"
5. "http://java.sun.com/dtd/web-facesconfig_1_0.dtd">
6.
7. <faces-config>
8.    <managed-bean>
9.       <managed-bean-name>tp</managed-bean-name>
10.       <managed-bean-class>com.corejsf.TabbedPane</managed-bean-class>
11.       <managed-bean-scope>session</managed-bean-scope>
12.    </managed-bean>
13. </faces-config>
```

Listing 7–28 tabbedpane/WEB-INF/classes/com/corejsf/TabbedPane.java

```
1. package com.corejsf;
2.
3. import javax.faces.event.ActionEvent;
4.
5. public class TabbedPane {
6.    private int index;
7.    private static final int JEFFERSON_INDEX = 0;
8.    private static final int ROOSEVELT_INDEX = 1;
9.    private static final int LINCOLN_INDEX = 2;
10.    private static final int WASHINGTON_INDEX = 3;
11.
12.    private String[] tabs = { "jeffersonTabText", "rooseveltTabText",
13.          "lincolnTabText",  "washingtonTabText", };
14.
15.    private String[] tabTooltips = { "jeffersonTooltip", "rooseveltTooltip",
16.          "lincolnTooltip",  "washingtonTooltip" };
17.
18.    public TabbedPane() {
19.       index = JEFFERSON_INDEX;
20.
```

Listing 7-28	tabbedpane/WEB-INF/classes/com/corejsf/TabbedPane.java (cont.)

```
21.    }
22.
23.    // action listeners that set the current tab
24.
25.    public void jeffersonAction(ActionEvent e) { index = JEFFERSON_INDEX;  }
26.    public void rooseveltAction(ActionEvent e) { index = ROOSEVELT_INDEX;  }
27.    public void lincolnAction(ActionEvent e) { index = LINCOLN_INDEX;     }
28.    public void washingtonAction(ActionEvent e) { index = WASHINGTON_INDEX; }
29.
30.    // CSS styles
31.
32.    public String getJeffersonStyle() { return getCSS(JEFFERSON_INDEX);  }
33.    public String getRooseveltStyle() { return getCSS(ROOSEVELT_INDEX);  }
34.    public String getLincolnStyle() { return getCSS(LINCOLN_INDEX);     }
35.    public String getWashingtonStyle() { return getCSS(WASHINGTON_INDEX); }
36.
37.    private String getCSS(int forIndex) {
38.       return forIndex == index ? "tabbedPaneTextSelected" : "tabbedPaneText";
39.    }
40.
41.    // methods for determining the current tab
42.
43.    public boolean isJeffersonCurrent() { return index == JEFFERSON_INDEX;  }
44.    public boolean isRooseveltCurrent() { return index == ROOSEVELT_INDEX;  }
45.    public boolean isLincolnCurrent() { return index == LINCOLN_INDEX;     }
46.    public boolean isWashingtonCurrent() { return index == WASHINGTON_INDEX; }
47.
48.    // methods that get tooltips for titles
49.
50.    public String getJeffersonTooltip() {
51.       return com.corejsf.util.Messages.getString(
52.          "com.corejsf.messages", tabTooltips[JEFFERSON_INDEX], null);
53.    }
54.    public String getRooseveltTooltip() {
55.       return com.corejsf.util.Messages.getString(
56.          "com.corejsf.messages", tabTooltips[ROOSEVELT_INDEX], null);
57.    }
58.    public String getLincolnTooltip() {
59.       return com.corejsf.util.Messages.getString(
60.          "com.corejsf.messages", tabTooltips[LINCOLN_INDEX], null);
61.    }
62.    public String getWashingtonTooltip() {
63.       return com.corejsf.util.Messages.getString(
64.          "com.corejsf.messages", tabTooltips[WASHINGTON_INDEX], null);
65.    }
66. }
```

SUBVIEWS AND TILES

Topics in This Chapter

Chapter 8

User interfaces are typically the most volatile aspect of web applications during development, so it's crucial to create flexible and extensible interfaces. This chapter shows you how to achieve that flexibility and extensibility by including common content. First we discuss standard JSP mechanisms—JSP includes and JSTL imports—you can use to include common content in a JSF application. Next we explore the use of Struts's Tiles package—which lets you encapsulate layout in addition to content, among other handy features—with JSF.

Common Layouts

Many popular web sites, such as nytimes.com, java.sun.com, or amazon.com, use a common layout for their web pages. For example, all three of the web sites listed above use a header-menu-content layout as depicted in Figure 8–1.

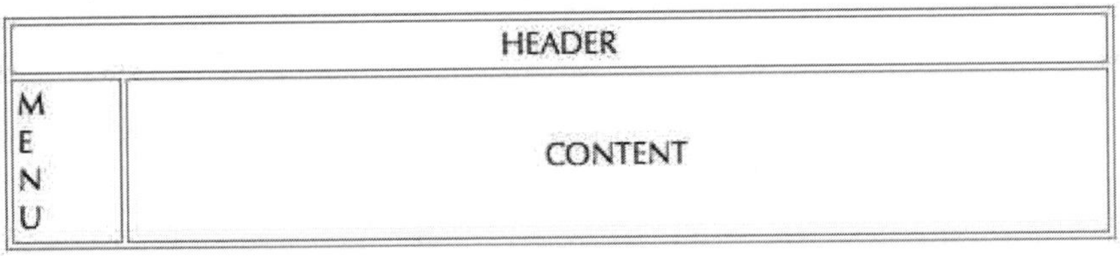

HEADER	
M E N U	CONTENT

Figure 8–1 A Typical Web Page Layout

You can use HTML frames to achieve the layout shown in Figure 8–1, but frames are undesirable for several reasons. For example, frames make it hard for users to bookmark pages. Frames also generate separate requests, which can be problematic for web applications. Including content, which is the focus of this chapter, is generally preferred over frames.

A Book Viewer and a Library

To illustrate implementing layouts, including common content, and using Tiles, we discuss two applications in this chapter: a book viewer and a library. Those applications are shown in Figure 8–2 and Figure 8–3, respectively.

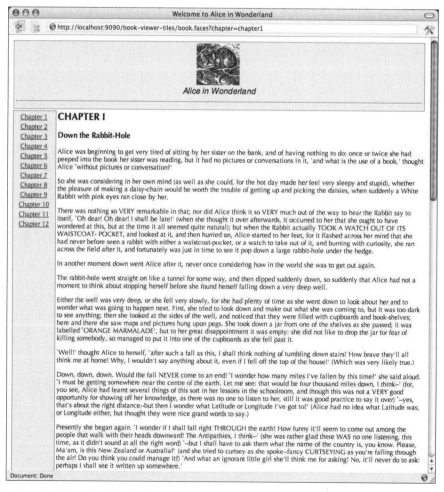

Figure 8–2 The Book Viewer

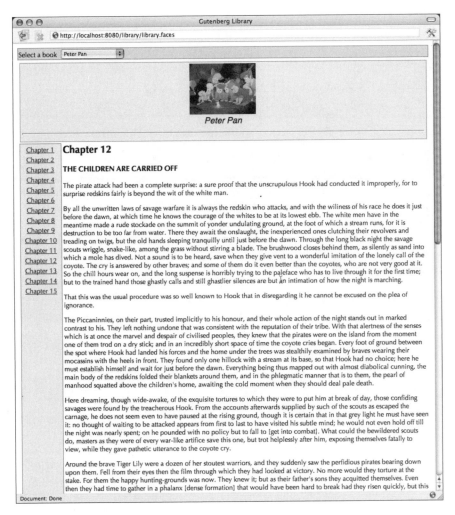

Figure 8–3   The Library

The book viewer is intuitive. If you click on a chapter link, that chapter is shown in the content region of the web page. The library is an extension of the book viewer that lets you view more than one book. You can select books from the menu at the top of the web page.

The book viewer addresses the following topics:

- "Monolithic JSF Pages" on page 320
- "Common Content Inclusion" on page 325
- "Looking at Tiles" on page 330

- "Parameterizing Tiles" on page 334
- "Extending Tiles" on page 335

The library illustrates these Tiles features:

- "Nested Tiles" on page 340
- "Tile Controllers" on page 340

Coverage of the book viewer begins in the next section. The library is discussed in "The Library" on page 338.

 NOTE: For the examples in this chapter, we downloaded Alice in Wonderland and Peter Pan from the Project Gutenberg web site—http://promo.net/pg/—chopped them up into chapters and converted them to HTML.

The Book Viewer

The book viewer is rather limited in scope. It supports only a single book, which is a bean that we define in the faces configuration file. The name of that bean is book.

The book bean has these properties:

- titleKey
- image
- numChapters
- chapterKeys

The titleKey property represents a key in a resource bundle for the book's title. In the book viewer's properties file we have the key/value pair titleKey=Alice in Wonderland. When we display the book's title, we use the titleKey property like this:

```
<h:outputText value="#{msgs[book.titleKey]}"/>
```

The image property is a string. The application interprets that string as a URL and loads it in the book viewer's header like this:

```
<h:graphicImage url="#{book.image}"/>
```

The chapterKeys property is a read-only list of keys, one for each chapter. The book viewer populates the book viewer's menu with corresponding values from a resource bundle:

```
<h:dataTable value="#{book.chapterKeys}" var="chapterKey">
    <h:commandLink>
        <h:outputText value="#{msgs[chapterKey]}"/>
        ...
    </h:commandLink>
</h:dataTable>
```

The Book class uses the numChapters property to compute the chapter keys.

The implementation of the Book class is rather mundane. You can see it in Listing 8–3 on page 323. Here's how we define an instance of the Book class in faces-config.xml:

```
<faces-config>
    <!-- The book -->
    <managed-bean>
        <managed-bean-name>book</managed-bean-name>
        <managed-bean-class>com.corejsf.Book</managed-bean-class>
        <managed-bean-scope>request</managed-bean-scope>

        <managed-property>
            <property-name>titleKey</property-name>
            <value>aliceInWonderland</value>
        </managed-property>

        <managed-property>
            <property-name>image</property-name>
            <value>cheshire.jpg</value>
        </managed-property>

        <managed-property>
            <property-name>numChapters</property-name>
            <property-class>java.lang.Integer</property-class>
            <value>12</value>
        </managed-property>
    </managed-bean>
</faces-config>
```

There are many ways to implement a header-menu-content layout, as shown in Figure 8–1 on page 315. In this section we look at three options: a monolithic JSF page, inclusion of common content, and Tiles.

NOTE: We don't set the book's chapterKeys property in faces-config.xml. That's because the Book class creates that list of chapter keys for us. All we have to do is define the numChapters property.

Monolithic JSF Pages

A monolithic JSF page is perhaps the quickest way to implement the book
viewer shown in Figure 8–2; for example, here's a naive implementation:

```
<%-- A panel grid, which resides in a form, for the entire page --%>
<h:panelGrid columns="2" styleClass="book"
    columnClasses="menuColumn, chapterColumn">

    <%-- The header, containing an image, title and horizontal rule --%>
    <f:facet name="header">
        <h:panelGrid columns="1" styleClass="bookHeader">
            <h:graphicImage value="#{book.image}"/>
            <h:outputText value="#{msgs[book.titleKey]}" styleClass='bookTitle'/>
            <f:verbatim><hr></f:verbatim>
        </h:panelGrid>
    </f:facet>

    <%-- Column 1: The menu, which consists of chapter links --%>
    <h:dataTable value="#{book.chapterKeys}" var="chapterKey"
                    styleClass="links" columnClasses="linksColumn">
        <h:column>
            <h:commandLink>
                <h:outputText value="#{msgs[chapterKey]}"/>
                <f:param name="chapter" value="#{chapterKey}"/>
            </h:commandLink>
        </h:column>
    </h:dataTable>

    <%-- Column 2: The chapter content --%>
    <f:verbatim>
        <c:import url="${param.chapter}.html"/>
    </f:verbatim>
</h:panelGrid>
```

The book viewer is implemented with a panel grid with two columns. The
header region is populated with an image, text, and HTML horizontal rule.
Besides the header, the panel grid has only one row—the menu occupies the
left column and the current chapter is displayed in the right column.

The menu is composed of chapter links. By default, Book.getChapterKeys() returns
a list of strings that look like this:

```
chapter1
chapter2
...
chapterN
```

Chapter N represents the last chapter in the book. In the book viewer's
resource bundle, we define values for those keys:

```
chapter1=Chapter 1
chapter2=Chapter 2
...
```

To create chapter links, we use h:dataTable to iterate over the book's chapter keys. For every chapter, we create a link whose text corresponds to the chapter key's value with this expression: #{msgs[chapterKey]}. So we wind up with Chapter 1 ... Chapter12 displayed in the menu when the number of chapters is 12.

The right column is reserved for chapter content. That content is included with JSTL's c:import tag.

The directory structure for the book viewer is shown in Figure 8–4. The monolithic JSF page version of the book viewer is listed in Listing 8–1 through Listing 8–5.

 NOTE: Notice the f:param tag inside h:commandLink. The JSF framework turns that parameter into a request parameter—named chapter—when the link is activated. When the page is reloaded, that request parameter is used to load the chapter's content like this: <c:import url="${param.chapter}"/>

 NOTE: When we import book chapters, we place the c:import tag in the body of an f:verbatim tag.

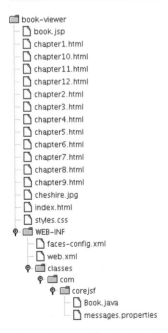

```
book-viewer
  book.jsp
  chapter1.html
  chapter10.html
  chapter11.html
  chapter12.html
  chapter2.html
  chapter3.html
  chapter4.html
  chapter5.html
  chapter6.html
  chapter7.html
  chapter8.html
  chapter9.html
  cheshire.jpg
  index.html
  styles.css
  WEB-INF
    faces-config.xml
    web.xml
    classes
      com
        corejsf
          Book.java
          messages.properties
```

Figure 8–4 The book-viewer Directory Structure

Listing 8–1 `book-viewer-monolith/book.jsp`

```
1. <html>
2.   <%@ taglib uri="http://java.sun.com/jstl/core" prefix="c" %>
3.   <%@ taglib uri="http://java.sun.com/jsf/core"  prefix="f" %>
4.   <%@ taglib uri="http://java.sun.com/jsf/html"  prefix="h" %>
5.   <f:view>
6.     <head>
7.       <link href="styles.css" rel="stylesheet" type="text/css"/>
8.       <f:loadBundle basename="com.corejsf.messages" var="msgs"/>
9.       <title><h:outputText value="#{msgs.bookWindowTitle}"/></title>
10.    </head>
11.    <body>
12.      <h:form>
13.        <h:panelGrid columns="2" styleClass="book"
14.             columnClasses="menuColumn, chapterColumn">
15.          <f:facet name="header">
16.            <h:panelGrid columns="1" styleClass="bookHeader">
17.              <h:graphicImage value="#{book.image}"/>
18.              <h:outputText value="#{msgs[book.titleKey]}"
19.                    styleClass='bookTitle'/>
20.
21.              <f:verbatim><hr/></f:verbatim>
22.            </h:panelGrid>
23.          </f:facet>
24.
25.          <h:dataTable value="#{book.chapterKeys}" var="chapterKey"
26.               styleClass="links" columnClasses="linksColumn">
27.            <h:column>
28.              <h:commandLink>
29.                <h:outputText value="#{msgs[chapterKey]}"/>
30.                <f:param name="chapter" value="#{chapterKey}"/>
31.              </h:commandLink>
32.            </h:column>
33.          </h:dataTable>
34.
35.          <f:verbatim>
36.            <c:import url="${param.chapter}.html"/>
37.          </f:verbatim>
38.        </h:panelGrid>
39.      </h:form>
40.    </body>
41.  </f:view>
42. </html>
```

Listing 8–2 `book-viewer-monolith/WEB-INF/faces-config.xml`

```
1. <?xml version="1.0"?>
2.
3. <!DOCTYPE faces-config PUBLIC
4.   "-//Sun Microsystems, Inc.//DTD JavaServer Faces Config 1.0//EN"
5.   "http://java.sun.com/dtd/web-facesconfig_1_0.dtd">
6.
7. <faces-config>
8.   <!-- The book -->
9.   <managed-bean>
10.      <managed-bean-name>book</managed-bean-name>
11.      <managed-bean-class>com.corejsf.Book</managed-bean-class>
12.      <managed-bean-scope>request</managed-bean-scope>
13.
14.      <managed-property>
15.         <property-name>titleKey</property-name>
16.         <value>aliceInWonderland</value>
17.      </managed-property>
18.
19.      <managed-property>
20.         <property-name>image</property-name>
21.         <value>cheshire.jpg</value>
22.      </managed-property>
23.
24.      <managed-property>
25.         <property-name>numChapters</property-name>
26.         <property-class>java.lang.Integer</property-class>
27.         <value>12</value>
28.      </managed-property>
29.   </managed-bean>
30. </faces-config>
```

Listing 8–3 `book-viewer-monolith/WEB-INF/classes/com/corejsf/Book.java`

```
1. package com.corejsf;
2.
3. import java.util.LinkedList;
4. import java.util.List;
5.
6. public class Book {
7.    private String titleKey;
8.    private String image;
9.    private int numChapters;
10.   private List chapterKeys = null;
```

Listing 8–3   book-viewer-monolith/WEB-INF/classes/com/corejsf/Book.java (cont.)

```java
11.
12.    // PROPERTY: titleKey
13.    public void setTitleKey(String titleKey) { this.titleKey = titleKey; }
14.    public String getTitleKey() { return titleKey; }
15.
16.    // PROPERTY: image
17.    public void setImage(String image) { this.image = image; }
18.    public String getImage() { return image; }
19.
20.    // PROPERTY: numChapters
21.    public void setNumChapters(int numChapters) { this.numChapters = numChapters;}
22.    public int getNumChapters() { return numChapters; }
23.
24.    // PROPERTY: chapterKeys
25.    public List getChapterKeys() {
26.       if(chapterKeys == null) {
27.          chapterKeys = new LinkedList();
28.          for(int i=1; i <= numChapters; ++i)
29.             chapterKeys.add("chapter" + i);
30.       }
31.       return chapterKeys;
32.    }
33. }
```

Listing 8–4   book-viewer-monolith/WEB-INF/classes/com/corejsf/
messages.properties

```
1. bookWindowTitle=Welcome to Alice in Wonderland
2. aliceInWonderland=Alice in Wonderland
3.
4. chapter1=Chapter 1
5. chapter2=Chapter 2
6. chapter3=Chapter 3
7. chapter4=Chapter 4
8. chapter5=Chapter 5
9. chapter6=Chapter 6
10. chapter7=Chapter 7
11. chapter8=Chapter 8
12. chapter9=Chapter 9
13. chapter10=Chapter 10
14. chapter11=Chapter 11
15. chapter12=Chapter 12
16. chapter13=Chapter 13
17. chapter14=Chapter 14
18. chapter15=Chapter 15
```

Listing 8–5	book-viewer-monolith/styles.css

```css
1.  .bookHeader {
2.      width: 100%;
3.      text-align: center;
4.      background-color: #eee;
5.      padding: 0 px;
6.      border: thin solid CornflowerBlue;
7.  }
8.  .bookTitle {
9.      text-align: center;
10.     font-style: italic;
11.     font-size: 1.3em;
12.     font-family: Helvetica;
13. }
14. .book {
15.     vertical-align: top;
16.     width: 100%;
17.     height: 100%;
18. }
19. .menuColumn {
20.     vertical-align: top;
21.     background-color: #eee;
22.     width: 100px;
23.     border: thin solid #777;
24. }
25. .chapterColumn {
26.     vertical-align: top;
27.     text-align: left;
28.     width: *;
29. }
```

Common Content Inclusion

A monolithic JSF page is a poor choice for the book viewer because the JSF page is difficult to modify. Also, realize that our monolithic JSF page represents two things: layout and content.

Layout is implemented with an h:panelGrid tag, and content is represented by various JSF tags, such as h:graphicImage, h:outputText, h:commandLink, and the book chapters. Realize that *with a monolithic JSF page, we cannot reuse content or layout.*

In the next section we concentrate on including content. In "Looking at Tiles" on page 330, we discuss including layout.

Content Inclusion in JSP-Based Applications

Instead of cramming a bunch of code into a monolithic JSF page, as we did in Listing 8–1 on page 322, it's better to include common content so you can reuse that content in other JSF pages. With JSP, you have three choices for including content:

- `<%@ include file="header.jsp"% >`
- `<jsp:include page="header.jsp"/>`
- `<c:import url="header.jsp"/>`

The first choice listed above—the JSP `include` directive—includes the specified file before the enclosing JSF page is compiled to a servlet. However, the `include` directive suffers from an important limitation: If the included file's content changes after the enclosing page was first processed, those changes are not reflected in the enclosing page. That means you must manually update the enclosing pages—whether the including pages changed or not—whenever included content changes.

The last two choices listed above include the content of a page at runtime and merge the included content with the including JSF page. Because the inclusion happens at runtime, changes to included pages are always reflected when the enclosing page is redisplayed. For that reason, `jsp:include` and `c:import` are usually preferred to the `include` directive.

The `c:import` tag works just like `jsp:include`, but it has more features; for example, `c:import` can import resources from another web application, whereas `jsp:include` cannot. Also, prior to JSP 2.0, you cannot use JSP expressions for `jsp:include` attributes, whereas you can with `c:import`. Remember that you must import the JSTL core tag library to use `c:import`.

Throughout this chapter, we use `c:import` for consistency. You can use either `jsp:include` or `c:import` to dynamically include content. If you don't need `c:import`'s extra features, then it's ever-so-slightly easier to use `jsp:include` because you don't need to import the JSTL core tag library.

JSF-Specific Considerations

Regardless of whether you include content with the `include` directive, `jsp:include`, or `c:import`, there are two special considerations that you must take into account when you include content in a JavaServer Faces application.

1. You must wrap included JSF tags in an `f:subview` tag.
2. Included JSF tags cannot contain f:view tags.

The first rule applies to included content that contains JSF tags. For example, the book viewer should encapsulate header content in its own JSF page so that we can reuse that content:

```
<%-- This is header .jsp --%>
<%@ taglib uri="http://java.sun.com/jsf/core" prefix="f" %>
<%@ taglib uri="http://java.sun.com/jsf/html" prefix="h" %>

<h:panelGrid columns="1" styleClass="header">
    <h:graphicImage value="books/book/cheshire.jpg"/>
    <h:outputText value="#{msgs.bookTitle}" styleClass="bookTitle"/>
    ...
</h:panelGrid>
```

Now we can include that content from the original JSF page:

```
<%-- This is from the original JSF page --%>
<f:view>

    ...
    <f:subview id="header">
        <c:import url="header.jsp"/>
    </f:subview>
    ...
</f:view>
```

You must assign an ID to each subview. The standard convention for including content is to name the subview after the imported JSF page.

JSF views, which are normally web pages, can contain an unlimited number of subviews. But there can be only one view. Because of that restriction, included JSF tags—which must be wrapped in a subview—cannot contain f:view tags.

CAUTION: The book-viewer-include application maps the Faces servlet to `*.faces`. That means you can start the application with this URL: http://www.localhost:8080/book-viewer-include/book.faces. The Faces servlet maps books.faces to books.jsp. However, you can't use the faces suffix when you use c:import. If you use c:import, you must use the jsp suffix.

Content Inclusion in the Book Viewer

To include content in the book viewer, we split our monolithic JSF page into four files: the original JSF page, /header.jsp, /menu.jsp, and /content.jsp. We include the header, menu, and content in the original JSF page:

```
<h:panelGrid columns="2" styleClass="book"
    columnClasses="menuColumn, contentColumn">

    <f:facet name="header">
        <f:subview id="header">
            <c:import url="header.jsp"/>
        </f:subview>
```

```
          </f:facet>

          <f:subview id="menu">
              <c:import url="menu.jsp"/>
          </f:subview>
          <f:subview id="content">
              <c:import url="content.jsp"/>
          </f:subview>
      </h:panelGrid>
      ...
```

This code is much cleaner than the original JSF page listed in Listing 8–1 on page 322, so it's easier to understand, maintain, and modify. But more importantly, we are now free to reuse the header, menu, and content for other views. For example, to use the book-viewer with another book, all we have to do is change the book's `titleKey`, `image`, and `numChapters` properties in `faces-config.xml`.

The directory structure for the book viewer with includes example is shown in Figure 8–5. Listing 8–6 through Listing 8–9 show the JSF pages for the book, its header, menu, and content.

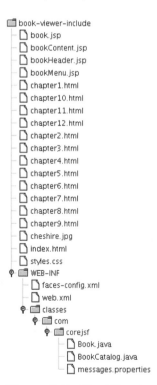

**Figure 8–5   The Directory Structure
                of the Book Viewer with Includes**

Listing 8–6   `book-viewer-include/book.jsp`

```
1.  <html>
2.     <%@ taglib uri="http://java.sun.com/jstl/core" prefix="c" %>
3.     <%@ taglib uri="http://java.sun.com/jsf/core"  prefix="f" %>
4.     <%@ taglib uri="http://java.sun.com/jsf/html"  prefix="h" %>
5.     <f:view>
6.        <head>
7.           <link href="styles.css" rel="stylesheet" type="text/css"/>
8.           <f:loadBundle basename="com.corejsf.messages" var="msgs"/>
9.           <title><h:outputText value="#{msgs.bookWindowTitle}"/></title>
10.       </head>
11.       <body>
12.          <h:form>
13.             <h:panelGrid columns="2" styleClass="book"
14.                   columnClasses="menuColumn, chapterColumn">
15.                <f:facet name="header">
16.                   <f:subview id="header">
17.                      <c:import url="/bookHeader.jsp"/>
18.                   </f:subview>
19.                </f:facet>
20.
21.                <f:subview id="menu">
22.                   <c:import url="/bookMenu.jsp"/>
23.                </f:subview>
24.
25.                <f:verbatim>
26.                   <c:import url="/bookContent.jsp"/>
27.                </f:verbatim>
28.             </h:panelGrid>
29.          </h:form>
30.       </body>
31.    </f:view>
32. </html>
```

Listing 8–7   `book-viewer-include/bookHeader.jsp`

```
1. <%@ taglib uri="http://java.sun.com/jsf/core" prefix="f" %>
2. <%@ taglib uri="http://java.sun.com/jsf/html" prefix="h" %>
3.
4. <h:panelGrid columns="1" styleClass="bookHeader">
5.    <h:graphicImage value="#{book.image}"/>
6.    <h:outputText value="#{msgs[book.titleKey]}" styleClass="bookTitle"/>
7.    <f:verbatim><hr></f:verbatim>
8. </h:panelGrid>
```

Listing 8–8   `book-viewer-include/bookMenu.jsp`

```
1. <%@ taglib uri="http://java.sun.com/jsf/core" prefix="f" %>
2. <%@ taglib uri="http://java.sun.com/jsf/html" prefix="h" %>
3.
4. <h:dataTable value="#{book.chapterKeys}" var="chapterKey"
5.       styleClass="links" columnClasses="linksColumn">
6.   <h:column>
7.     <h:commandLink>
8.       <h:outputText value="#{msgs[chapterKey]}"/>
9.       <f:param name="chapter" value="#{chapterKey}"/>
10.    </h:commandLink>
11.  </h:column>
12. </h:dataTable>
```

Listing 8–9   `book-viewer-include/bookContent.jsp`

```
1. <%@ taglib uri="http://java.sun.com/jstl/core" prefix="c" %>
2.
3. <c:import url="${param.chapter}.html"/>
```

Looking at Tiles

We've seen how to encapsulate and include content and how that strategy increases flexibility—it's much easier to reuse content if you include it rather than mixing it all in one file. Now that you can create user interfaces with pluggable content, you may be satisfied with that level of flexibility and reuse; but wait, there's more.

In addition to *encapsulating content*, you can use Tiles to *encapsulate layout*. For the application shown in Figure 8–2 on page 316, encapsulating layout means making the layout code—the h:panelGrid and its contents listed in Listing 8–6 on page 329—available for reuse. As it stands in Listing 8–6, that layout code can only be used by the JSF page shown in Figure 8–2. If you implement JSF pages with identical layouts, you must *replicate that layout code for every page*. With Tiles, you define a layout that can be reused by multiple *tiles*, which are nothing more mysterious than imported JSP pages. *Tiles lets you implement layout code once and reuse it among many pages.*

But reusing layout is just the beginning of the Tiles bag of tricks. You can do more:

- Nest tiles.
- Extend tiles.

- Restrict tiles to users of a particular role.
- Attach controllers (Java objects) to tiles that are invoked just before their tile is displayed.

Those are the core features that Tiles offers in the pursuit of the ultimate flexibility in crafting web-based user interfaces.

Installing Tiles

Tiles is distributed only with Struts 1.1, but it doesn't depend on Struts at all, so you can use it standalone or with other web application frameworks, such as JSF. Because Tiles comes with Struts, you must download Struts 1.1 from http://jakarta.apache.org/site/binindex.cgi.

Here is how you install Tiles:

1. Download Struts 1.1 from http://jakarta.apache.org/site/binindex.cgi.
2. Copy the following JAR files from $STRUTS_HOME/lib to /WEB-INF/lib: struts.jar, commons-beanutils.jar, commons-collections.jar, and commons-digester.jar
3. Add the Tiles servlet to your deployment descriptor (web.xml).
4. Set the Tiles configuration file to /WEB-INF/tiles.xml in web.xml.

Your deployment descriptor should look similar to the one listed in Listing 8–10.

Listing 8–10   /WEB-INF/web.xml

```
1. <?xml version="1.0"?>
2. <!DOCTYPE web-app PUBLIC
3.   "-//Sun Microsystems, Inc.//DTD Web Application 2.3//EN"
4.   "http://java.sun.com/dtd/web-app_2_3.dtd">
5.
6. <web-app>
7.   <servlet>
8.     <servlet-name>Tiles Servlet</servlet-name>
9.     <servlet-class>org.apache.struts.tiles.TilesServlet</servlet-class>
10.     <init-param>
11.       <param-name>definitions-config</param-name>
12.       <param-value>/WEB-INF/tiles.xml</param-value>
13.     </init-param>
14.     <load-on-startup>2</load-on-startup>
15.   </servlet>
16.
17.   <servlet>
18.     <servlet-name>Faces Servlet</servlet-name>
```

Listing 8–10	/WEB-INF/web.xml (cont.)

```
19.        <servlet-class>javax.faces.webapp.FacesServlet</servlet-class>
20.        <load-on-startup>1</load-on-startup>
21.    </servlet>
22.
23.    <servlet-mapping>
24.        <servlet-name>Faces Servlet</servlet-name>
25.        <url-pattern>*.faces</url-pattern>
26.    </servlet-mapping>
27.
28.    <welcome-file-list>
29.        <welcome-file>index.html</welcome-file>
30.    </welcome-file-list>
31. </web-app>
```

Notice that you must load the Tiles servlet when your application starts. You do that with the load-on-startup element, as we did in the preceding listing.

The definitions-config initialization parameter for the Tiles servlet specifies either a single configuration file—as we did in the preceding listing—or a comma-separated list of configuration files. Those configuration files contain your tile definitions. You can name those files anything you want as long as they end in .xml. In Listing 8–10 we specified a single file in /WEB-INF named tiles.xml. The following section shows you what to put in your Tiles configuration files.

Using Tiles with the Book Viewer

Using Tiles with JSF is a simple three-step process:

1. Use tiles:insert to insert a tile definition in a JSF page.

2. Define the tile in your Tiles configuration file.

3. Implement the tile's layout.

For the book viewer, we start in book.jsp, where we insert a tile named book:

```
...
<%@ taglib uri="http://jakarta.apache.org/struts/tags-tiles"
    prefix="tiles" %>
...
<h:form>
    <tiles:insert definition="book" flush="false"/>
</h:form>
...
```

We define the book tile in /WEB-INF/tiles.xml:

```
<definition name="book" path="/headerMenuContentLayout.jsp">
    <put name="header"  value="/bookHeader.jsp"/>
    <put name="menu" value="/bookMenu.jsp"/>
    <put name="content" value="/bookContent.jsp"/>
</definition>
```

The previous snippet of XML defines a tile. The tile's layout is specified with the definition element's path attribute. The tile attributes, specified with put elements, are used by the layout. That layout looks like this:

```
<%-- this is /headerMenuContentLayout.jsp --%>

<%@ taglib uri="http://java.sun.com/jsf/html" prefix="h"%>
<%@ taglib uri="http://java.sun.com/jsf/core" prefix="f"%>
<%@ taglib uri="http://jakarta.apache.org/struts/tags-tiles" prefix="tiles"%>

<h:panelGrid columns="2" styleClass="gridClass"
    headerClass="headerClass"
    columnClasses="menuClass, contentClass">

    <f:facet name="header">
        <f:subview id="header">
          <tiles:insert attribute="header" flush="false"/>
        </f:subview>
    </f:facet>

    <f:subview id="menu">
        <tiles:insert attribute="menu" flush="false"/>
    </f:subview>

    <f:subview id="content">
        <tiles:insert attribute="content" flush="false"/>
    </f:subview>
</h:panelGrid>
```

The tiles:insert tag dynamically includes content. That content is the value of the attribute tag of tiles:insert. For example, the preceding code inserts the header attribute. That attribute's value is /header.jsp, so tiles:insert dynamically includes that file.

Notice that we specified a flush="false" attribute for the tiles:insert tag. That is necessary for most modern servlet containers because those containers disallow buffer flushing inside custom tags. If your servlet container throws an exception stating that you cannot flush from a custom tag, then you know you've forgotten to specify that attribute, which is true by default.

What have we gained by using Tiles in this example? *We've encapsulated layout so that we can reuse it in other tiles, instead of replicating that layout code from one JSF page to another.* For example, you could reuse the book viewer's layout, implemented in /headerMenuContentLayout.jsp, for other pages in the application that have the same layout.

Parameterizing Tiles

There's one flaw to the layout listed in the previous section: it hardcodes CSS classes, namely gridClass, headerClass, menuClass, and contentClass. That means that every web page using the header-menu-content layout will have the same look and feel. It would be better if we could parameterize the CSS class names. That way, other tiles with a header-menu-content layout could define their own look and feel. Let's see how we can do that. First, we add three attributes to the book tile:

```
<definition name="book" path="/headerMenuContentLayout.jsp">
    <put name="headerClass"  value="headerClass"/>
    <put name="menuClass" value="menuClass"/>
    <put name="contentClass" value="contentClass"/>

    <put name="header" value="/bookHeader.jsp"/>
    <put name="menu" value="/bookMenu.jsp"/>
    <put name="content" value="/bookContent.jsp"/>
</definition>
```

Then we use those attributes in the layout:

```
<%-- this is an excerpt of /headerMenuContentLayout.jsp --%>
...
<tiles:importAttribute scope="request"/>

<h:panelGrid columns="2" styleClass="#{gridClass}"
    headerClass="#{headerClass}"
    columnClasses="#{menuClass}, #{contentClass}">
    ...
</h:panelGrid>
```

Tile attributes, such as headerClass, menuClass, etc., in the preceding code, exist in *tiles scope*, which is inaccessible to JavaServer Faces. To make our attributes accessible to the layout JSF page listed above, we use the tiles:importAttribute tag. That tag imports all tile attributes to the scope you specify with the scope attribute. In the preceding code, we imported them to request scope.

Now we can specify different CSS classes for other tiles:

```
<definition name="anotherTile" path="/headerMenuContentLayout.jsp">
    <put name="headerClass"  value="aDifferentHeaderClass"/>
    ...
</definition>
```

 NOTE: The tiles:importAttribute tag also lets you import one attribute at a time; for example: <tiles:importAttribute name="headerClass" scope="..."/>.

Extending Tiles

In "Parameterizing Tiles" on page 334 we defined a tile that looked like this:

```
<definition name="book" path="/headerMenuContentLayout.jsp">
    <put name="headerClass"  value="headerClass"/>
    <put name="menuClass" value="menuClass"/>
    <put name="contentClass" value="contentClass"/>

    <put name="header"  value="/bookHeader.jsp"/>
    <put name="menu" value="/bookMenu.jsp"/>
    <put name="content" value="/bookContent.jsp"/>
</definition>
```

There are two distinct types of attributes in that tile: CSS classes and included content. Although the latter is specific to the book tile, the former can be used by tiles that represent something other than books. Because of that generality, we split the book tile into two:

```
<definition name="header-menu-content" path="/headerMenuContentLayout.jsp">
    <put name="headerClass"  value="headerClass"/>
    <put name="menuClass" value="menuClass"/>
    <put name="contentClass" value="contentClass"/>
</definition
```

```
<definition name="book" extends="header-menu-content">
    <put name="header"  value="/bookHeader.jsp"/>
    <put name="menu" value="/bookMenu.jsp"/>
    <put name="content" value="/bookContent.jsp"/>
</definition>
```

Now the book tile *extends* the header-menu-content tile. When you extend a tile, you inherit its attributes, much the same as object-oriented inheritance. Because of that inheritance, both book tile definitions in this section have the same attributes. But now, part of the original book tile—the CSS class attributes—are available for reuse by other tiles that extend the header-menu-content tile.

> NOTE: Here's one more thing to consider about Tiles. Imagine the book
> viewer has been a huge success and Project Gutenberg has commissioned
> you to implement a library that can display all 6,000+ of their books. You define
> more than 6,000 tiles that reuse the same layout—one tile for each book—and
> present your finished product to the folks at Gutenberg. They think it's great, but
> they want you to add a footer to the bottom of the page. Since you've used Tiles,
> you only need to change the single layout used by all your tiles. Imagine the diffi-
> culty you would encounter making that change if you had replicated the layout
> code more than 6,000 times!

Figure 8–6 shows the directory structure for the "tileized" version of the book
viewer. That directory structure is the same as the previous version of the book
viewer, except that we've added a layout—headerMenuContentLayout.jsp—and the
tiles definition file, /WEB-INF/tiles.xml.

```
book-viewer-tiles-extends
├─ .classpath
├─ .project
├─ blank.jsp
├─ book.jsp
├─ bookContent.jsp
├─ bookHeader.jsp
├─ bookMenu.jsp
├─ chapter1.html
├─ chapter10.html
├─ chapter11.html
├─ chapter12.html
├─ chapter2.html
├─ chapter3.html
├─ chapter4.html
├─ chapter5.html
├─ chapter6.html
├─ chapter7.html
├─ chapter8.html
├─ chapter9.html
├─ cheshire.jpg
├─ headerMenuContentLayout.jsp
├─ index.html
├─ styles.css
├─ WEB-INF
│   ├─ faces-config.xml
│   ├─ tiles.xml
│   ├─ web.xml
│   ├─ classes
│   │   └─ com
│   │       └─ corejsf
│   │           ├─ Book.java
│   │           ├─ BookCatalog.java
│   │           └─ messages.properties
```

**Figure 8–6   Book Viewer with
Extended Tile Directory Structure**

Listing 8–11 through Listing 8–13 show the Tiles definition file, the book layout, and the JSF page that displays Alice in Wonderland. We left out the listings of the other files in the application because they are unchanged from the application discussed in "Content Inclusion in JSP-Based Applications" on page 326.

Listing 8–11 `book-viewer-tiles/WEB-INF/tiles.xml`

```
1. <!DOCTYPE tiles-definitions PUBLIC
2. "-//Apache Software Foundation//DTD Tiles Configuration//EN"
3. "http://jakarta.apache.org/struts/dtds/tiles-config.dtd">
4.
5. <tiles-definitions>
6.    <definition name="menu-header-content" path="/headerMenuContentLayout.jsp">
7.       <put name="gridClass"          value="headerMenuContent"/>
8.       <put name="headerClass"        value="header"/>
9.       <put name="menuColumnClass"    value="menuColumn"/>
10.      <put name="contentColumnClass" value="contentColumn"/>
11.   </definition>
12.
13.   <definition name="book" extends="menu-header-content">
14.      <put name="header"  value="/bookHeader.jsp"/>
15.      <put name="menu"    value="/bookMenu.jsp"/>
16.      <put name="content" value="/bookContent.jsp"/>
17.   </definition>
18. </tiles-definitions>
```

Listing 8–12 `book-viewer-tiles/headerMenuContentLayout.jsp`

```
1. <%@ taglib uri="http://java.sun.com/jsf/core"  prefix="f" %>
2. <%@ taglib uri="http://java.sun.com/jsf/html"  prefix="h" %>
3. <%@ taglib uri="http://jakarta.apache.org/struts/tags-tiles" prefix="tiles" %>
4.
5. <tiles:importAttribute scope="request"/>
6.
7. <h:panelGrid columns="2" styleClass="#{gridClass}"
8.    headerClass="#{headerClass}"
9.       columnClasses="#{menuColumnClass}, #{contentColumnClass}">
10.   <f:facet name="header">
11.      <f:subview id="header">
12.         <tiles:insert attribute="header" flush="false"/>
13.      </f:subview>
14.   </f:facet>
15.   <f:subview id="menu">
16.      <tiles:insert attribute="menu" flush="false"/>
```

Listing 8–12	book-viewer-tiles/headerMenuContentLayout.jsp (cont.)

```
17.     </f:subview>
18.
19.     <f:verbatim>
20.         <tiles:insert attribute="content" flush="false"/>
21.     </f:verbatim>
22.  </h:panelGrid>
```

Listing 8–13	book-viewer-tiles/book.jsp

```
1.  <html>
2.      <%@ taglib uri="http://java.sun.com/jstl/core" prefix="c" %>
3.      <%@ taglib uri="http://java.sun.com/jsf/core"  prefix="f" %>
4.      <%@ taglib uri="http://java.sun.com/jsf/html"  prefix="h" %>
5.      <%@ taglib uri="http://jakarta.apache.org/struts/tags-tiles" prefix="tiles" %>
6.
7.      <f:view>
8.          <head>
9.              <link href="styles.css" rel="stylesheet" type="text/css"/>
10.             <f:loadBundle basename="com.corejsf.messages" var="msgs"/>
11.             <title><h:outputText value="#{msgs.bookWindowTitle}"/></title>
12.         </head>
13.         <body>
14.             <f:subview id="book">
15.                 <h:form>
16.                     <tiles:insert definition="book" flush="false"/>
17.                 </h:form>
18.             </f:subview>
19.         </body>
20.     </f:view>
21.  </html>
```

The Library

In this section, we turn the book viewer into a library, shown in Figure 8–7.

The library application shown in Figure 8–7 contains a menu at the top of the page that lets you select a book, either Alice in Wonderland or Peter Pan. The rest of the application works like the book viewer we've discussed throughout this chapter.

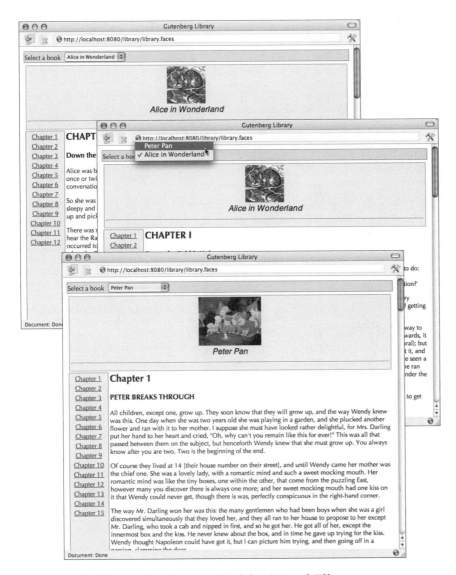

Figure 8–7 Library Implemented with JSF and Tiles

The library employs two Tiles techniques that are of interest to us: nesting tiles and using tile controllers.

Nested Tiles

The library shown in Figure 8–7 contains a book viewer. So does the library tile:

```
<definition name="book">
   ...
</definition>

<definition name="library" path="/libraryLayout.jsp"
      controllerClass="com.corejsf.LibraryTileController">
   <put name="header"  value="/bookSelector.jsp"/>
   <put name="book" value="book"/>
</definition>
```

Notice the value for the book attribute—it's a tile, not a JSP page. Using a tile name instead of a JSP page lets you nest tiles, as we did by nesting the book tile in the library.

Tile Controllers

In our book viewer application, we had one managed bean named book—see "The Book Viewer" on page 318 for more information about the book bean. The library, on the other hand, must be aware of more than one book.

In this section—with a sleight of hand—we show you how to support multiple books without having to change the book viewer. The book viewer will continue to manipulate a book bean, but that bean will no longer be a managed bean. Instead, it will be the book that was last selected in the library's pull-down menu at the top of the page.

We accomplish that sleight of hand with a Tiles controller. Tiles lets you attach a Java object, known as a tile controller, to a tile. That object's class must implement the org.apache.struts.tiles.Controller interface, which defines a single perform method. Tiles invokes that method just before it loads the controller's associated tile. Tile controllers have access to their tile's context, which lets the controller access the tile's attributes or create new attributes.

We attach a controller to the library tile. The controller looks for a library attribute in session scope. If the library's not there, the controller creates a library and stores it in session scope. The controller then consults the library's selectedBook property to see if a book has been selected. If so, the controller sets the value of the book session attribute to the selected book. If there is no selected book, the controller sets the book attribute to Alice in Wonderland. Subsequently, when the library tile is loaded, the book viewer accesses the selected book. The controller is listed in Listing 8–19 on page 345.

Figure 8–8 shows the directory structure for the library application. For brevity, we left out the book HTML files.

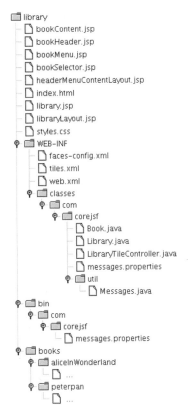

```
library
    bookContent.jsp
    bookHeader.jsp
    bookMenu.jsp
    bookSelector.jsp
    headerMenuContentLayout.jsp
    index.html
    library.jsp
    libraryLayout.jsp
    styles.css
    WEB-INF
        faces-config.xml
        tiles.xml
        web.xml
        classes
            com
                corejsf
                    Book.java
                    Library.java
                    LibraryTileController.java
                    messages.properties
                    util
                        Messages.java
    bin
        com
            corejsf
                messages.properties
    books
        aliceInWonderland
            ...
        peterpan
            ...
```

Figure 8–8   Library Directory Structure

The files shown in Figure 8–8 are listed in Listing 8–14 through Listing 8–27, with the exception of the HTML files. As you look through those listings, note the effort required to add a new book. All you have to do is modify the constructor in Library.java—see Listing 8–18 on page 343—to create your book and add it to the book map. You could even implement the Library class so that it reads XML book definitions. That way, you could add books without any programming. Digesting XML is an easy task with Tiles's distant cousin, the Apache Commons Digester. See http://jakarta.apache.org/commons/digester/ for more information about the Digester.

Listing 8–14   library/library.jsp

```
1.  <html>
2.    <%@ taglib uri="http://java.sun.com/jsf/core"  prefix="f" %>
3.    <%@ taglib uri="http://java.sun.com/jsf/html"  prefix="h" %>
4.    <%@ taglib uri="http://jakarta.apache.org/struts/tags-tiles" prefix="tiles" %>
5.
6.    <f:view>
7.      <head>
8.        <link href="styles.css" rel="stylesheet" type="text/css"/>
9.        <f:loadBundle basename="com.corejsf.messages" var="msgs"/>
10.       <title><h:outputText value="#{msgs.libraryWindowTitle}"/></title>
11.     </head>
12.     <body>
13.       <f:subview id="library">
14.         <h:form>
15.           <tiles:insert definition="library" flush="false"/>
16.         </h:form>
17.       </f:subview>
18.     </body>
19.   </f:view>
20. </html>
```

Listing 8–15   library/WEB-INF/tiles.xml

```
1.  <!DOCTYPE tiles-definitions PUBLIC
2.  "-//Apache Software Foundation//DTD Tiles Configuration//EN"
3.  "http://jakarta.apache.org/struts/dtds/tiles-config.dtd">
4.
5.  <tiles-definitions>
6.    <definition name="menu-header-content" path="/headerMenuContentLayout.jsp">
7.      <put name="gridClass"          value="headerMenuContent"/>
8.      <put name="headerClass"        value="header"/>
9.      <put name="menuColumnClass"    value="menuColumn"/>
10.     <put name="contentColumnClass" value="contentColumn"/>
11.   </definition>
12.
13.   <definition name="book" extends="menu-header-content">
14.     <put name="header"  value="/bookHeader.jsp"/>
15.     <put name="menu"    value="/bookMenu.jsp"/>
16.     <put name="content" value="/bookContent.jsp"/>
17.   </definition>
18.
19.   <definition name="library" path="/libraryLayout.jsp"
20.                 controllerClass="com.corejsf.LibraryTileController">
21.     <put name="header"  value="/bookSelector.jsp"/>
22.     <put name="book" value="book"/>
23.   </definition>
24. </tiles-definitions>
```

Listing 8–16 `library/libraryLayout.jsp`

```
1. <%@ taglib uri="http://java.sun.com/jsf/core"  prefix="f" %>
2. <%@ taglib uri="http://java.sun.com/jsf/html"  prefix="h" %>
3. <%@ taglib uri="http://jakarta.apache.org/struts/tags-tiles" prefix="tiles" %>
4.
5. <h:panelGrid columns="1" styleClass="book" headerClass="libraryHeader">
6.    <f:facet name="header">
7.       <f:subview id="header">
8.          <tiles:insert attribute="header" flush="false"/>
9.       </f:subview>
10.    </f:facet>
11.
12.    <f:subview id="book">
13.       <tiles:insert attribute="book" flush="false"/>
14.    </f:subview>
15. </h:panelGrid>
```

Listing 8–17 `library/bookSelector.jsp`

```
1. <%@ taglib uri="http://java.sun.com/jsf/core" prefix="f" %>
2. <%@ taglib uri="http://java.sun.com/jsf/html" prefix="h" %>
3.
4. <h:outputText value="#{msgs.selectABookPrompt}"/>
5.
6. <f:verbatim>  </f:verbatim>
7.
8. <h:selectOneMenu onchange="submit()" value="#{library.book}"
9.       valueChangeListener="#{library.bookSelected}">
10.    <f:selectItems value="#{library.bookItems}"/>
11. </h:selectOneMenu>
```

Listing 8–18 `library/WEB-INF/classes/com/corejsf/Library.java`

```
1. package com.corejsf;
2.
3. import java.util.*;
4. import javax.faces.model.SelectItem;
5. import javax.faces.event.ValueChangeEvent;
6.
7. public class Library {
8.    private Map bookMap = new HashMap();
9.    private Book initialBook = null;
10.    private List bookItems = null;
11.    private String book = null;
12.    private String selectedBook = null;
13.
14.    public Library() {
```

Listing 8–18 library/WEB-INF/classes/com/corejsf/Library.java (cont.)

```
15.        Book peterpan = new Book();
16.        Book aliceInWonderland = new Book();
17.
18.        initialBook = peterpan;
19.
20.        aliceInWonderland.setDirectory("books/aliceInWonderland");
21.        aliceInWonderland.setTitleKey("aliceInWonderland");
22.        aliceInWonderland.setImage("books/aliceInWonderland/cheshire.jpg");
23.        aliceInWonderland.setNumChapters(12);
24.
25.        peterpan.setDirectory("books/peterpan");
26.        peterpan.setTitleKey("peterpan");
27.        peterpan.setImage("books/peterpan/peterpan.jpg");
28.        peterpan.setNumChapters(15);
29.
30.        bookMap.put("aliceInWonderland", aliceInWonderland);
31.        bookMap.put("peterpan", peterpan);
32.     }
33.     public void setBook(String book) { this.book = book; }
34.     public String getBook() { return book; }
35.
36.     public Map getBooks() {
37.        return bookMap;
38.     }
39.     public void bookSelected(ValueChangeEvent e) {
40.        selectedBook = (String) e.getNewValue();
41.     }
42.     public Book getSelectedBook() {
43.        return selectedBook != null ? (Book) bookMap.get(selectedBook) :
44.                                      initialBook;
45.     }
46.     public List getBookItems() {
47.        if(bookItems == null) {
48.           bookItems = new LinkedList();
49.           Iterator it = bookMap.values().iterator();
50.           while(it.hasNext()) {
51.              Book book = (Book)it.next();
52.              bookItems.add(new SelectItem(book.getTitleKey(),
53.                                getBookTitle(book.getTitleKey())));
54.           }
55.        }
56.        return bookItems;
57.     }
58.     private String getBookTitle(String key) {
59.        return com.corejsf.util.Messages.
60.                   getString("com.corejsf.messages", key, null);
61.     }
62. }
```

Listing 8–19   library/WEB-INF/classes/com/corejsf/LibraryTileController.java

```
 1. package com.corejsf;
 2.
 3.
 4. import java.io.IOException;
 5. import javax.servlet.ServletContext;
 6. import javax.servlet.ServletException;
 7. import javax.servlet.http.HttpServletRequest;
 8. import javax.servlet.http.HttpServletResponse;
 9. import javax.servlet.http.HttpSession;
10. import org.apache.struts.tiles.ComponentContext;
11. import org.apache.struts.tiles.Controller;
12.
13. public class LibraryTileController implements Controller {
14.     public void perform(ComponentContext tilesContext,
15.                     HttpServletRequest request, HttpServletResponse response,
16.                     ServletContext context)
17.                                 throws IOException, ServletException {
18.         HttpSession session = request.getSession();
19.
20.         String chapter = (String) request.getParameter("chapter");
21.         session.setAttribute("chapter", chapter == null || "".equals(chapter) ?
22.                     "chapter1" : chapter);
23.
24.         Library library = (Library) session.getAttribute("library");
25.
26.         if(library == null) {
27.             library = new Library();
28.             session.setAttribute("library", library);
29.         }
30.
31.         Book selectedBook = library.getSelectedBook();
32.         if(selectedBook != null) {
33.             session.setAttribute("book", selectedBook);
34.         }
35.     }
36. }
```

Listing 8–20   library/WEB-INF/classes/com/corejsf/Book.java

```
 1. package com.corejsf;
 2.
 3. import java.util.LinkedList;
 4. import java.util.List;
 5.
 6. public class Book {
 7.     private String titleKey;
```

Listing 8–20 library/WEB-INF/classes/com/corejsf/Book.java (cont.)

```
8.    private String image;
9.    private String directory;
10.   private int numChapters;
11.   private List chapterKeys = null;
12.
13.   // PROPERTY: titleKey
14.   public void setTitleKey(String titleKey) { this.titleKey = titleKey; }
15.   public String getTitleKey() { return titleKey; }
16.
17.   // PROPERTY: image
18.   public void setImage(String image) { this.image = image; }
19.   public String getImage() { return image; }
20.
21.   // PROPERTY: directory
22.   public void setDirectory(String directory) { this.directory = directory; }
23.   public String getDirectory() { return directory; }
24.
25.   // PROPERTY: numChapters
26.   public void setNumChapters(int numChapters) { this.numChapters = numChapters; }
27.   public int getNumChapters() { return numChapters; }
28.
29.   // PROPERTY: chapterKeys
30.   public List getChapterKeys() {
31.      if(chapterKeys == null) {
32.         chapterKeys = new LinkedList();
33.         for(int i=1; i <= numChapters; ++i)
34.            chapterKeys.add("chapter" + i);
35.      }
36.      return chapterKeys;
37.   }
38. }
```

Listing 8–21 library/bookHeader.jsp

```
1. <%@ taglib uri="http://java.sun.com/jsf/core" prefix="f" %>
2. <%@ taglib uri="http://java.sun.com/jsf/html" prefix="h" %>
3.
4. <h:panelGrid columns="1" styleClass="bookHeader">
5.    <h:graphicImage value="#{book.image}"/>
6.    <h:outputText value="#{msgs[book.titleKey]}" styleClass="bookTitle"/>
7.    <f:verbatim><hr></f:verbatim>
8. </h:panelGrid>
```

Listing 8–22   `library/bookMenu.jsp`

```
1. <%@ taglib uri="http://java.sun.com/jsf/core" prefix="f" %>
2. <%@ taglib uri="http://java.sun.com/jsf/html" prefix="h" %>
3.
4. <h:dataTable value="#{book.chapterKeys}" var="chapterKey"
5.        styleClass="links" columnClasses="linksColumn">
6.   <h:column>
7.     <h:commandLink>
8.       <h:outputText value="#{msgs[chapterKey]}"/>
9.       <f:param name="chapter" value="#{chapterKey}"/>
10.    </h:commandLink>
11.  </h:column>
12. </h:dataTable>
```

Listing 8–23   `library/bookContent.jsp`

```
1. <%@ taglib uri="http://java.sun.com/jstl/core" prefix="c" %>
2.
3. <c:import url="${book.directory}/${chapter}.html"/>
```

Listing 8–24   `library/styles.css`

```
1. .library {
2.    vertical-align: top;
3.    width: 100%;
4.    height: 100%;
5. }
6. .libraryHeader {
7.    width: 100%;
8.    text-align: left;
9.    vertical-align: top;
10.   background-color: #ddd;
11.   font-weight: lighter;
12.   border: thin solid #777;
13. }
14. .bookHeader {
15.   width: 100%;
16.   text-align: center;
17.   background-color: #eee;
18.   border: thin solid CornflowerBlue;
19. }
20. .bookTitle {
21.   text-align: center;
22.   font-style: italic;
23.   font-size: 1.3em;
24.   font-family: Helvetica;
```

Listing 8–24   library/styles.css (cont.)

```
25. }
26. .menuColumn {
27.    vertical-align: top;
28.    background-color: #eee;
29.    border: thin solid #777;
30. }
31. .chapterColumn {
32.    vertical-align: top;
33.    text-align: left;
34.    width: *;
35.    padding: 3px;
36. }
37. .contentColumn {
38.    vertical-align: top;
39.    text-align: left;
40.    width: *;
41. }
42. .links {
43.    width: 85px;
44.    vertical-align: top;
45.    text-align: center;
46. }
47. .linksColumn {
48.    vertical-align: top;
49.    text-align: center;
50. }
```

Listing 8–25   library/WEB-INF/faces-config.xml

```
1. <?xml version="1.0"?>
2.
3. <!DOCTYPE faces-config PUBLIC
4.    "-//Sun Microsystems, Inc.//DTD JavaServer Faces Config 1.0//EN"
5.    "http://java.sun.com/dtd/web-facesconfig_1_0.dtd">
6.
7. <faces-config>
8.
9. </faces-config>
```

Listing 8–26   library/WEB-INF/web.xml

```
1. <?xml version="1.0"?>
2. <!DOCTYPE web-app PUBLIC
3.    "-//Sun Microsystems, Inc.//DTD Web Application 2.3//EN"
4.    "http://java.sun.com/dtd/web-app_2_3.dtd">
5. <web-app>
6.    <servlet>
```

Listing 8–26 `library/WEB-INF/web.xml (cont.)`

```
7.    <servlet-name>Tiles Servlet</servlet-name>
8.    <servlet-class>org.apache.struts.tiles.TilesServlet</servlet-class>
9.    <init-param>
10.      <param-name>definitions-config</param-name>
11.      <param-value>/WEB-INF/tiles.xml</param-value>
12.    </init-param>
13.    <load-on-startup>2</load-on-startup>
14.   </servlet>
15.
16.   <servlet>
17.    <servlet-name>Faces Servlet</servlet-name>
18.    <servlet-class>javax.faces.webapp.FacesServlet</servlet-class>
19.    <load-on-startup>1</load-on-startup>
20.   </servlet>
21.
22.   <servlet-mapping>
23.    <servlet-name>Faces Servlet</servlet-name>
24.    <url-pattern>*.faces</url-pattern>
25.   </servlet-mapping>
26.
27.   <welcome-file-list>
28.    <welcome-file>index.html</welcome-file>
29.   </welcome-file-list>
30. </web-app>
```

Listing 8–27 `library/classes/com/corejsf/messages.properties`

```
1. libraryWindowTitle=Gutenberg Library
2. aliceInWonderland=Alice in Wonderland
3. peterpan=Peter Pan
4. selectABookPrompt=Select a book
5.
6. chapter1=Chapter 1
7. chapter2=Chapter 2
8. chapter3=Chapter 3
9. chapter4=Chapter 4
10. chapter5=Chapter 5
11. chapter6=Chapter 6
12. chapter7=Chapter 7
13. chapter8=Chapter 8
14. chapter9=Chapter 9
15. chapter10=Chapter 10
16. chapter11=Chapter 11
17. chapter12=Chapter 12
18. chapter13=Chapter 13
19. chapter14=Chapter 14
20. chapter15=Chapter 15
```

CUSTOM
COMPONENTS

Topics in This Chapter

Chapter

9

JSF provides a basic set of components for building HTML-based web applications such as text fields, checkboxes, buttons, and so on. However, most user-interface designers will desire more advanced components, such as calendars, tabbed panes, or navigation trees, that are not part of the standard JSF component set. Fortunately, JSF makes it possible to build reusable JSF components with rich behavior.

This chapter shows you how to implement custom components. We use two custom components—a tabbed pane and a spinner, shown in Figure 9–1—to illustrate the various aspects of creating custom components.

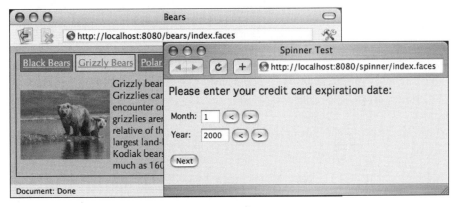

Figure 9–1   The TabbedPane and the Spinner

The JSF API lets you implement custom components and associated tags with the same features as the JSF standard tags. For example, h:input uses a value binding to associate a text field's value with a bean property—you could use value bindings to wire calendar cells to bean properties. JSF standard input components fire value change events when their value changes—you could fire value change events when a different date is selected in the calendar.

The first part of this chapter uses the spinner component to illustrate basic issúes that you encounter in all custom components. We then revisit the spinner to show more advanced issues:

- "Using an External Renderer" on page 378
- "Calling Converters from External Renderers" on page 384
- "Supporting Value Change Listeners" on page 385
- "Supporting Method Bindings" on page 386

The second half of the chapter examines a tabbed pane component that illustrates the following aspects of custom component development.

- "Processing SelectItem Children" on page 406
- "Processing Facets" on page 407
- "Encoding CSS Styles" on page 410
- "Using Hidden Fields" on page 411
- "Saving and Restoring State" on page 412
- "Firing Action Events" on page 414

Implementing Custom Components with Classes

In the following sections, we discuss the classes that you need to implement custom components.

To motivate the discussion, we will develop a spinner component. A spinner lets you enter a number in a text field, either by typing it directly in the field or by activating an increment or decrement button. Figure 9–2 shows an application that uses two spinners for a credit card's expiration date, one for the month and another for the year.

In Figure 9–2, from top to bottom, all proceeds as expected. The user enters valid values so navigation takes us to a designated JSF page that echoes those values.

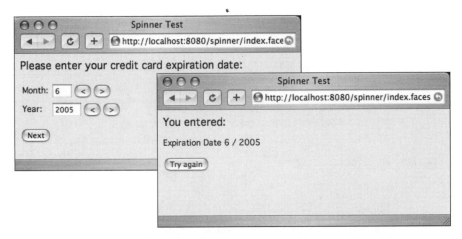

Figure 9–2 **Using the Spinner Component**

The spinner insists on integer values. Figure 9–3 shows an attempt to enter bad data. We let the standard integer converter handle conversion errors. You can see how we did it in "Using Converters" on page 364.

Here's how you use corejsf:spinner:

```
<%@ taglib uri="http://corejsf.com/spinner" prefix="corejsf" %>
...
<corejsf:spinner value="#{cardExpirationDate.month}"
    id="monthSpinner" minimum="1" maximum="12" size="3"/>
<h:message for="monthSpinner"/>
...
<corejsf:spinner value="#{cardExpirationDate.year}"
    id="yearSpinner" minimum="1900" maximum="2100" size="5"/>
<h:message for="yearSpinner"/>
```

The corejsf:spinner tag supports the following attributes.

- binding
- id
- minimum
- maximum
- rendered
- size
- value

Only one of the attributes—value—is required.

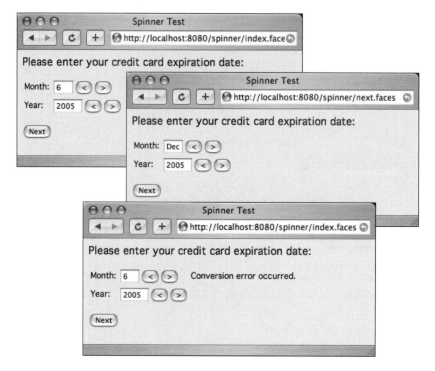

Figure 9–3 Handling Conversion Failures

The minimum and maximum attributes let you assign a range of valid values; for example, the month spinner has a minimum of 1 and a maximum of 12. You can also limit the size of the spinner's text field with the size attribute. The value attribute can take a literal string—for example, value="2"—or a value binding, for example, value="#{someBean.someProperty}".

Finally, the spinner supports the binding, id, and rendered attributes, which are discussed in Chapter 4. Support for those attributes is free because our tag class extends the javax.faces.webapp.UIComponentTag class.

In the preceding code fragment we assigned explicit identifiers to our spinners with the id attribute. We did that so we could display conversion errors with h:message. The spinner component doesn't require users to specify an identifier. If an identifier is not specified, JSF generates one automatically.

Users of JSF custom tags need not understand how those tags are implemented. Users simply need to know the functionality of a tag and the set of available attributes. Just as for any component model, the expectation is that a few skilled programmers will create tags that can be used by many page developers.

Tags and Components

Minimally, a tag for a JSF custom component requires two classes:

*   A class that processes tag attributes. By convention, the class name has a Tag suffix; for example, SpinnerTag.
*   A component class that maintains state, renders a user interface, and processes input. By convention, the class name has a UI prefix; for example, UISpinner.

The tag class is part of the plumbing. It creates the component and transfers tag attribute values to component properties and attributes. The implementation of the tag class is largely mechanical. See "Implementing Custom Component Tags" on page 367 for more information on tag classes.

The UI class does the important work. It has two separate responsibilities:

*   To *render* the user interface by encoding markup
*   To *process user input* by decoding the current HTTP request

Component classes can delegate rendering and processing input to a separate renderer. By using different renderers, you can support multiple clients such as web browsers and cell phones. Initially, our spinner component will render itself, but in "Using an External Renderer" on page 378, we show you how to implement a separate renderer for the spinner.

A component's UI class must extend the UIComponent class. That interface defines 36 methods, so you will want to extend an existing class that implements the interface. You can choose from the classes shown in Figure 9–4.

Our UISpinner class will extend UIInput, which extends UIOutput and implements the EditableValueHolder interface. Our UITabbedPane will extend UICommand, which implements the ActionSource interface.

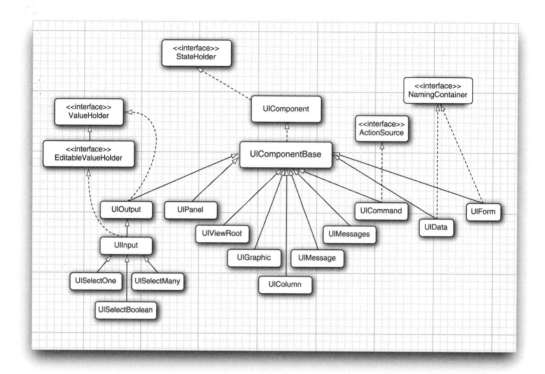

Figure 9–4 JSF Component Hierarchy (not all classes are shown)

The Custom Component Developer's Toolbox

When you implement custom components you will become very familiar with a handful of JSF classes:

- `javax.faces.component.UIComponent`
- `javax.faces.webapp.UIComponentTag`
- `javax.faces.context.FacesContext`
- `javax.faces.application.Application`
- `javax.faces.context.ResponseWriter`

`UIComponent` is an abstract class that defines what it means to be a component. Each component manages several important categories of data. These include:

- A list of *child components*. For example, the children of the `h:panelGrid` component are the components that are placed in the grid. However, a component need not have any children.
- A map of *facet components*. Facets are similar to child components, but each facet has a key, not a position in a list. It is up to the component how

to lay out its facets. For example, the h:dataTable component has header and footer facets.

- A map of *attributes*. This is a general-purpose map that you can use to store arbitrary key/value pairs.

- A map of *value bindings*. This is another general-purpose map that you can use to store arbitrary value bindings. For example, if the spinner tag has an attribute value="#{cardExpirationDate.month}", then the tag handler constructs a ValueBinding object for the given value binding expression and stores it under the key "value".

- A collection of *listeners*. This collection is maintained by the JSF framework.

When you define your own JSF components, you usually subclass one of the following three standard component classes:

- UICommand, if your component produces actions similar to a command button or link.

- UIOutput, if your component displays a value but does not allow the user to edit it.

- UIInput, if your component reads a value from the user (such as the spinner).

If you look at Figure 9–4, you will find that these three classes implement interfaces that specify these distinct responsibilities:

- ActionSource defines methods for managing action listeners and actions.

- ValueHolder defines methods for managing a component value, a local value, and a converter.

- EditableValueHolder extends ValueHolder and adds methods for managing validators and value change listeners.

TIP: You often need to cast a generic UIComponent parameter to a subclass in order to access values, converters, and so on. Rather than casting to a specific class such as UISpinner, cast to an interface type, such as ValueHolder. That makes it easier to reuse your code.

UIComponentTag is a superclass for the tags you implement for your custom components. It implements mundane things—like support for binding, id, and rendered attributes—so you can concentrate on supporting the attributes your tags require.

The FacesContext class contains JSF-related request information. Among other things, you can access request parameters through FacesContext, get a reference to the Application object, get the current view root component, or get a reference to the response writer, which you use to encode markup.

The Application class keeps track of objects shared by a single application—for example, the set of supported locales and available converters and validators. The Application class also serves as a factory, with factory methods for components, converters, validators, value bindings, and method bindings. In this chapter, we're mostly interested in using the Application class to create converters, value bindings, and method bindings.

Nearly all custom components generate markup, so you will want to use the ResponseWriter class to ease that task. Response writers have methods for starting and ending HTML elements and methods for writing element attributes.

We now return to the spinner implementation and view the spinner from a number of different perspectives. We start with every component's most basic tasks—generating markup and processing requests—and then turn to the more mundane issue of implementing the corresponding tag handler class.

Encoding: Generating Markup

JSF components generate markup for their user interfaces. By default, the standard JSF components generate HTML. Components can do their own encoding, or they can delegate encoding to a separate renderer. The latter is the more elegant approach because it lets you plug in different renderers, for example to encode markup in something other than HTML. However, for simplicity, we will start out with a spinner that renders itself.

Components encode markup with three methods:

- encodeBegin()
- encodeChildren()
- encodeEnd()

The methods are called by JSF at the end of the life cycle, in the order in which they are listed above. JSF invokes encodeChildren only if a component returns true from its getRendersChildren method. By default, getRendersChildren returns false for most components.

For simple components, like our spinner, that don't have children, you don't need to implement encodeChildren. The spinner also has no compelling reason for overriding both encodeBegin and encodeEnd, so we do all our encoding in encodeBegin.

The spinner generates HTML for a text field and two buttons; that HTML looks like this:

```
<input type="text" name="..." value="current value"/>
<input type="submit" name="..." value="<"/>
<input type="submit" name="..." value=">"/>
```

Here's how that HTML is encoded in UISpinner.

```java
public class UISpinner extends UIInput {
    private static final String MORE = ".more";
    private static final String LESS = ".less";
    ...
    public void encodeBegin(FacesContext context) throws IOException {
        ResponseWriter writer = context.getResponseWriter();
        String clientId = getClientId(context);

        encodeInputField(writer, clientId);
        encodeDecrementButton(writer, clientId);
        encodeIncrementButton(writer, clientId);
    }
    private void encodeInputField(ResponseWriter writer, String clientId)
            throws IOException {
        writer.startElement("input", this);
        writer.writeAttribute("name", clientId, "clientId");

        Object v = getValue();
        if (v != null)
            writer.writeAttribute("value", v.toString(), "value");

        Integer size = (Integer) getAttributes().get("size");
        if (size != null) writer.writeAttribute("size", size, "size");

        writer.endElement("input");
    }
    private void encodeDecrementButton(ResponseWriter writer, String clientId)
            throws IOException {
        writer.startElement("input", this);
        writer.writeAttribute("type", "submit", null);
        writer.writeAttribute("name", clientId + LESS, null);
        writer.writeAttribute("value", "<", "value");
        writer.endElement("input");
    }
    private void encodeIncrementButton(ResponseWriter writer, String clientId)
            throws IOException {
        writer.startElement("input", this);
        writer.writeAttribute("type", "submit", null);
        writer.writeAttribute("name", clientId + MORE, null);
        writer.writeAttribute("value", ">", "value");
        writer.endElement("input");
    }
    ...
}
```

The ResponseWriter class has convenience methods for writing markup. The start-Element and endElement methods produce the element delimiters. They keep track of child elements, so you don't have to worry about the distinction between <input .../> and <input ...>...</input>. The writeAttribute method writes an attribute name/value pair with the appropriate escape characters. The last parameter of the startElement and writeAttribute methods is intended for tool support, but it is not used by the JSF 1.0 reference implementation. You are supposed to pass the rendered component object or attribute name, or null if the output doesn't directly correspond to a component or attribute.

UISpinner.encodeBegin faces two challenges. First, it must get the current state of the spinner. The numerical value is easily obtained with the getValue method that the spinner inherits from UIInput. The size is retrieved from the component's attribute map, using the getAttributes method. (As you will see in the section "Implementing Custom Component Tags" on page 367, the SpinnerTag class stores the tag's size attribute in the component's attribute map.)

Second, the encoding method needs to come up with names for the HTML elements the spinner encodes. It calls the getClientId method to obtain the client ID of the component, which is composed of the ID of the enclosing form and the ID of this component, such as _id1:monthSpinner. That identifier is created by the JSF implementation. The increment and decrement button names start with the client ID and end in .more and .less, respectively. Here is a complete example of the HTML generated by the spinner:

```
<input type="text" name="_id1:monthSpinner" value="1" size="3"/>
<input type="submit" name="_id1:monthSpinner.less" value="<"/>
<input type="submit" name="_id1:monthSpinner.more" value=">"/>
```

In the next section we discuss how those names are used by the spinner's decode method.

 javax.faces.component.UIComponent

- void encodeBegin(FacesContext context) throws IOException
  JSF calls this method—in the "Render Response" phase of the JSF life cycle—only if the component's renderer type is null, signifying that the component renders itself.
- String getClientId(FacesContext context)
  Returns the client ID for this component. The JSF framework creates the client ID from the ID of the enclosing form (or, more generally, the enclosing *naming container*) and the ID of this component.

- Map getAttributes()

  Returns a mutable map of component attributes and properties. You use this method to view, add, update, or remove attributes from a component. You can also use this map to view or update properties. The map's get and put methods check whether the key matches a component property. If so, the property getter or setter is called.

> NOTE: The spinner is a simple component with no children, so its encoding is rather basic. For a more complicated example, see how the tabbed pane renderer encodes markup. That renderer is shown in Listing 9–18 on page 414.

> NOTE: The JSF 1.0 reference implementation invokes a component's encode-Children method if the component returns true from getRendersChildren. Interestingly, it doesn't matter whether the component actually has children—as long as the component's getRendersChildren method returns true, JSF calls encodeChildren even if the component has no children.

---

javax.faces.context.FacesContext

- ResponseWriter getResponseWriter()

  Returns a reference to the response writer. You can plug your own response writer into JSF if you want. By default, JSF uses a response writer that can write HTML tags.

javax.faces.context.ResponseWriter

- void startElement(String elementName, UIComponent component)

  Writes the start tag for the specified element. The component parameter lets tools associate a component and its markup. The 1.0 version of the JSF reference implementation ignores this attribute.

- void endElement(String elementName)

  Writes the end tag for the specified element.

- void writeAttribute(String attributeName, String attributeValue, String componentProperty)

  Writes an attribute and its value. This method must be called between calls to startElement() and endElement(). The componentProperty is the name of the component property that corresponds to the attribute. Its use is meant for tools. It is not supported by the 1.0 reference implementation.

Decoding: Processing Request Values

To understand the decoding process, keep in mind how a web application works. The server sends an HTML form to the browser. The browser sends back a POST request that consists of name/value pairs. That POST request is the only data that the server can use to interpret the user's actions inside the browser.

If the user clicks on the increment or decrement button, the ensuing POST request includes the names and values of *all* text fields, but only the name and value of the *clicked* button. For example, if the user clicks the month spinner's increment button in the application shown in Figure 9–1 on page 351, the following request parameters are transferred to the server from the browser:

Name	Value
_id1:monthSpinner	1
_id1:yearSpinner	12
_id1:monthSpinner.more	>

When our spinner decodes an HTTP request, it looks for the request parameter names that match its client ID and processes the associated values. The spinner's decode method is listed below.

```java
public void decode(FacesContext context) {
   Map requestMap = context.getExternalContext().getRequestParameterMap();
   String clientId = getClientId(context);

   int increment;
   if (requestMap.containsKey(clientId + MORE)) increment = 1;
   else if (requestMap.containsKey(clientId + LESS)) increment = -1;
   else increment = 0;

   try {
      int submittedValue
         = Integer.parseInt((String) requestMap.get(clientId));
      int newValue = getIncrementedValue(submittedValue, increment);
      setSubmittedValue("" + newValue);
      setValid(true);
   }
   catch(NumberFormatException ex) {
      // let the converter take care of bad input, but we still have
      // to set the submitted value or the converter won't have
      // any input to deal with
      setSubmittedValue((String) requestMap.get(clientId));
   }
}
```

The decode method looks at the request parameters to determine which of the spinner's buttons, if any, triggered the request. If a request parameter named *clientId*.less exists, where *clientId* is the client ID of the spinner we're decoding, then we know the decrement button was activated. If the decode method finds a request parameter named *clientId*.more, then we know the increment button was activated. If neither parameter exists, we know the request was not initiated by the spinner, so we set the increment to zero. We still need to update the value—the user might have typed a value into the text field and clicked the "Next" button.

Our naming convention works for multiple spinners in a page because each spinner is encoded with the spinner component's client ID, which is guaranteed to be unique. If you have multiple spinners in a single page, each spinner component decodes its own request.

Once the decode method determines that one of the spinner's buttons was clicked, it increments the spinner's value by 1 or –1, depending on which button the user activated. That incremented value is calculated by a private get-IncrementedValue method.

```
private int getIncrementedValue(int submittedValue, int increment) {
    Integer minimum = (Integer) getAttributes().get("minimum");
    Integer maximum = (Integer) getAttributes().get("maximum");
    int newValue = submittedValue + increment;

    if ((minimum == null || newValue >= minimum.intValue()) &&
        (maximum == null || newValue <= maximum.intValue()))
        return newValue;
    else
        return submittedValue;
}
```

The getIncrementedValue method checks the value the user entered in the spinner against the spinner's minimum and maximum attributes. Those attributes are set by the spinner's tag handler class.

After it gets the incremented value, the decode method calls the spinner component's setSubmittedValue method. That method stores the submitted value in the component. Subsequently, in the JSF life cycle, that submitted value will be converted and validated by the JSF framework.

> **CAUTION:** You must call setValid(true) after setting the submitted value. Otherwise, the input is not considered valid, and the current page is simply redisplayed.

---

javax.faces.component.UIComponent

- void decode(FacesContext context)

  JSF calls this method—at the beginning of the JSF life cycle—only if the component's renderer type is null, signifying that the component renders itself.

  The decode method decodes request parameters. Typically, components transfer request parameter values to component properties or attributes. Components that fire action events queue them in this method.

 javax.faces.context.FacesContext

- ExternalContext getExternalContext()

  Returns a reference to a context proxy. Typically, the real context is a servlet or portlet context. If you use the external context instead of using the real context directly, your applications can work with servlets and portlets.

 javax.faces.context.ExternalContext

- Map getRequestParameterMap()

  Returns a map of request parameters. Custom components typically call this method in decode() to see if they were the component that triggered the request.

 javax.faces.component.EditableValueHolder

- void setSubmittedValue(Object submittedValue)

  Sets a component's submitted value—input components have editable values, so UIInput implements the EditableValueHolder interface. The submitted value is the value the user entered, presumably in a web page. For HTML-based applications, that value is always a string, but the method accepts an Object reference in deference to other display technologies.

- void setValid(boolean valid)

  Custom components use this method to indicate their value's validity. If a component can't convert its value, it sets the valid property to false.

Using Converters

The spinner component uses the standard JSF integer converter to convert strings to Integer objects, and vice versa. The UISpinner constructor simply calls setConverter, like this:

```
public class UISpinner extends UIInput {
    ...
    public UISpinner() {
        setConverter(new IntegerConverter()); // to convert the submitted value
        setRendererType(null);                // this component renders itself
    }
```

The spinner's decode method traps invalid inputs in the NumberFormatException
catch clause. However, instead of reporting the error, it simply sets the component's submitted value to the user input. Later on in the JSF life cycle, the standard integer converter will try to convert that value and will generate an
appropriate error message for bad input.

Listing 9–1 contains the complete code for the UISpinner class.

Listing 9–1   spinner/WEB-INF/classes/com/corejsf/UISpinner.java

```
 1. package com.corejsf;
 2.
 3. import java.io.IOException;
 4. import java.util.Map;
 5. import javax.faces.component.UIInput;
 6. import javax.faces.context.FacesContext;
 7. import javax.faces.context.ResponseWriter;
 8. import javax.faces.convert.IntegerConverter;
 9.
10. public class UISpinner extends UIInput {
11.    private static final String MORE = ".more";
12.    private static final String LESS = ".less";
13.
14.    public UISpinner() {
15.       setConverter(new IntegerConverter()); // to convert the submitted value
16.       setRendererType(null);                // this component renders itself
17.    }
18.
19.    public void encodeBegin(FacesContext context) throws IOException {
20.       ResponseWriter writer = context.getResponseWriter();
21.       String clientId = getClientId(context);
22.
23.       encodeInputField(writer, clientId);
24.       encodeDecrementButton(writer, clientId);
25.       encodeIncrementButton(writer, clientId);
26.    }
27.
28.    public void decode(FacesContext context) {
29.       Map requestMap = context.getExternalContext().getRequestParameterMap();
30.       String clientId = getClientId(context);
31.
```

Listing 9–1 spinner/WEB-INF/classes/com/corejsf/UISpinner.java (cont.)

```
32.      int increment;
33.      if (requestMap.containsKey(clientId + MORE)) increment = 1;
34.      else if(requestMap.containsKey(clientId + LESS)) increment = -1;
35.      else increment = 0;
36.
37.      try {
38.        int submittedValue
39.          = Integer.parseInt((String) requestMap.get(clientId));
40.
41.        int newValue = getIncrementedValue(submittedValue, increment);
42.        setSubmittedValue("" + newValue);
43.        setValid(true);
44.      }
45.      catch(NumberFormatException ex) {
46.        // let the converter take care of bad input, but we still have
47.        // to set the submitted value, or the converter won't have
48.        // any input to deal with
49.        setSubmittedValue((String) requestMap.get(clientId));
50.      }
51.    }
52.
53.    private void encodeInputField(ResponseWriter writer, String clientId)
54.        throws IOException {
55.      writer.startElement("input", this);
56.      writer.writeAttribute("name", clientId, "clientId");
57.
58.      Object v = getValue();
59.      if (v != null)
60.        writer.writeAttribute("value", v.toString(), "value");
61.
62.      Integer size = (Integer)getAttributes().get("size");
63.      if(size != null)
64.        writer.writeAttribute("size", size, "size");
65.
66.      writer.endElement("input");
67.    }
68.
69.    private void encodeDecrementButton(ResponseWriter writer, String clientId)
70.        throws IOException {
71.      writer.startElement("input", this);
72.      writer.writeAttribute("type", "submit", null);
73.      writer.writeAttribute("name", clientId + LESS, null);
74.      writer.writeAttribute("value", "<", "value");
75.      writer.endElement("input");
76.    }
```

Listing 9–1   spinner/WEB-INF/classes/com/corejsf/UISpinner.java (cont.)

```
77.  private void encodeIncrementButton(ResponseWriter writer, String clientId)
78.                                                   throws IOException {
79.      writer.startElement("input", this);
80.      writer.writeAttribute("type", "submit", null);
81.      writer.writeAttribute("name", clientId + MORE, null);
82.      writer.writeAttribute("value", ">", "value");
83.      writer.endElement("input");
84.  }
85.
86.  private int getIncrementedValue(int submittedValue, int increment) {
87.      Integer minimum = (Integer) getAttributes().get("minimum");
88.      Integer maximum = (Integer) getAttributes().get("maximum");
89.      int newValue = submittedValue + increment;
90.
91.      if ((minimum == null || newValue >= minimum.intValue()) &&
92.          (maximum == null || newValue <= maximum.intValue()))
93.          return newValue;
94.      else
95.          return submittedValue;
96.  }
97. }
```

javax.faces.component.ValueHolder

* void setConverter(Converter converter)

  Input and output components both have values and therefore both implement the ValueHolder interface. Values must be converted, so the ValueHolder interface defines a method for setting the converter. Custom components use this method to associate themselves with standard or custom converters.

Implementing Custom Component Tags

Now that you have seen how to implement the spinner component, there is one remaining chore: to supply a tag handler. Component tag handlers are similar to the tag handlers for converters and validators that you saw in Chapter 6. A tag handler needs to gather the attributes that were supplied in the JSF tag and move them into the component object.

Follow these steps to create a tag handler for your custom component:

* Implement a tag class.
* Create (or update) a tag library descriptor (TLD).

JSF provides two tag superclasses, UIComponentTag and UIComponentBodyTag, that you can extend to implement your tag class. You extend the former if your component does not process its *body* (that is, the child tags and text between the start and end tag), and the latter if it does. Only four of the standard JSF tags extend UIComponentBodyTag: f:view, f:verbatim, h:commandLink, and h:outputLink. Our spinner component does not process its body, so it extends UIComponentTag.

> **NOTE:** A tag that implements UIComponentTag can *have* a body, provided that the body tags know how to process themselves. For example, you can add an f:attribute child to a spinner.

Let's look at the implementation of the SpinnerTag class:

```
public class SpinnerTag extends UIComponentTag {
   private String minimum = null;
   private String maximum = null;
   private String size = null;
   private String value = null;
   ...

}
```

The spinner tag class has an instance field for each attribute. The tag class should keep all attributes as String objects, so that the tag user can supply either value binding expressions or values.

Tag classes have five responsibilities:

- To identify a component type
- To identify a renderer type
- To provide setter methods for tag attributes
- To store tag attribute values in the tag's component
- To release resources

The SpinnerTag class identifies its component type as com.corejsf.Spinner and its renderer type as null. A null renderer type means that a component renders itself.

```
public String getComponentType() { return "com.corejsf.Spinner"; }
public String getRendererType()  { return null; }
```

SpinnerTag provides setter methods for the attributes it supports: minimum, maximum, value, and size.

```
public void setMinimum(String newValue) { minimum = newValue; }
public void setMaximum(String newValue) { maximum = newValue; }
public void setSize(String newValue) { size = newValue; }
public void setValue(String newValue) { value = newValue; }
```

Tags must override a setProperties method to copy tag attribute values to the
component. The method name is somewhat of a misnomer because it usually
sets component attributes or value bindings, not properties.

```
public void setProperties(UIComponent component) {
    // always call the superclass method
    super.setProperties(component);

    setInteger(component, "size", size);
    setInteger(component, "minimum", minimum);
    setInteger(component, "maximum", maximum);
    setString(component, "value", value);
}
```

The spinner tag's setInteger and setString methods are helper methods that set a
component attribute or value binding. Here is the setInteger method:

```
public void setInteger(UIComponent component,
        String attributeName, String attributeValue) {
    if (attributeValue == null) return;
    if (isValueReference(attributeValue))
        setValueBinding(component, attributeName, attributeValue);
    else
        component.getAttributes().put(attributeName,
                new Integer(attributeValue));
}
```

If the attribute value is a value reference (such as "#{cardExpirationDate.year}),
then we call the setValueBinding helper method. That method goes through the
usual laborious contortions to create a ValueBinding object and to pass it to the
component's map of value bindings.

```
public void setValueBinding(UIComponent component,
        String attributeName, String attributeValue) {
    FacesContext context = FacesContext.getCurrentInstance();
    Application app = context.getApplication();
    ValueBinding vb = app.createValueBinding(attributeValue);
    component.setValueBinding(attributeName, vb);
}
```

If the attribute value is not a value reference, we convert the attribute value to
the target type and put it into the component's attribute map.

> NOTE: The map returned by the UIComponent.getAttributes method is smart: it can access both attributes and properties. For example, if you call the map's put method with an attribute whose name is "value", the setValue method is called. If the attribute name is "minimum", the name/value pair is put into the component's attribute map since the UISpinner class doesn't have a setMinimum method. Unfortunately, the map isn't smart enough to deal with value bindings.

Finally, tags must implement the release method to release resources and reset all instance fields, so that the tag object can be reused for parsing other tags.

```
public void release() {
    // always call the superclass method
    super.release();

    minimum = null;
    maximum = null;
    size = null;
    value = null;
}
```

> NOTE: Tag classes must call superclass methods when they override set-Properties and release.

Listing 9–2 contains the complete code for the tag handler.

After you've created your tag class, you need to declare your new tag in a tag library descriptor. Listing 9–3 shows how the corejsf:spinner tag is defined. You might notice that we've declared three attributes in the TLD that are not in the SpinnerTag class: binding, id, and rendered. We don't need accessor methods for them in the SpinnerTag class, because those methods are implemented by UIComponentTag.

Listing 9–2   spinner/WEB-INF/classes/com/corejsf/SpinnerTag.java

```
 1. package com.corejsf;
 2.
 3. import javax.faces.application.Application;
 4. import javax.faces.component.UIComponent;
 5. import javax.faces.context.FacesContext;
 6. import javax.faces.el.ValueBinding;
 7. import javax.faces.webapp.UIComponentTag;
 8.
 9. public class SpinnerTag extends UIComponentTag {
10.     private String minimum = null;
11.     private String maximum = null;
```

Listing 9–2 spinner/WEB-INF/classes/com/corejsf/SpinnerTag.java (cont.)

```
12.   private String size = null;
13.   private String value = null;
14.
15.   public String getRendererType() { return null; }
16.   public String getComponentType() { return "com.corejsf.Spinner"; }
17.
18.   public void setMinimum(String newValue) { minimum = newValue; }
19.   public void setMaximum(String newValue) { maximum = newValue; }
20.   public void setSize(String newValue) { size = newValue; }
21.   public void setValue(String newValue) { value = newValue; }
22.
23.   public void setProperties(UIComponent component) {
24.      // always call the superclass method
25.      super.setProperties(component);
26.
27.      setInteger(component, "size", size);
28.      setInteger(component, "minimum", minimum);
29.      setInteger(component, "maximum", maximum);
30.      setString(component, "value", value);
31.   }
32.
33.   public void setInteger(UIComponent component,
34.         String attributeName, String attributeValue) {
35.      if (attributeValue == null) return;
36.      if (isValueReference(attributeValue))
37.         setValueBinding(component, attributeName, attributeValue);
38.      else
39.         component.getAttributes().put(attributeName,
40.               new Integer(attributeValue));
41.   }
42.
43.   public void setString(UIComponent component,
44.         String attributeName, String attributeValue) {
45.      if (attributeValue == null) return;
46.      if (isValueReference(attributeValue))
47.         setValueBinding(component, attributeName, attributeValue);
48.      else
49.         component.getAttributes().put(attributeName, attributeValue);
50.   }
51.
52.   public void setValueBinding(UIComponent component,
53.         String attributeName, String attributeValue) {
54.      FacesContext context = FacesContext.getCurrentInstance();
55.      Application app = context.getApplication();
56.      ValueBinding vb = app.createValueBinding(attributeValue);
```

Listing 9–2 spinner/WEB-INF/classes/com/corejsf/SpinnerTag.java (cont.)

```
57.  component.setValueBinding(attributeName, vb);
58.     }
59.
60.     public void release() {
61.        // always call the superclass method
62.        super.release();
63.
64.        minimum = null;
65.        maximum = null;
66.        size = null;
67.        value = null;
68.     }
69. }
```

Listing 9–3 spinner/WEB-INF/spinner.tld

```
1.  <?xml version="1.0" encoding="ISO-8859-1" ?>
2.  <!DOCTYPE taglib
3.    PUBLIC "-//Sun Microsystems, Inc.//DTD JSP Tag Library 1.2//EN"
4.    "http://java.sun.com/dtd/web-jsptaglibrary_1_2.dtd">
5.  <taglib>
6.     <tlib-version>0.03</tlib-version>
7.     <jsp-version>1.2</jsp-version>
8.     <short-name>spinner</short-name>
9.     <uri>http://corejsf.com/spinner</uri>
10.    <description>This tag library contains a spinner tag</description>
11.
12.    <tag>
13.       <name>spinner</name>
14.       <tag-class>com.corejsf.SpinnerTag</tag-class>
15.
16.       <attribute>
17.          <name>binding</name>
18.          <description>A value binding that points to a bean property</description>
19.       </attribute>
20.
21.       <attribute>
22.          <name>id</name>
23.          <description>The client id of this component</description>
24.       </attribute>
25.
```

Listing 9–3   spinner/WEB-INF/spinner.tld (cont.)

```
26.         <attribute>
27.           <name>rendered</name>
28.           <description>Is this component rendered?</description>
29.         </attribute>
30.
31.         <attribute>
32.           <name>minimum</name>
33.           <description>The spinner minimum value</description>
34.         </attribute>
35.
36.         <attribute>
37.           <name>maximum</name>
38.           <description>The spinner maximum value</description>
39.         </attribute>
40.
41.         <attribute>
42.           <name>size</name>
43.           <description>The size of the input field</description>
44.         </attribute>
45.
46.         <attribute>
47.           <name>value</name>
48.           <required>true</required>
49.           <description>The value of the spinner</description>
50.         </attribute>
51.     </tag>
52. </taglib>
```

`javax.faces.webapp.UIComponentTag`

- `void setProperties(UIComponent component)`

  Transfers tag attribute values to component properties, attributes, or both. Custom components must call the superclass `setProperties` method to make sure that properties are set for the attributes `UIComponentTag` supports: `binding`, `id`, and `rendered`.

`javax.faces.context.FacesContext`

- `static FacesContext getCurrentInstance()`

  Returns a reference to the current `FacesContext` instance.

API `javax.faces.application.Application`

- `ValueBinding createValueBinding(String valueReferenceExpression)`

  Creates a value binding and stores it in the application. The string must be a value reference expression of this form: #{...}

API `javax.faces.component.UIComponent`

- `void setValueBinding(String name, ValueBinding valueBinding)`

  Stores a value binding by name in the component.

API `javax.faces.webapp.UIComponentTag`

- `static boolean isValueReference(String expression)`

  Returns true if expression starts with "#{" and ends with "}".

The Spinner Application

After a number of different perspectives of the spinner component, it's time to take a look at the spinner example in its entirety. This section lists the code for the spinner test application shown in Figure 9–1 on page 351. The directory structure is shown in Figure 9–5 and the code is shown in Listing 9–4 through Listing 9–9.

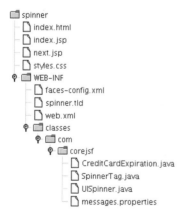

Figure 9–5   Spinner Directory Structure

Listing 9–4   spinner/index.jsp

```
1.  <html>
2.     <%@ taglib uri="http://java.sun.com/jsf/core" prefix="f" %>
3.     <%@ taglib uri="http://java.sun.com/jsf/html" prefix="h" %>
4.     <%@ taglib uri="http://corejsf.com/spinner" prefix="corejsf" %>
5.     <f:view>
6.        <head>
7.           <link href="styles.css" rel="stylesheet" type="text/css"/>
8.           <f:loadBundle basename="com.corejsf.messages" var="msgs"/>
9.           <title><h:outputText value="#{msgs.windowTitle}"/></title>
10.       </head>
11.       <body>
12.          <h:form id="spinnerForm">
13.             <h:outputText value="#{msgs.creditCardExpirationPrompt}"
14.                styleClass="pageTitle"/>
15.             <p/>
16.             <h:panelGrid columns="3">
17.                <h:outputText value="#{msgs.monthPrompt}"/>
18.                <corejsf:spinner value="#{cardExpirationDate.month}"
19.                   id="monthSpinner" minimum="1" maximum="12" size="3"/>
20.                <h:message for="monthSpinner"/>
21.                <h:outputText value="#{msgs.yearPrompt}"/>
22.                <corejsf:spinner value="#{cardExpirationDate.year}"
23.                   id="yearSpinner" minimum="1900" maximum="2100" size="5"/>
24.                <h:message for="yearSpinner"/>
25.             </h:panelGrid>
26.             <p/>
27.             <h:commandButton value="#{msgs.nextButtonPrompt}" action="next"/>
28.          </h:form>
29.       </body>
30.    </f:view>
31. </html>
```

Listing 9–5   spinner/next.jsp

```
1. <html>
2.    <%@ taglib uri="http://java.sun.com/jsf/core" prefix="f" %>
3.    <%@ taglib uri="http://java.sun.com/jsf/html" prefix="h" %>
4.
5.    <f:view>
6.       <head>
```

Listing 9–5 spinner/next.jsp (cont.)

```
7.          <link href="styles.css" rel="stylesheet" type="text/css"/>
8.          <f:loadBundle basename="com.corejsf.messages" var="msgs"/>
9.          <title><h:outputText value="#{msgs.windowTitle}"/></title>
10.       </head>
11.       <body>
12.          <h:form>
13.            <h:outputText value="#{msgs.youEnteredPrompt}" styleClass="pageTitle"/>
14.            <p>
15.            <h:outputText value="#{msgs.expirationDatePrompt}"/>
16.              <h:outputText value="#{cardExpirationDate.month}"/> /
17.              <h:outputText value="#{cardExpirationDate.year}"/>
18.            <p>
19.            <h:commandButton value="Try again" action="again"/>
20.          </h:form>
21.       </body>
22.    </f:view>
23. </html>
```

Listing 9–6 spinner/WEB-INF/classes/com/corejsf/CreditCardExpiration.java

```
1. package com.corejsf;
2.
3. public class CreditCardExpiration {
4.    private int month = 1;
5.    private int year = 2000;
6.
7.    // PROPERTY: month
8.    public int getMonth() { return month; }
9.    public void setMonth(int newValue) { month = newValue; }
10.
11.    // PROPERTY: year
12.    public int getYear() { return year; }
13.    public void setYear(int newValue) { year = newValue; }
14. }
```

Listing 9–7 spinner/WEB-INF/faces-config.xml

```
1. <?xml version="1.0"?>
2.
3. <!DOCTYPE faces-config PUBLIC
4.    "-//Sun Microsystems, Inc.//DTD JavaServer Faces Config 1.0//EN"
5.    "http://java.sun.com/dtd/web-facesconfig_1_0.dtd">
6.
```

| Listing 9–7 | spinner/WEB-INF/faces-config.xml (cont.) |

```
7.  <faces-config>
8.
9.      <navigation-rule>
10.         <from-view-id>/index.jsp</from-view-id>
11.         <navigation-case>
12.             <from-outcome>next</from-outcome>
13.             <to-view-id>/next.jsp</to-view-id>
14.         </navigation-case>
15.     </navigation-rule>
16.
17.     <navigation-rule>
18.         <from-view-id>/next.jsp</from-view-id>
19.         <navigation-case>
20.             <from-outcome>again</from-outcome>
21.             <to-view-id>/index.jsp</to-view-id>
22.         </navigation-case>
23.     </navigation-rule>
24.
25.     <component>
26.         <component-type>com.corejsf.Spinner</component-type>
27.         <component-class>com.corejsf.UISpinner</component-class>
28.     </component>
29.
30.     <managed-bean>
31.         <managed-bean-name>cardExpirationDate</managed-bean-name>
32.         <managed-bean-class>com.corejsf.CreditCardExpiration</managed-bean-class>
33.         <managed-bean-scope>session</managed-bean-scope>
34.     </managed-bean>
35.
36. </faces-config>
```

| Listing 9–8 | spinner/WEB-INF/classes/com/corejsf/messages.properties |

```
1. windowTitle=Spinner Test
2. creditCardExpirationPrompt=Please enter your credit card expiration date:
3. monthPrompt=Month:
4. yearPrompt=Year:
5. nextButtonPrompt=Next
6. youEnteredPrompt=You entered:
7. expirationDatePrompt=Expiration Date
8. changes=Changes:
```

Listing 9–9 `spinner/styles.css`

```
1. body {
2.   background: #eee;
3. }
4. .pageTitle {
5.   font-size: 1.25em;
6. }
```

Revisiting the Spinner

Let's revisit the spinner listed in the previous section. That spinner has two serious drawbacks. First, the spinner component renders itself, so you couldn't, for example, attach a separate renderer to the spinner when you migrate your application to cell phones. Second, the spinner requires a roundtrip to the server every time a user clicks on the increment or decrement button. Nobody would implement an industrial-strength spinner with those deficiencies. Let's see how to address them.

While we are at it, we will also add another feature to the spinner—the ability to attach value change listeners.

Using an External Renderer

In the preceding example, the UISpinner class was in charge of its own rendering. However, most UI classes delegate rendering to a separate class. Using separate renderers is a good idea: it becomes easy to replace renderers, to adapt to a different UI toolkit, or simply to achieve different HTML effects. In "Encoding JavaScript to Avoid Server Roundtrips" on page 396 we see how to use an alternative renderer that uses JavaScript to keep track of the spinner's value on the client.

Using an external renderer requires these steps:

- Define an ID string for your renderer.
- Declare the renderer in a JSF configuration file.
- Modify your tag class to return the renderer's ID from `getRendererType()`.
- Implement the renderer class.

The identifier—in our case, `com.corejsf.Spinner`—must be defined in a JSF configuration file, like this:

```
<faces-config>
    ...
    <component>
        <component-type>com.corejsf.Spinner</component-type>
        <component-class>com.corejsf.UISpinner</component-class>
    </component>

    <render-kit>
        <renderer>
            <component-family>javax.faces.Input</component-family>
            <renderer-type>com.corejsf.Spinner</renderer-type>
            <renderer-class>com.corejsf.SpinnerRenderer</renderer-class>
        </renderer>
    </render-kit>
</faces-config>
```

The `component-family` element serves to overcome a historical problem. The
names of the standard HTML tags are meant to indicate the component type
and the renderer type. For example, an `h:selectOneMenu` is a `UISelectOne` component
whose renderer has type `javax.faces.Menu`. That same renderer can also be used
for the `h:selectManyMenu` tag. But the scheme didn't work so well. The renderer for
`h:inputText` writes an HTML `input` text field. That renderer won't work for `h:out-`
`putText`—you don't want to use a text field for output. So, instead of identifying
renderers by individual components, renderers are determined by the renderer
type and the *component family*. Table 9–1 shows the component families of all
standard component classes. In our case, we use the component family
`javax.faces.Input` because `UISpinner` is a subclass of `UIInput`.

Table 9–1   Component Families of Standard Component Classes

Component Class	Component Family
UICommand	javax.faces.Command
UIData	javax.faces.Data
UIForm	javax.faces.Form
UIGraphic	javax.faces.Graphic
UIInput	javax.faces.Input
UIMessage	javax.faces.Message

Table 9–1   Component Families of Standard Component Classes (cont.)

Component Class	Component Family
UIMessages	javax.faces.Messages
UIOutput	javax.faces.Output
UIPanel	javax.faces.Panel
UISelectBoolean	javax.faces.SelectBoolean
UISelectMany	javax.faces.SelectMany
UISelectOne	javax.faces.SelectOne

The getRendererType of your tag class needs to return the renderer ID.

```
public class SpinnerTag extends UIComponentTag {
    ...
    public String getComponentType() { return "com.corejsf.Spinner"; }
    public String getRendererType()  { return "com.corejsf.Spinner"; }
    ...
}
```

 NOTE: Component IDs and Renderer IDs have separate name spaces. It is okay to use the same string as a component ID and a renderer ID.

It is also a good idea to set the renderer type in the component constructor:

```
public class UISpinner extends UIInput {
    public UISpinner() {
        setConverter(new IntegerConverter()); // to convert the submitted value
        setRendererType("com.corejsf.Spinner"); // this component has a renderer
    }
}
```

Then the renderer type is properly set if a component is programmatically constructed without the use of tags.

The final step is implementing the renderer itself. Renderers extend the javax.faces.render.Renderer class. That class has seven methods, four of which are familiar:

- void encodeBegin(FacesContext context, UIComponent component)
- void encodeChildren(FacesContext context, UIComponent component)
- void encodeEnd(FacesContext context, UIComponent component)
- void decode(FacesContext context, UIComponent component)

The renderer methods listed above are almost identical to their component counterparts except that the renderer methods take an additional argument: a reference to the component being rendered. To implement those methods for the spinner renderer, we move the component methods to the renderer and apply code changes to compensate for the fact that the renderer is passed a reference to the component. That's easy to do.

Here are the remaining Renderer methods:

- Object getConvertedValue(FacesContext context, UIComponent component, Object submittedValue)
- boolean getRendersChildren()
- String convertClientId(FacesContext context, String clientId)

The getConvertedValue method converts a component's submitted value from a string to an object. The default implementation in the Renderer class simply returns the value.

The getRendersChildren method specifies whether a renderer is responsible for rendering its component's children. If that method returns true, JSF will call the renderer's encodeChildren method; if it returns false (the default behavior), the JSF implementation won't call that method.

The convertClientId method converts an ID string (such as _id1:monthSpinner) so that it can be used on the client—some clients may place restrictions on IDs, such as disallowing special characters. However, the default implementation simply returns the ID string, unchanged.

If you have a component that renders itself, it's usually a simple task to move code from the component to the renderer. Listing 9–10 and Listing 9–11 show the code for the spinner component and renderer, respectively.

Listing 9–10   spinner2/WEB-INF/classes/com/corejsf/UISpinner.java

```
1. package com.corejsf;
2.
3. import javax.faces.component.UIInput;
4. import javax.faces.convert.IntegerConverter;
5.
6. public class UISpinner extends UIInput {
7.     public UISpinner() {
8.         setConverter(new IntegerConverter()); // to convert the submitted value
9.         setRendererType("com.corejsf.Spinner");  // this component has a renderer
10.     }
11. }
```

Listing 9-11   spinner2/WEB-INF/classes/com/corejsf/SpinnerRenderer.java

```java
1. package com.corejsf;
2.
3. import java.io.IOException;
4. import java.util.Map;
5. import javax.faces.component.UIComponent;
6. import javax.faces.component.EditableValueHolder;
7. import javax.faces.component.UIInput;
8. import javax.faces.context.FacesContext;
9. import javax.faces.context.ResponseWriter;
10. import javax.faces.convert.ConverterException;
11. import javax.faces.render.Renderer;
12.
13. public class SpinnerRenderer extends Renderer {
14.    private static final String MORE = ".more";
15.    private static final String LESS = ".less";
16.
17.    public Object getConvertedValue(FacesContext context, UIComponent component,
18.          Object submittedValue) throws ConverterException {
19.       return com.corejsf.util.Renderers.getConvertedValue(context, component,
20.          submittedValue);
21.    }
22.
23.    public void encodeBegin(FacesContext context, UIComponent spinner)
24.          throws IOException {
25.       ResponseWriter writer = context.getResponseWriter();
26.       String clientId = spinner.getClientId(context);
27.
28.       encodeInputField(spinner, writer, clientId);
29.       encodeDecrementButton(spinner, writer, clientId);
30.       encodeIncrementButton(spinner, writer, clientId);
31.    }
32.
33.    public void decode(FacesContext context, UIComponent component) {
34.       EditableValueHolder spinner = (EditableValueHolder) component;
35.       Map requestMap = context.getExternalContext().getRequestParameterMap();
36.       String clientId = component.getClientId(context);
37.
38.       int increment;
39.       if (requestMap.containsKey(clientId + MORE)) increment = 1;
40.       else if (requestMap.containsKey(clientId + LESS)) increment = -1;
41.       else increment = 0;
42.
43.       try {
44.          int submittedValue
45.             = Integer.parseInt((String) requestMap.get(clientId));
```

```
46.
47.        int newValue = getIncrementedValue(component, submittedValue,
48.           increment);
49.        spinner.setSubmittedValue("" + newValue);
50.        spinner.setValid(true);
51.     }
52.     catch(NumberFormatException ex) {
53.        // let the converter take care of bad input, but we still have
54.        // to set the submitted value, or the converter won't have
55.        // any input to deal with
56.        spinner.setSubmittedValue((String) requestMap.get(clientId));
57.     }
58.  }
59.
60.  private void encodeInputField(UIComponent spinner, ResponseWriter writer,
61.        String clientId) throws IOException {
62.     writer.startElement("input", spinner);
63.     writer.writeAttribute("name", clientId, "clientId");
64.
65.     Object v = ((UIInput)spinner).getValue();
66.     if(v != null)
67.        writer.writeAttribute("value", v.toString(), "value");
68.
69.     Integer size = (Integer)spinner.getAttributes().get("size");
70.     if(size != null)
71.        writer.writeAttribute("size", size, "size");
72.
73.     writer.endElement("input");
74.  }
75.
76.  private void encodeDecrementButton(UIComponent spinner,
77.        ResponseWriter writer, String clientId) throws IOException {
78.     writer.startElement("input", spinner);
79.     writer.writeAttribute("type", "submit", null);
80.     writer.writeAttribute("name", clientId + LESS, null);
81.     writer.writeAttribute("value", "<", "value");
82.     writer.endElement("input");
83.  }
84.
85.  private void encodeIncrementButton(UIComponent spinner,
86.        ResponseWriter writer, String clientId) throws IOException {
87.     writer.startElement("input", spinner);
88.     writer.writeAttribute("type", "submit", null);
89.     writer.writeAttribute("name", clientId + MORE, null);
90.     writer.writeAttribute("value", ">", "value");
```

Listing 9–11 `spinner2/WEB-INF/classes/com/corejsf/SpinnerRenderer.java (cont.)`

```
 91.      writer.endElement("input");
 92.    }
 93.
 94.    private int getIncrementedValue(UIComponent spinner, int submittedValue,
 95.        int increment) {
 96.      Integer minimum = (Integer) spinner.getAttributes().get("minimum");
 97.      Integer maximum = (Integer) spinner.getAttributes().get("maximum");
 98.      int newValue = submittedValue + increment;
 99.
100.      if ((minimum == null || newValue >= minimum.intValue()) &&
101.          (maximum == null || newValue <= maximum.intValue()))
102.        return newValue;
103.      else
104.        return submittedValue;
105.    }
106. }
```

Calling Converters from External Renderers

If you compare Listing 9–10 and Listing 9–11 with Listing 9–1, you'll see that we moved most of the code from the original component class to a new renderer class.

However, there is a hitch. As you can see from Listing 9–10, the spinner handles conversions simply by invoking `setConverter()` in its constructor. Because the spinner is an input component, its superclass—UIInput—uses the specified converter during the "Process Validations" phase of the life cycle.

But when the spinner delegates to a renderer, it's the renderer's responsibility to convert the spinner's value by overriding `Renderer.getConvertedValue()`. So we must replicate the conversion code from UIInput in a custom renderer. We placed that code—which is required in all renderers that use a converter—in the static `getConvertedValue` method of the class `com.corejsf.util.Renderers` (see Listing 9–12 on page 388).

NOTE: The `Renderers.getConvertedValue` method shown in Listing 9–12 is a necessary evil because `UIInput` does not make its conversion code publicly available. That code resides in `UIInput.validate`, which looks like this in the JSF 1.0 Reference Implementation:

```
// This code is from the javax.faces.component.UIInput class:

public void validate(FacesContext context) {
```

```
    if (renderer != null) {
        newValue = renderer.getConvertedValue(context, this,
                                                submittedValue);
    } else if (submittedValue instanceof String) {
        // If there's no Renderer and we've got a String,
        // run it through the Converter (if any)
        Converter converter = getConverterWithType(context);
        ...
        // much more code follows for converting the UIInput's value
        // and for dealing with conversion failures...
    }
}
```

Because UIInput's conversion code is buried in the validate method, it's not available for a renderer to reuse, as would be the case, for example, if UIInput implemented that code in a public getConvertedValue method. Because UIInput's conversion code can't be reused, you must reimplement it for custom components that use standard converters to convert their values. Fortunately, we've already done it for you.

Supporting Value Change Listeners

If your custom component is an input component, you can fire value change events to interested listeners. For example, in a calendar application, you may want to update another component whenever a month spinner value changes.

Fortunately, it is easy to support value change listeners. The UIInput class automatically generates value change events whenever the input value has changed. Recall that there are two ways of attaching a value change listener. You can add one or more listeners with f:valueChangeListener, like this:

```
<corejsf:spinner ...>
    <f:valueChangeListener type="com.corejsf.SpinnerListener"/>
    ...
</corejsf:spinner>
```

Or you can use a valueChangeListener attribute:

```
<corejsf:spinner value="#{cardExpirationDate.month}"
    id="monthSpinner" minimum="1" maximum="12" size="3"
    valueChangeListener="#{cardExpirationDate.changeListener}"/>
```

The first way doesn't require any effort on the part of the component implementor. The second way merely requires that your tag handler supports the valueChangeListener attribute. The attribute value is a method binding that requires special handling—the topic of the next section.

Supporting Method Bindings

Four commonly used attributes require method bindings—see Table 9–2. You create a MethodBinding object by calling the createMethodBinding method of the Application class. That method has two parameters: the method binding expression and an array of Class objects that describe the method's parameter types. For example, this code creates a method binding for a value change listener:

```
FacesContext context = FacesContext.getCurrentInstance();
Application app = context.getApplication();
Class[] paramTypes = new Class[] { ValueChangeListener.class };
MethodBinding mb = app.createMethodBinding(attributeValue, paramTypes);
```

You then store the MethodBinding object with the component in the usual way:

```
component.getAttributes().put("valueChangeListener", mb);
```

Alternatively, you can call the property setter directly:

```
((EditableValueHolder) component).setValueChangeListener(mb);
```

Table 9–2 Method Binding Attributes

Attribute Name	Method Parameters
valueChangeListener	ValueChangeEvent
validator	FacesContext, UIComponent, Object
actionListener	ActionEvent
action	*none*

Nobody likes to write this tedious code, so we bundled it with the setValueChangeListener method of the convenience class com.corejsf.util.Tags (see Listing 9–13 on page 390). The SpinnerTag class simply calls

```
com.corejsf.util.Tags.setValueChangeListener(component,
    valueChangeListener);
```

Action listeners and validators follow exactly the same pattern—see the setActionListener and setValidator methods in the com.corejsf.util.Tags class.

However, actions are slightly more complex. An action can either be a method binding or a fixed string, for example

```
<h:commandButton value="Login" action="#{loginController.verifyUser}"/>
```

or

```
<h:commandButton value="Login" action="login"/>
```

But the setAction method of the ActionSource interface requires a MethodBinding in all cases. Therefore, we must construct a MethodBinding object whose getExpression-String method returns the given string—see the setAction method of the Tags class.

In the next sample program, we demonstrate the value change listener by keeping a count of all value changes that we display on the form (see Figure 9–6).

```
public class CreditCardExpiration {
    private int changes = 0;
    // to demonstrate the value change listener
    public void changeListener(ValueChangeEvent e) {
        changes++;
    }
}
```

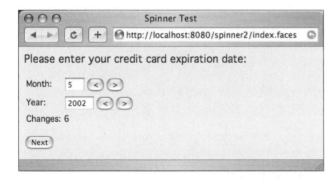

Figure 9–6   Counting the Value Changes

Figure 9–7 shows the directory structure of the sample application. As you can see, we rely on the Core JSF Renderers and Tags convenience classes that contain much of the repetitive code. (The Renderers class also contains a getSelectedItems method that we need later in this chapter—ignore it for now.) Listing 9–14 contains the revised SpinnerTag class, and Listing 9–15 shows the faces-config.xml file.

Figure 9–7 Directory Structure of the Revised Spinner Example

Listing 9–12 spinner2/WEB-INF/classes/com/corejsf/util/Renderers.java

```
1. package com.corejsf.util;
2.
3. import java.util.ArrayList;
4. import java.util.Arrays;
5. import java.util.Collection;
6. import java.util.Iterator;
7. import java.util.List;
8. import java.util.Map;
9.
10. import javax.faces.application.Application;
11. import javax.faces.component.UIComponent;
12. import javax.faces.component.UIForm;
13. import javax.faces.component.UISelectItem;
14. import javax.faces.component.UISelectItems;
15. import javax.faces.component.ValueHolder;
16. import javax.faces.context.FacesContext;
17. import javax.faces.convert.Converter;
18. import javax.faces.convert.ConverterException;
19. import javax.faces.el.ValueBinding;
20. import javax.faces.model.SelectItem;
21.
22. public class Renderers {
23.     public static Object getConvertedValue(FacesContext context,
24.         UIComponent component,
```

```
25.          Object submittedValue) throws ConverterException {
26.      if (submittedValue instanceof String) {
27.         Converter converter = getConverter(context, component);
28.         if (converter != null) {
29.            return converter.getAsObject(context, component,
30.                  (String) submittedValue);
31.         }
32.      }
33.      return submittedValue;
34.   }
35.
36.   public static Converter getConverter(FacesContext context,
37.      UIComponent component) {
38.      if (!(component instanceof ValueHolder)) return null;
39.      ValueHolder holder = (ValueHolder) component;
40.
41.      Converter converter = holder.getConverter();
42.      if (converter != null) return converter;
43.
44.      ValueBinding valueBinding = component.getValueBinding("value");
45.      if (valueBinding == null) return null;
46.
47.      Class targetType = valueBinding.getType(context);
48.      if (targetType == null) return null;
49.      // Version 1.0 of the reference implementation will not apply a converter
50.      // if the target type is String or Object, but that is a bug.
51.
52.      Application app = context.getApplication();
53.      return app.createConverter(targetType);
54.   }
55.
56.   public static String getFormId(FacesContext context, UIComponent component) {
57.      UIComponent parent = component;
58.      while (!(parent instanceof UIForm)) parent = parent.getParent();
59.      return parent.getClientId(context);
60.   }
61.
62.   public static List getSelectItems(UIComponent component) {
63.      ArrayList list = new ArrayList();
64.      Iterator children = component.getChildren().iterator();
65.      while (children.hasNext()) {
66.         UIComponent child = (UIComponent) children.next();
67.
68.         if (child instanceof UISelectItem) {
69.            Object value = ((UISelectItem) child).getValue();
```

```
70.            if (value == null) {
71.               UISelectItem item = (UISelectItem) child;
72.               list.add(new SelectItem(item.getItemValue(),
73.                     item.getItemLabel(),
74.                     item.getItemDescription(),
75.                     item.isItemDisabled()));
76.            } else if (value instanceof SelectItem) {
77.               list.add(value);
78.            }
79.         } else if (child instanceof UISelectItems) {
80.            Object value = ((UISelectItems) child).getValue();
81.            if (value instanceof SelectItem)
82.               list.add(value);
83.            else if (value instanceof SelectItem[])
84.               list.addAll(Arrays.asList((SelectItem[]) value));
85.            else if (value instanceof Collection)
86.               list.addAll((Collection) value);
87.            else if (value instanceof Map) {
88.               Iterator entries = ((Map) value).entrySet().iterator();
89.               while (entries.hasNext()) {
90.                  Map.Entry entry = (Map.Entry) entries.next();
91.                  list.add(new SelectItem(entry.getKey(),
92.                        "" + entry.getValue()));
93.               }
94.            }
95.         }
96.      }
97.      return list;
98.   }
99. }
```

Listing 9–13   spinner2/WEB-INF/classes/com/corejsf/util/Tags.java

```
1. package com.corejsf.util;
2.
3. import java.io.Serializable;
4. import javax.faces.application.Application;
5. import javax.faces.component.UIComponent;
6. import javax.faces.context.FacesContext;
7. import javax.faces.el.MethodBinding;
8. import javax.faces.el.ValueBinding;
9. import javax.faces.event.ActionEvent;
10. import javax.faces.event.ValueChangeEvent;
11. import javax.faces.webapp.UIComponentTag;
```

Listing 9–13 spinner2/WEB-INF/classes/com/corejsf/util/Tags.java (cont.)

```
12.
13. public class Tags {
14.    public static void setString(UIComponent component, String attributeName,
15.       String attributeValue) {
16.       if (attributeValue == null)
17.          return;
18.       if (UIComponentTag.isValueReference(attributeValue))
19.          setValueBinding(component, attributeName, attributeValue);
20.       else
21.          component.getAttributes().put(attributeName, attributeValue);
22.    }
23.
24.    public static void setInteger(UIComponent component,
25.       String attributeName, String attributeValue) {
26.       if (attributeValue == null) return;
27.       if (UIComponentTag.isValueReference(attributeValue))
28.          setValueBinding(component, attributeName, attributeValue);
29.       else
30.          component.getAttributes().put(attributeName,
31.             new Integer(attributeValue));
32.    }
33.
34.    public static void setBoolean(UIComponent component,
35.       String attributeName, String attributeValue) {
36.       if (attributeValue == null) return;
37.       if (UIComponentTag.isValueReference(attributeValue))
38.          setValueBinding(component, attributeName, attributeValue);
39.       else
40.          component.getAttributes().put(attributeName,
41.             new Boolean(attributeValue));
42.    }
43.
44.    public static void setValueBinding(UIComponent component, String attributeName,
45.       String attributeValue) {
46.       FacesContext context = FacesContext.getCurrentInstance();
47.       Application app = context.getApplication();
48.       ValueBinding vb = app.createValueBinding(attributeValue);
49.       component.setValueBinding(attributeName, vb);
50.    }
51.
52.    public static void setActionListener(UIComponent component,
53.       String attributeValue) {
54.       setMethodBinding(component, "actionListener", attributeValue,
55.          new Class[] { ActionEvent.class });
56.    }
```

Listing 9-13 spinner2/WEB-INF/classes/com/corejsf/util/Tags.java (cont.)

```
57.
58.    public static void setValueChangeListener(UIComponent component,
59.        String attributeValue) {
60.      setMethodBinding(component, "valueChangeListener", attributeValue,
61.          new Class[] { ValueChangeEvent.class });
62.    }
63.
64.    public static void setValidator(UIComponent component,
65.        String attributeValue) {
66.      setMethodBinding(component, "validator", attributeValue,
67.          new Class[] { FacesContext.class, UIComponent.class, Object.class });
68.    }
69.
70.    public static void setAction(UIComponent component, String attributeValue) {
71.      if (attributeValue == null) return;
72.      if (UIComponentTag.isValueReference(attributeValue))
73.        setMethodBinding(component, "action", attributeValue,
74.            new Class[] {});
75.      else {
76.        FacesContext context = FacesContext.getCurrentInstance();
77.        Application app = context.getApplication();
78.        MethodBinding mb = new ActionMethodBinding(attributeValue);
79.        component.getAttributes().put("action", mb);
80.      }
81.    }
82.
83.    public static void setMethodBinding(UIComponent component, String attributeName,
84.        String attributeValue, Class[] paramTypes) {
85.      if (attributeValue == null)
86.        return;
87.      if (UIComponentTag.isValueReference(attributeValue)) {
88.        FacesContext context = FacesContext.getCurrentInstance();
89.        Application app = context.getApplication();
90.        MethodBinding mb = app.createMethodBinding(attributeValue, paramTypes);
91.        component.getAttributes().put(attributeName, mb);
92.      }
93.    }
94.
95.    private static class ActionMethodBinding
96.        extends MethodBinding implements Serializable {
97.      private String result;
98.
99.      public ActionMethodBinding(String result) { this.result = result; }
100.      public Object invoke(FacesContext context, Object params[]) {
101.        return result;
```

Listing 9–13 spinner2/WEB-INF/classes/com/corejsf/util/Tags.java (cont.)

```
102.      }
103.      public String getExpressionString() { return result; }
104.      public Class getType(FacesContext context) { return String.class; }
105.   }
106. }
```

Listing 9–14 spinner2/WEB-INF/classes/com/corejsf/SpinnerTag.java

```
1. package com.corejsf;
2.
3. import javax.faces.component.UIComponent;
4. import javax.faces.webapp.UIComponentTag;
5.
6. public class SpinnerTag extends UIComponentTag {
7.    private String minimum = null;
8.    private String maximum = null;
9.    private String size = null;
10.    private String value = null;
11.    private String valueChangeListener = null;
12.
13.    public String getRendererType() { return "com.corejsf.Spinner"; }
14.    public String getComponentType() { return "com.corejsf.Spinner"; }
15.
16.    public void setMinimum(String newValue) { minimum = newValue; }
17.    public void setMaximum(String newValue) { maximum = newValue; }
18.    public void setSize(String newValue) { size = newValue; }
19.    public void setValue(String newValue) { value = newValue; }
20.    public void setValueChangeListener(String newValue)  {
21.       valueChangeListener = newValue;
22.    }
23.
24.    public void setProperties(UIComponent component) {
25.       // always call the superclass method
26.       super.setProperties(component);
27.
28.       com.corejsf.util.Tags.setInteger(component, "size", size);
29.       com.corejsf.util.Tags.setInteger(component, "minimum", minimum);
30.       com.corejsf.util.Tags.setInteger(component, "maximum", maximum);
31.       com.corejsf.util.Tags.setString(component, "value", value);
32.       com.corejsf.util.Tags.setValueChangeListener(component,
33.          valueChangeListener);
34.    }
35.
36.    public void release() {
```

Listing 9–14   spinner2/WEB-INF/classes/com/corejsf/SpinnerTag.java (cont.)

```
37.     // always call the superclass method
38.     super.release();
39.
40.     minimum = null;
41.     maximum = null;
42.     size = null;
43.     value = null;
44.     valueChangeListener = null;
45.   }
46. }
```

Listing 9–15   spinner2/WEB-INF/faces-config.xml

```
1. <?xml version="1.0"?>
2.
3. <!DOCTYPE faces-config PUBLIC
4.   "-//Sun Microsystems, Inc.//DTD JavaServer Faces Config 1.0//EN"
5.   "http://java.sun.com/dtd/web-facesconfig_1_0.dtd">
6.
7. <faces-config>
8.
9.    <navigation-rule>
10.      <from-view-id>/index.jsp</from-view-id>
11.      <navigation-case>
12.        <from-outcome>next</from-outcome>
13.        <to-view-id>/next.jsp</to-view-id>
14.      </navigation-case>
15.    </navigation-rule>
16.
17.    <navigation-rule>
18.      <from-view-id>/next.jsp</from-view-id>
19.      <navigation-case>
20.        <from-outcome>again</from-outcome>
21.        <to-view-id>/index.jsp</to-view-id>
22.      </navigation-case>
23.    </navigation-rule>
24.
25.    <managed-bean>
26.      <managed-bean-name>cardExpirationDate</managed-bean-name>
27.      <managed-bean-class>com.corejsf.CreditCardExpiration</managed-bean-class>
28.      <managed-bean-scope>session</managed-bean-scope>
29.    </managed-bean>
30.
```

| Listing 9–15 | spinner2/WEB-INF/faces-config.xml (cont.) |

```
31.    <component>
32.        <component-type>com.corejsf.Spinner</component-type>
33.        <component-class>com.corejsf.UISpinner</component-class>
34.    </component>
35.
36.    <render-kit>
37.        <renderer>
38.            <component-family>javax.faces.Input</component-family>
39.            <renderer-type>com.corejsf.Spinner</renderer-type>
40.            <renderer-class>com.corejsf.SpinnerRenderer</renderer-class>
41.        <renderer>
42.    <render-kit>
43. </faces-config>
```

 javax.faces.context.FacesContext

- Application getApplication()
  Returns a reference to the application object.

 javax.faces.application.Application

- ValueBinding createMethodBinding(String valueReferenceExpression, Class[] arguments)
  Creates a method binding and stores it in the application. The valueReferenceExpression must be a value reference expression. The Class[] represents the types of the arguments passed to the method.

 javax.faces.component.EditableValueHolder

- void setValueChangeListener(MethodBinding listenerMethod)
  Sets a method binding for a component that implements the EditableValueHolder interface. That method must return void and is passed a ValueChangeEvent.

 javax.faces.event.ValueChangeEvent

- Object getOldValue()
  Returns the component's old value.
- Object getNewValue()
  Returns the component's new value.

`javax.faces.component.ValueHolder`

• `Converter getConverter()`

Returns the converter associated with a component. The `ValueHolder` interface is implemented by input and output components.

 `javax.faces.component.UIComponent`

• `ValueBinding getValueBinding(String valueBindingName)`

Returns a value binding previously set by calling `UIComponent.setValueBinding()`. That method is discussed on page 374.

 `javax.faces.el.ValueBinding`

• `Class getType(FacesContext context) throws EvaluationException, PropertyNotFoundException`

Returns the class of the object to which a value binding applies. That class can subsequently be used to access a converter with `Application.createConverter()`.

 `javax.faces.application.Application`

• `Converter createConverter(Class targetClass) throws FacesException, NullPointerException`

Creates a converter, given its target class. JSF implementations maintain a map of valid converter types, which are typically specified in a faces configuration file. If `targetClass` is a key in that map, this method creates an instance of the associated converter (specified as the value for the target-Class key) and returns it. If `targetClass` is not in the map, this method searches the map for a key that corresponds to `targetClass`'s interfaces and superclasses, in that order, until it finds a matching class. Once a matching class is found, this method creates an associated converter and returns it. If no converter is found for the `targetClass`, it's interfaces, or it's superclasses, this method returns `null`.

Encoding JavaScript to Avoid Server Roundtrips

The spinner component performs a roundtrip to the server every time you click one of its buttons. That roundtrip updates the spinner's value on the server. Those roundtrips can take a severe bite out of the spinner's performance, so in almost all circumstances, it's better to store the spinner's value on the client and update the component's value only when the form in which the spinner resides is submitted. We can do that with JavaScript that looks like this:

```
<input type="text" name="_id1:monthSpinner" value="0"/>

<script language="JavaScript">
   document['_id1']['_id1:monthSpinner'].spin = function (increment) {
      var v = parseInt(this.value) + increment;
      if (isNaN(v)) return;
      if ('min' in this && v < this.min) return;
      if ('max' in this && v > this.max) return;
         this.value = v;
   };
   document['_id1']['_id1:monthSpinner'].min = 0;
</script>

<input type="button" value="<"
      onclick="document['_id1']['_id1:monthSpinner'].spin(-1);"/>
<input type="button" value=">"
      onclick="document['_id1']['_id1:monthSpinner'].spin(1);"/>
```

When you write JavaScript code that accesses fields in a form, you need to have access to the form ID, such as '_id1' in the expression

```
document['_id1']['_id1:monthSpinner']
```

The second array index is simply the client ID of the component.

Obtaining the form ID is a common task, and we added a convenience method to the com.corejsf.util.Renderers class for this purpose:

```
public static String getFormId(FacesContext context, UIComponent component) {
   UIComponent parent = component;
   while (!(parent instanceof UIForm)) parent = parent.getParent();
   return parent.getClientId(context);
}
```

We won't go into the details of JavaScript programming here, but note that we are a bit paranoid about injecting global JavaScript functions into an unknown page. We don't want to risk name conflicts. Fortunately, JavaScript is a well-designed language with a flexible object model. Rather than writing a global spin function, we define spin to be a method of the text field object. JavaScript lets you enhance the capabilities of objects on-the-fly, simply by adding methods and fields. We use the same approach with the minimum and maximum values of the spinner, adding min and max fields if they are required.

The spinner renderer that encodes the preceding JavaScript is shown in Listing 9–16.

Note that the UISpinner component is completely unaffected by this change. Only the renderer has been updated, thus demonstrating the power of plug-gable renderers.

Listing 9–16   spinner-js/WEB-INF/classes/com/corejsf/JSSpinnerRenderer.java

```
1. package com.corejsf;
2.
3. import java.io.IOException;
4. import java.text.MessageFormat;
5. import java.util.Map;
6. import javax.faces.component.EditableValueHolder;
7. import javax.faces.component.UIComponent;
8. import javax.faces.component.UIInput;
9. import javax.faces.context.FacesContext;
10. import javax.faces.context.ResponseWriter;
11. import javax.faces.convert.ConverterException;
12. import javax.faces.render.Renderer;
13.
14. public class JSSpinnerRenderer extends Renderer {
15.     private static final String MORE = ".more";
16.     private static final String LESS = ".less";
17.
18.     public Object getConvertedValue(FacesContext context, UIComponent component,
19.         Object submittedValue) throws ConverterException {
20.       return com.corejsf.util.Renderers.getConvertedValue(context, component,
21.         submittedValue);
22.     }
23.
24.     public void encodeBegin(FacesContext context, UIComponent component)
25.         throws IOException {
26.       ResponseWriter writer = context.getResponseWriter();
27.       String clientId = component.getClientId(context);
28.       String formId = com.corejsf.util.Renderers.getFormId(context, component);
29.
30.       UIInput spinner = (UIInput)component;
31.       Integer min = (Integer) component.getAttributes().get("minimum");
32.       Integer max = (Integer) component.getAttributes().get("maximum");
33.       Integer size = (Integer) component.getAttributes().get("size");
34.
35.       writer.write(MessageFormat.format(
36.         "<input type=\"text\" name=\"{0}\" value=\"{1}\"",
37.         new Object[] { clientId, spinner.getValue().toString() } ));
38.
39.       if (size != null)
```

Listing 9–16	spinner-js/WEB-INF/classes/com/corejsf/JSSpinnerRenderer.java (cont.)

```
40.         writer.write(MessageFormat.format(
41.            " size=\"{0}\"", new Object[] { size } ));
42.      writer.write(MessageFormat.format("/>"
43.         + "<script language=\"JavaScript\">"
44.         + "document.forms[''{0}''][''{1}''].spin = function (increment) '{'"
45.         + "var v = parseInt(this.value) + increment;"
46.         + "if (isNaN(v)) return;"
47.         + "if (\"min\" in this && v < this.min) return;"
48.         + "if (\"max\" in this && v > this.max) return;"
49.         + "this.value = v;"
50.         + "};",
51.         new Object[] { formId, clientId } ));
52.
53.      if (min != null) {
54.         writer.write(MessageFormat.format(
55.            "document.forms[''{0}''][''{1}''].min = {2};",
56.            new Object[] { formId, clientId, min }));
57.      }
58.      if (max != null) {
59.         writer.write(MessageFormat.format(
60.            "document.forms[''{0}''][''{1}''].max = {2};",
61.            new Object[] { formId, clientId, max }));
62.      }
63.      writer.write(MessageFormat.format(
64.         "</script>"
65.         + "<input type=\"button\" value=\"<\""
66.         + " onclick=\"document.forms[''{0}''][''{1}''].spin(-1); \"/>"
67.         + "<input type=\"button\" value=\">\""
68.         + " onclick=\"document.forms[''{0}''][''{1}''].spin(1); \"/>"
69.         new Object[] { formId, clientId }));
70.   }
71.
72.   public void decode(FacesContext context, UIComponent component) {
73.      EditableValueHolder spinner = (EditableValueHolder) component;
74.      Map requestMap = context.getExternalContext().getRequestParameterMap();
75.      String clientId = component.getClientId(context);
76.
77.      int increment;
78.      if (requestMap.containsKey(clientId + MORE)) increment = 1;
79.      else if (requestMap.containsKey(clientId + LESS)) increment = -1;
80.      else increment = 0;
81.
82.      try {
83.         int submittedValue
```

Listing 9–16	spinner-js/WEB-INF/classes/com/corejsf/JSSpinnerRenderer.java (cont.)

```
84.              = Integer.parseInt((String) requestMap.get(clientId));
85.
86.          int newValue = getIncrementedValue(component, submittedValue,
87.             increment);
88.          spinner.setSubmittedValue("" + newValue);
89.          spinner.setValid(true);
90.       }
91.       catch(NumberFormatException ex) {
92.          // let the converter take care of bad input, but we still have
93.          // to set the submitted value, or the converter won't have
94.          // any input to deal with
95.          spinner.setSubmittedValue((String) requestMap.get(clientId));
96.       }
97.    }
98.
99.    private void encodeDecrementButton(UIComponent spinner,
100.         ResponseWriter writer, String clientId) throws IOException {
101.      writer.startElement("input", spinner);
102.      writer.writeAttribute("type", "submit", null);
103.      writer.writeAttribute("name", clientId + LESS, null);
104.      writer.writeAttribute("value", "<", "value");
105.      writer.endElement("input");
106.    }
107.
108.    private void encodeIncrementButton(UIComponent spinner,
109.         ResponseWriter writer, String clientId) throws IOException {
110.      writer.startElement("input", spinner);
111.      writer.writeAttribute("type", "submit", null);
112.      writer.writeAttribute("name", clientId + MORE, null);
113.      writer.writeAttribute("value", ">", "value");
114.      writer.endElement("input");
115.    }
116.
117.    private int getIncrementedValue(UIComponent spinner, int submittedValue,
118.         int increment) {
119.      Integer minimum = (Integer) spinner.getAttributes().get("minimum");
120.      Integer maximum = (Integer) spinner.getAttributes().get("maximum");
121.      int newValue = submittedValue + increment;
122.
123.      if ((minimum == null || newValue >= minimum.intValue()) &&
124.          (maximum == null || newValue <= maximum.intValue()))
125.         return newValue;
126.      else
127.         return submittedValue;
128.    }
129. }
```

Using Child Components and Facets

The spinner discussed in the first half of this chapter is a simple component that nonetheless illustrates a number of useful techniques for implementing custom components. To illustrate more advanced custom component techniques, we switch to a more complicated component: a tabbed pane, as shown in Figure 9–8.

Figure 9–8 The Tabbed Pane Component

In Chapter 7, we showed you how to create an ad hoc tabbed pane with standard JSF tags such as h:graphicImage and h:commandLink. In this chapter we show you how to implement a tabbed pane component.

Of course, the advantage of a custom component over an ad hoc implementation is that the former is reusable. For example, we can easily reuse the tabbed pane component to create a tabbed pane just like the ad hoc version, as shown in Figure 9–9.

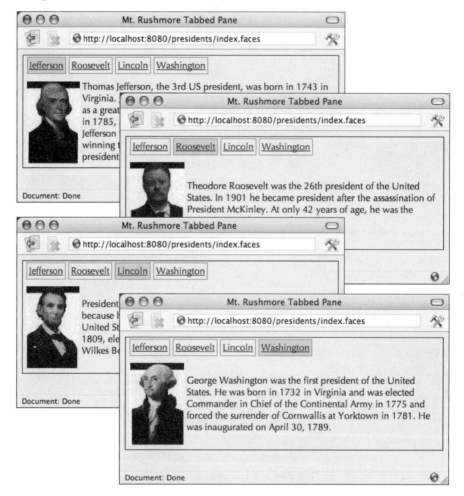

Figure 9–9   Reusing the Tabbed Pane Component

The tabbed pane component has some interesting features:

*   You can *use CSS classes* for the tabbed pane as a whole and also for selected and unselected tabs.
*   You *specify tabs* with f:selectItem tags (or f:selectItems), like the standard JSF menu and listbox tags specify menu or listbox items.

- You can *specify tabbed pane content* (for example, the picture and description in Figure 9–9) *with a URL* (which the tabbed pane renderer includes) *or a facet* (which the renderer renders). For example, you could specify the content for the Washington tab in Figure 9–9 as /washington.jsp or washington. If you use the former, the tabbed pane renderer includes the response from the specified JSP page. If you use the latter, the renderer looks for a facet of the tabbed pane named washington. (This use of facets is similar to the use of header and footer facets in the h:dataTable tag.)

- The tabbed pane renderer *uses the servlet request dispatcher* to include the content associated with a tab if that content is a URL.

- You can *add an action listener* to the tabbed pane. That listener is notified whenever a tab is selected.

- You can *localize tab text* by specifying keys from a resource bundle instead of the actual text displayed in the tab.

- The tabbed pane *uses hidden fields* to transmit the selected tab and its content from the client to the server.

Because the tabbed pane has so many features, there are several ways in which you can use it. Here's a simple use:

```
<corejsf:tabbedPane>
    <f:selectItem itemLabel="Jefferson"  itemValue="/jefferson.jsp"/>
    <f:selectItem itemLabel="Roosevelt"  itemValue="/roosevelt.jsp"/>
    <f:selectItem itemLabel="Lincoln"    itemValue="/lincoln.jsp"/>
    <f:selectItem itemLabel="Washington" itemValue="/washington.jsp"/>
</corejsf:tabbedPane>
```

The preceding code results in a rather plain-looking tabbed pane, as shown in Figure 9–10.

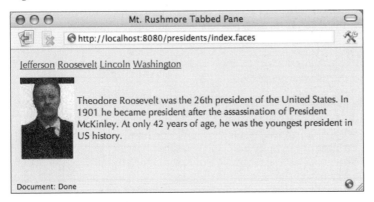

Figure 9–10   A Plain Tabbed Pane

To get the effect shown in Figure 9–9, you can use CSS styles, like this:

```
<corejsf:tabbedPane styleClass="tabbedPane"
      tabClass="tab" selectedTabClass="selectedTab">
    <f:selectItem itemLabel="Jefferson"  itemValue="/jefferson.jsp"/>
    <f:selectItem itemLabel="Roosevelt"  itemValue="/roosevelt.jsp"/>
    <f:selectItem itemLabel="Lincoln"    itemValue="/lincoln.jsp"/>
    <f:selectItem itemLabel="Washington" itemValue="/washington.jsp"/>
</corejsf:tabbedPane>
```

You can also use a single f:selectItems tag in lieu of multiple f:selectitem tags, like this:

```
<corejsf:tabbedPane styleClass="tabbedPane"
      tabClass="tab" selectedTabClass="selectedTab">
    <f:selectItems value="#{tabbedPaneBean.tabs}"/>
</corejsf:tabbedPane>
```

The preceding items are created by a bean:

```
public class TabbedPaneBean {
    private static final SelectItem[] tabs = {
        new SelectItem("/jefferson.jsp",  "Jefferson"),
        new SelectItem("/roosevelt.jsp",  "Roosevelt"),
        new SelectItem("/lincoln.jsp",    "Lincoln"),
        new SelectItem("/washington.jsp", "Washington"),
    };

    public SelectItem[] getTabs() {
        return tabs;
    }
}
```

In the previous example we directly specified the text displayed in each tab as select item labels: Jefferson, Roosevelt, etc. Before the tabbed pane renderer encodes a tab, it looks to see if those labels are keys in a resource bundle—if so, the renderer encodes the key's value. If the labels are not keys in a resource bundle, the renderer just encodes the labels as they are. You specify the resource bundle with the resourceBundle attribute, like this:

```
<corejsf:tabbedPane resourceBundle="com.corejsf.messages">
    <f:selectItem itemLabel="jeffersonTabKey"  itemValue="/jefferson.jsp"/>
    <f:selectItem itemLabel="rooseveltTabKey"  itemValue="/roosevelt.jsp"/>
    <f:selectItem itemLabel="lincolnTabKey"    itemValue="/lincoln.jsp"/>
    <f:selectItem itemLabel="washingtonTabKey" itemValue="/washington.jsp"/>
</corejsf:tabbedPane>
```

Notice the item labels—they are all keys in the messages resource bundle:

```
...
jeffersonTabText=Jefferson
rooseveltTabText=Roosevelt
lincolnTabText=Lincoln
washingtonTabText=Washington
...
```

There's one more way to specify tabs: with a facet, like this:

```
<corejsf:tabbedPane >

   ...
   <f:selectItem itemLabel="Jefferson"  itemValue="jefferson"/>

   ...
   <f:facet name="jefferson">
      <h:panelGrid columns="2">
         <h:graphicImage value="/images/jefferson.jpg"/>
         <h:outputText value="#{msgs.jeffersonDiscussion}"/>
      </h:panelGrid>
   </f:facet>
</corejsf:tabbedPane>
```

Up to now we've used URLs for item values. The contents of that URL are included by the tabbed pane renderer. But in the preceding code we specify a facet instead of a URL—the Jefferson select item's value is jefferson, which corresponds to a facet of the same name. Because we specified a facet, the tabbed pane renderer renders the facet instead of including content.

Finally, the tabbed pane component fires an action event when a user selects a tab. You can use the f:actionListener tag to add one or more action listeners, or you can specify a method that handles action events with the tabbed pane's actionListener attribute, like this:

```
<corejsf:tabbedPane ... actionListener="#{tabbedPaneBean.presidentSelected}">
   <f:selectItems value="#{tabbedPaneBean.tabs}"/>
</corejsf:tabbedPane>
```

Now that we have an overview of the tabbed pane component, let's take a closer look at how it implements advanced features. Here's what we'll cover in this section.

- "Processing SelectItem Children" on page 406
- "Processing Facets" on page 407
- "Including Content" on page 409
- "Encoding CSS Styles" on page 410
- "Using Hidden Fields" on page 411

- "Saving and Restoring State" on page 412
- "Firing Action Events" on page 414

Processing SelectItem Children

The tabbed pane lets you specify tabs with f:selectItem or f:selectItems. Those tags create UISelectItem components and add them to the tabbed pane as children. Because the tabbed pane renderer has children and because it renders those children, it overrides rendersChildren() and encodeChildren().

```
public boolean rendersChildren() {
    return true;
}
public void encodeChildren(FacesContext context, UIComponent component)
        throws java.io.IOException {
    // if the tabbedpane component has no children, this method is still called
    if (component.getChildCount() == 0) {
        return;
    }
    ...
    List items = com.corejsf.util.Renderers.getSelectItems(context, component);
    Iterator it = items.iterator();
    while (it.hasNext())
        encodeTab(context, writer, (SelectItem) it.next(), component);
    ...
    }
    ...
}
```

Generally, a component that processes its children contains code such as the following:

```
Iterator children = component.getChildren().iterator();
while (children.hasNext()) {
    UIComponent child = (UIComponent) children.next();
    processChild(context, writer, child, component);
}
```

However, our situation is more complex. Recall from Chapter 4 that you can specify a single select item, a collection of select items, an array of select items, or a map of Java objects as the value for the f:selectItems tag. Whenever your class processes children that are of type SelectItem or SelectItems, you need to deal with this mix of possibilities. The com.corejsf.util.Renderers.getSelectItems method accounts for all those data types and synthesizes them into a list of SelectItem objects. Here is the code for the helper method:

```
public static List getSelectItems(UIComponent component) {
    ArrayList list = new ArrayList();
    Iterator children = component.getChildren().iterator();
    while (children.hasNext()) {
        UIComponent child = (UIComponent) children.next();

        if (child instanceof UISelectItem) {
            Object value = ((UISelectItem) child).getValue();
            if (value == null) {
                UISelectItem item = (UISelectItem) child;
                list.add(new SelectItem(item.getItemValue(),
                        item.getItemLabel(),
                        item.getItemDescription(),
                        item.isItemDisabled()));
            } else if (value instanceof SelectItem) {
                list.add(value);
            }
        } else if (child instanceof UISelectItems) {
            Object value = ((UISelectItems) child).getValue();
            if (value instanceof SelectItem)
                list.add(value);
            else if (value instanceof SelectItem[])
                list.addAll(Arrays.asList((SelectItem[]) value));
            else if (value instanceof Collection)
                list.addAll((Collection) value);
            else if (value instanceof Map) {
                Iterator entries = ((Map) value).entrySet().iterator();
                while (entries.hasNext()) {
                    Map.Entry entry = (Map.Entry) entries.next();
                    list.add(new SelectItem(entry.getKey(),
                            "" + entry.getValue()));
                }
            }
        }
    }
    return list;
}
```

The encodeChildren method of the TabbedPaneRenderer calls this method and encodes
each child into a tab. You will see the details in "Using Hidden Fields" on
page 411.

Processing Facets

The tabbed pane lets you specify URLs or facet names for the content associated with a particular tag. The renderer accounts for that duality in its encodeEnd
method:

```
public void encodeEnd(FacesContext context, UIComponent component)
                                         throws java.io.IOException {
   ResponseWriter writer = context.getResponseWriter();
   UITabbedPane tabbedPane = (UITabbedPane) component;
   String content = tabbedPane.getContent();
   ...
   if (content != null) {
     UIComponent facet = component.getFacet(content);
     if (facet != null) {
       if (facet.isRendered()) {
          facet.encodeBegin(context);
          if (facet.getRendersChildren())
             facet.encodeChildren(context);
          facet.encodeEnd(context);
       }
     }
     else
        includePage(context, component);
   }
}
...
}
```

The UITabbedPane class has a field content that stores the facet name or URL of the currently displayed tab.

The encodeEnd method checks to see whether the content of the currently selected tab is the name of a facet of this component. If so, it encodes the facet by invoking its encodeBegin, encodeChildren, and encodeEnd methods. Whenever a renderer renders its own children, it needs to take over this responsibility.

If the content of the current tab is not a facet, the renderer assumes the content is a URL and includes it, as shown in the following section.

API `javax.faces.component.UIComponent`

- `UIComponent getFacet(String facetName)`

  Returns a reference to the facet if it exists. If the facet does not exist, the method returns null.

- `boolean getRendersChildren()`

  Returns a boolean that's true if the component renders its children, false otherwise. A component's encodeChildren method won't be called if this method does not return true. By default, getRendersChildren returns false.

- boolean isRendered()

    Returns the rendered property. The component is only rendered if the rendered property is true.

Including Content

As you saw in the preceding section, the tabbed pane renderer's encodeEnd method calls the includePage method when the content is described by a URL.

Here's the includePage method:

```
private void includePage(FacesContext fc, UIComponent component) {
    ExternalContext ec = fc.getExternalContext();
    ServletContext sc = (ServletContext) ec.getContext();
    UITabbedPane tabbedPane = (UITabbedPane) component;
    String content = tabbedPane.getContent();

    ServletRequest request = (ServletRequest) ec.getRequest();
    ServletResponse response = (ServletResponse) ec.getResponse();
    try {
        sc.getRequestDispatcher(content).include(request, response);
    }
    catch(Exception ex) {
        System.out.println("Couldn't load page: " + content);
    }
}
```

The includePage method uses the servlet request dispatcher to include the response from the specified URL. The request dispatcher reads the requested URL and writes its content to the response writer.

---

javax.servlet.ServletContext

- RequestDispatcher getRequestDispatcher(String path)

    Returns a reference to a request dispatcher, given a path to a resource.

---

javax.servlet.RequestDispatcher

- void include(ServletRequest request, ServletResponse response) throws IllegalStateException, IOException, ServletException

    Includes the content of some resource. The path to that resource is passed to the RequestDispatcher constructor.

Encoding CSS Styles

You can support CSS styles in two steps:

*   Add an attribute to the tag library descriptor.

*   Encode the component's attribute in your renderer's encode methods.

First, we add attributes styleClass, tabClass, and selectedTabClass to the TLD:

```
<taglib>
   ...
   <tag>
      ...
      <attribute>
        <name>styleClass</name>
        <description>The CSS style for this component</description>
      </attribute>
      ...
   </tag>
</taglib>
```

We then write attributes for the CSS classes:

```
public class TabbedPaneRenderer extends Renderer {
   ...
   public void encodeBegin(FacesContext context, UIComponent component)
         throws java.io.IOException {
      ResponseWriter writer = context.getResponseWriter();
      writer.startElement("table", component);

      String styleClass = (String) component.getAttributes().get("styleClass");
      if (styleClass != null)
         writer.writeAttribute("class", styleClass, "styleClass");

      writer.write("\n"); // to make generated HTML easier to read
   }
   public void encodeChildren(FacesContext context, UIComponent component)
            throws java.io.IOException {
      ...
      encodeTab(context, responseWriter, selectItem, component);
      ...
   }
   ...
   private void encodeTab(FacesContext context, ResponseWriter writer,
         SelectItem item, UIComponent component) throws java.io.IOException {
      ...
      String tabText = getLocalizedTabText(component, item.getLabel());
      ...
```

```
        String tabClass = null;
        if (content.equals(selectedContent))
            tabClass = (String) component.getAttributes().get("selectedTabClass");
        else
            tabClass = (String) component.getAttributes().get("tabClass");

        if (tabClass != null)
            writer.writeAttribute("class", tabClass, "tabClass");
        ...
    }
    ...
}
```

We encode the styleClass attribute for the tabbed pane's outer table and encode
the tabClass and selectedTabClass attribute for each individual tag.

  javax.faces.model.SelectItem

- Object getValue()
  Returns the select item's value.

Using Hidden Fields

Each tab in the tabbed pane is encoded as a hyperlink, like this:

```
<a href="#" onclick="document.forms[formId][clientId].value=content;
    document.forms[formId].submit();"/>
```

When a user clicks on a particular hyperlink, the form is submitted (The href
value corresponds to the current page). Of course, the server needs to know
which tab was selected. This information is stored in a *hidden field* that is placed
after all the tabs:

```
<input type="hidden" name="clientId"/>
```

When the form is submitted, the name and value of the hidden field are sent
back to the server, allowing the decode method to activate the selected tab.

The renderer's encodeTab method produces the hyperlink tags. The encodeEnd
method calls encodeHiddenFields(), which encodes the hidden field. You can see
the details in Listing 9–18 on page 414.

When the tabbed pane renderer decodes the incoming request, it uses the
request parameter, associated with the hidden field, to set the tabbed pane
component's content.

```
public void decode(FacesContext context, UIComponent component) {
    Map requestParams = context.getExternalContext().getRequestParameterMap();
    String clientId = component.getClientId(context);
    String content = (String) (requestParams.get(clientId));
```

```
      if (content != null && !content.equals("")) {
         UITabbedPane tabbedPane = (UITabbedPane) component;
         tabbedPane.setContent(content);
      }
      ...
   }
   ...
}
```

Saving and Restoring State

The UITabbedPane class has an instance field that stores the facet name or URL of the currently displayed tab. Whenever your components have instance fields and there is a possibility that they are used in a web application that saves state on the client, then you need to implement the saveState and restoreState methods of the StateHolder interface.

These methods have the following form:

```
public Object saveState(FacesContext context) {
   Object values[] = new Object[n];
   values[0] = super.saveState(context);
   values[1] = instance field #1;
   values[2] = instance field #2;
   ...
   return values;
}

public void restoreState(FacesContext context, Object state) {
   Object values[] = (Object[]) state;
   super.restoreState(context, values[0]);
   instance field #1 = (Type) values[1];
   instance field #2 = (Type) values[2];
   ...
}
```

Listing 9–17 shows how the UITabbedPane class saves and restores its state.

To test why state saving is necessary, run this experiment:

- Comment out the saveState and restoreState methods.
- Activate client-side state saving by adding these lines to web.xml:

```
<context-param>
   <param-name>javax.faces.STATE_SAVING_METHOD</param-name>
   <param-value>client</param-value>
</context-param>
```

- Add a button to the index.jsp page of the bears application:

```
<h:commandButton value="Redisplay"/>
```

- Run the application and click on a tab.
- Click the "Redisplay" button. The current page is redisplayed, but no tab is selected!

This problem occurs because the state of the page is saved on the client, encoded as the value of a hidden field. When the page is redisplayed, a new UITabbedPane object is constructed and its restoreState method is called. If the UITabbedPane class does not override the restoreState method, the content field is not restored.

> **NOTE:** In Chapter 6, you saw that you could save the state of converters and validators simply by making the converter or validator class serializable. This approach does not work for components—you must use the StateHolder methods.

> **TIP:** If you store all of your component state as *attributes*, you don't have to implement the saveState and restoreState methods because component attributes are automatically saved by the JSF implementation. For example, the tabbed pane can simply use a "content" attribute instead of the content field.
>
> Then you don't need the UITabbedPane class at all. Simply use the UICommand super-class and declare the component class like this:
>
> ```
> <component>
>     <component-type>com.corejsf.TabbedPane</component-type>
>     <component-class>javax.faces.component.UICommand</component-class>
> </component>
> ```
>
> Frankly, that's what we do in our own code. You will find several examples in Chapters 11 and 12. The standard JSF components use the more elaborate mechanism to minimize the size of the state information.

Listing 9–17　　bears/WEB-INF/classes/com/corejsf/UITabbedPane.java

```
1. package com.corejsf;
2.
3. import javax.faces.component.UICommand;
4. import javax.faces.context.FacesContext;
5.
6. public class UITabbedPane extends UICommand {
7.     private String content;
8.
9.     public String getContent() { return content; }
```

Listing 9-17	bears/WEB-INF/classes/com/corejsf/UITabbedPane.java (cont.)

```
10.    public void setContent(String newValue) { content = newValue; }
11.
12.    public Object saveState(FacesContext context) {
13.        Object values[] = new Object[2];
14.        values[0] = super.saveState(context);
15.        values[1] = content;
16.        return values;
17.    }
18.
19.    public void restoreState(FacesContext context, Object state) {
20.        Object values[] = (Object[]) state;
21.        super.restoreState(context, values[0]);
22.        content = (String) values[1];
23.    }
24. }
```

Firing Action Events

When your component handles action events or actions, you need to take the following steps:

- Your component should extend UICommmand.

- You need to queue an ActionEvent in the decode method of your renderer.

The tabbed pane component fires an action event when a user selects one of its tabs. That action is queued by TabbedPaneRenderer in the decode method.

```
public void decode(FacesContext context, UIComponent component) {
    ...
    UITabbedPane tabbedPane = (UITabbedPane) component;
    ...
    component.queueEvent(new ActionEvent(tabbedPane));
}
```

This completes the discussion of the TabbedPaneRenderer class. You will find the complete code in Listing 9–18. The TabbedPaneTag class is as boring as ever, and we do not show it here.

Listing 9-18	bears/WEB-INF/classes/com/corejsf/TabbedPaneRenderer.java

```
1. package com.corejsf;
2.
3. import java.io.IOException;
4. import java.util.Iterator;
5. import java.util.List;
6. import java.util.Map;
7. import java.util.logging.Level;
```

Listing 9–18   bears/WEB-INF/classes/com/corejsf/TabbedPaneRenderer.java (cont.)

```
 8. import java.util.logging.Logger;
 9. import javax.faces.component.UIComponent;
10. import javax.faces.context.ExternalContext;
11. import javax.faces.context.FacesContext;
12. import javax.faces.context.ResponseWriter;
13. import javax.faces.event.ActionEvent;
14. import javax.faces.model.SelectItem;
15. import javax.faces.render.Renderer;
16. import javax.servlet.ServletContext;
17. import javax.servlet.ServletException;
18. import javax.servlet.ServletRequest;
19. import javax.servlet.ServletResponse;
20.
21. // Renderer for the UITabbedPane component
22.
23. public class TabbedPaneRenderer extends Renderer {
24.    private static Logger logger = Logger.getLogger("com.corejsf.util");
25.
26.    // By default, getRendersChildren() returns false, so encodeChildren()
27.    // won't be invoked unless we override getRendersChildren() to return true
28.
29.    public boolean getRendersChildren() {
30.       return true;
31.    }
32.
33.    // The decode method gets the value of the request parameter whose name
34.    // is the client Id of the tabbedpane component. The request parameter
35.    // is encoded as a hidden field by encodeHiddenField, which is called by
36.    // encodeEnd. The value for the parameter is set by JavaScript generated
37.    // by the encodeTab method. It is the name of a facet or a JSP page.
38.
39.    // The decode method uses the request parameter value to set the
40.    // tabbedpane component's content attribute.
41.    // Finally, decode() queues an action event that's fired to registered
42.    // listeners in the Invoke Application phase of the JSF lifecycle. Action
43.    // listeners can be specified with the <corejsf:tabbedpane>'s actionListener
44.    // attribute or with <f:actionListener> tags in the body of the
45.    // <corejsf:tabbedpane> tag.
46.
47.    public void decode(FacesContext context, UIComponent component) {
48.       Map requestParams = context.getExternalContext().getRequestParameterMap();
49.       String clientId = component.getClientId(context);
50.
51.       String content = (String) (requestParams.get(clientId));
52.       if (content != null && !content.equals("")) {
53.          UITabbedPane tabbedPane = (UITabbedPane) component;
```

Listing 9–18   bears/WEB-INF/classes/com/corejsf/TabbedPaneRenderer.java (cont.)

```
54.           tabbedPane.setContent(content);
55.       }
56.
57.       component.queueEvent(new ActionEvent(component));
58.   }
59.
60.   // The encodeBegin method writes the starting <table> HTML element
61.   // with the CSS class specified by the <corejsf:tabbedpane>'s styleClass
62.   // attribute (if supplied)
63.
64.   public void encodeBegin(FacesContext context, UIComponent component)
65.           throws java.io.IOException {
66.       ResponseWriter writer = context.getResponseWriter();
67.       writer.startElement("table", component);
68.
69.       String styleClass = (String) component.getAttributes().get("styleClass");
70.       if (styleClass != null)
71.           writer.writeAttribute("class", styleClass, null);
72.
73.       writer.write("\n"); // to make generated HTML easier to read
74.   }
75.
76.   // encodeChildren() is invoked by the JSF implementation after encodeBegin().
77.   // The children of the <corejsf:tabbedpane> component are UISelectItem
78.   // components, set with one or more <f:selectItem> tags or a single
79.   // <f:selectItems> tag in the body of <corejsf:tabbedpane>
80.
81.   public void encodeChildren(FacesContext context, UIComponent component)
82.           throws java.io.IOException {
83.       // if the tabbedpane component has no children, this method is still
84.       // called
85.       if (component.getChildCount() == 0) {
86.           return;
87.       }
88.
89.       ResponseWriter writer = context.getResponseWriter();
90.       writer.startElement("thead", component);
91.       writer.startElement("tr", component);
92.       writer.startElement("th", component);
93.
94.       writer.startElement("table", component);
95.       writer.startElement("tbody", component);
96.       writer.startElement("tr", component);
97.
98.       List items = com.corejsf.util.Renderers.getSelectItems(component);
```

Listing 9–18 bears/WEB-INF/classes/com/corejsf/TabbedPaneRenderer.java (cont.)

```
 99.        Iterator it = items.iterator();
100.        while (it.hasNext())
101.           encodeTab(context, writer, (SelectItem) it.next(), component);
102.
103.        writer.endElement("tr");
104.        writer.endElement("tbody");
105.        writer.endElement("table");
106.
107.        writer.endElement("th");
108.        writer.endElement("tr");
109.        writer.endElement("thead");
110.        writer.write("\n"); // to make generated HTML easier to read
111.     }
112.
113.     // encodeEnd() is invoked by the JSF implementation after encodeChildren().
114.     // encodeEnd() writes the table body and encodes the tabbedpane's content
115.     // in a single table row.
116.
117.     // The content for the tabbed pane can be specified as either a URL for
118.     // a JSP page or a facet name, so encodeEnd() checks to see if it's a facet;
119.     // if so, it encodes it; if not, it includes the JSP page
120.
121.     public void encodeEnd(FacesContext context, UIComponent component)
122.           throws java.io.IOException {
123.        ResponseWriter writer = context.getResponseWriter();
124.        UITabbedPane tabbedPane = (UITabbedPane) component;
125.        String content = tabbedPane.getContent();
126.
127.        writer.startElement("tbody", component);
128.        writer.startElement("tr", component);
129.        writer.startElement("td", component);
130.
131.        if (content != null) {
132.           UIComponent facet = component.getFacet(content);
133.           if (facet != null) {
134.              if (facet.isRendered()) {
135.                 facet.encodeBegin(context);
136.                 if (facet.getRendersChildren())
137.                    facet.encodeChildren(context);
138.                 facet.encodeEnd(context);
139.              }
140.           } else
141.              includePage(context, component);
142.        }
143.
```

```
144.        writer.endElement("td");
145.        writer.endElement("tr");
146.        writer.endElement("tbody");
147.
148.        // Close off the column, row, and table elements
149.        writer.endElement("table");
150.
151.        encodeHiddenField(context, writer, component);
152.      }
153.
154.    // The encodeHiddenField method is called at the end of encodeEnd().
155.    // See the decode method for an explanation of the field and its value.
156.
157.    private void encodeHiddenField(FacesContext context, ResponseWriter writer,
158.          UIComponent component) throws java.io.IOException {
159.      // write hidden field whose name is the tabbedpane's client Id
160.      writer.startElement("input", component);
161.      writer.writeAttribute("type", "hidden", null);
162.      writer.writeAttribute("name", component.getClientId(context), null);
163.      writer.endElement("input");
164.    }
165.
166.    // encodeTab, which is called by encodeChildren, encodes an HTML anchor
167.    // element with an onclick attribute which sets the value of the hidden
168.    // field encoded by encodeHiddenField and submits the tabbedpane's enclosing
169.    // form. See the decode method for more information about the hidden field.
170.    // encodeTab also writes out a class attribute for each tab corresponding
171.    // to either the tabClass attribute (for unselected tabs) or the
172.    // selectedTabClass attribute (for the selected tab).
173.
174.    private void encodeTab(FacesContext context, ResponseWriter writer,
175.          SelectItem item, UIComponent component) throws java.io.IOException {
176.      String tabText = getLocalizedTabText(component, item.getLabel());
177.      String content = (String) item.getValue();
178.
179.      writer.startElement("td", component);
180.      writer.startElement("a", component);
181.      writer.writeAttribute("href", "#", "href");
182.
183.      String clientId = component.getClientId(context);
184.      String formId = com.corejsf.util.Renderers.getFormId(context, component);
185.
186.      writer.writeAttribute("onclick",
187.      // write value for hidden field whose name is the tabbedpane's client Id
188.
```

Listing 9–18 bears/WEB-INF/classes/com/corejsf/TabbedPaneRenderer.java (cont.)

```
189.            "document.forms['" + formId + "']['" + clientId + "'].value='"
190.                + content + "'; " +
191.
192.                // submit form in which the tabbedpane resides
193.                "document.forms['" + formId + "'].submit(); ", null);
194.
195.        UITabbedPane tabbedPane = (UITabbedPane) component;
196.        String selectedContent = tabbedPane.getContent();
197.
198.        String tabClass = null;
199.        if (content.equals(selectedContent))
200.            tabClass = (String) component.getAttributes().get("selectedTabClass");
201.        else
202.            tabClass = (String) component.getAttributes().get("tabClass");
203.
204.        if (tabClass != null)
205.            writer.writeAttribute("class", tabClass, null);
206.
207.        writer.write(tabText);
208.
209.        writer.endElement("a");
210.        writer.endElement("td");
211.        writer.write("\n"); // to make generated HTML easier to read
212.    }
213.
214.    // Text for the tabs in the tabbedpane component can be specified as
215.    // a key in a resource bundle, or as the actual text that's displayed
216.    // in the tab. Given that text, the getLocalizedTabText method tries to
217.    // retrieve a value from the resource bundle specified with the
218.    // <corejsf:tabbedpane>'s resourceBundle attribute. If no value is found,
219.    // getLocalizedTabText just returns the string it was passed.
220.
221.    private String getLocalizedTabText(UIComponent tabbedPane, String key) {
222.        String bundle = (String) tabbedPane.getAttributes().get("resourceBundle");
223.        String localizedText = null;
224.
225.        if (bundle != null) {
226.            localizedText = com.corejsf.util.Messages.getString(bundle, key, null);
227.        }
228.        if (localizedText == null)
229.            localizedText = key;
230.        // The key parameter was not really a key in the resource bundle,
231.        // so just return the string as is
232.        return localizedText;
233.    }
```

| **Listing 9-18** | bears/WEB-INF/classes/com/corejsf/TabbedPaneRenderer.java (cont.) |

```
234.
235.    // includePage uses the servlet request dispatcher to include the page
236.    // corresponding to the selected tab.
237.
238.    private void includePage(FacesContext fc, UIComponent component) {
239.        ExternalContext ec = fc.getExternalContext();
240.        ServletContext sc = (ServletContext) ec.getContext();
241.        UITabbedPane tabbedPane = (UITabbedPane) component;
242.        String content = tabbedPane.getContent();
243.
244.        ServletRequest request = (ServletRequest) ec.getRequest();
245.        ServletResponse response = (ServletResponse) ec.getResponse();
246.        try {
247.            sc.getRequestDispatcher(content).include(request, response);
248.        } catch (ServletException ex) {
249.            logger.log(Level.WARNING, "Couldn't load page: " + content, ex);
250.        } catch (IOException ex) {
251.            logger.log(Level.WARNING, "Couldn't load page: " + content, ex);
252.        }
253.    }
254. }
```

Using the Tabbed Pane

The bears application shown in Figure 9–8 on page 401 uses a bean to specify the URLs for the tabs. The bean code is in Listing 9–19. Companion code also contains a presidents application that specifies the tabs with facets.

The directory structure for the application is shown in Figure 9–11. Listing 9–20 shows the index.jsp page, and Listing 9–21 shows one of the pages that make up the tab content. The other pages look similar and are omitted. Listing 9–22 through Listing 9–25 show the tag library descriptor, tag class, faces configuration file and the stylesheet for the tabbed pane application.

You have now seen how to implement custom components. We covered all essential issues that you will encounter as you develop your own components. The code in this chapter should make a good starting point for your component implementations.

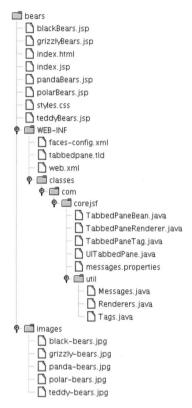

```
bears
    blackBears.jsp
    grizzlyBears.jsp
    index.html
    index.jsp
    pandaBears.jsp
    polarBears.jsp
    styles.css
    teddyBears.jsp
    WEB-INF
        faces-config.xml
        tabbedpane.tld
        web.xml
        classes
            com
                corejsf
                    TabbedPaneBean.java
                    TabbedPaneRenderer.java
                    TabbedPaneTag.java
                    UITabbedPane.java
                    messages.properties
                    util
                        Messages.java
                        Renderers.java
                        Tags.java
    images
        black-bears.jpg
        grizzly-bears.jpg
        panda-bears.jpg
        polar-bears.jpg
        teddy-bears.jpg
```

Figure 9–11 The Bears Directory Structure

Listing 9–19   bears/WEB-INF/classes/com/corejsf/TabbedPaneBean.java

```
1. package com.corejsf;
2.
3. import javax.faces.model.SelectItem;
4.
5. public class TabbedPaneBean {
6.    private static final SelectItem[] tabs = {
7.       new SelectItem("/blackBears.jsp",   "blackTabText"),
8.       new SelectItem("/grizzlyBears.jsp", "grizzlyTabText"),
```

Listing 9–19   bears/WEB-INF/classes/com/corejsf/TabbedPaneBean.java (cont.)

```
9.       new SelectItem("/polarBears.jsp",  "polarTabText"),
10.      new SelectItem("/pandaBears.jsp",  "pandaTabText"),
11.      new SelectItem("/teddyBears.jsp",  "teddyTabText"),
12.    };
13.
14.    public SelectItem[] getTabs() {
15.      return tabs;
16.    }
17.  }
```

Listing 9–20   bears/index.jsp

```
1.  <html>
2.    <%@ taglib uri="http://java.sun.com/jsf/core" prefix="f" %>
3.    <%@ taglib uri="http://java.sun.com/jsf/html" prefix="h" %>
4.    <%@ taglib uri="http://corejsf.com/tabbedpane" prefix="corejsf" %>
5.
6.    <f:view>
7.      <head>
8.        <link href="styles.css" rel="stylesheet" type="text/css"/>
9.        <f:loadBundle basename="com.corejsf.messages" var="msgs"/>
10.       <title>
11.         <h:outputText value="#{msgs.windowTitle}"/>
12.       </title>
13.     </head>
14.     <body>
15.       <h:form>
16.         <corejsf:tabbedPane styleClass="tabbedPane" tabClass="tab"
17.           selectedTabClass="selectedTab"
18.           resourceBundle="com.corejsf.messages">
19.           <f:selectItems value="#{tabbedPaneBean.tabs}"/>
20.         </corejsf:tabbedPane>
21.       </h:form>
22.     </body>
23.   </f:view>
24. </html>
```

Listing 9–21 bears/blackBears.jsp

```
1. <%@ taglib uri="http://java.sun.com/jsf/html" prefix="h" %>
2. <%@ taglib uri="http://java.sun.com/jsf/core" prefix="f" %>
3.
4. <f:subview id="blackBear">
5.    <h:panelGrid columns='2' columnClasses='bearDiscussionColumn'>
6.       <h:graphicImage value='/images/black-bears.jpg'/>
7.       <h:outputText value='#{msgs.blackBearDiscussion}'
8.                 styleClass='tabbedPaneContent'/>
9.    </h:panelGrid>
10. </f:subview>
```

Listing 9–22 bears/WEB-INF/tabbedpane.tld

```
1. <?xml version="1.0" encoding="ISO-8859-1" ?>
2.
3. <!DOCTYPE taglib
4.   PUBLIC "-//Sun Microsystems, Inc.//DTD JSP Tag Library 1.2//EN"
5.   "http://java.sun.com/dtd/web-jsptaglibrary_1_2.dtd">
6.
7. <taglib>
8.    <tlib-version>0.03</tlib-version>
9.    <jsp-version>1.2</jsp-version>
10.   <short-name>corejsf</short-name>
11.   <uri>http://corejsf/components</uri>
12.   <description>A library containing a tabbed pane</description>
13.
14.   <tag>
15.      <name>tabbedPane</name>
16.      <tag-class>com.corejsf.TabbedPaneTag</tag-class>
17.      <body-content>JSP</body-content>
18.      <description>A tag for a tabbed pane component</description>
19.
20.      <attribute>
21.         <name>id</name>
22.         <required>false</required>
23.         <rtexprvalue>false</rtexprvalue>
24.         <description>Component id of this component</description>
25.      </attribute>
26.
```

Listing 9–22 bears/WEB-INF/tabbedpane.tld (cont.)

```
27.        <attribute>
28.          <name>binding</name>
29.          <required>false</required>
30.          <rtexprvalue>false</rtexprvalue>
31.          <description>Component reference expression for this component
32.          </description>
33.        </attribute>
34.
35.        <attribute>
36.          <name>rendered</name>
37.          <required>false</required>
38.          <rtexprvalue>false</rtexprvalue>
39.          <description>
40.            A flag indicating whether or not this component should be rendered.
41.            If not specified, the default value is true.
42.          </description>
43.        </attribute>
44.
45.        <attribute>
46.          <name>style</name>
47.          <required>false</required>
48.          <rtexprvalue>false</rtexprvalue>
49.          <description>The CSS style for this component</description>
50.        </attribute>
51.
52.        <attribute>
53.          <name>styleClass</name>
54.          <required>false</required>
55.          <rtexprvalue>false</rtexprvalue>
56.          <description>The CSS class for this component</description>
57.        </attribute>
58.
59.        <attribute>
60.          <name>tabClass</name>
61.          <required>false</required>
62.          <rtexprvalue>false</rtexprvalue>
63.          <description>The CSS class for unselected tabs</description>
64.        </attribute>
65.
```

Listing 9–22 bears/WEB-INF/tabbedpane.tld (cont.)

```
65.        <attribute>
66.          <name>selectedTabClass</name>
67.          <required>false</required>
68.          <rtexprvalue>false</rtexprvalue>
69.          <description>The CSS class for the selected tab</description>
70.        </attribute>
71.
72.        <attribute>
73.          <name>resourceBundle</name>
74.          <required>false</required>
75.          <rtexprvalue>false</rtexprvalue>
76.          <description>
77.            The resource bundle used to localize select item labels
78.          </description>
79.        </attribute>
80.
81.        <attribute>
82.          <name>actionListener</name>
83.          <required>false</required>
84.          <rtexprvalue>false</rtexprvalue>
85.          <description>
86.            A method reference that's called when a tab is selected
87.          </description>
88.        </attribute>
89.      </tag>
90.    </taglib>
```

Listing 9–23 tabbedpane/WEB-INF/classes/com/corejsf/TabbedPaneTag.java

```
1. package com.corejsf;
2.
3. import javax.faces.application.Application;
4. import javax.faces.context.FacesContext;
5. import javax.faces.component.UIComponent;
6. import javax.faces.el.MethodBinding;
7. import javax.faces.event.ActionEvent;
8. import javax.faces.webapp.UIComponentBodyTag;
9.
```

Listing 9–23	tabbedpane/WEB-INF/classes/com/corejsf/TabbedPaneTag.java (cont.)

```java
10. import com.corejsf.util.Tags;
11.
12. // This tag supports the following attributes
13. //
14. // binding (supported by UIComponentBodyTag)
15. // id (supported by UIComponentBodyTag)
16. // style (supported by UIComponentBodyTag)
17. // rendered (supported by UIComponentBodyTag)
18. // styleClass
19. // tabClass
20. // selectedTabClass
21. // resourceBundle
22. // actionListener
23.
24. public class TabbedPaneTag extends UIComponentBodyTag {
25.    private String style, styleClass, tabClass, selectedTabClass, resourceBundle,
26.                   actionListener;
27.
28.    public String getRendererType () {
29.       return "TabbedPaneRenderer";
30.    }
31.    public String getComponentType() {
32.       return "Tabbed Pane";
33.    }
34.
35.    // tabClass attribute
36.    public String getTabClass() { return tabClass; }
37.    public void setTabClass(String tabClass) { this.tabClass= tabClass; }
38.
39.    // selectedTabClass attribute
40.    public String getSelectedTabClass() { return selectedTabClass; }
41.    public void setSelectedTabClass(String selectedTabClass) {
42.       this.selectedTabClass= selectedTabClass;
43.    }
44.
45.    // styleClass attribute
```

Listing 9–23	tabbedpane/WEB-INF/classes/com/corejsf/TabbedPaneTag.java (cont.)

```
46.   public String getStyle() { return style; }
47.   public void setStyle(String style) { this.style= style; }
48.
49.   // styleClass attribute
50.   public String getStyleClass() { return styleClass; }
51.   public void setStyleClass(String styleClass) { this.styleClass = styleClass; }
52.
53.   // resourceBundle attribute
54.   public String getResourceBundle() { return resourceBundle; }
55.   public void setResourceBundle(String resourceBundle) {
56.       this.resourceBundle = resourceBundle;
57.   }
58.
59.   // actionListener attribute
60.   public String getActionListener() { return resourceBundle; }
61.   public void setActionListener(String actionListener) {
62.       this.actionListener = actionListener;
63.   }
64.
65.   protected void setProperties(UIComponent component) {
66.       // make sure you always call the superclass
67.       super.setProperties(component);
68.
69.       com.corejsf.util.Tags.setComponentAttribute(component, "style", style);
70.       com.corejsf.util.Tags.setComponentAttribute(component, "styleClass",
71.                                                   styleClass);
72.       com.corejsf.util.Tags.setComponentAttribute(component, "tabClass",
73.                                                   tabClass);
74.       com.corejsf.util.Tags.setComponentAttribute(component, "selectedTabClass",
75.                                                   selectedTabClass);
76.       com.corejsf.util.Tags.setComponentAttribute(component, "resourceBundle",
77.                                                   resourceBundle);
78.       com.corejsf.util.Tags.setComponentAttribute(component, "actionListener",
79.                                                   actionListener);
80.   }
81. }
```

Listing 9–24 tabbedpane/WEB-INF/faces-config.xml

```
1. <?xml version="1.0"?>
2.
3. <!DOCTYPE faces-config PUBLIC
4. "-//Sun Microsystems, Inc.//DTD JavaServer Faces Config 1.0//EN"
5. "http://java.sun.com/dtd/web-facesconfig_1_0.dtd">
6.
7. <faces-config>
8.    <managed-bean>
9.       <managed-bean-name>tabbedPaneBean</managed-bean-name>
10.      <managed-bean-class>com.corejsf.TabbedPaneBean</managed-bean-class>
11.      <managed-bean-scope>session</managed-bean-scope>
12.   </managed-bean>
13.
14.   <navigation-rule>
15.      <from-view-id>/index.jsp</from-view-id>
16.         <navigation-case>
17.            <to-view-id>/welcome.jsp</to-view-id>
18.         </navigation-case>
19.   </navigation-rule>
20.
21.   <component>
22.      <description>A tabbed pane</description>
23.      <component-type>Tabbed Pane</component-type>
24.      <component-class>com.corejsf.UITabbedPane</component-class>
25.   </component>
26.
27.   <!-- order is important within elements -->
28.   <render-kit>
29.      <renderer>
30.         <component-family>javax.faces.Command</component-family>
31.         <renderer-type>TabbedPaneRenderer</renderer-type>
32.         <renderer-class>com.corejsf.TabbedPaneRenderer</renderer-class>
33.      </renderer>
34.   </render-kit>
35. </faces-config>
```

Listing 9–25   tabbedpane/styles.css

```css
1. body {
2.    background: #ccc;
3. }
4. .emphasis {
5.    font-size: 3.5em;
6.    font-style: italic;
7. }
8. .tabbedPane {
9.    vertical-align: top;
10.    border: thin solid Blue;
11.    width: 96%;
12.    height 96%;
13. }
14. .tab {
15.    vertical-align: top;
16.    padding: 3px;
17.    border: thin solid Red;
18.    color: Yellow;
19.    background: LightSlateGray;
20. }
21. .selectedTab {
22.    vertical-align: top;
23.    padding: 3px;
24.    border: thin solid Black;
25.    color: LightSlateGray;
26.    background: Yellow;
27. }
28. .tabbedPaneContent {
29.    vertical-align: top;
30.    width: *;
31.    height: *;
32. }
```

EXTERNAL SERVICES

Topics in This Chapter

Chapter 10

In this chapter, you learn how to access external services from your JSF application. We show you how to connect to databases, directories, and web services. Our primary interest lies in the clean separation between the application logic and the configuration of resources.

Accessing a Database

In this section, we assume that you are familiar with basic database commands in SQL (the Structured Query Language), as well as the JDBC (Java Database Connectivity) API. A good introduction to these topics can be found in *Horstmann & Cornell, Core Java, Vol. 2, ch. 4, Sun Microsystems Press, 2002.* For your convenience, here is a brief refresher of the basics.

Issuing SQL Statements

To issue SQL statements to a database, you need a *connection* object. There are various methods of obtaining a connection. The most elegant one is to make a *directory lookup*, using the Java Naming and Directory Interface (JNDI).

```
Context ctx = new InitialContext();
DataSource source = (DataSource) ctx.lookup("java:comp/env/jdbc/mydb");
Connection conn = source.getConnection();
```

Later in this chapter we show you how to configure the data source in the Tomcat container. For now, let's assume that the data source is properly configured to connect to your favorite database.

Once you have the Connection object, you create a Statement object that you use to send SQL statements to the database. You use the executeUpdate method for SQL statements that update the database, and the executeQuery method for queries that return a result set.

```
Statement stat = conn.createStatement();
stat.executeUpdate("INSERT INTO Users VALUES ('troosevelt', 'jabberwock')");
ResultSet result = stat.executeQuery("SELECT * FROM Users");
```

The ResultSet class has an unusual iteration protocol. You first call the next method to advance the cursor to the first row. (The next method returns false if no further rows are available.) Then you call the getString method to get a field value as a string. For example,

```
while (result.next()) {
    username = result.getString("username");
    password = result.getString("password");
    . . .
}
```

When you are done using the database, be certain that you close the connection. To ensure that the connection is closed under all circumstances, even when an exception occurs, wrap the query code inside a try/finally block, like this:

```
Connection conn = source.getConnection();
try {
    . . .
}
finally {
    conn.close();
}
```

Of course, there is much more to the JDBC API, but these simple concepts are sufficient to get you started.

Connection Management

One of the more vexing issues for the web developer is the management of database connections. There are two conflicting concerns. First, opening a connection to a database can be time consuming. Several seconds may elapse for the processes of connecting, authenticating, and acquiring resources to be completed. Thus, you cannot simply open a new connection for every page request.

On the flip side, you cannot keep open a huge number of connections to the database. Connections consume resources, both in the client program and in the database server. Commonly, a database puts a limit on the maximum number of concurrent connections that it allows. Thus, your application cannot simply open a connection whenever a user logs in and leave it open until the user logs off. After all, your user might walk away and never log off.

One common mechanism for solving these concerns is to *pool* the database connections. A connection pool holds database connections that are already opened. Application programs obtain connections from the pool. When the connections are no longer needed, they are returned to the pool, but they are not closed. Thus, the pool minimizes the time lag of establishing database connections.

Implementing a database connection pool is not easy, and it certainly should not be the responsibility of the application programmer. As of version 2.0, JDBC supports pooling in a pleasantly transparent way. When you receive a pooled Connection object, it is actually instrumented so that its close method merely returns it to the pool. It is up to the application server to set up the pool and to give you a data source whose getConnection method yields pooled connections.

Each application server has its own way of configuring the database connection pool. The details are not part of any Java standard—the JDBC specification is completely silent on this issue. In the next section, we describe how to configure Tomcat for connection pooling. The basic principle is the same with other application servers, but of course the details may differ considerably.

To maintain the pool, it is still essential that you close every connection object when you are done using it. Otherwise the pool will run dry, and new physical connections to the database will need to be opened. Properly closing connections is the topic of the next section.

Plugging Connection Leaks

Consider this simple sequence of statements:

```
DataSource source = ...
Connection conn = source.getConnection();
Statement stat = conn.createStatement();
String command = "INSERT INTO Users VALUES ('troosevelt', 'jabberwock')";
stat.executeUpdate(command);
conn.close();
```

The code looks clean—we open a connection, issue a command, and immediately close the connection. But there is a fatal flaw. If one of the method calls throws an exception, the call to the close method never happens!

In that case, an irate user may resubmit the request many times in frustration, leaking another connection object with every click.

To overcome this issue, *always* place the call to close inside a finally block:

```
DataSource source = ...
Connection conn = source.getConnection();
try {
   Statement stat = conn.createStatement();
   String command = "INSERT INTO Users VALUES ('troosevelt', 'jabberwock')";
   stat.executeUpdate(command);
}
finally {
   conn.close();
}
```

This simple rule completely solves the problem of leaking connections.

The rule is most effective if you *do not combine* this try/finally construct with any other exception handling code. In particular, do not attempt to catch a SQLException in the same try block:

```
// we recommend that you do NOT do this
Connection conn = null;
try {
   conn = source.getConnection();
   Statement stat = conn.createStatement();
   String command = "INSERT INTO Users VALUES ('troosevelt', 'jabberwock')";
   stat.executeUpdate(command);
}
catch (SQLException) {
   // log error
}
finally {
   conn.close(); // ERROR
}
```

That code has two subtle mistakes. First, if the call to getConnection throws an exception, then conn is still null, and you can't call close. Moreover, the call to close can also throw a SQLException. You could clutter up the finally clause with more code, but the result is a mess. Instead, use two separate try blocks:

```
// we recommend that you use separate try blocks
try {
   Connection conn = source.getConnection();
   try {
      Statement stat = conn.createStatement();
      String command = "INSERT INTO Users VALUES ('troosevelt', 'jabberwock')";
      stat.executeUpdate(command);
```

```
   }
   finally {
      conn.close();
   }
}
catch (SQLException) {
   // log error
}
```

The inner try block ensures that the connection is closed. The outer try block ensures that the exception is logged.

 NOTE: Of course, you can also tag your method with throws SQLException and leave the outer try block to the caller. That is often the best solution.

Using Prepared Statements

A common optimization technique for JDBC programs is the use of the Prepared-Statement class. You use a *prepared statement* to speed up database operations if your code issues the same type of query multiple times. Consider the lookup of user passwords. You will repeatedly need to issue a query of the form

```
SELECT password FROM Users WHERE username=...
```

A prepared statement asks the database to precompile a query, that is, parse the SQL statement and compute a query strategy. That information is kept with the prepared statement and reused whenever the query is reissued.

You create a prepared statement with the prepareStatement method of the Connection class. Use a ? character for each parameter.

```
PreparedStatement stat = conn.prepareStatement(
   "SELECT password FROM Users WHERE username=?");
```

When you are ready to issue a prepared statement, first set the parameter values.

```
stat.setString(1, name);
```

(Note that the index value 1 denotes the first parameter.) Then issue the statement in the usual way:

```
ResultSet result = stat.executeQuery();
```

At first glance, it appears as if prepared statements would not be of much benefit in a web application. After all, you close the connection whenever you complete a user request. A prepared statement is tied to a database connection, and all the work of establishing it is lost when the physical connection to the database is terminated.

However, if the physical database connections are kept in a pool, then there is a good chance that the prepared statement is still usable when you retrieve a connection. Many connection pool implementations will cache prepared statements. When you call prepareStatement, the pool will first look inside the statement cache, using the query string as a key. If the prepared statement is found, then it is reused. Otherwise, a new prepared statement is created and added to the cache.

All this activity is transparent to the application programmer. You simply request PreparedStatement objects and hope that, at least some of the time, the pool can retrieve an existing object for the given query.

You will see in the next section how to configure the connection pool in the Tomcat container to cache prepared statements.

CAUTION: You cannot keep a PreparedStatement object and reuse it beyond a single request scope. Once you close a pooled connection, all associated PreparedStatement objects also revert to the pool. Thus, you should not hang on to PreparedStatement objects beyond the current request. Instead, keep calling the prepareStatement method with the same query string, and chances are good that you'll get a cached statement object.

Configuring a Database Resource in Tomcat

In this section, we walk you through the steps of configuring a database resource pool in the Tomcat 5 container.

Locate the conf/server.xml file and look for the element that describes the host that will contain your web application, such as

```
<!-- Define the default virtual host -->
<Host name="localhost" debug="0" appBase="webapps"
    unpackWARs="false" autoDeploy="true">
...
</Host>
```

Inside this element, place a DefaultContext element that specifies both the database details (driver, URL, username, and password) and the desired characteristics of the pool.

Here is a typical example, specifying a connection pool to a PostgreSQL database. The values that you need to customize are highlighted.

```
<DefaultContext>
   <Resource name="jdbc/mydb" auth="Container"
      type="javax.sql.DataSource"/>
   <ResourceParams name="jdbc/mydb">
      <parameter>
         <name>factory</name>
           <value>org.apache.commons.dbcp.BasicDataSourceFactory</value>
      </parameter>
      <parameter>
         <name>driverClassName</name>
         <value>org.postgresql.Driver</value>
      </parameter>
      <parameter>
         <name>url</name>
         <value>jdbc:postgresql://127.0.0.1:5432/postgres</value>
      </parameter>
      <parameter>
        <name>username</name>
         <value>dbuser</value>
      </parameter>
      <parameter>
         <name>password</name>
         <value>dbpassword</value>
      </parameter>
      <parameter>
         <name>maxActive</name>
         <value>20</value>
      </parameter>
      <parameter>
         <name>maxIdle</name>
         <value>10</value>
      </parameter>
      <parameter>
         <name>poolPreparedStatements</name>
         <value>true</value>
      </parameter>
   </ResourceParams>
</DefaultContext>
```

> NOTE: You can also add the Resource and ResourceParams elements into the context of a specific web application. Then the data source is available only to that application.

Note the name of the resource: jdbc/mydb. That name is used to obtain the data source from the JNDI directory service:

```
DataSource source = (DataSource) ctx.lookup("java:comp/env/jdbc/mydb");
```

The java:comp/env prefix is the standard JNDI directory lookup path to the component environment in a J2EE container. By convention, you place JDBC resources in the jdbc subpath. It is up to you how to name the individual resources.

To configure the pool, you specify a sequence of parameters—see Table 10–1 for the most common ones. A complete description of all valid parameters can be found at http://jakarta.apache.org/commons/dbcp/configuration.html.

Table 10–1   Common Tomcat Database Pool Parameters

Parameter Name	Description
driverClassName	The name of the JDBC driver, such as org.postgresql.Driver
url	The database URL, such as jdbc:postgresql:mydb
username	The database user name
password	The password of the database user
maxActive	The maximum number of simultaneous active connections, or zero for no limit.
maxIdle	The maximum number of active connections that can remain idle in the pool without extra ones being released, or zero for no limit.
poolPreparedStatements	true if prepared statements are pooled (default: false)
removeAbandoned	true if the pool should remove connections that appear to be abandoned (default: false)
removeAbandonedTimeout	The number of seconds after which an unused connection is considered abandoned (default: 300)
logAbandoned	true to log a stack trace of the code that abandoned the connection (default: false)

To activate the pooling of prepared statements, be sure to set poolPreparedStatements to true.

The last three parameters in Table 10–1 refer to a useful feature of the Tomcat pool. The pool can be instructed to monitor and remove connections that appear to be abandoned. If a connection has not been used for some time, then it is likely that an application forgot to close it. After all, a web application should always close its database connections after rendering the response to a user request. The pool can recycle unused connections and optionally log these events. The logging is useful for debugging since it allows the application programmer to plug connection leaks.

The J2EE specification requires that resources are declared in the web.xml file of your web application. Add the following entry to your web.xml file:

```
<resource-ref>
    <res-ref-name>jdbc/mydb</res-ref-name>
    <res-type>javax.sql.DataSource</res-type>
    <res-auth>Container</res-auth>
</resource-ref>
```

Finally, you need to place the database driver file (such as pg73jdbc3.jar for the PostgreSQL database) into Tomcat's common/lib directory. If the database driver file has a .zip extension, you need to rename it to .jar, such as classes12.jar for the Oracle database.

TIP: You can find detailed configuration instructions for a number of popular databases at http://jakarta.apache.org/tomcat/tomcat-5.0-doc/jndi-data-source-examples-howto.html.

A Complete Database Example

In this example, we show how to verify a username/password combination. As with the example program in Chapter 1, we start with a simple login screen (Figure 10–1). If the username/password combination is correct, we show a welcome screen (Figure 10–2). Otherwise, we prompt the user to try again (Figure 10–3). Finally, if a JNDI or database error occurred, we show an error screen (Figure 10–4).

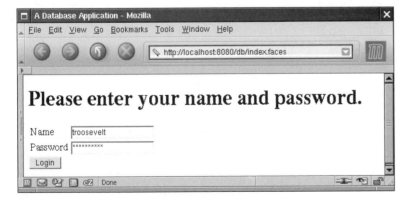

Figure 10–1   Login Screen

Figure 10-2   Welcome Screen

Figure 10-3   Authentication Error Screen

Figure 10-4   Internal Error Screen

Thus, we have four JSF pages, shown in Listings 10–1 through 10–4. Listing 10–5 shows the faces-config.xml file with the navigation rules. The navigation rules use the loginAction and logoutAction properties of the UserBean class. Listing 10–6 gives the code for the UserBean.

In our simple example, we add the database code directly into the UserBean class. It would also be possible to have two layers of objects: beans for communication with the JSF pages, and data access objects that represent entities in the database.

We place the code for database access into the separate method

```
public void doLogin() throws SQLException, NamingException
```

That method queries the database for the username/password combination and sets the loggedIn field to true if the username and password match.

The button on the index.jsp page references the login method of the user bean. That method calls the doLogin method and returns a result string for the navigation handler. The login method also deals with exceptions that the doLogin method reports. We assume that the doLogin method is focused on the database, not the user interface. If an exception occurs, doLogin should simply report it and take no further action. The login method, on the other hand, logs exceptions and returns a result string "internalError" to the navigation handler.

```
public String login() {
   try {
      doLogin();
   }
   catch (SQLException ex) {
      logger.log(Level.SEVERE, "loginAction", ex);
      return "internalError";
   }
   catch (NamingException ex) {
      logger.log(Level.SEVERE, "loginAction", ex);
      return "internalError";
   }
   if (loggedIn)
      return "loginSuccess";
   else
      return "loginFailure";
}
```

Before running this example, you need to carry out several housekeeping chores.

- Start your database.
- Create a table named Users and add one or more username/password entries:

```
CREATE TABLE Users (username CHAR(20), password CHAR(20))
INSERT INTO Users VALUES ('troosevelt', 'jabberwock')
```

- Place the database driver file into Tomcat's common/lib directory.
- Modify conf/server.xml and add the database resource.
- Restart Tomcat.

You can then deploy and test your application.

Figure 10–5 shows the directory structure for this application, and Figure 10–6 shows the navigation map.

> **NOTE:** Lots of things can go wrong with database configurations. If the application has an internal error, look at the Tomcat logs (by default, in Tomcat's logs/catalina.out).

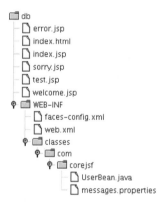

```
📁 db
├─ 📄 error.jsp
├─ 📄 index.html
├─ 📄 index.jsp
├─ 📄 sorry.jsp
├─ 📄 test.jsp
├─ 📄 welcome.jsp
└─ 📁 WEB-INF
   ├─ 📄 faces-config.xml
   ├─ 📄 web.xml
   └─ 📁 classes
      └─ 📁 com
         └─ 📁 corejsf
            ├─ 📄 UserBean.java
            └─ 📄 messages.properties
```

Figure 10–5   Directory Structure of the Database Application

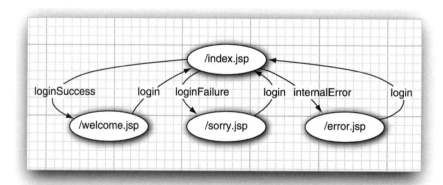

Figure 10–6   Navigation Map of the Database Application

Listing 10–1   db/index.jsp

```
1. <html>
2.    <%@ taglib uri="http://java.sun.com/jsf/core" prefix="f" %>
3.    <%@ taglib uri="http://java.sun.com/jsf/html" prefix="h" %>
4.    <f:view>
5.       <head>
6.          <f:loadBundle basename="com.corejsf.messages" var="msgs"/>
7.          <title><h:outputText value="#{msgs.title}"/></title>
8.       </head>
9.       <body>
10.          <h:form>
11.             <h1><h:outputText value="#{msgs.enterNameAndPassword}"/></h1>
12.             <h:panelGrid columns="2">
13.                <h:outputText value="#{msgs.name}"/>
14.                <h:inputText value="#{user.name}"/>
15.
16.                <h:outputText value="#{msgs.password}"/>
17.                <h:inputSecret value="#{user.password}"/>
18.             </h:panelGrid>
19.             <h:commandButton value="#{msgs.login}" action="#{user.login}"/>
20.          </h:form>
21.       </body>
22.    </f:view>
23. </html>
```

Listing 10–2   db/welcome.jsp

```
1. <html>
2.    <%@ taglib uri="http://java.sun.com/jsf/core" prefix="f" %>
3.    <%@ taglib uri="http://java.sun.com/jsf/html" prefix="h" %>
4.    <f:view>
5.       <head>
6.          <f:loadBundle basename="com.corejsf.messages" var="msgs"/>
7.          <title><h:outputText value="#{msgs.title}"/></title>
8.       </head>
9.       <body>
10.          <h:form>
11.             <p>
12.                <h:outputText value="#{msgs.welcome}"/>
13.                <h:outputText value="#{user.name}"/>!
14.             </p>
15.             <p>
16.                <h:commandButton value="#{msgs.logout}" action="#{user.logout}"/>
17.             </p>
18.          </h:form>
19.       </body>
20.    </f:view>
21. </html>
```

Listing 10–3 db/sorry.jsp

```
1.  <html>
2.  <%@ taglib uri="http://java.sun.com/jsf/core" prefix="f" %>
3.  <%@ taglib uri="http://java.sun.com/jsf/html" prefix="h" %>
4.  <f:view>
5.    <head>
6.      <f:loadBundle basename="com.corejsf.messages" var="msgs"/>
7.      <title><h:outputText value="#{msgs.title}"/></title>
8.    </head>
9.    <body>
10.     <h:form>
11.       <h1><h:outputText value="#{msgs.authError}"/></h1>
12.       <p>
13.         <h:outputText value="#{msgs.authError_detail}"/>!
14.       </p>
15.       <p>
16.         <h:commandButton value="#{msgs.continue}" action="login"/>
17.       </p>
18.     </h:form>
19.   </body>
20. </f:view>
21. </html>
```

Listing 10–4 db/error.jsp

```
1.  <html>
2.  <%@ taglib uri="http://java.sun.com/jsf/core" prefix="f" %>
3.  <%@ taglib uri="http://java.sun.com/jsf/html" prefix="h" %>
4.  <f:view>
5.    <head>
6.      <f:loadBundle basename="com.corejsf.messages" var="msgs"/>
7.      <title><h:outputText value="#{msgs.title}"/></title>
8.    </head>
9.    <body>
10.     <h:form>
11.       <h1><h:outputText value="#{msgs.internalError}"/></h1>
12.       <p><h:outputText value="#{msgs.internalError_detail}"/></p>
13.       <p>
14.         <h:commandButton value="#{msgs.continue}" action="login"/>
15.       </p>
16.     </h:form>
17.   </body>
18. </f:view>
19. </html>
```

Listing 10–5 db/WEB-INF/faces-config.xml

```
1. <?xml version="1.0"?>
2. <!DOCTYPE faces-config PUBLIC
3.   "-//Sun Microsystems, Inc.//DTD JavaServer Faces Config 1.0//EN"
4.   "http://java.sun.com/dtd/web-facesconfig_1_0.dtd">
5. <faces-config>
6.   <navigation-rule>
7.     <from-view-id>/index.jsp</from-view-id>
8.     <navigation-case>
9.       <from-outcome>loginSuccess</from-outcome>
10.       <to-view-id>/welcome.jsp</to-view-id>
11.     </navigation-case>
12.     <navigation-case>
13.       <from-outcome>loginFailure</from-outcome>
14.       <to-view-id>/sorry.jsp</to-view-id>
15.     </navigation-case>
16.     <navigation-case>
17.       <from-outcome>internalError</from-outcome>
18.       <to-view-id>/error.jsp</to-view-id>
19.     </navigation-case>
20.   </navigation-rule>
21.   <navigation-rule>
22.     <from-view-id>/welcome.jsp</from-view-id>
23.     <navigation-case>
24.       <from-outcome>login</from-outcome>
25.       <to-view-id>/index.jsp</to-view-id>
26.     </navigation-case>
27.   </navigation-rule>
28.   <navigation-rule>
29.     <from-view-id>/sorry.jsp</from-view-id>
30.     <navigation-case>
31.       <from-outcome>login</from-outcome>
32.       <to-view-id>/index.jsp</to-view-id>
33.     </navigation-case>
34.   </navigation-rule>
35.   <navigation-rule>
36.     <from-view-id>/error.jsp</from-view-id>
37.     <navigation-case>
38.       <from-outcome>login</from-outcome>
39.       <to-view-id>/index.jsp</to-view-id>
40.     </navigation-case>
41.   </navigation-rule>
42.
43.   <managed-bean>
44.     <managed-bean-name>user</managed-bean-name>
45.     <managed-bean-class>com.corejsf.UserBean</managed-bean-class>
46.     <managed-bean-scope>session</managed-bean-scope>
47.   </managed-bean>
48. </faces-config>
```

Listing 10–6 db/WEB-INF/classes/com/corejsf/UserBean.java

```
1. package com.corejsf;
2.
3. import java.sql.Connection;
4. import java.sql.PreparedStatement;
5. import java.sql.ResultSet;
6. import java.sql.SQLException;
7. import java.util.logging.Level;
8. import java.util.logging.Logger;
9. import javax.naming.Context;
10. import javax.naming.InitialContext;
11. import javax.naming.NamingException;
12. import javax.sql.DataSource;
13.
14. public class UserBean {
15.    private String name;
16.    private String password;
17.    private boolean loggedIn;
18.    private Logger logger = Logger.getLogger("com.corejsf");
19.
20.    public String getName() { return name; }
21.    public void setName(String newValue) { name = newValue; }
22.
23.    public String getPassword() { return password; }
24.    public void setPassword(String newValue) { password = newValue; }
25.
26.    public String login() {
27.       try {
28.          doLogin();
29.       }
30.       catch (SQLException ex) {
31.          logger.log(Level.SEVERE, "loginAction", ex);
32.          return "internalError";
33.       }
34.       catch (NamingException ex) {
35.          logger.log(Level.SEVERE, "loginAction", ex);
36.          return "internalError";
37.       }
38.       if (loggedIn)
39.          return "loginSuccess";
40.       else
41.          return "loginFailure";
42.    }
43.
44.    public String logout() {
45.       loggedIn = false;
```

Listing 10–6	db/WEB-INF/classes/com/corejsf/UserBean.java (cont.)

```java
46.        return "login";
47.    }
48.
49.    public void doLogin() throws SQLException, NamingException {
50.        Context ctx = new InitialContext();
51.        if (ctx == null) throw new NamingException("No initial context");
52.
53.        DataSource ds = (DataSource) ctx.lookup("java:comp/env/jdbc/mydb");
54.        if (ds == null) throw new NamingException("No data source");
55.
56.        Connection conn = ds.getConnection();
57.        if (conn == null) throw new SQLException("No connection");
58.
59.        try {
60.            PreparedStatement passwordQuery = conn.prepareStatement(
61.                "SELECT password from Users WHERE username = ?");
62.
63.            passwordQuery.setString(1, name);
64.
65.            ResultSet result = passwordQuery.executeQuery();
66.
67.            if (!result.next()) return;
68.            String storedPassword = result.getString("password");
69.            loggedIn = password.equals(storedPassword.trim());
70.        }
71.        finally {
72.            conn.close();
73.        }
74.    }
75. }
```

Using LDAP for Authentication

In the preceding section, you have seen how to read a username and password from a database. In this section, we look at LDAP, the Lightweight Directory Access Protocol. LDAP servers are more flexible and efficient for managing user information than are database servers. Particularly in large organizations, in which data replication is an issue, LDAP is preferred over relational databases for storing directory information.

Because LDAP is less commonly used than relational database technology, we briefly introduce it here. For an in-depth discussion of LDAP, we recommend the "LDAP bible": *Timothy Howes et al., Understanding and Deploying LDAP Directory Services, 2nd ed., Macmillan 2003.*

LDAP Directories

LDAP uses a *hierarchical* database. It keeps all data in a tree structure, not in a set of tables as a relational database would. Each entry in the tree has

- zero or more *attributes*. An attribute has a key and a value. An example attribute is cn=John Q. Smith. (The key cn stores the "common name." See Table 10–2 for the meaning of commonly used LDAP attributes.)
- one or more *object classes*. An object class defines the set of required and optional attributes for this element. For example, the object class person defines a required attribute cn and an optional attribute telephoneNumber. Of course, the object classes are different from Java classes, but they also support a notion of inheritance. For example, inetOrgPerson is a subclass of person with additional attributes.
- a *distinguished name* (for example, uid=troosevelt,ou=people, dc=corejsf,dc=com). The distinguished name is a sequence of attributes that trace a path joining the entry with the root of the tree. There may be alternate paths, but one of them must be specified as distinguished.

Table 10–2   Commonly Used LDAP Attributes

Attribute Name	Meaning
dc	Domain Component
cn	Common Name
sn	Surname
dn	Distinguished Name
o	Organization
ou	Organizational Unit
uid	Unique Identifier

Figure 10–7 shows an example of a directory tree.

How to organize the directory tree, and what information to put in it, can be a matter of intense debate. We do not discuss the issues here. Instead, we simply assume that an organizational scheme has been established and that the directory has been populated with the relevant user data.

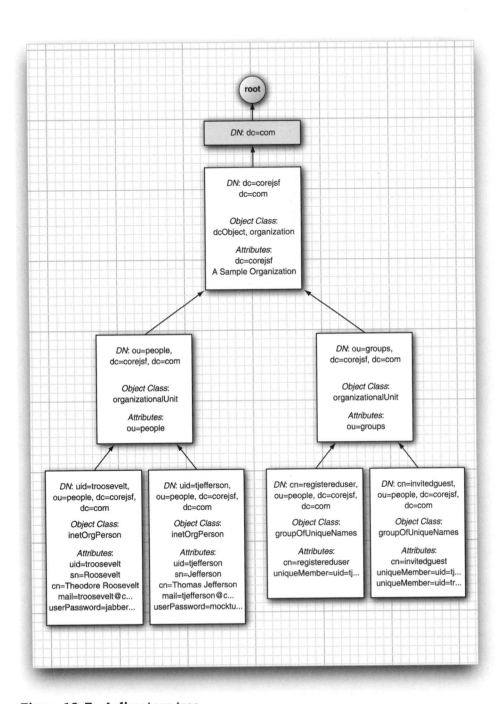

Figure 10–7   A directory tree

Configuring an LDAP Server

You have several options for running an LDAP server to try out the programs in this section. Here are the most popular choices:

- The free OpenLDAP server (http://openldap.org), available for Linux and Windows and built into Mac OS X.
- A high-performance server such as the Sun Java System Directory Server (http://www.sun.com/software/products/directory_srvr/home_directory.html), which is available on a variety of platforms
- Microsoft Active Directory

We give you brief instructions for configuring OpenLDAP. If you use another directory server, the basic steps are similar.

Our sample directory uses the standard object class inetOrgPerson. (We use that class because it has useful attributes such as uid and mail.) You should make sure that your LDAP server recognizes this object class.

If you use OpenLDAP, you need to edit the slapd.conf file before starting the LDAP server. Locate the line that includes the core.schema file, and add lines to include the cosine.schema and inetorgperson.schema files. (On Linux, the default location for the slapd.conf file is /usr/local/etc/openldap. The schema files are in the schema subdirectory.)

> NOTE: Alternatively, you can make adjustments to our sample data. For example, you can change inetOrgPerson to the more commonly available person, omit the uid and mail attributes, and use the sn attribute as the login name. If you follow that approach, you will need to change the attributes in the sample programs as well.

In OpenLDAP, edit the suffix entry in slapd.conf to match the sample data set. This entry specifies the distinguished name suffix for this server. It should read

```
suffix  "dc=corejsf,dc=com"
```

You also need to configure an LDAP user with administrative rights to edit the directory data. In OpenLDAP, add these lines to slapd.conf:

```
rootdn  "cn=Manager,dc=corejsf,dc=com"
rootpw  secret
```

We recommend that you specify authorization settings, although they are not strictly necessary for running the examples in this sections. The following settings in slapd.conf permit the Manager user to read and write passwords, and everyone else to read all other attributes.

```
access to attr=userPassword
            by dn.base="cn=Manager,dc=corejsf,dc=com" write
            by * none
access to *
            by dn.base="cn=Admin,dc=corejsf,dc=com" write
            by * read
```

You can now start the LDAP server. On Linux, run /usr/local/libexec/slapd.

Next, populate the server with the sample data. Most LDAP servers allow the import of LDIF (Lightweight Directory Interchange Format) data. LDIF is a humanly readable format that simply lists all directory entries, including their distinguished names, object classes, and attributes. Listing 10–7 shows an LDIF file that describes our sample data:

. ldap/misc/sample.ldif

For example, with OpenLDAP, you use the ldapadd tool to add the data to the directory:

```
ldapadd -f sample.ldif -x -D "cn=Manager,dc=corejsf,dc=com" -w secret
```

Before proceeding, it is a good idea to double-check that the directory contains the data that you need. We suggest that you download Jarek Gawor's LDAP Browser\Editor from http://www.mcs.anl.gov/~gawor/ldap/. This convenient Java program lets you browse the contents of any LDAP server. Launch the program and configure it with the following options:

- Host: localhost
- Base DN: dc=corejsf,dc=com
- Anonymous bind: unchecked
- User DN: cn=Manager
- Append base DN: checked
- Password: secret

Make sure the LDAP server has started, then connect. If everything is in order, you should see a directory tree similar to that shown in Figure 10–8.

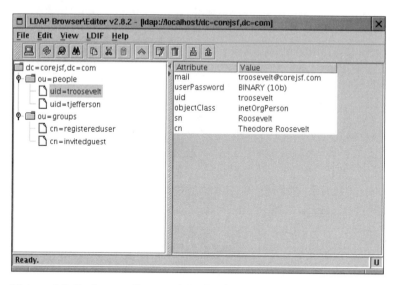

Figure 10–8   Inspecting an LDAP Directory Tree

Listing 10–7 ldap/misc/sample.ldif

```
1. # Define top-level entry
2. dn: dc=corejsf,dc=com
3. objectClass: dcObject
4. objectClass: organization
5. dc: corejsf
6. o: A Sample Organization
7.
8. # Define an entry to contain people
9. # searches for users are based on this entry
10. dn: ou=people,dc=corejsf,dc=com
11. objectClass: organizationalUnit
12. ou: people
13.
14. # Define a user entry for Theodore Roosevelt
15. dn: uid=troosevelt,ou=people,dc=corejsf,dc=com
16. objectClass: inetOrgPerson
17. uid: troosevelt
18. sn: Roosevelt
19. cn: Theodore Roosevelt
20. mail: troosevelt@corejsf.com
21. userPassword: jabberwock
22.
```

Listing 10–7 ldap/misc/sample.ldif (cont.)

```
23. # Define a user entry for Thomas Jefferson
24. dn: uid=tjefferson,ou=people,dc=corejsf,dc=com
25. objectClass: inetOrgPerson
26. uid: tjefferson
27. sn: Jefferson
28. cn: Thomas Jefferson
29. mail: tjefferson@corejsf.com
30. userPassword: mockturtle
31.
32. # Define an entry to contain LDAP groups
33. # searches for roles are based on this entry
34. dn: ou=groups,dc=corejsf,dc=com
35. objectClass: organizationalUnit
36. ou: groups
37.
38. # Define an entry for the "registereduser" role
39. dn: cn=registereduser,ou=groups,dc=corejsf,dc=com
40. objectClass: groupOfUniqueNames
41. cn: registereduser
42. uniqueMember: uid=tjefferson,ou=people,dc=corejsf,dc=com
43.
44. # Define an entry for the "invitedguest" role
45. dn: cn=invitedguest,ou=groups,dc=corejsf,dc=com
46. objectClass: groupOfUniqueNames
47. cn: invitedguest
48. uniqueMember: uid=troosevelt,ou=people,dc=corejsf,dc=com
49. uniqueMember: uid=tjefferson,ou=people,dc=corejsf,dc=com
```

Accessing LDAP Directory Information

Once you have your LDAP database populated, it is time to connect to it with a
Java program. You use the Java Naming and Directory Interface (JNDI), an
interface that unifies various directory protocols.

Start by getting a *directory context* to the LDAP directory, with the following
incantation:

```
Hashtable env = new Hashtable();
env.put(Context.SECURITY_PRINCIPAL, userDN);
env.put(Context.SECURITY_CREDENTIALS, password);
DirContext initial = new InitialDirContext(env);
DirContext context = (DirContext) initial.lookup("ldap://localhost:389");
```

Here, we connect to the LDAP server at the local host. The port number 389 is
the default LDAP port.

If you connect to the LDAP database with an invalid user/password combination, an AuthenticationException is thrown.

 NOTE: Sun's JNDI tutorial suggests an alternative way to connect to the server:

```
Hashtable env = new Hashtable();
env.put(Context.INITIAL_CONTEXT_FACTORY, "com.sun.jndi.ldap.LdapCtxFactory");
env.put(Context.PROVIDER_URL, "ldap://localhost:389");
env.put(Context.SECURITY_PRINCIPAL, userDN);
env.put(Context.SECURITY_CREDENTIALS, password);
DirContext context = new InitialDirContext(env);
```

However, it seems undesirable to hardwire the Sun LDAP provider into your code. JNDI has an elaborate mechanism for configuring providers, and you should not lightly bypass it.

To list the attributes of a given entry, specify its distinguished name and then use the getAttributes method:

```
Attributes answer
   = context.getAttributes("uid=troosevelt,ou=people,dc=corejsf,dc=com");
```

You can get a specific attribute with the get method, for example:

```
Attribute commonNameAttribute = answer.get("cn");
```

To enumerate all attributes, you use the NamingEnumeration class. The designers of this class felt that they too could improve on the standard Java iteration protocol, and they gave us this usage pattern:

```
NamingEnumeration attrEnum = answer.getAll();
while (attrEnum.hasMore()) {
   Attribute attr = (Attribute) attrEnum.next();
   String id = attr.getID();
   ...
}
```

Note the use of hasMore instead of hasNext.

Since an attribute can have multiple values, you need to use another Naming-Enumeration to list them all:

```
NamingEnumeration valueEnum = attr.getAll();
while (valueEnum.hasMore()) {
   Object value = valueEnum.next();
   ...
}
```

However, if you know that the attribute has a single value, you can call the get method to retrieve it:

```
String commonName = (String) commonNameAttribute.get();
```

You now know how to query the directory for user data. Next, let us take up operations for modifying the directory contents.

To add a new entry, gather the set of attributes in a BasicAttributes object. (The BasicAttributes class implements the Attributes interface.)

```
Attributes attrs = new BasicAttributes();
attrs.put("objectClass", "inetOrgPerson");
attrs.put("uid", "alincoln");
attrs.put("sn", "Lincoln");
attrs.put("cn", "Abraham Lincoln");
attrs.put("mail", "alincoln@corejsf.com");
String pw = "redqueen";
attrs.put("userPassword", pw.getBytes());
```

Then call the createSubcontext method. Provide the distinguished name of the new entry and the attribute set.

```
context.createSubcontext(
    "uid=alincoln,ou=people,dc=corejsf,dc=com", attrs);
```

CAUTION: When assembling the attributes, remember that the attributes are checked against the schema. Don't supply unknown attributes, and be sure to supply all attributes that are required by the object class. For example, if you omit the sn of person, the createSubcontext method will fail.

To remove an entry, call destroySubcontext:

```
context.destroySubcontext(
    "uid=alincoln,ou=people,dc=corejsf,dc=com");
```

Finally, you may want to edit the attributes of an existing entry. You call the method

```
context.modifyAttributes(distinguishedName, flag, attrs);
```

Here, flag is one of

```
DirContext.ADD_ATTRIBUTE
DirContext.REMOVE_ATTRIBUTE
DirContext.REPLACE_ATTRIBUTE
```

The attrs parameter contains a set of the attributes to be added, removed, or replaced.

Conveniently, the BasicAttributes(String, Object) constructor constructs an attribute set with a single attribute. For example,

```
context.modifyAttributes(
    "uid=alincoln,ou=people,dc=corejsf,dc=com",
    DirContext.ADD_ATTRIBUTE,
    new BasicAttributes("telephonenumber", "+18005551212"));
```

```
context.modifyAttributes(
    "uid=alincoln,ou=people,dc=corejsf,dc=com",
    DirContext.REMOVE_ATTRIBUTE,
    new BasicAttributes("mail", "alincoln@coresjf.com"));
```

```
context.modifyAttributes(
    "uid=alincoln,ou=people,dc=corejsf,dc=com",
    DirContext.REPLACE_ATTRIBUTE,
    new BasicAttributes("userPassword", newpw.getBytes()));
```

Finally, when you are done with a context, you should close it:

```
context.close();
```

You now know enough about directory operations to carry out the tasks that you will commonly need when working with LDAP directories. A good source for more advanced information is the JNDI tutorial at http://java.sun.com/products/jndi/tutorial.

However, we are not quite ready to put together a JSF application that uses LDAP. It would be extremely unprofessional to hardcode the directory URL and the manager password into a program. Instead, these values should be specified in a configuration file. The next section discusses various options for the management of configuration parameters. We put the alternatives to work with an application that allows users to self-register on a web site; we use LDAP to store the user information.

---

javax.naming.directory.InitialDirContext [SDK 1.3]

• InitialDirContext(Hashtable env)

Constructs a directory context, using the given environment settings. The hash table can contain bindings for Context.SECURITY_PRINCIPAL, Context.SECURITY_CREDENTIALS, and other keys—see the API documentation for the javax.naming.Context interface for details.

API **javax.naming.Context [SDK 1.3]**

- Object lookup(String name)

  Looks up the object with the given name. The return value depends on the nature of this context. It commonly is a subtree context or a leaf object.

- Context createSubcontext(String name)

  Creates a subcontext with the given name. The subcontext becomes a child of this context. All path components of the name, except for the last one, must exist.

- void destroySubcontext(String name)

  Destroys the subcontext with the given name. All path components of the name, except for the last one, must exist.

- void close()

  Closes this context.

API **javax.naming.directory.DirContext [SDK 1.3]**

- Attributes getAttributes(String name)

  Gets the attributes of the entry with the given name.

- void modifyAttributes(String name, int flag, Attributes modes)

  Modifies the attributes of the entry with the given name. The value flag is one of DirContext.ADD_ATTRIBUTE, DirContext.REMOVE_ATTRIBUTE, or DirContext.REPLACE_ATTRIBUTE

API **javax.naming.directory.Attributes [SDK 1.3]**

- Attribute get(String id)

  Gets the attribute with the given ID.

- NamingEnumeration getAll()

  Yields an enumeration that iterates through all attributes in this attribute set.

- void put(String id, Object value)

  Adds an attribute to this attribute set.

API **javax.naming.directory.BasicAttributes [SDK 1.3]**

- BasicAttributes(String id, Object value)

  Constructs an attribute set that contains a single attribute with the given ID and value.

API · **javax.naming.directory.Attribute [SDK 1.3]**

- `String getID()`
  Gets the ID of this attribute.

- `Object get()`
  Gets the first attribute value of this attribute if the values are ordered or an arbitrary value if they are unordered.

- `NamingEnumeration getAll()`
  Yields an enumeration that iterates through all values of this attribute.

API · **javax.naming.NamingEnumeration [SDK 1.3]**

- `boolean hasMore()`
  Returns `true` if this enumeration object has more elements.

- `Object next()`
  Returns the next element of this enumeration.

Managing Configuration Information

Whenever your application interfaces with external services, you need to specify configuration parameters: URLs, usernames, passwords, and so on. You should never hardcode these parameters inside your application classes—doing so would make it difficult to update passwords, switch to alternative servers, and so on.

In the section on database services, you saw a reasonable approach for managing the database configuration. The configuration information is placed inside `server.xml`. The servlet container uses this information to construct a data source and bind it to a well-known name. The classes that need to access the database use JNDI look up the data source.

Placing configuration information into `server.xml` is appropriate for a *global* resource such as a database. This resource can be used by all web applications inside the container. On the other hand, application-specific configuration information should be placed inside `web.xml` or `faces-config.xml`. Using the example of an LDAP connection, we explore all three possibilities.

Configuring a Bean

Whenever you define a bean in faces-config.xml, you can provide initialization parameters by using the managed-property element. Here is how we can initialize a bean that connects to an LDAP directory:

```
<managed-bean>
    <managed-bean-name>userdir</managed-bean-name>
    <managed-bean-class>com.corejsf.UserDirectoryBean</managed-bean-class>
    <managed-bean-scope>application</managed-bean-scope>
    <managed-property>
        <property-name>URL</property-name>
        <value>ldap://localhost:389</value>
    </managed-property>
    <managed-property>
        <property-name>managerDN</property-name>
        <value>cn=Manager,dc=corejsf,dc=com</value>
    </managed-property>
    <managed-property>
        <property-name>managerPassword</property-name>
        <value>secret</value>
    </managed-property>
</managed-bean>
```

You see the familiar managed-bean-name and managed-bean-class elements. However, this bean is given *application scope*. The bean object stays alive for the duration of the entire application, and it can serve multiple sessions. Finally, we used the managed-property settings to initialize the bean. Thus, we achieved our goal of placing these initialization parameters inside a configuration file rather than hardwiring them into the bean code.

Of course, our bean needs setters for these properties:

```
public class UserDirectoryBean {
    private String url;
    private String managerDN;
    private String managerPW;

    public void setManagerDN(String newValue) { managerDN = newValue; }
    public void setManagerPassword(String newValue) { managerPW = newValue; }
    public void setURL(String newValue) { url = newValue; }

    public DirContext getRootContext() throws NamingException { ... }
}
```

When the bean is constructed, the setters are invoked with the values specified in `faces-config.xml`.

Finally, client code needs to have access to the bean object. For example, suppose the `UserBean` class wants to connect to the directory:

```
UserDirectoryBean userdir = ... // how?
DirContext context = userdir.connect(dn, pw);
```

To look up a JSF bean, you use its value binding of its name, as in the following statements:

```
FacesContext context = FacesContext.getCurrentInstance();
Application app = context.getApplication();
ValueBinding binding = app.createValueBinding("#{userdir}");
UserDirectoryBean dir = (UserDirectoryBean) binding.getValue(context);
```

In summary, here are the steps for configuring a JSF bean:

1. Place the configuration parameters inside `managed-property` elements in the `faces-config.xml` file.
2. Provide property setters for these properties in the bean class.
3. Look up the bean object through its value binding.

This configuration method is straightforward and convenient. However, it is not suitable for configuring objects that should be available to multiple web applications. Moreover, purists might argue that `faces-config.xml` is intended to describe the logic of a web application, not its interface with external resources, and that `web.xml` would be more appropriate for the latter. Read on if either of these objections matters to you.

Configuring the External Context

In this section, we assume that your JSF application is launched as a servlet. You can supply parameters in `web.xml` by providing a set of `context-param` elements inside the `web-app` element:

```
<web-app>
   <context-param>
      <param-name>URL</param-name>
      <param-value>ldap://localhost:389</param-value>
   </context-param>
   <context-param>
      <param-name>managerDN</param-name>
      <param-value>cn=Manager,dc=corejsf,dc=com</param-value>
   </context-param>
```

```
<context-param>
    <param-name>managerPassword</param-name>
    <param-value>secret</param-value>
</context-param>
    ...
</web-app>
```

To read a parameter, get the *external context* object. That object describes the execution environment that launched your JSF application. If you use a servlet container, then the external context is a wrapper around the ServletContext object. The ExternalContext class has a number of convenience methods to access properties of the underlying servlet context. The getInitParameter method retrieves a context parameter value with a given name.

> CAUTION: Do not confuse context-param with init-param. The latter tag is used for parameters that a servlet can process at startup. It is unfortunate that the method for reading a context parameter is called getInitParameter.

Here is the code for getting an LDAP context from configuration parameters in web.xml:

```
public DirContext getRootContext() throws NamingException {
    ExternalContext external
        = FacesContext.getCurrentInstance().getExternalContext();

    String managerDN = external.getInitParameter("managerDN");
    String managerPW = external.getInitParameter("managerPassword");
    String url = external.getInitParameter("URL");

    Hashtable env = new Hashtable();
    env.put(Context.SECURITY_PRINCIPAL, managerDN);
    env.put(Context.SECURITY_CREDENTIALS, managerPW);
    DirContext initial = new InitialDirContext(env);

    Object obj = initial.lookup(url);
    if (!(obj instanceof DirContext))
        throw new NamingException("No directory context");
    return (DirContext) obj;
}
```

Follow these steps for accessing resources through the external context:

1. Place the configuration parameters inside context-param elements in the web.xml file.

2. Use the ExternalContext to look up the parameter values.

3. Turn the parameters into objects for your application.

As you can see, this configuration method works at a lower level than the configuration of a JSF bean. The web.xml file simply contains an unstructured list of parameters. It is up to you to construct objects that make use of these parameters.

 javax.faces.context.FacesContext

- ExternalContext getExternalContext()

  Gets the external context, a wrapper such as a servlet or portlet context around the execution environment of this JSF application.

 javax.faces.context.ExternalContext

- String getInitParameter(String name)

  Gets the initialization parameter with the given name.

Configuring a Container-Managed Resource

We now discuss how to specify container-wide resources. The information in this section is specific to Tomcat. Other containers will have similar mechanisms, but the details will differ.

Earlier in this chapter, we showed you how to configure a JDBC data source by specifying the database URL and login parameters in Tomcat's server.xml file. We simply used a JNDI lookup to obtain the data source object. This is an attractive method for specifying systemwide resources. Fortunately, Tomcat lets you fit your own resources into the same mechanism.

As with JDBC data sources, you specify a Resource and its ResourceParams in server.xml. For example, here is the configuration information for an LDAP directory.

```
<Resource name="ldap/mydir" auth="Container"
   type="javax.naming.directory.DirContext"/>

<ResourceParams name="ldap/mydir">
   <parameter>
      <name>factory</name>
      <value>com.corejsf.DirContextFactory</value>
   </parameter>
   <parameter>
      <name>URL</name>
      <value>ldap://localhost:389</value>
   </parameter>
   <parameter>
      <name>java.naming.security.principal</name>
```

```
    <value>cn=Manager,dc=corejsf,dc=com</value>
  </parameter>
  <parameter>
    <name>java.naming.security.credentials</name>
    <value>secret</value>
  </parameter>
</ResourceParams>
```

However, Tomcat has no standard "factory" for LDAP directories. This class uses the custom factory com.corejsf.DirContextFactory. All factories need to implement the ObjectFactory interface type and implement the getObjectInstance method.

```
public class DirContextFactory implements ObjectFactory {

  public Object getObjectInstance(Object obj,
      Name n, Context nameCtx, Hashtable environment)
      throws NamingException {
    ...
  }
}
```

This method, defined in glorious generality, can be used to produce any object from arbitrary configuration information. There is quite a bit of variability in how the parameters are used, but fortunately we only need to understand what parameters Tomcat supplies when requesting a resource. Tomcat places the configuration parameters into a Reference object, a kind of hash table on a megadose of steroids. Our factory simply places the parameters into a plain hash table and then gets the directory context—see Listing 10–8 for the complete source code.

> NOTE: The class com.sun.jndi.ldap.LdapCtxFactory (which is explicitly invoked in Sun's JNDI tutorial) also implements the ObjectFactory interface. Could you use that class as a factory for LDAP connections in Tomcat's server.xml file? Sadly, the answer is no. The getObjectInstance method of com.sun.jndi.ldap.LdapCtxFactory expects an Object parameter that is either an URL string, an array of URL strings, or a Reference object containing values with key "URL". The other environment settings must be provided in the Hashtable parameter. That's not what Tomcat supplies.

Note that we simply use the standard JNDI environment names for the principal and credentials in the server.xml file. The Context interface constants that we used previously are merely shortcuts for the environment names. For example, Context.SECURITY_PRINCIPAL is the string "java.naming.security.principal". (Admittedly, the constant names aren't much shorter, but they are safer. If you misspell the constant, then the compiler will warn you. If you misspell the environment name, your application will mysteriously fail.)

Now that you have completed the configuration, the remainder is smooth sailing. Your program simply accesses the resource through its JNDI name:

```
public DirContext getRootContext() throws NamingException {
   Context ctx = new InitialContext();
   return (DirContext) ctx.lookup("java:comp/env/ldap/mydir");
}
```

In summary, here are the steps for configuring a container-wide resource:

1. Place the configuration parameters inside the ResourceParams section that has the same name as the Resource element for your resource.

2. If you use a custom resource factory, deploy the class so that the container can load it (for example, in a JAR file that you place inside the common/lib directory).

3. Look up the resource object through its JNDI name.

Listing 10–8   ldap3/misc/com/corejsf/DirContextFactory.java

```
 1. package com.corejsf;
 2.
 3. import java.util.Enumeration;
 4. import java.util.Hashtable;
 5. import javax.naming.Context;
 6. import javax.naming.Name;
 7. import javax.naming.NamingException;
 8. import javax.naming.RefAddr;
 9. import javax.naming.Reference;
10. import javax.naming.directory.DirContext;
11. import javax.naming.directory.InitialDirContext;
12. import javax.naming.spi.ObjectFactory;
13.
14. public class DirContextFactory implements ObjectFactory {
15.    public Object getObjectInstance(Object obj,
16.       Name n, Context nameCtx, Hashtable environment)
17.       throws NamingException {
18.
19.       Hashtable env = new Hashtable();
20.       String url = null;
21.       Reference ref = (Reference) obj;
22.       Enumeration addrs = ref.getAll();
23.       while (addrs.hasMoreElements()) {
```

| Listing 10–8 | ldap3/misc/com/corejsf/DirContextFactory.java (cont.) |

```
24.          RefAddr addr = (RefAddr) addrs.nextElement();
25.          String name = addr.getType();
26.          String value = (String) addr.getContent();
27.          if (name.equals("URL")) url = value;
28.          else env.put(name, value);
29.       }
30.       DirContext initial = new InitialDirContext(env);
31.       if (url == null) return initial;
32.       else return initial.lookup(url);
33.    }
34. }
```

 NOTE: Compile this file, place it inside a JAR file, and put the JAR file into the common/lib directory of Tomcat.

```
cd corejsf-examples/ch10/ldap3/misc
javac com/corejsf/DirContextFactory.java
jar cvf tomcat/common/lib/dirctxfactory.jar com/corejsf/*.class
```

Remember to restart the server.

Creating an LDAP Application

We now put together a complete application that stores user information in an LDAP directory.

The application simulates a news web site that gives users free access to news as long as they provide some information about themselves. We do not actually provide any news. We simply provide a screen to log in (Figure 10–9) and a separate screen to register for the service (Figure 10–10). Upon successful login, users can read news and update their personal information (Figure 10–11).

The update screen is similar to the registration screen, and we do not show it. Figure 10–12 shows the directory structure, and Figure 10–13 shows the page flow between the news service pages.

We provide three versions of this application, with configuration information in faces-config.xml, web.xml, and server.xml, respectively.

All three versions have identical web pages—see Listings 10–9 through 10–12. (We omit the listings of repetitive pages.) The primary difference between the versions is the implementation of the getRootContext method in the UserBean class (Listing 10–13). The first application has a UserDirectoryBean class (Listing 10–14) that is configured in faces-config.xml (Listing 10–15). The second application makes an ad hoc lookup of servlet initialization parameters. The third version makes a JNDI lookup, using the class of Listing 10–8. See the preceding sections for details. Finally, for completeness, Listing 10–16 contains the code for the Name class that is used in the UserBean class.

Figure 10–9   Logging In to the News Service

Figure 10–10   Registering for the News Service

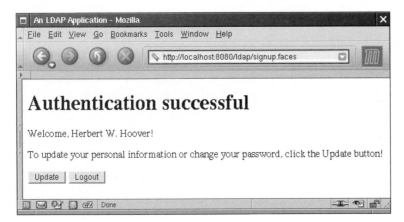

Figure 10–11   Main Screen of the News Service

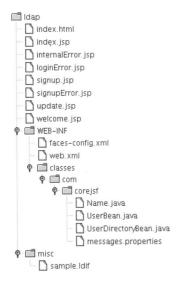

Figure 10–12   The Directory
Structure of the LDAP Example

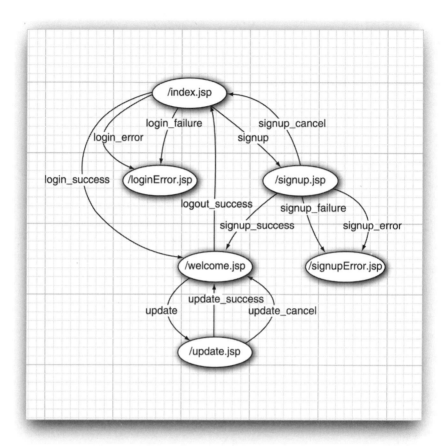

Figure 10–13   Page Flow of the News Service

Listing 10–9   ldap/index.jsp

```
1.  <html>
2.     <%@ taglib uri="http://java.sun.com/jsf/core" prefix="f" %>
3.     <%@ taglib uri="http://java.sun.com/jsf/html" prefix="h" %>
4.     <f:view>
5.        <head>
6.           <f:loadBundle basename="com.corejsf.messages" var="msgs"/>
7.           <title><h:outputText value="#{msgs.title}"/></title>
8.        </head>
9.        <body>
10.          <h:form>
11.             <h1><h:outputText value="#{msgs.enterNameAndPassword}"/></h1>
12.             <h:panelGrid columns="2">
```

Listing 10–9   ldap/index.jsp (cont.)

```
13.                 <h:outputText value="#{msgs.loginID}"/>
14.                 <h:inputText value="#{user.id}"/>
15.
16.                 <h:outputText value="#{msgs.password}"/>
17.                 <h:inputSecret value="#{user.password}"/>
18.             </h:panelGrid>
19.             <h:commandButton value="#{msgs.login}" action="#{user.login}"/>
20.             <br/>
21.             <h:outputText value="#{msgs.signupNow}"/>
22.             <h:commandButton value="#{msgs.signup}" action="signup"/>
23.         </h:form>
24.     </body>
25.   </f:view>
26. </html>
```

Listing 10–10   ldap/signup.jsp

```
1. <html>
2.     <%@ taglib uri="http://java.sun.com/jsf/core" prefix="f" %>
3.     <%@ taglib uri="http://java.sun.com/jsf/html" prefix="h" %>
4.     <f:view>
5.         <head>
6.             <f:loadBundle basename="com.corejsf.messages" var="msgs"/>
7.             <title><h:outputText value="#{msgs.title}"/></title>
8.         </head>
9.         <body>
10.             <h:form>
11.                 <h1><h:outputText value="#{msgs.newUserSignup}"/></h1>
12.                 <p><h:outputText value="#{msgs.newUserSignup_detail}"/></p>
13.                 <h:panelGrid columns="2">
14.                     <h:outputText value="#{msgs.firstName}"/>
15.                     <h:inputText value="#{user.name.first}"/>
16.
17.                     <h:outputText value="#{msgs.middleInitial}"/>
18.                     <h:inputText value="#{user.name.middle}"/>
19.
20.                     <h:outputText value="#{msgs.lastName}"/>
21.                     <h:inputText value="#{user.name.last}"/>
22.
23.                     <h:outputText value="#{msgs.email}"/>
24.                     <h:inputText value="#{user.email}"/>
25.
```

Listing 10–10   ldap/signup.jsp (cont.)

```
26.                <h:outputText value="#{msgs.loginID}"/>
27.                <h:inputText value="#{user.id}"/>
28.
29.                <h:outputText value="#{msgs.password}"/>
30.                <h:inputSecret value="#{user.password}"/>
31.             </h:panelGrid>
32.             <h:commandButton value="#{msgs.submit}" action="#{user.signup}"/>
33.             <h:commandButton value="#{msgs.cancel}" action="signup_cancel"/>
34.          </h:form>
35.       </body>
36.    </f:view>
37. </html>
```

Listing 10–11   ldap/welcome.jsp

```
1. <html>
2.    <%@ taglib uri="http://java.sun.com/jsf/core" prefix="f" %>
3.    <%@ taglib uri="http://java.sun.com/jsf/html" prefix="h" %>
4.    <f:view>
5.       <head>
6.          <f:loadBundle basename="com.corejsf.messages" var="msgs"/>
7.          <title><h:outputText value="#{msgs.title}"/></title>
8.       </head>
9.       <body>
10.          <h:form>
11.             <h1><h:outputText value="#{msgs.success}"/></h1>
12.             <p>
13.                <h:outputText value="#{msgs.welcome}"/>
14.                <h:outputText value="#{user.name}"/>!
15.             </p>
16.             <p>
17.                <h:outputText value="#{msgs.success_detail}"/>
18.             </p>
19.             <h:commandButton value="#{msgs.update}" action="update"/>
20.             <h:commandButton value="#{msgs.logout}" action="#{user.logout}"/>
21.          </h:form>
22.       </body>
23.    </f:view>
24. </html>
```

Listing 10–12   ldap/loginError.jsp

```
1.  <html>
2.    <%@ taglib uri="http://java.sun.com/jsf/core" prefix="f" %>
3.    <%@ taglib uri="http://java.sun.com/jsf/html" prefix="h" %>
4.    <f:view>
5.      <head>
6.        <f:loadBundle basename="com.corejsf.messages" var="msgs"/>
7.        <title><h:outputText value="#{msgs.title}"/></title>
8.      </head>
9.      <body>
10.       <h:form>
11.         <h1><h:outputText value="#{msgs.loginError}"/></h1>
12.         <p>
13.           <h:outputText value="#{msgs.loginError_detail}"/>
14.         </p>
15.         <p>
16.           <h:commandButton value="#{msgs.tryAgain}" action="login"/>
17.           <h:commandButton value="#{msgs.signup}" action="signup"/>
18.         </p>
19.       </h:form>
20.     </body>
21.   </f:view>
22. </html>
```

Listing 10–13   ldap/WEB-INF/classes/com/corejsf/UserBean.java

```
1.  package com.corejsf;
2.
3.  import java.util.logging.Level;
4.  import java.util.logging.Logger;
5.  import javax.faces.application.Application;
6.  import javax.faces.context.FacesContext;
7.  import javax.faces.el.ValueBinding;
8.  import javax.naming.NameNotFoundException;
9.  import javax.naming.NamingException;
10. import javax.naming.directory.Attributes;
11. import javax.naming.directory.BasicAttributes;
12. import javax.naming.directory.DirContext;
13.
14. public class UserBean {
15.   private Name name;
16.   private String id;
17.   private String email;
18.   private String password;
```

Listing 10–13   ldap/WEB-INF/classes/com/corejsf/UserBean.java (cont.)

```java
19.     private Logger logger = Logger.getLogger("com.corejava");
20.
21.     public UserBean() { name = new Name(); }
22.
23.     public DirContext getRootContext() throws NamingException {
24.        FacesContext context = FacesContext.getCurrentInstance();
25.        Application app = context.getApplication();
26.        ValueBinding binding = app.createValueBinding("#{userdir}");
27.        UserDirectoryBean dir =
28.           (UserDirectoryBean) binding.getValue(context);
29.        return dir.getRootContext();
30.     }
31.
32.     public Name getName() { return name; }
33.     public void setName(Name newValue) { name = newValue; }
34.
35.     public String getEmail() { return email; }
36.     public void setEmail(String newValue) { email = newValue; }
37.
38.     public String getId() { return id; }
39.     public void setId(String newValue) { id = newValue; }
40.
41.     public String getPassword() { return password; }
42.     public void setPassword(String newValue) { password = newValue; }
43.
44.     public String login() {
45.        try {
46.           DirContext context = getRootContext();
47.           try {
48.              String dn = "uid=" + id + ",ou=people,dc=corejsf,dc=com";
49.              Attributes userAttributes = context.getAttributes(dn);
50.              String cn = (String) userAttributes.get("cn").get();
51.              name.parse(cn);
52.              email = (String) userAttributes.get("mail").get();
53.              byte[] pw = (byte[])
54.                 userAttributes.get("userPassword").get();
55.              if (password.equals(new String(pw)))
56.                 return "login_success";
57.              else
58.                 return "login_failure";
59.           } finally {
60.              context.close();
61.           }
62.        }
63.        catch (NamingException ex) {
```

Listing 10–13 ldap/WEB-INF/classes/com/corejsf/UserBean.java (cont.)

```
64.          logger.log(Level.SEVERE, "loginAction", ex);
65.          return "login_error";
66.       }
67.    }
68.
69.    public String signup() {
70.       try {
71.          DirContext context = getRootContext();
72.          try {
73.             String dn = "uid=" + id + ",ou=people,dc=corejsf,dc=com";
74.
75.             try {
76.                context.lookup(dn);
77.                return "signup_failure";
78.             }
79.             catch (NameNotFoundException ex) {}
80.
81.             Attributes attrs = new BasicAttributes();
82.             attrs.put("objectClass", "inetOrgPerson");
83.             attrs.put("uid", id);
84.             attrs.put("sn", name.getLast());
85.             attrs.put("cn", name.toString());
86.             attrs.put("mail", email);
87.             attrs.put("userPassword", password.getBytes());
88.             context.createSubcontext(dn, attrs);
89.          } finally {
90.             context.close();
91.          }
92.       }
93.       catch (NamingException ex) {
94.          logger.log(Level.SEVERE, "loginAction", ex);
95.          return "signup_error";
96.       }
97.
98.       return "signup_success";
99.    }
100.
101.   public String update() {
102.      try {
103.         DirContext context = getRootContext();
104.         try {
105.            String dn = "uid=" + id + ",ou=people,dc=corejsf,dc=com";
106.            Attributes attrs = new BasicAttributes();
107.            attrs.put("sn", name.getLast());
108.            attrs.put("cn", name.toString());
```

Listing 10–13 ldap/WEB-INF/classes/com/corejsf/UserBean.java (cont.)

```
109.            attrs.put("mail", email);
110.            attrs.put("userPassword", password.getBytes());
111.            context.modifyAttributes(dn,
112.               DirContext.REPLACE_ATTRIBUTE, attrs);
113.         } finally {
114.            context.close();
115.         }
116.      }
117.      catch (NamingException ex) {
118.         logger.log(Level.SEVERE, "updateAction", ex);
119.         return "internal_error";
120.      }
121.
122.      return "update_success";
123.   }
124.
125.   public String logout() {
126.      password = "";
127.      return "logout_success";
128.   }
129. }
```

Listing 10–14 ldap/WEB-INF/classes/com/corejsf/UserDirectoryBean.java

```
 1. package com.corejsf;
 2.
 3. import java.util.Hashtable;
 4. import javax.naming.Context;
 5. import javax.naming.NamingException;
 6. import javax.naming.directory.DirContext;
 7. import javax.naming.directory.InitialDirContext;
 8.
 9. public class UserDirectoryBean {
10.    private String url;
11.    private String managerDN;
12.    private String managerPW;
13.
14.    public void setManagerDN(String newValue) { managerDN = newValue; }
15.    public void setManagerPassword(String newValue) {
16.       managerPW = newValue; }
17.    public void setURL(String newValue) { url = newValue; }
18.
```

Listing 10–14 ldap/WEB-INF/classes/com/corejsf/UserDirectoryBean.java (cont.)

```
19.  public DirContext getRootContext() throws NamingException {
20.      Hashtable env = new Hashtable();
21.      env.put(Context.SECURITY_PRINCIPAL, managerDN);
22.      env.put(Context.SECURITY_CREDENTIALS, managerPW);
23.      DirContext initial = new InitialDirContext(env);
24.
25.      Object obj = initial.lookup(url);
26.      if (!(obj instanceof DirContext))
27.          throw new NamingException("No directory context");
28.      return (DirContext) obj;
29.  }
30. }
```

Listing 10–15 ldap/WEB-INF/faces-config.xml

```
1. <?xml version="1.0"?>
2.
3. <!DOCTYPE faces-config PUBLIC
4.   "-//Sun Microsystems, Inc.//DTD JavaServer Faces Config 1.0//EN"
5.   "http://java.sun.com/dtd/web-facesconfig_1_0.dtd">
6.
7. <faces-config>
8.
9.    <navigation-rule>
10.       <from-view-id>/index.jsp</from-view-id>
11.       <navigation-case>
12.          <from-outcome>login_success</from-outcome>
13.          <to-view-id>/welcome.jsp</to-view-id>
14.       </navigation-case>
15.       <navigation-case>
16.          <from-outcome>login_error</from-outcome>
17.          <to-view-id>/loginError.jsp</to-view-id>
18.       </navigation-case>
19.       <navigation-case>
20.          <from-outcome>login_failure</from-outcome>
21.          <to-view-id>/loginError.jsp</to-view-id>
22.       </navigation-case>
23.       <navigation-case>
24.          <from-outcome>signup</from-outcome>
25.          <to-view-id>/signup.jsp</to-view-id>
26.       </navigation-case>
27.    </navigation-rule>
28.    <navigation-rule>
29.       <from-view-id>/signup.jsp</from-view-id>
```

Listing 10–15   ldap/WEB-INF/faces-config.xml (cont.)

```
30.      <navigation-case>
31.         <from-outcome>signup_success</from-outcome>
32.         <to-view-id>/welcome.jsp</to-view-id>
33.      </navigation-case>
34.      <navigation-case>
35.         <from-outcome>signup_failure</from-outcome>
36.         <to-view-id>/signupError.jsp</to-view-id>
37.      </navigation-case>
38.      <navigation-case>
39.         <from-outcome>signup_error</from-outcome>
40.         <to-view-id>/signupError.jsp</to-view-id>
41.      </navigation-case>
42.      <navigation-case>
43.         <from-outcome>signup_cancel</from-outcome>
44.         <to-view-id>/index.jsp</to-view-id>
45.      </navigation-case>
46.   </navigation-rule>
47.   <navigation-rule>
48.      <from-view-id>/welcome.jsp</from-view-id>
49.      <navigation-case>
50.         <from-outcome>update</from-outcome>
51.         <to-view-id>/update.jsp</to-view-id>
52.      </navigation-case>
53.      <navigation-case>
54.         <from-outcome>logout_success</from-outcome>
55.         <to-view-id>/index.jsp</to-view-id>
56.      </navigation-case>
57.   </navigation-rule>
58.   <navigation-rule>
59.      <from-view-id>/update.jsp</from-view-id>
60.      <navigation-case>
61.         <from-outcome>update_success</from-outcome>
62.         <to-view-id>/welcome.jsp</to-view-id>
63.      </navigation-case>
64.      <navigation-case>
65.         <from-outcome>update_cancel</from-outcome>
66.         <to-view-id>/welcome.jsp</to-view-id>
67.      </navigation-case>
68.   </navigation-rule>
69.   <navigation-rule>
70.      <navigation-case>
71.         <from-outcome>login</from-outcome>
72.         <to-view-id>/index.jsp</to-view-id>
73.      </navigation-case>
74.      <navigation-case>
```

Listing 10–15 ldap/WEB-INF/faces-config.xml (cont.)

```
75.         <from-outcome>internal_error</from-outcome>
76.         <to-view-id>/internalError.jsp</to-view-id>
77.      </navigation-case>
78.   </navigation-rule>
79.
80.   <managed-bean>
81.      <managed-bean-name>user</managed-bean-name>
82.      <managed-bean-class>com.corejsf.UserBean</managed-bean-class>
83.      <managed-bean-scope>session</managed-bean-scope>
84.   </managed-bean>
85.
86.   <managed-bean>
87.      <managed-bean-name>userdir</managed-bean-name>
88.      <managed-bean-class>com.corejsf.UserDirectoryBean</managed-bean-class>
89.      <managed-bean-scope>application</managed-bean-scope>
90.      <managed-property>
91.         <property-name>URL</property-name>
92.         <value>ldap://localhost:389</value>
93.      </managed-property>
94.      <managed-property>
95.         <property-name>managerDN</property-name>
96.         <value>cn=Manager,dc=corejsf,dc=com</value>
97.      </managed-property>
98.      <managed-property>
99.         <property-name>managerPassword</property-name>
100.        <value>secret</value>
101.     </managed-property>
102.  </managed-bean>
103.
104. </faces-config>
```

Listing 10–16 ldap/WEB-INF/classes/com/corejsf/Name.java

```
1. package com.corejsf;
2.
3. public class Name {
4.    private String first;
5.    private String middle;
6.    private String last;
7.
8.    public Name() { first = ""; middle = ""; last = ""; }
9.
10.   public String getFirst() { return first; }
11.   public void setFirst(String newValue) { first = newValue; }
```

Listing 10–16   ldap/WEB-INF/classes/com/corejsf/Name.java (cont.)

```
12.
13.    public String getMiddle() { return middle; }
14.    public void setMiddle(String newValue) { middle = newValue; }
15.
16.    public String getLast() { return last; }
17.    public void setLast(String newValue) { last = newValue; }
18.
19.    public void parse(String fullName) {
20.       int firstSpace = fullName.indexOf(' ');
21.       int lastSpace = fullName.lastIndexOf(' ');
22.       if (firstSpace == -1) {
23.          first = "";
24.          middle = "";
25.          last = fullName;
26.       }
27.       else {
28.          first = fullName.substring(0, firstSpace);
29.          if (firstSpace < lastSpace)
30.             middle = fullName.substring(firstSpace + 1, lastSpace);
31.          else
32.             middle = "";
33.          last = fullName.substring(lastSpace + 1, fullName.length());
34.       }
35.    }
36.
37.    public String toString() {
38.       StringBuffer buffer = new StringBuffer();
39.       buffer.append(first);
40.       buffer.append(' ');
41.       if (middle.length() > 0) {
42.          buffer.append(middle.charAt(0));
43.          buffer.append(". ");
44.       }
45.       buffer.append(last);
46.       return buffer.toString();
47.    }
48. }
```

Container-Managed Authentication and Authorization

In the preceding sections you saw how a web application can use an LDAP directory to look up user information. It is up to the application to use that information appropriately, to allow or deny users access to certain resources. In this section, we discuss an alternative approach: *container-managed authentica-*

tion. This mechanism puts the burden of authenticating users on the servlet container (such as Tomcat). It is much easier to ensure that security is handled consistently for an entire Web application if the container manages autentication and authorization. The application programmer can then focus on the flow of the web application without worrying about user privileges.

Most of the configuration details in this chapter are specific to Tomcat, but other servlet containers have similar mechanisms.

To protect a set of pages, you specify access control information in the web.xml file. For example, the following security constraint restricts all pages in the protected subdirectory to authenticated users that have the role registereduser or invitedguest.

```
<security-constraint>
   <web-resource-collection>
      <url-pattern>/protected/*</url-pattern>
   </web-resource-collection>
   <auth-constraint>
      <role-name>registereduser</role-name>
      <role-name>invitedguest</role-name>
   </auth-constraint>
</security-constraint>
```

The role of a user is assigned during authentication. Roles are stored in the user directory together with user names and passwords.

NOTE: If JSF is configured to use a /faces prefix for JSF pages, then you must add a corresponding URL pattern to the security constraint, such as /faces/protected/* in the preceding example.

Next, you need to specify how users authenticate themselves. The most flexible approach is form-based authentication. Add the following entry to web.xml:

```
<login-config>
   <auth-method>FORM</auth-method>
   <form-login-config>
      <form-login-page>/login.html</form-login-page>
      <form-error-page>/noauth.html</form-error-page>
   </form-login-config>
</login-config>
```

The form login configuration specifies a web page into which the user types in the username and password. You are free to design any desired appearance for the login page, but you must include a mechanism to submit a request to j_security_check with request parameters named j_username and j_password. The following form will do the job:

```
<form method="POST" action="j_security_check">
  User name: <input type="text" name="j_username"/>
  Password:  <input type="password" name="j_password"/>
  <input type="submit" value="Login"/>
</form>
```

The error page can be any page at all.

When the user requests a protected resource, the login page is displayed (see Figure 10–14). If the user supplies a valid username and password, then the requested page appears. Otherwise, the error page is shown.

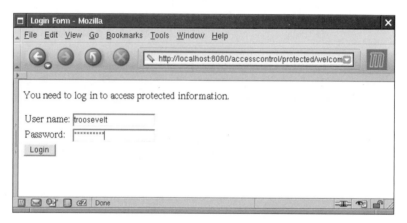

Figure 10–14   Requesting a Protected Resource

NOTE: To securely transmit the login information from the client to the server, you should use SSL. Configuring a server for SSL is beyond the scope of this book. For more information, turn to http://jakarta.apache.org/tomcat/tomcat-5.0-doc/ssl-howto.html.

You can also specify "basic" authentication by placing the following login configuration into web.xml:

```
<login-conf>
  <auth-method>BASIC</auth-method>
  <realm-name>This string shows up in the dialog</realm-name>
</login-conf>
```

In that case, the browser pops up a password dialog (see Figure 10–15). However, a professionally designed web site will probably use form-based authentication.

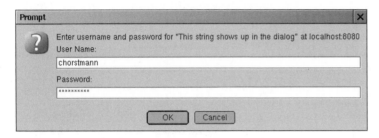

Figure 10–15 Basic Authentication

The web.xml file only describes which resources have access restrictions and which roles are allowed access. It is silent on how users, passwords, and roles are stored. You configure that information by specifying a *realm* for the web application. A realm is any mechanism for looking up user names, passwords, and roles. Tomcat supports several standard realms that access user information from one of the following sources:

- An LDAP directory
- A relational database
- An XML file (by default, conf/tomcat-users.xml) that is read when the server starts

To configure a realm, you supply a Realm element. Listing10–17 shows a typical example, a JNDI realm.

Listing 10–17 accesscontrol/META-INF/context.xml

```
1. <Context path="/accesscontrol" docbase="webapps/accesscontrol.war">
2. <Realm className="org.apache.catalina.realm.JNDIRealm"
3.    debug="99"
4.    connectionURL="ldap://localhost:389"
5.    connectionName="cn=Manager,dc=corejsf,dc=com"
6.    connectionPassword="secret"
7.    userPattern="uid={0},ou=people,dc=corejsf,dc=com"
8.    userPassword="userPassword"
9.    roleBase="ou=groups,dc=corejsf,dc=com"
10.   roleName="cn"
11.   roleSearch="(uniqueMember={0})"/>
12. </Context>
```

The configuration lists the URL and login information and describes how to look up users and roles.

In this example, the Realm element is placed inside a Context element in the file META-INF/context.xml. This is the preferred mechanism for supplying an application-specific realm.

◆ CAUTION: You can also configure a realm in the Engine or Host element of the server.xml file. However, that realm is then used by the manager application in addition to your regular web application. If you want to use the manager application to install your web applications, then you must make sure that the username and password that you use for installation is included in the realm, with a role of manager.

Since the servlet container is in charge of authentication and authorization, there is nothing for you to program. Nevertheless, you may want to have programmatic access to the user information. The HttpServletRequest yields a small amount of information, in particular, the name of the user who logged in. You get the request object from the external context:

```
ExternalContext external
    = FacesContext.getCurrentInstance().getExternalContext();
HttpServletRequest request
  = (HttpServletRequest) external.getRequest();
String user = request.getRemoteUser();
```

You can also test whether the current user belongs to a given role. For example,

```
String role = "admin";
boolean isAdmin = request.isUserInRole(role);
```

▤ NOTE: Currently, there is no specification for logging off or for switching identities when using container-managed security. This is a problem, particularly for testing web applications. Tomcat uses cookies to represent the current user, and you need to quit and restart your browser whenever you want to switch your identity. We resorted to using Lynx for testing because it starts up much faster than a graphical web browser—see Figure 10–16.

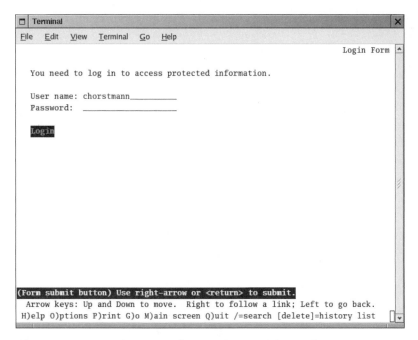

Figure 10–16   Using Lynx for Testing a Web Application

We give you a skeleton application that shows container-managed security at work. When you access the protected resource protected/welcome.jsp (Listing 10–18), then the authentication dialog of Listing 10–21 is displayed. You can proceed only if you enter a username and password of a user belonging to the registereduser or invitedguest role.

Just to demonstrate the servlet API, the welcome page shows the name of the registered user and lets you test for role membership (see Figure 10–16).

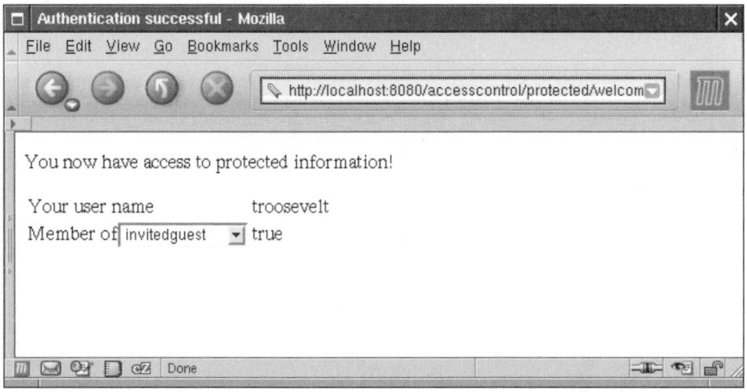

Figure 10–17   Welcome Page of the Authentication Test Application

Listing 10–18 accesscontrol/protected/welcome.jsp

```
1.  <html>
2.    <%@ taglib uri="http://java.sun.com/jsf/core" prefix="f" %>
3.    <%@ taglib uri="http://java.sun.com/jsf/html" prefix="h" %>
4.    <f:view>
5.      <head>
6.        <f:loadBundle basename="com.corejsf.messages" var="msgs"/>
7.        <title><h:outputText value="#{msgs.title}"/></title>
8.      </head>
9.      <body>
10.       <h:form>
11.         <p><h:outputText value="#{msgs.youHaveAccess}"/></p>
12.         <h:panelGrid columns="2">
13.           <h:outputText value="#{msgs.yourUserName}"/>
14.           <h:outputText value="#{user.name}"/>
15.
16.           <h:panelGroup>
17.             <h:outputText value="#{msgs.memberOf}"/>
18.             <h:selectOneMenu onchange="submit()" value="#{user.role}">
19.               <f:selectItem itemValue="" itemLabel="Select a role"/>
20.               <f:selectItem itemValue="admin" itemLabel="admin"/>
21.               <f:selectItem itemValue="manager" itemLabel="manager"/>
22.               <f:selectItem itemValue="registereduser"
23.                   itemLabel="registereduser"/>
24.               <f:selectItem itemValue="invitedguest"
25.                   itemLabel="invitedguest"/>
26.             </h:selectOneMenu>
27.           </h:panelGroup>
28.           <h:outputText value="#{user.inRole}"/>
29.         </h:panelGrid>
30.       </h:form>
31.     </body>
32.   </f:view>
33. </html>
```

Listing 10–19 accesscontrol/WEB-INF/web.xml

```
1.  <?xml version="1.0"?>
2.  <!DOCTYPE web-app PUBLIC
3.    "-//Sun Microsystems, Inc.//DTD Web Application 2.3//EN"
4.    "http://java.sun.com/dtd/web-app_2_3.dtd">
5.
6.  <web-app>
7.    <servlet>
8.      <servlet-name>Faces Servlet</servlet-name>
```

Listing 10–19 accesscontrol/WEB-INF/web.xml (cont.)

```
 9.      <servlet-class>javax.faces.webapp.FacesServlet</servlet-class>
10.      <load-on-startup>1</load-on-startup>
11.    </servlet>
12.
13.    <servlet-mapping>
14.      <servlet-name>Faces Servlet</servlet-name>
15.      <url-pattern>*.faces</url-pattern>
16.    </servlet-mapping>
17.
18.    <welcome-file-list>
19.      <welcome-file>index.html</welcome-file>
20.    </welcome-file-list>
21.
22.    <security-constraint>
23.      <web-resource-collection>
24.        <web-resource-name>Protected Pages</web-resource-name>
25.        <url-pattern>/protected/*</url-pattern>
26.      </web-resource-collection>
27.      <auth-constraint>
28.        <role-name>registereduser</role-name>
29.      <role-name>invitedguest</role-name>
30.      </auth-constraint>
31.     </security-constraint>
32.
33.    <login-config>
34.      <auth-method>FORM</auth-method>
35.      <form-login-config>
36.        <form-login-page>/login.html</form-login-page>
37.        <form-error-page>/noauth.html</form-error-page>
38.      </form-login-config>
39.    </login-config>
40.
41.    <security-role>
42.      <role-name>registereduser</role-name>
43.    </security-role>
44.    <security-role>
45.      <role-name>invitedguest</role-name>
46.    </security-role>
47. </web-app>
```

Listing 10–20 accesscontrol/WEB-INF/classes/com/corejsf/UserBean.java

```
 1. package com.corejsf;
 2.
 3. import java.util.logging.Logger;
 4. import javax.faces.context.ExternalContext;
 5. import javax.faces.context.FacesContext;
 6. import javax.servlet.http.HttpServletRequest;
 7.
 8. public class UserBean {
 9.    private String name;
10.    private String role;
11.    private Logger logger = Logger.getLogger("com.corejsf");
12.
13.    public String getName() {
14.       if (name == null) getUserData();
15.       return name == null ? "" : name;
16.    }
17.
18.    public String getRole() { return role == null ? "" : role; }
19.    public void setRole(String newValue) { role = newValue; }
20.
21.    public boolean isInRole() {
22.       ExternalContext context
23.          = FacesContext.getCurrentInstance().getExternalContext();
24.       Object requestObject = context.getRequest();
25.       if (!(requestObject instanceof HttpServletRequest)) {
26.          logger.severe("request object has type " + requestObject.getClass());
27.          return false;
28.       }
29.       HttpServletRequest request = (HttpServletRequest) requestObject;
30.       return request.isUserInRole(role);
31.    }
32.
33.    private void getUserData() {
34.       ExternalContext context
35.          = FacesContext.getCurrentInstance().getExternalContext();
36.       Object requestObject = context.getRequest();
37.       if (!(requestObject instanceof HttpServletRequest)) {
38.          logger.severe("request object has type " + requestObject.getClass());
39.          return;
40.       }
41.       HttpServletRequest request = (HttpServletRequest) requestObject;
42.       name = request.getRemoteUser();
43.    }
44. }
```

Listing 10–21	accesscontrol/login.html

```
 1.  <html>
 2.     <head>
 3.        <title>Login Form</title>
 4.     </head>
 5.
 6.     <body>
 7.        <form method="POST" action="j_security_check">
 8.           <p>You need to log in to access protected information.</p>
 9.           <table>
10.              <tr>
11.                 <td>User name:</td>
12.                 <td>
13.                    <input type="text" name="j_username"/>
14.                 </td>
15.              </tr>
16.              <tr>
17.                 <td>Password:</td>
18.                 <td>
19.                    <input type="password" name="j_password"/>
20.                 </td>
21.              </tr>
22.           </table>
23.           <input type="submit" value="Login"/>
24.        </form>
25.     </body>
26.  </html>
```

Figure 10–18 shows the directory structure of the application. The web.xml file in Listing 10–22 restricts access to the protected directory. Listing 10–23 contains the page that is displayed when authorization fails. Listing 10–25 contains the protected page. You can find the message strings in Listing 10–26 and the code for the user bean in Listing 10–24.

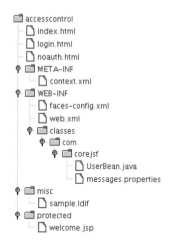

accesscontrol
├── index.html
├── login.html
├── noauth.html
├── META-INF
│   └── context.xml
├── WEB-INF
│   ├── faces-config.xml
│   ├── web.xml
│   └── classes
│   └── com
│   └── corejsf
│   ├── UserBean.java
│   └── messages.properties
├── misc
│   └── sample.ldif
└── protected
        └── welcome.jsp

**Figure 10–18   Directory Structure
of the Access Control Application**

Listing 10–22   accesscontrol/WEB-INF/web.xml

```
1. <?xml version="1.0"?>
2. <!DOCTYPE web-app PUBLIC
3.    "-//Sun Microsystems, Inc.//DTD Web Application 2.3//EN"
4.    "http://java.sun.com/dtd/web-app_2_3.dtd">
5.
6. <web-app>
7.    <servlet>
8.       <servlet-name>Faces Servlet</servlet-name>
9.       <servlet-class>javax.faces.webapp.FacesServlet</servlet-class>
10.       <load-on-startup>1</load-on-startup>
11.    </servlet>
12.
13.    <servlet-mapping>
14.       <servlet-name>Faces Servlet</servlet-name>
15.       <url-pattern>*.faces</url-pattern>
16.    </servlet-mapping>
17.
18.    <welcome-file-list>
19.       <welcome-file>index.html</welcome-file>
20.    </welcome-file-list>
21.
```

Listing 10–22   accesscontrol/WEB-INF/web.xml (cont.)

```
22.    <security-constraint>
23.      <web-resource-collection>
24.        <web-resource-name>Protected Pages</web-resource-name>
25.        <url-pattern>/protected/*</url-pattern>
26.      </web-resource-collection>
27.      <auth-constraint>
28.        <role-name>registereduser</role-name>
29.      <role-name>invitedguest</role-name>
30.      </auth-constraint>
31.    </security-constraint>
32.
33.    <login-config>
34.      <auth-method>FORM</auth-method>
35.      <form-login-config>
36.        <form-login-page>/login.html</form-login-page>
37.        <form-error-page>/noauth.html</form-error-page>
38.      </form-login-config>
39.    </login-config>
40.
41.    <security-role>
42.      <role-name>registereduser</role-name>
43.    </security-role>
44.    <security-role>
45.      <role-name>invitedguest</role-name>
46.    </security-role>
47. </web-app>
```

Listing 10–23   accesscontrol/noauth.html

```
1. <html>
2.   <head>
3.     <title>Authentication failed</title>
4.   </head>
5.
6.   <body>
7.     <p>Sorry--authentication failed. Please try again.</p>
8.   </body>
9. </html>
```

Listing 10–24   accesscontrol/WEB-INF/classes/com/corejsf/UserBean.java

```
 1. package com.corejsf;
 2.
 3. import java.util.logging.Logger;
 4. import javax.faces.context.ExternalContext;
 5. import javax.faces.context.FacesContext;
 6. import javax.servlet.http.HttpServletRequest;
 7.
 8. public class UserBean {
 9.    private String name;
10.    private String role;
11.    private Logger logger = Logger.getLogger("com.corejsf");
12.
13.    public String getName() {
14.       if (name == null) getUserData();
15.       return name == null ? "" : name;
16.    }
17.
18.    public String getRole() { return role == null ? "" : role; }
19.    public void setRole(String newValue) { role = newValue; }
20.
21.    public boolean isInRole() {
22.       ExternalContext context
23.          = FacesContext.getCurrentInstance().getExternalContext();
24.       Object requestObject =  context.getRequest();
25.       if (!(requestObject instanceof HttpServletRequest)) {
26.          logger.severe("request object has type " + requestObject.getClass());
27.          return false;
28.       }
29.       HttpServletRequest request = (HttpServletRequest) requestObject;
30.       return request.isUserInRole(role);
31.    }
32.
33.    private void getUserData() {
34.       ExternalContext context
35.          = FacesContext.getCurrentInstance().getExternalContext();
36.       Object requestObject =  context.getRequest();
37.       if (!(requestObject instanceof HttpServletRequest)) {
38.          logger.severe("request object has type " + requestObject.getClass());
39.          return;
40.       }
41.       HttpServletRequest request = (HttpServletRequest) requestObject;
42.       name = request.getRemoteUser();
43.    }
44. }
```

Listing 10–25   accesscontrol/protected/welcome.jsp

```
1. <html>
2.    <%@ taglib uri="http://java.sun.com/jsf/core" prefix="f" %>
3.    <%@ taglib uri="http://java.sun.com/jsf/html" prefix="h" %>
4.    <f:view>
5.       <head>
6.          <f:loadBundle basename="com.corejsf.messages" var="msgs"/>
7.          <title><h:outputText value="#{msgs.title}"/></title>
8.       </head>
9.       <body>
10.          <h:form>
11.             <p><h:outputText value="#{msgs.youHaveAccess}"/></p>
12.             <h:panelGrid columns="2">
13.                <h:outputText value="#{msgs.yourUserName}"/>
14.                <h:outputText value="#{user.name}"/>
15.
16.                <h:panelGroup>
17.                   <h:outputText value="#{msgs.memberOf}"/>
18.                   <h:selectOneMenu onchange="submit()" value="#{user.role}">
19.                      <f:selectItem itemValue="" itemLabel="Select a role"/>
20.                      <f:selectItem itemValue="admin" itemLabel="admin"/>
21.                      <f:selectItem itemValue="manager" itemLabel="manager"/>
22.                      <f:selectItem itemValue="registereduser"
23.                         itemLabel="registereduser"/>
24.                      <f:selectItem itemValue="invitedguest"
25.                         itemLabel="invitedguest"/>
26.                   </h:selectOneMenu>
27.                </h:panelGroup>
28.                <h:outputText value="#{user.inRole}"/>
29.             </h:panelGrid>
30.          </h:form>
31.       </body>
32.    </f:view>
33. </html>
```

Listing 10–26   accesscontrol/WEB-INF/classes/com/corejsf/messages.properties

```
1. title=Authentication successful
2. youHaveAccess=You now have access to protected information!
3. yourUserName=Your user name
4. memberOf=Member of
```

API `javax.servlet.HttpServletRequest`

- `String getRemoteUser() [Servlet 2.2]`

  Gets the name of the user who is currently logged in, or `null` if there is no such user.

- `boolean isUserInRole(String role) [Servlet 2.2]`

  Tests whether the current user belongs to the given role.

Using Web Services

When a web application needs to get information from an external source, it typically uses a remote procedure call mechanism. In recent years, *web services* have emerged as a popular technology for this purpose.

Technically, a web service has two components:

- A server that can be accessed with the SOAP (Simple Object Access Protocol) transport protocol

- A description of the service in the WSDL (Web Service Description Language) format

Fortunately, you can use web services, even if you know nothing at all about SOAP and just a little about WSDL.

To make web services easy to understand, we look at a concrete example: the Amazon Web Services, described at http://www.amazon.com/gp/aws/landing.html. The Amazon Web Services allow a programmer to interact with the Amazon system for a wide variety of purposes. For example, you can get listings of all books with a given author or title, or you can fill shopping carts and place orders. Amazon makes these services available for use by companies that want to sell items to their customers, using the Amazon system as a fulfillment back-end. To run our example program, you will need to sign up with Amazon and get a free developer token that lets you connect to the service.

You also need to download and install the Java Web Services Developer Pack (JWSDP) from http://java.sun.com/webservices/webservicespack.html.

NOTE: You may already use the JWSDP for the examples in this book—it bundles JSF, Tomcat, and Ant. If so, there is no need to reinstall it. If you use standalone versions of JSF, Tomcat, and Ant, you can install the JWSDP and continue to use the standalone versions to run this example.

A primary attraction of web services is that they are language-neutral. We will access the Amazon Web Services by using the Java programming language, but other developers can equally well use C++ or Visual Basic. The WSDL descriptor describes the services in a language-independent manner. For example, the WSDL for the Amazon Web Services (located at http://soap.amazon.com/schemas3/AmazonWebServices.wsdl) describes an AuthorSearchRequest operation as follows:

```
<operation name="AuthorSearchRequest">
   <input message="typens:AuthorSearchRequest"/>
   <output message="typens:AuthorSearchResponse"/>
</operation>
...
<message name="AuthorSearchRequest">
   <part name="AuthorSearchRequest" type="typens:AuthorRequest"/>
</message>
<message name="AuthorSearchResponse">
   <part name="return" type="typens:ProductInfo"/>
</message>
```

Elsewhere, it defines the data types. Here is the definition of AuthorRequest:

```
<xsd:complexType name="AuthorRequest">
   <xsd:all>
      <xsd:element name="author" type="xsd:string"/>
      <xsd:element name="page" type="xsd:string"/>
      <xsd:element name="mode" type="xsd:string"/>
      <xsd:element name="tag" type="xsd:string"/>
      <xsd:element name="type" type="xsd:string"/>
      <xsd:element name="devtag" type="xsd:string"/>
      <xsd:element name="sort" type="xsd:string" minOccurs="0"/>
      <xsd:element name="locale" type="xsd:string" minOccurs="0"/>
      <xsd:element name="keywords" type="xsd:string" minOccurs="0"/>
      <xsd:element name="price" type="xsd:string" minOccurs="0"/>
   </xsd:all>
</xsd:complexType>
```

When this description is translated into the Java programming language, the AuthorRequest type becomes a class.

```
public class AuthorRequest {
   public AuthorRequest(String author, String page, String mode, String tag,
      String type, String devtag, String sort, String locale, String keyword,
         String price) { ... }
   public String getAuthor() { ... }
   public void setAuthor(String newValue) { ... }
   public String getPage() { ... }
   public void setPage(String) { ... }
   ...
}
```

To call the search service, construct an `AuthorRequest` object and call the `authorSearchRequest` of a "port" object.

```
AmazonSearchPort asp = (AmazonSearchPort)
   (new AmazonSearchService_Impl().getAmazonSearchPort());
AuthorRequest req = new AuthorRequest(name,
   "1", "books", "", "lite", "", token, "", "", "");
ProductInfo pinfo = asp.authorSearchRequest(req);
```

The port object translates the Java object into a SOAP message, passes it to the Amazon server, and translates the returned message into a `ProductInfo` object. The port classes are automatically generated.

 NOTE: The WSDL file does not specify *what* the service does. It only specifies the parameter and return types.

To generate the required Java classes, place into an empty directory a `config.xml` file with the following contents:

```
<?xml version="1.0" encoding="UTF-8"?>
<configuration
   xmlns="http://java.sun.com/xml/ns/jax-rpc/ri/config">
      <wsdl
         location="http://soap.amazon.com/schemas3/AmazonWebServices.wsdl"
         packageName="com.corejsf.amazon" />
</configuration>
```

Then run these commands:

```
jwsdp/jaxrpc/bin/wscompile.sh -import config.xml
jwsdp/jaxrpc/bin/wscompile.sh -gen config.xml
jar cvf aws.jar .
```

Here, *jwsdp* is the directory into which you installed the JWSDP, such as /usr/local/jwsdp-1.3 or c:\jwsdp-1.3. (As usual, Windows users need to use \ instead of /.)

Place the resulting JAR file into the `WEB-INF/lib` directory of any JSF application that uses the Amazon Web Services.

 NOTE: If you like, you can also run the wscompile program from inside Ant. See the *jwsdp*/jaxrpc/samples/HelloWorld directory for an example.

Our sample application is straightforward. The user specifies an author name and clicks the "Search" button (see Figure 10–19).

Figure 10–19   Searching for Books with a Given Author

We simply show the first page of the response in a data table (see Figure 10–20). This shows that the web service is successful. We leave it as the proverbial exercise for the reader to extend the functionality of the application.

Search Result

First Author	Title	Publisher	Publication Date
Lewis Carroll	Euclid and His Modern Rivals	Dover Pubns	29 March, 2004
David Carroll	World of Darkness: Time of Judgment (World of Darkness)	White Wolf Publishing Inc.	March, 2004
Lewis Carroll	Alicia En El Pais De Las Maravillas/Alice in Wonderland	Editorial Juventud, S.A.	October, 2001
Lewis Carroll	Ninas	Lumen Espana	August, 1998
Lewis Carroll	Alicia En El Pais De Las Maravillas, a Traves Del Espejo Y LA Caza Del Snark/Alice's Adventures in Wonderland, Alice Through the Mirror and the hunti	Edhasa	April, 2002
Lewis Carroll	Alicia En El Pais de Las Maravillas - A Traves del	Ediciones Catedra S.A.	August, 1999
Lewis Carroll	Through the Looking-Glass, and What Alice Found There (Collected Works of Lewis Carroll)	Classic Books	May, 2000
Lewis Carroll	The New Belfry of Christ Church, Ocford (Collected Works of Lewis Carroll)	Classic Books	May, 2000
Lectorum Publications	A Traves Del Espejo Trebol	Everest De Ediciones Y Distribucion	January, 2002
Lewis Carroll	The Vision of the Three T's (Collected Works of Lewis Carroll)	Classic Books	May, 2000

Figure 10–20   A Search Result

Figure 10–21 shows the directory structure of the application. Note the JAR file in the WEB-INF/lib directory.

You need different build files for this application since a large number of additional libraries are required for the SOAP calls—see Listings 10–27 and 10–28. As always, you need to customize build.properties. If you use the JWSDP instead of the standalone Tomcat server, you don't need to include the jwsdp-shared files in the copy target.

The bean class in Listing 10–29 contains the call to the web service. The call returns an object of type ProductInfo. We stash away the Details array contained in the returned object.

Note how the developer token is set in faces-config.xml (Listing 10–30). Be sure to supply your own ID in that file.

Listings 10–31 through 10–33 show the JSF pages. The result.jsp page contains a data table that displays information from the Details array that was returned by the search service.

Finally, Listing 10–34 is the message bundle.

**Figure 10–21   Directory Structure
of the Web Service Test Application**

Listing 10–27   amazon/build.xml

```
1. <project default="install">
2.
3.    <property file="build.properties"/>
4.    <property name="appdir" value="${basedir}"/>
5.    <property name="builddir" value="${appdir}/build"/>
6.    <property name="appname" value="amazon"/>
7.    <property name="warfile" value="${builddir}/${appname}.war"/>
```

Listing 10–27 amazon/build.xml (cont.)

```
8.
9.      <path id="classpath">
10.         <pathelement location="${servlet.api.jar}"/>
11.         <pathelement location="${jsp.api.jar}"/>
12.         <fileset dir="${builddir}/WEB-INF/lib">
13.             <include name="*.jar"/>
14.         </fileset>
15.     </path>
16.
17.     <target name="init">
18.         <tstamp/>
19.     </target>
20.
21.     <target name="copy" depends="init"
22.         description="Copy files to build directory.">
23.         <mkdir dir="${builddir}"/>
24.         <copy todir="${builddir}">
25.             <fileset dir="${appdir}">
26.                 <exclude name="**/*.java"/>
27.                 <exclude name="build/**"/>
28.                 <!-- for Eclipse -->
29.                 <exclude name="bin/**"/>
30.                 <exclude name=".*"/>
31.             </fileset>
32.         </copy>
33.         <copy todir="${builddir}/WEB-INF/lib">
34.             <fileset dir="${jsf.lib.dir}" includes="${jsf.libs}"/>
35.             <fileset dir="${jstl.lib.dir}" includes="${jstl.libs}"/>
36.             <fileset dir="${commons.lib.dir}" includes="${commons.libs}"/>
37.             <fileset dir="${jaxrpc.lib.dir}" includes="*.jar"/>
38.             <fileset dir="${saaj.lib.dir}" includes="*.jar"/>
39.             <fileset dir="${jwsdp-shared.lib.dir}" includes="${jwsdp-shared.libs}"/>
40.         </copy>
41.     </target>
42.
43.     <target name="compile" depends="copy"
44.         description="Compile source files.">
45.         <javac
46.             srcdir="${appdir}/WEB-INF/classes"
47.             destdir="${builddir}/WEB-INF/classes"
48.             debug="true"
49.             deprecation="true">
50.             <include name="**/*.java"/>
51.             <classpath refid="classpath"/>
52.         </javac>
```

Listing 10–27 amazon/build.xml (cont.)

```
53.    </target>
54.
55.    <target name="war" depends="compile"
56.       description="Build WAR file.">
57.       <delete file="${warfile}"/>
58.       <jar jarfile="${warfile}" basedir="${builddir}"/>
59.    </target>
60.
61.    <target name="install" depends="war"
62.       description="Deploy web application.">
63.       <copy file="${warfile}" todir="${tomcat.dir}/webapps"/>
64.    </target>
65.
66. </project>
```

Listing 10–28 amazon/build.properties

```
 1. jsf.dir=/usr/local/jsf-1_0
 2. tomcat.dir=/usr/local/jakarta-tomcat-5.0.19
 3.
 4. username=me
 5. password=secret
 6. manager.url=http://localhost:8080/manager
 7.
 8. servlet.api.jar=${tomcat.dir}/common/lib/servlet-api.jar
 9. jsp.api.jar=${tomcat.dir}/common/lib/jsp-api.jar
10.
11. jsf.lib.dir=${jsf.dir}/lib
12. jstl.lib.dir=${tomcat.dir}/webapps/jsp-examples/WEB-INF/lib
13. commons.lib.dir=${tomcat.dir}/server/lib
14.
15. jsf.libs=jsf-api.jar,jsf-impl.jar
16. jstl.libs=jstl.jar,standard.jar
17. commons.libs=commons-beanutils.jar,commons-digester.jar
18.
19. jwsdp.dir=/home/apps/jwsdp-1.3
20. jaxp.lib.dir=${jwsdp.dir}/jaxp/lib
21. jaxrpc.lib.dir=${jwsdp.dir}/jaxrpc/lib
22. saaj.lib.dir=${jwsdp.dir}/saaj/lib
23. jwsdp-shared.lib.dir=${jwsdp.dir}/jwsdp-shared/lib
24. jaxp.api.jar=${jaxp.lib.dir}/jaxp-api.jar
25. jwsdp-shared.libs=jax-qname.jar,namespace.jar,activa-
tion.jar,jaas.jar,mail.jar,xsdlib.jar,providerutil.jar
```

Listing 10–29 amazon/WEB-INF/classes/com/corejsf/AmazonSearchBean.java

```java
 1. package com.corejsf;
 2.
 3. import com.corejsf.amazon.AmazonSearchPort;
 4. import com.corejsf.amazon.AmazonSearchService_Impl;
 5. import com.corejsf.amazon.AuthorRequest;
 6. import com.corejsf.amazon.Details;
 7. import com.corejsf.amazon.ProductInfo;
 8.
 9. public class AuthorSearchBean {
10.    private String name;
11.    private String type;
12.    private Details[] details;
13.    private String token;
14.
15.    public String getName() { return name; }
16.    public void setName(String newValue) { name = newValue; }
17.
18.    public void setToken(String newValue) { token = newValue; }
19.
20.    public String search() {
21.       try{
22.          AmazonSearchPort asp = (AmazonSearchPort)
23.             (new AmazonSearchService_Impl().getAmazonSearchPort());
24.
25.          AuthorRequest req = new AuthorRequest(name,
26.             "1", "books", "", "lite", "", token, "", "", "");
27.          ProductInfo pinfo = asp.authorSearchRequest(req);
28.          details = pinfo.getDetails();
29.          return "success";
30.       } catch(Exception e) {
31.          e.printStackTrace();
32.          return "failure";
33.       }
34.    }
35.
36.    public Details[] getDetails() { return details; }
37. }
```

Listing 10–30   amazon/WEB-INF/faces-config.xml

```
 1. <?xml version="1.0"?>
 2.
 3. <!DOCTYPE faces-config PUBLIC
 4.    "-//Sun Microsystems, Inc.//DTD JavaServer Faces Config 1.0//EN"
 5.    "http://java.sun.com/dtd/web-facesconfig_1_0.dtd">
 6.
 7. <faces-config>
 8.
 9.    <navigation-rule>
10.       <from-view-id>/index.jsp</from-view-id>
11.       <navigation-case>
12.          <from-outcome>success</from-outcome>
13.          <to-view-id>/result.jsp</to-view-id>
14.       </navigation-case>
15.       <navigation-case>
16.          <from-outcome>failure</from-outcome>
17.          <to-view-id>/error.jsp</to-view-id>
18.       </navigation-case>
19.    </navigation-rule>
20.    <navigation-rule>
21.       <from-view-id>/result.jsp</from-view-id>
22.       <navigation-case>
23.          <from-outcome>back</from-outcome>
24.          <to-view-id>/index.jsp</to-view-id>
25.       </navigation-case>
26.    </navigation-rule>
27.    <navigation-rule>
28.       <from-view-id>/error.jsp</from-view-id>
29.       <navigation-case>
30.          <from-outcome>continue</from-outcome>
31.          <to-view-id>/index.jsp</to-view-id>
32.       </navigation-case>
33.    </navigation-rule>
34.
35.    <managed-bean>
36.       <managed-bean-name>authorSearch</managed-bean-name>
37.       <managed-bean-class>com.corejsf.AuthorSearchBean</managed-bean-class>
38.       <managed-bean-scope>session</managed-bean-scope>
39.       <managed-property>
40.          <property-name>token</property-name>
41.          <value>Your token goes here</value>
42.       </managed-property>
43.    </managed-bean>
44.
45. </faces-config>
```

Listing 10-31 amazon/index.jsp

```
1.  <html>
2.  <%@ taglib uri="http://java.sun.com/jsf/core" prefix="f" %>
3.  <%@ taglib uri="http://java.sun.com/jsf/html" prefix="h" %>
4.  <f:view>
5.     <head>
6.        <f:loadBundle basename="com.corejsf.messages" var="msgs"/>
7.        <link href="styles.css" rel="stylesheet" type="text/css"/>
8.        <title><h:outputText value="#{msgs.title}"/></title>
9.     </head>
10.    <body>
11.       <h:form>
12.          <h1><h:outputText value="#{msgs.authorSearch}"/></h1>
13.          <h:outputText value="#{msgs.author}"/>
14.          <h:inputText value="#{authorSearch.name}"/>
15.          <h:commandButton value="#{msgs.search}"
16.             action="#{authorSearch.search}"/>
17.       </h:form>
18.    </body>
19.  </f:view>
20. </html>
```

Listing 10-32 amazon/result.jsp

```
1.  <html>
2.  <%@ taglib uri="http://java.sun.com/jsf/core" prefix="f" %>
3.  <%@ taglib uri="http://java.sun.com/jsf/html" prefix="h" %>
4.  <f:view>
5.     <head>
6.        <f:loadBundle basename="com.corejsf.messages" var="msgs"/>
7.        <title><h:outputText value="#{msgs.title}"/></title>
8.     </head>
9.     <body>
10.       <h:form>
11.          <h1><h:outputText value="#{msgs.searchResult}"/></h1>
12.          <h:dataTable value="#{authorSearch.details}" var="detail"
13.             border="1">
14.             <h:column>
15.                <f:facet name="header">
16.                   <h:outputText value="#{msgs.author1}"/>
1.
```

Listing 10–32   amazon/result.jsp (cont.)

```
2.              </f:facet>
3.              <h:outputText value="#{detail.authors[0]}"/>
4.            </h:column>
5.            <h:column>
6.              <f:facet name="header">
7.                <h:outputText value="#{msgs.title}"/>
8.              </f:facet>
9.              <h:outputText value="#{detail.productName}"/>
10.           </h:column>
11.           <h:column>
12.             <f:facet name="header">
13.               <h:outputText value="#{msgs.publisher}"/>
14.             </f:facet>
15.             <h:outputText value="#{detail.manufacturer}"/>
16.           </h:column>
17.           <h:column>
18.             <f:facet name="header">
19.               <h:outputText value="#{msgs.pubdate}"/>
20.             </f:facet>
21.             <h:outputText value="#{detail.releaseDate}"/>
22.           </h:column>
23.         </h:dataTable>
24.         <h:commandButton value="#{msgs.back}" action="back"/>
25.       </h:form>
26.     </body>
27.   </f:view>
28. </html>
```

Listing 10–33   amazon/error.jsp

```
1. <html>
2.   <%@ taglib uri="http://java.sun.com/jsf/core" prefix="f" %>
3.   <%@ taglib uri="http://java.sun.com/jsf/html" prefix="h" %>
4.   <f:view>
5.     <head>
6.       <f:loadBundle basename="com.corejsf.messages" var="msgs"/>
7.       <title><h:outputText value="#{msgs.title}"/></title>
8.     </head>
9.     <body>
10.      <h:form>
11.        <h1><h:outputText value="#{msgs.internalError}"/></h1>
12.        <p><h:outputText value="#{msgs.internalError_detail}"/></p>
13.        <p>
```

Listing 10–33 amazon/error.jsp (cont.)

```
14.                 <h:commandButton value="#{msgs.continue}" action="login"/>
15.             </p>
16.         </h:form>
17.       </body>
18.     </f:view>
19. </html>
```

Listing 10–34 amazon/WEB-INF/classes/com/corejsf/messages.properties

```
1. title=A Faces Application that Invokes a Web Service
2. authorSearch=Author Search at Amazon
3. author=Author
4. format=Format
5. search=Search
6. searchResult=Search Result
7. internalError=Internal Error
8. internalError_detail=To our chagrin, an internal error has occurred. \
9.     Please report this problem to our technical staff.
10. continue=Continue
11. author1=First Author
12. title=Title
13. publisher=Publisher
14. pubdate=Publication Date
15. back=Back
```

You have now seen how your web applications can connect to external services, such as databases, directories, and web services. Here are some general considerations to keep in mind.

- Libraries are placed either in the WEB-INF/lib directory of the web application or in the common/lib directory of the servlet container. You would do the latter only for libraries that are used by many applications, such as JDBC drivers.

- Servlet containers typically provide common services for database connection pooling, authentication realms, and so on. JNDI provides a convenient mechanism for locating the classes that are needed to access these services.

- Configuration parameters can be placed into faces-config.xml or web.xml. The former is more appropriate for parameters that are intrinsic to the web application; the latter should be used for parameters that are determined at deployment time.

WIRELESS CLIENTS

Chapter

In recent years, there has been much excitement about accessing web pages through mobile devices such as cell phones or personal digital assistants. These devices have small screens and limited keyboards, making it difficult or impossible to display and navigate regular web pages.

In this chapter, we show you how to write JSF applications that support alternative clients. We focus on cell phones and the Java 2 Platform Micro Edition (J2ME) technology, but the same principles apply to other client technologies.

Rendering Technologies for Mobile Clients

To focus on a specific—and very useful—scenario, let us suppose that we want to deploy a web-based application on a cell phone. Four rendering technologies are supported to various degrees at the time at which we write this book.

1. WAP/WML: The Wireless Access Protocol and the Wireless Markup Language
2. XHTML: The XML representation of HTML, or a subset thereof
3. XUL: The XML User Interface Language
4. J2ME: The Java 2 Micro Edition

WAP is a protocol stack for wireless devices, and WML is a markup language that is loosely equivalent to HTML. However, WML is optimized for cell phones with a small display. WAP/WML enjoys wide device support, but it has had only limited commercial success. WML user interfaces tend to be rather cumbersome and unattractive. We do not discuss WAP/WML in this chapter, but you will find that the techniques that we introduce can be easily modified to render WML.

Mobile phones that render an XHTML subset in "micro browsers" are becoming more common. There is no technical challenge in rendering XHTML for phones in a JSF implementation. You merely need to keep in mind that pages destined for cell phones need to be fairly simple, with small amounts of text and graphics.

XUL is an XML dialect for defining interactive user interfaces. The poster child of XUL is the Mozilla browser (as well as its mail and composer components). Micro implementations of XUL are available on handheld devices, but they are not common. The web site http://xul.sourceforge.net contains a good overview of XUL technologies.

NOTE: The JSF reference implementation contains a XUL demo. The purpose of that demo is *not* to show how to deliver an XUL application from a web server. Instead, the demo proves that you can host the JSF engine inside an XUL container, *replacing* the servlet container.

The Java 2 Platform Micro Edition (J2ME) is a version of Java that is optimized for small devices. J2ME affords different flavors for cell phones, cable television boxes, car computers, and so on. Cell phones are supported by the MIDP (Mobile Information Device Profile) library. That library is tailored for devices with limited memory, small screens, and a numeric keypad.

MIDP applications can use the power of Java to produce user interfaces that take optimal advantage of the limited screen size. For example, the "Smart-Ticket" application from the Java blueprint series paints a seating chart for a theater, allowing the customer to pick a seat (see Figure 11–1). It would be difficult to realize such an effective interface on a micro browser.

Network transmission is far slower and more expensive in cell phones than in desktops. For that reason, MIDP applications typically place more application logic onto the client than a browser-based application would. For example, validation and simple navigation logic should be handled on the client.

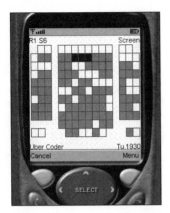

Figure 11–1   The SmartTicket application

In this chapter, we focus on the development of J2ME-based applications. The server-side techniques that are necessary to support these applications can easily be adapted to support other mobile technologies.

MIDP Basics

In this section, we briefly review the building of a MIDP application. For more information, see *Jonathan Knudsen, Wireless Java: Developing with J2ME, Second Edition, Apress 2003.*

Canvases and Forms

MIDP supports a graphic library that is similar to the AWT from the prehistoric time before Swing. That library is even simpler than AWT, and it is intended for small screens and numeric keypads.

A MIDP application extends the MIDlet class and minimally extends the three methods startApp, pauseApp, and destroyApp.

The user interface is composed of *displayables*, each of which fills the screen of the device. The most common displayables are the Canvas and Form classes. A canvas is used for painting of a full-size drawing (such as a theater seating chart or a game board). To create a drawing, subclass Canvas and override the paint method:

```
public MyCanvas extends Canvas {
   public void paint(Graphics g) {
      g.drawLine(x1, y1, x2, y2);
      ...
   }
   ...
}
```

A form contains a vertically arranged sequence of Item objects. Items are user interface components such as TextField and ChoiceGroup. Figure 11–2 shows a typical form.

Figure 11–2 A MIDP Form

To define a form, simply construct a form object and append items.

```
Form myForm = new Form("Search Flight");
TextField text = new TextField("Airport", "JFK", 3,
   TextField.ANY);
ChoiceGroup choices = new ChoiceGroup("Time", Choice.EXCLUSIVE);
choices.append("am", null /* no image */);
choices.append("pm", null);
myForm.append(text);
myForm.append(choices);
```

You switch to a particular displayable by calling the setCurrent method of the Display class:

```
public class MyMIDlet extends MIDlet {
   public void startApp() {
      ...
      Display display = Display.getDisplay(this);
      display.setCurrent(myForm);
   }
   ...
}
```

Commands and Keys

To switch between displayables and to initiate network activity, you define commands. A command has a name, a semantic hint that describes the nature of the command (such as OK, BACK, or EXIT), and a priority. The MIDP environment binds the command to a key or a voice action. Most cell phones have two "soft keys" below the display; these can be mapped to arbitrary commands (see Figure 11–3). If a screen has many commands, the MIDP environment constructs a menu and programs a key to pop up the menu. The priority value gives a hint to the environment whether a command should be bound to an easily accessible key or whether it can be buried inside a menu.

NOTE: The MIDP environment is in charge of binding commands to keys or menus. Using a high priority value does not guarantee that a command is bound to a key.

soft keys

Figure 11–3   The Soft Keys of a Cell Phone

Each displayable needs to specify a CommandListener. When the user executes the command, the commandAction method of the listener is executed. As with Swing applications, you can specify a separate listener for each command, or you can provide a single listener that dispatches all commands. For simplicity, we do the latter in our sample application.

```
public class MyMIDlet extends MIDlet implements CommandListener {
    private Command nextCommand;
    private Command exitCommand;

    ...
    public void startApp() {
```

```
    nextCommand = new Command("Next", Command.OK, 0);
    exitCommand = new Command("Exit", Command.EXIT, 1);
    myscreen.addCommand(nextCommand);
    myscreen.setCommandListener(this);
    ...
  }

  public void commandAction(Command c, Displayable d) {
    if (c == nextCommand) doNext();
    else if (c == exitCommand) notifyDestroyed();
    else ...
  }

  private void doNext() { ... }
  ...
}
```

In a canvas, you can listen to arbitrary keystrokes. However, not all devices have dedicated cursor keys, so it is best to let the MIDP environment map keys to *game actions* such as LEFT or FIRE.

```
public class MyCanvas extends Canvas {
  ...
  public void keyPressed(int keyCode) {
    int action = getGameAction(keyCode);
    if (action == LEFT) ...
    else ...
  }
}
```

Networking

MIDP contains an HttpConnection class that is similar to its J2SE counterpart. This class manages the details of the HTTP protocol, such as request and response headers. Follow these steps to get information from a web server.

First, you obtain an HttpConnection object:

```
HttpConnection conn = (HttpConnection) Connector.open(url);
```

Next, set the request headers:

```
conn.setRequestMethod(HttpConnection.POST);
conn.setRequestProperty("User-Agent",
    "Profile/MIDP-2.0 Configuration/CLDC-1.0");
conn.setRequestProperty("Content-Type",
    "application/x-www-form-urlencoded");
```

Now get the output stream of the connection and send your data to the stream. If you issue a POST command, you need to send URL-encoded name/value pairs. If you issue a GET command, you need not send any data.

 CAUTION: If you send POST data to a web server, remember to set the content type to `application/x-www-form-urlencoded`.

Here we read the POST data from a hash table. Unfortunately, MIDP has no built-in method for URL encoding, so we had to write our own. You can find the code in Listing 11–19 at the end of this chapter.

```
Hashtable request = ...;
OutputStream out = conn.openOutputStream();
Enumeration keys = request.keys();
while (keys.hasMoreElements()) {
    String key = (String) keys.nextElement();
    String value = (String) request.get(key);
    urlEncode(key, out);
    out.write('=');
    urlEncode(value, out);
    if (keys.hasMoreElements()) out.write('&');
}
```

Getting the response code automatically closes the output stream.

```
int rc = conn.getResponseCode();
if (rc != HttpConnection.HTTP_OK)
    throw new IOException("HTTP response code: " + rc);
```

You can now read the response headers and the server reply.

```
String cookie = conn.getHeaderField("Set-cookie");
int length = conn.getLength();
InputStream in = conn.openInputStream();
byte[] data = new byte[length];
in.read(data, 0, length);
```

If the server does not report the content length, you will need to manually read until EOF—see the code in Listing 11–1 on page 520.

Close the connection when you are done.

```
conn.close();
```

The principal challenge with MIDP networking is to analyze the response data. If the server sends HTML or XML, the client needs to parse the response. The current version of MIDP has no support for XML. We examine this issue on page 515.

Multithreading

When a MIDP application makes a network connection, it needs to use a separate thread. Particularly on a cell phone, network connections can be slow and flaky. Moreover, you cannot freeze the user-interface thread, since the UI may pop up a permission dialog when the network connection is about to be initiated (see Figure 11–4).

Figure 11–4   Network Permission Dialog

It would be nice if the MIDP library had explicit support for this issue, but unfortunately you need to implement the threading yourself. On a resource-constrained virtual machine, thread creation is expensive, so you want to create one thread for all your connections.

Here is the outline of the threading code:

```
public class MyMIDlet extends MIDlet {
    public void startApp() {
        worker = new ConnectionWorker();
        workerThread = new Thread(worker);
        workerThread.start();
        waitForm = new Form("Waiting...");
        ...
    }
    ...
    public void connect(String url, Hashtable request) {
        display.setCurrent(waitForm);
        worker.connect(url, request);
    }

    public void connectionCompleted(data[] response) {
        // analyze response
```

```
        // switch to the next screen
    }
    ...
    private class ConnectionWorker implements Runnable {
        private String url;
        private Hashtable request;
        private byte[] data;
        private boolean busy;

        public synchronized void run() {
            try {
                for (;;) {
                    while (!busy) wait();
                    try { data = post(); }
                    catch (IOException ex) { ... }
                    busy = false;
                    connectionCompleted(data);
                }
            }
            catch (InterruptedException ex) {}
        }

        public synchronized void connect(String url, Hashtable request) {
            this.url = url;
            this.request = request;
            busy = true;
            notify();
        }
        private byte[] post(String url, Hashtable request) { ... }
    }
}
```

The user interface thread calls the connect method, which notifies the worker thread that another connection job is available. As long as there is no possibility that the user interface issues multiple connection commands at the same time, this simple synchronization scheme suffices.

In our sample application, we avoid all the nasty issues of synchronization and cancellation by switching to a wait screen whenever the network connection is in progress. The run method calls the connectionCompleted method of the midlet after the data has been read from the network connection. (We made the connection worker into an inner class to simplify this callback. Note that the callback runs on the worker thread. It should only configure and display the next screen.)

For a more sophisticated implementation, with an animated wait screen and an option to cancel the connection, see the excellent article http://developers.sun.com/techtopics/mobility/midp/articles/threading.

The MIDP Emulator

Sun Microsystems makes available a convenient toolkit for testing wireless applications (see Figure 11–5). The toolkit includes an environment for compiling and packaging wireless applications, as well as emulators for cell phones and other handheld devices. You can download the wireless toolkit from http://java.sun.com/products/j2mewtoolkit/.

Installing and using the toolkit is straightforward. A tutorial is available at http://developers.sun.com/techtopics/mobility/midp/articles/wtoolkit/.

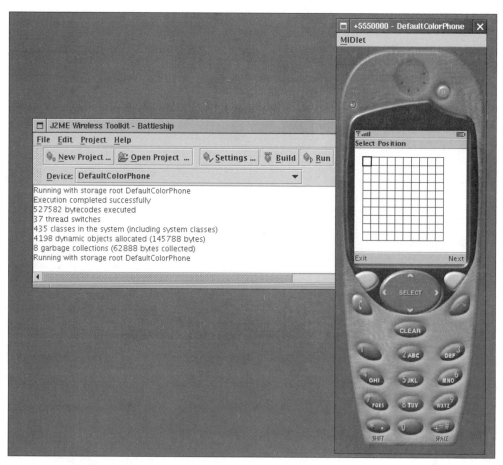

Figure 11–5   Wireless Toolkit

Mobile Communication and Control Flow

Now that you have seen the basics of MIDP programming, let us consider the communication between a MIDP program and a JavaServer Faces application. What data needs to be transferred, and how should the data be formatted?

Let's start at the beginning. The midlet requests a page from the JSF application. Had the request come from a browser, the result would be a page description in HTML. However, a midlet doesn't render HTML. It renders a set of predefined forms and canvases. Thus, the JSF application should tell the midlet

- which form to display next
- how to populate the form items (text fields, choice groups, etc.)

If the next displayable is a canvas, the midlet needs information that is customized for the canvas (such as the seating pattern and the set of available seats for a seating chart).

How should that information be formatted? There are a number of choices.

- An XML document
- A serialized Java object
- An ad hoc format

Unfortunately, the current version of MIDP does not include an XML parser. Lightweight XML parsers that you can bundle with your application are available. A popular choice is the kXML parser, available at http://kxml.org. However, parsers with a small footprint tend to have painful APIs, lacking amenities such as XPath. And XML files tend to be verbose, with higher transmission costs than strictly necessary. Many MIDP developers shy away from XML for these reasons.

Communication through Java serialization certainly avoids all parsing overhead since the Java library already knows how to do the parsing. However, the CLDC technology, which underlies MIDP on cell phones, does not currently support serialization. It would also take quite a bit of effort to produce JSF renderers for this purpose.

In our sample application, we use an ad hoc format. We simply send a set of URL encoded name/value pairs, such as

```
form=login
user=John+Q%2e+Public
password=
```

This format is easily achieved with custom JSF components whose renderers produce the name/value pairs.

For instance, the preceding example is the output of the JSF page

```
<j2me:form id="login">
  <j2me:input id="uname" value="#{user.name}"/>
  <j2me:input id="password" value="#{user.password}"/>
</j2me:form>
```

The indentation in the JSF page produces additional white space that the client must ignore.

Note that the j2me:form and j2me:input components are not a part of any standard. Later in this chapter we show you how to implement them.

> **NOTE:** You may wonder why we don't simply use the time-honored Proper-ties format to encode name/value pairs. The reason is that the MIDP library does not include the Properties class, so we would have to produce our own decoder. Moreover, the Properties format doesn't escape trailing spaces.

Conversely, the MIDP application needs to send user input to the web application. The easiest method is a simple HTTP POST of URL-encoded form data. A JSF application is prepared to process POST data and to present the request parameters to the various component decoders.

For example, if the user fills in a login screen, the client simply posts data such as

```
form=login&uname=John+Q%2e+Public&password=secret
```

You may wonder why you should bother with JSF when the entire presentation logic appears to be located in the client. Perhaps the client should communicate directly with the server-side business logic, using a protocol such as RMI or SOAP?

Actually, as you will see in our sample application, JSF adds a lot of value. JSF has a well-developed model for the binding between presentation and business logic. It is better to reuse this model than to try to reinvent it. Moreover, many navigation decisions are best handled on the server. For example, if a customer places an order and an item is out of stock, the server is best equipped to determine the impact on navigation. JSF has a good navigation model, so why not take advantage of it?

Of course, some of the presentation logic is best handled by the client. Simple validation and navigation between data entry screens need not involve the server at all. This is not a problem. The midlet can gather user data, using as many screens and validation steps as necessary, and then post all data to the server in one step.

In summary, here are the main points to keep in mind when you are developing a MIDP application with JSF.

- The midlet draws predefined screens rather than rendering arbitrary markup.
- As with HTML rendering, the JSF components are proxies for the client-side components.
- The controller is split between the midlet and the JSF application. Fine-grained navigation and validation decisions are handled by the midlet, and all other presentation logic is handled by the JSF application in the usual way.

Component Implementation for Mobile Clients

The JSF specification specifies a standard set of presentation-neutral components such as UIInput, UIForm, and UICommand, and an HTML-specific set of tags and renderers. There is no standard implementation for non-HTML clients. Thus, we need to develop our own set of tags and renderers to communicate with a midlet.

Let us first review what exactly happens when you put an HTML component tag such as h:inputText into your JSF page.

- The standard tag library file html_basic.tld maps the inputText tag to the class com.sun.faces.taglib.html_basic.InputTextTag. The tag handler class is called whenever the JSF file parser encounters an inputText tag. The tag handler stashes away the tag attributes (such as value and validator) inside the associated component object.
- The getComponentType method of that class returns the string "javax.faces.HtmlInputText", and the getRendererType method returns the string "javax.faces.Text".
- The file jsf-ri-config.xml maps these strings to classes javax.faces.component.html.HtmlInputText and com.sun.faces.renderkit.html_basic.TextRenderer.
- The HtmlInputText class is a subclass of UIInput. It merely adds getter and setter methods for the "pass through" attributes (such as onMouseOver, alt, and so on). The UIInput class carries out validation, manages value change events, and updates model values.
- The com.sun.faces.renderkit.html_basic.TextRenderer class does a fair amount of heavy lifting. Its decode method fetches the value that the user supplied

and sets it as the current value of the component. Its encode methods produce a string of the form `<input type="text" .../>`. Moreover, these methods handle data conversion and value binding lookup.

When we implement our own components, we can reuse component classes such as `UIInput`. However, the JSF framework gives very limited support for tags and renderers. Much of the essential work is carried out by classes in the `com.sun.faces` packages. We need to replicate that work in our own tags and renderers.

We designed a tag library with five tags: `input`, `select`, `output`, `form`, and `command`. On the JSF side, they correspond to the `UIInput`, `UISelectOne`, `UIOutput`, `UIForm`, and `UICommand` classes. On the MIDP side, the first two correspond to `TextField` and `ChoiceGroup` items. The `form` tag identifies the form that the client should display. The client uses the `command` tag to invoke JSF actions.

Let's walk through the `input` tag in detail. Consider the following tag:

```
<j2me:input id="uname" value="#{user.name}"
    validator="#{loginform.authenticate}"/>
```

The tag class for the `input` tag processes the `id`, `value`, and `validator` attributes and set the appropriate values in the `UIInput` component.

When the client requests this page for the first time, the renderer for this tag produces a string such as

```
uname=John+Q%2e+Public
```

The renderer simply looks up the ID and the value of the `UIInput` component.

When the MIDP client receives this string, it places the value of the `uname` key inside the matching text field. Note again that the client does its own rendering. The server doesn't tell it where to place the text field, only what value it should contain.

When the client posts the form contents to the server, it sends POST data that contain the new value of the text field, such as

```
...&uname=Jane+Doe&...
```

Now the renderer for the `input` tag kicks in again, fetching the request parameter value and setting the value of the `UIInput` component.

We don't need to worry about invoking the validator or evaluating the value binding expression—those tasks are handled by the JSF framework.

Now let's look at the code in detail.

As always, we start with a tag library descriptor file (see Listing 11–1). That file lists the tags, their valid attributes, and the handler classes.

For simplicity, all tag handlers extend the J2meComponentTag class shown in Listing 11–3. That class processes the value, action, and validator attributes. The id and binding attributes are handled by the UIComponentTag superclass.

The InputTag class (Listing 11–4) merely defines the getComponentType and getRendererType methods. The first method returns the string "Input", which is mapped by the standard JSF configuration to the UIInput component. The second method returns the string J2meText, which we will map to the TextRenderer class of Listing 11–5.

The decode method of the renderer simply sets the new value of the component:

```
Map requestMap = context.getExternalContext()
    .getRequestParameterMap();
if (requestMap.containsKey(id)) {
    String newValue = (String) requestMap.get(id);
    ((ValueHolder) component).setValue(newValue);
}
```

The encodeBegin method writes out the current value:

```
ResponseWriter writer = context.getResponseWriter();
String id = component.getId();
String value = ((ValueHolder) component).getValue().toString();
writer.write(id + "=" + URLEncoder.encode(value, "UTF8") + "\n");
```

Moreover, the encodeBegin method produces a name/value pair with all messages that may have queued up for this component. For example, if during validation, an error was found in the uname field, the resulting output would be

```
uname.messages=No+such+user
```

It is up to the client to decide what to do with these messages.

The remaining component implementations are similar. A few issues are worth noting.

- The renderer for the command tag queues an action event instead of setting a component value. The associated UICommand component automatically processes the event, using its action property. See Listing 11–6.

- The renderer for the selectOne tag (shown in Listing 11–7) encodes the labels for the choices in the following format:

```
direction.label.0=horizontal
direction.label.1=vertical
```

It needs to carry out this in the encodeEnd method rather than encodeBegin since the enclosed f:selectItem or f:selectItems values are not available at the beginning!

- Finally, the form renderer needs to call the setSubmitted method of the UIForm and to indicate whether the form is requested for the first time or whether it is posted again with new values. (See Listing 11–8.) There is a technical reason for this requirement. When the form is rendered for the first time, the component values may be defaults that do not pass validation. Validation should only occur when the renderer processes form data that are posted from the client. The submitted property regulates this behavior. We simply require the client to include the form ID when posting form data.

As you can see, implementing these renderers is fairly straightforward. Moreover, you gain some insight into the rendering process that is helpful for understanding any JSF application.

To separate the configuration information for these renderers from the application-specific configuration, we use an auxiliary file j2me-config.xml (see Listing 11–2). To add this file to your web application, include the following parameter definition in your web.xml file:

```
<context-param>
  <param-name>
    javax.faces.application.CONFIG_FILES</param-name>
  <param-value>
    /WEB-INF/faces-config.xml,
    /WEB-INF/j2me-config.xml
  </param-value>
</context-param>
```

In the next section, we put our tags to work in a complete application.

Listing 11–1 phonebattle/WEB-INF/j2me.tld

```
 1. <?xml version="1.0" encoding="ISO-8859-1" ?>
 2. <!DOCTYPE taglib
 3.   PUBLIC "-//Sun Microsystems, Inc.//DTD JSP Tag Library 1.2//EN"
 4.   "http://java.sun.com/dtd/web-jsptaglibrary_1_2.dtd">
 5. <taglib>
 6.   <tlib-version>0.03</tlib-version>
 7.   <jsp-version>1.2</jsp-version>
 8.   <short-name>j2me</short-name>
 9.   <uri>http://corejsf.com/j2me</uri>
10.   <description>
11.     This tag library contains J2ME component tags.
12.   </description>
13.
```

Listing 11–1   phonebattle/WEB-INF/j2me.tld (cont.)

```
14.    <tag>
15.       <name>form</name>
16.       <tag-class>com.corejsf.j2me.FormTag</tag-class>
17.       <attribute>
18.
19.          <name>id</name>
20.       </attribute>
21.    </tag>
22.    <tag>
23.       <name>input</name>
24.       <tag-class>com.corejsf.j2me.InputTag</tag-class>
25.       <attribute>
26.          <name>id</name>
27.       </attribute>
28.       <attribute>
29.          <name>value</name>
30.       </attribute>
31.       <attribute>
32.          <name>validator</name>
33.       </attribute>
34.    </tag>
35.    <tag>
36.       <name>output</name>
37.       <tag-class>com.corejsf.j2me.OutputTag</tag-class>
38.       <attribute>
39.          <name>id</name>
40.       </attribute>
41.       <attribute>
42.          <name>value</name>
43.       </attribute>
44.    </tag>
45.    <tag>
46.       <name>selectOne</name>
47.       <tag-class>com.corejsf.j2me.SelectOneTag</tag-class>
48.       <attribute>
49.          <name>id</name>
50.       </attribute>
51.       <attribute>
52.          <name>binding</name>
53.       </attribute>
54.       <attribute>
55.          <name>value</name>
56.       </attribute>
57.    </tag>
58.    <tag>
```

Listing 11–1 phonebattle/WEB-INF/j2me.tld (cont.)

```
59.    <name>command</name>
60.    <tag-class>com.corejsf.j2me.CommandTag</tag-class>
61.    <attribute>
62.       <name>id</name>
63.    </attribute>
64.    <attribute>
65.       <name>action</name>
66.    </attribute>
67.  </tag>
1.  </taglib>
```

Listing 11–2 phonebattle/WEB-INF/j2me-config.xml

```
1.  <?xml version="1.0"?>
2.
3.  <!DOCTYPE faces-config PUBLIC
4.    "-//Sun Microsystems, Inc.//DTD JavaServer Faces Config 1.0//EN"
5.    "http://java.sun.com/dtd/web-facesconfig_1_0.dtd">
6.
7.  <faces-config>
8.    <render-kit>
9.      <renderer>
10.        <component-family>javax.faces.Input</component-family>
11.        <renderer-type>com.corejsf.j2me.Text</renderer-type>
12.        <renderer-class>com.corejsf.j2me.TextRenderer</renderer-class>
13.      </renderer>
14.      <renderer>
15.        <component-family>javax.faces.Output</component-family>
16.        <renderer-type>com.corejsf.j2me.Text</renderer-type>
17.        <renderer-class>com.corejsf.j2me.TextRenderer</renderer-class>
18.      </renderer>
19.      <renderer>
20.        <component-family>javax.faces.Form</component-family>
21.        <renderer-type>com.corejsf.j2me.Form</renderer-type>
22.        <renderer-class>com.corejsf.j2me.FormRenderer</renderer-class>
23.      </renderer>
24.      <renderer>
25.        <component-family>javax.faces.SelectOne</component-family>
26.        <renderer-type>com.corejsf.j2me.Choice</renderer-type>
27.        <renderer-class>com.corejsf.j2me.ChoiceRenderer</renderer-class>
28.      </renderer>
29.      <renderer>
30.        <component-family>javax.faces.Command</component-family>
31.        <renderer-type>com.corejsf.j2me.Command</renderer-type>
32.        <renderer-class>com.corejsf.j2me.CommandRenderer</renderer-class>
33.      </renderer>
34.    </render-kit>
35.  </faces-config>
```

Listing 11–3   phonebattle/WEB-INF/classes/com/corejsf/j2me/
J2meComponentTag.java

```
1. package com.corejsf.j2me;
2.
3. import javax.faces.component.UIComponent;
4. import javax.faces.webapp.UIComponentTag;
5.
6. public abstract class J2meComponentTag extends UIComponentTag {
7.    private String value;
8.    private String action;
9.    private String validator;
10.
11.    // PROPERTY: value
12.    public void setValue(String newValue) { value = newValue; }
13.
14.    // PROPERTY: action
15.    public void setAction(String newValue) { action = newValue; }
16.
17.    // PROPERTY: validator
18.    public void setValidator(String newValue) { validator = newValue; }
19.
20.    public void setProperties(UIComponent component) {
21.       super.setProperties(component);
22.       com.corejsf.util.Tags.setString(component, "value", value);
23.       com.corejsf.util.Tags.setAction(component, action);
24.       com.corejsf.util.Tags.setValidator(component, validator);
25.    }
26.
27.    public void release() {
28.       value = null;
29.       validator = null;
30.       action = null;
31.    }
32. }
```

Listing 11–4   phonebattle/WEB-INF/classes/com/corejsf/j2me/InputTag.java

```
1. package com.corejsf.j2me;
2.
3.
4. public class InputTag extends J2meComponentTag {
5.    public String getComponentType() { return "javax.faces.Input"; }
6.    public String getRendererType() { return "com.corejsf.j2me.Text"; }
7. }
```

Listing 11–5   phonebattle/WEB-INF/classes/com/corejsf/j2me/TextRenderer.java

```
 1. package com.corejsf.j2me;
 2.
 3. import java.io.IOException;
 4. import java.net.URLEncoder;
 5. import java.util.Map;
 6. import javax.faces.component.UIComponent;
 7. import javax.faces.component.ValueHolder;
 8. import javax.faces.context.FacesContext;
 9. import javax.faces.context.ResponseWriter;
10. import javax.faces.render.Renderer;
11.
12. public class TextRenderer extends Renderer {
13.    public void encodeBegin(FacesContext context, UIComponent component)
14.       throws IOException {
15.       ResponseWriter writer = context.getResponseWriter();
16.       String id = component.getId();
17.       String value = "" + ((ValueHolder) component).getValue();
18.       writer.write(id + "=" + URLEncoder.encode(value, "UTF8") + "\n");
19.    }
20.
21.    public void decode(FacesContext context, UIComponent component) {
22.       if (context == null || component == null) return;
23.
24.       String id = component.getId();
25.       Map requestMap
26.          = context.getExternalContext().getRequestParameterMap();
27.       if (requestMap.containsKey(id)
28.          && component instanceof ValueHolder) {
29.          String newValue = (String) requestMap.get(id);
30.          ((ValueHolder) component).setValue(newValue);
31.       }
32.    }
33. }
```

Listing 11–6 phonebattle/WEB-INF/classes/com/corejsf/j2me/ CommandRenderer.java

```
1. package com.corejsf.j2me;
2.
3. import java.util.Map;
4. import javax.faces.component.UIComponent;
5. import javax.faces.context.FacesContext;
6. import javax.faces.event.ActionEvent;
7. import javax.faces.render.Renderer;
8.
9. public class CommandRenderer extends Renderer {
10.    public void decode(FacesContext context, UIComponent component) {
11.       if (context == null || component == null) return;
12.
13.       String id = component.getId();
14.       Map requestMap
15.          = context.getExternalContext().getRequestParameterMap();
16.       if (requestMap.containsKey(id)) {
17.          component.queueEvent(new ActionEvent(component));
18.       }
19.    }
20. }
```

Listing 11–7 phonebattle/WEB-INF/classes/com/corejsf/j2me/ChoiceRenderer.java

```
1. package com.corejsf.j2me;
2.
3. import java.io.IOException;
4. import java.net.URLEncoder;
5. import java.util.List;
6. import java.util.Map;
7. import javax.faces.component.UIComponent;
8. import javax.faces.component.EditableValueHolder;
9. import javax.faces.component.ValueHolder;
10. import javax.faces.context.FacesContext;
11. import javax.faces.context.ResponseWriter;
12. import javax.faces.model.SelectItem;
13. import javax.faces.render.Renderer;
14.
15. public class ChoiceRenderer extends Renderer {
16.    public void encodeEnd(FacesContext context, UIComponent component)
17.       throws IOException {
18.       ResponseWriter writer = context.getResponseWriter();
19.       EditableValueHolder input = (EditableValueHolder) component;
```

Listing 11-7   phonebattle/WEB-INF/classes/com/corejsf/j2me/ChoiceRenderer.java (cont.)

```
20.      String id = component.getId();
21.      List items = com.corejsf.util.Renderers.getSelectItems(component);
22.      String value = input.getValue().toString();
23.      String label = findLabel(items, value);
24.      writer.write(id + "=" + URLEncoder.encode(label, "UTF8") + "\n");
25.      for (int i = 0; i < items.size(); i++) {
26.         SelectItem item = (SelectItem) items.get(i);
27.         writer.write(id + ".label." + i
28.            + "=" + URLEncoder.encode(item.getLabel(), "UTF8") + "\n");
29.      }
30.   }
31.
32.   public void decode(FacesContext context, UIComponent component) {
33.      if (context == null || component == null) return;
34.
35.      String id = component.getId();
36.      Map requestMap
37.         = context.getExternalContext().getRequestParameterMap();
38.      if (requestMap.containsKey(id)
39.         && component instanceof ValueHolder) {
40.         String label = (String) requestMap.get(id);
41.         List items = com.corejsf.util.Renderers.getSelectItems(component);
42.         Object value = findValue(items, label);
43.         ((ValueHolder) component).setValue(value);
44.      }
45.   }
46.
47.   private static Object findValue(List list, String label) {
48.      for (int i = 0; i < list.size(); i++) {
49.         SelectItem item = (SelectItem) list.get(i);
50.         if (item.getLabel().equals(label)) return item.getValue();
51.      }
52.      return null;
53.   }
54.
55.   private static String findLabel(List list, Object value) {
56.      for (int i = 0; i < list.size(); i++) {
57.         SelectItem item = (SelectItem) list.get(i);
58.         if (item.getValue().equals(value)) return item.getLabel();
59.      }
60.      return null;
61.   }
62. }
```

```
63. package com.corejsf.j2me;
64.
65. import java.io.IOException;
66. import java.net.URLEncoder;
67. import java.util.Iterator;
68. import java.util.Map;
69. import javax.faces.application.FacesMessage;
70. import javax.faces.component.UIComponent;
71. import javax.faces.component.UIForm;
72. import javax.faces.context.FacesContext;
73. import javax.faces.context.ResponseWriter;
74. import javax.faces.render.Renderer;
75.
76. public class FormRenderer extends Renderer {
77.    public void encodeBegin(FacesContext context,
78.       UIComponent component) throws IOException {
79.       ResponseWriter writer = context.getResponseWriter();
80.       writer.write("form=" + component.getId() + "\n");
81.
82.       Iterator ids = context.getClientIdsWithMessages();
83.       while (ids.hasNext()) {
84.          String id = (String) ids.next();
85.          Iterator messages = context.getMessages(id);
86.          String msg = null;
87.          while (messages.hasNext()) {
88.             FacesMessage m = (FacesMessage) messages.next();
89.             if (msg == null) msg = m.getSummary();
90.             else msg = msg + "," + m.getSummary();
91.          }
92.          if (msg != null) {
93.             writer.write("messages");
94.             if (id != null) writer.write("." + id);
95.             writer.write("=" + URLEncoder.encode(msg, "UTF8") + "\n");
96.          }
97.       }
98.    }
99.
100.    public void decode(FacesContext context, UIComponent component) {
101.       Map map = context.getExternalContext().getRequestParameterMap();
102.       ((UIForm)component).setSubmitted(
103.          component.getId().equals(map.get("form")));
104.    }
```

The Battleship Game

In this section, we put together a simple wireless application that plays the Battleship game against a simulated opponent on a server. We chose this game because it demonstrates a mix of text and graphical components on the handheld device. As a practical matter, customers would probably not want to pay for airtime to play such a simple game against a remote computer. However, with the same implementation techniques, you can implement more complex games and business applications with rich user interfaces.

The Game Rules

In Battleship, each player has a battleground—a rectangular grid. At the start of the game, the players arrange sets of ships on their battlegrounds. In the United States, the traditional arrangement is a 10 by 10 grid, with one ship each of sizes 2, 4, and 5, and two ships of size 3. Players do not see each other's battleground. Players take turns, firing at each other's battlegrounds (see Figure 11–6). The other player announces whether a shot hits a ship or misses. The first player who sinks all ships of the opponent wins the game.

Figure 11–6   The Battleship Game

The User Interface

In the setup phase, the player selects the starting position of the next ship, then moves to a form for choosing the ship's direction and size (see Figure 11–7). Clicking the soft button labeled "Add" sends the form data to the server (see Figure 11–8). The process repeats until all ships are placed.

NOTE: It would have been nicer to put the direction and size items on the same screen as the grid. This is possible in MIDP 2.0, by implementing a `CustomItem`. For simplicity, we do not use this technique.

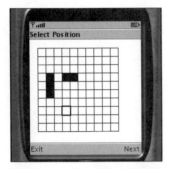

Figure 11–7   Selecting the Ship Position

Figure 11–8   Adding a Ship

In each turn of the battle, the player first sees the damage done by the opponent and then gets to fire a shot by selecting the target position and pressing the soft button labeled "Fire" (see Figure 11–9). When the game is over, the winner is announced (see Figure 11–10).

Figure 11–9   Firing a Shot

Figure 11–10   Winning the Game

Implementation

To implement this game, we use two standard components on the server side: `UIInput` (for the position) and `UISelectOne` (for the direction and size). We also use a custom BattleGround component, for displaying boats and firing shots. A Game-Bean manages the battlegrounds of the two opponents, and a SetupForm coordinates the components used during game setup. The SetupForm validates the placement of a new boat, and it determines when all boats have been placed. We do not discuss the code of these classes in detail; much of it is concerned with the tedium of arranging the boats and playing the game. See Listings 11–14 through 11–18 at the end of this section. Figure 11–11 shows the files that make up the application.

Figure 11–11   Files of the Wireless Battleship Program

Let us turn to the interesting part of the implementation, starting with the first page, setup.jsp (Listing 11–9). The page contains four components: a map of the battleground, a text field for the position of the next boat, and two selection components for the boat's size and position.

Listing 11–9 phonebattle/setup.jsp

```
1. <%@ taglib uri="http://java.sun.com/jsf/core" prefix="f" %>
2. <%@ taglib uri="http://corejsf.com/j2me" prefix="j2me" %>
3. <%@ taglib uri="http://corejsf.com/battleship" prefix="battleship" %>
4. <f:view>
5.   <j2me:form id="setup">
6.     <battleship:map id="own" value="#{game.own}" own="true"
7.           validator="#{setupform.validate}"/>
8.     <j2me:selectOne id="direction"
9.           binding="#{setupform.directionComponent}"
10.          value="#{setupform.horizontal}">
11.       <f:selectItem itemValue="true" itemLabel="horizontal"/>
12.       <f:selectItem itemValue="false" itemLabel="vertical"/>
13.     </j2me:selectOne>
14.     <j2me:selectOne id="size"
15.           binding="#{setupform.sizeComponent}"
16.          value="#{setupform.size}">
17.       <f:selectItems value="#{game.own.availableSizes}"/>
18.     </j2me:selectOne>
19.     <j2me:command id="submit" action="#{setupform.submitAction}"/>
20.   </j2me:form>
21. </f:view>
```

Note that the client UI shows this information on two separate screens.

Also note that the two selection components are managed by the SetupForm class. This arrangement simplifies the implementation of the validate method. (Since the validator is attached to the text input component, it is passed as a parameter to the validate call.)

We discussed the renderers for the standard components in the preceding section. Let us briefly look at the renderer for the battleground (Listing 11–18 on page 546). The encodeBegin method produces a string that describes the battle map. The own property determines whether to include boats that haven't yet been hit. They are shown only if own is true. Each position is encoded as one of the following values:

- 0 = water, not hit, or unknown if not owner
- 1 = ship, not hit
- 2 = water, hit
- 3 = ship, hit

Rows are separated by URL-encoded spaces. A typical rendering result looks like this:

```
own=0010000000+0010000000+0000001100+...+0000000000
```

When the user selects a position, the client sends back a request value of the form

```
...&opponent=C4&...
```

The decode method calls the setCurrent method of the battleground and fires an action event. In the setup phase, the event handler adds a boat at the specified position. In the play phase, the event handler fires a shot at that position.

When all boats have been added, the navigation handler selects the turn.jsp page (Listing 11–10). It simply shows both boards. The action event handler of the second board triggers the game.move method. That method fires on the opponent's board, lets the opponent fire on the player's board, and checks whether either contender has won the game.

Listing 11–10 phonebattle/turn.jsp

```
1. <%@ taglib uri="http://java.sun.com/jsf/core" prefix="f" %>
2. <%@ taglib uri="http://corejsf.com/j2me" prefix="j2me" %>
3. <%@ taglib uri="http://corejsf.com/battleship" prefix="battleship" %>
4. <f:view>
5.    <j2me:form id="turn">
6.        <battleship:map id="own" value="#{game.own}" own="true"/>
7.        <battleship:map id="opponent" value="#{game.opponent}" own="false"/>
8.        <j2me:command id="fire" action="#{game.move}"/>
9.    </j2me:form>
10. </f:view>
```

If a player has won, then either the win.jsp or lose.jsp page is displayed. (See Listings 11–11 and 11–12 for these pages.) Note that these pages, unlike all other pages of this application, actually render some contents. They set a value for the result key, which is displayed by the client.

Listing 11–11 phonebattle/win.jsp

```
1. <%@ taglib uri="http://java.sun.com/jsf/core" prefix="f" %>
2. <%@ taglib uri="http://corejsf.com/j2me" prefix="j2me" %>
3. <f:view>
4.    <f:loadBundle basename="com.corejsf.messages" var="msgs"/>
5.    <j2me:form id="win">
6.        <j2me:output id="result" value="#{msgs.youWon}"/>
7.        <j2me:command id="newgame" action="#{game.initialize}"/>
8.    </j2me:form>
9. </f:view>
```

Listing 11–12   phonebattle/lose.jsp

```
1. <%@ taglib uri="http://java.sun.com/jsf/core" prefix="f" %>
2. <%@ taglib uri="http://corejsf.com/j2me" prefix="j2me" %>
3. <f:view>
4.    <f:loadBundle basename="com.corejsf.messages" var="msgs"/>
5.    <j2me:form id="lose">
6.       <j2me:output id="result" value="#{msgs.youLost}"/>
7.       <j2me:command id="newgame" action="#{game.initialize}"/>
8.    </j2me:form>
9. </f:view>
```

Listing 11–13 contains the navigation handler; see Figure 11–12 for the navigation map.

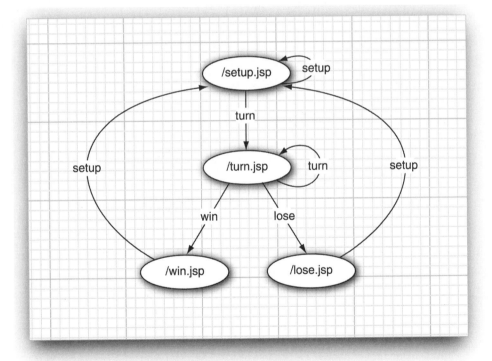

Figure 11–12   Navigation Map of the Battleship Application

The client is shown in Listing 11–19. Its implementation is fairly straightforward. From the perspective of interfacing a midlet with JSF, the most important piece is the handled of the server response. The connectionCompleted method is called after the server response has been decoded and placed in a hash table. The value of the `form` key determines the next form to be displayed.

```
public void connectionCompleted(Hashtable response) {
    webform = (String) response.get("form");
    if (webform.equals("add")) showAdd(response);
    else if (webform.equals("turn")) showTurn(response);
    else if (webform.equals("win")) showGameOver(response);
    else if (webform.equals("lose")) showGameOver(response);
}
```

The `connectionCompleted` method simply branches to a separate method for each form. Each method is responsible for applying the response parameters and switching the display. For example, here is the `showGameOver` method:

```
public void showGameOver(Hashtable response) {
    result.setText((String) response.get("result"));
    display.setCurrent(gameOverForm);
}
```

Conversely, when the server is contacted, the contents of the various components are packaged in a request data table. For example, the following method is called when the user adds a new boat.

```
public void doAdd() {
    Hashtable request = new Hashtable();
    request.put("size", size.getString(size.getSelectedIndex()));
    request.put("direction",
        direction.getString(direction.getSelectedIndex()));
    request.put("position", position.getString());
    request.put("form", "setup");
    request.put("submit", "");
    connect("setup.jsp", request);
}
```

Note the `form` and `submit` parameters. The `form` parameter is required so that the `FormRenderer` treats the submitted values as updates to an existing form, as discussed in the preceding section. The `submit` parameter must be present so that the renderer of the server-side `UICommand` component fires an action event.

> 🖫 TIP: It can be frustrating to debug the server-side portion of a mobile application through the phone emulator. We found it much easier to use a browser (see Figure 11–13). Simply make a GET request (such as http://localhost:8080/phonebattle/setup.faces?form=setup&direction=vertical&own=A4&size=3&submit=) and see the server response (or, sadly, more often than not, a stack trace).

As you can see, it is reasonably simple to combine the MIDP and JSF technologies to develop mobile applications. Here is the approach that we have taken in this chapter:

- Use HTTP POST to send data from a midlet to the web server.
- Encode the navigation and rendering information in URL-encoded name/value pairs instead of HTML.
- Provide a simple JSF tag library that renders the standard JSF components in this format.

We hope that someday a standard mechanism will be provided for sending data from a JSF application to a midlet.

Once the plumbing is in place, there is very little difference between wireless and browser clients on the JSF side. Of course, the client midlet needs to render the UI, but that's the MIDP way.

NOTE: It is a simple matter to reimplement the battleship game for a browser client (see Figure 11–14). All the "business logic" in the form and game bean is unchanged. The only real work is to implement an HTML renderer for the battle map. You can find the code for this application on the web site for this book.

Given the similarities between the phone and web versions, you may wonder whether you could produce a unified version of the code and automatically switch renderers, depending on the User-agent field of the request. We don't think that is very practical. Page layout is always going to be different for different devices.

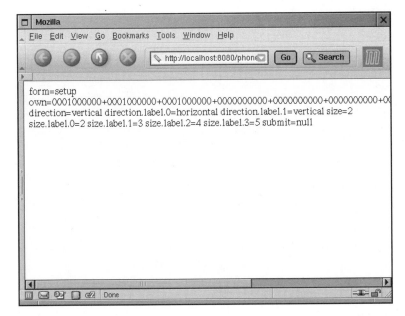

Figure 11–13 Debugging a Wireless Application with a Browser

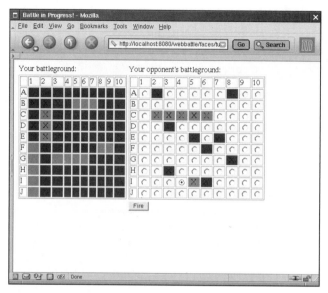

Figure 11–14   A Browser-Based Battle Game

Listing 11–13   phonebattle/WEB-INF/faces-config.xml

```
1. <?xml version="1.0"?>
2.
3. <!DOCTYPE faces-config PUBLIC
4.   "-//Sun Microsystems, Inc.//DTD JavaServer Faces Config 1.0//EN"
5.   "http://java.sun.com/dtd/web-facesconfig_1_0.dtd">
6.
7. <faces-config>
8.
9.    <navigation-rule>
10.       <from-view-id>/setup.jsp</from-view-id>
11.       <navigation-case>
12.          <from-outcome>setup</from-outcome>
13.          <to-view-id>/setup.jsp</to-view-id>
14.       </navigation-case>
15.       <navigation-case>
16.          <from-outcome>turn</from-outcome>
17.          <to-view-id>/turn.jsp</to-view-id>
18.       </navigation-case>
19.    </navigation-rule>
20.    <navigation-rule>
21.       <from-view-id>/turn.jsp</from-view-id>
22.       <navigation-case>
23.          <from-outcome>turn</from-outcome>
24.          <to-view-id>/turn.jsp</to-view-id>
```

Listing 11–13   phonebattle/WEB-INF/faces-config.xml (cont.)

```
25.    </navigation-case>
26.    <navigation-case>
27.      <from-outcome>win</from-outcome>
28.      <to-view-id>/win.jsp</to-view-id>
29.    </navigation-case>
30.    <navigation-case>
31.      <from-outcome>lose</from-outcome>
32.      <to-view-id>/lose.jsp</to-view-id>
33.    </navigation-case>
34.  </navigation-rule>
35.  <navigation-rule>
36.    <from-view-id>/win.jsp</from-view-id>
37.    <navigation-case>
38.      <from-outcome>setup</from-outcome>
39.      <to-view-id>/setup.jsp</to-view-id>
40.    </navigation-case>
41.  </navigation-rule>
42.  <navigation-rule>
43.    <from-view-id>/lose.jsp</from-view-id>
44.    <navigation-case>
45.      <from-outcome>setup</from-outcome>
46.      <to-view-id>/setup.jsp</to-view-id>
47.    </navigation-case>
48.  </navigation-rule>
49.
50.  <component>
51.    <component-type>com.corejsf.BattleMap</component-type>
52.    <component-class>javax.faces.component.UIInput</component-class>
53.  </component>
54.
55.  <render-kit>
56.    <renderer>
57.      <component-family>javax.faces.Input</component-family>
58.      <renderer-type>com.corejsf.BattleMap</renderer-type>
59.      <renderer-class>com.corejsf.BattleMapRenderer</renderer-class>
60.    </renderer>
61.  </render-kit>
62.
63.  <managed-bean>
64.    <managed-bean-name>game</managed-bean-name>
65.    <managed-bean-class>com.corejsf.GameBean</managed-bean-class>
66.    <managed-bean-scope>session</managed-bean-scope>
67.  </managed-bean>
68.  <managed-bean>
69.    <managed-bean-name>setupform</managed-bean-name>
```

Listing 11–13   phonebattle/WEB-INF/faces-config.xml (cont.)

```
70.        <managed-bean-class>com.corejsf.SetupForm</managed-bean-class>
71.        <managed-bean-scope>session</managed-bean-scope>
72.        <managed-property>
73.           <property-name>battleGround</property-name>
74.           <value>#{game.own}</value>
75.        </managed-property>
76.     </managed-bean>
77. </faces-config>
```

Listing 11–14   phonebattle/WEB-INF/classes/com/corejsf/BattleGround.java

```
1. package com.corejsf;
2.
3. import java.util.ArrayList;
4. import java.util.List;
5. import java.util.Random;
6. import javax.faces.model.SelectItem;
7.
8. public class BattleGround {
9.    public static final int OCCUPIED = 1;
10.    public static final int HIT = 2;
11.
12.    private int rows;
13.    private int columns;
14.    private int currentRow;
15.    private int currentColumn;
16.    private int[][] positions;
17.    private int[] sizes;
18.    private static final int[] INITIAL_SIZES = { 2, 3, 3, 4, 5 };
19.    private static Random generator = new Random();
20.
21.    // PROPERTY: rows
22.    public void setRows(int newValue) { rows = newValue; }
23.    public int getRows() { return rows; }
24.
25.    // PROPERTY: columns
26.    public void setColumns(int newValue) { columns = newValue; }
27.    public int getColumns() { return columns; }
28.
29.    public void initialize() {
30.       sizes = (int[]) INITIAL_SIZES.clone();
31.       positions = new int[rows][columns];
32.    }
33.
```

Listing 11–14 phonebattle/WEB-INF/classes/com/corejsf/BattleGround.java

```java
34.    public void initializeRandomly() {
35.        initialize();
36.        for (int i = 0; i < sizes.length; i++)
37.            addRandomBoat(sizes[i]);
38.    }
39.
40.    public int getValueAt(int i, int j) {
41.        if (positions == null) return 0;
42.        if (0 <= i && i < rows && 0 <= j && j < columns)
43.            return positions[i][j];
44.        else
45.            return 0;
46.    }
47.
48.    public void setCurrent(String pos) {
49.        if (pos == null || pos.length() < 2)
50.            throw new IllegalArgumentException();
51.        int r = pos.charAt(0) - 'A';
52.        int c = Integer.parseInt(pos.substring(1)) - 1;
53.        if (r < 0 || r >= rows || c < 0 || c >= columns)
54.            throw new IllegalArgumentException();
55.        currentRow = r;
56.        currentColumn = c;
57.    }
58.
59.    public void fire() {
60.        if (positions == null) return;
61.        positions[currentRow][currentColumn] |= HIT;
62.    }
63.
64.    public void addBoat(int size, boolean horizontal) {
65.        addBoat(size, currentRow, currentColumn, horizontal);
66.    }
67.
68.    public boolean boatFits(int size, boolean horizontal) {
69.        return boatFits(size, currentRow, currentColumn, horizontal);
70.    }
71.
72.    public void makeRandomMove() {
73.        // try to find a neighbor of an occupied+hit cell that hasn't
74.        // been fired on
75.        for (int i = 0; i < rows; i++)
76.            for (int j = 0; j < columns; j++)
77.                if (positions[i][j] == (OCCUPIED | HIT))
78.                    for (int m = i - 1; m <= i + 1; m++)
```

Listing 11–14   phonebattle/WEB-INF/classes/com/corejsf/BattleGround.java

```
79.              for (int n = j - 1; n <= j + 1; n++)
80.                 if (m >= 0 && m < rows && n >= 0 && n < columns
81.                    && (positions[m][n] & HIT) == 0) {
82.                    positions[m][n] |= HIT;
83.                    return;
84.                 }
85.       // pick a random cell that hasn't yet been hit
86.       int m = generator.nextInt(rows);
87.       int n = generator.nextInt(columns);
88.       for (int i = 0; i < rows; i++)
89.          for (int j = 0; j < columns; j++) {
90.             int r = (i + m) % rows;
91.             int s = (j + n) % columns;
92.             if ((positions[r][s] & HIT) == 0) {
93.                positions[r][s] |= HIT;
94.                return;
95.             }
96.          }
97.    }
98.
99.    public List getAvailableSizes() {
100.      List availableSizes = new ArrayList();
101.      for (int i = 0; i < sizes.length; i++)
102.         if (sizes[i] > 0) {
103.            // is it a duplicate?
104.            boolean found = false;
105.            for (int j = 0; j < i && !found; j++)
106.               if (sizes[i] == sizes[j]) found = true;
107.            if (!found) {
108.               String sz = "" + sizes[i];
109.               availableSizes.add(new SelectItem(sz, sz, null));
110.            }
111.         }
112.      return availableSizes;
113.   }
114.
115.   public boolean isGameOver() {
116.      for (int i = 0; i < rows; i++)
117.         for (int j = 0; j < columns; j++)
118.            if (positions[i][j] == OCCUPIED /* and not hit */)
119.               return false;
120.      return true;
121.   }
122.
123.   private void addBoat(int size, int i, int j, boolean horizontal) {
```

Listing 11-14   phonebattle/WEB-INF/classes/com/corejsf/BattleGround.java

```
124.        if (!boatFits(size, i, j, horizontal)) return;
125.        boolean found = false;
126.        for (int k = 0; !found && k < sizes.length; k++) {
127.            if (sizes[k] == size) {
128.                found = true;
129.                sizes[k] = 0;
130.            }
131.        }
132.        if (!found) return;
133.
134.        for (int k = 0; k < size; k++)
135.            positions[i + (horizontal ? 0 : k)]
136.                [j + (horizontal ? k : 0)] = OCCUPIED;
137.    }
138.
139.    private boolean boatFits(int size, int i, int j,
140.        boolean horizontal) {
141.        boolean found = false;
142.        for (int k = 0; !found && k < sizes.length; k++) {
143.            if (sizes[k] == size) found = true;
144.        }
145.        if (!found) return false;
146.        if (horizontal && j + size > columns
147.            || !horizontal && i + size > rows)
148.            return false;
149.        for (int k = 0; k < size; k++)
150.            if (positions[i + (horizontal ? 0 : k)]
151.                [j + (horizontal ? k : 0)] != 0)
152.                return false;
153.        return true;
154.    }
155.
156.    private void addRandomBoat(int size) {
157.        if (rows < size || columns < size) return;
158.        int i;
159.        int j;
160.        boolean horizontal;
161.        boolean fits;
162.        do {
163.            horizontal = generator.nextBoolean();
164.            i = generator.nextInt(rows - (horizontal ? 0 : size ));
165.            j = generator.nextInt(columns - (horizontal ? size : 0));
166.        } while (!boatFits(size, i, j, horizontal));
167.        addBoat(size, i, j, horizontal);
168.    }
169. }
```

Listing 11–15   phonebattle/WEB-INF/classes/com/corejsf/GameBean.java

```java
1. package com.corejsf;
2.
3. public class GameBean {
4.     private BattleGround own;
5.     private BattleGround opponent;
6.
7.     public GameBean() { initialize(); }
8.
9.     // PROPERTY: own
10.    public BattleGround getOwn() { return own; }
11.    public void setOwn(BattleGround newValue) { own = newValue; }
12.
13.    // PROPERTY: opponent
14.    public BattleGround getOpponent() { return opponent; }
15.    public void setOpponent(BattleGround newValue) { opponent = newValue; }
16.
17.    public String initialize() {
18.        own = new BattleGround();
19.        own.setRows(10);
20.        own.setColumns(10);
21.        own.initialize();
22.        opponent = new BattleGround();
23.        opponent.setRows(10);
24.        opponent.setColumns(10);
25.        opponent.initializeRandomly();
26.        return "setup";
27.    }
28.
29.    public String move() {
30.        opponent.fire();
31.        if (opponent.isGameOver()) return "win";
32.        own.makeRandomMove();
33.        if (own.isGameOver()) return "lose";
34.        return "turn";
35.    }
36. }
```

Listing 11–16   phonebattle/WEB-INF/classes/com/corejsf/SetupForm.java

```
1. package com.corejsf;
2.
3. import javax.faces.application.FacesMessage;
4. import javax.faces.component.UIInput;
5. import javax.faces.component.UISelectOne;
6. import javax.faces.context.FacesContext;
7. import javax.faces.model.SelectItem;
8.
9. public class SetupForm {
10.    private boolean horizontal = true;
11.    private String size = "2";
12.    private String position = "";
13.    private UISelectOne directionComponent;
14.    private UISelectOne sizeComponent;
15.    private BattleGround battleGround;
16.
17.    // PROPERTY: size
18.    public String getSize() {
19.       if (battleGround.getAvailableSizes().size() > 0)
20.          size = ((SelectItem)
21.             battleGround.getAvailableSizes().get(0)).getLabel();
22.       return size;
23.    }
24.    public void setSize(String newSize) { this.size = newSize; }
25.
26.    // PROPERTY: horizontal
27.    public String getHorizontal() { return "" + horizontal; }
28.    public void setHorizontal(String newHorizontal) {
29.       this.horizontal = Boolean.valueOf(newHorizontal).booleanValue();
30.    }
31.
32.    // PROPERTY: position
33.    public String getPosition() { return position; }
34.    public void setPosition(String newPosition) { this.position = newPosition; }
35.
36.    // PROPERTY: directionComponent
37.    public UISelectOne getDirectionComponent() { return directionComponent; }
38.    public void setDirectionComponent(UISelectOne newValue) {
39.       directionComponent = newValue;
40.    }
41.
42.    // PROPERTY: sizeComponent
43.    public UISelectOne getSizeComponent() { return sizeComponent; }
```

Listing 11–16 phonebattle/WEB-INF/classes/com/corejsf/SetupForm.java (cont.)

```
44.    public void setSizeComponent(UISelectOne newValue) {
45.       sizeComponent = newValue;
46.    }
47.
48.    // PROPERTY: battleGround
49.    public void setBattleGround(BattleGround newBattleGround) {
50.       this.battleGround = newBattleGround;
51.    }
52.
53.    public void validate(FacesContext context, UIInput input) {
54.       String dval = (String) directionComponent.getValue();
55.       boolean horiz = Boolean.valueOf(dval).booleanValue();
56.
57.       String sval = (String) sizeComponent.getValue();
58.       int sz = Integer.parseInt(sval);
59.       if(!battleGround.boatFits(sz, horiz)) {
60.          input.setValid(false);
61.          context.addMessage(input.getId(),
62.             new FacesMessage(FacesMessage.SEVERITY_ERROR,
63.                "Boat doesn't fit",
64.                "The boat that you specified doesn't fit"));
65.       }
66.    }
67.
68.    public String submitAction() {
69.       battleGround.addBoat(Integer.parseInt(size), horizontal);
70.       if (battleGround.getAvailableSizes().size() == 0)
71.          return "turn";
72.       SelectItem item
73.          = (SelectItem) battleGround.getAvailableSizes().get(0);
74.       size = item.getLabel();
75.       return "setup";
76.    }
77. }
1.
```

Listing 11–17   phonebattle/WEB-INF/classes/com/corejsf/BattleMapTag.java

```
2. package com.corejsf;
3.
4. import javax.faces.component.UIComponent;
5. import javax.faces.webapp.UIComponentTag;
6.
7. public class BattleMapTag extends UIComponentTag {
8.    private String own;
9.    private String value;
10.   private String validator;
11.
12.   // PROPERTY: own
13.   public void setOwn(String newValue) { own = newValue; }
14.
15.   // PROPERTY: value
16.   public void setValue(String newValue) { value = newValue; }
17.
18.   // PROPERTY: validator
19.   public void setValidator(String newValue) { validator = newValue; }
20.
21.   public void setProperties(UIComponent component) {
22.      super.setProperties(component);
23.
24.      com.corejsf.util.Tags.setString(component, "value", value);
25.      com.corejsf.util.Tags.setBoolean(component, "own", own);
26.      com.corejsf.util.Tags.setValidator(component, validator);
27.   }
28.
29.   public void release() {
30.      own = null;
31.      value = null;
32.      validator = null;
33.   }
34.
35.   public String getRendererType() { return "com.corejsf.BattleMap"; }
36.   public String getComponentType() { return "com.corejsf.BattleMap"; }
37. }
```

```
38. package com.corejsf;
39.
40. import java.io.IOException;
41. import java.util.Map;
42. import javax.faces.application.FacesMessage;
43. import javax.faces.component.UIComponent;
44. import javax.faces.component.UIInput;
45. import javax.faces.component.ValueHolder;
46. import javax.faces.context.FacesContext;
47. import javax.faces.context.ResponseWriter;
48. import javax.faces.event.ActionEvent;
49. import javax.faces.render.Renderer;
50.
51. public class BattleMapRenderer extends Renderer {
52.    public void encodeBegin(FacesContext context, UIComponent component)
53.       throws IOException {
54.       ResponseWriter writer = context.getResponseWriter();
55.       String id = component.getId();
56.       Object value = ((ValueHolder) component).getValue();
57.       BattleGround ground = (BattleGround) value;
58.       writer.write(id + "=");
59.
60.       boolean own = ((Boolean)
61.          component.getAttributes().get("own")).booleanValue();
62.       /*
63.        0 = water, not hit, or unknown if not owner
64.        1 = ship, not hit
65.        2 = water, hit
66.        3 = ship, hit
67.       */
68.       for (int i = 0; i < ground.getRows(); i++) {
69.          if (i > 0) writer.write("+");
70.          for (int j = 0; j < ground.getColumns(); j++) {
71.             int v = ground.getValueAt(i, j);
72.             boolean hit = (v & BattleGround.HIT) != 0;
73.             if (own || hit) {
74.                writer.write('0' + v);
75.             } else
76.                writer.write('0');
77.          }
78.       }
79.    }
80.
```

Listing 11–18	phonebattle/WEB-INF/classes/com/corejsf/BattleMapRenderer.java (cont.)

```
81.    public void decode(FacesContext context, UIComponent component) {
82.        if (context == null || component == null) return;
83.
84.        UIInput input = (UIInput) component;
85.        String id = input.getId();
86.        Object value = input.getValue();
87.        BattleGround ground = (BattleGround) value;
88.
89.        // if we don't do the following, then the local value is null
90.        input.setValue(value);
91.
92.        Map parameters
93.            = context.getExternalContext().getRequestParameterMap();
94.        String coords = (String) parameters.get(id);
95.        if (coords == null) return;
96.
97.        try {
98.            ground.setCurrent(coords);
99.            input.queueEvent(new ActionEvent(input));
100.       } catch (Exception ex) {
101.           input.setValid(false);
102.           context.addMessage(id,
103.               new FacesMessage(FacesMessage.SEVERITY_ERROR,
104.                   "Invalid position",
105.                   "The boat position that you specified is invalid"));
106.       }
107.   }
108. }
```

Listing 11–19	phonebattle/misc/BattleshipMIDlet.java

```
1. import java.io.IOException;
2. import java.io.InputStream;
3. import java.io.OutputStream;
4. import java.io.UnsupportedEncodingException;
5. import java.util.Enumeration;
6. import java.util.Hashtable;
7. import javax.microedition.io.Connector;
8. import javax.microedition.io.HttpConnection;
9. import javax.microedition.lcdui.Canvas;
10. import javax.microedition.lcdui.Choice;
11. import javax.microedition.lcdui.ChoiceGroup;
12. import javax.microedition.lcdui.Command;
```

Listing 11–19 phonebattle/misc/BattleshipMIDlet.java (cont.)

```java
13. import javax.microedition.lcdui.CommandListener;
14. import javax.microedition.lcdui.Display;
15. import javax.microedition.lcdui.Displayable;
16. import javax.microedition.lcdui.Form;
17. import javax.microedition.lcdui.Graphics;
18. import javax.microedition.lcdui.StringItem;
19. import javax.microedition.midlet.MIDlet;
20.
21. public class BattleshipMIDlet extends MIDlet implements CommandListener {
22.     private Display display;
23.     private Form addBoatForm;
24.     private StringItem position;
25.     private ChoiceGroup size;
26.     private ChoiceGroup direction;
27.     private StringItem message;
28.     private StringItem result;
29.     private Command exitCommand;
30.     private Command startCommand;
31.     private Command nextCommand;
32.     private Command addCommand;
33.     private Command opponentCommand;
34.     private Command fireCommand;
35.     private Command continueCommand;
36.     private Command newGameCommand;
37.     private BattleCanvas addBoatCanvas;
38.     private BattleCanvas own;
39.     private BattleCanvas opponent;
40.     private Form startForm;
41.     private Form messageForm;
42.     private Form waitForm;
43.     private Form gameOverForm;
44.     private String webform;
45.     private ConnectionWorker worker;
46.     private Thread workerThread;
47.
48.     // Required methods
49.
50.     public void startApp() {
51.         display = Display.getDisplay(this);
52.         exitCommand = new Command("Exit", Command.EXIT, 1);
53.         createStartForm();
54.         createAddBoatForms();
55.         createBattleCanvases();
56.         createMessageForm();
57.         createGameOverForm();
58.
```

Listing 11–19 | phonebattle/misc/BattleshipMIDlet.java (cont.)

```
59.      worker = new ConnectionWorker();
60.      workerThread = new Thread(worker);
61.      workerThread.start();
62.      waitForm = new Form("Waiting...");
63.
64.      display.setCurrent(startForm);
65.    }
66.
67.    public void pauseApp() {}
68.
69.    public void destroyApp(boolean unconditional) {}
70.
71.    // Initialization
72.
73.    public void createStartForm() {
74.      startForm = new Form("Start");
75.      startForm.setTitle("Welcome");
76.      startForm.append("Start the Battleship Game");
77.      startCommand = new Command("Start", Command.OK, 0);
78.      startForm.addCommand(startCommand);
79.      startForm.addCommand(exitCommand);
80.      startForm.setCommandListener(this);
81.    }
82.
83.    public void createAddBoatForms() {
84.      addBoatCanvas = new BattleCanvas();
85.      addBoatCanvas.setTitle("Select Position");
86.      nextCommand = new Command("Next", Command.OK, 0);
87.      addBoatCanvas.addCommand(nextCommand);
88.      addBoatCanvas.addCommand(exitCommand);
89.      addBoatCanvas.setCommandListener(this);
90.
91.      addBoatForm = new Form("Add Boat");
92.      direction = new ChoiceGroup("Direction", Choice.EXCLUSIVE);
93.      size = new ChoiceGroup("Size", Choice.EXCLUSIVE);
94.      position = new StringItem("", null);
95.      addBoatForm.append(direction);
96.      addBoatForm.append(size);
97.      addBoatForm.append(position);
98.      addCommand = new Command("Add", Command.OK, 0);
99.      addBoatForm.addCommand(addCommand);
100.     addBoatForm.addCommand(exitCommand);
101.     addBoatForm.setCommandListener(this);
102.   }
103.
```

Listing 11–19 phonebattle/misc/BattleshipMIDlet.java (cont.)

```
104.   public void createBattleCanvases() {
105.     own = new BattleCanvas();
106.     own.setTitle("Your battleground");
107.
108.     opponent = new BattleCanvas();
109.     opponent.setTitle("Your opponent");
110.
111.     opponentCommand = new Command("Opponent", Command.OK, 0);
112.     own.addCommand(opponentCommand);
113.     own.addCommand(exitCommand);
114.     own.setCommandListener(this);
115.     fireCommand = new Command("Fire", Command.OK, 0);
116.     opponent.addCommand(fireCommand);
117.     opponent.addCommand(exitCommand);
118.     opponent.setCommandListener(this);
119.   }
120.
121.   public void createMessageForm() {
122.     messageForm = new Form("Message");
123.     message = new StringItem("", null);
124.     messageForm.append(message);
125.     continueCommand = new Command("Continue", Command.OK, 0);
126.     messageForm.addCommand(continueCommand);
127.     messageForm.addCommand(exitCommand);
128.     messageForm.setCommandListener(this);
129.   }
130.
131.   public void createGameOverForm() {
132.     gameOverForm = new Form("Game Over");
133.     result = new StringItem("", null);
134.     gameOverForm.append(result);
135.     newGameCommand = new Command("New Game", Command.OK, 0);
136.     gameOverForm.addCommand(newGameCommand);
137.     gameOverForm.addCommand(exitCommand);
138.     gameOverForm.setCommandListener(this);
139.   }
140.
141.   // Commands
142.
143.   public void commandAction(Command c, Displayable s) {
144.     if (c == startCommand) doStart();
145.     else if (c == nextCommand) doNext();
146.     else if (c == addCommand) doAdd();
147.     else if (c == continueCommand) doContinue();
148.     else if (c == opponentCommand) doOpponent();
```

Listing 11–19 phonebattle/misc/BattleshipMIDlet.java (cont.)

```
149.    else if (c == fireCommand) doFire();
150.    else if (c == newGameCommand) doNewGame();
151.    else if (c == exitCommand) notifyDestroyed();
152.  }
153.
154.  public void doStart() {
155.    connect("setup.faces", null);
156.  }
157.
158.  public void doNext() {
159.    position.setText("Position: " + addBoatCanvas.getString());
160.    display.setCurrent(addBoatForm);
161.  }
162.
163.  public void doAdd() {
164.    Hashtable request = new Hashtable();
165.    request.put("size", size.getString(size.getSelectedIndex()));
166.    request.put("direction",
167.       direction.getString(direction.getSelectedIndex()));
168.    request.put("own", addBoatCanvas.getString());
169.    request.put("form", "setup");
170.    request.put("submit", "");
171.    connect("setup.faces", request);
172.  }
173.
174.  public void doContinue() {
175.    display.setCurrent(addBoatCanvas);
176.  }
177.
178.  public void doOpponent() {
179.    display.setCurrent(opponent);
180.  }
181.
182.  public void doFire() {
183.    Hashtable request = new Hashtable();
184.    request.put("own", own.getString());
185.    request.put("opponent", opponent.getString());
186.    request.put("form", "turn");
187.    request.put("fire", "");
188.    connect("turn.faces", request);
189.  }
190.
191.  public void doNewGame() {
192.    Hashtable request = new Hashtable();
193.    request.put("form", webform);
```

Listing 11-19 phonebattle/misc/BattleshipMIDlet.java (cont.)

```
194.      request.put("newgame", "");
195.      connect(webform + ".faces", request);
196.  }
197.
198.  // Connection
199.
200.  public void connect(String url, Hashtable request) {
201.      display.setCurrent(waitForm);
202.      worker.connect(url, request);
203.  }
204.
205.  public void connectionCompleted(Hashtable response) {
206.      webform = (String) response.get("form");
207.      if (webform.equals("setup")) showSetup(response);
208.      else if (webform.equals("turn")) showTurn(response);
209.      else if (webform.equals("win")) showGameOver(response);
210.      else if (webform.equals("lose")) showGameOver(response);
211.  }
212.
213.  // Navigation
214.
215.  public void showSetup(Hashtable response) {
216.      select(size, response, "size");
217.      select(direction, response, "direction");
218.      addBoatCanvas.parse((String) response.get("own"));
219.      String msg = (String) response.get("messages.own");
220.      if (msg != null) {
221.          message.setText(msg);
222.          display.setCurrent(messageForm);
223.          return;
224.      }
225.      display.setCurrent(addBoatCanvas);
226.  }
227.
228.  public void showGameOver(Hashtable response) {
229.      result.setText((String) response.get("result"));
230.      display.setCurrent(gameOverForm);
231.  }
232.
233.  public void showTurn(Hashtable response) {
234.      own.parse((String) response.get("own"));
235.      opponent.parse((String) response.get("opponent"));
236.      display.setCurrent(own);
237.  }
238.
```

Listing 11-19 phonebattle/misc/BattleshipMIDlet.java (cont.)

```java
239.    private static void select(ChoiceGroup group,
240.        Hashtable response, String name) {
241.        String value = (String) response.get(name);
242.        int i = 0;
243.        String label;
244.        group.deleteAll();
245.        while ((label = (String) response.get(name + ".label." + i))
246.            != null) {
247.            group.append(label, null);
248.            if (label.equals(value))
249.                group.setSelectedIndex(i, true);
250.            i++;
251.        }
252.    }
253.
254.    private class ConnectionWorker implements Runnable {
255.        private String url;
256.        private String urlPrefix = "http://localhost:8080/phonebattle/";
257.        private Hashtable request;
258.        private Hashtable response;
259.        private String sessionCookie;
260.        private boolean busy = false;
261.
262.        public synchronized void run() {
263.            try {
264.                for (;;) {
265.                    while (!busy)
266.                        wait();
267.                    try {
268.                        byte[] data = post();
269.                        response = decode(data);
270.
271.                    }
272.                    catch (IOException ex) {
273.                        ex.printStackTrace();
274.                    }
275.                    busy = false;
276.                    connectionCompleted(response);
277.                }
278.            }
279.            catch (InterruptedException ie) {}
280.        }
281.
282.        public synchronized void connect(String url, Hashtable request) {
283.            this.url = url;
```

Listing 11–19   phonebattle/misc/BattleshipMIDlet.java (cont.)

```
284.        this.request = request;
285.        if (busy) return;
286.        busy = true;
287.        notify();
288.      }
289.
290.      private void urlEncode(String s, OutputStream out)
291.        throws IOException {
292.        byte[] bytes = s.getBytes("UTF8");
293.        for (int i = 0; i < bytes.length; i++) {
294.          byte b = bytes[i];
295.          if (b == ' ')
296.            out.write('+');
297.          else if ('0' <= b && b <= '9'
298.            || 'A' <= b && b <= 'Z'
299.            || 'a' <= b && b <= 'z'
300.            || "-_.!~*'(),".indexOf(b) >= 0)
301.            out.write(b);
302.          else {
303.            out.write('%');
304.            int b1 = (b & 0xF0) >> 4;
305.            out.write((b1 < 10 ? '0' : 'a' - 10) + b1);
306.            int b2 = b & 0xF;
307.            out.write((b2 < 10 ? '0' : 'a' - 10) + b2);
308.          }
309.        }
310.      }
311.
312.      private boolean isspace(byte b) {
313.        return " \n\r\t".indexOf(b) >= 0;
314.      }
315.
316.      private Hashtable decode(byte[] data) {
317.        if (data == null) return null;
318.        Hashtable table = new Hashtable();
319.        try {
320.          int start = 0;
321.          for (;;) {
322.            while (start < data.length && isspace(data[start]))
323.              start++;
324.            if (start >= data.length) return table;
325.            int end = start + 1;
326.            int count = 0;
327.            while (end < data.length && data[end] != '=') end++;
328.            String key =
```

Listing 11–19   phonebattle/misc/BattleshipMIDlet.java (cont.)

```
329.                    new String(data, start, end - start, "ASCII");
330.                start = end + 1;
331.                end = start;
332.                while (end < data.length && !isspace(data[end])) {
333.                    count++;
334.                    if (data[end] == '%') end += 3; else end++;
335.                }
336.                byte[] b = new byte[count];
337.                int k = start;
338.                int c = 0;
339.                while (k < end) {
340.                    if (data[k] == '%') {
341.                        int h = data[k + 1];
342.                        if (h >= 'a') h = h - 'a' + 10;
343.                        else if (h >= 'A') h = h - 'A' + 10;
344.                        else h = h - '0';
345.                        int l = data[k + 2];
346.                        if (l >= 'a') l = l - 'a' + 10;
347.                        else if (l >= 'A') l = l - 'A' + 10;
348.                        else l = l - '0';
349.                        b[c] = (byte) ((h << 4) + l);
350.                        k += 3;
351.                    }
352.                    else if (data[k] == '+') {
353.                        b[c] = ' ';
354.                        k++;
355.                    }
356.                    else {
357.                        b[c] = data[k];
358.                        k++;
359.                    }
360.                    c++;
361.                }
362.                String value = new String(b, "UTF8");
363.                table.put(key, value);
364.                start = end + 1;
365.            }
366.        }
367.        catch (UnsupportedEncodingException ex) {
368.        }
369.        return table;
370.    }
371.
372.    private byte[] post() throws IOException {
373.        HttpConnection conn = null;
```

Listing 11-19   phonebattle/misc/BattleshipMIDlet.java (cont.)

```java
374.        byte[] data = null;
375.
376.        try {
377.            conn = (HttpConnection) Connector.open(urlPrefix + url);
378.
379.            conn.setRequestMethod(HttpConnection.POST);
380.            conn.setRequestProperty("User-Agent",
381.                "Profile/MIDP-2.0 Configuration/CLDC-1.0");
382.            conn.setRequestProperty("Content-Language", "en-US");
383.            conn.setRequestProperty("Content-Type",
384.                "application/x-www-form-urlencoded");
385.            if (sessionCookie != null)
386.                conn.setRequestProperty("Cookie", sessionCookie);
387.
388.            OutputStream out = conn.openOutputStream();
389.            if (request != null) {
390.                Enumeration keys = request.keys();
391.                while (keys.hasMoreElements()) {
392.                    String key = (String) keys.nextElement();
393.                    String value = (String) request.get(key);
394.                    urlEncode(key, out);
395.                    out.write('=');
396.                    urlEncode(value, out);
397.                    if (keys.hasMoreElements()) out.write('&');
398.                }
399.            }
400.
401.            int rc = conn.getResponseCode();
402.            if (rc != HttpConnection.HTTP_OK)
403.                throw new IOException("HTTP response code: " + rc);
404.
405.            InputStream in = conn.openInputStream();
406.
407.            // Read the session ID--it's the first cookie
408.            String cookie = conn.getHeaderField("Set-cookie");
409.            if (cookie != null) {
410.                int semicolon = cookie.indexOf(';');
411.                sessionCookie = cookie.substring(0, semicolon);
412.            }
413.
414.            // Get the length and process the data
415.            int len = (int) conn.getLength();
416.            int actual = 0;
417.            int bytesread = 0 ;
418.            if (len > 0) {
```

Listing 11–19   phonebattle/misc/BattleshipMIDlet.java (cont.)

```
419.          data = new byte[len];
420.          while ((bytesread != len) && (actual != -1)) {
421.              actual = in.read(data, bytesread, len - bytesread);
422.              if (actual != -1) bytesread += actual;
423.          }
424.        } else {
425.          final int BLOCKSIZE = 1024;
426.          data = new byte[BLOCKSIZE];
427.          while (actual != -1) {
428.              if (bytesread == data.length) {
429.                  byte[] bigger = new byte[data.length + BLOCKSIZE];
430.                  System.arraycopy(data, 0, bigger, 0, data.length);
431.                  data = bigger;
432.              }
433.              actual = in.read(data, bytesread,
434.                  data.length - bytesread);
435.              if (actual != -1) bytesread += actual;
436.          }
437.          if (bytesread < data.length) {
438.              byte[] smaller = new byte[bytesread];
439.              System.arraycopy(data, 0, smaller, 0, bytesread);
440.              data = smaller;
441.          }
442.        }
443.      } catch (ClassCastException e) {
444.        throw new IOException("Not an HTTP URL");
445.      } finally {
446.        if (conn != null) conn.close();
447.      }
448.      return data;
449.    }
450.  }
451. }
452.
453. class BattleCanvas extends Canvas {
454.    public static final int ROWS = 10;
455.    public static final int COLUMNS = 10;
456.    public static final int OCCUPIED = 1;
457.    public static final int HIT = 2;
458.
459.    private int[][] positions = new int[ROWS][COLUMNS];
460.    private int currentRow = 0;
461.    private int currentColumn = 0;
462.
463.    public void parse(String state) {
```

Listing 11-19 phonebattle/misc/BattleshipMIDlet.java (cont.)

```
464.      int n = 0;
465.      for (int i = 0; i < ROWS; i++) {
466.         for (int j = 0; j < COLUMNS; j++) {
467.            char c = state.charAt(n);
468.            n++;
469.            positions[i][j] = c - '0';
470.         }
471.         n++;
472.      }
473.   }
474.
475.   public String getString() {
476.      return "" + (char) ('A' + currentRow) + (1 + currentColumn);
477.   }
478.
479.   public void paint(Graphics g) {
480.      int width = getWidth();
481.      int height = getHeight();
482.      int oldColor = g.getColor();
483.      g.setColor(0xFFFFFF);
484.      g.fillRect(0, 0, width, height);
485.      g.setColor(oldColor);
486.      int cellWidth = width / (COLUMNS + 2);
487.      int cellHeight = height / (ROWS + 2);
488.      int cellSize = Math.min(cellWidth, cellHeight);
489.      for (int i = 0; i <= ROWS; i++) {
490.         int y = (i + 1) * cellSize;
491.         g.drawLine(cellSize, y, (COLUMNS + 1) * cellSize, y);
492.      }
493.      for (int j = 0; j <= COLUMNS; j++) {
494.         int x = (j + 1) * cellSize;
495.         g.drawLine(x, cellSize, x, (ROWS + 1) * cellSize);
496.      }
497.      for (int i = 0; i < ROWS; i++) {
498.         int y = (i + 1) * cellSize;
499.         for (int j = 0; j < COLUMNS; j++) {
500.            int x = (j + 1) * cellSize;
501.            int p = positions[i][j];
502.            if ((p & OCCUPIED) != 0)
503.               g.fillRect(x, y, cellSize, cellSize);
504.            if ((p & HIT) != 0) {
505.               if (p == (HIT | OCCUPIED)) {
506.                  oldColor = g.getColor();
507.                  g.setColor(0xFFFFFF);
508.               }
```

Listing 11–19   phonebattle/misc/BattleshipMIDlet.java (cont.)

```
509.              g.drawLine(x, y, x + cellSize, y + cellSize);
510.              g.drawLine(x + cellSize, y, x, y + cellSize);
511.              if (p == (HIT | OCCUPIED)) g.setColor(oldColor);
512.            }
513.          }
514.        }
515.        int x = (currentColumn + 1) * cellSize;
516.        int y = (currentRow + 1) * cellSize;
517.        g.drawRect(x - 1, y - 1, cellSize + 2, cellSize + 2);
518.    }
519.
520.    public void keyPressed(int keyCode) {
521.        int action = getGameAction(keyCode);
522.        if (action == LEFT)
523.            currentColumn = (currentColumn + COLUMNS - 1) % COLUMNS;
524.        else if (action == RIGHT)
525.            currentColumn = (currentColumn + 1) % COLUMNS;
526.        else if (action == UP)
527.            currentRow = (currentRow + ROWS - 1) % ROWS;
528.        else if (action == DOWN)
529.            currentRow = (currentRow + 1) % ROWS;
530.        repaint();
531.    }
532. }
```

HOW DO I...

Topics in This Chapter

Chapter 12

The preceding chapters covered the JSF technology in a systematic manner, organized by core concepts. However, every technology has certain aspects that defy systematic exposure, and JSF is no exception. At times, you will ask yourself "How do I..." and not find an answer, perhaps because JSF doesn't really offer support for the feature or because the solution is unintuitive. This chapter was designed to help out. We answer, in somewhat random order, common questions that we found on discussion groups or that we received from readers.

Web User Interface Design

In this section, we show you how to use features such as popups, applets, and file upload dialogs in your web pages. We hope that future versions of JSF will include ready-made components to achieve these tasks. Here we show you how to implement and configure the required components.

How do I support file uploads?

The users of your application may want to upload files, such as photos or documents—see Figures 12–1 and 12–2.

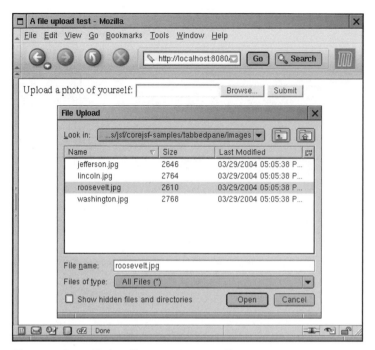

Figure 12–1   Uploading an Image File

Figure 12–2   Uploaded Image

Unfortunately, there is no standard file upload component in JSF 1.0/1.1. How-ever, it turns out that it is fairly straightforward to implement one. The hard work has already been done by the folks at the Apache organization in the Commons file upload library—see http://jakarta.apache.org/commons/fileupload. We will show you how to incorporate the library into a JSF component.

A file upload is different from all other form requests. When the form data (including the uploaded file) is sent from the client to the server, it is encoded with the "multipart/form-data" encoding instead of the usual "application/x-www-form-urlencoded" encoding. Unfortunately, JSF does not handle this encoding at all. To overcome this issue, we install a *servlet filter* that intercepts a file upload and turns uploaded files into request attributes and all other form data into request parameters. (We use a utility method in the Commons file upload library for the dirty work of decoding a multipart/form-data request.) The JSF application then processes the request parameters, blissfully unaware that they were not URL encoded. The decode method of the file upload component either places the uploaded data into a disk file or stores it in a value reference.

The code for the servlet filter is in Listing 12–1.

 NOTE: You can find general information about servlet filters at http://java.sun.com/products/servlet/Filters.html.

You need to install the filter in the web-inf.xml file, using this syntax:

```
<filter>
   <filter-name>Upload Filter</filter-name>
   <filter-class>com.corejsf.UploadFilter</filter-class>
   <init-param>
      <param-name>com.corejsf.UploadFilter.sizeThreshold</param-name>
      <param-value>1024</param-value>
   </init-param>
</filter>

<filter-mapping>
   <filter-name>Upload Filter</filter-name>
   <url-pattern>/upload/*</url-pattern>
</filter-mapping>
```

The filter uses the sizeThreshold initialization parameter to configure the file upload object: files > 1024 bytes are saved to a temporary disk location rather than being held in memory. Our filter supports two additional initialization parameters: com.corejsf.UploadFilter.sizeMax (the maximum permitted size of an uploaded file) and com.corejsf.UploadFilter.repositoryPath (the temporary location for uploaded files before they are moved to a permanent place). The filter simply sets the corresponding properties of the DiskFileUpload object of the Commons file-upload library.

The filter mapping restricts the filter to URLs that start with /upload/. Thus, we avoid unnecessary filtering of other requests.

Figure 12–3 shows the directory structure of the sample application.

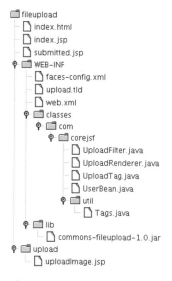

**Figure 12–3   The Directory Structure
of the File Upload Application**

Listing 12–1   fileupload/WEB-INF/classes/com/corejsf/UploadFilter.java

```
1. package com.corejsf;
2.
3. import java.io.IOException;
4. import java.util.Collections;
5. import java.util.Enumeration;
6. import java.util.HashMap;
7. import java.util.List;
8. import java.util.Map;
9. import javax.servlet.Filter;
10. import javax.servlet.FilterChain;
11. import javax.servlet.FilterConfig;
12. import javax.servlet.ServletException;
13. import javax.servlet.ServletRequest;
```

```java
14. import javax.servlet.ServletResponse;
15. import javax.servlet.http.HttpServletRequest;
16. import javax.servlet.http.HttpServletRequestWrapper;
17. import org.apache.commons.fileupload.DiskFileUpload;
18. import org.apache.commons.fileupload.FileItem;
19. import org.apache.commons.fileupload.FileUpload;
20. import org.apache.commons.fileupload.FileUploadException;
21.
22.
23. public class UploadFilter implements Filter {
24.    private int sizeThreshold = -1;
25.    private long sizeMax = -1;
26.    private String repositoryPath;
27.
28.    public void init(FilterConfig config) throws ServletException {
29.       repositoryPath = config.getInitParameter(
30.          "com.corejsf.UploadFilter.repositoryPath");
31.       try {
32.          String paramValue = config.getInitParameter(
33.             "com.corejsf.UploadFilter.sizeThreshold");
34.          if (paramValue != null)
35.             sizeThreshold = Integer.parseInt(paramValue);
36.          paramValue = config.getInitParameter(
37.             "com.corejsf.UploadFilter.sizeMax");
38.          if (paramValue != null)
39.             sizeMax = Long.parseLong(paramValue);
40.       }
41.       catch (NumberFormatException ex) {
42.          ServletException servletEx = new ServletException();
43.          servletEx.initCause(ex);
44.          throw servletEx;
45.       }
46.    }
47.
48.    public void destroy() {
49.    }
50.
51.    public void doFilter(ServletRequest request,
52.       ServletResponse response, FilterChain chain)
53.       throws IOException, ServletException {
54.
55.       if (!(request instanceof HttpServletRequest)) {
56.          chain.doFilter(request, response);
57.          return;
58.       }
```

Listing 12–1 fileupload/WEB-INF/classes/com/corejsf/UploadFilter.java (cont.)

```
59.
60.        HttpServletRequest httpRequest = (HttpServletRequest) request;
61.
62.        boolean isMultipartContent = FileUpload.isMultipartContent(httpRequest);
63.        if (!isMultipartContent) {
64.          chain.doFilter(request, response);
65.          return;
66.        }
67.
68.        DiskFileUpload upload = new DiskFileUpload();
69.        if (repositoryPath != null)
70.          upload.setRepositoryPath(repositoryPath);
71.
72.        try {
73.          List list = upload.parseRequest(httpRequest);
74.          final Map map = new HashMap();
75.          for (int i = 0; i < list.size(); i ++) {
76.            FileItem item = (FileItem) list.get(i);
77.            String str = item.getString();
78.            if (item.isFormField())
79.              map.put(item.getFieldName(), new String[] { str });
80.            else
81.              httpRequest.setAttribute(item.getFieldName(), item);
82.          }
83.
84.          chain.doFilter(new
85.            HttpServletRequestWrapper(httpRequest) {
86.              public Map getParameterMap() {
87.                return map;
88.              }
89.              // busywork follows ... should have been part of the wrapper
90.              public String[] getParameterValues(String name) {
91.                Map map = getParameterMap();
92.                return (String[]) map.get(name);
93.              }
94.              public String getParameter(String name) {
95.                String[] params = getParameterValues(name);
96.                if (params == null) return null;
97.                return params[0];
98.              }
99.              public Enumeration getParameterNames() {
100.               Map map = getParameterMap();
101.               return Collections.enumeration(map.keySet());
102.             }
103.           }, response);
```

Listing 12–1 fileupload/WEB-INF/classes/com/corejsf/UploadFilter.java (cont.)

```
104.        } catch (FileUploadException ex) {
105.            ServletException servletEx = new ServletException();
106.            servletEx.initCause(ex);
107.            throw servletEx;
108.        }
109.    }
110. }
```

Now let's move on to the upload component. It supports two attributes: value and target. The value simply denotes a value reference into which the file contents are stored. This makes sense for short files. More commonly, you will use the target attribute to specify the target location of the file.

The implementation of the FileUploadRenderer class in Listing 12–2 is straightforward. The encodeBegin method renders the HTML element. The decode method retrieves the file items that the servlet filter placed into the request attributes and disposes of them as directed by the tag attributes. The target attribute denotes a file relative to the server directory containing the root of the web application.

The associated tag handler class, in Listing 12–3, is as dull as ever.

Finally, when using the file upload tag, you need to remember to set the form encoding to "multipart/form-data"—see Listing 12–4.

Listing 12–2 fileupload/WEB-INF/classes/com/corejsf/UploadRenderer.java

```
 1. package com.corejsf;
 2.
 3. import java.io.File;
 4. import java.io.IOException;
 5. import java.io.InputStream;
 6. import java.io.UnsupportedEncodingException;
 7. import javax.faces.FacesException;
 8. import javax.faces.component.EditableValueHolder;
 9. import javax.faces.component.UIComponent;
10. import javax.faces.context.ExternalContext;
11. import javax.faces.context.FacesContext;
12. import javax.faces.context.ResponseWriter;
13. import javax.faces.el.ValueBinding;
14. import javax.faces.render.Renderer;
15. import javax.servlet.ServletContext;
16. import javax.servlet.http.HttpServletRequest;
17. import org.apache.commons.fileupload.FileItem;
```

Listing 12–2 fileupload/WEB-INF/classes/com/corejsf/UploadRenderer.java (cont.)

```
18.
19. public class UploadRenderer extends Renderer {
20.    public void encodeBegin(FacesContext context, UIComponent component)
21.       throws IOException {
22.       if (!component.isRendered()) return;
23.       ResponseWriter writer = context.getResponseWriter();
24.
25.       String clientId = component.getClientId(context);
26.
27.       writer.startElement("input", component);
28.       writer.writeAttribute("type", "file", "type");
29.       writer.writeAttribute("name", clientId, "clientId");
30.       writer.endElement("input");
31.       writer.flush();
32.    }
33.
34.    public void decode(FacesContext context, UIComponent component) {
35.       ExternalContext external = context.getExternalContext();
36.       HttpServletRequest request = (HttpServletRequest) external.getRequest();
37.       String clientId = component.getClientId(context);
38.       FileItem item = (FileItem) request.getAttribute(clientId);
39.
40.       Object newValue;
41.       ValueBinding binding = component.getValueBinding("value");
42.       if (binding != null) {
43.          if (binding.getType(context) == byte[].class) {
44.             newValue = item.get();
45.          }
46.          if (binding.getType(context) == InputStream.class) {
47.             try {
48.                newValue = item.getInputStream();
49.             } catch (IOException ex) {
50.                throw new FacesException(ex);
51.             }
52.          }
53.          else {
54.             String encoding = request.getCharacterEncoding();
55.             if (encoding != null)
56.                try {
```

Listing 12–2	fileupload/WEB-INF/classes/com/corejsf/UploadRenderer.java (cont.)

```
57.                  newValue = item.getString(encoding);
58.              } catch (UnsupportedEncodingException ex) {
59.                  newValue = item.getString();
60.              }
61.          else
62.              newValue = item.getString();
63.          }
64.          ((EditableValueHolder) component).setSubmittedValue(newValue);
65.      }
66.
67.      Object target;
68.      binding = component.getValueBinding("target");
69.      if (binding != null) target = binding.getValue(context);
70.      else target = component.getAttributes().get("target");
71.
72.      if (target != null) {
73.          File file;
74.          if (target instanceof File)
75.              file = (File) target;
76.          else {
77.              ServletContext servletContext
78.                  = (ServletContext) external.getContext();
79.              file = new File(servletContext.getRealPath("/"),
80.                  target.toString());
81.          }
82.
83.          try { // ugh--write is declared with "throws Exception"
84.              item.write(file);
85.          } catch (Exception ex) {
86.              throw new FacesException(ex);
87.          }
88.      }
89.   }
90. }
```

Listing 12–3   fileupload/WEB-INF/classes/com/corejsf/UploadTag.java

```
1. package com.corejsf;
2.
3. import javax.faces.component.UIComponent;
4. import javax.faces.webapp.UIComponentTag;
5.
6.
7. public class UploadTag extends UIComponentTag {
8.    private String value;
9.    private String target;
10.
11.    public void setValue(String newValue) { value = newValue; }
12.    public void setTarget(String newValue) { target = newValue; }
13.
14.    public void setProperties(UIComponent component) {
15.       super.setProperties(component);
16.       com.corejsf.util.Tags.setString(component, "target", target);
17.       com.corejsf.util.Tags.setString(component, "value", value);
18.    }
19.
20.    public void release() {
21.       super.release();
22.       value = null;
23.       target = null;
24.    }
25.
26.    public String getRendererType() { return "com.corejsf.Upload"; }
27.    public String getComponentType() { return "com.corejsf.Upload"; }
28. }
```

| **Listing 12–4** | `fileupload/upload/uploadImage.jsp` |

```
1.  <html>
2.    <%@ taglib uri="http://java.sun.com/jsf/core" prefix="f" %>
3.    <%@ taglib uri="http://java.sun.com/jsf/html" prefix="h" %>
4.    <%@ taglib uri="http://java.sun.com/upload" prefix="corejsf" %>
5.
6.    <f:view>
7.      <head>
8.        <title>A file upload test</title>
9.      </head>
10.     <body>
11.       <h:form enctype="multipart/form-data">
12.         Upload a photo of yourself:
13.         <corejsf:upload target="upload/#{user.id}_image.jpg"/>
14.         <h:commandButton value="Submit" action="submit"/>
15.       </h:form>
16.     </body>
17.   </f:view>
18. </html>
```

How do I show an image map?

To implement a client-side image map, supply the `usemap` attribute with the
`h:outputImage` element:

```
<h:outputImage value="image location" usemap="#aLabel"/>
```

You can then specify the map in HTML in the JSF page:

```
<map name="aLabel">
   <area shape="polygon" coords="..." href="...">
   <area shape="rect" coords="..." href="...">
   ...
</map>
```

However, this approach does not integrate well with JSF navigation. It would
be nicer if the map areas acted like command buttons or links.

The JSF reference implementation includes sample `map` and `area` tags that overcome this limitation. The implementation is described in detail in the JSF tutorial, which was last seen as Chapters 17–21 of http://java.sun.com/j2ee/1.4/docs/
tutorial/doc/index.html.

To see the image map in action, load the web application that displays the sample components. If you use Tomcat, simply point your browser to

http://localhost:8080/manager/deploy?war=file:/jsf/samples/jsf-components.war

Replace /jsf with the path to your JSF installation directory. Load

```
http://localhost:8080/jsf-components
```

Then investigate the image map component (see Figure 12–4).

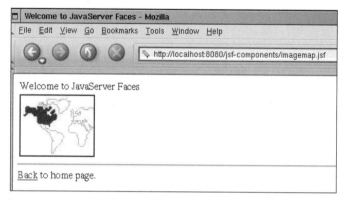

Figure 12–4   Image Map Sample Component

Alternatively, you can use a technique that we showed in Chapter 7. Put the image inside a command button, and process the x- and y-coordinates on the server side:

```
<h:commandButton image="..." actionListener="..."/>
```

Attach an action listener that gets the client ID of the button, attaches the suffixes .x and .y, and looks up the coordinate values in the request map. Process the values in any desired way. With this technique, the server application needs to know the geometry of the image.

How do I include an applet in my page?

Simply include the applet tag in the usual way—see, for example, Listing 12–5. This page displays the chart applet from *Horstmann & Cornell, Core Java vol. 1, ch. 10, Sun Microsystems Press 2002* (see Figure 12–5).

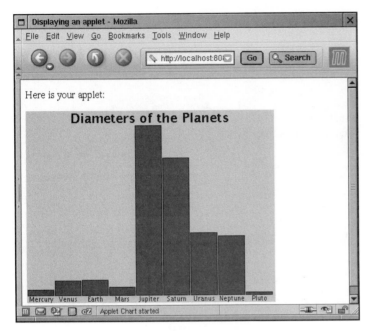

Figure 12–5 The Chart Applet

Just keep a couple of points in mind.

- If you include the applet tag inside a panel grid (as in our example), then you need to enclose it inside

  ```
  <f:verbatim escape="false">...</f:verbatim>
  ```

- You may want to consider using the jsp:plugin tag instead of the applet tag. That tag generates the appropriate markup for the Java Plug-in. For example,

  ```
  <jsp:plugin type="applet" code="Chart.class"
     width="400" height="300">
     <jsp:params>
        <jsp:param name="title" value="Diameters of the Planets"/>
        <jsp:param name="values" value="9"/>
        ...
     </jsp:params>
  </jsp:plugin>
  ```

  See http://java.sun.com/products/plugin for more information on the Java Plug-in.

Listing 12–5   applet/index.jsp

```
1.  <html>
2.    <%@ taglib uri="http://java.sun.com/jsf/core" prefix="f" %>
3.    <%@ taglib uri="http://java.sun.com/jsf/html" prefix="h" %>
4.    <f:view>
5.      <head>
6.        <f:loadBundle basename="com.corejsf.messages" var="msgs"/>
7.        <title><h:outputText value="#{msgs.title}"/></title>
8.      </head>
9.      <body>
10.       <h:form>
11.         <h:panelGrid columns="1">
12.           <h:column>
13.             <h:outputText value="#{msgs.header}"/>
14.           </h:column>
15.
16.           <h:column>
17.             <f:verbatim escape="false">
18.               <applet code="Chart.class" width="400" height="300">
19.                 <param name="title" value="Diameters of the Planets"/>
20.                 <param name="values" value="9"/>
21.                 <param name="name.1" value="Mercury"/>
22.                 <param name="name.2" value="Venus"/>
23.                 <param name="name.3" value="Earth"/>
24.                 <param name="name.4" value="Mars"/>
25.                 <param name="name.5" value="Jupiter"/>
26.                 <param name="name.6" value="Saturn"/>
27.                 <param name="name.7" value="Uranus"/>
28.                 <param name="name.8" value="Neptune"/>
29.                 <param name="name.9" value="Pluto"/>
30.                 <param name="value.1" value="3100"/>
31.                 <param name="value.2" value="7500"/>
32.                 <param name="value.3" value="8000"/>
33.                 <param name="value.4" value="4200"/>
34.                 <param name="value.5" value="88000"/>
35.                 <param name="value.6" value="71000"/>
36.                 <param name="value.7" value="32000"/>
37.                 <param name="value.8" value="30600"/>
38.                 <param name="value.9" value="1430"/>
39.               </applet>
40.             </f:verbatim>
41.           </h:column>
42.         </h:panelGrid>
43.       </h:form>
44.     </body>
45.   </f:view>
46. </html>
```

How do I produce binary data in a JSF page?

It is possible to use JSF to create a binary response instead of a web page. Follow these steps:

- Take over the creation of the response headers and content by manipulating the response object returned by `ExternalContext.getResponse`.
- Suppress the generation of the JSF response by calling the `responseComplete` method on the current `FacesContext`.

As an example, we implement a JSF tag that creates a chart image—see Figure 12–6. The image contains JPEG formatted data that were dynamically generated.

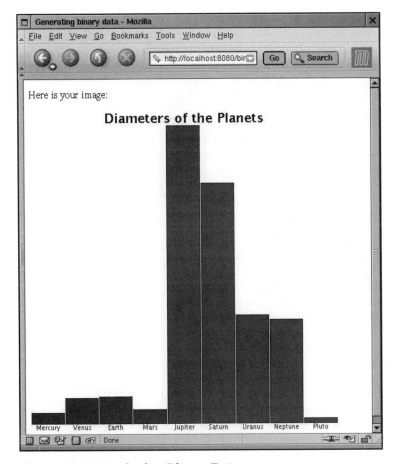

Figure 12–6   Producing Binary Data

Listing 12–6 contains an h:graphicImage tag that includes an image generated by the JSF page in Listing 12–7. The chart tag is mapped to an UIOutput component and the renderer in Listing 12–8.

The important activity occurs in the encodeBegin method. First, we get the HttpServletResponse object and set the content type to image/jpeg. Then we get the output stream object.

```
HttpServletResponse response
   = (HttpServletResponse) context.getExternalContext().getResponse();
response.setContentType("image/jpeg");
OutputStream stream = response.getOutputStream();
```

Next, we gather the parameters that describe the chart and call the drawChart method. That method draws the chart on the Graphics2D object of a BufferedImage.

```
BufferedImage image = new BufferedImage(width, height, BufferedImage.TYPE_INT_RGB);
Graphics2D g2 = (Graphics2D) image.getGraphics();
drawChart(g2, width, height, title, names, values);
```

The drawChart method was taken from the chart applet in *Horstmann & Cornell, Core Java Vol. 1, Ch. 10, Sun Microsystems Press, 2002.*

Next, we use the ImageIO class to get a writer for the JPEG format. The writer sends the image data to the output stream to the stream that we obtained from the HttpServletResponse.

```
Iterator iter = ImageIO.getImageWritersByFormatName("jpeg");
ImageWriter writer = (ImageWriter) iter.next();
writer.setOutput(ImageIO.createImageOutputStream(stream));
writer.write(image);
```

Finally, we terminate the response processing:

```
context.responseComplete();
```

The JSF implementation simply sends the output data to the browser and terminates this request.

You use the same approach to generate any kind of binary data. The only difference is the code for sending data to the output stream.

Listing 12–6   binary/index.jsp

```
1. <html>
2.    <%@ taglib uri="http://java.sun.com/jsf/core" prefix="f" %>
3.    <%@ taglib uri="http://java.sun.com/jsf/html" prefix="h" %>
4.    <f:view>
5.       <head>
6.          <title>Generating binary data</title>
7.       </head>
8.       <body>
9.          <h:form>
10.             <p>Here is your image:</p>
11.             <h:graphicImage url="chart.faces"/>
12.          </h:form>
13.       </body>
14.    </f:view>
15. </html>
```

Listing 12–7   binary/chart.jsp

```
1. <%@ taglib uri="http://java.sun.com/jsf/core" prefix="f" %>
2. <%@ taglib uri="http://corejsf.com/chart" prefix="corejsf" %>
3. <f:view>
4.    <corejsf:chart width="500" height="500"
5.       title="Diameters of the Planets"
6.       names="#{planets.names}" values="#{planets.values}"/>
7. </f:view>
```

Listing 12–8   binary/WEB-INF/classes/com/corejsf/ChartRenderer.java

```
1. package com.corejsf;
2.
3. import java.awt.Color;
4. import java.awt.Font;
5. import java.awt.Graphics2D;
6. import java.awt.font.FontRenderContext;
7. import java.awt.font.LineMetrics;
8. import java.awt.geom.Rectangle2D;
9. import java.awt.image.BufferedImage;
10. import java.io.IOException;
11. import java.io.OutputStream;
12. import java.util.Iterator;
13. import java.util.Map;
14. import javax.faces.component.UIComponent;
15. import javax.faces.context.FacesContext;
16. import javax.faces.el.ValueBinding;
17. import javax.faces.render.Renderer;
```

```
18. import javax.imageio.ImageIO;
19. import javax.imageio.ImageWriter;
20. import javax.servlet.http.HttpServletResponse;
21.
22. public class ChartRenderer extends Renderer {
23.    public void encodeBegin(FacesContext context, UIComponent component)
24.       throws IOException {
25.       if (!component.isRendered()) return;
26.
27.       HttpServletResponse response
28.          = (HttpServletResponse) context.getExternalContext().getResponse();
29.       response.setContentType("image/jpeg");
30.       OutputStream stream = response.getOutputStream();
31.
32.       Map attributes = component.getAttributes();
33.
34.       int width = parseInt(attributes, "width", DEFAULT_WIDTH);
35.       int height = parseInt(attributes, "height", DEFAULT_HEIGHT);
36.       String title = parseString(attributes, "title", "");
37.
38.       ValueBinding vb = component.getValueBinding("names");
39.       String[] names = vb == null ? null : (String[]) vb.getValue(context);
40.       vb = component.getValueBinding("values");
41.       double[] values = vb == null ? null : (double[]) vb.getValue(context);
42.
43.       BufferedImage image = new BufferedImage(width, height,
44.          BufferedImage.TYPE_INT_RGB);
45.       Graphics2D g2 = (Graphics2D) image.getGraphics();
46.       drawChart(g2, width, height, title, names, values);
47.
48.       Iterator iter = ImageIO.getImageWritersByFormatName("jpeg");
49.       ImageWriter writer = (ImageWriter) iter.next();
50.       writer.setOutput(ImageIO.createImageOutputStream(stream));
51.       writer.write(image);
52.
53.       context.responseComplete();
54.    }
55.
56.    private static int parseInt(Map attributes, String name, int defaultValue) {
57.       String value = (String) attributes.get(name);
58.       if (value != null)
59.          try {
60.             return Integer.parseInt(value);
61.          } catch (NumberFormatException ex) {
62.          }
63.       return defaultValue;
```

```
64.    }
65.
66.    private static String parseString(Map attributes, String name,
67.       String defaultValue) {
68.       String value = (String) attributes.get(name);
69.       if (value != null) return value;
70.       return defaultValue;
71.    }
72.
73.    private static void drawChart(Graphics2D g2, int width, int height,
74.       String title, String[] names, double[] values)
75.    {
76.       // clear the background
77.       g2.setPaint(Color.WHITE);
78.       g2.fill(new Rectangle2D.Double(0, 0, width, height));
79.       g2.setPaint(Color.BLACK);
80.
81.       if (names == null || values == null || names.length != values.length)
82.          return;
83.
84.       // compute the minimum and maximum values
85.       if (values == null) return;
86.       double minValue = 0;
87.       double maxValue = 0;
88.       for (int i = 0; i < values.length; i++) {
89.          if (minValue > values[i]) minValue = values[i];
90.          if (maxValue < values[i]) maxValue = values[i];
91.       }
92.       if (maxValue == minValue) return;
93.
94.       Font titleFont = new Font("SansSerif", Font.BOLD, 20);
95.       Font labelFont = new Font("SansSerif", Font.PLAIN, 10);
96.
97.       // compute the extent of the title
98.       FontRenderContext context = g2.getFontRenderContext();
99.       Rectangle2D titleBounds
100.          = titleFont.getStringBounds(title, context);
101.       double titleWidth = titleBounds.getWidth();
102.       double top = titleBounds.getHeight();
103.
104.       // draw the title
105.       double y = -titleBounds.getY(); // ascent
106.       double x = (width - titleWidth) / 2;
107.       g2.setFont(titleFont);
108.       g2.drawString(title, (float)x, (float)y);
109.
```

Listing 12–8   binary/WEB-INF/classes/com/corejsf/ChartRenderer.java (cont.)

```
110.      // compute the extent of the bar labels
111.      LineMetrics labelMetrics
112.         = labelFont.getLineMetrics("", context);
113.      double bottom = labelMetrics.getHeight();
114.
115.      y = height - labelMetrics.getDescent();
116.      g2.setFont(labelFont);
117.
118.      // get the scale factor and width for the bars
119.      double scale = (height - top - bottom)
120.         / (maxValue - minValue);
121.      int barWidth = width / values.length;
122.
123.      // draw the bars
124.      for (int i = 0; i < values.length; i++) {
125.         // get the coordinates of the bar rectangle
126.         double x1 = i * barWidth + 1;
127.         double y1 = top;
128.         double barHeight = values[i] * scale;
129.         if (values[i] >= 0)
130.            y1 += (maxValue - values[i]) * scale;
131.         else {
132.            y1 += maxValue * scale;
133.            barHeight = -barHeight;
134.         }
135.
136.         // fill the bar and draw the bar outline
137.         Rectangle2D rect = new Rectangle2D.Double(x1, y1,
138.            barWidth - 2, barHeight);
139.         g2.setPaint(Color.RED);
140.         g2.fill(rect);
141.         g2.setPaint(Color.BLACK);
142.         g2.draw(rect);
143.
144.         // draw the centered label below the bar
145.         Rectangle2D labelBounds
146.            = labelFont.getStringBounds(names[i], context);
147.
148.         double labelWidth = labelBounds.getWidth();
149.         x = i * barWidth + (barWidth - labelWidth) / 2;
150.         g2.drawString(names[i], (float)x, (float)y);
151.      }
152.   }
153.
154.   private static int DEFAULT_WIDTH = 200;
155.   private static int DEFAULT_HEIGHT = 200;
156. }
```

How do I show a large data set one page at a time?

As you saw in Chapter 5, you can add scroll bars to a table. But if the table is truly large, you don't want it sent to the client in its entirety. Downloading the table takes a long time, and chances are that the application user only wants to see the first few rows anyway.

The standard user interface for navigating large table is a "pager," a set of links to each page of the table, to the next and previous page, and if there are a great number of pages, to the next and previous batch of pages. Figure 12–7 shows a pager that scrolls through a large data set—the predefined time zones, obtained by a call to java.util.TimeZone.getAvailableIDs().

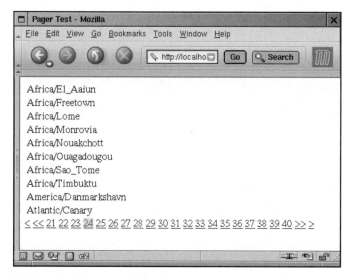

Figure 12–7   Table with a Pager

Unfortunately, JSF 1.0/1.1 does not include a pager component. However, it is fairly easy to write one, and we give you the code to use or modify in your own applications.

The pager is a companion to a data table. You specify the ID of the data table, the number of pages that the pager displays, and the styles for the selected and unselected links. For example,

```
<h:dataTable id="timezones" value="#{bb.data}" var="row" rows="10">
    ...
```

```
</h:dataTable>
<corejsf:pager dataTableId="timezones" showpages="20"
    selectedStyleClass="currentPage"/>
```

Suppose the user clicks on the ">"link to move to the next page. The pager locates the data table and updates its first property, adding the value of the rows property. You will find that code in the decode method of the PagerRenderer in Listing 12–9.

The encode method is a bit more involved. It generates a set of links. Similarly to a commandLink, clicking the link activates JavaScript code that sets a value in a hidden field and submits the form.

Listing 12–10 shows the index.jsp page that generates the table and the pager. Listing 12–11 shows the trivial backing bean.

Listing 12–9   pager/WEB-INF/classes/com/corejsf/PagerRenderer.java

```java
1.  package com.corejsf;
2.
3.  import java.io.IOException;
4.  import java.util.Iterator;
5.  import java.util.Map;
6.  import javax.faces.component.NamingContainer;
7.  import javax.faces.component.UIComponent;
8.  import javax.faces.component.UIData;
9.  import javax.faces.component.UIForm;
10. import javax.faces.context.FacesContext;
11. import javax.faces.context.ResponseWriter;
12. import javax.faces.el.ValueBinding;
13. import javax.faces.render.Renderer;
14.
15. public class PagerRenderer extends Renderer {
16.     public void encodeBegin(FacesContext context, UIComponent component)
17.         throws IOException {
18.         String id = component.getClientId(context);
19.         UIComponent parent = component;
20.         while (!(parent instanceof UIForm)) parent = parent.getParent();
21.         String formId = parent.getClientId(context);
22.
23.         ResponseWriter writer = context.getResponseWriter();
24.
25.         String styleClass = (String) get(context, component, "styleClass");
26.         String selectedStyleClass = (String) get(context, component,
27.             "selectedStyleClass");
28.         String dataTableId = (String) get(context, component, "dataTableId");
```

Listing 12–9 pager/WEB-INF/classes/com/corejsf/PagerRenderer.java (cont.)

```
29.        Integer a = (Integer) get(context, component, "showpages");
30.        int showpages = a == null ? 0 : a.intValue();
31.
32.        // find the component with the given ID
33.
34.        UIData data = (UIData) findComponent(context.getViewRoot(),
35.           getId(dataTableId, id), context);
36.
37.        int first = data.getFirst();
38.        int itemcount = data.getRowCount();
39.        int pagesize = data.getRows();
40.        if (pagesize <= 0) pagesize = itemcount;
41.
42.        int pages = itemcount / pagesize;
43.        if (itemcount % pagesize != 0) pages++;
44.
45.        int currentPage = first / pagesize;
46.        if (first >= itemcount - pagesize) currentPage = pages - 1;
47.        int startPage = 0;
48.        int endPage = pages;
49.        if (showpages > 0) {
50.           startPage = (currentPage / showpages) * showpages;
51.           endPage = Math.min(startPage + showpages, pages);
52.        }
53.
54.        if (currentPage > 0)
55.           writeLink(writer, component, formId, id, "<", styleClass);
56.
57.        if (startPage > 0)
58.           writeLink(writer, component, formId, id, "<<", styleClass);
59.
60.        for (int i = startPage; i < endPage; i++) {
61.           writeLink(writer, component, formId, id, "" + (i + 1),
62.              i == currentPage ? selectedStyleClass : styleClass);
63.        }
64.
65.        if (endPage < pages)
66.           writeLink(writer, component, formId, id, ">>", styleClass);
67.
68.        if (first < itemcount - pagesize)
69.           writeLink(writer, component, formId, id, ">", styleClass);
70.
71.        // hidden field to hold result
72.        writeHiddenField(writer, component, id);
73.     }
74.
```

Listing 12-9   pager/WEB-INF/classes/com/corejsf/PagerRenderer.java (cont.)

```
75.    private void writeLink(ResponseWriter writer, UIComponent component,
76.       String formId, String id, String value, String styleClass)
77.       throws IOException {
78.       writer.writeText(" ", null);
79.       writer.startElement("a", component);
80.       writer.writeAttribute("href", "#", null);
81.       writer.writeAttribute("onclick", onclickCode(formId, id, value), null);
82.       if (styleClass != null)
83.          writer.writeAttribute("class", styleClass, "styleClass");
84.       writer.writeText(value, null);
85.       writer.endElement("a");
86.    }
87.
88.    private String onclickCode(String formId, String id, String value) {
89.       StringBuffer buffer = new StringBuffer();
90.       buffer.append("document.forms[");
91.       buffer.append("'");
92.       buffer.append(formId);
93.       buffer.append("'");
94.       buffer.append("]['");
95.       buffer.append(id);
96.       buffer.append("'].value='");
97.       buffer.append(value);
98.       buffer.append("';");
99.       buffer.append(" document.forms[");
100.      buffer.append("'");
101.      buffer.append(formId);
102.      buffer.append("'");
103.      buffer.append("].submit()");
104.      buffer.append("; return false;");
105.      return buffer.toString();
106.   }
107.
108.   private void writeHiddenField(ResponseWriter writer, UIComponent component,
109.      String id) throws IOException {
110.      writer.startElement("input", component);
111.      writer.writeAttribute("type", "hidden", null);
112.      writer.writeAttribute("name", id, null);
113.      writer.endElement("input");
114.   }
115.
116.   public void decode(FacesContext context, UIComponent component) {
117.      String id = component.getClientId(context);
118.      Map parameters = context.getExternalContext()
119.         .getRequestParameterMap();
```

Listing 12-9 pager/WEB-INF/classes/com/corejsf/PagerRenderer.java (cont.)

```
120.        String response = (String) parameters.get(id);
121.
122.        String dataTableId = (String) get(context, component, "dataTableId");
123.        Integer a = (Integer) get(context, component, "showpages");
124.        int showpages = a == null ? 0 : a.intValue();
125.
126.        UIData data = (UIData) findComponent(context.getViewRoot(),
127.           getId(dataTableId, id), context);
128.
129.        int first = data.getFirst();
130.        int itemcount = data.getRowCount();
131.        int pagesize = data.getRows();
132.        if (pagesize <= 0) pagesize = itemcount;
133.
134.        if (response.equals("<")) first -= pagesize;
135.        else if (response.equals(">")) first += pagesize;
136.        else if (response.equals("<<")) first -= pagesize * showpages;
137.        else if (response.equals(">>")) first += pagesize * showpages;
138.        else {
139.           int page = Integer.parseInt(response);
140.           first = (page - 1) * pagesize;
141.        }
142.        if (first + pagesize > itemcount) first = itemcount - pagesize;
143.        if (first < 0) first = 0;
144.        data.setFirst(first);
145.     }
146.
147.     private static Object get(FacesContext context, UIComponent component,
148.        String name) {
149.        ValueBinding binding = component.getValueBinding(name);
150.        if (binding != null) return binding.getValue(context);
151.        else return component.getAttributes().get(name);
152.     }
153.
154.     private static UIComponent findComponent(UIComponent component, String id,
155.        FacesContext context) {
156.        String componentId = component.getClientId(context);
157.        if (componentId.equals(id)) return component;
158.        Iterator kids = component.getChildren().iterator();
159.        while (kids.hasNext()) {
160.           UIComponent kid = (UIComponent) kids.next();
161.           UIComponent found = findComponent(kid, id, context);
162.           if (found != null) return found;
163.        }
164.        return null;
```

Listing 12–9	pager/WEB-INF/classes/com/corejsf/PagerRenderer.java (cont.)

```
165.    }
166.
167.    private static String getId(String id, String baseId) {
168.       String separator = "" + NamingContainer.SEPARATOR_CHAR;
169.       String[] idSplit = id.split(separator);
170.       String[] baseIdSplit = baseId.split(separator);
171.       StringBuffer buffer = new StringBuffer();
172.       for (int i = 0; i < baseIdSplit.length - idSplit.length; i++) {
173.          buffer.append(baseIdSplit[i]);
174.          buffer.append(separator);
175.       }
176.       buffer.append(id);
177.       return buffer.toString();
178.    }
179. }
```

Listing 12–10	pager/index.jsp

```
1. <html>
2.    <%@ taglib uri="http://java.sun.com/jsf/core" prefix="f" %>
3.    <%@ taglib uri="http://java.sun.com/jsf/html" prefix="h" %>
4.    <%@ taglib uri="http://corejsf.com/pager" prefix="corejsf" %>
5.
6.    <f:view>
7.       <head>
8.          <link href="styles.css" rel="stylesheet" type="text/css"/>
9.          <title>Pager Test</title>
10.       </head>
11.       <body>
12.          <h:form>
13.             <h:dataTable id="timezones" value="#{bb.data}" var="row" rows="10">
14.                <h:column>
15.                   <h:outputText value="#{row}" />
16.                </h:column>
17.             </h:dataTable>
18.             <corejsf:pager dataTableId="timezones"
19.                showpages="20" selectedStyleClass="currentPage"/>
20.          </h:form>
21.       </body>
22.    </f:view>
23. </html>
```

Listing 12–11   pager/WEB-INF/classes/com/corejsf/BackingBean.java

```java
1. package com.corejsf;
2.
3. public class BackingBean {
4.     private String[] data = java.util.TimeZone.getAvailableIDs();
5.     public String[] getData() { return data; }
6. }
```

How do I generate a popup window?

The basic method for a popup window is simple. Use the JavaScript calls

```
popup = window.open(url, name, features);
popup.focus();
```

The features parameter is a string such as "height=300,width=200,tool-bar=no,menubar=no".

The popup window should be displayed when the user clicks a button or link. Attach a function to the onclick handler of the button or link, and have the function return false so that the browser doesn't submit the form or follow the link. For example,

```
<h:commandButton value="..." onclick="doPopup(this); return false;"/>
```

The doPopup function contains the JavaScript instructions for popping up the window. It is contained in a script tag inside the page header.

However, challenges arise when you need to transfer data between the main window and the popup.

Let us look at a specific example. Figure 12–8 shows a page with a popup window that lists the states of the USA or the provinces of Canada, depending on the setting of the radio buttons. The list is generated by a backing bean on the server.

How does the backing bean know which state was selected? After all, the form has not yet been posted back to the server when the user requests the popup. We show you two solutions—each of them is interesting in its own right and may give you ideas for solving similar problems.

In the first solution, we pass the selection parameter to the popup URL, like this:

```
window.open("popup.faces?country=" + country[i].value, "popup", features);
```

The popup.faces page retrieves the value of the country request parameter as param.country:

```
<h:dataTable value="#{bb.states[param.country]}" var="state">
```

Here, the states property of the backing bean bb yields a map whose index is the country name.

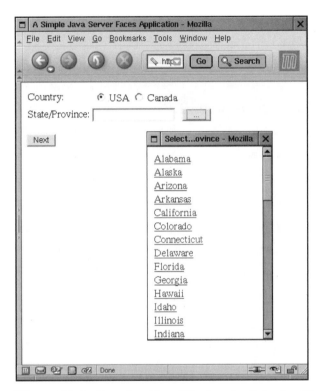

Figure 12–8 Popping Up a Window to Select a State or Province

The second solution (suggested by Marion Bass and Sergey Smirnov) is more involved but also more powerful. In this technique, the popup window is first created as a blank window and then filled with the response to a JSF command.

The JSF command is issued by a form that contains a hidden field and an invisible link, like this:

```
<h:form id="hidden" target="popup">
  <h:inputHidden id="country" value="#{bb.country}"/>
  <h:commandLink id="go" action="showStates" value="">
    <f:verbatim></f:verbatim>
  </h:commandLink>
</h:form>
```

Note the following details:

*   The target of the form has the same name as the popup window. Therefore, the browser will show the result of the action inside the popup.

- The hidden country field will be populated before the form is submitted. It sets the bb.country value binding. This enables the backing bean to return the appropriate set of states or provinces.
- The action attribute of the command link is used by the navigation handler to select the JSF page that generates the popup contents.

The doPopup function initializes the hidden field and fires the link action:

```
var hidden = document.forms.hidden;
hidden["hidden:go"].value = "x"; // any value will do
hidden["hidden:country"].value = country[selected].value;
hidden.submit();
```

The value of the selected radio button is transferred into the hidden field. When the hidden form is submitted, that value will be stored in the backing bean.

The value of the link element can be any nonblank entry. It is used by the decode method of the UICommandLink renderer to check that this link was activated.

In this solution, the JSF page for the popup is more straightforward. The table of states or provinces is simply populated by the bean property call

```
<h:dataTable value="#{bb.statesForCountry}" var="state">
```

The statesForCountry property takes the country property into account—it was set when the hidden form was decoded. This approach is more flexible than the first approach because it allows arbitrary bean properties to be set before the popup contents are computed.

With both approaches, it is necessary to send the popup data back to the original page. However, this can be achieved with straightforward JavaScript. The popup's opener property is the window that opened the popup. When the user clicks a link in the popup, we simply set the value of the corresponding text field in the original page:

```
opener.document.forms[formId][formId + ":state"].value = value;
```

How does the popup know the form ID of the original form? Here we take advantage of the flexibility of JavaScript. You can add instance fields to any object on-the-fly. We set an openerFormId field in the popup window when it is constructed:

```
popup = window.open(...);
popup.openerFormId = source.form.id;
```

When we are ready to modify the form variables, we retrieve it from the popup window like this:

```
var formId = window.openerFormId;
```

These are the tricks that you need to know in order to deal with popup windows. The following example shows the two approaches that we discussed. The index.jsp and popup.jsp files in Listings 12–12 and 12–13 show the first approach, using a request parameter to configure the popup page. The index2.jsp and popup2.jsp files in Listings 12–14 and 12–15 show the second approach, filling the popup page with the result of a JSF action. Listing 12–16 shows the backing bean, and Listing 12–17 shows the configuration file. Note how the showStates action leads to the popup2.jsp page.

Listing 12–12   popup/index.jsp

```
1.  <html>
2.     <%@ taglib uri="http://java.sun.com/jsf/core" prefix="f" %>
3.     <%@ taglib uri="http://java.sun.com/jsf/html" prefix="h" %>
4.
5.     <f:view>
6.        <head>
7.           <script language="JavaScript1.1">
8.              function doPopup(source) {
9.                 country = source.form[source.form.id + ":country"];
10.                for (var i = 0; i < country.length; i++) {
11.                   if (country[i].checked) {
12.                      popup = window.open("popup.faces?country="
13.                         + country[i].value, "popup",
14.                         "height=300,width=200,toolbar=no,menubar=no,"
15.                         + "scrollbars=yes");
16.                      popup.openerFormId = source.form.id;
17.                      popup.focus();
18.                   }
19.                }
20.             }
21.          </script>
22.          <title>A Simple Java Server Faces Application</title>
23.       </head>
24.       <body>
25.          <h:form>
26.             <table>
27.                <tr>
28.                   <td>Country:</td>
29.                   <td>
30.                      <h:selectOneRadio id="country" value="#{bb.country}">
31.                         <f:selectItem itemLabel="USA"  itemValue="USA"/>
32.                         <f:selectItem itemLabel="Canada"  itemValue="Canada"/>
33.                      </h:selectOneRadio>
34.                   </td>
35.                </tr>
36.                <tr>
37.                   <td>State/Province:</td>
38.                   <td>
```

Listing 12–12   popup/index.jsp (cont.)

```
39.                <h:inputText id="state" value="#{bb.state}"/>
40.             </td>
41.             <td>
42.                <h:commandButton value="..."
43.                   onclick="doPopup(this); return false;"/>
44.             </td>
45.          </tr>
46.       </table>
47.       <p>
48.          <h:commandButton value="Next" action="next"/>
49.       </p>
50.    </h:form>
51.    </body>
52. </f:view>
53. </html>
```

Listing 12–13   popup/popup.jsp

```
1.  <html>
2.  <%@ taglib uri="http://java.sun.com/jsf/core" prefix="f" %>
3.  <%@ taglib uri="http://java.sun.com/jsf/html" prefix="h" %>
4.
5.  <f:view>
6.     <head>
7.        <script type="text/javascript" language="JavaScript1.2">
8.           function doSave(value) {
9.              var formId = window.openerFormId;
10.             opener.document.forms[formId][formId + ":state"].value = value;
11.             window.close();
12.          }
13.       </script>
14.       <title>Select a state/province</title>
15.    </head>
16.    <body>
17.       <h:form>
18.          <h:dataTable value="#{bb.states[param.country]}" var="state">
19.             <h:column>
20.                <h:outputLink value="#"
21.                   onclick="doSave('#{state}');">
22.                   <h:outputText value="#{state}" />
23.                </h:outputLink>
24.             </h:column>
25.          </h:dataTable>
26.       </h:form>
27.    </body>
28. </f:view>
29. </html>
```

Listing 12–14 popup/index2.jsp

```
1.  <html>
2.    <%@ taglib uri="http://java.sun.com/jsf/core" prefix="f" %>
3.    <%@ taglib uri="http://java.sun.com/jsf/html" prefix="h" %>
4.
5.    <f:view>
6.      <head>
7.        <script language="JavaScript1.1">
8.          function doPopup(source) {
9.            country = source.form[source.form.id + ":country"];
10.           for (var i = 0; i < country.length; i++) {
11.             if (country[i].checked) {
12.               popup = window.open("",
13.                 "popup",
14.                 "height=300,width=200,toolbar=no,menubar=no,"
15.                 + "scrollbars=yes");
16.               popup.openerFormId = source.form.id;
17.               popup.focus();
18.               var hidden = document.forms.hidden;
19.               hidden["hidden:go"].value = "x"; // any value will do
20.               hidden["hidden:country"].value = country[i].value;
21.               hidden.submit();
22.             }
23.           }
24.         }
25.       </script>
26.       <title>A Simple Java Server Faces Application</title>
27.     </head>
28.     <body>
29.       <h:form>
30.         <table>
31.           <tr>
32.             <td>Country:</td>
33.             <td>
34.               <h:selectOneRadio id="country" value="#{bb.country}">
35.                 <f:selectItem itemLabel="USA"  itemValue="USA"/>
36.                 <f:selectItem itemLabel="Canada"  itemValue="Canada"/>
37.               </h:selectOneRadio>
38.             </td>
39.           </tr>
40.           <tr>
41.             <td>State/Province:</td>
42.             <td>
43.               <h:inputText id="state" value="#{bb.state}"/>
44.             </td>
45.             <td>
46.               <h:commandButton value="..."
47.                 onclick="doPopup(this); return false;"/>
48.             </td>
49.           </tr>
```

Listing 12–14   popup/index2.jsp (cont.)

```
50.              </table>
51.              <p>
52.                 <h:commandButton value="Next" action="next"/>
53.              </p>
54.           </h:form>
55.
56.           <%-- This hidden form sends a request to a popup window. --%>
57.           <h:form id="hidden" target="popup">
58.              <h:inputHidden id="country" value="#{bb.country}"/>
59.              <h:commandLink id="go" action="showStates" value="">
60.                 <f:verbatim/>
61.              </h:commandLink>
62.           </h:form>
63.        </body>
64.     </f:view>
65. </html>
```

Listing 12–15   popup/popup2.jsp

```
1. <html>
2.    <%@ taglib uri="http://java.sun.com/jsf/core" prefix="f" %>
3.    <%@ taglib uri="http://java.sun.com/jsf/html" prefix="h" %>
4.
5.    <f:view>
6.       <head>
7.          <script language="JavaScript1.1">
8.             function doSave(value) {
9.                var formId = window.openerFormId;
10.               opener.document.forms[formId][formId + ":state"].value = value;
11.               window.close();
12.            }
13.         </script>
14.         <title>Select a state/province</title>
15.      </head>
16.      <body>
17.         <h:form>
18.            <h:dataTable value="#{bb.statesForCountry}" var="state">
19.               <h:column>
20.                  <h:outputLink value="#"
21.                     onclick="doSave('#{state}');">
22.                     <h:outputText value="#{state}" />
23.                  </h:outputLink>
24.               </h:column>
25.            </h:dataTable>
26.         </h:form>
27.      </body>
28.   </f:view>
29. </html>
```

Listing 12–16 popup/WEB-INF/classes/com/corejsf/BackingBean.java

```java
 1. package com.corejsf;
 2.
 3. import java.util.HashMap;
 4. import java.util.Map;
 5.
 6. public class BackingBean {
 7.    private String country = "USA";
 8.    private String state = "";
 9.    private static Map states;
10.
11.    // PROPERTY: country
12.    public String getCountry() { return country; }
13.    public void setCountry(String newValue) { country = newValue; }
14.
15.    // PROPERTY: state
16.    public String getState() { return state; }
17.    public void setState(String newValue) { state = newValue; }
18.
19.    public Map getStates() { return states; }
20.
21.    public String[] getStatesForCountry() { return (String[]) states.get(country); }
22.
23.    static {
24.       states = new HashMap();
25.       states.put("USA",
26.          new String[] {
27.             "Alabama", "Alaska", "Arizona", "Arkansas", "California",
28.             "Colorado", "Connecticut", "Delaware", "Florida", "Georgia",
29.             "Hawaii", "Idaho", "Illinois", "Indiana", "Iowa", "Kansas",
30.             "Kentucky", "Louisiana", "Maine", "Maryland", "Massachusetts",
31.             "Michigan", "Minnesota", "Mississippi", "Missouri", "Montana",
32.             "Nebraska", "Nevada", "New Hampshire", "New Jersey", "New Mexico",
33.             "New York", "North Carolina", "North Dakota", "Ohio", "Oklahoma",
34.             "Oregon", "Pennsylvania", "Rhode Island", "South Carolina",
35.             "South Dakota", "Tennessee", "Texas", "Utah", "Vermont",
36.             "Virginia", "Washington", "West Virginia", "Wisconsin", "Wyoming"
37.          });
38.
39.       states.put("Canada",
40.          new String[] {
41.             "Alberta", "British Columbia", "Manitoba", "New Brunswick",
42.             "Newfoundland and Labrador", "Northwest Territories",
43.             "Nova Scotia", "Nunavut", "Ontario", "Prince Edward Island",
44.             "Quebec", "Saskatchewan", "Yukon"
45.          });
46.    }
47. }
```

Listing 12-17 popup/WEB-INF/faces-config.xml

```
1.  <?xml version="1.0"?>
2.
3.  <!DOCTYPE faces-config PUBLIC
4.    "-//Sun Microsystems, Inc.//DTD JavaServer Faces Config 1.0//EN"
5.    "http://java.sun.com/dtd/web-facesconfig_1_0.dtd">
6.
7.  <faces-config>
8.     <navigation-rule>
9.        <navigation-case>
10.           <from-outcome>next</from-outcome>
11.           <to-view-id>/welcome.jsp</to-view-id>
12.        </navigation-case>
13.        <navigation-case>
14.           <from-outcome>showStates</from-outcome>
15.           <to-view-id>/popup2.jsp</to-view-id>
16.        </navigation-case>
17.        <navigation-case>
18.           <from-outcome>technique1</from-outcome>
19.           <to-view-id>/index.jsp</to-view-id>
20.        </navigation-case>
21.        <navigation-case>
22.           <from-outcome>technique2</from-outcome>
23.           <to-view-id>/index2.jsp</to-view-id>
24.        </navigation-case>
25.     </navigation-rule>
26.
27.     <managed-bean>
28.        <managed-bean-name>bb</managed-bean-name>
29.        <managed-bean-class>com.corejsf.BackingBean</managed-bean-class>
30.        <managed-bean-scope>session</managed-bean-scope>
31.     </managed-bean>
32.  </faces-config>
```

How do I customize error pages?

You probably don't want your users to see scary stack traces when they run into an error in your web application. There are two mechanisms for customizing the display of errors.

You can specify an error page for a specific JSF page with the following JSP directive:

```
<%@ page errorPage="error.jsp" %>
```

When an error occurs during execution of the page, the error.jsp page is displayed. However, if the error occurs before the page has been compiled, then this mechanism doesn't work.

You can specify generic error pages with the error-page tag in the web.xml file. Specify either a Java exception class or an HTTP error code. For example,

```
<error-page>
   <exception-type>java.lang.Exception</exception-type>
   <location>/exception.jsp</location>
</error-page>
<error-page>
   <error-code>500</error-code>
   <location>/error.jsp</location>
</error-page>
<error-page>
   <error-code>404</error-code>
   <location>/notfound.jsp</location>
</error-page>
```

If an exception occurs and an error page matches its type, then the matching error page is displayed. Otherwise, an HTTP error 500 is generated.

If an HTTP error occurs and there is a matching error page, it is displayed. Otherwise, the default error page is displayed.

CAUTION: If an error occurs while trying to display a custom error page, the default error page is displayed instead. If your custom error page stubbornly refuses to appear, check the log files for messages relating to your error page.

If you use the JSP errorPage directive, the exception object is available in the request map with the key "javax.servlet.jsp.jspException". If you use the servlet error-page mechanism, several objects related to the error are placed in the request map—see Table 12–1. You can use these values to display information that describes the error.

Table 12–1   Servlet Exception Attributes

Key	Value	Type
javax.servlet.error.status_code	The HTTP error code	Integer
javax.servlet.error.message	A description of the error	String
javax.servlet.error. exception_type	The class of the exception	Class
javax.servlet.error.exception	The exception object	Throwable
javax.servlet.error.request_uri	The path to the application resource that encountered the error	String

Table 12–1 Servlet Exception Attributes (cont.)

Key	Value	Type
javax.servlet.error.servlet_name	The name of the servlet that encountered the error	String

The following sample application uses this technique. We purposely produce a null pointer exception in the password property of the UserBean. Listing 12–18 shows the web.xml file that sets the error page to errorDisplay.jsp (Listing 12–19). Listing 12–20 shows the ErrorBean class. Its getStackTrace method assembles a complete stack trace that contains all nested exceptions.

> NOTE: The errorDisplay.jsp page uses a f:subview tag. This is a workaround for an anomaly in the JSF reference implementation—using f:view in an error page causes an assertion error in the framework code.

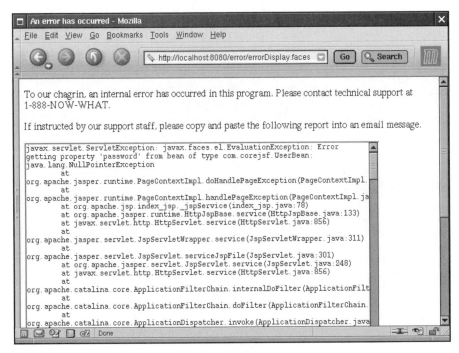

Figure 12–9 A Customized Error Display

Listing 12-18   error/WEB-INF/web.xml

```
1. <?xml version="1.0"?>
2.
3. <!DOCTYPE web-app PUBLIC
4.    "-//Sun Microsystems, Inc.//DTD Web Application 2.3//EN"
5.    "http://java.sun.com/dtd/web-app_2_3.dtd">
6.
7. <web-app>
8.    <servlet>
9.       <servlet-name>Faces Servlet</servlet-name>
10.      <servlet-class>javax.faces.webapp.FacesServlet</servlet-class>
11.      <load-on-startup>1</load-on-startup>
12.   </servlet>
13.
14.   <servlet-mapping>
15.      <servlet-name>Faces Servlet</servlet-name>
16.      <url-pattern>*.faces</url-pattern>
17.   </servlet-mapping>
18.
19.   <welcome-file-list>
20.      <welcome-file>/index.html</welcome-file>
21.   </welcome-file-list>
22.
23.   <error-page>
24.      <error-code>500</error-code>
25.      <location>/errorDisplay.faces</location>
26.   </error-page>
27. </web-app>
```

Listing 12-19   error/errorDisplay.jsp

```
1. <html>
2.    <%@ taglib uri="http://java.sun.com/jsf/core" prefix="f" %>
3.    <%@ taglib uri="http://java.sun.com/jsf/html" prefix="h" %>
4.
5.    <f:subview id="dummy">
6.       <head>
7.          <f:loadBundle basename="com.corejsf.messages" var="msgs"/>
8.          <title><h:outputText value="#{msgs.title}"/></title>
9.       </head>
10.      <body>
11.         <h:form>
12.            <p><h:outputText value="#{msgs.errorOccurred}"/></p>
```

Listing 12–19 error/errorDisplay.jsp (cont.)

```
13.              <p><h:outputText value="#{msgs.copyReport}"/></p>
14.              <h:inputTextarea value="#{error.stackTrace}"
15.                 rows="40" cols="80" readonly="true"/>
16.          </h:form>
17.       </body>
18.    </f:subview>
19. </html>
```

Listing 12–20 error/WEB-INF/classes/com/corejsf/ErrorBean.java

```
 1. package com.corejsf;
 2.
 3. import java.io.PrintWriter;
 4. import java.io.StringWriter;
 5. import java.sql.SQLException;
 6. import java.util.Map;
 7. import javax.faces.context.FacesContext;
 8. import javax.servlet.ServletException;
 9.
10. public class ErrorBean {
11.    public String getStackTrace() {
12.       FacesContext context = FacesContext.getCurrentInstance();
13.       Map request = context.getExternalContext().getRequestMap();
14.       Throwable ex = (Throwable) request.get("javax.servlet.error.exception");
15.       StringWriter sw = new StringWriter();
16.       PrintWriter pw = new PrintWriter(sw);
17.       fillStackTrace(ex, pw);
18.       return sw.toString();
19.    }
20.
21.    private static void fillStackTrace(Throwable t, PrintWriter w) {
22.       if (t == null) return;
23.       t.printStackTrace(w);
24.       if (t instanceof ServletException) {
25.          Throwable cause = ((ServletException) t).getRootCause();
26.          if (cause != null) {
27.             w.println("Root cause:");
28.             fillStackTrace(cause, w);
29.          }
30.       } else if (t instanceof SQLException) {
31.          Throwable cause = ((SQLException) t).getNextException();
32.          if (cause != null) {
33.             w.println("Next exception:");
```

Listing 12–20 `error/WEB-INF/classes/com/corejsf/ErrorBean.java (cont.)`

```
34.                fillStackTrace(cause, w);
35.            }
36.        } else {
37.            Throwable cause = t.getCause();
38.            if (cause != null) {
39.                w.println("Cause:");
40.                fillStackTrace(cause, w);
41.            }
42.        }
43.    }
44. }
```

Validation

JSF 1.0/1.1 has strong support for server-side validation of a single component. However, if you want to carry out client-side validation or to validate relationships among components, you are on your own. The following sections tell you how you can overcome these issues.

How do I use the Struts framework for client-side validation?

A web application can validate user input inside the browser client or on the server. Client-side validation is more efficient. Users don't have to wait for the server to diagnose the error and render a response page. However, client-side validation requires downloading validation code into browsers, typically using JavaScript. Unfortunately, producing JavaScript code that runs in multiple browsers is a bit of a black art.

The HTML tags in JSF 1.0/1.1 do not provide client-side validation. If you want to add client-side validation to your application, you have two choices: use a third-party library or implement a custom solution.

In this section, we show you how you can use the client-side validator in the Struts framework together with JSF. You can download Struts from http:// jakarta.apache.org/struts.

Using Struts gives you the advantage of using a set of well-debugged Java-Script routines. You will see on page 606 how you can write a validator that uses your own JavaScript code.

Here is an overview of the required steps for using Struts validation in a JSF application.

1. Add the files struts.jar, commons-validator.jar, commons-lang.jar, and jakarta-oro.jar from the Struts distribution to the WEB-INF/lib directory of your web application.

2. Add the following entry to your web.xml file:

    ```
    <servlet>
      <servlet-name>action</servlet-name>
      <servlet-class>org.apache.struts.action.ActionServlet</servlet-class>
      <init-param>
        <param-name>config</param-name>
        <param-value>/WEB-INF/struts-config.xml</param-value>
      </init-param>
      <load-on-startup>2</load-on-startup>
    </servlet>
    ```

3. Add a file WEB-INF/struts-config.xml that specifies the location of the validator configuration files and message bundles (see Listing 12–21).

4. Add the file validator-rules.xml from the Struts distribution to the WEB-INF directory of your web application.

5. Add a message bundle that specifies the text of the error messages (see Listing 12–22).

6. In each JSF page that uses client-side validation, import the Struts HTML tag library:

    ```
    <%@ taglib uri="http://jakarta.apache.org/struts/tags-html" prefix="html" %>
    ```

    Add the following tag inside the head element of each form that requires client-side validation:

    ```
    <html:javascript formName="myForm"/>
    ```

    Here, *myForm* is a form name that you need to choose. Set the same form name as the ID of the h:form element. Also add an onsubmit attribute that calls the JavaScript function validate*MyForm*, like this:

    ```
    <h:form id="myForm" onsubmit="return validateMyForm(this);">
    ```

    Listing 12–24 shows an example.

7. Provide a file validation.xml that contains all client-side validation rules of your application. You can see an example in Listing 12–24 on page 606. The file format is explained in http://jakarta.apache.org/struts/userGuide/dev_validator.html. Table 12–2 describes the client-side validators.

Table 12–2   Struts Client-Side Validators

Validator Name	Parameters	Purpose
`required`	none	Checks that the field has characters other than white space
`maxlength`	`maxlength`	Checks that the field length is at most the value of the `maxlength` parameter
`minlength`	`minlength`	Checks that the field length is at least the value of the `minlength` parameter
`byte`	none	Checks that the field contains an integer between −128 and 127
`short`	none	Checks that the field contains an integer between −32768 and 32767
`integer`	none	Checks that the field contains an integer between −2147483648 and 2147483647
`float`	none	Checks that the field contains a floating-point number
`intRange`	`min, max`	Checks that the field contains an integer between `min` and `max`. Both must be specified.
`floatRange`	`min, max`	Checks that the field contains a floating-point number between `min` and `max`. Both must be specified.
`date`	`datePatternStrict`	Checks that the field contains a date with the given pattern
`email`	none	Checks that the field contains a syntactically correct email address
`creditCard`	none	Checks that the field contains a credit card number that passes the Luhn check
`mask`	`mask`	Checks that the field matches the regular expression given in the `mask` parameter

To demonstrate this technique, we added client-side validators to the validator application of Chapter 6. Figure 12–10 shows a validation error message.

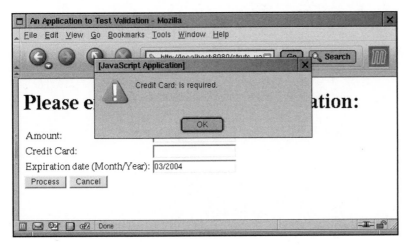

Figure 12–10   Client-Side Validation

Figure 12–11 shows the directory structure of the application.

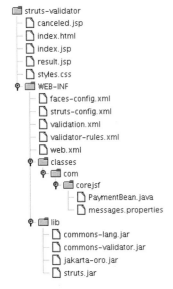

Figure 12–11   Directory Structure
of the struts-validator **Application**

Using the Struts validator is an attractive option if you are already familiar with Struts. However, it is quite a bother to specify the validation rules in an external file that is completely separate from your JSF pages. You can do better than that with a couple of custom tags—see the next section.

Listing 12–21 struts-validator/WEB-INF/struts-config.xml

```
 1. <?xml version="1.0" encoding="ISO-8859-1" ?>
 2.
 3. <!DOCTYPE struts-config PUBLIC
 4.         "-//Apache Software Foundation//DTD Struts Configuration 1.1//EN"
 5.         "http://jakarta.apache.org/struts/dtds/struts-config_1_1.dtd">
 6.
 7. <struts-config>
 8.
 9.    <message-resources parameter="com.corejsf.messages"/>
10.    <plug-in className="org.apache.struts.validator.ValidatorPlugIn">
11.       <set-property property="pathnames"
12.          value="/WEB-INF/validator-rules.xml,/WEB-INF/validation.xml"/>
13.    </plug-in>
14.
15. </struts-config>
```

Listing 12–22 struts-validator/WEB-INF/classes/com/corejsf/messages.properties

```
 1. title=An Application to Test Validation
 2. enterPayment=Please enter the payment information:
 3. amount=Amount:
 4. creditCard=Credit Card:
 5. expirationDate=Expiration date (Month/Year):
 6. paymentInformation=Payment information
 7. canceled=The transaction has been canceled.
 8. back=Back
 9.
10. errors.required={0} is required.
11. errors.minlength={0} can not be less than {1} characters.
12. errors.maxlength={0} can not be greater than {1} characters.
13. errors.invalid={0} is invalid.
14.
15. errors.byte={0} must be a byte.
16. errors.short={0} must be a short.
17. errors.integer={0} must be an integer.
18. errors.long={0} must be a long.
19. errors.float={0} must be a float.
20. errors.double={0} must be a double.
21.
22. errors.date={0} is not a date.
23. errors.range={0} is not in the range {1} through {2}.
24. errors.creditcard={0} is an invalid credit card number.
25. errors.email={0} is an invalid e-mail address.
```

Listing 12–23 struts-validator/index.jsp

```
1. <html>
2.    <%@ taglib uri="http://java.sun.com/jsf/core" prefix="f" %>
3.    <%@ taglib uri="http://java.sun.com/jsf/html" prefix="h" %>
4.    <%@ taglib uri="http://jakarta.apache.org/struts/tags-html" prefix="html" %>
5.
6.    <f:view>
7.       <head>
8.          <link href="styles.css" rel="stylesheet" type="text/css"/>
9.          <f:loadBundle basename="com.corejsf.messages" var="msgs"/>
10.          <html:javascript formName="paymentForm"/>
11.          <title><h:outputText value="#{msgs.title}"/></title>
12.       </head>
13.       <body>
14.          <h:form id="paymentForm" onsubmit="return validatePaymentForm(this);">
15.             <h1><h:outputText value="#{msgs.enterPayment}"/></h1>
16.             <h:panelGrid columns="3">
17.                <h:outputText value="#{msgs.amount}"/>
18.                <h:inputText id="amount" value="#{payment.amount}"
19.                   required="true">
20.                   <f:convertNumber minFractionDigits="2"/>
21.                   <f:validateDoubleRange minimum="10" maximum="10000"/>
22.                </h:inputText>
23.                <h:message for="amount" styleClass="errorMessage"/>
24.
25.                <h:outputText value="#{msgs.creditCard}"/>
26.                <h:inputText id="card" value="#{payment.card}"
27.                   required="true">
28.                   <f:validateLength minimum="13"/>
29.                </h:inputText>
30.                <h:message for="card" styleClass="errorMessage"/>
31.
32.                <h:outputText value="#{msgs.expirationDate}"/>
33.                <h:inputText id="date" value="#{payment.date}"
34.                   required="true">
35.                   <f:convertDateTime pattern="MM/yyyy"/>
36.                </h:inputText>
37.                <h:message for="date" styleClass="errorMessage"/>
38.             </h:panelGrid>
39.             <h:commandButton value="Process" action="process"/>
40.             <h:commandButton value="Cancel" action="cancel" immediate="true"/>
41.          </h:form>
42.       </body>
43.    </f:view>
44. </html>
```

Listing 12–24   struts-validator/WEB-INF/validation.xml

```xml
1. <?xml version="1.0" encoding="ISO-8859-1" ?>
2. <!DOCTYPE form-validation PUBLIC "-//Apache Software Foundation//DTD Commons
3.    Validator Rules Configuration 1.0//EN"
4.    "http://jakarta.apache.org/commons/dtds/validator_1_0.dtd">
5. <form-validation>
6.    <formset>
7.       <form name="paymentForm">
8.          <field property="paymentForm:amount" depends="required">
9.             <arg0 key="amount"/>
10.         </field>
11.         <field property="paymentForm:card" depends="required,minlength">
12.            <arg0 key="creditCard"/>
13.            <arg1 key="${var:minlength}" resource="false"/>
14.            <var>
15.               <var-name>minlength</var-name>
16.               <var-value>13</var-value>
17.            </var>
18.         </field>
19.         <field property="paymentForm:date" depends="required,date">
20.            <arg0 key="expirationDate"/>
21.            <var>
22.               <var-name>datePatternStrict</var-name>
23.               <var-value>MM/yyyy</var-value>
24.            </var>
25.         </field>
26.      </form>
27.   </formset>
28. </form-validation>
```

How do I write my own client-side validation tag?

Let us suppose you have developed a JavaScript function for validation and tested it on multiple browsers. Now you would like to use it in your JSF applications. You need two tags:

1.   A validator tag that is attached to each component that requires validation.

2.   A component tag that generates the JavaScript code for validating all components on the form. The component tag must be added to the end of the form. Note that we cannot use a validator tag for this purpose. Only components can render output.

As an example, we show you how to make use of the credit card validation code in the Struts Validator (see Listing 12–25 on page 609). We produce two tags: a creditCardValidator tag that can be added to any JSF input component, and a component tag validatorScript that generates the required JavaScript code.

The `creditCardValidator` tag has two attributes. The `message` attribute specifies the error message template, such as

```
{0} is not a valid credit card number
```

The `arg` attribute is the value that should be filled in for {0}, usually the field name. For example,

```
<corejsf:creditCardValidator
    message="#{msgs.invalidCard}" arg="#{msgs.primaryCard}"/>
```

The code for the validator is in Listing 12–26 on page 610. The validator class has two unrelated purposes: validation and error message formatting.

The class carries out a traditional server-side validation, independent of the client-side JavaScript code. After all, it is not a good idea to solely rely on client-side validation. Users may have deactivated JavaScript in their browsers. Also, automated scripts or web-savvy hackers may send unvalidated HTTP requests to your web application.

The `getErrorMessage` method formats an error message that will be included in the client-side JavaScript code. The error message is constructed from the `message` and `arg` attributes.

The `validatorScript` component is far more interesting—see Listing 12–27 on page 612. Its `encodeBegin` method calls the recursive `findCreditCardValidators` method, which walks the component tree, locates all components, enumerates their validators, checks which ones are credit card validators, and gathers them in a map object. The `writeValidationFunctions` method writes the JavaScript code that invokes the validation function on all fields with credit card validators.

You must place the `validatorScript` tag at the *end* of the form, like this:

```
<h:form id="paymentForm" onsubmit="return validatePaymentForm(this);">
    ...
    <corejsf:validatorScript functionName="validatePaymentForm"/>
</h:form>
```

Listing 12–28 on page 614 shows a sample JSF page.

CAUTION: If you place the `validatorScript` tag before the tags for the components that need to be validated, then the code that traverses the form component may not find the validators! This unintuitive and annoying behavior is a consequence of the JSP mechanism on which the JSF reference implementation is based. When a JSP-based implementation renders a JSF page *for the first time*, the component tree does not yet exist. Instead, it intermingles rendering and construction of the component tree.

The details of the `writeValidationFunctions` depend on the intricacies of the JavaScript code used by the Struts validator, which is taken from the Commons Validator project—see http://jakarta.apache.org/commons/validator.

> NOTE: As we write this book, the JavaScript functions are not a part of the source or binary distribution of the Commons Validator project. You can get them from CVS at http://cvs.apache.org/viewcvs.cgi/jakarta-commons/validator/ src/javascript. The development of this library is still in flux—you may need to tweak our code to match later versions.

First, the `writeValidationFunctions` method produces the validation function that is called in the `onsubmit` handler of the form:

```
var bCancel = false;
function functionName(form) { return bCancel || validateCreditCard(form); }
```

If a form contains "Cancel" or "Back" buttons, their `onclick` handlers should set the `bCancel` variable to `true`, in order to bypass validation.

The `validateCreditCard` function is the entry point into the Commons Validator code. It expects to find a function named `creditCard` that constructs a configuration object. The `writeValidationFunctions` method generates the code for the `creditCard` function.

Unfortunately, the details are rather convoluted. The `creditCard` function returns an object with one instance field for each validated form element. Each instance field contains an array with two values: the ID of the form element and the error message to display when validation fails. The instance field names don't matter. In the `writeValidationFunctions` method, we take advantage of the flexibility of JavaScript and simply call the fields 0, 1, 2, and so on. For example,

```
function creditCard() {
    this[0] = new Array("paymentForm:primary",
        "Primary Credit Card is not a valid card number");
    this[1] = new Array("paymentForm:backup",
        "Backup Credit Card is not a valid card number");
}
```

If you design your own JavaScript functions, you can provide a saner mechanism for bundling up the parameters.

Listing 12–25 clientside-validator/scripts/validateCreditCard.js

```
1.   /*$RCSfile: validateCreditCard.js,v $ $Revision: 1.5 $ $Date: 2003/12/15 02:56:57 $ */
2.   /**
3.    * Check to see if fields are a valid creditcard number based on Luhn checksum.
4.    * Fields are not checked if they are disabled.
5.    * <p>
6.    * @param form The form validation is taking place on.
7.    */
8.   function validateCreditCard(form) {
9.       var bValid = true;
10.      var focusField = null;
11.      var i = 0;
12.      var fields = new Array();
13.      oCreditCard = new creditCard();
14.      for (x in oCreditCard) {
15.          if ((form[oCreditCard[x][0]].type == 'text' ||
16.              form[oCreditCard[x][0]].type == 'textarea') &&
17.              (form[oCreditCard[x][0]].value.length > 0)  &&
18.              form[oCreditCard[x][0]].disabled == false) {
19.              if (!luhnCheck(form[oCreditCard[x][0]].value)) {
20.                  if (i == 0) {
21.                      focusField = form[oCreditCard[x][0]];
22.                  }
23.                  fields[i++] = oCreditCard[x][1];
24.                  bValid = false;
25.              }
26.          }
27.      }
28.      if (fields.length > 0) {
29.          focusField.focus();
30.          alert(fields.join('\n'));
31.      }
32.      return bValid;
33.  }
34.
35.  /**
36.   * Checks whether a given credit card number has a valid Luhn checksum.
37.   * This allows you to spot most randomly made-up or garbled credit card
38.   * numbers immediately.
39.   * Reference: http://www.speech.cs.cmu.edu/~sburke/pub/luhn_lib.html
40.   */
41.  function luhnCheck(cardNumber) {
42.      if (isLuhnNum(cardNumber)) {
43.          var no_digit = cardNumber.length;
44.          var oddoeven = no_digit & 1;
```

Listing 12–25 clientside-validator/scripts/validateCreditCard.js (cont.)

```
45.              var sum = 0;
46.              for (var count = 0; count < no_digit; count++) {
47.                  var digit = parseInt(cardNumber.charAt(count));
48.                  if (!((count & 1) ^ oddoeven)) {
49.                      digit *= 2;
50.                      if (digit > 9) digit -= 9;
51.                  };
52.                  sum += digit;
53.              };
54.              if (sum == 0) return false;
55.              if (sum % 10 == 0) return true;
56.          };
57.      return false;
58.  }
59.
60.  function isLuhnNum(argvalue) {
61.      argvalue = argvalue.toString();
62.      if (argvalue.length == 0) {
63.          return false;
64.      }
65.      for (var n = 0; n < argvalue.length; n++) {
66.          if ((argvalue.substring(n, n+1) < "0") ||
67.              (argvalue.substring(n,n+1) > "9")) {
68.              return false;
69.          }
70.      }
71.      return true;
72.  }
```

Listing 12–26 clientside-validator/WEB-INF/classes/com/corejsf/
CreditCardValidator.java

```java
1. package com.corejsf;
2.
3. import java.io.Serializable;
4. import java.text.MessageFormat;
5. import java.util.Locale;
6. import javax.faces.application.FacesMessage;
7. import javax.faces.component.UIComponent;
8. import javax.faces.context.FacesContext;
9. import javax.faces.validator.Validator;
10. import javax.faces.validator.ValidatorException;
11.
```

Listing 12–26   clientside-validator/WEB-INF/classes/com/corejsf/
CreditCardValidator.java (cont.)

```
12. public class CreditCardValidator implements Validator, Serializable {
13.    private String message;
14.    private String arg;
15.
16.    // PROPERTY: message
17.    public void setMessage(String newValue) { message = newValue; }
18.
19.    // PROPERTY: arg
20.    public void setArg(String newValue) { arg = newValue; }
21.    public String getArg() { return arg; }
22.
23.    public void validate(FacesContext context, UIComponent component,
24.       Object value) {
25.       if(value == null) return;
26.       String cardNumber;
27.       if (value instanceof CreditCard)
28.          cardNumber = value.toString();
29.       else
30.          cardNumber = getDigitsOnly(value.toString());
31.       if(!luhnCheck(cardNumber)) {
32.          FacesMessage message = new FacesMessage(FacesMessage.SEVERITY_ERROR,
33.             getErrorMessage(value, context), null);
34.          throw new ValidatorException(message);
35.       }
36.    }
37.
38.    public String getErrorMessage(Object value, FacesContext context) {
39.       Object[] params = new Object[] { value };
40.       if (message == null)
41.          return com.corejsf.util.Messages.getString(
42.             "com.corejsf.messages", "badLuhnCheck", params);
43.       else {
44.          Locale locale = context.getViewRoot().getLocale();
45.          MessageFormat formatter = new MessageFormat(message, locale);
46.          return formatter.format(params);
47.       }
48.    }
49.
50.    private static boolean luhnCheck(String cardNumber) {
51.       int sum = 0;
52.
53.       for(int i = cardNumber.length() - 1; i >= 0; i -= 2) {
54.          sum += Integer.parseInt(cardNumber.substring(i, i + 1));
55.          if(i > 0) {
```

| Listing 12–26 | clientside-validator/WEB-INF/classes/com/corejsf/
CreditCardValidator.java (cont.) |

```
56.          int d = 2 * Integer.parseInt(cardNumber.substring(i - 1, i));
57.          if(d > 9) d -= 9;
58.          sum += d;
59.        }
60.      }
61.
62.    return sum % 10 == 0;
63.  }
64.
65.  private static String getDigitsOnly(String s) {
66.    StringBuffer digitsOnly = new StringBuffer ();
67.    char c;
68.    for(int i = 0; i < s.length (); i++) {
69.      c = s.charAt (i);
70.      if (Character.isDigit(c)) {
71.        digitsOnly.append(c);
72.      }
73.    }
74.    return digitsOnly.toString ();
75.  }
76. }
```

| Listing 12–27 | clientside-validator/WEB-INF/classes/com/corejsf/
UIValidatorScript.java |

```
1. package com.corejsf;
2.
3. import java.io.IOException;
4. import java.util.Iterator;
5. import java.util.List;
6. import java.util.Map;
7. import java.util.TreeMap;
8. import javax.faces.component.EditableValueHolder;
9. import javax.faces.component.UIComponent;
10. import javax.faces.component.UIComponentBase;
11. import javax.faces.context.FacesContext;
12. import javax.faces.context.ResponseWriter;
13. import javax.faces.validator.Validator;
14.
15. public class UIValidatorScript extends UIComponentBase {
16.    private Map validators = new TreeMap();
17.    // a map from IDs to CreditCardValidator objects
18.
```

Listing 12-27 clientside-validator/WEB-INF/classes/com/corejsf/ UIValidatorScript.java (cont.)

```
19.   public String getRendererType() { return null; }
20.   public String getFamily() { return null; }
21.
22.   private void findCreditCardValidators(UIComponent c, FacesContext context) {
23.      if (c instanceof EditableValueHolder) {
24.         EditableValueHolder h = (EditableValueHolder) c;
25.         Validator[] vs = h.getValidators();
26.         for (int i = 0; i < vs.length; i++) {
27.            if (vs[i] instanceof CreditCardValidator) {
28.               CreditCardValidator v = (CreditCardValidator) vs[i];
29.               String id = c.getClientId(context);
30.               validators.put(id, v);
31.            }
32.         }
33.      }
34.
35.      List children = c.getChildren();
36.      for (int i = 0; i < children.size(); i++) {
37.         UIComponent child = (UIComponent) children.get(i);
38.         findCreditCardValidators(child, context);
39.      }
40.   }
41.
42.   private void writeScriptStart(ResponseWriter writer) throws IOException {
43.      writer.startElement("script", this);
44.      writer.writeAttribute("type", "text/javascript", null);
45.      writer.writeAttribute("language", "Javascript1.1", null);
46.      writer.write("\n<!--\n");
47.   }
48.
49.   private void writeScriptEnd(ResponseWriter writer) throws IOException {
50.      writer.write("\n-->\n");
51.      writer.endElement("script");
52.   }
53.
54.   private void writeValidationFunctions(ResponseWriter writer,
55.      FacesContext context) throws IOException {
56.      writer.write("var bCancel = false;\n");
57.      writer.write("function " );
58.      writer.write(getAttributes().get("functionName").toString());
59.      writer.write("(form) { return bCancel || validateCreditCard(form); }\n");
60.
61.      writer.write("function creditCard() { \n");
62.      // for each field validated by this type, add configuration object
```

Listing 12-27	clientside-validator/WEB-INF/classes/com/corejsf/ UIValidatorScript.java (cont.)

```
63.      Iterator iter = validators.keySet().iterator();
64.      int k = 0;
65.      while (iter.hasNext()) {
66.         String id = (String) iter.next();
67.         CreditCardValidator v = (CreditCardValidator) validators.get(id);
68.         writer.write("this[" + k + "] = ");
69.         k++;
70.
71.         writer.write("new Array('");
72.         writer.write(id);
73.         writer.write("', '");
74.         writer.write(v.getErrorMessage(v.getArg(), context));
75.         writer.write("');\n");;
76.      }
77.      writer.write("}\n");
78.   }
79.
80.   public void encodeBegin(FacesContext context) throws IOException {
81.      String id = getClientId(context);
82.      ResponseWriter writer = context.getResponseWriter();
83.
84.      validators.clear();
85.      findCreditCardValidators(context.getViewRoot(), context);
86.
87.      writeScriptStart(writer);
88.      writeValidationFunctions(writer, context);
89.      writeScriptEnd(writer);
90.   }
91. }
```

Listing 12-28	clientside-validator/index.jsp

```
1. <html>
2.    <%@ taglib uri="http://java.sun.com/jsf/core" prefix="f" %>
3.    <%@ taglib uri="http://java.sun.com/jsf/html" prefix="h" %>
4.    <%@ taglib uri="http://corejsf.com/creditcard" prefix="corejsf" %>
5.    <f:view>
6.       <head>
7.          <link href="styles.css" rel="stylesheet" type="text/css"/>
8.          <f:loadBundle basename="com.corejsf.messages" var="msgs"/>
9.
```

Listing 12–28 clientside-validator/index.jsp (cont.)

```
10.         <script src="scripts/validateCreditCard.js"
11.             type="text/javascript" language="JavaScript1.1">
12.         </script>
13.         <title><h:outputText value="#{msgs.title}"/></title>
14.     </head>
15.     <body>
16.         <h:form id="paymentForm" onsubmit="return validatePaymentForm(this);">
17.             <h1><h:outputText value="#{msgs.enterPayment}"/></h1>
18.             <h:panelGrid columns="3">
19.                 <h:outputText value="#{msgs.amount}"/>
20.                 <h:inputText id="amount" value="#{payment.amount}">
21.                     <f:convertNumber minFractionDigits="2"/>
22.                 </h:inputText>
23.                 <h:message for="amount" styleClass="errorMessage"/>
24.
25.                 <h:outputText value="#{msgs.creditCard}"/>
26.                 <h:inputText id="card" value="#{payment.card}" required="true">
27.                     <corejsf:creditCardValidator
28.                         message="#{msgs.unknownType}"arg="#{msgs.creditCard}"/>
29.                 </h:inputText>
30.                 <h:message for="card" styleClass="errorMessage"/>
31.
32.                 <h:outputText value="#{msgs.expirationDate}"/>
33.                 <h:inputText id="date" value="#{payment.date}">
34.                     <f:convertDateTime pattern="MM/dd/yyyy"/>
35.                 </h:inputText>
36.                 <h:message for="date" styleClass="errorMessage"/>
37.             </h:panelGrid>
38.             <h:commandButton value="Process" action="process"/>
39.             <corejsf:validatorScript functionName="validatePaymentForm"/>
40.         </h:form>
41.     </body>
42.     </f:view>
43. </html>
```

How do I use the Jakarta Commons Validator for client-side validation?

In the preceding section, you saw how to write your own validator tag that puts a validation script from the Commons Validator project to work. If you like that approach, there is no need to get busy and replicate that work for all of the other validators. We supply a custom tag library for this purpose.

To use our wrapper around Commons Validator, follow these instructions:

1. Place the library file `corejsf-validator.jar` into the `WEB-INF/lib` directory of your web application. Place the file `validation-rules.xml` into the `WEB-INF/lib` directory of your web application. Both files are included in the companion code for this book.

2. Place the library files `commons-validator.jar` and `jakarta-oro.jar` into the `WEB-INF/lib` directory of your web application. The files are available at http://jakarta.apache.org/commons/validator and http://jakarta.apache.org/oro.

3. Include a tag library declaration such as

   ```
   <%@ taglib uri="http://corejsf.com/validator" prefix="v" %>
   ```

   Here, we use v as a prefix. As always, you can use any prefix of your choice.

4. Include a call to the validation method in the `onsubmit` handler of your form, like this:

   ```
   <h:form id="paymentForm" onsubmit="return validatePaymentForm(this);">
   ```

   Just before the `</h:form>` tag, add a `v:validatorScript` tag:

   ```
   <v:validatorScript functionName="validatePaymentForm"/>
   ```

   The function name must match the function in the `onsubmit` handler.

5. Add validators to your components, for example:

   ```
   <h:inputText id="amount" value="#{payment.amount}">
     <v:commonsValidator type="floatRange"
         min="10" max="10000" arg="#{msgs.amount}"/>
   </h:inputText>
   ```

   The type argument is the validator type. It should be one of the types of Table 12–2. Supply attributes `min`, `max`, `minlength`, `maxlength`, `mask`, and `datePatternStrict` as required by the validation method that you choose. Supply the argument for the error message in the `arg` attribute. Typically, this is the name of the field.

How do I validate relationships between components?

In JSF, validators are intended to check the validity of a single component. However, you often need to test relationships between components. For example, it is common to ask users to reenter a password. You'd like to show a validation error if the two passwords are not identical.

The sophisticated approach is to design a custom component that renders two input fields, one for the password and one for the confirmed password. That is quite elegant, but of course it is a lot of work.

The other approach is simply to let the *last* of the related components do the validation. The preceding components will have their local values set, and your validator code can read them. For the last component only, you need to use the value that was passed by the validation method.

The validation method is most conveniently placed in a backing bean that also holds the components of the form. For example,

```
public class BackingBean
{
  . private UIInput passwordField;
    private UIInput confirmField;
    ...
    public void validateConfirmField(FacesContext context, UIComponent component,
        Object value) {
        if (!passwordField.getLocalValue().equals(value))
            throw new ValidatorException(...);
}
```

You then simply attach the validator to the confirmation field:

```
<h:inputText binding="#{bb.confirmField}" required="true"
    validator="#{bb.validateConfirmField}"/>
```

For a more complete example of this technique, see Chapter 6.

Programming

In the following sections, we discuss issues that are of interest to JSF programmers. We show you how to use Eclipse with JSF, how to reduce the drudgery of common implementation tasks, how to initialize your application, and how to package components into a reusable JAR file.

How do I use JSF with Eclipse?

You can use Eclipse to edit JSF pages and to compile the code for beans, converters, validators, and components. We assume that you are familiar with the basic operation of Eclipse and so we cover only the special configuration details for JSF programming.

The principal issue is the installation of JSF and Ant libraries. It would be rather tedious to install the libraries separately for each project.

Let us consider the JSF libraries first. The trick is to make a project that contains the libraries, and to use it as a base for all JSF projects. Here is how you set up the base project (which we will call jsflibs).

1. Select File->New->Project from the menu and supply the project name, jsflibs.

2. In the "Java Build Settings" screen of the project wizard, click on the "Libraries" tab, then click on the "Add External JARs" button. Add the jsf-api.jar file from the jsf/lib directory.

3. Repeat to add the servlet-api.jar and jsp-api.jar files from *tomcat*/common/lib (see Figure 12–12).

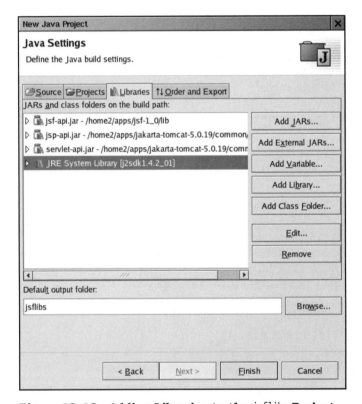

Figure 12–12   Adding Libraries to the jsflibs **Project**

4. Click on the "Order and Export" button and check the three libraries that you just added (see Figure 12–13).

5. Click the "Finish" button.

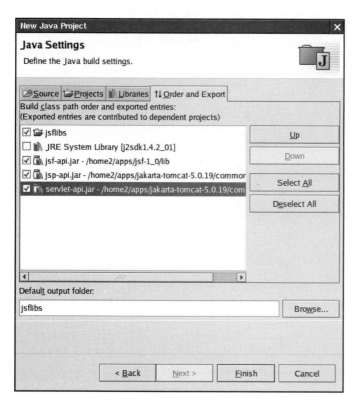

Figure 12–13   Exporting Libraries in the jsflibs **Project**

Whenever you set up your JSF projects, start with the "New Java Project" wizard in the usual way. However, when you get the "Java Build Settings" screen, click on the "Projects" tab and check the jsflibs project (see Figure 12–14). Now all the required libraries are automatically included in your project.

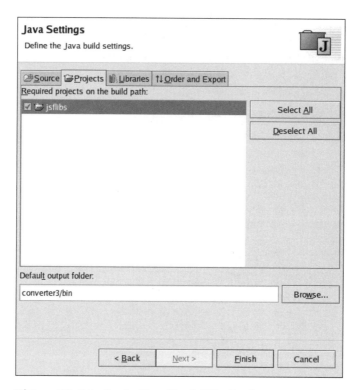

Figure 12–14   Including the `jsflibs` **Project**

Now let us turn to the Ant setup. Our Ant script uses the `catalina-ant` and `ant-contrib` libraries. If you want to run Ant inside Eclipse, you need to add these libraries to the Ant configuration. Follow these steps.

1.   Select the Window -> Preferences menu option.
2.   Select the Ant -> Runtime tree node.
3.   Click on "Ant Home Entries" (see Figure 12–15).
4.   Then click on the "Add External JARs" button to add *tomcat*/`server/lib/catalina-ant.jar`.
5.   Repeat to add the `ant-contrib` JAR file.
6.   Click the "OK" button.

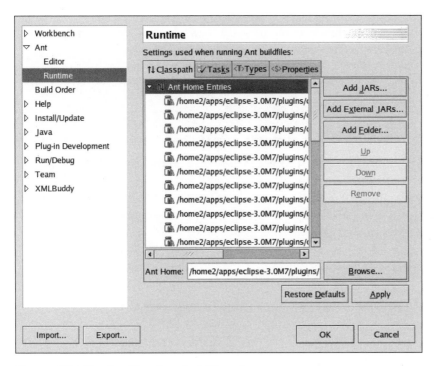

Figure 12–15   Configuring Ant libraries

For easy invocation of Ant, the build.xml file must be included in the project directory. This differs from the setup of our sample applications for which we use a single build.xml file for all applications. If you like our setup, simply add the following build.xml file into each Eclipse project directory:

```
<project default="build.war">
    <basename property="app" file="${basedir}"/>
    <property file="../build.properties"/>
    <property name="appdir" value="${basedir}"/>
    <import file="../build.xml"/>
</project>
```

Or, if you prefer, copy the build.xml and build.properties files into each project.

To run Ant, simply right-click on the build.xml file and select "Run Ant...". The Ant messages show up in the console.

> TIP: We recommend that you install the XML Buddy plugin and make it the default editor for JSF pages. You can download the plugin from http://xml-buddy.com. Of course, since XML Buddy is a real XML editor, it will frown upon <%...%> delimiters. We suggest that you use proper XML syntax—see the note on page 15.

How do I locate a configuration file?

Some applications prefer to process their own configuration files rather than using faces-config.xml or web.xml. The challenge is to locate the file since you don't know where the web container stores the files of your web application. In fact, the web container need not physically store your files at all—it can choose to read them out of the WAR file.

Instead, use the getResourceAsStream method of the ExternalContext class. For example, suppose you want to read app.properties in the WEB-INF directory of your application. Here is the required code:

```
FacesContext context = FacesContext.getCurrentInstance();
ExternalContext external = context.getExternalContext();
InputStream in = external.getResourceAsStream("/WEB-INF/app.properties");
```

How do I get the form ID for generating document.forms[id] in JavaScript?

Some components will need to generate JavaScript code to access the current form, either to submit it or to access fields contained in the form.

The JSF API has no convenience method for finding the form ID. Use the following code:

```
UIComponent parent = component;
while (!(parent instanceof UIForm)) parent = parent.getParent();
String formId = parent.getClientId(context);
```

(We supply this code in the getFormId method of the com.corejsf.util.Renderers class.)

You can now render JavaScript commands like this:

```
String command = "document.forms['" + formId + "'].submit()";
```

How do I make a JavaScript function appear only once per page?

Some components require substantial amounts of client-side JavaScript. If you have multiple instances of such a component in your page, you do not want to render multiple copies of the function.

To suppress multiple copies of the same code, your renderer can get the request map (`facesContext.getExternalContext().getRequestMap()`) and put a value of `Boolean.TRUE` with a key that indicates the component type. Next time the renderer is called, it can retrieve the key to find out if it has run previously in the same request.

How do I package a set of tags into a JAR file?

If you designed components, validators, or converters that are reusable across multiple projects, you will want to package them into JAR files so that they can be added to the `WEB-INF/lib` directory of any web application.

You will want to make the JAR file self-contained so that users don't have to worry about editing tag library descriptor or configuration files. Follow these steps:

1. Place a TLD file into the `META-INF` directory. The TLD file should contain a `uri` element that users of your library can reference in their JSF pages.

2. Place a file named `faces-config.xml` into the `META-INF` directory that contains the required `component`, `validator`, and `converter` elements.

3. Place any resource bundles and configuration files together with your classes. Load them with `ResourceBundle.getBundle` or `Class.getResourceAsStream`.

4. Avoid name clashes by using an appropriate prefix for the global names, such as component names, message keys, or loggers, used by your implementation.

Let us look at an example: the `corejsf-validator.jar` file described on page 615. Figure 12–16 shows the directory structure. Listings 12–29 and 12–30 show the tag library descriptor and configuration files.

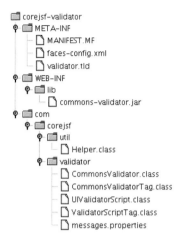

Figure 12–16   Directory Structure
of corejsf-validator.jar

Listing 12–29   commons-validator-lib/META-INF/validator.tld

```
1. <?xml version="1.0" encoding="ISO-8859-1" ?>
2. <!DOCTYPE taglib
3.   PUBLIC "-//Sun Microsystems, Inc.//DTD JSP Tag Library 1.2//EN"
4.   "http://java.sun.com/dtd/web-jsptaglibrary_1_2.dtd">
5. <taglib>
6.   <tlib-version>1.0</tlib-version>
7.   <jsp-version>1.2</jsp-version>
8.   <uri>http://corejsf.com/validator</uri>
9.   <tag>
10.     <name>commonsValidator</name>
11.     <tag-class>com.corejsf.validator.CommonsValidatorTag</tag-class>
12.     <attribute>
13.        <name>type</name>
14.     </attribute>
15.     <attribute>
16.        <name>min</name>
17.     </attribute>
18.     <attribute>
19.        <name>max</name>
20.     </attribute>
21.     <attribute>
22.        <name>minlength</name>
23.     </attribute>
24.     <attribute>
25.        <name>maxlength</name>
26.     </attribute>
27.     <attribute>
28.        <name>mask</name>
```

Listing 12–29 `commons-validator-lib/META-INF/validator.tld (cont.)`

```
29.      </attribute>
30.      <attribute>
31.        <name>datePatternStrict</name>
32.      </attribute>
33.      <attribute>
34.        <name>message</name>
35.      </attribute>
36.      <attribute>
37.        <name>arg</name>
38.      </attribute>
39.      <attribute>
40.        <name>client</name>
41.      </attribute>
42.      <attribute>
43.        <name>server</name>
44.      </attribute>
45.    </tag>
46.    <tag>
47.      <name>validatorScript</name>
48.      <tag-class>com.corejsf.validator.ValidatorScriptTag</tag-class>
49.      <attribute>
50.        <name>functionName</name>
51.      </attribute>
52.    </tag>
53. </taglib>
```

Listing 12–30 `commons-validator-lib/META-INF/faces-config.xml`

```
1. <?xml version="1.0"?>
2.
3. <!DOCTYPE faces-config PUBLIC
4.   "-//Sun Microsystems, Inc.//DTD JavaServer Faces Config 1.0//EN"
5.   "http://java.sun.com/dtd/web-facesconfig_1_0.dtd">
6.
7. <faces-config>
8.    <validator>
9.      <validator-id>com.corejsf.validator.CommonsValidator</validator-id>
10.     <validator-class>com.corejsf.validator.CommonsValidator</validator-class>
11.   </validator>
12.
13.   <component>
14.     <component-type>com.corejsf.validator.ValidatorScript</component-type>
15.     <component-class>com.corejsf.validator.UIValidatorScript</component-class>
16.   </component>
17. </faces-config>
```

How do I carry out initialization or cleanup work?

You have several choices, depending on the timing of your tasks.

- To manage application scope objects, attach a ServletContextListener. Implement the contextInitialized and contextDestroyed methods. Add the listener class to the web.xml file like this:

```
<listener>
   <listener-class>mypackage.MyListener</listener-class>
</listener>
```

- To manage session scope objects, attach an HttpSessionListener. Implement the sessionCreated and sessionDestroyed methods. Add the listener class to the web.xml file as in the preceding case.

- To manage request scope objects, attach a PhaseListener. (Phase listeners were discussed in Chapter 7.) You can initialize objects in the beforePhase method when the phase ID is APPLY_REQUEST_VALUES. You can clean up in the afterPhase method when the phase ID is RENDER_RESPONSE.

How do I extend the JSF expression language?

You can supply your own *variable resolver* and *property resolver* for evaluating value binding expressions. The variable resolver determines the value of the first variable in an expression. For example, the standard variable resolver looks up managed beans and handles the predefined variables such as cookie or view. The property resolver takes an object and a property value and looks up the result. For example, if the getValue method of the standard property resolver is given the UIView object corresponding to the view variable and the string locale, the result is the return value of view.getLocale().

If you want to introduce your own variables, you supply your own variable resolver and install it in an application resource file. If you package your custom classes in a JAR file, place a faces-config.xml file into the META-INF directory. Include a variable-resolver element like this:

```
<application>
   <variable-resolver>
      com.corejsf.CustomVariableResolver
   </variable-resolver>
   ...
</application>
```

Since you probably don't want to reimplement the existing lookup rules, you should use the decorator pattern for your own variable resolver. Apply your lookup rules and defer to the original resolver for all other cases.

If you supply a constructor with a single parameter of type VariableResolver, then the JSF implementation passes you its default variable resolver. This makes it straightforward to use the decorator pattern. Here is an example of a variable resolver that recognizes the variable name sysprop:

```
public class CustomVariableResolver extends VariableResolver {
    private VariableResolver original;

    public CustomVariableResolver(VariableResolver original) {
        this.original = original;
    }

    public Object resolveVariable(FacesContext context, String name) {
        if (name.equals("sysprop")) return System.getProperties();
        return original.resolveVariable(context, name);
    }
}
```

Once you install this variable resolver, the expression #{sysprop['java.version']} yields the version of the virtual machine.

Installing a property resolver is similar. You add a property-resolver element to the application configuration, like this:

```
<application>
    ...
    <property-resolver>
        com.corejsf.CustomPropertyResolver
    </property-resolver>
</application>
```

The PropertyResolver class has eight abstract methods that look up and set indexed and named properties. As with variable resolvers, you will want to decorate the standard property resolver. The following example lets you look up components by their ID.

```
public class CustomPropertyResolver extends PropertyResolver {
    private PropertyResolver original;

    public CustomPropertyResolver(PropertyResolver original) {
        this.original = original;
    }

    public Class getType(Object base, int index) {
        return original.getType(base, index);
    }

    public Class getType(Object base, Object property) {
```

```
      if (base instanceof UIComponent && property instanceof String) {
        UIComponent c = ((UIComponent) base).findComponent((String) property);
        if (c != null) return c.getClass();
      }
      return original.getType(base, property);
    }

    public Object getValue(Object base, int index) {
      return original.getValue(base, index);
    }


    public Object getValue(Object base, Object property) {
      if (base instanceof UIComponent && property instanceof String) {
        UIComponent c = ((UIComponent) base).findComponent((String) property);
        if (c != null) return c;
      }
      Object r = original.getValue(base, property);
      return r;
    }

    public boolean isReadOnly(Object base, int index) {
      return original.isReadOnly(base, index);
    }

    public boolean isReadOnly(Object base, Object property) {
      if (base instanceof UIComponent && property instanceof String) {
        UIComponent c = ((UIComponent) base).findComponent((String) property);
        if (c != null) return true;
      }
      return original.isReadOnly(base, property);
    }

    public void setValue(Object base, int index, Object value) {
      original.setValue(base, index, value);
    }

    public void setValue(Object base, Object property, Object value) {
      if (base instanceof UIComponent && property instanceof String) {
        UIComponent c = ((UIComponent) base).findComponent((String) property);
        if (c != null) return;
      }
      original.setValue(base, property, value);
    }
  }
}
```

Consider, for example, the expression

```
view.loginForm.password.value
```

It finds the component with ID loginForm inside the view root, then finds the component with ID password inside the form, and then calls its getValue method.

How do I choose different render kits?

You may want to render your pages with the default render kit for browser clients and with a custom render kit for other client technologies such as mobile devices.

To switch between render kits based on the incoming request, install a custom view handler. Add a view-handler element to a JSF configuration file:

```
<application>
  <view-handler>
      com.corejsf.CustomViewHandler
  </view-handler>
  ...
</application>
```

As in the preceding section, use the decorator pattern to extend the regular view handler. In the calculateRenderKit method, select the appropriate render kit, depending on the incoming request:

```
public class CustomViewHandler extends ViewHandler {
   private ViewHandler original;
   public CustomViewHandler(ViewHandler original) {
      this.original = original;
   }
   public String calculateRenderKitId(FacesContext context) {
      ExternalContext external = context.getExternalContext();
      String userAgent = (String) external.getRequestHeaderMap().get("User-Agent");
      if (...) return WIRELESS_KIT_ID;
      else return RenderKitFactory.HTML_BASIC_RENDER_KIT;
   }
   public Locale calculateLocale(FacesContext context) {
      return original.calculateLocale(context);
   }
   ...
}
```

You specify the render kit IDs when you set up the render kits in a JSF configuration file, for example,

```
<render-kit>
   <render-kit-id>com.corejsf.WIRELESS_KIT</render-kit-id>
   <renderer>...</renderer>
   <renderer>...</renderer>
   ...
</render-kit>
```

Debugging and Logging

Troubleshooting a JSF application can be painful. So many minor details must be just right or your application won't work. Error messages can be hard to find or nonexistent. Minor typos can give rise to an application that simply doesn't start or that seems to get stuck. The items in this section contain some tips to help you out.

How do I decipher a stack trace?

When you see a screen such as the one in Figure 12–17, count yourself lucky.

Figure 12–17   Error Page

Read the first line (or the first line that seems to make some sense), and correlate it with your JSF file. In this case, there is an illegal tag (inputTaxt instead of inputText) in line 16, column 21, or hopefully somewhere near there.

The error report may also indicate a problem with your code. For example,

```
java.lang.ClassCastException
    com.corejsf.UploadRenderer.decode(UploadRenderer.java:73)
    javax.faces.component.UIComponentBase.decode(UIComponentBase.java:658)
    javax.faces.component.UIInput.decode(UIInput.java:464)
    javax.faces.component.UIComponentBase.processDecodes(UIComponentBase.java:878)
    javax.faces.component.UIInput.processDecodes(UIInput.java:380)
    javax.faces.component.UIForm.processDecodes(UIForm.java:139)
    javax.faces.component.UIComponentBase.processDecodes(UIComponentBase.java:873)
    javax.faces.component.UIViewRoot.processDecodes(UIViewRoot.java:305)
    com.sun.faces.lifecycle.ApplyRequestValuesPhase.execute(ApplyRequestValuesPhase.java:79)
    com.sun.faces.lifecycle.LifecycleImpl.phase(LifecycleImpl.java:200)
    com.sun.faces.lifecycle.LifecycleImpl.execute(LifecycleImpl.java:90)
    javax.faces.webapp.FacesServlet.service(FacesServlet.java:197)
    com.corejsf.UploadFilter.doFilter(UploadFilter.java:68)
```

The remedy is straightforward. Have a look at line 73 of UploadRenderer.java and find out what caused the bad cast.

> **!** TIP: If your stack trace states that errors in your code are in unknown source locations, compile with debugging on. If you use Ant, add the attribute debug="true" to the javac task.

Sometimes, the situation is not so rosy. Consider this report:

```
javax.servlet.ServletException: javax.faces.el.EvaluationException: Error getting property 'password' from
bean of type com.corejsf.UserBean: java.lang.NullPointerException
    org.apache.jasper.runtime.PageContextImpl.doHandlePageException(PageContextImpl.java:864)
    org.apache.jasper.runtime.PageContextImpl.handlePageException(PageContextImpl.java:800)
    org.apache.jsp.index_jsp._jspService(index_jsp.java:78)
    org.apache.jasper.runtime.HttpJspBase.service(HttpJspBase.java:133)
    javax.servlet.http.HttpServlet.service(HttpServlet.java:856)
    org.apache.jasper.servlet.JspServletWrapper.service(JspServletWrapper.java:311)
    org.apache.jasper.servlet.JspServlet.serviceJspFile(JspServlet.java:301)
    org.apache.jasper.servlet.JspServlet.service(JspServlet.java:248)
    javax.servlet.http.HttpServlet.service(HttpServlet.java:856)
    com.sun.faces.context.ExternalContextImpl.dispatch(ExternalContextImpl.java:322)
    com.sun.faces.application.ViewHandlerImpl.renderView(ViewHandlerImpl.java:142)
    com.sun.faces.lifecycle.RenderResponsePhase.execute(RenderResponsePhase.java:87)
    com.sun.faces.lifecycle.LifecycleImpl.phase(LifecycleImpl.java:200)
    com.sun.faces.lifecycle.LifecycleImpl.render(LifecycleImpl.java:117)
    javax.faces.webapp.FacesServlet.service(FacesServlet.java:198)
```

Here, the subsystem that evaluates the expression language has wrapped an exception in the bean code inside an EvaluationException. You get to know where the EvaluationException is thrown, but that doesn't help you—you need the location of the NullPointerException that caused it.

Your next step is to inspect the log files. In this case, the log contains a more detailed report:

```
Caused by: javax.faces.el.EvaluationException: Error getting property 'password' from bean of type
com.corejsf.UserBean: java.lang.NullPointerException
        at com.sun.faces.el.PropertyResolverImpl.getValue(PropertyResolverImpl.java:89)
        at com.sun.faces.el.impl.ArraySuffix.evaluate(ArraySuffix.java:162)
        at com.sun.faces.el.impl.ComplexValue.evaluate(ComplexValue.java:146)
        at com.sun.faces.el.impl.ExpressionEvaluatorImpl.evaluate(ExpressionEvaluatorImpl.java:238)
        at com.sun.faces.el.ValueBindingImpl.getValue(ValueBindingImpl.java:155)       ... 55 more
Caused by: java.lang.NullPointerException
        at com.corejsf.UserBean.getPassword(UserBean.java:12)
        at sun.reflect.NativeMethodAccessorImpl.invoke0(Native Method)
        at sun.reflect.NativeMethodAccessorImpl.invoke(NativeMethodAccessorImpl.java:39)
        at sun.reflect.DelegatingMethodAccessorImpl.invoke(DelegatingMethodAccessorImpl.java:25)
        at java.lang.reflect.Method.invoke(Method.java:324)
        at com.sun.faces.el.PropertyResolverImpl.getValue(PropertyResolverImpl.java:79)
        ... 59 more
```

Finally, information you can use: Line 12 of UserBean.java caused the problem.

Unfortunately, sometimes the stack trace gives you no useful information at all. Here is an example of a bad case.

```
javax.servlet.ServletException: Cannot find FacesContext
        org.apache.jasper.runtime.PageContextImpl.doHandlePageException(PageContextImpl.java:867)
        org.apache.jasper.runtime.PageContextImpl.handlePageException(PageContextImpl.java:800)
        org.apache.jsp.index_jsp._jspService(index_jsp.java:78)
        org.apache.jasper.runtime.HttpJspBase.service(HttpJspBase.java:133)
        javax.servlet.http.HttpServlet.service(HttpServlet.java:856)
        org.apache.jasper.servlet.JspServletWrapper.service(JspServletWrapper.java:311)
        org.apache.jasper.servlet.JspServlet.serviceJspFile(JspServlet.java:301)
        org.apache.jasper.servlet.JspServlet.service(JspServlet.java:248)
        javax.servlet.http.HttpServlet.service(HttpServlet.java:856)
```

What caused this error? Misalignment of the planets? No—the problem was a bad URL: http://localhost:8080/login/index.**jsp** instead of http://localhost:8080/login/index.**faces**.

How do I find the logs?

The details depend on your JSF container. Tomcat 5 keeps logs in the *tomcat*/logs directory. The standard Tomcat log files are

*   catalina.out
*   localhost_log.*date*.log

Here *date* is a date stamp such as 2003-06-30. The catalina.out file contains all output that was sent to System.out and System.err. The localhost_log.*date*.log files contain the logging messages that were generated by the servlet context.

NOTE: Both Tomcat and the JSF reference implementation use Apache Commons logging (see http://jakarta.apache.org/commons/logging.html). This logging library is merely a bridge to various logging libraries, in particular the java.util.logging library that was introduced in SDK version 1.4, and the Apache Log4J library (http://logging.apache.org/log4j/docs/). There are religious wars over which logging library is better and whether Commons logging is a good idea—see, for example, http://www.qos.ch/logging/thinkAgain.html. We must admit to a slight preference for java.util.logging. It may not be perfect, but it's good enough, and it is a standard part of Java.

By default, Tomcat is configured to map Commons logging to the java.util.logging package. By default, that package is configured so that all messages with level INFO and higher are sent to System.out. Thus, most Tomcat messages end up in catalina.out. A much smaller number of messages are sent to the servlet context log, another logging facility that is completely unrelated to Commons logging. Therefore, you should check the localhost_log.*date*.log if catalina.out doesn't have the message you are looking for.

The catalina.out file is specified in the startup script (catalina.sh or catalina.bat in the *tomcat/bin* directory). The localhost_log.*date*.log files are configured in *tomcat/conf/server.xml*.

If you use the Tomcat implementation in the Java Web Services Development Pack, then the files are called launcher.server.log and jwsdp_log.*date*.log.

How do I find out what parameters my page received?

It is often helpful to know what parameters the client sent back to the server when a form was submitted. Here is a quick and dirty method for logging the request parameters.

Insert this snippet of code on top of the JSF file that receives the request:

```
<%
java.util.Enumeration e = request.getParameterNames();
while (e.hasMoreElements())
{
   String n = (String) e.nextElement();
   String[] v = request.getParameterValues(n);
   for (int i = 0; v != null && i < v.length; i++)
      java.util.logging.Logger.global.info("name=" + n + ",value=" + v[i]);
}
%>
```

Then catalina.out will contain entries such as

```
Apr 2, 2004 12:50:45 PM org.apache.jsp.welcome_jsp _jspService
INFO: name=_id0,value=_id0
```

```
Apr 2, 2004 12:50:45 PM org.apache.jsp.welcome_jsp _jspService
INFO: name=_id0:_id1,value=me
Apr 2, 2004 12:50:45 PM org.apache.jsp.welcome_jsp _jspService
INFO: name=_id0:_id2,value=secret
Apr 2, 2004 12:50:45 PM org.apache.jsp.welcome_jsp _jspService
INFO: name=_id0:_id3,value=Login
```

How do I turn on logging of the JSF container?

The JSF reference implementation contains copious logging statements whose output can be very helpful in tracking down problems with your applications.

Here, we assume that Tomcat has been configured to use the java.util.logging library that was introduced in SDK 1.4. This is the default setting for Tomcat.

1. Edit the startup script catalina.sh or catalina.bat in the *tomcat*/bin directory. At the top, add a line that sets the variable CATALINA_OPTS to the following parameter definition:

   -Djava.util.logging.config.file=*tomcat*/conf/logging.properties

   In Unix/Linux, use this syntax:

   CATALINA_OPTS="-Djava.util.logging.config.file=*tomcat*/conf/logging.properties"

   In Windows, use this syntax:

   set CATALINA_OPTS=-Djava.util.logging.config.file=*tomcat*\conf\logging.properties

   (As always, *tomcat* denotes the name of the Tomcat installation such as /usr/local/jakarta-tomcat-5.0.19 or c:\jakarta-tomcat-5.0.19.)

2. Copy the file logging.properties from the subdirectory jre/lib inside your Java SDK to the *tomcat*/conf directory.

3. Edit the file *tomcat*/conf/logging.properties. Locate the line

   java.util.logging.ConsoleHandler.level = INFO

   and change INFO to FINEST. At the end of the file, add a line

   com.sun.faces.level=FINEST

4. Restart Tomcat and run a JSF application. Then inspect the file *tomcat*/logs/catalina.out. It will contain messages such as

```
FINEST: End execute(phaseId=RESTORE_VIEW 1)
Jan 27, 2004 6:57:04 PM com.sun.faces.lifecycle.LifecycleImpl hasPostDataOrQueryParams
FINEST: Request Method: POST/PUT
Jan 27, 2004 6:57:04 PM com.sun.faces.lifecycle.LifecycleImpl execute
FINEST: execute(phaseId=APPLY_REQUEST_VALUES 2)
Jan 27, 2004 6:57:04 PM com.sun.faces.lifecycle.LifecycleImpl execute
FINEST: Begin execute(phaseId=APPLY_REQUEST_VALUES 2)
Jan 27, 2004 6:57:04 PM com.sun.faces.lifecycle.ApplyRequestValuesPhase execute
FINE: Entering ApplyRequestValuesPhase
Jan 27, 2004 6:57:04 PM com.corejsf.UploadRenderer decode
```

To turn off JSF container logging, simply edit *tomcat*/conf/logging.properties and change com.sun.faces.level to INFO.

> **NOTE:** If Tomcat finds the Apache Log4J library on the classpath, then it will use that logging library unless you specifically add the following definition to CATALINA_OPTS:
>
> -Dorg.apache.commons.logging.Log=org.apache.commons.logging.impl.Jdk14Logger

---

How do I replace catalina.out *with rotating logs?*

Again, we assume that Tomcat has been configured to use the java.util.logging library that was introduced in SDK 1.4. This is the default setting for Tomcat.

1. Edit the startup script catalina.sh or catalina.bat in the *tomcat*/bin directory. At the top, add a line that sets the variable CATALINA_OPTS to the following parameter definition:

    -Djava.util.logging.config.file=*tomcat*/conf/logging.properties

    In Unix/Linux, use this syntax:

    CATALINA_OPTS="-Djava.util.logging.config.file=*tomcat*/conf/logging.properties"

    In Windows, use this syntax:

    set CATALINA_OPTS=-Djava.util.logging.config.file=*tomcat*\conf\logging.properties

    (As always, *tomcat* denotes the name of the Tomcat installation such as /usr/local/jakarta-tomcat-5.0.19 or c:\jakarta-tomcat-5.0.19.)

2. Copy the file logging.properties from the subdirectory jre/lib inside your Java SDK to the *tomcat*/conf directory.

3. Edit the file *tomcat*/conf/logging.properties and make the following changes:

Change the value of...	from	to
handlers	java.util.log-ging.ConsoleHandler	java.util.logging.FileHandler, java.util.logging.ConsoleHandle
java.util.logging.FileHandler.pattern	%h/java%u.log	*tomcat*/logs/tomcat%u.log
java.util.logging.FileHandler.formatter	java.util.log-ging.XMLFormatter	java.util.logging.SimpleFormatter
java.util.logging.ConsoleHandler.level	INFO	NONE

4. Restart Tomcat. The logs will now be in files tomcat0.log.0, tomcat0.log.1, and so on, inside the *tomcat*/logs directory. The newest log is always tomcat0.log.0.

How do I find the library source?

You can download the library source from http://www.sun.com/software/communitysource/jsf. The library source can be very helpful for troubleshooting, and to clarify opaque points of the specification.

The library code is organized in four directories:

*   jsf-api, the documented API classes whose package names start with javax.faces

*   jsf-ri, the reference implementation classes whose package names start with com.sun.faces

*   jsf-tools, the tools that mechanically generate tag handlers and renderers

*   jsf-demo, the demo applications

In order to get a complete set of source files, you must run the Ant script in the jsf-tools directory.

1. Edit the build.properties file in the jsf-tools directory and supply the settings for tomcat.home and jsf.home.

2. If you use the standalone version of Tomcat, you also need to modify build.xml and change the correct locations for the commons-logging.jar, commons-digester.jar, commons-collections.jar, and commons-beanutils.jar files to ${tomcat.home}/server/lib.

3.   In the `jsf-tools` directory, run Ant without any arguments.

4.   The source code is produced in the `jsf-tools/build/generate` directory.

Finally, it is sometimes useful to find configuration details of the JSF implementation, such as the names of the standard components, renderers, converters, and validators. Look inside the files `jsf-ri/src/com/sun/faces/jsf-ri-config.xml` and `jsf-api/doc/standard-xml-renderkit.xml`.

Index

informIT

YOUR GUIDE TO IT REFERENCE

Articles

Keep your edge with thousands of free articles, in-depth features, interviews, and IT reference recommendations – all written by experts you know and trust.

Online Books

Answers in an instant from **InformIT Online Book's** 600+ fully searchable on line books. Sign up now and get your first 14 days **free**.

POWERED BY

Safari™

Catalog

Review online sample chapters, author biographies and customer rankings and choose exactly the right book from a selection of over 5,000 titles.

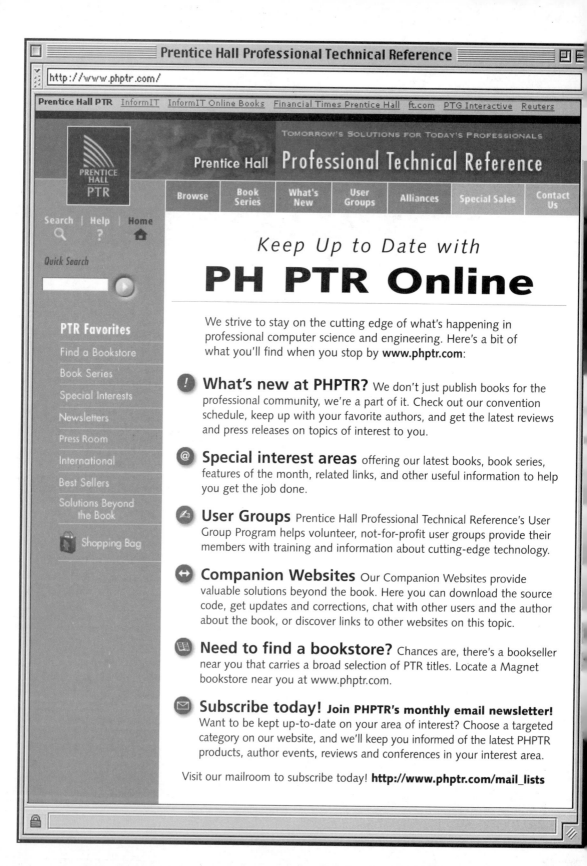

Prentice Hall Professional Technical Reference

http://www.phptr.com/

Prentice Hall PTR   InformIT   InformIT Online Books   Financial Times Prentice Hall   ft.com   PTG Interactive   Reuters

TOMORROW'S SOLUTIONS FOR TODAY'S PROFESSIONALS

Prentice Hall **Professional Technical Reference**

Browse | Book Series | What's New | User Groups | Alliances | Special Sales | Contact Us

Search | Help | Home

Quick Search

PTR Favorites

Find a Bookstore

Book Series

Special Interests

Newsletters

Press Room

International

Best Sellers

Solutions Beyond the Book

Shopping Bag

Keep Up to Date with
PH PTR Online

We strive to stay on the cutting edge of what's happening in professional computer science and engineering. Here's a bit of what you'll find when you stop by **www.phptr.com**:

What's new at PHPTR? We don't just publish books for the professional community, we're a part of it. Check out our convention schedule, keep up with your favorite authors, and get the latest reviews and press releases on topics of interest to you.

Special interest areas offering our latest books, book series, features of the month, related links, and other useful information to help you get the job done.

User Groups Prentice Hall Professional Technical Reference's User Group Program helps volunteer, not-for-profit user groups provide their members with training and information about cutting-edge technology.

Companion Websites Our Companion Websites provide valuable solutions beyond the book. Here you can download the source code, get updates and corrections, chat with other users and the author about the book, or discover links to other websites on this topic.

Need to find a bookstore? Chances are, there's a bookseller near you that carries a broad selection of PTR titles. Locate a Magnet bookstore near you at www.phptr.com.

Subscribe today! Join PHPTR's monthly email newsletter! Want to be kept up-to-date on your area of interest? Choose a targeted category on our website, and we'll keep you informed of the latest PHPTR products, author events, reviews and conferences in your interest area.

Visit our mailroom to subscribe today! **http://www.phptr.com/mail_lists**